ARTICLE 4. Utilization of Proper Means to Gain Proper Ends

The law enforcement officer shall be mindful of his responsibility to pay strict heed to the selection of means in discharging the duties of his office. Violations of laws or disregard for public safety and property on the part of the officer are intrinsically wrong; they are self-defeating in that they instill in the public mind a like disposition. The employment of illegal means, no matter how worthy the end, is certain to encourage disrespect for the law and its officer. If the law is to be honored, it must first be honored by those who enforce it.

ARTICLE 5. Cooperation with Public Officials in the Discharge of Their Authorized Duties

The law enforcement officer shall cooperate fully with other public officials in the discharge of authorized duties, regardless of party affiliation or personal prejudice. He shall be meticulous in assuring himself of the propriety, under the law, of such actions and shall guard against the use of his office or person, whether knowingly, or unknowingly, in any improper or illegal action. In any situation open to question, he shall seek authority from his superior officer, giving him a full report of the proposed service or action.

ARTICLE 6. Private Conduct

The law enforcement officer shall be mindful of his special identification by the public as an upholder of the law. Laxity of conduct or manner in private life, expressing either disrespect for the law or seeking to gain special privilege, cannot but reflect upon the police officer and the police service. The community and the service require that the law enforcement officer lead the life of a decent and honorable man. Following the career of a policeman gives no man special perquisites. It does give the satisfaction of safeguarding the American republic. The officer who reflects upon this tradition will not degrade it. Rather, he will so conduct his private life that the public will regard him as an example of stability, fidelity, and morality.

ARTICLE 7. Conduct Toward the Public

The law enforcement officer, mindful of his responsibility to the whole community, shall deal with individuals of the community in a manner such as will inspire confidence and trust. Thus, he will be neither overbearing nor subservient, as the individual citizen has neither an obligation to stand in awe of him nor a right to command him. The officer will give service where he can, and require compliance with the law. He will do neither from personal preference or prejudice but only as a duly appointed officer of the law discharging his sworn obligation.

ARTICLE 8. Conduct and Dealing with Violators

The law enforcement officer shall use his powers of arrest in accordance with the law and with due regard to the right of the citizen concerned. His office gives him no right to prosecute the violator nor to mete out punishment for the offense. He shall, at all times, have a clear appreciation of his responsibilities and limitations regarding detention of the violator; he shall conduct himself in such a manner as will minimize the possibility of having to use force. To this end he shall cultivate a dedication to the service of the people and the equitable upholding of their laws whether in the handling of law violators or in dealing with the law abiding.

ARTICLE 9. Gifts and Favors

The law enforcement officer, representing government, bears the heavy responsibility of maintaining, in his own conduct, the honor and integrity of all governmental institutions. He shall, therefore, guard against placing himself in a position which any person can reasonably assume that special consideration is being given. Thus, he should be firm in refusing gifts, favors, or gratuities, large or small, which can, in the public mind, be interpreted as capable of influencing his judgment in the discharge of his duties.

ARTICLE 10. Presentation of Evidence

The law enforcement officer shall be concerned equally in the prosecution of the wrong doer and the defense of the innocent. He shall ascertain what constitutes evidence and shall present such evidence impartially and without malice. In so doing, he will ignore social, political, and other distinctions among the persons involved, strengthening the tradition of the reliability and integrity of an officer's word.

ARTICLE 11. Attitude Toward Profession

The law enforcement officer shall regard the discharge of his duties as a public trust and recognize his responsibility as a public servant. By diligent study and sincere attention to self-improvement he shall strive to make the best possible application of science to the solution of crime and, in the field of human relationships, strive for effective leadership and public influence in matters affecting public safety. He shall appreciate the importance and responsibility of his office, hold police work to be an honorable profession rendering valuable service to his community and the country.

SOURCE: International Association of Chiefs of Police. Reprinted by permission of IACP.

Ethical Dilemmas and Decisions in Criminal Justice

SIXTH EDITION

Joycelyn M. Pollock
Texas State University–San Marcos

 WADSWORTH
CENGAGE Learning™

Australia • Brazil • Japan • Korea • Mexico • Singapore •
Spain • United Kingdom • United States

WADSWORTH
CENGAGE Learning

Ethical Dilemmas and Decisions in Criminal Justice, **Sixth Edition**

Joycelyn M. POLLOCK

Senior Acquisitions Editor: Carolyn Henderson Meier

Senior Development Editor: Bob Jucha

Assistant Editor: Meaghan Banks

Editorial Assistant: John Chell

Technology Project Manager: Bessie Weiss

Marketing Manager: Michelle Williams

Marketing Assistant: Jillian Myers

Marketing Communications Manager: Tami Strang

Project Manager, Editorial Production: Jennie Redwitz

Creative Director: Rob Hugel

Art Director: Maria Epes

Print Buyer: Paula Vang

Permissions Editor, Text: Bob Kauser

Production Service: Antima Gupta, ICC Macmillan Inc.

Photo Researcher: Pre-Press PMG

Copy Editor: Carolyn Acheson Blaney

Cover Designer: Dustin York, Riezebos Holzbaur Design Group

Cover Image: Istockphoto.com and Fotolia.com

Compositor: ICC Macmillan Inc.

For product information and technology assistance, contact us at **Cengage Learning Customer & Sales Support, 1-800-354-9706.**
For permission to use material from this text or product, submit all requests online at **www.cengage.com/permissions.**
Further permissions questions can be e-mailed to **permissionrequest@cengage.com.**

Library of Congress Control Number: 2008938390

Student Edition:

ISBN-13: 978-0-495-60033-6

ISBN-10: 0-495-60033-4

Wadsworth
10 Davis Drive
Belmont, CA 94002-3098
USA

Cengage Learning is a leading provider of customized learning solutions with office locations around the globe, including Singapore, the United Kingdom, Australia, Mexico, Brazil, and Japan. Locate your local office at **international.cengage.com/region.**

Cengage Learning products are represented in Canada by Nelson Education, Ltd.

For your course and learning solutions, visit **www.cengage.com.**
Purchase any of our products at your local college store or at our preferred online store **www.ichapters.com.**

Printed in Canada
1 2 3 4 5 6 7 12 11 10 09 08

To Greg and Eric, as always

ABOUT THE AUTHOR

Joycelyn M. Pollock received her Ph.D. in Criminal Justice at the State University of New York at Albany. She also obtained a J.D. at the University of Houston, and passed the Texas Bar in 1991.

The first edition of *Ethics in Crime and Justice: Dilemmas and Decisions* was published in 1986 and continues to be one of the leading texts in the field. Dr. Pollock has also published *Crime and Justice in America: An Introduction* (2008), *Criminal Law* (with John Klotter, 2007); *Morality Stories*, Second Edition (2007); *Prisons and Prison Life: Costs and Consequences* (2003); *Women, Prison and Crime*, Second Edition (2002); *Sex and Supervision: Guarding Male and Female Inmates* (1986); *Counseling Women Prisoners* (1999); *Criminal Women* (2000); *Prison: An American Institution* (editor; 1997); and is co-editor with Alida Merlo of *Women, Law and Social Control*, Second Edition (2004).

In addition to teaching at Texas State University (formerly Southwest Texas State University), she has delivered training to police officers, probation officers, parole officers, constables, and other groups in the areas of sexual harassment, ethics, criminology, and other subjects. She has taught at the Houston Police Academy, the Bill Blackwood Law Enforcement Management Institute, and has been a guest speaker for the International Association of Policewomen, the Texas Juvenile Justice Association, and the Southwest Legal Institute, among other groups. In 1998 she was awarded a Fulbright Teaching Fellowship to Turku School of Law in Turku, Finland. She was also a recipient of a Senior Scholar Justice award from the Open Society Institute. She has served as President of the Southwest Association of Criminal Justice and a Trustee-at-Large for the Academy of Criminal Justice Sciences. In 2007 she was awarded the Bruce Smith Award from ACJS for outstanding contributions to the field of criminology, and in 2008 she was awarded the Distinguished Alumni award from the State University at Albany, School of Criminal Justice.

Brief Contents

Contents

INTRODUCING THE WADSWORTH CENGAGE LEARNING CRIMINAL JUSTICE ADVISORY BOARD

The entire Criminal Justice team at Wadsworth Cengage Learning wishes to express its sincere gratitude to the hardworking members of our Criminal Justice Advisory Board. This group of skilled, experienced instructors comes together once a year to further their driving mission, which can be summed up as follows:

> This collaborative group of publishing professionals and instructors from traditional and nontraditional educational institutions is designed to foster development of exceptional educational and career opportunities in the field of criminal justice by providing direction and assistance to the faculty and administrators charged with training tomorrow's criminal justice professionals. The Advisory Board offers peer support and advice, consults from both the academic and publishing communities, and serves as a forum for creating and evolving best practices in the building of successful criminal justice programs.

The members of our Advisory Board have the wisdom, expertise, and vision to set goals that empower students, setting them up to capitalize on the field's tremendous growth and expanding job opportunities. According to the U.S. Bureau of Labor Statistics, employment for correctional officers, law enforcement officers, investigators, and security officers is projected to increase at a rate of 9–26% over the next eight years. Add to that the growing number of jobs available in other parts of the criminal justice system—case officer, youth specialist, social services, and more—and one can begin to get a true sense of the vast employment opportunity in the field. Helping today's students unlock the door to exciting and secure futures is the ultimate goal of everyone associated with the Wadsworth Cengage Learning Criminal Justice Advisory Board.

Included on the board are faculty and administrators from schools such as:

Brown College	John Jay College of Criminal Justice
Florida Metropolitan University	Rasmussen College
Globe University/Minnesota School of Business	South University
Hesser College	Western Career College
Kaplan University	Western Carolina University
Keiser University	Westwood College

Again, the Wadsworth Cengage Learning Criminal Justice Team would like to extend our personal and professional thanks for all that the Advisory Board has enabled us to accomplish over the past few years. We look forward to continuing our successful collaboration in the years ahead.

We are always looking to add like-minded instructors to the Advisory Board; if you would like to be considered for inclusion on the Board, please contact Michelle Williams (michelle.williams@cengage.com).

Preparing Students for a Lifetime of Service

PREFACE

The first edition of this book was published in 1986, when there were very few texts for a course covering criminal justice ethics. Over the many years and editions, the book has been shaped by current events, reviewers' comments, and the many individuals who have read the book and provided feedback. I want to thank each and every person who has contacted me through e-mail, letters, or personally at conferences. I welcome and appreciate all feedback. Please continue to let me know what you think and help me make the book better and more accurate.

In each edition there have been important events that have shaped the content. For instance, the Rodney King incident occurred between the second and third editions; the Ramparts scandal occurred between the third and fourth editions; and the fifth edition included a discussion of the Abu Ghraib incident. In this edition, recent events such as corruption scandals in the police departments of Boston and Chicago, the resignation of the governor of New York for wiring money to a call girl, the misguided prosecution of the Duke University lacrosse team members, and the U.S. Justice Department's memoranda concerning methods of torture in Guantanamo Bay Detention Camp are mentioned.

Since the first edition, this text has provided the basic philosophical principles necessary to analyze ethical dilemmas, and it has also included current news events in criminal justice to show that these are not "ivory tower" discussions but are applicable to daily events. The newspaper and online news sources should be integral instructional tools in every ethics course.

This book offers an approach that is "ripped from the headlines," so to speak, covering real-life examples of misconduct, the effects of misconduct, research on criminal justice ethics, and the various policy issues in criminal justice. The book also identifies themes that run through the entire criminal justice system so, for instance, issues such as discretion and due process are discussed in chapters concerning practitioners in law enforcement, the courts, and corrections. This text offers the reader an essential primer on ethical systems before addressing the dilemmas of practitioners. There are also expanded chapters on justice and the law. It is important to understand not just the dilemmas that criminal justice professionals may face but also how their experiences relate to larger questions, such as the definition of justice.

NEW TO THIS EDITION

Since the first edition, each chapter has posed ethical dilemmas to students so they can apply the principles of ethical decision making. Many of these dilemmas have been supplied by police officers, probation officers, students, and others who work in the field, or have been adapted from current events. In this edition we have kept these dilemmas as well as some of the expanded learning tools created in the last edition, including a list of key terms, enhanced reading lists, and study review questions. We have, however, transformed the discussion questions into writing exercises for instructors who would like to use them for class assignments.

Also in this edition we collected all the key term definitions into a glossary at the back of the book, and moved all of the exercises that were in the chapters to the Instructor's Resource Manual. We have changed a few of the Policy Boxes that show how policy issues in criminal justice always have ethical implications. We have kept the Quote and Query boxes, and either replaced or added to them with new quotations.

We have also created two new features designed to enhance the book's real-world orientation. First, to bring the discussion of ethics to a more personal level, we introduce each chapter with a real-life example of a person who has experienced an ethical challenge related to that chapter's central topic. Second, we created a new chapter feature called "Walking the Walk," which highlights an individual who exemplifies a strong ethical role model as a professional. We hope these additions will help to show that the principles discussed are not just something to learn for tests but have relevance to how to live one's life.

The fourth edition was published close on the heels of the tragedy of the World Trade Center attack. That event forever destroyed this country's sense of invulnerability and created fear and disquiet that continue to affect people's lives. The world seems to be a more dangerous place. The result has been a reordering of the nation's priorities and the federalization of law enforcement. Before September 11, 2001, the issues that might have been at the forefront of a discussion of ethics in the criminal justice system would have been racial profiling, how to address the drug problem, corruption by public or private leaders, and how to treat juvenile offenders. After the beginning of the "war on terror," our discussion has been expanded to the techniques, tactics, and policies employed to combat this threat.

In the last edition I added a discussion of what is acceptable in war and in our fight against terrorism. Do these "ends" justify torture? Do they justify curtailing the civil liberties of resident aliens? Of citizens? Although one might argue that these issues are peripheral to the subject of criminal justice, nothing could be further from the truth. Every day we can read about situations where local law enforcement and our court system are faced with challenges based on their role as the first line of defense of this nation's security. It is the local police who had to decide whether questioning Arab-Americans after 9/11 without probable cause was appropriate and legal; it is the local police who are asked to or told not to help identify illegal aliens. It is judges in federal courts who are asked to decide issues concerning the detainees in Guantanamo. It is American citizens who might be the targets of federal wiretapping. As in the last edition, Chapter 15 presents an expanded discussion of the means–end argument as related to terrorism—i.e., the idea that it is acceptable to use any means to fight terrorism is similar to earlier argument when the "end" was crime control.

Here are some of the changes and additions to each chapter in this edition:

- **Chapter 1, Morality, Ethics, and Human Behavior:** "Walking the Walk" box featuring Lt. Col. Scott Waddle.
- **Chapter 2, Determining Moral Behavior:** "Walking the Walk" box on Sgt. Joe Darby; "In the News" box on Barack Obama and Reverend Wright; discussion of the Josephson Institute's 6 Pillars of Character.
- **Chapter 3, Making Ethical Decisions:** Discussion of ex-governor Elliot Spitzer; expanded discussion of biological bases of morality; expanded discussion of Bandura's research.
- **Chapter 4, The Origins and Concept of Justice:** Expanded discussion of affirmative action; updated discussion of 100:1 ratio for sentencing powder and crack cocaine users; updated discussion of the *Hamdan v. Rumsfeld* (2006) case and the Military Commissions Act.
- **Chapter 5, Law and the Individual:** "Walking the Walk" box on Charles Swift; updated discussion of federal sentencing guidelines; updated discussion of *Roper v. Simmons* (2005); Policy Box on law enforcement and illegal immigration.
- **Chapter 6, Ethics and the Criminal Justice Professional:** "In the News" boxes on Winter Soldiers and on corruption at the U.S.–Mexico border; updated information on Lynddie England; box on whistleblowers in the news; discussion of Howard Gardner's Good Works Foundation; discussion of recent scandals, e.g. Hewlett Packard's "Spy Scandal."
- **Chapter 7, The Police Role in Society: Crime Fighter or Public Servant?:** Discussion of the "Oakland Riders"; discussion of recent cases of police use of force; discussion of the May 2007 MacArthur Park "riot"; "Walking the Walk" box on Anthony Bouza.
- **Chapter 8, Corruption and the "Code":** Discussion of Fyfe and Kane's 2006 N.Y.P.D. study; "In the News" boxes on the Chicago police scandal involving Officer Anthony Abbate and Boston's police drug scandal involving Officer Roberto Pulido; discussion of tazer use; discussion of Gilmartin and Harris's Continuum of Coercion.
- **Chapter 9, Investigative Methods, Noble-Cause, and Reducing Police Corruption:** Discussion of Kim Rossmo's research on failed police investigations; "In the News" boxes on two recently exonerated men who served time because FBI agents protected an informant and a scandal involving the Atlanta police department; "Walking the Walk" box on Keith Batt; expanded discussion of police ethics training.

- **Chapter 10, Ethics and Legal Professionals:** Updated discussion of exonerated inmates; expanded discussion of the Model Rules of Professional Responsibility; "Walking the Walk" box on Frank Armani; discussions of the Genarlow Wilson case, Prosecutor Mike Nifong and the Duke University lacrosse team members' prosecution, and U.S. Attorney Johnny Sutton's prosecution of border agents Jose Alonso Compean and Ignacio Ramos; updated discussion of forensic evidence and recent news items on prosecutor misconduct.
- **Chapter 11, Justice and Judicial Ethics:** Updated discussion of indigent defense appointment, *Kimbrough v. U.S.* (2007), *Gall v. U.S.* (2007), and the 2007 Model Code of Judicial Conduct; "In the News" box on judicial misconduct; update on the Innocence Commissions; discussion of the firing of federal prosecutors and judicial independence.
- **Chapter 12, The Ethics of Punishment and Corrections:** Expanded discussion of changes in habeas corpus appeals for death penalty cases and *Baze v. Rees* (2008); updated discussion of privatization.
- **Chapter 13, Ethics and Institutional Corrections:** Discussions of correctional officers called "Cowboys" in the federal prison in Arizona and "Green Wall" guards in California; discussion of the Prison Rape Elimination Act; expanded discussion of prison psychologists.
- **Chapter 14, Ethics and Community Corrections:** Expanded discussion of sex offender registries; discussion of forgiveness in context of Amish school shooting.
- **Chapter 15, Ethical Choices and the "War on Terror":** "Walking the Walk" box on Chaplain Yee; expanded discussion of "just war" debate; expanded and updated discussion of government actions in response to 9/11; boxes on the timeline of activities related to Military Commissions and government use of coercive interrogation techniques; a box on individuals who have been in the news for their moral stands against governmental actions in the war on terror.

Changes in this edition are, as always, reflective of the concerns expressed by the book's reviewers, although it was impossible to respond to all of the diverse points of view expressed by them. The fifth edition was a fairly dramatic reorganization of the book, done only three years ago; therefore, I have kept the chapters substantially the same in this edition so instructors who are using the book do not have to change their course organization.

In every edition I must balance the discussion of ethical systems and the philosophy of ethics with a discussion of issues and events. In the last several years, several new ethics texts have been published. I am happy to welcome these books into the field because some provide a greater emphasis on the philosophical issues of criminal justice ethics, some concentrate almost exclusively on law enforcement, and some are oriented to training. The instructor can decide which approach best suits his or her course. It is a constant struggle to keep the page count about the same even though every edition must cover several years of new events and new research in the field. Contrary to some reviewers' suggestions, however, I hesitate to take out older examples because these show the constancy of key problems. Serpico's experiences in the 1970s are similar to those of Keith Batt in his dilemma to expose the Oakland Riders over thirty years later. My main objective in this text and in teaching is to show that the questions of ethics are not new, nor are the means to answer them.

SUPPLEMENTS

The following supplemental aids are available to qualified adopters to assist instructors and students. Please consult your local sales representative for details.

eBank Instructor's Resource Manual with Test Bank This helpful manual provides resources that will maximize your time and minimize your effort in preparing for your course. The Instructor's Resource Manual section includes detailed Chapter Outlines, Learning Objectives, Key Terms, and Classroom Exercises. The Test Bank has been reviewed for accuracy by professors in the field. It consists of questions in multiple choice, true/false, fill-in-the-blank, and essay formats, coded to the Learning Objectives of the book. Our Instructor Approved Seal, which appears on the front cover, is our assurance that you are working with an assessment and grading resource of the highest calibre.

The Instructor's Resource Manual section of this supplement will be posted on the password-protected website for the book. To protect the integrity of our testing materials, we avoid posting test questions online. If you wish to obtain a copy of the Instructor's Resource Manual with Test Bank, please contact your local Cengage Learning representative.

eBank PowerPoint Presentations These handy Microsoft® PowerPoint® slides, which outline the chapters of the main text in a classroom-ready presentation, will help you in making your lectures engaging and in reaching your visually oriented students. The presentations are available for download on the password-protected website, and can also be obtained by e-mailing your local Cengage Learning representative.

Book Companion Website The book-specific website at www.cengage.com/criminaljustice/pollock offers students a variety of study tools and useful resources such as a glossary and flash cards. Instructor resources, including Microsoft® PowerPoint® slides and the Instructor's Resource Manual, are also available for download from the site with an instructor login.

ACKNOWLEDGMENTS

It is impossible to remember all the people who contribute to one's thinking in a field of study as rich as ethics. I am continuously impressed with the work of others and enriched by their contributions. If I list some—e.g., John Crank, Michael Caldero, Mickey Braswell, Carl Klockars, Tim Prenzler, Sam Souryal, and Vic Kappeler—unfortunately, I will forget others unfairly. I also thank those who have contacted me after using the book in a college classroom or training course. Such feedback is always welcome. Some of these individuals have provided commentary or criticism that has been very helpful. I thank, for instance, Michael

Geary, Tom Martinelli, Jack Van Steenburg, and Matthew Hickman who have shared with me their thoughts and experiences. The anonymous reviewers provided astute, comprehensive feedback that greatly assisted me in creating this new edition. They are:

Susan Brinkley, University of Tampa

Craig Campbell, St. Edward's University

Duane Everhart, Wayne Community College

Lori Guevara, Fayetteville State University

Curtis Hayes, Western New Mexico University

Stephen Hennessy, St. Cloud State University

William McCamey, Western Illinois University

Stephen Mallory, University of Mississippi

Rebecca Anne Mercier, Bluegrass Community and Technical College

Thomas Nolan, Boston University

Angela Simon, University of Dubuque

Sharon Tracy, Georgia Southern University

The staff members at Wadsworth have been integral to the development of this edition as well. They are: Carolyn Henderson Meier, Senior Acquisitions Editor; Robert Jucha, Senior Development Editor; Michelle Williams, Marketing Manager; Jennie Redwitz, Senior Content Project Manager; Bob Kauser, Senior Rights Acquisitions Account Manager; and Meaghan Banks, Assistant Editor. Thanks also to Antima Gupta at ICC Macmillan Inc. and copy editor Carolyn Acheson.

I thank Quint Thurman, the chair of my department at Texas State University–San Marcos. He continues to try his best to make the environment conducive to productivity and professionalism.

As always, I am grateful for my husband, Eric, and my son, Greg. They are eternally patient and never complain about the time I spend on writing instead of cooking, cleaning, walking the dogs, watering the yard, or spending time with them.

Joycelyn Pollock
jp12@txstate.edu

MORALITY, ETHICS, AND HUMAN BEHAVIOR

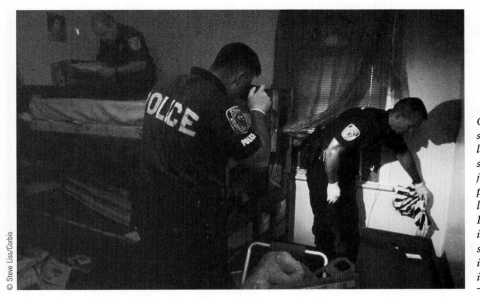

CHAPTER 1

© Steve Liss/Corbis

Criminal justice professionals face ethical dilemmas in each subsystem of the criminal justice system, including police officers who collect and analyze evidence. Professionals follow ethical codes that are designed to identify and illustrate ethical behavior in that profession.

CHAPTER OBJECTIVES

1. Become acquainted with the major arguments supporting the importance of studying ethics in the criminal justice field.

2. Learn the vocabulary of ethics: morals, ethics, values, ethical codes, ethical standards, and dilemmas.

3. Understand how to analyze an ethical dilemma.

4. Become sensitive to the types of ethical dilemmas faced in one's professional life.

Consider the following dilemma: You are a police officer patrolling late at night and see a car weaving back and forth across lanes of traffic. You turn on your siren, and the car pulls over. The driver stumbles out of the car, obviously intoxicated. There is no question that the driver meets the legal definition of intoxication. He also happens to be your father. What would you do?

Or decide what you would do in this case: You are a correctional officer working the late-night shift. Your sergeant and another officer from the day shift come onto the tier where you are working and ask you to open up an inmate's cell. After you do so, they enter the cell. Then you hear a series of sounds— grunts, cries, and moans. They leave, muttering about how the inmate has been taught a lesson. You believe that you have been a party to an assault, but you say nothing. The next night you find out that the inmate did not report the incident, nor did any other inmates. You believe that if you come forward and report what you saw, you will be severely ostracized. You may not be believed (especially if the inmate doesn't back you up). You might even lose your job. What would you do?

Finally, consider this scenario: You are a student interning in a criminal defense lawyer's office. As part of your duties, you sit in court with the lawyer you are working with, help her with legal research, and assist in interviewing witnesses. During the course of the internship, you conclude that the lawyer, in your opinion, is extremely negligent. She does not return clients' calls, she misses appeal deadlines, and she ignores or does not follow up on promising leads that might lead to exculpatory evidence. You are appalled that several of her clients are advised to plead guilty even though you think that the evidence against them is weak. After bringing up these issues with her, she fires you on the spot and tells you that all her clients are guilty anyway and that she is just another "cog in the wheel" of the justice machine. What, if anything, would you do?

WHY STUDY ETHICS?

How would you go about deciding what to do in these situations? Learning how to determine the "right thing to do" is the central purpose of this book. We make ethical decisions all the time, whether we recognize them or not. Think about some ethical choices you have been faced with in the last couple of weeks or months. Perhaps you have been faced with one of the following ethical choices:

- At work you were asked to cover for a friend who wanted to go home early and not report the time lost.
- A co-worker took something from the store where you both worked and expected you to say nothing.
- A friend asked you to lie for him to his girlfriend to cover up the fact that he went out with another girl.
- You felt compelled to tell a professor a "white lie" when asking for an extension on an assignment or for a different test time.

All of us make choices that can be judged under ethical standards. Further, we frequently judge other people's behaviors as right or wrong. Criminal justice professionals, whether they work in law enforcement, the courts, or corrections, encounter a multitude of situations in which they must make choices that can be judged after the fact as right or wrong. A characteristic of every criminal justice profession is that the role entails a public trust that involves power over others. Those who have such power must be especially sensitive to the ethical issues that may arise in their professional lives.

The criminal justice system often is examined using political, organizational, or sociological approaches. Let us shift the lens somewhat and look at the system through an ethics perspective. Asking whether something is legal, for instance, is not necessarily the same question as asking whether something is right. Actors at every stage in the justice process make decisions that can be analyzed and judged as ethical or unethical. Although the decisions faced by these professionals—ranging from legislators who write the laws to correctional professionals who supervise prisoners—may be different, they also have similarities, especially in the use of **discretion** and the presence of authority and power.

Legislators have the power to define behavior as illegal and, therefore, punishable. They also have the power to set the amount of punishment. They criminalize behavior usually because it threatens public safety but sometimes also employ moral definitions for deciding which behaviors should be legal and which should be illegal. "Protection of public morality" is the rationale for a number of laws, including those involving drugs, gambling, and prostitution. How do legislators use their great discretion to balance the rights of *all* people? Further, how do criminal justice leaders guide their subordinates in implementing the laws in a fair and just manner? Chapters 4 and 5 explore these questions in more detail.

Police officers, who enforce the laws created by legislators, have a great deal of discretionary power. For instance, they have

1. the power to deprive people of their liberty (through arrest),
2. the power to decide which individuals to investigate and perhaps target for undercover operations, and
3. the power to issue a ticket or provide "mercy" and let a driver off with a warning.

Police serve as the interface between the awesome power of the state and the citizenry governed. In some countries police operate as a fearsome coercive force for a controlling political body. In the United States a small number of people believe that our police operate in a similar way; however, we enjoy constitutional protections against untrammeled police power, and police act as the guardians of the law, not merely enforcers for those in power. In Chapters 7, 8 and 9 the ethical use of police discretion is discussed in more detail.

Prosecutors probably face the least public scrutiny of all criminal justice professionals—which is ironic because they possess a great deal of discretion in deciding who and how to prosecute.

1. They decide which charges to pursue and which to drop.
2. They decide which cases to take to a grand jury.
3. They decide how to prosecute a case and whether to pursue the death penalty in homicide cases.
4. They make decisions about the types of crimes to pursue, which affects police officers' enforcement decisions.

Although prosecutors have ethical duties to pursue "justice" rather than conviction, some critics argue that, at times, their decision making seems to be influenced by politics or factors other than the goal of justice.

Judges also possess incredible power, typically employed through decision making in the following areas:

1. Denying or accepting plea bargains.
2. Decisions regarding rules of evidence.
3. Decisions about sentencing.

Chapters 10 and 11 explore the ethical issues of legal professionals in the criminal justice system.

Finally, correctional officials have the following immense powers over the lives of some citizens.

1. Probation officers make recommendations in pre-sentence reports and violation reports that affect whether an individual goes to prison.
2. Prison officials decide to award or take away "good time," and they may punish an inmate with segregation; both types of decisions affect the individual's liberty.
3. Correctional officers make daily decisions that affect the life and health of the prisoners they supervise.
4. Parole officials decide when to file a violation report, as well as make less serious decisions regarding the parolee's life.

In short, all correctional professionals have a great deal of discretion over the lives of those they control. The ethical issues of correctional professionals are discussed in Chapters 12, 13 and 14.

Although the professionals discussed face different dilemmas, they also have the following common elements:

1. *They each have discretion, that is, the power to make a decision.* Although the specific decisions are different, they all involve power over others and the potential deprivation of life, liberty, or property.

2. *They each have the duty of enforcing the law.* Although this concept is obvious with police, it is also clear that each of the professionals mentioned has a basic duty to uphold and enforce all laws; they serve the law in their professional lives.

3. *They must accept that their duty is to protect the constitutional safeguards that are the cornerstone of our legal system—specifically, due process and equal protection.* Due process protects each of us from error in any governmental deprivation of life, liberty, or property. We recognize the right of government to control and even to punish, but we have certain protections against arbitrary or unlawful use of that power. Due process protects us against such abuses. We also expect that the power of our government will be used fairly and in an unbiased manner. Equal protection should ensure that what happens to us is not determined by the color of our skin, our gender, nationality, or the religion we practice. Laws are for everyone, and the protection of the law extends to all of us. Although a fair amount of evidence indicates that different treatment does exist, the ideal of equal protection is an essential element of our legal system and should be an operating principle for everyone working in this system.

4. *They are **public servants**.* Their salaries come from the public purse. Public servants possess more than a job; they have taken on special duties involving the public trust. Individuals such as legislators, public officials, police officers, judges, and prosecutors are either elected or appointed guardians of the public's interests. Arguably, they must be held to *higher standards* than those they guard or govern. Temptations are many, and, unfortunately, we find examples of *double standards*, in which public servants take advantage of their positions for special favors, rather than *higher* standards of exemplary behavior.

Obviously, the law governs many of the decisions that public servants make, but because of the discretion at every step of the criminal justice process, the possibility of an unethical use of such discretion remains. Understanding the ethical issues involved in one's profession might help to guide such discretion and prevent abuse. Therefore, all professionals in the criminal justice field must be sensitive to ethical issues. These issues may involve their relationships with citizens and others over whom they have power, their relationships with their agency, or their relationships with one another. The Quote and Query box gives the qualities of public servants. Box 1.1, "Principles of Public Service Ethics," considers the ethical duties of public servants.

QUOTE AND QUERY

Part of what is needed [for public servants] is a public sense of what Madison meant by wisdom and good character: balanced perception and integrity. Integrity means wholeness in public and private life consisting of habits of justice, temperance, courage, compassion, honesty, fortitude, and disdain for self-pity.

Delattre, 1989: 78–83.

How do you define integrity? Do you feel it is necessary that public servants be better than the rest of us?

BOX 1.1 | PRINCIPLES OF PUBLIC SERVICE ETHICS

1. *Public service.* Public servants should treat their office as a public trust, using the power and resources of public office only to advance public interests and not to attain personal benefit or pursue any other private interest incompatible with the public good.
2. *Objective judgment.* Public servants should employ independent objective judgment in performing their duties, deciding all matters on the merits, free from avoidable conflicts of interest and both real and apparent improper influences.
3. *Accountability.* Public servants should ensure that government is conducted openly, efficiently, equitably, and honorably in a manner that permits the citizenry to make informed judgments and hold government officials accountable.
4. *Democratic leadership.* Public servants should honor and respect the principles and spirit of representative democracy and set a positive example of good citizenship by scrupulously observing the letter and spirit of laws and rules.
5. *Respectability.* Public servants should safeguard public confidence in the integrity of government by being honest, fair, caring, and respectful, and by avoiding conduct creating the appearance of impropriety or that is otherwise unbefitting a public official.

Source: Adapted from Josephson Institute of Ethics, 2005.

Felkenes (1987: 26) explained why the study of ethics is important for criminal justice professionals.

1. Professionals are recognized as such in part because [a] "profession" normally includes a set of ethical requirements as part of its meaning....Professionalism among all actors at all levels of the criminal justice system depends upon their ability to administer policy effectively in a morally and ethically responsible manner.
2. Training in critical ethics helps to develop analytical skills and reasoning abilities needed to understand the pragmatic and theoretical aspects of the criminal justice system.
3. Criminal justice professionals should be able to recognize quickly the ethical consequences of various actions, and the moral principles involved.
4. Ethical considerations are central to decisions involving discretion, force, and due process which require people to make enlightened moral judgments.
5. Ethics is germane to most management and policy decisions concerning such penal issues as rehabilitation, deterrence, and just deserts.
6. Ethical considerations are essential aspects of criminal justice research.

In answer to a similar question, Braswell (1996/2002: 8) explained the following five goals of a study of ethics.

1. Become aware of and open to ethical issues.
2. Begin developing critical thinking skills.
3. Become more personally responsible.
4. Understand how the criminal justice system is engaged in a process of coercion.
5. Develop **wholesight** (which roughly means exploring with one's heart as well as one's mind).

The comprehensive nature of these two lists requires few additions; however, we also could note that individuals who ignore ethics do so at their peril. They may find themselves sliding down a slippery slope of behaviors that threaten their career and personal well-being. Even if their actions are not discovered, many people suffer from personal crises when their actions are in conflict with their conscience. Three basic points are reiterated below.

1. We study ethics because criminal justice is uniquely involved in coercion, which means there are many and varied opportunities to abuse such power.
2. Almost all criminal justice professionals are public servants and, thus, owe special duties to the public they serve.
3. We study ethics to sensitize students to ethical issues and provide tools to help identify and resolve the ethical dilemmas that they may face in their professional lives.

DEFINING TERMS

The words **morals** and **ethics** are often used in daily conversations. For example, when public officials use their offices for personal profit or when politicians accept bribes from special interest groups, they are described as unethical. When an individual does a good deed, engages in charitable activities or personal sacrifice, or takes a stand against wrongdoing, we might describe that individual as a moral person. Often, the terms *morals* and *ethics* are used interchangeably. This makes sense because they both come from similar root meanings. The Greek word *ethos* pertains to custom (behavioral practices) or character, and *morals* is a Latin-based word with a similar meaning.

MORALS AND ETHICS

Morals and morality refer to what is judged as good conduct. (Immorality refers to bad conduct.) The term *moral* also is used to describe someone who has the capacity to make value judgments and discern right from wrong (Souryal, 1992: 12). The term *ethics* refers to the study and analysis of what constitutes good or bad conduct (Barry, 1985: 5; Sherman, 1981: 8).

There are several branches, or schools, of ethics.

1. **Meta-ethics** is the discipline that investigates the meaning of ethical systems and whether they are relative or are universal, and are self-constructed or are independent of human creation.
2. **Normative ethics** determines what people ought to do and defines moral duties based on ethical systems or other means of analysis.
3. **Applied ethics** is the application of ethical principles to specific issues.
4. **Professional ethics** is an even more specific type of applied ethics relating to the behavior of certain professions or groups.

To many people, ethics has come to mean the definition of specific behaviors as right and wrong within a profession. Often, in common usage, *morality* is used to speak of the total person, or the sum of a person's actions in every sphere of life, and *ethics* is used to refer to behaviors relating to a profession and is an analysis of behavior relevant to a certain profession. For instance, the medical profession follows the Hippocratic Oath, a declaration of rules and principles of conduct for doctors to follow in their daily practices; it dictates appropriate behavior and goals. In fact, most professions have their own set of ethical standards or canons of ethics.

Even though professional ethics typically restricts attention to areas of behavior relevant to the profession, these can be fairly inclusive and enter into what we might consider the private life of the individual. For instance, doctors are judged harshly if they engage in romantic relationships with their patients, as are professors if they become involved with students. These rules usually are included in codes of ethics for these professions. We are very much aware of how politicians' private behavior can affect their career in politics. When politicians are embroiled in controversial love affairs or are exposed as spouse abusers, such a revelation has a definite effect on their future. Clearly, in professions involving the public trust, such as politics, education, and the clergy, there is a thin line between one's private life and one's public life.

For our purposes it does not make a great deal of difference whether we use the formal or colloquial definitions of *morals* and *ethics*. This text is an applied ethics text, in that we will be concerned with what is defined as right and wrong behavior in the professions relevant to the criminal justice system and how people in these professions make decisions in the course of their careers. It also is a professional ethics text, because we are concerned primarily with professional ethics in criminal justice.

MAKING MORAL JUDGMENTS

We make moral or ethical judgments all the time: "Abortion is wrong." "Capital punishment is just." "It's good to give to charity." "It's wrong to hit your spouse." These are all judgments of good and bad behavior. We also make choices that can be judged as right or wrong. Should you call-in sick to your boss, even though you aren't sick, to get a day in the sun? Should you give back extra change that a clerk gave you by mistake? Should you tell a friend that her husband is having an affair even though he asked you not to tell?

Not all behaviors involve questions of ethics. To draw the boundaries of our ethical discussion more specifically, we need to know which behavioral decisions might be judged under ethical standards. Decisions that can be judged involve four elements: (1) acts that are (2) human, and (3) of free will (4) that affect others.

Act   First of all, some act must be present to judge. For instance, we are concerned with the *act* of stealing or the *act* of contributing to charity, rather than an idle thought that stealing a lot of money would enable us to buy a sailboat or a vague intention to be more generous. We are not necessarily concerned with how people feel or what they think about a particular action unless it has some bearing on what they do. The intention or motive behind a behavior is an important component of that behavior. For instance, in ethical formalism (which we will discuss in Chapter 2), one must know the intent of an action to be able to judge it as moral or immoral, but one also must have some action to examine before making a moral judgment.

WALKING THE WALK

Scott Waddle was the captain of the *U.S.S. Greenville* in 2001, a former Eagle Scout whose career in the Navy saw a steady progression of successes resulting in his command of the *Greenville*. A tireless promoter of the Navy and the giant submarine he captained, Waddle sent autographed pictures of the sub to schoolchildren, and he enthusiastically participated in the "distinguished visitor" program, which allowed civilians to accompany the submarine crew on cruises.

During one of these public relations cruises, on February 9, 2001, the submarine captain gave the order for an "emergency blow," a maneuver in which the submarine comes up out of the depths at great speed, breaking the surface of the water like a breaching whale before settling back onto the surface. In a tragic accident, the probabilities of which boggle the mind, the submarine came up under a Japanese trawler, smashing it to bits and sending the crew who survived the initial impact into the ocean. The accident killed nine people and cost more than $100 million in damages and compensation costs.

The ensuing investigation and testimony determined that the person in charge of the radar deferred to Waddle's visual inspection of the surface and didn't tell him of a sonar contact that was within 4,000 yards. Waddle and other officers who manned the periscope had scanned the surface too quickly and missed the small ship in the turbulent swells. Testimony indicated that after the crash, Waddle grimly kept the crew focused and announced over the intercom. "Remember what you saw, remember what happened, do not embellish," he instructed. "Tell the truth and maintain your dignity."

Against his lawyer's advice, Waddle gave up his right to silence in the military tribunal that was held to assess whether to court martial him. He was reported to have said, "This court needs to hear from me—It's the right thing to do." In his testimony he refused to shift responsibility to others and accepted all blame for the accident. He said, "I'm solely responsible for this truly tragic accident, and for the rest of my life I will have to live with the horrible consequences."

One of the fathers of the Japanese fishermen was sitting in the room when Waddle testified, and his anger was overcome by Waddle's tearful apology. Waddle ultimately accepted a letter of reprimand that ended his career with the Navy. Then he went to Japan to apologize to the victims' families personally.

In the aftermath of his decision to testify and not fight to keep his career, Waddle reported that he considered suicide, but he moved past his shame and guilt. Today he gives speeches on the experience and advises others of the importance of dealing with failure honestly, one of which was to a Boy Scout awards ceremony in Chattanooga, Tennessee. Speaking to the 500 attendees, he said that the values of honesty and responsibility he learned in Scouting helped him make the decisions he did during the aftermath of the accident.

Sources: "Hight, 2005: A11; Putman, 2008; "Waddle's PR Savvy," *Newsweek*, April 2, 2001; retrieved on 3/19/2008 from http://timesfreepress.com/news/2008/feb/27/retired-navy-officer-reflects-honesty-responsibility; http://www.accessmylibrary.com/coms2/summary_0286-10978509_ITM

Only Human Acts Second, judgments of moral or ethical behavior are directed specifically to human behavior. A dog that bites is not considered immoral or evil, although we may criticize pet owners who allow their dogs the opportunity to bite. Nor do we consider drought, famine, floods, or other natural disasters immoral even though they result in death, destruction, and misery. Philosophers widely believe that only humans can be moral (or immoral) because of our capacity to reason. Because only humans have the capacity to be "good"—which involves a voluntary, rational decision and subsequent action—only humans, of all members of the animal kingdom, have the capacity to be "bad."

There is much more to this argument of course, and some argue that some mammals show moral traits, if not moral sensibilities. Shermer (2004: 27–28), for instance, recognizes a pre-moral sense in animals, including shame or guilt in dogs, food sharing in bats, comforting and cooperative behaviors in chimpanzees, life-saving behaviors in dolphins and elephants, and defending behaviors in whales. Mammals, especially apes, monkeys, dolphins, and whales, exhibit attachment and bonding, cooperation and mutual aid, sympathy and empathy, direct and indirect reciprocity, altruism and reciprocal altruism, conflict resolution and peacemaking, deception and deception detection, community concern and caring about what others think, and awareness of and response to the social rules of the group.

Does this mean, then, that these mammals can be considered moral or immoral? Although they may be placed on the continuum of moral awareness closer to humans than other species, one could also argue that they, at least as far as we know, do not possess the moral rationality of humans. They do not have the ability to think through their actions and freely choose to be good or bad.

Free Will   In addition to limiting discussions of morality to human behavior, we usually further restrict our discussion to behavior that stems from free will and free action. Culpability is not assigned to persons who are not sufficiently aware of the world around them to be able to decide rationally what is good or bad. The two groups traditionally exempt from responsibility in this sense are the young and the insane.

Arguably, we do not judge the morality of their behavior because we do not believe that they have the capacity to reason and, therefore, cannot choose to be moral or immoral. Although we may punish a two-year-old for hitting a baby, we do so to educate or socialize, not to punish, as we would an older child or adult. We incapacitate the mentally ill to protect ourselves against their violence and strange behavior, but we consider them sick, not evil. This is true even if their actual behavior is indistinguishable from that of other individuals we do punish. For example, a murder may result in a death sentence or a hospital commitment, depending on whether the person is judged to be sane or insane, responsible or not responsible.

Affects Others   Finally, we usually discuss moral or immoral behavior only in cases in which the behavior significantly affects others. For instance, throwing a rock off a bridge would be neither good nor bad unless you could possibly hit or were aiming at a person below. If no one is there, your behavior is neutral. If someone is below, however, you might endanger that person's life, so your behavior is judged as "bad."

All the moral dilemmas we will discuss in this book involve at least two parties, and the decision to be made affects at least one other individual in every case.

In reality, it is difficult to think of an action that does not affect others, however indirectly. Even self-destructive behavior is said to harm the people who love us and who would be hurt by such actions.

We sense that these elements are important in judging morality when we hear the common rationale of those who, when judged as doing something wrong, protest, "But nobody was hurt!" or "I didn't mean to." Indeed, even a hermit living alone on a desert island may engage in immoral or unethical actions. Whether he wants to be or not, the hermit is part of human society; therefore, some people would say that even he might engage in actions that could be judged immoral if they degrade or threaten the future of humankind, such as committing suicide or polluting the ocean.

One's actions toward nature also might be defined as immoral, so relevant actions include not only actions done to people but also to animals and to nature. To abuse or exploit animals can be defined as immoral. Judgments can be made against cockfighting, dog racing, laboratory experimentation on animals, and hunting. The growing area of environmental ethics reflects increasing concern for the future of the planet. The rationale for environmental ethics may be that any actions that harm the environment affect all humans. It also might be justified by the belief that humankind is a part of nature—not superior to it—and part of natural law should be to protect, not exploit, our world.

Thus far, we know that morality and ethics concern the judgment of behavior as right or wrong. Furthermore, such judgments are directed only at voluntary human behavior that affects other people, the Earth, and living things. We can further restrict our inquiries regarding ethics to those behavioral decisions that are relevant to one's profession in the criminal justice system. Discussions regarding the ethics of police officers, for instance, would concern issues such as the following:

1. Whether to take gratuities
2. Whether to cover up the wrongdoing of a fellow officer
3. Whether to sleep on duty
4. Whether to call-in sick when one wants to play golf or go fishing
5. Whether to lie on an expense sheet.

Discussions regarding the ethics of defense attorneys might revolve around the following:

1. Whether to devote more effort to private cases than appointed cases
2. Whether to allow perjury
3. Whether to attack the character of a victim in order to defend a client.

Of course, all of these actions affect other people, as do most actions taken as a professional. Review the "Inventory of Ethical Issues" (Box 1.2). Notice that the ethical issues fall into three major categories:

1. Effects on citizenry
2. Effects on other employees
3. Effects on one's organization

BOX 1.2	INVENTORY OF ETHICAL ISSUES

The Individual and the Organization
work ethic (a day's work for a day's pay)
petty theft of supplies or cash
overtime abuse
gifts and gratuities
falsifying reports
misuse of sick days
personal use of supplies or equipment

The Organization and Employees
sexual or racial harassment by supervisors
discouraging honest criticism or feedback
arbitrary or unfair decisions
inadequate compensation
inadequate training
unrealistic or inappropriate demands
putting employees in unnecessary danger

The Individual and Other Employees
backstabbing and lack of support
gossip
sexual or racial harassment
lying to cover up blame
taking credit for others' work

The Individual and the Public
misuse of authority
inadequate performance of duty
sexual, racial, ethnic harassment
special treatment
lack of expertise (not keeping up with training)
malfeasance or misfeasance of duties
rudeness or incivility

DUTIES

Another comment we should make about behavior and morality is that philosophers distinguish between moral duties and superogatories. **Duties** refer to those actions that an individual must perform to be considered moral. For instance, everyone might agree that one has a duty to support one's parents if able to do so; one has a duty to obey the law (unless it is an immoral law); and a police officer has a moral and ethical duty to tell the truth on a police report. Duties are what you must do in order to be good.

Other actions, considered **superogatories**, are commendable but not required. A Good Samaritan who jumps into a river to save a drowning person, risking his or her own life to do so, has performed a superogatory action. Those who stood on the bank received no moral condemnation, because risking one's life is above and beyond anyone's moral duty. Of course, if one can help save a life with no great risk to oneself, a moral duty does exist in that situation.

Police officers have an ethical duty to get involved when others do not. Consider the 2001 attack on the World Trade Centers. One of the most moving images of that tragedy was of police officers and firefighters running toward danger while others ran away. This professional duty to put oneself in harm's way is why we revere and pay homage to these public servants. Many civilians also put themselves in harm's way in this disaster, and because they had no professional duty to do so, they could be said to be performing superogatory actions.

There are also **imperfect duties**, general duties that one should uphold but do not have a specific application as to when or how. For instance, most ethical systems support a general duty of generosity but have no specific duty demanding a certain type or manner of generosity. Another imperfect duty might be to be honest. Generally, one should be honest, but, as we will see in Chapter 2, some ethical systems allow for exceptions to the general rule.

VALUES

Values are defined as elements of desirability, worth, or importance. Values and judgments of worth are often equated with moral judgments of goodness. We see that both can be distinguished from factual judgments, which can be empirically verified. Note the difference between these factual judgments:

1. "He is lying" and
2. "It is raining"

and these value judgments:

1. "She is a good woman" and
2. "That was a wonderful day."

The last two judgments are more similar to moral judgments. "Facts" are capable of scientific proof, but values and moral judgments are not.

Some writers think that value judgments and moral judgments are indistinguishable because neither can be verified (Mackie, 1977; Margolis, 1971). Some also think that values and morals are relativistic and individual. These people have no universal values; their values are all subjective. Values, then, are merely opinions (Mackie, 1977: 22–24). In this view, because they are only opinions, no value is more important than any other value.

In contrast, others believe that not all values are equal, and that some values, such as honesty, are always more important than values such as pleasure. Are values such as charity and altruism "more important" or "better" than pleasure or wealth? This question is related to a later discussion in Chapter 2 concerning whether ethics are relative or absolute.

Discussions concerning values imply a choice or a judgment. If, for instance, you were confronted with an opportunity to cheat on an exam, your values of academic success and honesty would be directly at odds. Values and morals are similar, although values merely indicate *relative* importance, whereas morals prescribe or proscribe behavior. The value of honesty is conceptually distinct from the moral rule against lying.

Individual values form value systems. All people prioritize certain things that they consider important in life. Behavior is generally consistent with values. For instance, some individuals believe that financial success is more important than family or health. In this case, we may assume that their behavior will reflect the importance of that value and that these persons will be workaholics, spending more time at work than with family and endangering their health with long hours, stress, and lack of exercise. Others place a higher priority on religious faith, wisdom, honesty, and/or independence than financial success or status.

Most of us live our lives in rough accordance with our values, but we often live our lives without taking a close look at the value system that influences our behavior.

Can you identify any decisions you have made recently that were based on your value system?

This concept of a value system is fairly explicit in Messner and Rosenfeld's (1994) theory of crime. In their explanation of why the United States has a higher rate of violent crime than other Western countries, they propose that the U.S. value system, which emphasizes consumerism over family and money over honesty, creates an environment in which crime results. In the United States success is defined almost exclusively by the accumulation of material goods, not by doing "good." Because behavior is influenced by one's value system, individuals who place material success over any other value will behave dishonestly or even violently in the pursuit of such goods.

An explicit value system is a part of every ethical system, as we will see in Chapter 2. Certain values hold special relevance to the criminal justice system. Privacy, freedom, public order, justice, duty, and loyalty are all values that will come up again in later discussions. The values of life, respect for the person, and survival can be found in all ethical systems.

MORALITY AND THE LAW

Laws govern many aspects of our behavior. **Laws,** in the form of statutes and ordinances, tell us how to drive, how to operate our business, and what we can and cannot do in public and even in private. They are the formal, written rules of society. Yet, they are not comprehensive in defining moral behavior. There is a law against hitting one's mother (assault) but no law against financially abandoning her, yet both are considered morally wrong. We have laws against "bad" behavior, such as burglarizing a house or embezzling from our employer, but we have few laws prescribing "good" behavior, such as helping a victim or contributing to a charity.

The exception to this consists of **Good Samaritan laws**, which exist in some states and are common in Europe. These laws make it a crime to pass by an accident scene or witness a crime without rendering assistance.

Some actions prohibited by law are thought to be private decisions of the individual and not especially wrong or harmful. In the past, many people objected to sodomy laws and other laws regulating sexual behavior between consenting adults because they believed that private behavior was outside the parameters of social control. Eventually, in *Lawrence v. Texas,* 539 U.S. 558 (2003), the Supreme Court agreed that no state could criminalize homosexuality between consenting adults. When laws prohibit behaviors that are not universally condemned, such as laws prohibiting alcohol, drugs, gambling and prostitution, enforcement is more subject to criticism and, not incidentally, more prone to corruption because of the greater ability to rationalize under-enforcement or preferential treatment.

Consider, for instance, the argument that organized crime grew tremendously during Prohibition and that an unknown number of law enforcement officers accepted bribes or were involved in protection rackets. Some argue that the same scenario occurred during the war on drugs. The rationalization of authorities who are inclined to accept protection money or bribes is that the offenders are engaged in providing a commodity that the public desires.

Among the laws of the past that were or are now considered immoral are

1. the internment of Japanese Americans during World War II
2. "Jim Crow" laws before the civil rights era
3. pre–Civil War laws that mandated the return of runaway slaves to their owners.

More recently, legal authorities have authorized forms of interrogation that many argue constitute torture and are morally and ethically wrong, even if lawful.

An important question in the study of ethics is whether one can be a good person while obeying a bad law. Civil disobedience occurs when people voluntarily disobey what they consider to be an unjust or immoral law. In Chapters 4 and 5 we discuss morality and immorality in relation to law and the concept of justice.

A crime is composed of the following three elements:

1. An *actus reus*
2. A *mens rea* (with concurrence between the two)
3. Causation

The *actus reus* is the physical act that is defined as the crime. Further, the act must have been the result of the defendant's own volition. If, for instance, the act was performed while sleepwalking or when the person was not fully conscious, there was no *actus reus*. The *mens rea* is the mental element involved in the crime. Different levels of culpability are based on the level of intent versus lack of intent for the act and the consequence. The four levels of legal culpability are:

1. negligence
2. recklessness
3. knowing
4. intentional (or purposive).

Causation is when the *actus reus* creates the result prohibited or described by the law. **Proximate cause** is the law's attempt to use common sense to limit a defendant's culpability. Even if the defendant's act was the "but for" cause of the end result, the defendant will not be held responsible if what occurs was not predictable or foreseeable. For instance, if the defendant's assault puts the victim in the hospital, and then the person is killed in an accidental fire, even though death ultimately resulted from the assault, the defendant is not guilty of homicide because the assault was not the proximate cause of the death (a foreseeable or predictable result). But if the victim dies from an infection acquired in the hospital, the defendant would be held legally culpable because it was foreseeable. What about moral culpability? Is it the same?

CRIMINAL CULPABILITY/MORAL CULPABILITY

The law recognizes different levels of responsibility based on *mens rea*, or the mental state of the offender. First-degree homicide, for instance, requires proof of **intent**, whereas second-degree homicide requires only evidence of **knowing** that one is performing the *actus reus* of the crime. Crimes that require only evidence of **negligence** (when the defendant should have known the danger of the act) or **recklessness** (when the defendant did know the danger of the act) have less severe punishments attached to them because the level of culpability, fault, or blame is less. Careless actions, such as driving while intoxicated or killing someone while playing with a loaded weapon, are judged as less "bad" than actions performed with deliberation and intent. An individual who has weighed the consequences and knows the outcome and all the ramifications of the action and then proceeds has greater legal culpability than someone who has proceeded without such deliberation, albeit with a negligent disregard for potential or probable consequences.

So, too, in discussions of moral culpability, we are interested in the mental state of the person: Did he or she mean to do the act, or was it an accident? Possibly one's mental state prevents the prosecutor from considering any level of guilt. If one is found "incompetent to stand trial," this means that there has been a legal determination that the individual is incapable of understanding the proceedings and assisting in his or her own defense. We have a long legal tradition of requiring the defendant to be at least minimally competent and rational, and we recognize different levels of culpability.

Historically, two groups have been considered "excused" from criminal culpability: the insane and juveniles. This is because of a belief that individuals in these groups are not rational; they cannot weigh the consequences of their actions and, therefore, should not be held accountable. Thus, even those who are found competent to stand trial may be acquitted by reason of insanity. Or they may not. We continue to imprison and even execute those who show obvious signs of mental illness, despite our legal tradition of holding only "rational" people legally culpable.

The other group that traditionally has been excused from criminal culpability consists of the young. Attitudes toward the **age of reason** and when a child is said to have reached this age seem to be changing. In the early twentieth century, there was a concerted effort to remove juveniles from the adult legal system and to create a legal system for juveniles that would include protection as part of its mission. The system would adhere to a *parens patriae* model (standing in the stead of a parent) rather than act purely as punisher. This philosophy was based on the belief that the juvenile acted with less rationality than the adult. Today that trend seems to be reversing itself. States have reduced the age at which a child is considered to be an adult, have developed procedures allowing youngsters to be remanded to adult courts for trial and sentencing, and have allowed juveniles, even though sentenced in the juvenile system, to be held in facilities for adults.

Insane persons and juveniles traditionally have been excused because they lack the ability to weigh their actions. Some argue that others, too, are not fully responsible for their actions. For instance, the myriad "abuse excuses" dominate the legal landscape today. These defenses argue that the defendant might have committed the crime but did so because of some compelling reason or excuse, such as those listed below.

1.   They were battered or abused.
2.   They suffered from post-traumatic stress syndrome.

IN THE NEWS | A SCORNED WOMAN

In Houston, Clara Harris, an upper-middle-class professional woman, found her husband at a hotel with his mistress after he had sworn to her that he had broken off the affair. She was devastated because the couple had young twins and she had attempted to save her marriage by changing her appearance and deemphasizing her career. She fought with the mistress in the hotel lobby and was dragged off the woman and pushed down by her husband. Then, in the parking lot of the hotel where the confrontation occurred, in front of many witnesses and with his daughter in the car, she ran over her husband and killed him.

Would you find this woman guilty of first-degree murder, second-degree murder, or some other crime? What punishment does she deserve?

Source: Associated Press, 2005a.

---

3. They experienced harassment.
4. They were under the influence of alcohol or drugs.
5. They were unduly influenced by music, television, or movies.
6. They were affected by sugar or food additives.
7. They were driven to desperate acts by the actions of a spouse.

Dershowitz (1994) has argued that we have gone too far in allowing a multitude of excuses for criminal behavior—a conclusion that is somewhat ironic because, as a criminal defense attorney, he has helped introduce some of these defenses. The "In the News" box illustrates the "scorned woman" defense. Should there be consideration of the mental anguish that the cheating husband caused to his wife? Is she less blameworthy because she was upset?

Although they are related, the moral culpability of an actor is not necessarily equivalent to legal culpability. A person might not be guilty of a crime and still might be considered morally culpable. Alternatively, one might be guilty of a crime and be considered morally blameless. A dilemma later in this chapter involves a loving mother who killed her suffering sons. Is she legally culpable but morally blameless, both legally and morally culpable, or some other combination?

We are all bound by limitations (or opportunities) of birth and circumstance. If we were to analyze moral culpability on the basis of life choices, it might be that, because of their respective life positions, some people who commit serious crimes are less blameworthy than others who come from better backgrounds and commit less serious crimes.

Do all people truly have freedom of choice? It is illegal for a rich man or a poor man to steal a loaf of bread, but a rich man doesn't have to, nor does he have to engage in armed robbery to obtain goods. But he might commit tax evasion, toxic waste dumping, or embezzlement. Who is more culpable, the executives of a company such as Enron who were paid extremely high salaries but broke the law to make even more money, or the burglar who has no job and steals your television set? Is there ever a good enough reason for committing a crime? Also remember that the idea of moral culpability may be quite different from legal responsibility. We will explore some of these concepts more fully in Chapters 4 and 5.

REGULATIONS, STANDARDS, AND GUIDELINES

In addition to laws, we have examples of behavioral rules that lead to a judgment of wrong and, in most cases, some form of punishment.

1. **Regulations** govern the activities of occupations from physician to plumber and organizations from governmental agencies to private clubs. Regulations typically come from a governmental authority and often specify sanctions for noncompliance.
2. **Standards** may come from private or public bodies and often are used as a basis for some type of accreditation.
3. **Guidelines** may come from a professional group and usually are recommendations rather than directions.

Distinctions can be made among these terms, although they often are used interchangeably. These rules for behavior usually do not carry the formal sanctions of criminal law, but some may carry civil liabilities.

Most regulations are set by state and federal governments. For instance, consider the following:

1. The Food and Drug Administration (FDA) prescribes certain procedures and rules for pharmaceutical companies to follow in developing, testing, and distributing drugs.
2. The Environmental Protection Agency (EPA) watches over industry to make sure that safe methods for disposal of hazardous wastes are implemented.
3. The Occupational Safety and Health Agency (OSHA) sets safety standards for the workplace to avoid or reduce the number of workplace injuries.

Noncompliance with standards and regulations is not equated with immoral behavior as readily as is criminal lawbreaking. Although fines may be levied against the construction supervisor who ignores Occupational Safety and Health Agency standards or the automaker who violates standards of the Consumer Safety Board, these people ordinarily are not considered criminals even when their actions result in injury or death. This concept is illustrated in the Quote and Query box.

QUOTE AND QUERY

Why do 26 dead miners amount to a "disaster" and six dead suburbanites a "mass murder?" "Murder" suggests a murderer, and "disaster" suggests the work of impersonal forces. But if over 1,000 safety violations had been found in the mine— three the day before the first explosion—was no one responsible for failing to eliminate those hazards? And if someone could have prevented the hazards and did not, does that person not bear responsibility for the deaths of 26 men? Is he less evil because he did not want them to die, although he chose to leave them in jeopardy? Is he not a murderer, perhaps even a mass murderer?

Reiman, 1984: 23.

Do you think that employers who put their employees in harm's way should be prosecuted for manslaughter?

When rules or standards are violated, criminal charges may be imposed. For instance, if a company blatantly violates safety regulations by forcing employees to work with toxic chemicals, company officials may be charged with negligent manslaughter if a worker dies. This situation is extremely rare, however, and there is usually a great deal of difference between the sanctions related to a violation of regulations and criminal lawbreaking. Some of the individuals who are caught and punished are truly surprised that their actions could result in criminal punishment. They also typically do not consider themselves to be criminals, even after they put on a prison uniform.

In addition to guidelines and standards, professions usually have a code of ethics or set of professional rules to educate and encourage their members to perform in accordance with an ideal of behavior. These guidelines may be general or specific. For instance, lawyers have extensive written rules, but some other professions have only a one-page code of ethics. Laws, standards, regulations, guidelines, and codes of ethics are all designed to control and guide behavior.

It is interesting to observe that regulations and rules for behavior often seem to expand in inverse relation to the practiced ethics of a specific profession or organization. Frequently, when a breakdown in ethical behavior is detected, there is an attempt to bring people back in line by the use of rules. In any profession, though, the most effective ethical guides would seem not to be those that specify behavior but, rather, those that are consistent with and support an organizational ideal.

People can find many ways of violating the spirit of an administrative rule while complying with its exact wording. There always seem to be politicians who engage in behavior involving conflicts of interest but argue that they are not breaking any laws, and lawyers who get around their ethical responsibilities by complying with the letter but not the spirit of the rules. Decision makers in organizations often think they must give employees extensive lists of rules. In an office these may include injunctions not to take supplies, not to make personal telephone calls, and not to spend more than fifteen minutes on breaks. Enforcing rules is very different from promoting an ethical standard of honesty and integrity in the workplace. Where ethical standards are nonexistent, multitudinous rules of behavior are unlikely to eliminate wrongdoing.

MORALITY AND BEHAVIOR

One of the most difficult things to understand about human behavior is the disjunction between moral beliefs and behavior. We all can attest to the reality that believing something is wrong does not always prevent us from doing it. Often, we engage in acts that we believe are bad, such as lying, stealing, and cheating. In any group of people (such as a college class), a majority will have engaged in some type of wrongful act at least once.

Why do people engage in behavior that they believe to be wrong? Criminology attempts to explain why people commit unlawful acts, but the larger question is this: Why do any of us engage in wrongful acts? Psychological experiments show that a large percentage of schoolchildren will cheat when given the opportunity to do so, even though they know it is wrong (e.g., Lickona, 1976). In a later chapter, we will review police integrity stings revealing that even police officers sometimes steal or keep things that don't belong to them. Some looters in New Orleans after

Hurricane Katrina may have been stealing food as a matter of necessity, but many others exploited the natural disaster to take what they knew wasn't theirs. Theories abound endorsing everything from learning and role modeling to biological predisposition, but we still haven't answered fundamental questions of causation. Even with all the scientific and philosophical attempts to explain human action, we are left with troubling questions when we read or hear about people who kill, steal, or otherwise offend our sense of morality. Evil is still one of the great mysteries of life.

In discussions concerning these questions, basic beliefs about the nature of humankind must be considered. Are people fundamentally bad and held in check only by rules and fear of punishment? Or are people fundamentally good and commit bad acts because of improper upbringing or events that subvert their natural goodness? Or are there fundamentally bad and fundamentally good people who are just "born that way" for no reason? We explore some of these questions in Chapter 3.

ANALYZING ETHICAL DILEMMAS

Ethical discussions in criminal justice focus on issues or dilemmas. **Ethical issues** are broad social questions, often concerning the government's social control mechanisms and the impact on those governed—for example, what laws to pass, what sentences to attach to certain crimes, whether to abolish the death penalty, and whether to build more prisons or use community correctional alternatives. The typical individual does not have much control over these issues. The ethical issues that arise in relation to criminal justice are serious, difficult, and affect people's lives in fundamental ways. These are just a sample of some criminal justice issues that have ethical implications:

1. Decriminalization of soft drugs
2. Megan's Law and other sex-offender registry statutes
3. The death penalty
4. Mandatory DNA registries
5. Three-strikes legislation
6. Racial profiling
7. Law-enforcement corruption
8. Waiver of juveniles to adult courts
9. Citizen oversight committees for police departments
10. The Patriot Act and other challenges to civil liberties in the wake of terrorism.

Periodically we will highlight a criminal justice policy issue in this text to illustrate the relationships among law, policy, and ethics. The Policy Box examines the issue of the medical use of marijuana.

Ethical dilemmas are situations in which one person must make a decision about what to do. Either the choice is unclear or the "right" choice will be difficult because of the costs involved. Ethical dilemmas involve the individual struggling with personal decision making, whereas ethical issues are topics for which one might have an opinion but rarely a chance to take a stand that has much impact (unless one happens to be a Supreme Court judge or a state governor).

At times, one's belief regarding an ethical issue gives rise to a personal dilemma. In 2000, George Ryan, then governor of Illinois, declared a moratorium

POLICY BOX	MEDICAL USE OF MARIJUANA

Periodically, controversy arises over whether marijuana should be legalized for the limited use of pain relief and nausea control for seriously ill individuals, including cancer patients and those individuals suffering from AIDS. Many medical professionals have testified in state and federal hearings that they believe that marijuana is more effective and has fewer side-effects than other forms of legal relief. Others dispute the findings.

Laws: The federal government's drug laws do not make an exception for the medical use of marijuana. California passed a law allowing certain uses of marijuana to be regulated but decriminalized. The Supreme Court held that the federal laws "trumped" California law.

Policy: Federal drug officials made it clear that they would enforce the federal laws against doctors and medical co-ops that distribute the drugs. State officials were upset that the Supreme Court overturned the mandate of the people, but these officials had no power to control federal law enforcement.

Individual ethics: Some people, including doctors, have decided to continue their distribution and use of marijuana. They have utilized their own ethical system to decide that enforcement of the law is wrong in these circumstances, which creates the possibility that they will be arrested for their actions. (See *Raich v. Ashcroft*, 248 F.Supp. 2d 918 [N.D. Cal. 2003].)

on use of the death penalty in his state when at least five individuals on Death Row were exonerated through the use of DNA evidence. One of his last acts as he left office in 2003 was to commute the sentences of all 160 prisoners on Death Row to life without parole.

Governor Ryan faced a difficult personal dilemma because he was in a position to do something about his belief that the death penalty was implemented in a way that could never be just. The strong support *and* strong opposition to his action indicates the depth of his dilemma and the seriousness of the issue. In a sad and ironic footnote to this story, Ryan was indicted and convicted of federal racketeering charges, and sentenced to a six and one-half year sentence in a federal prison. Evidence proved that he had been involved in a system of "sweetheart deals" and backroom bribes selling government contracts since he had been Secretary of State (Schaper, 2007).

Sadly, there are additional examples of public figures whose private lives aren't consistent with their public actions. Elliot Spitzer, governor of New York who was elected on a law-and-order platform, resigned in March of 2008 after it was revealed that he had paid thousands of dollars to prostitutes. Even though he consistently took courageous stands to promote the public good as part of his professional duties, his private decisions led him to break the law and engage in marital infidelity. Then, Lieutenant Governor David Patterson, who stepped in as governor after Spitzer's resignation, admitted that both he and his wife had extramarital affairs, and that he had tried marijuana and cocaine in the 1970s when he was in college. Later it was revealed that he helped his lover get a government job. How professionals make decisions in both their public and private lives is the topic of Chapter 6.

Although most of us do not have the power to commute death sentences or sign laws into effect, we can do something about our beliefs. Writing letters, petitioning our legislators, marching in demonstrations, and working to pass (or overturn) laws are examples of acting on our moral beliefs. Personal ethical dilemmas arise when the individual is forced to choose between two or more behaviors. In applied ethics texts, various authors set out the steps to take when facing ethical dilemmas. For instance, Ruggiero (2004) advises us to study the details of the case, identify the relevant criteria (obligations, ideals, consequences), determine possible courses of action, and decide which is the most ethical.

To be able to analyze ethical dilemmas, one must discover all relevant information. Here are the some steps to clarify the dilemma:

1. Review all the facts. Make sure that one has all the facts that are known—not future predictions, not suppositions, not probabilities.
2. Identify all the potential values of each party that might be relevant; in addition, identify all concepts (things that cannot be proven empirically).
3. Identify all possible moral issues for each party involved, to help us see that sometimes one's own moral or ethical dilemma is caused by others' actions. For instance, a police officer's ethical dilemma when faced with the wrongdoing of a fellow officer is a direct result of that other officer making a bad choice. It is helpful to see all the moral issues involved to be able to address the central issue.
4. Decide what is the most immediate moral or ethical issue facing the individual. This is always a behavior choice, not an opinion. For example, the moral issue of whether abortion should be legalized is quite different from the moral dilemma of whether I should have an abortion if I find myself pregnant. Obviously, one affects the other, but they are conceptually distinct.
5. Resolve the ethical or moral dilemma by using an ethical system or some other means of decision making (these ethical systems are discussed in Chapter 2).

Let us refer to the dilemma, at the beginning of this chapter, of the correctional officer who must decide what to do about the possible beating he observed.

1. This officer has to make sure that he has all the facts. Was the inmate hurt? Did his injuries occur during the time the two other officers were in his cell? Is the officer sure that no one reported it? Would the inmate come forward if he believed that someone would testify against the other two officers, or would he deny the assault (if there was one)? What other facts are important to know? Remember that facts are those things that can be proven; however, this does not necessarily mean that the individual facing the dilemma has the proof.
2. The officer might examine the relevant values. In this situation, one can identify duty, legality, honesty, integrity, safety, protection, loyalty, self-preservation, and trust. Are any other values important to resolve the dilemma? Concepts also are important. They are like values in that they are not susceptible to empirical proof, but they are not necessarily values. Although this dilemma may not have any relevant concepts, others do. For instance, the issue of abortion revolves around the value of life, but it is also a concept in that there is no proof of when life begins or ends (although there are facts regarding

respiration, brain activity, etc.). Many arguments surrounding ethical issues are really arguments about concepts, not necessarily values or ethical judgments.

3. Several ethical issues come into play here. The first is whether the other officers should have entered the prisoner's cell. There is probably an earlier issue involving whatever the prisoner did to warrant the visit. There is obviously the issue of whether the officer should have let off-duty officers into the cell in the first place. Finally, there is the issue of what the officer should do now that he believes an injustice may have taken place.

4. Resolve the immediate dilemma—whether to come forward with the information. For this step, it is helpful to work through Chapter 2 first because one way to resolve ethical dilemmas is to decide on an ethical system. If the officer was a utilitarian, he would weigh the costs and benefits for all concerned in coming forward and in staying quiet. If he followed duty-based ethics (ethical formalism), he would find the answer once he determined his duty.

To resolve any dilemma, think of ethical judgments as a pyramid, as indicated in Figure 1.1. The tip of the Ethical Pyramid is the judgment itself. We make ethical judgments all the time. The moral rules that support such judgments make up the body of the pyramid. Suppose someone were to say, "Capital punishment is wrong." If one asks, "Why is capital punishment wrong?" the answer might take the form of **moral rules**, which are general rules of right and wrong, or value statements. In this case, the rules cited might include the following: One should never take a life. One should preserve life. One should abhor violence. Two wrongs don't make a right. And so on.

These rules, in turn, must be supported by ethical systems, which will be covered in Chapter 2. Some rules, however, are inconsistent with some ethical systems. For instance, "One must always follow the law" may be consistent with ethical formalism but be inconsistent with ethics of care. That is why law is not part of the ethical

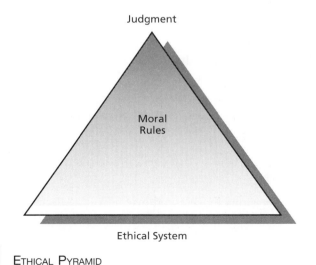

Judgment

Moral
Rules

Ethical System

FIGURE 1.1 | ETHICAL PYRAMID

pyramid. Although most of the time asking the question "Is it against the law?" answers the question of what is right, in some situations the law either is not relevant or it may even be inconsistent with one's ethical system. In the movie *Schlinder's List*, for instance, we commend his lawbreaking as moral courage.

These concepts will be clearer after the ethical systems are described in Chapter 2. Suffice to say for now that ethical judgments always have some rationale behind them. These rationales tend to be consistent with traditional and historical ethical systems. In Chapter 2 we will explore some of these traditional ethical systems and revisit the Ethical Pyramid.

CONCLUSION

In this chapter we defined the terms *morals* and *ethics* as both relating to standards of behavior. We noted why a study of ethics is important to criminal justice professionals. It also was noted that not all behaviors would be subject to ethical judgments—only those that are performed by humans who are acting with free will and that affect others. Professional ethics deals with only those behaviors relevant to one's profession.

We also discussed the relationship between law and ethics and discovered that although there is an overlap, the two are not synonymous. We make ethical judgments (what we consider right and wrong) using rationales derived from historical and traditional ethical systems. These ethical systems will be described in Chapter 2.

This chapter closes with some Review Questions to answer in class or in a journal. These can be helpful to check your understanding of the issues. These are followed by Writing/Discussion Exercises, which have no right or wrong answers and can be the basis for classroom discussions or individual writing assignments. Finally, Ethical Dilemmas are presented to encourage the reader to practice ethical analysis. Working through at least some of these dilemmas using the Ethical Pyramid and applying one or more of the ethical systems described in Chapter 2 will be helpful.

Key Terms

actus reus 15	Good Samaritan laws 14	meta-ethics 7	public servants 5
age of reason 16		moral rules 23	recklessness 16
applied ethics 7	guidelines 18	morals 7	regulations 18
discretion 3	imperfect duties 12	negligence 16	standards 18
duties 12	intent 15	normative ethics 7	superogatories 12
ethical dilemmas 20	knowing 15	*parens patriae* 16	values 13
ethical issues 20	laws 14	professional ethics 7	wholesight 6
ethics 7	*mens rea* 15	proximate cause 15	

Review Questions

1. What are some decisions by criminal justice professionals that may be evaluated under ethical criteria? What do all professionals in the criminal justice system have in common?

2. Discuss Felkenes's reasons for why it is important for criminal justice professionals to study ethics.

3. Define *morals, ethics, values, duties,* and *ethical systems.*

4. What are the four elements that specify the types of behaviors that are judged under ethical criteria?
5. Which groups traditionally have been exempt from legal and moral culpability? Why?
6. What is the difference between duties and superogatories?
7. Do laws cover all moral rules? If your answer is no, explain why.

8. What are the elements of a crime? What are the levels of legal culpability? Do they always equate to moral culpability?
9. Define regulations, standards, and guidelines. Are violations of these rules the same as lawbreaking?
10. What is the difference between an ethical issue and an ethical dilemma? What are the steps in analyzing an ethical dilemma?

Writing/Discussion Exercises

1. Write an essay (or discuss) whether public servants should be held to higher standards than the rest of us. Touch on the following questions in your response: Should we be concerned with a politician who has extra-marital affairs? Drinks to excess? Gambles? Uses drugs? Abuses his or her spouse? What if the person is a police officer? A judge? Should a female police officer be sanctioned for posing naked in a men's magazine, using pieces of her uniform as "props?" Should a probation officer socialize in bars that his or her probationers are likely to frequent? Should a prosecutor be extremely active in a political party and then make decisions regarding targets of "public integrity" investigations of politicians?
2. Write an essay (or discuss) whether anyone should be excused legally and/or morally for his or her behavior. In your response, touch on the following questions: Is a child before the legal age of reason morally culpable for

his or her actions? Why or why not? What should be the age of reason? What are some situations in which the individual cannot be considered rational or, alternatively, is not acting from free will? Can the behavior that results be defined as moral or immoral? What about a person who says that he "couldn't help himself"? Do you think there is such a thing as an "irresistible impulse"? Do you hold someone just as accountable for acts that are reckless and acts that are deliberate?
3. Write an essay (or discuss) whether or not the state should regulate private behavior. Touch on the following: Do you believe the state should regulate behavior that arguably doesn't hurt anyone else (such as laws regarding the wearing of motorcycle or bicycle helmets)? Prostitution? Gambling? Which, if any, laws do you believe legislate what should be private decisions of individuals?

Ethical Dilemmas

Situation 1

A rich businessman's daughter, Patty had the best of everything all her life. Her future would have been college, a good marriage to a successful young man, and a life of comparative luxury— except that she was kidnapped by a small band of radical extremists who sought to overthrow the government by terror, intimidation, and robbery. After being raped, beaten, and locked in a small, dark closet for many days, continually taunted and threatened, she was told that she must participate with the terrorist gang in a bank robbery; otherwise, she and her family would be killed. During the course of the robbery, a bank guard was shot.

Was her action immoral? What if she had killed the guard? What if the terrorists had kidnapped her mother or father, too, and told her if she didn't cooperate, they would kill her parents immediately?

What would you have done in her place? (Readers might recognize this dilemma as the Patty Hearst case. In the 1970s the Symbionese Liberation Army, a terrorist group, kidnapped the daughter of Randolph Hearst, the tycoon of a large newspaper chain. Her subsequent capture, trial, conviction, and prison sentence have been portrayed in books and movies and provide ripe material for questions of free will and legal and moral culpability.)

Situation 2

You are taking an essay exam in a college classroom. The test is closed-book and closed-notes, yet you look up and see that the person sitting next to you has hidden under his blue book a piece of paper filled with notes, which he is using to answer some questions. What would you do? Would your answer change if the test were graded on a curve? What if the student is a friend? What would you do if the student were flunking the course and was going to lose the scholarship he needed to stay in school?

Situation 3

You are selected for a jury in a trial of a sixty-four-year-old mother who killed her two adult sons. The two men had Huntington's disease, a degenerative brain disease, and were institutionalized. They were certain to die and would endure much pain and suffering before they expired. Her husband had died from this same disease, and she had nursed him throughout.

She took a gun into the nursing home, kissed her sons good-bye, and then shot them both through the head. She was arrested for first-degree murder. The prosecutor informs you that there is no "mercy killing" defense in the law as it is written.

If you were on the jury, how would you decide this case? What punishment does she deserve? (See "Justice Tempered with Mercy," by K. Ellington, *Houston Chronicle*, January 30, 2003: 10A. The prosecutor accepted a plea of guilty to assisting suicide.)

Situation 4

You are completing an internship with a juvenile probation agency and truly have enjoyed the experience. Although working with the kids is challenging, you see many rewards in the job, especially when you sense that you are reaching a client and making a difference. Mr. Childers, the probation officer with whom you work, is less optimistic about the kids and operates in a strictly by-the-book legalistic manner. He is burned out and basically does his job without getting too involved. Although you respect him, you know you would approach the clients differently if you were to be hired fulltime.

One weekend you are out with friends in a downtown bar frequented by college students. To your surprise, you see Sarah, a sixteen-year-old probationer, dancing. In watching her, you realize that she is drunk and, in fact, is holding a beer and drinking it while she is dancing with a man who is obviously much older than she is. You go over to her, and she angrily tells you to mind your own business and immediately leaves with the guy. Later she comes back into the bar and pleads with you to keep quiet. She is tearfully apologetic and tells you that she already has had several violations of her probation and at the last hearing was told that if she has one more violation, she will be sent to a juvenile detention center. You know that Sarah has been doing much better in school and plans to graduate and even go to college.

On Monday morning you sit in Mr. Childers's office. What should you tell him?

Situation 5

All your life you have played by the rules. Even after you went to college, you studied hard and didn't party to the extent that it hurt your grades. During your senior year you began to make plans to graduate and begin your career. One Friday night you were in a car with four other students heading home from a bar. Before you knew what happened, the car was hit head on, and all of you were injured seriously. You now are paralyzed and facing the rest of your life in a wheelchair. The car that hit you was driven by a drunken student who, ironically, was in several of your classes. Several days after you return home from the hospital, he wants to see you. Despite your anger, you do see him, and he begs for your forgiveness. He totally breaks down and cries and tells you that he had never done anything like that before and wishes he were dead.

Can you forgive him? When he is prosecuted, what would your sentence recommendation be? Would your answers be different if someone had died? What if he had prior drunk-driving incidents? What if he also had committed other crimes and was not a fellow college student?

Suggested Readings

Braswell, M., McCarthy, B., and McCarthy, B. (Eds.). 2002. *Justice, Crime and Ethics,* 3rd ed. Cincinnati: Anderson.

Dershowitz, A. 1994. *The Abuse Excuse and Other Cop-Outs, Sob Stories, and Evasions of Responsibility.* Boston: Little, Brown.

Fieser, J. 1999. *Metaethics, Normative Ethics, and Applied Ethics: Contemporary and Historical Readings.* Belmont, CA: Wadsworth.

Leighton, P., and Reiman, J. 2001. *Criminal Justice Ethics.* Upper Saddle River, NJ: Prentice-Hall.

Miller, K., and Radelet, M. 1993. *Executing the Mentally Ill.* Newbury Park, CA: Sage.

Muraskin, R., and Muraskin, M. 2001. *Morality and the Law.* Upper Saddle River, NJ: Prentice-Hall.

Ruggiero, V. 2004. *Thinking Critically About Ethical Issues* (5th ed.). New York: McGraw-Hill.

Shermer, M. 2004. *The Science of Good and Evil: Why People Cheat, Gossip, Care, Share, and Follow the Golden Rule.* New York: Times Books, Holt & Co.

Solomon, R. 2006. *The Big Questions: A Short Introduction to Philosophy.* Belmont, CA: Wadsworth.

Thiroux, J., and Kraseman, K. 2006. *Ethics: Theory and Practice.* Upper Saddle River, NJ: Prentice Hall.

DETERMINING MORAL BEHAVIOR

© Vatican Museums and Galleries, Vatican City, Italy/The Bridgeman Art Library International

Even though every age perceives their dilemmas as unique, ethical issues are not new. Socrates, Plato, and Aristotle attempted to answer the question, "What is good?"

CHAPTER OBJECTIVES

1. Become familiar with the major ethical systems and the criticisms leveled against each.

2. Become familiar with ways to resolve ethical dilemmas in addition to the ethical systems.

3. Understand the controversy between relativism and absolutism.

4. Become familiar with how the major ethical systems have relevance to issues in criminal justice.

5. Learn how to apply the major ethical systems to ethical dilemmas.

CHAPTER OUTLINE

Detective Russell Poole was a Robbery–Homicide Division investigator with the Los Angeles Police Department. In 1998 he was assigned an investigation regarding the alleged beating of Ismael Jimenez, a reputed gang member, by L.A.P.D. officers, and a suspected cover-up of the incident. In his investigation he uncovered a pattern of complaints of violence by the anti-gang task force in the Ramparts Division. Gang members told Poole and his partners that a number of officers harassed them, assaulted them, and pressured them to provide untraceable guns. The beating occurred because Jimenez would not provide the officers with a gun. In a search of the house of Rafael Perez, a member of the anti-gang task force, Poole found a box with a half-dozen realistic replica toy guns. He concluded that a number of the officers in the division were "vigilante cops" and requested that the investigation proceed further.

Bernard Parks, the L.A.P.D. chief at the time, ordered Poole to limit his investigation solely to the Jimenez beating after Poole had informed his superiors of what his investigation had uncovered. Poole prepared a forty-page report on the Jimenez case for the district attorney's office, detailing the pattern of complaints, alleged assaults, and other allegations of serious wrongdoing on the part of the Rampart officers. Poole's report never reached the district attorney's office because his lieutenant, enforcing the chief's orders, replaced his detailed report with a two-page report written by the lieutenant and another supervisor. Poole knew that in not providing the district attorney's office with all the information he uncovered, he could be charged with obstruction of justice, and the report provided so little information that the officer probably would not even be charged. Poole's lieutenant then asked him to put his name on the report (Golab, 2000).

How did Sergeant Poole decide what was the right thing to do in this situation? He had conflicting duties and conflicting values. He knew that not signing the report might have serious consequences for his career. How would you determine the right thing to do if you were in a similar situation?

As discussed in Chapter 1, if confronted with an ethical dilemma, one can follow a series of steps to help in coming to an ethical resolution:

1. *Identify the facts.* Identifying all relevant facts is essential as a first step.
2. *Identify relevant values and concepts.* One's values of duty, friendship, loyalty, honesty, and self-preservation are usually at the heart of professional ethical dilemmas. Concepts are like values in that neither is subject to empirical proof.
3. *Identify the possible choices one might make.* To resolve the dilemma, one must first clearly understand the possible choices.
4. *Analyze the choices under an ethical system.* Possible choices of behavior can be analyzed using basic moral rules that are embedded in ethical systems. This chapter presents descriptions of a number of ethical systems.

ETHICAL SYSTEMS

Our principles of right and wrong form a framework for the way we live our lives. But where do these principles come from? Before you read on, answer the following question: If you believe that stealing is wrong, why do you believe this to be so? You probably said it is because your parents taught you or because your religion forbids it—or maybe because society cannot tolerate people harming one another. Your answer is an indication of your **ethical system**. Ethical systems have a number of characteristics:

1. They are the source of moral beliefs.
2. They are the underlying premises from which you make judgments.
3. They are beyond argument. That is, although ethical decisions may become the basis of debate, the decisions are based on fundamental truths or propositions that are taken as a given by the individual employing the ethical system.

C. E. Harris (1986: 33) referred to such ethical systems as *moral theories* or *moral philosophies* and defined them as a systematic ordering of moral principles. To be accepted as an ethical system, the system of principles must be internally consistent, must be consistent with generally held beliefs, and must possess a type of "moral common sense." Baelz (1977: 19) further described ethical systems as having the following characteristics:

1. *They are prescriptive.* Certain behavior is demanded or proscribed. They are not just abstract principles of good and bad but have substantial impact on what we do.
2. *They are authoritative.* They are not ordinarily subject to debate. Once an ethical framework has been developed, it is usually beyond question.

3. *They are logically impartial or universal.* Moral considerations arising from ethical systems are not relative. The same rule applies in all cases and for everyone.

4. *They are not self-serving.* They are directed toward others; what is good is good for everyone, not just the individual.

We don't consciously think of ethical systems, but we use them to make judgments. For instance, we might say that a woman who leaves her children alone to go out drinking has committed an immoral act. That would be a *moral judgment.* *Moral rules* that underlie this judgment might include the following:

"Children should be looked after."

"One shouldn't drink to excess."

"Mothers should be good role models for their children."

These basic moral rules are derived from an *ethical system.* The Ethical Pyramid in Chapter 1 (Figure 1.1) is a visual representation of this discussion. In this pyramid the ethical system is the basis for moral rules or principles. In Figure 2.1 we revisit the ethical pyramid, but this time it includes the moral judgment discussed above, along with the moral rules on which the judgment is based. Setting up this ethical pyramid is helpful when discussing the ethical dilemmas at the back of each chapter.

In this chapter we will not discuss all possible ethical systems, nor are the brief descriptions here enough to fully explain each of the systems mentioned. The reader would be well advised to consult texts in philosophy and ethics for more detail. However, we will explore and provide brief summaries of the most often used ethical systems.

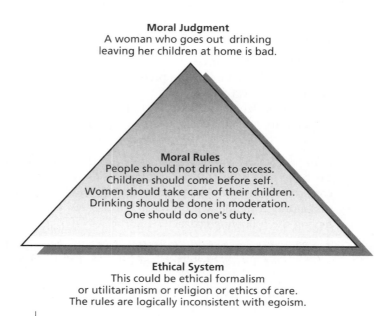

Moral Judgment
A woman who goes out drinking
leaving her children at home is bad.

Moral Rules
People should not drink to excess.
Children should come before self.
Women should take care of their children.
Drinking should be done in moderation.
One should do one's duty.

Ethical System
This could be ethical formalism
or utilitarianism or religion or ethics of care.
The rules are logically inconsistent with egoism.

FIGURE 2.1 | ETHICAL PYRAMID: EXAMPLE

DEONTOLOGICAL AND TELEOLOGICAL ETHICAL SYSTEMS

Deontological and *teleological* may be unfamiliar words, but the concepts that underlie them will be familiar to you. The two basic types of ethical systems are deontological systems and teleological systems.

A **deontological ethical system** is one that is concerned solely with the inherent nature of the act being judged. If an act or intent is inherently good (coming from a good will), it is still considered a good act even if it results in bad consequences. A **teleological ethical system** judges the consequences of an act. Even a bad act, if it results in good consequences, can be defined as good under a teleological system. The saying "the end justifies the means" is a teleological statement. The clearest examples of these two approaches are ethical formalism (a deontological or "nonconsequentialist" system) and utilitarianism (a teleological or "consequentialist" system).

ETHICAL FORMALISM

Ethical formalism is a deontological system because the important determinant for judging whether an act is moral is not its consequence, but only the motive or intent of the actor. According to the philosopher Emmanuel Kant (1724–1804), the only thing that is intrinsically good is a *good will*. On the one hand, if someone does an action from a good will, it can be considered a moral action even if it results in bad consequences. On the other hand, if someone performs some activity that looks on the surface to be altruistic but does it with an ulterior motive—for instance, to curry favor or gain benefit—that act is not moral. Gold, Braswell, and McCarthy (1991) offer the example of a motorist stranded by the side of the road; another driver who comes along has a decision to help or to pass by. If the driver makes a decision to stop and help, this would seem to be a good act. Not so, according to ethical formalism, unless it is done from a good will. If the helper stops because he or she expects payment, wants a return favor, or for any reason other than a good will, the act is only neutral—not moral. Only if the help springs from a good will can we say that it is truly good.

Kant (1949) believed that moral worth comes from doing one's duty. Just as there is the law of the family (father's rule), the law of the state and country, and the law of international relations, there is also a universal law of right and wrong. Morality, according to Kant, arises from the fact that humans, as rational beings, impose these laws and strictures of behavior upon themselves.

The following constitute the principles of Kant's ethical formalism (Bowie, 1985: 157):

1. *Act only on that maxim through which you can at the same time will that it should become a universal law.* In other words, for any decision of behavior to be made, examine whether that behavior would be acceptable if it were a universal law to be followed by everyone. For instance, a student might decide to cheat on a test, but for this action to be moral, the student would have to agree that everyone should be able to cheat on tests.

2. *Act in such a way that you always treat humanity, whether in your own person or that of any other, never simply as a means but always at the same time as an end.* In other words, one should not use people for one's own purposes.

For instance, being friendly to someone so that you can use her car is using her as a means to one's own ends. Even otherwise moral actions, such as giving to charity or doing charitable acts for others, would be considered immoral if done for ulterior motives such as self-aggrandizement.

3. *Act as if you were, through your maxims, a lawmaking member of a kingdom of ends.* This principle directs that the individual's actions should contribute to and be consistent with universal law. However, the good act must be done freely. If one is compelled to do a good act, the compulsion removes the moral nature of the act. Only when we freely choose to abide by moral law and these laws are self-imposed rather than imposed from the outside are they a reflection of the higher nature of humans.

These are absolute commands—together, they form the categorical imperative. According to Kant, **hypothetical imperatives** are commands that designate certain actions to attain certain ends. An example is, "*If* I want to be a success, *then* I must do well in college." By contrast, **categorical imperatives** command action that is necessary without any reference to intended purposes or consequences. The "imperative of morality" according to Kant needed no further justification. Further, the good of morality lies in one's intent, not in the consequence (Kant, 1949: 76).

A system such as ethical formalism is considered to be an *absolutist system*—if something is wrong, it is wrong all the time, such as murder or lying. To assassinate evil tyrants such as Adolf Hitler, Saddam Hussein, or Osama Bin Laden might be considered moral under a teleological system because of the action's consequence of ridding the world of dangerous people. However, in the deontological view, if the act and intent of killing are wrong, then killing is always wrong; thus, assassination must be considered immoral in all cases, regardless of the good consequences that might result. Even lying is deemed to be immoral in this system, despite some good arguments for the case that, at times, lying might be beneficial.

For instance, Kant argued that if someone asked to be hidden from an attacker in close pursuit and then the attacker asked where the potential victim was hiding, it would be immoral to lie about the victim's location. This seems wrong to many and serves to dissuade people from seeing the value of ethical formalism. However, according to Kant, lying or not lying is not the determining factor in that scenario or in any other. An individual cannot control consequences, only actions; therefore, one must act in a moral fashion without regard to potential consequences. In the example, the attacker may not kill the potential victim; the victim may still be able to get away; the attacker may be justified. The point is that no one person can control anything in life, so the only thing that makes sense is to live by the categorical imperative.

Kant also defended his position with semantics—distinguishing untruths from lies with the explanation that a lie is a lie only when the recipient is led to believe or has a right to believe that he or she is being told the truth. The attacker in the previous scenario or an attacker who has one "by the throat" demanding one's money has no right to expect the truth; thus, it would not be immoral not to tell this person the truth. Only if one led the attacker to believe that one were going to tell the truth and then did not would one violate the categorical imperative. In other words, Kant distinguishes untruths from lies. To not tell the truth when the attacker doesn't deserve the truth is not a lie, but if one intentionally and deliberately sets out to deceive, then that is a lie—even if it is being told to a person who doesn't deserve the truth (Kant, 1981).

This ethical framework follows simply from the beliefs that an individual must follow a self-imposed moral law and that one is capable of using reason to determine right actions because any action can be evaluated by using the principles just listed. Criticisms of ethical formalism include the following (Maestri, 1982: 910):

1. *Ethical formalism seems to be unresponsive to extreme circumstances.* If something is wrong in every circumstance regardless of the good that results or good reasons for the action, otherwise good people might be judged immoral or unethical.
2. *Morality is limited to duty.* One might argue that duty is the baseline of morality, not the highest aspiration of it. Further, it is not always clear where one's duty lies. At times one might face a dilemma where two duties conflict with each other.
3. *The priority of motive and intent over result is problematic in some instances.* It may be seriously questioned whether the intention to do good, regardless of result or perhaps with negative result, is always moral. Many would argue that the consequences of an action and the actual result must be evaluated to determine morality.

How would ethical formalism help resolve the dilemma faced by Sergeant Poole when he was asked to sign the "doctored" report for the district attorney's office? First, what was his duty? His duty was obviously to uphold the law. Did he also have a duty to obey his superiors? Did he have a duty to protect the police department from scandal? Did he have a duty to serve the public? Could he perform all these duties at the same time, or are they inconsistent with one another?

Applying the principles of ethical formalism to the dilemma, we can make the following observations:

1. *Act in such a way that the behavior could be universal.* Would covering up potential police misconduct be a rule that we would want to endorse universally? Probably not. It seems that if evidence is routinely held back from prosecutors, they would not be able to do their job.
2. *Do not treat others as a means to an end.* It seems clear that Poole's superiors were attempting to use him to further their own interest. Would he be using someone as a means to an end by signing the shortened report? Would he be using someone as a means to an end by not signing the shortened report?
3. *Behavior must be autonomous and freely chosen to be judged as moral.* If Poole was frightened or pressured into doing something, then the action would not be moral regardless of what it was. If, for instance, he believed that the district attorney would find out and come after him for falsifying a legal document, then he might not sign it, but it would not be because of a good will and therefore could not be considered a moral act.

Other writers present variations of deontological ethics that do not depend so heavily on Kant (Braswell, McCarthy, and McCarthy, 2002/2007). The core elements of any deontological or duty-based ethical system are the importance placed on intention and the use of a predetermined set of principles to judge morality rather than looking at the consequences of an act.

UTILITARIANISM

Utilitarianism is a teleological ethical system: What is good is determined by the consequences of the action. Jeremy Bentham (1748–1832), a major proponent of utilitarianism, believed that the morality of an action should be determined by how much it contributes to the good of the majority. According to Bentham, human nature seeks to maximize pleasure and avoid pain, and a moral system must be consistent with this natural fact.

The "utilitarian doctrine asserts that we should always act so as to produce the greatest possible ratio of good to evil for everyone concerned" (Barry, 1985: 65). That is, if one can show that an action significantly contributes to the general good, then it is good. In situations where one must decide between a good for an individual and a good for society, then society should prevail, despite the wrong being done to an individual. This is because the utility or good derived from that action generally outweighs the small amount of harm done (because the harm is done only to one, whereas the good is multiplied by the many). For instance, if it could be shown that using someone as an example would be an effective deterrent to crime, whether or not the person was actually guilty, the wrong done to that person by this unjust punishment might be outweighed by the good resulting for society. This assumes that citizens would not find out about the injustice and lose respect for the authority of the legal system, which would be a negative effect for all concerned. The Quote and Query box illustrates the principle of utility.

Although utilitarianism is quite prevalent in our thinking about ethical decision making, there are some serious criticisms of the system:

QUOTE AND QUERY

Nature has placed mankind under the governance of two sovereign masters, pain and pleasure. It is for them alone to point out what we ought to do, as well as to determine what we shall do. On the one hand, the standard of right and wrong, on the other the chain of causes and effects, are fastened to their throne. They govern us in all we do, in all we say, in all we think; every effort we can make to throw off our subjection, will serve but to demonstrate and confirm it. In words, a man may pretend to abjure their empire: but in reality he will remain subject to it all the while. The principle of utility recognizes the subjection, and assumes it for the foundation of that system.

Jeremy Bentham, quoted in Borchert and Stewart (1986: 183).

What is Bentham saying in this passage? Do you believe that all decisions are based fundamentally in seeking pleasure and avoiding pain?

1. *All "pleasures" or benefits are not equal.* Bentham did not judge the relative weight of utility. He considered pleasure to be a good whether it derived from vice, such as avarice or greed, or from virtue, such as charity and kindness. Later utilitarians, primarily John Stuart Mill (1806–1873), believed that utilities (benefits) had different weights or values. In other words, some were better than others. For instance, art offers a different utility for society than alcohol; altruism carries more benefit than pleasure, and so on. But who is to determine which is better? (Borchert and Stewart, 1986: 190). Although the concept of weighing utilities to decide what action to take makes sense, the actual exercise is sometimes very difficult.

2. *The system presumes that one can predict the consequences of one's actions.* In the well-known "lifeboat" dilemma, five people are in a lifeboat with enough food and water only for four. It is certain that they will survive if there are only four; it is also certain that they will all perish if one does not go overboard. What should be done? Under ethical formalism, it would be unthinkable to sacrifice an innocent, even if it means that all will die. Under utilitarian ethics, it is conceivable that the murder of one might be justified to save the others. But this hypothetical situation points out the fallacy of the utilitarian argument. In reality, it is not known whether any will survive. The fifth might be murdered, and five minutes later a rescue ship appears on the horizon. The fifth might be murdered, but then the remaining four are still eaten by sharks. Only in unrealistic hypothetical situations does one absolutely know the consequences of one's action. In real life, one never knows if an action will result in a greater good or ultimate harm.

3. *There is little concern for individual rights in utilitarianism.* Ethical formalism demands that each individual must be treated with respect and not be used as a means to an end. However, under utilitarianism, the rights of one individual may be sacrificed for the good of many. For instance, in World War II, Winston Churchill allowed Coventry to be bombed so the Germans would not know the Allies had cracked the Germans' secret military radio code. Several hundred English people were killed in the bombing raid of Coventry. Many might have been saved if they had been warned. It was a calculated loss for greater long-term gains—bringing the war to an end sooner. This could be justified under utilitarianism but perhaps not under ethical formalism. The Iraq war has been justified by the argument that it will save the lives of countless American citizens from some future terrorist acts and also protect Iraqi citizens from a brutal dictator, but there is no question that to bring about this good end, innocent Iraqi citizens have died, as have thousands of American soldiers. A utilitarian argument is used to justify these deaths.

Utilitarianism has two forms: act utilitarianism and rule utilitarianism. The basic difference between the two can be summarized as follows: In **act utilitarianism,** only the basic utility derived from an action is examined. We look at the consequences of any action for all involved and weigh the units of utility accordingly. In **rule utilitarianism,** one judges that action in reference to the precedent it sets and the long-term utility of the rule set by that action.

On the one hand, act utilitarianism might support stealing food when one is hungry and has no other way to eat because the utility of survival would outweigh the loss to the store owner. On the other hand, rule utilitarianism would be concerned with the effect that the action would have if made into a rule for behavior: "Any time an individual cannot afford food, he or she can steal it" would contribute to a state of lawlessness and a general disrespect for the law. Such a rule would probably not result in the greatest utility for the greatest number. With rule utilitarianism, then, we are concerned not only with the immediate utility of the action but also with the long-term utility or harm if the action were to be a rule for all similar circumstances. Note the similarity between rule utilitarianism and the first principle of the categorical imperative. In both approaches, one must judge as good only those actions that can be universalized.

Applying utilitarianism to Detective Russell Poole's dilemma, it seems clear that his superiors were engaged in damage control. They did not want a scandal, especially considering that it had not been that long since the Rodney King incident. By suppressing evidence of further wrongdoing, they probably assumed that they could keep the information from the public and deal with it internally. In fact, Chief Parks fired more than 100 officers during his time as chief, but he did so in a way that the district attorney's office was unable to prosecute any of the officers for their alleged crimes. Internal Affairs routinely used a practice of compelling testimony without reading the officer his rights before questioning. This meant that the evidence obtained could be used to discipline the officer but not to prosecute him or her. The result was that officers were fired but their cases never ended up in court—or in the newspaper.

If Detective Poole used utilitarian reasoning, where did the greatest benefit lie? Was there greater benefit to all concerned in opposing his superiors' attempts to suppress the investigation, or with going along with the cover-up? Actually, the attempt to suppress the actions of the Ramparts Division officers was unsuccessful anyway. A year after Poole refused to sign the report, Rafael Perez was prosecuted for stealing a large amount of cocaine from the evidence room. In a plea arrangement, he told investigators from the D.A.'s office the whole story of the Ramparts Division officers, leading to the biggest scandal in L.A.P.D.'s history (Golab, 2000; Boyer, 2001). This illustrates one of the problems with utilitarianism: If people sacrifice their integrity for what they consider is a good cause, the result may be that they lose their integrity and still not achieve their good cause.

In summary, utilitarianism holds that morality must be determined by the consequences of an action. Society and the survival and benefit of all are more important than any individual. This is a functional theory of right and wrong: Something is right when it benefits the continuance and good health of society. Rule utilitarianism may be closer to the principles of ethical formalism because it looks at general universal laws. The difference between the two is that the actions themselves are judged right or wrong depending on the motives behind them under ethical formalism, whereas utilitarianism looks to the long-term consequences of the behavior created by the prescribed rule to determine its morality. The "Walking the Walk" box is the first of several throughout this book that illustrates an individual who faced an ethical dilemma and made a difficult decision or decisions.

WALKING THE WALK

Joe Darby was a military reservist from a low-income family who grew up in Pennsylvania and settled in Maryland. The 372nd was a military police unit based in his town, and almost everyone had some ties to the military. Darby's unit was deployed to Iraq.

One fateful day in January of 2004, Darby began his march into the history books by asking Spc. Charles Graner for some pictures of the surrounding countryside. Graner gave him a CD of pictures. Clicking through the pictures to decide which ones to send home, he stumbled on some that, at first, made him laugh; then, as others appeared on the computer screen, he grew more and more disgusted. "They just didn't sit right with me," he said later.

The pictures were the infamous torture photos taken in the Abu Ghraib prison by Graner and others. Whether Graner didn't remember that they were on the CD or didn't care will never be known; however, once Darby saw the pictures, he couldn't stop thinking about them. He had not been present and did not know that soldiers had been posing the prisoners nude, forcing them to simulate masturbation and homosexual acts, using dogs to intimidate and attack the naked prisoners, and placing them on stools and telling them if they fell off they would be electrocuted.

Darby had seen other things at the prison though, which he related years later in news accounts—things like a helicopter flying into the prison grounds in the middle of the night with a prisoner being hustled into the interrogation room by men who not only were nameless but who never revealed whether they were military intelligence, CIA, or civilian contractors. When they left the next morning, the prisoner was dead and the soldiers were told to "clean it up."

The pictures of Charles Graner and Sabrina Harmon, posing next to the body of this man, are part of the group of photos that were plastered across newspapers, shown on televisions, and appeared in internet sites across the world. The scandal tarnished the reputation of the United States, probably contributed to an increase in the insurgency, ruined careers, and ended up with the soldiers in the pictures serving prison time.

So why did Darby do it? Why did he burn copies of the pictures onto a disk and give them to the CID (Criminal Intelligence Division) rather than to his commanding officer? He said later that it was because things had been reported to his superiors before and nothing happened, and, besides, Ivan Frederick, one of those who appeared in the pictures, was the commanding officer of the night shift. Darby first turned in the envelope with the photos to CID investigators and said he didn't know where it came from, but then he admitted that he had gotten the pictures from Graner. He was promised that his name would be kept confidential.

Once investigators obtained the photos, they immediately began an investigation and questioned all those in the pictures who were then, inexplicably, allowed to remain in the compound. Tension and paranoia was intense, and Darby said he literally feared for his life, hoping that no one would discover that it was he who had turned them in. "I'm not the kind of guy to rat somebody out," he said later. "I've kept a lot of secrets for soldiers...but this crossed the line to me. I had the choice between what I knew was morally right and my loyalty to other soldiers. I couldn't have it both ways."

At some point his name was leaked to the press, and then Secretary of Defense Donald Rumsfeld announced in the Congressional hearing about Abu Ghraib that Darby was the one who turned in the photos. He was sitting in a crowded messhall in Iraq when the hearing was being aired on the television. The room became quiet. Although some soldiers shook Darby's hand, many regarded him as a traitor. So did

(Continued)

most of his neighbors and even some of his family. His wife endured weeks of threats and vandalism before she was taken into protective custody by the military. Neighbors said he was a rat, a traitor, and should fear for his life. Darby, too, was removed from Iraq ahead of his unit and reunited with his wife in seclusion and under heavy guard. He was told that it wasn't safe to return to their hometown, and he had not, as of March 2008. They are not welcome there. His tour of duty was extended through the trials that lasted through 2006. In 2005 Darby received the Kennedy *Profiles in Courage* award.

Today, the media storm that Darby created has finally died down and he is a civilian trying to create a new life. He does not regret what he did. "I've always had a moral sense of right and wrong. And I knew that, you know, friends or not, it had to stop," Darby says.

Sources: Hylton, 2006; CBS.news. 2007; CBS.news.com. 2005; Gourevitch and Morris, 2008.

OTHER ETHICAL SYSTEMS

Although utilitarianism and ethical formalism are arguably the two best representatives of the contrast, the following ethical systems can be described as deontological or teleological as well,. As you read through these systems, apply the definitions of teleological systems and deontological systems to determine if you can categorize each. Some, such as egoism, are easy to categorize: It is clearly teleological. The others might not be so easy.

RELIGION

Probably the most frequently used source of individual ethics is religion. Religion might be defined as a body of beliefs that addresses fundamental issues such as, "What is life?" and "What are good and evil?" A religion also provides moral guidelines and directions on how to live one's life. For instance, Christians and Jews are taught the Ten Commandments, which prohibit certain behaviors defined as wrong. The authority of **religious ethics**, in particular Judeo-Christian ethics, stems from a willful and rational God. For believers, the authority of God's will is beyond question, and there is no need for further examination because of His perfection. The only possible controversy comes from human interpretation of God's commands. Indeed, these differences in interpretation are the source of most religious strife.

Religious ethics is, of course, much broader than simply Judeo-Christian ethics. Religions such as Buddhism, Confucianism, and Islam also provide a basis for ethics because they offer explanations of how to live the "good life" and address other philosophical issues, such as "What is reality?" Pantheistic religions—those of primitive hunter–gatherer societies—promote the belief that there is a living spirit in all things. A basic principle follows from this belief that life is important and one must have respect for all things, including trees, rivers, and animals. There must be a willful and rational god or god figure before there can be a judgment of right and wrong, thus providing a basis for an ethical system. Those religions that do have a god figure consider that figure to be the source of principles of ethics and morality.

It is also true that of the religions we might discuss, many have similar basic moral principles. Many religions have their own version of the Ten Commandments. In this regard, Islam is not too different from Judaism, which is not too different from Christianity. What Christians know as the Golden Rule actually predates Christianity, and the principle can be found in all the major religions, as well as offered by ancient philosophers:

1. Christianity: "Do unto others as you would have them do unto you."
2. Hinduism: "Do naught to others which, if done to thee, would cause thee pain: this is the sum of duty."
3. Buddhism: "In five ways should a clansman minister to his friends and familiars...by treating them as he treats himself."
4. Confucianism: "What you do not want done to yourself, do not do unto others."
5. Judaism: "Whatsoever thou wouldest that men should not do unto thee, do not do that to them." (Reiman, 1990: 147)
6. Isocrates: "Do not do to others what would anger you if done to you by others." (Shermer, 2004: 25)
7. Diogenes Laertius, *Lives of the Philosophers*: "The question was once put to Aristotle how we ought to behave to our friends; and his answer was, 'As we should wish them to behave to us.'" (Shermer, 2004: 25)
8. The Mahabharata: "This is the sum of all true righteousness, deal with others as thou wouldst thyself be dealt by. Do nothing to thy neighbor which thou wouldst not have him do to thee hereafter." (Shermer, 2004: 25)

A fundamental question discussed by philosophers and religious scholars is whether God commands us not to commit an act because it is inherently wrong (e.g., "Thou shalt not kill"), or whether an act acquires its "badness" or "goodness" solely from God's definition of it. This is a thorny issue and one that continues to be debated.

Another issue in Western religious ethics is how to determine God's will. Some believe that God is inviolable and that positions on moral questions are absolute. This is a legalist position. Others believe that God's will varies according to time and place—the situationalist position. According to this position, situational factors are important in determining the rightness of a particular action. Something may be right or wrong depending on the circumstances (Borchert and Stewart, 1986: 157). For instance, lying may be wrong unless it is to protect an innocent, or stealing may be wrong unless it is to protest injustice and to help unfortunates. Some would say that it is impossible to have an *a priori* knowledge of God's will because that would put us above God's law: We ourselves cannot be "all-knowing." Thus, for any situation, if we are prepared to receive God's divine commands, we can know them through faith and conscience. Box 2.1 briefly describes some of the major world religions other than to Judeo-Christianity.

According to Barry (1985, 51–54), human beings can "know" God's will in three ways:

1. *Individual conscience.* An individual's conscience is the best source for discovering what God wants one to do. If one feels uncomfortable about a certain action, it is probably wrong.

BOX 2.1 | OVERVIEW OF MAJOR WORLD RELIGIONS

Islam

One of the newest, yet largest, religions is Islam. Like Christianity, this religion recognizes one god, Allah. Jesus and other religious figures are recognized as prophets, as is Muhammed, who is considered to be the last and greatest prophet. Islam is based on the Koran, which is taken much more literally as the word of Allah than the Bible is taken by most Christians. There is a great deal of fatalism in Islam: *In Shallah,* meaning, "If God wills it," is a prevalent theme in Muslim societies, but there is recognition that if people choose evil, they do so freely. The five pillars of Islam are (1) repetition of the creed (*Shahada*), (2) daily prayer (*Salah*), (3) almsgiving (*Zakah*), (4) fasting (*Sawm*), and (5) pilgrimage (*Haj*).

Another feature of Islam is the idea of the holy war. In this concept, the faithful who die defending Islam against infidels will be rewarded in the afterlife (Hopfe, 1983). This is not to say that Islam provides a legitimate justification for terroristic acts. Devout Muslims protest that terrorists have subverted the teachings of Islam and do not follow its precepts, one of which is never to harm innocents.

Buddhism

Siddhartha Gautama (Buddha) attained enlightenment and preached to others how to do the same and achieve release from suffering. He taught that good behavior is that which follows the "middle path" between hedonistic pursuit of sensual pleasure and asceticism. Essentials of Buddhist teachings are ethical conduct, mental discipline, and wisdom. Ethical conduct is based on universal love and compassion for all living beings. Compassion and wisdom are needed in equal measures. Ethical conduct can be broken into right speech (refraining from lies, slander, enmity, and rude speech), right action (abstaining from destroying life, stealing, and dishonest dealings, and helping others lead peaceful and honorable lives), and right livelihood (abstaining from occupations that bring harm to others, such as arms dealing and killing animals). To follow the "middle path," one must abide by these guidelines (Kessler, 1992).

Confucianism

Confucius taught a humanistic social philosophy that included central concepts such as *Ren,* which is human virtue and humanity at its best, as well as the source of moral principles; *Li,* which is traditional order, ritual, or custom; *Xiao,* which is familial love; and *Yi,* which is rightness, both a virtue and a principle of behavior—that is, one should do what is right because it is right. The *doctrine of the mean* exemplifies one aspect of Confucianism that emphasizes a cosmic or natural order. Humans are a part of nature and are included in the scheme of life. Practicing moderation in one's life is part of this natural order and reflects a "way to Heaven" (Kessler, 1992).

Hinduism

In Hinduism the central concept of *Karma* can be understood as consequence. Specifically, what one does in one's present life will determine what happens in a future life. The goal is to escape the eternal birth–rebirth cycle by living one's life in a moral manner so no bad Karma will occur (Kessler, 1992). People start out life in the lowest caste, but if they live a good life, they will be reborn as members of a higher caste, until they reach the highest Brahman caste, and at that point the cycle can end. An early source for Hinduism was the Code of Manu. In this code are found the ethical ideals of Hinduism, which include pleasantness, patience, control of mind, nonstealing, purity, control of the senses, intelligence, knowledge, truthfulness, and nonirritability (Hopfe, 1983).

2. *Religious authorities.* These authorities can interpret right and wrong for us and are our best source if we are confused about certain actions.
3. *Holy scriptures.* The third way is to go directly to the Bible, Koran, or Torah as the source of God's law. Some believe that the written word of God holds the answers to all moral dilemmas.

Strong doubts exist as to whether any of these methods are true indicators of divine command. Our consciences may be no more than the products of our psychological development, influenced by our environment. Religious authorities are, after all, only human, with human failings. Even the Bible seems to support contradictory principles. For instance, advocates of capital punishment can find passages in the Bible that support it (such as Genesis 9:6: "Whoever sheds the blood of man, by man shall his blood be shed..."), but opponents to capital punishment argue that the New Testament offers little direct support for execution and has many more passages that direct one to forgive, such as Matthew 5:38--40: "... Offer no resistance to injury. When a person strikes you on the right cheek, turn and offer him the other."

The question of whether people can ever know God's will has been explored through the ages. Thomas Aquinas (1225–1274) believed that human reason was sufficient not only to prove the existence of God but also to discover God's divine commands (Borchert and Stewart, 1986: 159). Others believe that reason is not sufficient to know God and that it comes down to unquestioning belief, so reason and knowledge must always be separate from faith. These people believe that one can know whether an action is consistent with God's will only if it contributes to general happiness, because God intends for us to be happy, or when the action is done through the *holy spirit*—that is, when someone performs the action under the influence of true faith (Borchert and Stewart, 1986: 164–171).

To summarize, the religious ethics system is widely used and accepted. The authority of the god figure is the root of all morality; basic conceptions of good and evil, or right and wrong come from interpretations of the god figure's will. Many people throughout history have wrestled with the problem of determining what is right according to God. Current controversies within and between religious groups are illustrated by the "In the News" example on page 44.

NATURAL LAW

The **natural law** ethical system holds that there is a universal set of rights and wrongs that is similar to many religious beliefs, but without reference to a specific supernatural figure. Originating with the Stoics, natural law is an ethical system wherein no difference is recognized between physical laws—such as the law of gravity—and moral laws. Morality is part of the natural order of the universe. Further, this morality is the same across cultures and times. In this view, Christians simply added God as a source of law (as other religions added their own prophets and gods), but there is no intrinsic need to resort to a supernatural figure because these universal laws exist quite apart from any religion (Maestri, 1982).

The natural law ethical system presupposes that what is good is what is natural and what is natural is what is good. The essence of morality is what conforms to

---

IN THE NEWS | BARACK OBAMA AND REVEREND WRIGHT

In March of 2008, Barack Obama was criticized heavily for being associated with his pastor, Reverend Jeremiah Wright. The pastor's sermons often included criticism of America, including the following quote:

> We bombed Hiroshima, we bombed Nagasaki, and we nuked far more than the thousands in New York and the Pentagon, and we never batted an eye. We have supported state terrorism against the Palestinians and black South Africans, and now we are indignant because the stuff we have done overseas is now brought right back into our own front yards. America's chickens are coming home to roost.

In a speech distancing himself from Wright, Obama explained that he believed the comments were absolutely wrong but explained them as coming from an anger that whites may not understand. He ultimately rejected the Reverend's views absolutely. The situation does raise an interesting question, however, in how much authority religious leaders should have in their interpretation of God's will. Another issue, of course, is whether politics and religion should be so intertwined.

Do you think that ministers should be making political comments or remarking on national policies? What is the proper relationship between politics and religion?

Source: Saslow, E. 2008: A01.

---

the natural world; thus, there are basic inclinations that form the core of moral principles. For instance, the preservation of one's own being is a natural inclination and thus is a basic principle of morality. Actions consistent with this natural inclination would be those that preserve one's own life, such as in self-defense, but also those that preserve or maintain the species, such as a prohibition against murder. Other inclinations are peculiar to one's species—for instance, humans are social animals; thus, sociability is a natural inclination that leads to altruism and generosity. These are natural and thus moral. The pursuit of knowledge or understanding of the universe might also be recognized as a natural inclination of humans; thus, actions that conform to this natural inclination are moral.

Souryal (2007: 86) described natural law as the "steward" of natural rights. The U.S. founders might be described as natural law theorists. The Constitution recognizes "natural rights" endowed by the Creator. However, Fishman (1994) explained that Thomas Hobbes and John Locke transformed the original natural law theory that emphasized duties or obligations of humans in the natural order to one that emphasized "natural" human rights. To stay true to the internal consistency and historical legacy of natural rights theory, one must balance the emphasis on rights with an emphasis on obligations. For instance, the protection of individual freedoms as natural rights is an important component of any democracy, but democracy can exist only when citizens accept and perform the obligations of citizenship. Citizens who are not vigilant in protecting their freedoms through the political process risk losing them. In this sense, natural law theory echoes the emphasis on duty found in ethical formalism.

Natural law theory defines good as that which is natural. The difficulty of this system is identifying what is consistent and congruent with the natural inclinations of humankind. How do we know which acts are in accordance with the natural order of things? Who determines the natural laws?

Natural law can be employed to restrict the rights and liberties of groups of people. In *Bradwell v. Illinois* 83 US 130 (1873), the Supreme Court upheld Indiana's right to prevent Myra Bradwell from becoming a member of the bar. The state's argument, which the Supreme Court endorsed, was the woman's "natural" role was childbearer. In the famous "mother of the species" holding, the Court decided that the women's childbearing role was her natural destiny and that the sordid world of the courtroom was no place for a woman. The fundamental problem with this ethical system is: How does one know whether something is a natural law or human perception?

THE ETHICS OF VIRTUE

Each of the foregoing ethical systems asks, "What is a good action?" The **ethics of virtue** instead asks, "What is a good person?" This ethical system rejects the approach that one might use reason to discover what is good. Instead, the principle is that to be good, one must do good. Virtues that a good person possesses include thriftiness, temperance, humility, industriousness, and honesty. It may be considered a teleological system because it is concerned with acting in such a way as to achieve a good end (Prior, 1991). The specific "end" is happiness, or *eudaimonia*, but the meaning of this word is not the same as the meaning given by utilitarians. This version of happiness does not mean simply having pleasure but also living a good life, reaching achievements, and attaining moral excellence.

The roots of this system are in the work of Aristotle, who defined virtues as "excellences." These qualities are what enable an individual to move toward the achievement of what it takes to be human. Aristotle distinguished intellectual virtues (wisdom, understanding) from moral virtues (generosity, self-control). The moral virtues are not sufficient for "the good life"; one must also have the intellectual virtues, primarily "practical reason." Aristotle believed that we are, by nature, neither good nor evil but become so through training and the acquisition of habits:

> [T]he virtues are implanted in us neither by nature nor contrary to nature: we are by nature equipped with the ability to receive them and habit brings this ability to completion and fulfillment. (Aristotle, quoted in Prior, 1991: 156–157)

Habits of moral virtue are obtained by following the example of a moral *exemplar*. These habits are also more easily instilled when "right" or just laws also exist. Moral virtue is a state of character in which choices are consistent with the **principle of the golden mean**. This principle states that virtue is always the median between two extremes of character. For instance, liberality is the mean between prodigality and meanness; proper pride is the mean between empty vanity and undue humility, and so on (Albert, Denise, and Peterfreund, 1984). The "Catalog of Virtues" (Box 2.2) lists others.

Moral virtue comes from habit, which is why this system emphasizes character. The idea here is that one does not do good because of reason; rather, one does good because of the patterns of a lifetime. Those with good character will do the right thing, and those with bad character usually will choose the immoral path. Every day we are confronted with numerous opportunities to lie, cheat, and steal. When a cashier looks the other way, we could probably filch a $20 bill from the

BOX 2.2	CATALOG OF VIRTUES

Area	Defect	Mean	Excess
fear	cowardice	courage	recklessness
pleasure	insensitivity	self-control	self-indulgence
money	stinginess	generosity	extravagance
honor	small-mindedness	high-mindedness	vain
anger	apathy	gentleness	short temper
truth	self-depreciation	truthfulness	boastfulness
shame	shamelessness	modesty	self-hate

Source: Adapted from Prior (1991: 165).

cash drawer; or when a clerk gives us a $10 bill instead of a $1.00 bill by mistake, we could keep it instead of hand it back, or when we come into a store to find that the clerk has left for a few minutes, we could grab a few things and quickly depart. We don't because, generally, it does not even occur to us to steal. We do not have to go through any deep ethical analysis in most instances when we have the opportunity to do bad things, because our habits of a lifetime dictate our actions.

Somewhat related to the ethics of virtue ethical system are the "6 Pillars of Character" promulgated by the Josephson Institute of Ethics (2008), a private foundation dedicated to teaching and training in the field of ethics. The 6 Pillars of Character are somewhat similar to Aristotle's virtues.

1. *Trustworthiness*: This concept encompasses honesty and meeting one's obligations. Honesty means to be truthful, forthright, and sincere, and the pillar also involves loyalty, living up to one's beliefs, and having values.
2. *Respect*: This pillar is similar to the second portion of the categorical imperative, which admonishes to treat each person with respect and not as a means to an end. It also encompasses the Golden Rule.
3. *Responsibility*: This means standing up for one's choices and being accountable. Everyone has a moral duty to pursue excellence, but, if one fails, the duty is to take responsibility for the failure.
4. *Fairness*: This concept involves issues of equality, impartiality, and due process. To treat everyone fairly doesn't necessarily mean to treat everyone the same but, rather, to apply fairness in one's dealings with everyone.
5. *Caring*: This pillar encompasses the ideas of altruism and benevolence.
6. *Citizenship*: This includes the duties of every citizen, including voting, obeying the law, being a good steward of the natural resources of one's country, and doing one's fair share.

It should also be noted that most of us have some virtues and not others. There are many other virtues besides those already mentioned, including compassion, courage, conscientiousness, and devotion. Some of us may be completely honest in all of our dealings but not generous. Some may be courageous but not compassionate. Therefore, we all are moral to the extent that we possess moral virtues, but some of us are more moral than others by having more virtues. One difficulty is in judging the primacy of moral virtues. For instance, in professional ethics there are often conflicts that involve honesty and loyalty. If both are virtues, how does one resolve a dilemma in which one virtue must be sacrificed?

The ethics of virtue probably explains more individual behavior than other ethical systems because most of the time, if we have developed habits of virtue, we do not even think about the possible "bad" acts we might do. For instance, most of us do not have to analyze the "rightness" or "wrongness" of stealing every time we go into a store. We do not automatically consider lying every time a circumstance arises. Most of the time we do the right thing without thinking about it a great deal. However, when faced with a true dilemma—that is, a choice where the "right" decision is unclear—the ethics of virtue may be less helpful as an ethical system.

Alasdair MacIntyre (1991: 204), a current philosopher, defines virtues as those dispositions that will sustain us in the relevant "quest for the good, by enabling us to overcome the harms, dangers, temptations and distractions which we encounter, and which will furnish us with increasing self-knowledge and increasing knowledge of the good." MacIntyre (1999) also seems to endorse an ethics-of-care approach because he discusses virtue as necessary to care for the next generation. He sees life as one of "reciprocal indebtedness" and emphasizes "networks of relationships" as the locale of giving and receiving the benefits of virtues. This language is similar to the ethical system of the ethics of care, which will be discussed next.

In our opening case, Detective Poole reported that he never considered putting his name on a report he knew was wrong. His superiors, co-workers, and colleagues describe him as "professional," "hard working," "loyal, productive, thorough and reliable," "diligent," "honest," and "extremely credible." He was known as a first-rate investigator and trusted by the D.A.'s office to provide thorough and credible testimony. In other words, his habits in his professional life were directly contrary to participating in a cover-up. Those who advocate the ethics of virtue would predict that Poole would not participate in a cover-up because of his character—and they would be right because he did not sign the report (Golab, 2000).

THE ETHICS OF CARE

The **ethics of care** is another ethical system that does not depend on universal rules or formulas to determine morality. The emphasis is on human relationships and needs. The ethics of care has been described as a feminine morality because women in all societies are the childbearers and consequently seem to have a greater sensitivity to issues of care. Noddings (1986: 1) points out that the "mother's voice" has been silent in Western, masculine analysis: "One is tempted to say that ethics has so far been guided by Logos, the masculine spirit, whereas the more natural and perhaps stronger approach would be through Eros, the feminine spirit."

The ethics of care is founded in the natural human response to care for a newborn child, the ill, and the hurt. There are similarities in the ethics of care's idea that morals derive from natural human impulses of compassion and Jean-Jacques Rousseau's (1712–1778) argument that it is human's natural compassion that is the basis of human action and the idea that morality is based in emotion rather than rationality, i.e. "What I feel is right is right, what I feel is wrong is wrong" (Rousseau, as cited by Ruggiero, 2004: 28).

Carol Gilligan's work on moral development in psychology, which will be discussed in more detail in Chapter 3, identified a feminine approach to ethical dilemmas that focuses on relationships and needs instead of rights and universal laws. The most interesting feature of this approach is that while a relatively small number of women emphasized needs over rights, no men did. She attributed this to Western society, in which men and women both are socialized to Western ethics, which are primarily concerned with issues of rights, laws, and universalism (Gilligan, 1982).

Applying the ethics of care does not necessarily lead to different solutions, but perhaps to different questions. In an ethical system based on care, we would be concerned with issues of needs rather than rights. Other writers point to some Eastern religions, such as Taoism, as illustrations of the ethics of care (Gold et al., 1991). In these religions a rigid, formal, rule-based ethics is rejected in favor of gently leading the individual to follow a path of caring for others. In criminal justice, the ethics of care is represented to some extent by the rehabilitative ethic rather than the just-deserts model. Certainly the "restorative justice" movement is consistent with the ethics of care because of its emphasis on the motives and needs of all concerned, rather than simply retribution. In personal relationships the ethics of care would promote empathy and treating others in a way that does not hurt them. In this view, meeting needs is more important than securing rights.

In their text, Braswell and Gold (2002) discuss a concept called **peacemaking justice**. They show that the concept is derived from ancient principles, and it concerns care as well as other concepts: "Peacemaking, as evolved from ancient spiritual and wisdom traditions, has included the possibility of mercy and compassion within the framework of justice" (2002: 25). They propose that the peacemaking process is composed of three parts: connectedness, caring, and mindfulness.

1. "Connectedness" has to do with the interrelationships we have with one another and all of us have with the Earth.
2. "Caring" is similar to Noddings's concept that the "natural" inclination of humans is to care for one another.
3. "Mindfulness" involves being aware of others and the world in all personal decision making (Braswell and Gold, 2002: 25–37).

The Policy Box on "Peacemaking Justice" explores this approach as a policy decision.

To summarize, the ethics of care approach identifies the needs of all individuals in any ethical situation and attempts to maximize them. It is different from utilitarianism, however, in that one person cannot be sacrificed for others. Also, there is an attempt to resolve situations through human relationships and a sense that decisions should come from compassion rather than attention to rights or duties.

POLICY BOX | **PEACEMAKING JUSTICE**

Whether one calls the approach peacemaking justice, restorative justice, or some other term, there are many examples across the nation of a different approach to lawbreaking. It is more often used with juvenile offenders and emphasizes the needs of both parties in the criminal event—the victim and the offender. Often, the offender and the victim meet in some type of mediation setting. Frequently, the offender is asked to agree to some form of restitution, in many cases specifically to the victim. It could be the case that the offender meets with not just the victim but also with family members, teachers, and neighbors in an intervention designed to identify the cause of the wrongdoing. Some people, particularly prosecutors and victims' rights advocates, are not in favor of the justice system moving in this direction.

Law: There may be a need for enabling laws that allow for certain types of sentences developed under restorative justice programs. In general, the discretion of the judge would probably allow for any form of resolution that was arranged.

Policy: In general, prosecutors' offices have policies that require that the victim be involved and agree to any sentence. This is not contradictory to restorative justice. If the policy of the prosecutor's office was to pursue the harshest sentence possible for all offenders, that policy would be counter to the restorative approach.

Individual ethics: District attorneys set the policy of the office. Their definitions of justice play an important role. They may create an environment in which their jurisdiction is a model for restorative justice programs, or they may discourage or forbid such programs from being implemented.

EGOISM

Very simply, **egoism** postulates that what is good for one's survival and personal happiness is moral. The extreme of this position is that all people should operate on the assumption that they can do whatever benefits themselves. Others become the means to ensure happiness and have no meaning or rights as autonomous individuals.

Psychological egoism is a descriptive principle rather than an ethical prescription. Psychological egoism holds that humans are naturally egoists and that it would be unnatural for them to be any other way. All species have instincts for survival, and self-preservation and self-interest are merely part of that instinct. Therefore, it is not only moral to be egoistic, but it is the only way we can be, and any other explanations of behavior are mere rationalizations. In behaviors that appear to be altruistic, such as giving to charity or volunteering, the argument goes that these acts provide psychic and emotional pleasure to the individual and that is why they do them, not for some other selfless reason. Even though acts such as running into a burning building or jumping into a river to save victims seem altruistic, psychological egoists believe that these acts occur because of the personality make-up of individuals who derive greater pleasure from being considered heroes, or enjoy the adrenalin rush of the dangerous act more than the feeling of security derived from staying on the sidelines.

Enlightened egoism is a slight revision of this basic principle, adding that each person's objective is long-term welfare. This may mean that we should treat others as we would want them to treat us to ensure cooperative relations. Even seemingly selfless and altruistic acts are consistent with egoism because these acts benefit the individual by ensuring reciprocal assistance. Under egoism, it would be not only impossible but also immoral for someone to perform a completely selfless act. Even those who give their lives to save others do so perhaps with the expectation of rewards in the afterlife. Egoism completely turns around the priorities of utilitarianism to put the individual first, before anyone else and before society as a whole; however, because long-term interests often dictate meeting obligations and helping others, enlightened egoists might look like altruists.

Ayn Rand (1905–1982) is perhaps the best-known modern writer/philosopher associated with egoism. She promoted both psychological egoism (that humans *are* naturally selfish), and ethical egoism (that humans *should be* self-interested). It should also be noted that our capitalistic economic system is, to some extent, premised upon egoism. Capitalism is based on the premise that everyone pursuing self-interest will create a healthy economy: Workers will work harder to get more pay; owners will not exploit workers too badly because they might quit; merchants will try to get the highest price for items whereas consumers will shop for the lowest price; and so on. Only when government or liberal do-gooders manipulate the market, some argue, does capitalism not work optimally.

Most philosophers reject egoism because it violates the basic tenets of an ethical system. Universalism is inconsistent with egoism, because to approve of all people acting in their own self-interest is not a logical or feasible position. It cannot be right for both me and you to maximize our own self-interests because it would inevitably lead to conflict. Egoism would support exploitative actions by the strong against the weak, which seems wrong under all other ethical systems. However, psychological egoism is a relevant concept in natural law (self-preservation is natural) and utilitarianism (hedonism is a natural inclination). But if it is true that humans are *naturally* selfish and self-serving, one can point to examples that indicate that humans are also altruistic and self-sacrificing. What is the true nature of humankind?

OTHER METHODS OF ETHICAL DECISION MAKING

There are other approaches to ethical analysis in addition to the ethical systems discussed thus far. John Rawls (1957) presents a somewhat abstract procedure for deciding moral issues. He explains that moral principles can be developed through inductive logic. The method to discover these moral principles is through the considered moral judgments of a number of cases by a number of moral judges. These individuals would have the following characteristics:

1. They would possess common sense—they would not intellectualize the problem but apply common reason to arrive at a resolution.
2. They would have open minds.

3. They would know their own emotions.
4. They would have a sympathetic knowledge of humans.

The cases given them to decide would be such that the judges would not be harmed or benefited in any way by their decision, to ensure neutrality. The cases would present real conflicts of interest, but conflicts that are not too difficult and that are likely to present themselves in ordinary life. The judges would be presented with all relevant facts in the matter so they could make a reasoned judgment. The judgments should be certain, and they should be stable; that is, other judges at other times should arrive at the same judgments. Finally, the judgments should be intuitive. The reason is that ethical principles are to be derived from a series of judgments, and if judges were already using predetermined rules, there would be no way to derive general rules from the judgments (Rawls, 1957: 180).

The next step is to formulate an explication of the total range of judgments. An **explication** is a set of principles described as follows (Rawls, 1957: 182):

> [I]f any competent man were to apply them intelligently and consistently to the same cases under review, his judgments, made systematically nonintuitive by the explicit and conscious use of the principles, would be, nevertheless identical, case by case, with the considered judgments of the group of competent judges.

These explications must be written in ordinary language, be written in the form of principles, and be comprehensive in solving the range of moral judgments. In other words, common principles are extrapolated from the decisions of the moral judges, and these common principles are then used by the rest of us in decision making (Rawls, 1957).

Obviously, Rawls's proposal is more a rhetorical device than a useful tool for deciding ethical issues. However, the basic premise of his approach is to discover common principles that can be used to decide moral questions. This is fundamental to any logical solution to moral dilemmas. The ethical systems present principles similar to the explications that Rawls seeks through moral judges.

Another principle that one can derive from Rawls's discussion is that only neutral judges can develop objective and fair moral principles. His idea of a "veil of ignorance" attempts to create judges who are not personally invested in their decisions by their not knowing which actor they might be in any given dilemma. So, for instance, if the judges had to decide whether or not to lie, they would not know whether they were the liar or the person being lied to.

Basic moral or ethical principles can also be found in more pragmatic guidelines for use in decision making. A method proposed by Laura Nash (1981) helps individuals make business decisions, and these same questions seem applicable to situations faced by criminal justice professionals (see Box 2.3). Basically, the questions are designed to lead individuals to analyze their behavior and its implications. There is an assumption that exposure of unethical conduct will make the individual feel uneasy. To some extent, there is an assumption that a commonly agreed-upon definition of right and wrong exists.

The general principles that can be drawn from these questions are obvious:

1. We are interested in attaining all the facts of the situation; this includes the effects of the decision on oneself and others. It is important to understand hidden motivations and indirect effects.

BOX 2.3	HOW TO MAKE AN ETHICAL DECISION

1. Have you defined the problem accurately?
2. How would you define the problem if you were standing on the other side of the fence?
3. How did the situation arise in the first place?
4. To whom and to what do you give your loyalty as a person and as a member of the corporation?
5. What is your intention in making this decision?
6. How does this intention compare with the probable result?
7. Whom could your decision or action injure?
8. Can you discuss the problem with the affected parties before you make your decision?
9. Are you confident that your position will be as valid over a long period of time as it seems now?
10. Could you disclose without qualms your decision or action to your boss, your CEO, the board of directors, your family, your society as a whole?
11. What is the symbolic potential of your action if understood? If misunderstood?
12. Under what conditions would you allow exceptions to your stand?

Source: Nash, 1981: 81.

2. The concept of scrutiny works well to evaluate the decision taken; one must be comfortable with public disclosure. Along with this concept is the notion that others should be able to make the same decision and have it be judged acceptable.
3. Finally, the concept of rationale or reason implies that the individual decision is based on a more fundamental set of moral or ethical principles.

Let us apply these guidelines to a criminal justice example. If a police officer were confronted with an opportunity to accept some type of gratuity, either a dinner or a more expensive present, the officer could go through these steps:

1. First, evaluate all facts. Is anything expected in return? Is the gift really a gift, or is it a payment for some service? Do others receive the same gratuity?
2. Would the officer be comfortable if others knew of the gift or gratuity? Would he feel comfortable if other officers or other citizens knew he received the gift or gratuity?
3. Could the officer reconcile the decision to take the gratuity with a larger set of moral principles, such as the Law Enforcement Code of Ethics or his own department's rule book? What is the "symbolic potential" of the gratuity to the community?

Krogstand and Robertson (1979) described three principles of ethical decision making:

1. The **imperative principle** directs a decision maker to act according to a specific, unbending rule.
2. The **utilitarian principle** determines the ethics of conduct by the good or bad consequences of the action.
3. The **generalization principle** is based on this question: "What would happen if all similar persons acted this way under similar circumstances?"

These should sound familiar because they are, respectively, religious or absolutist ethics, utilitarianism, and ethical formalism. If one is familiar with these ethical principles, any specific dilemma can be analyzed using an ethical framework as a guideline.

Ruggiero (2004) proposes that ethical dilemmas be evaluated using three basic criteria. The first principle is to examine one's obligations and duties and what one has promised to do by contract or by taking on a role (this is similar to ethical formalism). The second principle is to examine moral ideals such as how one's decision squares with prudence, temperance, justice, honesty, compassion and other ideals (this is similar to Aristotle's Ethics of Virtue). The third principle is to evaluate the act to determine if it would result in good consequences (this is utilitarianism).

Close and Meier (1995: 130) provide a set of questions more specific to criminal justice professionals and sensitive to the due-process protections that are often discarded in a decision to commit an unethical act. They propose that the individual decision maker should ask the following questions:

1. Does the action violate another person's constitutional rights, including the right of due process?
2. Does the action involve treating another person only as a means to an end?
3. Is the action illegal?
4. Do you predict that your action will produce more bad than good for all persons affected?
5. Does the action violate department procedure or professional duty?

Finally, the simplest formulation of questions on which to base an ethical decision is as follows:

1. Does it affect others?
2. Does it hurt others?
3. Would I want it done if I were on the other side?
4. Would I be proud of the decision if it was made public?

These four simple questions may be sufficient to address most ethical dilemmas. In the end, most of us seek to make good decisions when confronted with moral or ethical dilemmas. Whichever decision-making method one chooses, the first step is to recognize that there is a choice to be made. The set of questions takes a general approach to evaluating one's ethics. It comes from the American Society for Public Administration (1979: 22–23) but has been adapted where necessary to apply to those who work in the criminal justice field.

RELATIVISM AND ABSOLUTISM

Ethical relativism describes the position that what is good or bad changes depending on the individual or group, and that there are no moral absolutes. What is right is determined by culture and/or individual belief; there are no universal laws.

The two main arguments for relativism are the following:

1. There are many different moral standards of behavior. According to Stace (1995: 26), "We find that there is nothing, or next to nothing, which has always and everywhere been regarded as morally good by all men."
2. Humans are incapable of determining what, if anything, is an absolute rule of morality. Who is to say what is right and what is wrong?

One may look to anthropology and the rise of social science to explain the popularity of moral relativism. Over the course of studying different societies—past and present, primitive and sophisticated—anthropologists have found that there are very few universals across cultures. Even those behaviors often believed to be universally condemned, such as incest, have been institutionalized and encouraged in some societies (Kottak, 1974: 307). Basically, **cultural relativism** defines good as that which contributes to the health and survival of society. As examples, societies where women are in ample supply may endorse polygyny, and societies that have a shortage of women may accept polyandry; hunting and gathering societies that must contend with harsh environments may hold beliefs allowing for the euthanasia of burdensome elderly, whereas agricultural societies that depend on knowledge passed down through generations may revere their elderly and accord them an honored place in society.

In criminology, cultural differences in perceptions of right and wrong are important to the subcultural deviance theory of crime, wherein some deviant activity is explained by subcultural approval of that behavior. The example typically used to illustrate this concept is that of the Sicilian father who kills the man who raped his daughter, because to do otherwise would violate values of his subculture emphasizing personal honor and retaliation (Sellin, 1970: 187). A more recent case of subcultural differences involves a father who sold his fourteen-year-old daughter into marriage. Because he lived in Chicago, he was arrested; if he had lived in his homeland of India, he would have been conforming to accepted norms of behavior. In a recent case in Texas, state officials seized all the children of a polygamous religious sect called the Fundamentalist Church of Jesus Christ of Latter Day Saints, because they allegedly required under-age girls to be married to the men in the sect. Because neither consent nor marriage is a defense to statutory rape, Texas laws were allegedly broken by the religious and cultural practices of the sect (Associated Press, 2008).

We should also note how governments attempt to change culture through the criminal law. The cultural support in India for killing wives whose families do not provide the dowry is being slowly eroded by the current legal system that (albeit halfheartedly) investigates and punishes those responsible. Cultural relativists recognize that cultures have very different definitions of right and wrong, and moral relativists argue that there are no fundamental or absolute definitions of right and wrong. Absolutists argue that just because there may be cultural norms endorsing such things as cannibalism, slavery, or having sex with six-year-olds, the norms do not make these acts moral.

Although cultural relativism holds that different societies may have different moral standards, it also dictates that individuals within a culture conform to the standards of their culture. Therein lies a fundamental flaw in the relativist approach:

If there are no universal norms, why should individuals be required to conform to societal or cultural norms? If their actions are not accepted today, it might be argued, they could be accepted tomorrow—if not by their society, perhaps by some other.

An additional inconsistency in cultural relativism is the corresponding prohibition against interfering in another culture's norms. The argument goes as follows: Because every culture is correct in its definitions of morality, another culture should not step in to change those definitions. However, if what is right is determined by which culture one happens to belong to, why then, if that culture happens to be imperialistic, would it be wrong to force cultural norms on other cultures? Cultural relativism attempts to combine an absolute (no interference) with a relativistic "truth" (there are no absolutes). This is logically inconsistent (Foot, 1982).

Cultural relativism usually concerns behaviors that are always right in one society and always wrong in another. Of course, what is more common is behavior that is judged to be wrong most of the time, but acceptable in certain instances. As examples: Killing is wrong except possibly in self-defense and war; lying is wrong except when one lies to protect another. Occupational subcultures also support standards of behavior that are acceptable only for those within the occupation. For instance, some police officers believe that it is wrong to break the speed limit unless one happens to be a police officer—even an off-duty one. Some politicians believe that certain laws don't apply to them because they are the ones who create the laws or because they can substitute their own judgment about what is best for the country. Some of these occupational ethics may be justified, but others may not be by any of the ethical decision-making methods we have discussed in this chapter.

It must be noted that even absolutist systems may accept some exceptions. The **principle of forfeiture** associated with deontological ethical systems holds that people who treat others as means to an end or take away or inhibit their freedom and well-being forfeit the right to protection of their own freedom and well-being (Harris, 1986: 136). Therefore, people who aggress first forfeit their own right to be protected from harm. This could permit self-defense (despite the moral proscription against taking life) and possibly provide justification for lying to a person who threatens harm. Critics of an absolutist system see this exception as a rationalization and a fatal weakness to the approach; in effect, moral rules are absolute *except* for those exceptions allowed by some "back-door" argument.

Alan Dershowitz, a well-known criminal defense attorney, has written a book of ethics in an attempt to explain how one should determine right and wrong. He argues that rights do not come from God because He does not speak to everyone in a single voice; they are not derived from natural law because nature is value-neutral; and they do not come from positive (man-made) law because it is subject to political influence. Dershowitz further disputes whether absolute rules can ever be sufficient to answer the questions of right and wrong. His conclusion is that our morals come from our experiences: Morality is evolving and changes when major events change our thinking about actions. His example is that when something like the Holocaust occurs, there is an evolution of rights such that new and greater rights are recognized.

According to Dershowitz, this moral evolution occurs in fits and starts and is not gradual or consistent; however, once something has been lived through, there is a new way of thinking about rights. He uses the example that after 9/11 we didn't put Middle Eastern visitors and citizens of Middle Eastern heritage in internment camps like we did with Japanese citizens in World War II (Dershowitz, 2004: 9, 94). One might argue with his facts, however, in that many after 9/11 did advocate internment and thousands of Middle Easterners who were in this country on visas or green cards were detained by authorities. Furthermore, it is interesting that Dershowitz has come out more recently in support of torture in certain circumstances, arguing that it is better to have rules and laws allowing torture in limited circumstances than to let it occur with no legal authority and, therefore, no legal oversight. His rationale, of course, is based on act utilitarianism: There is a greater good for everyone if the torture may reveal information that could save large numbers of people from harm. Perhaps he would agree that there may be some future time where we recognize the essential human right of anyone not to be tortured, but that time is not now.

Absolutists would argue, however, that the reason that things like the Holocaust, slavery, the slaughter of Native American Indians, the Armenian genocide, Japanese internment, the Bataan Death March, and torture in Abu Ghraib and Guantanamo happen is because people promoting their personal interests do not apply absolute rules of morality and ethics and, instead, utilize relativism: It is OK for me to do this, at this time, because of this reason.

Relativism allows for different rules for specific circumstances. Universalists would argue that if moral absolutes are removed, subjective moral discretion leads to egoistic (and nationalistic) rationalizations.

TOWARD A RESOLUTION: SITUATIONAL ETHICS

Situational ethics is often used as a synonym for *relativism*; however, if we clarify the term to include certain fundamental absolute elements, it might serve as a resolution to the problems inherent in both an absolutist and a relativist approach to ethics. Recall that relativism, on the one hand, is criticized because it must allow any practice to be considered "good" if it is considered good by some people; therefore, even human sacrifice and cannibalism would have to be considered moral—a thoroughly unpalatable consequence of accepting the doctrine. Absolutism, on the other hand, is also less than satisfactory because we all can think of some examples when the "rule" must be broken. Even Kant declined to be purely absolutist in his argument that lying isn't really lying if told to a person who is trying to harm us. What is needed, then, is an approach that resolves both problems.

Hinman (1998) resolves this debate by defining the balance between absolutism and relativism as **moral pluralism**. In his elaboration of this approach, he stops short of an "anything goes" rationale but does recognize multicultural "truths" that affect moral perceptions. The solution that will be offered here, whether one calls it situational ethics or some other term, is as follows:

1. There are basic principles of right and wrong.
2. These principles can be applied to ethical dilemmas and moral issues.

3. These principles may call for different results in different situations, depending on the needs, concerns, relationships, resources, weaknesses, and strengths of the individual actors.

Situational ethics is different from relativism because absolute laws are recognized, whereas under relativism there are no laws. What are absolute laws that can be identified as transcendent? Natural law, the Golden Rule, and the ethics of care could help us fashion a set of moral absolutes that might be general enough to ensure universal agreement. For instance, we could start with the following propositions:

1. Treat each person with the utmost respect and care.
2. Do one's duty or duties in such a way that one does not violate the first principle.

These principles would not have anything to say about dancing (as immoral or moral), but they would definitely condemn human sacrifice, child molestation, slavery, and a host of other practices that have been part of human society. Practices could be good in one society and bad in another. For instance, if polygamy was necessary to ensure the survival of society, it might be acceptable; if it was to serve the pleasure of some by using and treating others as mere objects, it would be immoral. Selling daughters into marriage to enrich the family would never be acceptable because that is not treating them with respect and care; however, arranged marriages might be acceptable if all parties agree and the motives are consistent with care.

To resolve the dilemma from Chapter 1 of the police officer who stops his father for DWI, one might argue that the officer can do his duty and still respect and care for his father. He could help his father through the arrest process, treat him with care, and make sure that he receives help, if needed, for his drinking. Although this might not be enough to placate his father and the father might still be angry with him, as would others, their reaction could then be analyzed: Are they treating the officer with care and respect? Does the father respect him if he expects his son to ignore a lawful duty?

This system is not too different from a flexible interpretation of Kant's categorical imperative, a strict interpretation of rule-based utilitarianism, or an inclusive application of the Golden Rule. All ethical systems (except egoism) struggle with objectivity and subjectivity, along with respect for the individual and concern for society. Interestingly, situational ethics seems to be entirely consistent with the ethics of care, especially when one contrasts this ethical system with a rule-based, absolutist system. In the ethics of care, you will recall, each individual is considered in the equation of what would be the "good." The schemata in Figure 2.2 may help to isolate the differences and similarities between these concepts.

Utilitarianism is arguably on the legal/rule side because the absolute rule of "the greatest utility for all" is often at the expense of the individual. Interestingly, the ethics of virtue, at least Aristotle's version, might be placed on the situational side, even though Aristotle believed that "practical reason" was more important than "moral virtues." This is because he recognized the concept of individuality in the "Golden Mean." In other words, one person's "mean" of courage might be different from another's, and this would have to be taken into account before judging behavior.

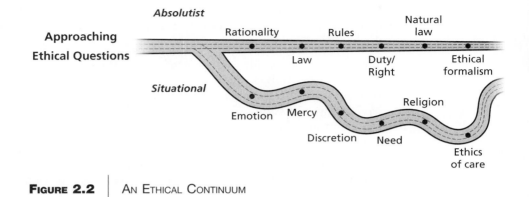

FIGURE 2.2 | AN ETHICAL CONTINUUM

RESULTING CONCERNS

As mentioned previously, ethical systems are not moral decisions as such; rather, they provide the guidelines or principles to make moral decisions. Box 2.4 ("The Major Ethical Systems") summarizes the key principles of these ethical systems.

It can happen that moral questions are decided in different ways under the same ethical system. For instance, if facts are in dispute, two people using utilitarianism may "weigh" the utilities of an act differently. Capital punishment is supported by some because of a belief that it is a deterrent to people who might commit murder; others argue it is wrong because it does not deter (this is an argument about facts between two utilitarians). Others believe that capital punishment is wrong regardless of its efficacy in deterrence. Most arguments about capital punishment get confused during the factual argument about the effectiveness of deterrence. "Is capital punishment wrong or right?" is a different question than "Does capital punishment deter?"

Another thing to consider is that none of us is perfect; we all have committed immoral or unethical acts that we know were wrong. Ethical systems help us to understand or analyze morality, but knowing what is right is no guarantee that we will always do the right thing. Few people follow such strong moral codes that they *never* lie or *never* cause other people harm. One can condemn the act and not the

---

BOX 2.4 | **THE MAJOR ETHICAL SYSTEMS**

Ethical formalism: What is good is that which conforms to the categorical imperative.

Utilitarianism: What is good is that which results in the greatest utility for the greatest number.

Religion: What is good is that which conforms to God's will.

Natural law: What is good is that which is natural.

Ethics of virtue: What is good is that which conforms to the Golden Mean.

Ethics of care: What is good is that which meets the needs of those concerned.

Egoism: What is good is that which benefits me.

person. The point is that just because some behaviors are understandable and perhaps even excusable does not make them moral or ethical. Few people consistently use just one ethical system in making moral decisions. Some of us are fundamentally utilitarian and some predominantly religious, but we may make decisions using other ethical frameworks as well.

Most of us try to behave ethically most of the time. Dilemmas arise when we are confused about the right thing to do or when the right thing to do carries considerable cost. Detective Poole knew what the right course of action was. He also knew that he would pay a price for doing it. In fact, he was transferred to a less prestigious position and denied a promotion. He was vilified and treated as a traitor by some officers when he went public with his evidence of a cover-up. Ultimately, he resigned from the Los Angeles Police Department (Golab, 2000). This illustrates the sad fact that doing the right thing sometimes comes at a high cost.

CONCLUSION

In this chapter we have explored some of the major ethical systems. Ethical systems are ordered principles that define what is right or good. Each of these ethical systems answers the question "What is good?" in a different way. Sometimes the same conclusion to an ethical dilemma can be reached using several different ethical systems, but sometimes using different ethical systems can result in contradictory answers to the determination of goodness.

Ethical systems are more complex to apply than they are to explain. For instance, utilitarianism is fairly easy to understand, but the measurement of utility for any given act is often quite difficult. Ethical formalism says to "do one's duty," but it does not help us when there are conflicting duties. The ethics of care emphasizes relationships but is vague in providing the steps necessary to resolve ethical dilemmas. The concept of situational ethics may help to reconcile the question as to whether ethics are ultimately relativistic or universal.

Key Terms

act utilitarianism 37

categorical
  imperatives 34

cultural relativism 54

deontological ethical
  system 33

egoism 49

enlightened egoism 50

ethical formalism 33

ethical system 31

ethics of care 47

ethics of virtue 45

explication 51

generalization
  principle 52

hypothetical
  imperatives 34

imperative principle 52

moral pluralism 56

natural law 43

peacemaking justice 48

principle of
  forfeiture 55

principle of the golden
  mean 45

psychological
  egoism 49

religious ethics 40

rule utilitarianism 37

situational ethics 56

teleological ethical
  system 33

utilitarian principle 52

utilitarianism 36

Review Questions

1. Discuss the differences between teleological systems and deontological systems.
2. Describe two teleological ethical systems, and describe two deontological systems.
3. What seems to be one similarity among all religious systems?
4. Contrast the ethics of care and utilitarianism. Compare the natural law system with religion.
5. If you had to choose one ethical system, which one most closely conforms to your own beliefs? Be explicit.
6. Instead of the ethical systems, describe another way of resolving ethical dilemmas using one of the other methods (e.g., Nash's set of questions) discussed in this chapter.
7. Provide some examples of cultural relativism. Discuss the arguments against and supporting relativism. Do the same for absolutism.
8. Is there a universal truth relating to right and wrong, moral and immoral? If you answered yes, what are the principles of such a system?
9. Explain the differences between situational ethics and relativism.
10. Determine which ethical system(s) support the questions in Nash's "How to Make an Ethical Decision."

Writing/Discussion Questions

1. Write an essay (or discuss) the ethical systems in regard to the following situations:

   a. In the movie *Sophie's Choice*, a woman is forced to choose which one of her children to send to the gas chamber. If she does not decide, both will be killed. How would ethical formalism resolve this dilemma? How would utilitarianism resolve it?

   b. There is a continuing debate over whether the United States had to bomb Hiroshima and Nagasaki at the end of World War II. Present the arguments on both sides. Now consider this: Are they utilitarian arguments, ethical formalist arguments, or some other?

2. Write an essay on (or discuss) the basic nature of humans. Are we basically altruistic? Basically egoistic? Include in this essay responses to the following and examples to support your answer: What are the "natural" inclinations of human beings? Do you think most people do the right thing out of habit or out of reason?

3. Write an essay (or discuss) whether ethics and morals are relative or absolute. Are there absolute moral truths, or is morality simply an individual's definition of right and wrong? Should everyone have the right to decide which behaviors are acceptable for them? Should all cultures have the right to decide what is right? If you believe there are absolute definitions of right and wrong, what are they?

Ethical Dilemmas

Situation 1

You are the manager of a retail store. The owner of the store gives you permission to hire a fellow classmate to help out. One day you see the classmate take some clothing from the store. When confronted by you, the peer laughs it off and says the owner is insured, no one is hurt, and it was under $100. "Besides," says your acquaintance, "friends stick together, right?" What would you do?

Situation 2

You are in a lifeboat along with four others. You have enough food and water to keep only four people alive for the several weeks you expect to be adrift until you float into a shipping lane and can be discovered and rescued. You will definitely all perish if the five of you consume all the food and water. There is the suggestion that one of you should die so the other four can live. Would you volunteer to commit suicide? Would you vote to have one go overboard if you choose by straws? Would you vote to throw overboard the weakest and least healthy of the five? If you were on a jury judging the behavior of four who did murder a fifth in order to stay alive, would you acquit them or convict them of murder? Would your answer be different if the murdered victim was your son or daughter?

Situation 3

You aspire to be a police officer and are about to graduate from a criminal justice department. Your best friend has just been hired by a local law enforcement agency, and you are applying as well. When you were both freshmen, you were caught with marijuana in your dorm room. Although you were arrested, the charges were dismissed because it turned out that the search was illegal. The application form includes a question that asks if you have ever been arrested. Your friend told you that he answered no because he knew this agency did not use polygraphs as part of the hiring process. You must now decide whether to also lie on the form. If you lie, you may be found out eventually, but there is a good chance that the long-ago arrest will never come to light. If you don't lie, you will be asked to explain the circumstances of the arrest, and your friend will be implicated as well. What should you do?

Situation 4

You have a best friend who has confessed a terrible secret to you. Today the man is married and has two children. He has a good family, a good life, and is a good citizen. However, fourteen years earlier he killed a woman. A homeless person was accused of the crime but died before he could be tried and punished. Nothing good can come of this man's confession. His family will suffer; and no one is at risk of being mistaken as the murderer. What would you advise him to do? (Some may recognize this dilemma as coming from Dostoyevsky's *The Brothers Karamazov*.)

Situation 5

You are working in Internal Affairs, and through the course of another investigation, you discover disturbing evidence regarding the police chief's son, who is also an officer in the department. Several informants have confided in you that this individual has roughed them up and taken their drugs, yet you find no record of arrest or the drugs being logged in the evidence room. When you write your report, your sergeant tears it up and tells you that there is not enough evidence to justify an investigation and for you to stick to what you are told to do. What would you do? What would you do if the chief calls you into his office the next day and offers you a transfer to a high-status position that will definitely lead to a promotion?

Suggested Readings

Associated Press 2008. Deal to Return Children To Parents Collapses. AP, reported by MSNBC.com, May 30, 2008; Retrieved 6/11/2008 from http://www.msnbc.msn.com/id/24887140.

Braswell, M., McCarthy, B., and McCarthy, B., eds.. 2002. *Justice, Crime, and Ethics,* 3rd ed. Cincinnati, OH: Anderson Publishing Company.

Dershowitz, A. 2004. *Rights From Wrongs: A Secular Theory of the Origins of Rights.* New York: Basic Books, 2004.

Foot, P. 1982. "Moral Relativism." In *Relativism: Cognitive and Moral,* eds, J. Meiland and M. Krausz, 152–167. Notre Dame, IN: University of Notre Dame Press.

Harman, G. and Thomson, J. 1996. *Moral relativism and Moral Objectivity.* London: Blackwell.

Hinman, L. 1998. *Ethics: A Pluralistic Approach to Moral Theory,* 2d Ed. Fort Worth, TX: Harcourt Brace.

Prior, W. (Ed.). 1991. From *Virtue and Knowledge: An Introduction to Ancient Greek Ethics.* New York: Routledge, Kegan Paul.

Rousseau, J. 1983. *Discourse on the Origins of Inequality.* Indianapolis, IN: Hackett Publishing.

Ruggiero, V. 2004. *Thinking Critically About Ethical Issues,* 5th ed. New York: McGraw-Hill.

Shermer, M. 2004. *The Science of Good and Evil: Why People Chat, Gossip, Care, Share, and Follow the Golden Rule.* New York: Times Books/Holt & Co.

Stace, W. 1995. "Ethical Relativity and Ethical Absolutism." In *Morality in Criminal Justice,* eds. D. Close and N. Meier, 25–32. Belmont, CA: Wadsworth.

Streiffer, R. 2003. *Moral Relativism and Reasons for Action.* New York: Routledge.

MAKING ETHICAL DECISIONS

CHAPTER **3**

PERSONS OF THE YEAR

TIME

The Whistleblowers

CYNTHIA COOPER
OF WORLDCOM

COLEEN ROWLEY
OF THE FBI

SHERRON WATKINS
OF ENRON

© Gregory Heisler/Getty Images

What makes people do things they know are wrong? What makes people stand up and expose wrongdoing? In 2002, instead of identifying the "Person of the Year," TIME Magazine identified three: Cynthia Cooper, who exposed fraud at WorldCom; Sherron Watkins, who warned of Enron's imminent collapse; and Colleen Rowley, who attempted to get FBI leaders to understand the internal failings that contributed to the 9/11 disaster.

CHAPTER OBJECTIVES

1. Become familiar with the major theories regarding the development of moral behavior.

2. Become familiar with Carol Gilligan's research exploring gender differences in moral development.

3. Recognize the difficulty associated with the relationship between moral beliefs and behavior.

4. Become familiar with some of the applications of moral development theory to criminal offenders.

5. Understand the range of answers to the question "Why be ethical?"

CHAPTER OUTLINE

In 2008 New York was rocked with a series of articles concerning Elliot Spitzer, a law-and-order governor who was caught on tape setting up a liaison with a high-priced call girl. His "fall from grace" was precipitous; he quickly resigned in the wake of a firestorm of publicity and faced potential federal charges. Critics were stunned because Spitzer's career had been a steady series of successes, first at Princeton, then Harvard, where he obtained his juris doctorate. He spent several years as a district attorney in Manhattan, then ran for and was elected Attorney General in 1998. He honed his political reputation as a fearless advocate for law and order who targeted white collar criminals on Wall Street and in the banking industry.

When Spitzer was elected governor in 2006, he pledged to clean up the corruption in Albany and alienated opponents and supporters alike with his "take no prisoners" approach to changing the back scratching and questionable ethics of the capital city. How could a moral crusader, who campaigned on the promise to clean up the corruption in Albany and who tirelessly prosecuted criminal offenders, betray his wife, lie to the voters, and break federal and state laws? Was he a good man who made mistakes, a bad man who did good things, or are moral character and moral behavior much more complicated than simple dichotomies of good and bad?

In Chapter 1 we explored the question "How does one determine what is good?" In this chapter we will discuss the questions "How does one become a good person?" and "Why be ethical?" As we have seen, philosophers have looked to God, natural law, reason, intuition, and emotion to determine moral truths. The fundamental question regarding the nature of humans is whether we are born good or evil, or whether we become that way through life circumstances. Philosophers, psychologists, sociologists, and criminologists have addressed this question, and sometimes argue over which field offers the best understanding of human nature.

Karl Menninger (1973), a psychiatrist, argued that the fields of psychiatry and psychology usurped and undercut earlier beliefs and judgments of sin. More than three decades ago he observed that sin had become a character disorder that had to be treated or a crime to be punished, but "treatment" or "punishment" didn't carry the same moral opprobrium as when such acts were considered sins; and, therefore, the moral decay of society was accelerating. The sins he described included group sins of slavery, corporate greed, and environmental damage; and individual sins consisted of pride, sensuality (adultery and pornography), gluttony (excessive food, drugs, and drink), sloth, envy, affluence, waste, cheating and stealing, lying, and cruelty.

Even though Menninger wrote about the "dissolution" of morality more than three decades ago, his words sound similar to those who conclude that we are experiencing a decline of morals today. It is also interesting to note that earlier in his career as a psychologist, he advocated diagnosis and classification of all criminals so they could be "treated" for the underlying pathology that caused them to commit crime. Thus, science was supplanted by moral judgment in his own approach to understanding and responding to bad behavior. This dichotomy between scientific determinism, which looks for causes of people's actions, and philosophical discussions of free will and human agency, which support moral judgments, are constant themes in any attempt to understand and explain human behavior.

THEORIES OF MORAL DEVELOPMENT

Psychology seeks to understand why people behave the way we do. If someone is a chronic liar, why is he that way? If someone is aggressive and takes what she wants regardless of other people's needs or desires, why does she behave that way? It should also be noted that *beliefs* and *actions* are related but that one does not necessarily predict the other. As stated before, just because we know something is wrong does not mean that we never do it. The most important contributions to this discussion involve biological theories, learning theory, and development theories. Simple definitions of the approaches are as follows.

1. *Biological theories* propose that we commit good or bad acts because of biological predispositions. Another biological explanation comes from sociobiology which looks at human behaviors—both good and bad—as evidence of traits that are selected for species survival in our evolution.
2. *Learning theory*, a psychological theory, argues that our behavior is based on the rewards we have received in our past. What we do and what we believe is based on what we have been rewarded for. More sophisticated social learning theories present the individual as an active participant in adapting and interpreting the rewards of his or her environment.
3. *Developmental theories* explain that people's behavior is influenced by the intellectual and emotional stage of development, and that one reaches or does not reach higher stages of development based on environmental factors.

BIOLOGICAL THEORIES

The most controversial theories of human behavior point to biological predeterminers. Biological criminologists have discovered correlations between delinquency/criminology and a range of human traits, including impulsivity and aggressiveness (Fishbein, 2000). Researchers who study the brain have also discovered a possible linkage between the brain and the development of moral behavior. The frontal lobes of the brain seem to be implicated in feelings of empathy, shame, and moral reasoning. Ellis and Pontus (1989: 6) presented a theory postulating the influence of the frontal lobe and the limbic system on the individual's capacity for moral reasoning, in which individuals with frontal-lobe damage display these characteristics:

1. increased impulsiveness
2. decreased attention span
3. difficulty in logical reasoning
4. difficulty adjusting to new events
5. tendency toward apathy and erratic mood shifts
6. tendency toward rude, unrestrained, tactless behavior
7. tendency to not be able to follow instructions, even after verbalizing what is required.

These authors also proposed that biological sex differences in brain activity support the notion that women are more inclined to empathy and sensitivity to human relationships. More than seventy studies examining sex differences in brain functioning found evidence that men are more antisocial, commit more serious types of offenses, and more often have serious childhood conduct disorders. There are also sex differences in delinquency, school performance, hyperactivity, impulsivity, and attention deficit disorders. Some analysts propose that these differences are associated with sex-linked brain activity, specifically in the frontal lobes and limbic regions. They claim that males' sex hormones influence brain development pre-natally and during puberty. Further, although there is a great deal of overlap between male and female populations in brain development and activity, there are also distinct and measurable differences; specifically, these differences may influence the brain's ability to absorb "moral messages" or act upon them. This research offers intriguing explanations of why some people (more often men) act in ways that are harmful to others.

Biological criminology looks at biological traits that predispose someone to commit crimes, and a separate, but related question as to whether an identified biological feature is inherited. Fishbein's (2000) review of bio-behavioral influences on criminality found numerous possible linkages between behavioral traits and potential criminality. Violence, for instance, seems to be linked to low serotonin levels. Low serotonin levels may be genetic, or they may be the result of post-natal influences, such as long-term drug use, situational depression, and so on. While impulsivity is an inherited trait and seems to be correlated with delinquency, research in this area uniformly indicates that environmental factors are just as or more important than biological factors. Others argue that the link between genetics and criminal behavior is unclear and suffers from extreme methodological issues (Wasserman and Wachbroit, 2001).

A somewhat different biological approach to understanding human behavior comes from socio-biology, which looks at how certain human traits have been selected because of their value in species survival. A detailed explanation of how biology might be used to help us understand why people engage in bad behaviors is offered by Walsh (1995, 2001/2002), who looks at certain types of crimes and whether or not an evolutionary rationale might exist. For instance, he observes that stepfathers are more likely than biological fathers to kill their stepchildren, and parallels this behavior to other species of animals, in which males kill the off-spring of other males—evidently a trait hardwired to perpetuate his progeny rather than others.

Wilson (1993) has argued that values such as sympathy, fairness, self-control, and duty are moral "senses" that are inherent in humans and arise through a com-bination of genetics and socialization. Shermer (2004) also argues that these traits have been inherited, although he supports a group selection argument—specifically, that eons ago those human groups that held these traits were more likely to survive than groups that did not, and quotes Darwin to support the view that:

> ...There can be no doubt that a tribe including many members who, from possessing in a high degree the spirit of patriotism, fidelity, obedience, courage and sympathy, were always ready to aid one another, and to sacrifice themselves for the common good, would be victorious over most other tribes; and this would be natural selection....
> (Darwin, quoted in Shermer, 2004: 51)

In an interesting twist to the debate as to whether morals exist apart from humans or are created by them, Shermer argues that they are both: They transcend humans in the sense that our moral senses have been created by evolutionary fac-tors that have taken place over the millennia; however, they are "of us" in the sense that they are human emotions, sentiments, and behaviors.

Shermer (2004: 37) states that asking why humans should be moral is like ask-ing why we should be hungry or jealous. We are because we are hardwired for these feelings and emotions. Drawing a parallel between humans and foxes, he relates research that showed breeding foxes for docility also resulted in other phys-ical changes, including more juvenile features and smaller jaws and teeth. Shermer argues that the same evolutionary trend occurred with humans. He compared humans to bonobos (a type of chimp that is much less aggressive, more sexual, and more social than its close genetic cousins). He suggested that the different behavioral patterns may be a result of their higher levels of serotonin than their more aggressive cousin chimps. The greater sexual activity is said to generate oxy-tocin (OT), a feel-good hormone that increases with sexual activity, and oxytocin is related to serotonin (2004: 227)

Shermer also places morality in the intuitive and emotional capacities of humans, rather than the rational (2004: 177, 257). He points out research showing that moral emotions activate the amygdale, the emotion module in the brain, as well as the orbital and medial prefrontal cortex, which are the centers of cognitive processing. Arguably, dilemmas arise when these two areas of the brain are in con-flict. For instance, in a well-known hypothetical moral dilemma, a woman is hiding from enemy soldiers with others in a cellar when her baby starts crying. Asked to imagine what they would do in this situation, two areas of the subjects' brains in

MRIs light up—the inferior parietal lobe, which is related to rational, but impersonal, thinking, and the "emotion" centers of the brain, which evidently react with horror to the alternative of smothering the baby (Vedantam, 2007).

Researchers found that when subjects performed altruistic acts, their behavior triggered the "pleasure" center of the brain, connected with food and sex. This indicates that moral behaviors are hardwired into humans' basic impulses. Other research indicated that those with damage to the ventromedial prefrontal cortex, which is related to emotions, were unable to have any feelings regarding moral judgments (e.g., sympathy for others pain and suffering or good feelings from altruism), although they were quite able to impersonally and coldly evaluate costs and benefits. The argument of some researchers is that morality lies in empathy, which derives from the emotional center of the brain. They say that only much later in evolution did the reasoning area of the brain become developed and involved in moral decision making (Vedantam, 2007).

This area of research is fascinating, not only to help us understand why humans act the way we do but also to help us understand in what specific ways we are similar to and different from other species in the animal kingdom. With continuing research in brain chemistry and with the work of the human genome project that has been "mapping" human DNA to discover our genetic heritage, fundamental questions of morality, culpability, and responsibility will arise. Biologists, anthropologists, sociologists, and philosophers all have participated in the resulting discussion of how and why humans decide to commit immoral or moral acts. The discussion below, however, turns to two other approaches taken by psychologists.

LEARNING THEORY

Learning theorists believe that children learn what they are taught, including morals and values as well as behavior. In other words, right or wrong is not discovered through reasoning; rather, all humans are shaped by the world around us, and we form completely subjective opinions about morality and ethics. This learning can take place through modeling or by reinforcement.

In **modeling**, values and moral beliefs come from those whom one admires and aspires to identify with. If that role model happens to be a priest, one will probably develop a religious ethical system; if the role model happens to be a pimp or a sociopath, an egoistic ethical system may develop. If the identification is broken, moral beliefs may change. It is no surprise that, when asked who has been important in their moral development, most people say it is their parents, because parents are the most significant people in life during the important formative years. Although we may not hold exactly the same views and have exactly the same values as our parents, they without a doubt are influential in our value formation.

Another way that learning theorists explain moral development is through **reinforcement**. This theory holds that behaviors and beliefs that are reinforced (either through material rewards or through more subjective rewards, such as praise) are repeated and eventually become permanent. Behavior is completely neutral; an infant can be taught any behavior desired, and the moral beliefs consistent with that belief. In one experiment children were told a hypothetical story in which an adult punished a neutral act, such as a child practicing a musical instrument. The children later defined that act as bad, despite the intrinsic neutrality of the action. This indicates the power of adult definitions and punishment in the child's moral development (Boyce and Jensen, 1978: 133–170).

Because behavior is more easily stabilized and tends to come before permanent attitude change, behavior often leads to the development of consistent beliefs. On the one hand, one child is rewarded for sharing (by parental praise or a realization of reciprocity) and eventually develops the belief that "sharing is good." On the other hand, a different child is rewarded for being selfish and bullying others to gain what he or she wants. On the playground other children are afraid of this child, who uses their fear to demand toys or extra turns. No adults reprimand the child, or they do so inconsistently, so the rewards far outweigh the negative consequences of the behavior. Eventually the child may develop a "me first" and "every person for himself/herself" philosophy of life.

Quite a bit of research supports a learning theory of moral development. For instance, it was found that large gains in moral maturity (at least as measured by paper-and-pencil tests of expression of beliefs) could be achieved by direct manipulation of rewards for such beliefs (Boyce and Jensen, 1978: 143). Contrary to the view that an individual comes to a realization of moral principles through cognitive development, this theory proposes that one can encourage or create moral beliefs simply through rewards.

When behavior is not consistent with beliefs, the discomfort that results is called **cognitive dissonance**. This leads to the development of attitudes to support one's behavior. The child who is constantly told to share toys and is disciplined upon refusing to do so is learning not just the desired behavior, but also the values of cooperation and charity. In an adult these values may be manifested by lending one's lawn mower to a neighbor or by contributing to charities. In contrast, if a child is never punished for aggressive behavior and instead is rewarded by always getting the desired object, aggressiveness and the accompanying moral principle of "might makes right" develop. If we do acts that are contrary to the beliefs that we have been taught, we will feel discomfort. Therefore, we will either stop doing the acts or change our beliefs to reduce the dissonance.

Albert Bandura (1925), one of the most cited psychologists of this era, developed social learning theory and the idea of modeling as the mechanism of development. In his early career he described how the successful use of rewards is related to the child's age. As the child matures, concrete rewards and external sanctions are replaced by symbolic and internal controls (one's conscience) (Bandura, 1964). Eventually Bandura described the individual as not simply a passive recipient of rewards but, rather, as an active participant in the construction and meaning of rewards (Bandura 1969, 1971). In this view, individuals are active, not passive; self-reflective, not merely acted upon; and self-regulating, not merely controlled by external forces. Bandura's later work revolved around his development of the concept of self-efficacy. **Self-efficacy** can be defined as the individual's feelings of competence, and this sense is developed by comparing the self to others.

Bandura has had quite a bit to say about the subject of morality. He believes that moral values can be most effectively instilled by a combination of direct influence (modeling) and reinforcement. Further, he argues that reinforcement (negative sanctions), accompanied by reasons that encourage empathy for the victims, produces greater abilities to self-regulate than those utilizing negative sanctions alone (1991: 53). Bandura sees social and moral maturity as constantly changing, reacting to outside influences (involving family, peers, and social institutions).

Moral standards are constructed by the individual, not merely mimicked as some of the more simplistic descriptions of learning theory would indicate. Moral behavior results from self-regulation and social sanctions, both of which work anticipatorily, meaning that one does or does not do an immoral act because of the internal or external sanctions that one expects (will they feel bad if they do it?) (Bandura, 1991: 68). Self-regulation works best when one has a strong belief in one's personal control; thus, self-efficacy is related to morality (Bandura, 2002).

Bandura also has developed a theory of when self-regulating controls are "turned off," leading to inhumane acts. This "selective disengagement" can occur through cognitive restructuring via several different mechanisms, as follows (Bandura, 1991; 1990; 2002).

1. *Moral justification*: This is an appeal to a higher or more important end to justify the act (e.g., terrorists who are fighting for a cause). Similar to utilitarianism, the idea here is that the end justifies the means.
2. *Euphemistic labeling*: By using words that downplay the seriousness of actions, the true moral nature of such actions is ignored (e.g., sanitizing language, such as "wasting" or "whacking" instead of killing, and the term "collateral damage" for killing civilians in times of war).
3. *Advantageous comparison*: This is an argument that the action may be wrong but it isn't as bad as some other actions (e.g., "What was done at Abu Ghraib wasn't as bad as the actions of insurgents who cut off the heads of civilian contractors.")
4. *Displacement of responsibility*: This argument basically removes the individual as a free-thinking agent of his or her own actions in order to deny culpability (e.g., "I was only following orders.").
5. *Diffusion of responsibility*: In this situation the individual can redefine his or her responsibility for an action by diffusing it among a number of people (e.g., when a number of people are engaged in morally questionable behavior such as a mob action).
6. *Disregard or distortion of the consequences*: By misidentifying the consequences of one's actions, one can deny one's responsibility for harm (e.g., when the executioner is hidden behind a curtain or when the CEO who gives the order to pollute merely requests that the problem be "taken care of").
7. *Dehumanization*: Humans feel the most sympathy/empathy for those who are most like us and who are closest to us, and we feel the least for those who are most unlike us; therefore, dehumanization is a process to strip the victim of any qualities of similarity that may create sympathy (e.g., the use of terms such as gooks, slant-eyes, pigs, wetbacks, and even worse words used to dehumanize groups).

Bandura argues that it takes a certain constellation of conditions to create human atrocities, not necessarily "monstrous" people (Bandura, 1991: 89). Also, he purports that the shift to immoral acts and attendant justifications is probably gradual, not immediate. Inhibitions are lessened when there is social support for inhuman acts. Finally, external conditions are not all-powerful; the individual adapts and reinterprets them within his or her own internal cognitive processes (Bandura, 2002).

Early learning theorists believed that honesty, integrity, and fairness exist only because they have been rewarded and are part of the individual's behavioral repertoire. According to learning theorists, the moral principles of "honesty is right," "integrity is good," and "fairness is ethical" come *after* the behavior has been stabilized, not before. This theory is very different from the view that moral beliefs come before actions. Current social learning theory is more sophisticated and views the individual as an active player in the construction of moral values; it is more accurately a dynamic between the individual and the world around him or her that combine to form moral beliefs, but these are not monolithic and consistent and can change given a change of social circumstances.

Learning theory leaves little room for universalism, absolutism, or the idea that a moral truth exists apart from humans that is not of their construction but that awaits their discovery. The theory is completely humanistic in that morality is considered to be a creation of humans that explains and provides a rationale for learned behavior.

DEVELOPMENTAL THEORIES

Developmental theories propose that individuals mature physically, cognitively, and emotionally. Think about it in this way:

1. Normal *physical* development can be charted by a pediatrician. We discover at the pediatrician's office whether the height and weight of our child are in the "normal curve" of development.
2. *Intellectual* development also is measured by a variety of intelligence tests and is charted against a normal curve of development. We do not expect the child to understand concepts before attaining certain developmental markers.
3. *Emotional or social* development also progresses at a predictable and normal pace, although it may be more difficult to measure.

Social maturity is marked by the ability to empathize with others and a willingness to compromise one's desires with others' needs. An emotionally mature person neither abandons self for others nor puts oneself above others but, rather, balances individual needs with others' demands; however, that development might be stunted by negative environmental influences.

Kohlberg's Moral Stages   The contributions of Jean Piaget and Lawrence Kohlberg have become essential to any discussion of moral development. Piaget believed that we all go through stages of cognitive, or intellectual, growth. These stages parallel moral stages of development, and together they describe a systematic way of perceiving the world. Piaget studied the rules that children develop in their play. These rules reflect the perceptions that children hold of themselves and others and move from egocentrism to cooperativeness.

Kohlberg carried on with Piaget's work and more fully described the stages that each individual passes through in moral and cognitive development (Kohlberg, 1984). In this conception, two-year-olds do not understand the world in the same way as twenty-year-olds do. This difference in understanding affects their moral reasoning ability. The infant lacks sensitivity toward others and is supremely selfish regarding his or her needs and wants. Infants are not concerned with others because they are only vaguely aware of their existence. The infant's world is confined to what is within reach of his or her hands and mouth. Even a mother is important only as the source of comfort and food. Slowly the infant becomes aware that others also have feelings and needs. This awareness leads to empathy and the recognition of right and wrong.

At later stages, abstract reasoning develops, which leads to the ability to understand more difficult moral concepts. **Kohlberg's moral stages** consist of three levels of moral reasoning, with two stages in each level. Some characteristics of these cognitive and moral stages are the following (Hersh, 1979: 52):

1. *The stages involve qualitative differences, as opposed to quantitative differences, in modes of thinking.* The child undergoes dramatic changes in perceptions; the child realizes that what he or she does has an impact on others. An infant realizes that when she pulls someone's hair, the person reacts. When an infant cries, someone comes. When he performs certain behaviors, he is praised.
2. *Each stage forms a structured whole; cognitive development and moral growth are integrated.* All individuals at a particular stage have similar perceptions of the world and the corresponding moral framework. Simplistically, this means that children cannot be sensitive to larger issues such as world hunger until they are able to grasp the reality of such conditions.
3. *The stages form an invariant sequence; no one bypasses any stage, and not all people develop to the higher stages.* According to Kohlberg, few individuals reach the post-conventional level; the majority of people reach the conventional level and stay there.
4. *Stages are hierarchical integrations.* Each succeeding stage encompasses and is more comprehensive and complicated than the stage that precedes it.

At the *pre-conventional level* the person approaches a moral issue motivated purely by personal interests. The major concern is the consequence of the action for the individual. For instance, young children do not share toys with others because they see no reason to do so. They derive pleasure from their toys, so to give the toys to others does not make sense to them. Even if the toys belong to others, children are predisposed to appropriate them. Parents are aware of the tears and tantrums associated with teaching a child that toys belonging to others must be given back. Young children first start sharing when they perceive benefit to themselves, such as giving someone their doll in exchange for a game or a ball, or they grudgingly share because they fear punishment from an adult if they do not.

Stage 1 has a punishment and obedience orientation. What is right is that which is praised; what is wrong is that which is punished. The child submits to an authority figure's definition and is concerned only with the consequences attached to certain behaviors, not with the behavior itself.

Stage 2 has an instrument-and-relativity orientation. The child becomes aware of and is concerned with others' needs. What is right is still determined by self-interest, but the concept of self-interest is broadened to include those who are within the child's sphere of relationships. Relationships are important to the child, and he or she is attached to parents, siblings, and best friends, who are included in the ring of self-interest. There is also the emerging concept of fairness and a recognition that others deserve to have their needs met.

At the *conventional level* people perceive themselves as members of society, and living up to role responsibilities is paramount in believing oneself to be good. Children enter this level when they are capable of playing with other children according to rules. Games and play are training grounds for moral development because they teach the child that there are defined roles and rules of behavior. For instance, a game of softball becomes a microcosm of real life when a child realizes that he or she is not only acting as self but also as a first baseman, a role that includes certain specific tasks. Before this stage, the child runs to the ball regardless of where it is hit. Thus, in a softball game with very young children playing, one may see all the players running after the ball and abandoning their bases because they have difficulty grasping the concept of role responsibilities. Further, although it would be more expeditious to trip the runners as they leave the base so they can be tagged "out," the child learns that such behavior is not "fair play" and is against the rules of the game. Thus, children learn to submerge individual interest to conform to rules and role expectations.

Stage 3 has an interpersonal concordance orientation. The individual performs conventionally determined good behavior to be considered a good person. The views of "significant others" are important to self-concept. Thus, individuals will control their behavior so as to not hurt others' feelings or be thought of as bad.

Stage 4 has a law-and-order orientation. The individual is concerned not just with interpersonal relationships but also with the rules set down by society. The law becomes all-important. Even if the laws themselves are wrong, one cannot disregard them, for that would invite social chaos.

At the *post-conventional level* a person moves beyond the norms and laws of a society to determine universal good—that is, what is good for all societies. Few people reach this level, and their actions are observably different from the majority. For instance, Mahatma Gandhi might be described as having a post-conventional morality. He did not subscribe to the idea that laws must be obeyed, and he carried out peaceful noncompliance against established laws to conform to his belief in a higher order of morality. At this level of moral development, the individual assumes the responsibility of judging laws and conventions.

Stage 5 has a social contract orientation. The person recognizes interests larger than current laws. This individual is able to evaluate the morality of laws in a historical context and feels an obligation to the law because of its benefits to societal survival.

Stage 6 centers on universal ethical principles. The person who has reached this stage bases moral judgments on the higher abstract laws of truth, justice, and morality.

A seventh stage? Kohlberg advanced the possibility of a seventh stage, which has been described as a "soft" stage of ethical awareness with an orientation of cosmic or religious thinking. It is not a higher level of reasoning, but is qualitatively different. According to Kohlberg, in this highest stage individuals have come to terms with questions such as, "Why be just in a universe that is largely unjust?" This is a different question than the definition of justice that forms the content of the other stages. In this stage one sees oneself as part of a larger whole, and humanity as only part of a larger cosmic structure. This stage focuses on *agape*—a nonexclusive love and acceptance of the cosmos and one's place in it (Kohlberg, 1983; Power and Kohlberg, 1980).

Critics of Kohlberg   Some believe that Kohlberg's theory of moral development has several serious flaws, of which the most prevalent criticisms are as follows.

1. The stages tend to center too much on the concept of justice, ignoring other aspects of morality.
2. The stages, especially stages 5 and 6, may be nothing more than culturally based beliefs regarding the highest level of morality. Many philosophers and other psychologists argue that Kohlberg's definition of deontological ideas of justice as higher levels of morality merely reflect the Judeo-Christian heritage of Kohlberg and his followers.
3. Justice, rules, and rights are emphasized as higher values than are caring and relationships—contrary to later research that shows the importance of emotion in moral decision making. In response to critics who argue that morality is not only about reasoning ability, Kohlberg and his associates assert that the theory is a measurement of "justice reasoning," not an attempt to present the "total complexity of the moral domain" (Levine, Kohlberg, and Hewer, 1985: 99).
4. Studies have found significant cultural differences in the age at which children reach different stages of moral development. This does not necessarily negate the validity of a stage sequence theory; however, it does call into question the specifics of movement through the stages (Boyce and Jensen, 1978). Further, research has indicated that people do display multiple moral rationales, indicating that it is possible to be "in" more than one stage level at a time—contrary to Kohlberg's description of the stage theory (Bandura, 1991: 49).
5. Some criticize the lack of connection between reasoning levels and moral action in specific situations. There does not seem to be a strong correlation between one's moral stage, as measured by the interview format of Kohlberg's research or more recently devised paper-and-pencil tests of recognition, and how one will respond when faced with a moral dilemma (Lutwak and Hennessy, 1985).
6. Kohlberg's research can be described as sexually biased because he interviewed boys almost exclusively in early research. Subsequent studies have found that women tend to cluster in Stage 3 because of their greater sensitivity to and emphasis on human relationships. Stage 3 is lower than Stage 4, the law-and-order stage, where men tend to be clustered. Unless one believes that women are generally less moral or less intellectually developed than men, this is a troubling finding that calls into question the hierarchical nature of the theory.

A Different Morality?   Carol Gilligan (1982, 1987), one of Kohlberg's students, researched the apparent sex difference in moral reasoning and proposed that women may possess a morality *different* from men. Most men, it seems, analyze moral decisions with a rules or justice orientation (Stage 4), whereas many women see the same moral dilemma with an orientation toward needs and relationships (Stage 3). Gilligan labeled this a *care perspective*. A morality based on the care perspective would be more inclined to look at how a decision affects relationships and addresses needs, whereas the justice perspective is concerned with notions of equality, rights, and universality. (Ethics of care is described in Chapter 2 as one of the ethical frameworks.)

In Gilligan's study, although both men and women raised justice and care concerns in responses to moral dilemmas, among those who focused on one or the other, men focused exclusively on justice whereas half of the women who exhibited a focus did so on justice concerns and the other half on care concerns (Gilligan, 1987). She also found that male and female respondents alike were able to switch from a justice perspective to a care perspective (or back again) when asked to do so; thus, their orientation was more a matter of perspective than an inability to see the other side. What Gilligan points out in her research is that the care perspective completely drops out when one uses only male subjects—which is what Kohlberg did in his early research for the moral stage theory.

A study of fifty college students (half men, half women) tested the subjects' orientation to three moral dilemmas, and the results were consistent with Gilligan's findings. However, the content of the dilemma evidently influenced whether care considerations would be found. The dilemmas involving interpersonal relationships were more likely than those without interpersonal relationships to stimulate care considerations (Rothbart, Hanley, and Albert, 1986; Flanagan and Jackson, 1987). More recent studies have continued to investigate sex differences in measurements of moral development. A study of male and female Coast Guard members revealed that, when utilizing an identification measure of morality, women scored statistically higher than did men (White, 1999); and a study of lawyers revealed that women were significantly less likely to be brought up on disciplinary charges (Hatamyar and Simmons, 2002).

Other studies have failed to find any differences between men and women in their responses to moral dilemmas (see reviews in Walker, 1986; Thoma, 1986; Loo, 2003). Critics of Gilligan argue that her work is more art than science in that she used small sample sizes and her results have not been widely replicated in larger studies. Further, similar to the criticisms directed to Kohlberg, the approach of measuring one's morality as a hierarchical stage, regardless of whether Stage 4 is higher or lower than Stage 3, has been criticized by those who argue that there is not necessarily a linear progression in one's moral development. Gilligan's most extreme critics, however, have been largely polemical, accusing her of stereotyping women by describing them as being more emotional and nurturing than men, which, critics argue, hark back to the days of stereotyping women as being "naturally" suited only to motherhood (Larrabee, 1993).

Teaching Moral Reasoning   The importance of Kohlberg's work is the link he makes between moral development and reason. Although this concept originated with Kant and even earlier philosophers, Kohlberg provides a psychological analysis that sheds light on *how* reason influences moral judgments. Also important in Kohlberg's work is the guidance it provides to education. According to the theory of moral stages, one can encourage movement through the stages by exposing the individual to higher-stage reasoning. The procedures for encouraging moral growth include presenting moral dilemmas and allowing the individual to support his or her position. Through exposure to higher reasoning, one sees the weaknesses and inconsistencies of lower-level reasoning (Hersh, 1979).

Kohlberg clearly indicated what was needed for moral growth. Even if one has reservations about the specific descriptions of the moral stages, the proposed guidelines to encourage moral development seem valid and are supported by others. Kohlberg (1976) described the following as necessary for moral growth:

1. *Being in a situation where seeing things from other points of view is encouraged.* This is important because upward-stage movement is a process of getting better at reconciling conflicting perspectives on a moral problem.
2. *Engaging in logical thinking, such as reasoned argument and consideration of alternatives.* This is essential because one cannot attain a given stage of moral reasoning before attaining the supporting Piagetian stage of logical reasoning.
3. *Having the responsibility to make moral decisions and to influence one's moral world.* This responsibility is necessary for developing a sense of moral agency and for learning to apply moral reasoning to situations.
4. *Being exposed to moral controversy and to conflict in moral reasoning that challenges the structure of one's present stage.* This is important for questioning one's moral beliefs and forcing a look at alternatives.
5. *Being exposed to the reasoning of individuals whose thinking is one stage higher than one's own.* The importance here is in offering a new moral structure for resolving the disequilibrium caused by moral conflict.
6. *Participating in creating and maintaining a just community whose members pursue common goals and resolve conflict in accordance with the ideals of mutual respect and fairness.*

People may become stuck at a certain point in moral development for several reasons, including not having sufficiently developed cognitive skills and/or living in a social environment that does not allow for role-taking opportunities or personal growth. For instance, a child growing up in a family that repeats basic moral views with little attempt to explain or defend them will learn to be closed to other viewpoints. A child who is never given responsibility or is never forced to take responsibility for his or her own actions will have difficulty developing moral reasoning skills and will not advance to higher stages. These children will be stunted, in a sense, at the Kohlberg pre-conventional level of an infant, constantly fed and cared for, but not allowed to discover that other people exist and must be considered. As adults, if we surround ourselves only with people who think as we do, we are unlikely to develop moral growth or even consider other positions.

ETHICS, BEHAVIOR, AND CRIMINALITY

Can one predict behavior from moral beliefs? Psychologists who have studied "immoral" behavior, such as lying and cheating by adults and children, have found it hard to predict who will perform these behaviors. There is not a strong correlation between beliefs and behaviors.

Some studies do find beliefs and actions to be correlated. In one study, "honesty scores" for people in three organizations were compiled from an attitudinal questionnaire about beliefs. It was found that the organization with the highest average honesty score had the least employee theft and the organization with the lowest average honesty score had the most employee theft (Adams, 1981). In contrast, Kohlberg cites the Hartshone and May study, which found no correlation between different tests of honesty and behavior, and another study in which female prisoners were found to have the same rank orderings of values as female college students. Kohlberg uses these studies as support for the proposition that one cannot measure a trait in isolation and expect to find consistency between values and action (Kohlberg and Candel, 1984: 499–503).

Recall that learning theory proposes that behavior precedes moral beliefs. Good behavior is created by external rewards, and then one develops the beliefs that go along with such behavior. However, some evidence indicates that compliance gained from external rewards is not stable until it becomes internalized, which involves adaptation to existing personality structures (Borchert and Stewart, 1986: 133–145). The question of when and why beliefs and values are internalized is not as easy to research. Even if ethical behavior could be ensured by providing rewards, this would not necessarily develop "moral character" or moral principles unless the beliefs were somehow internalized.

Part of the problem is the difficulty in measuring moral beliefs and the validity of the instruments used. Kohlberg's work has been so influential in this field that it is difficult to find any measurement of morality that does not directly or indirectly use his stage definitions. In attempting to examine whether bad behavior is associated with lower-stage scores, there is the assumption that lower-stage scores mean that the person has less developed moral reasoning. We have discussed Carol Gilligan's challenge to this conception, yet practically all studies that examine the correlation between behavior and belief continue to use stage scores as a measure of moral development.

Measurement of moral stages was accomplished in Kohlberg's work by interviews with subjects who were questioned using hypothetical moral dilemmas. Their responses then were rated by interviewers, with emphasis placed not necessarily on the answer given but, rather, on the reasoning for the answer. The individual was given a stage score based on what factors were emphasized. This procedure is time-consuming and expensive, so paper-and-pencil tests were devised, arguably measuring the same type of reasoning but through simpler, quicker means. Much criticism is directed at these so-called "recognition" tests, which require the subject merely to recognize and identify certain moral principles and agree with them, as opposed to "production" measures, which require the subject actually to reason through a dilemma and provide some rationale, which is then analyzed.

It may be that **recognition measures** are less reliable in predicting behavior. For instance, Gavaghan, Arnold, and Gibbs (1983) reported that although production measures were able to distinguish between a group of delinquents and nondelinquents, recognition measures could not. A later study was also unsuccessful in finding a correlation between the level of delinquency (self-reported) and moral development scores (Aleixo and Norris, 2000).

A logical approach to measuring morality and developing an approach that can predict behavior is to utilize criminal and delinquent populations; therefore, the fields of moral development and criminology are naturally related. One assumes that delinquent and criminal populations should have lower moral scores than law-abiding citizens, but this doesn't seem to be the case. Those who subscribe to a stage theory of moral development would argue that if delinquents score as high as law-abiding people, they may not have fully incorporated the higher-levelreasoning.

By contrast, learning theorists would propose that the rewards for good behavior are weak or not immediate. For instance, individuals who believe that stealing is wrong may nevertheless be tempted because of the immediacy of the reward (the coveted item). If they have internalized a strict sense of morality regarding stealing that would result in unpleasant feelings of guilt, then that immediate punishment will counteract the immediate reward. If, however, they had not been punished enough in the past (either physically or emotionally) for such action, then the guilt feelings will not occur quickly enough to counteract the temptation.

A huge body of literature is attempting to identify those elements and characteristics related to predicting future violence or future criminality. Tonry, Ohlin, and Farrington (1991) proposed three major theoretical perspectives that address the origins of delinquency—temperament, attachment, and social learning. After exploring the relative merits of these approaches, those authors postulated that temperament and attachment are interrelated in that the child's personality may affect parental interaction, which in turn affects attachment. Alternatively, parents themselves may be poor or inconsistent caregivers, in which case attachment will be weak. Not rejecting any of the three perspectives, the researchers state that although parental childrearing methods (attachment) may affect the age of onset of delinquency, peer influence (social learning) may affect continuation or intensity of delinquency.

Parental practices such as the use of affection and **inductive discipline** rather than power assertion or the withdrawal of affection have been identified as important in the moral development of adolescents (Leahy, 1981). Whether the association of parental practices and moral development (as measured by paper-and-pencil tests) operates in the same way that parental practices influence delinquent behavior is a separate question.

The other natural linkage between moral development and criminology is which interventions are most effective to change offenders' behaviors. Typically, the social sciences have generally avoided using moral definitions for wrongdoing, even though most criminal behavior—stealing, killing, assaulting, bribing, and so on—can also be defined as immoral or unethical. However, if the current science of criminology has avoided questions of morality, there was no such hesitation in early corrections.

Historically, criminality and sin were associated, and correctional practitioners were concerned primarily with reformation in a religious sense. Hence, early prisons were built to help the individual achieve redemption. There was a heavy dose of moral instruction in corrections; those who were said to lead dissolute and immoral lives were also targeted for reform. Society approved of official attempts to intervene in individuals' lives to help them become moral and productive citizens. For instance, the juvenile court system was given the mission to reform and educate youth (primarily those from immigrant groups) in a manner consistent with societal beliefs (Platt, 1977).

The orientation of corrections in the latter part of the twentieth century (1950s–1970s) became more scientific than religious, and intervention adopted the aim of psychological readjustment rather than personal redemption. After the rehabilitative era (1960–1970s), however, the rationale for corrections and punishment seemed to return to a moral orientation.

It is interesting that "faith-based" correctional programs are experiencing a resurgence, with the support of the White House. Religious instruction and correctional programs that use a religious orientation have emerged as options for correctional administrators seeking programs. Critics argue that public finances should not be used for such programs because the First Amendment prohibits state endorsement of any religion, but their popularity seems to be growing. Inner-Change Freedom Initiative, a private organization started by Chuck Colson of Watergate infamy, now provides programming in eight states, sometimes with multiple prisons participating. The state of Florida has developed its own program and now has transformed three prisons to "faith- and character-based" institutions. A task force is advocating opening five more, although Florida is facing a lawsuit by a group of citizens who allege that these programs are in violation of the separation of church and state by using public money for the programming (Associated Press, 2007b).

There have been various attempts to introduce offenders to "moral education." Hickey and Scharf (1980), who studied under Kohlberg, undertook an early attempt to apply moral development theory to corrections by introducing a therapeutic community in a Connecticut prison. Eventually they had "just communities" for men and women, run according to principles of fairness, justice, and rights. Prisoners were exposed to moral analysis in discussions and group meetings. Increases in stage scores were measured as averaging one-and-one-half stages after prisoners had lived in the just community.

It appears that simply offering moral discussion groups may also result in an increase in stage scores. Gibbs and his colleagues (1984) reported on an intervention involving sixty incarcerated juvenile delinquents. After eight weeks of discussion groups using moral dilemmas, socio-moral reasoning improved significantly. Whereas 87.5 percent of the treatment group moved from Stage 2 to Stage 3, only 14.3 percent of the control group moved to Stage 3.

Wiley (1988) reported on a more modest application of moral development education in the Texas Department of Corrections, in which teacher style was seen to influence gains in moral development scores. Specifically, inmate–students in prison classrooms where the teacher employed an interactive style (challenging and allowing active participation) showed significant gains in post-tests of moral development, unlike inmate–students in classrooms where the teaching style was authoritarian and teacher-centered. Interestingly, the course content was less important. These were not moral development classes but, instead, standard social science classes.

Arbuthnot and Gordon (1988) reviewed findings from several studies in which interventions with delinquents and adult offenders using socio-moral reasoning resulted in stage score improvement and also behavioral change. In one program for delinquents, for instance, subjects were monitored for one year, and significant differences in post-experimental problem behaviors were realized between the experimental group and the control group. Arbuthnot (1984) also discussed the interplay of environment and **socio-moral reasoning programs**. He pointed out that some prisoners find no rewards for expressing higher-stage reasoning, much less acting upon such reasoning. Therefore, any gains made in reasoning through an intervention, such as a moral analysis discussion group, would be unlikely to result in changes in behavior unless the environments were more supportive of higher stages.

It seems fairly clear that for such programs to work in prisons, an isolated living situation must be created to insulate participants from the negative reward structure of the prison. Also, if the intervention is in the community, attention must be given to the social environment of the participants. If stage improvements have no social supports, the gains may not be expressed in behavioral choices. Arbuthnot's discussion, then, combined Kohlberg's stage theory with a type of reinforcement theory.

More recently, moral reasoning programs have been used with sex offenders (Buttell, 2002). It was found that sex offenders tested at significantly lower moral stage development than a control sample. In a review of cognitive programs, including moral reasoning programs, Pearson (2002) concluded that such programs did decrease recidivism when compared to control groups.

TEACHING ETHICS

Many people believe that the general morality of this nation is declining. In a survey of 1,139 students at 27 universities, no less than 60 percent admitted cheating (Ryan, 2002: A11). Transparency International (2003) is an organization that compiles evidence of corruption from across the world and rates countries on how much corruption exists. The United States scored in sixteenth place, with more corruption than countries such as Finland, Denmark, New Zealand, Iceland, Singapore, Sweden, Canada, Australia, and the United Kingdom. Third-world countries such as Bangladesh, Nigeria, Uganda, Indonesia, Kenya, Cameroon, Bolivia, and Azerbaijan were rated as having the most corruption. In their latest 2007 report, the United States dropped down to 20 of the countries surveyed (Transparency International 2008).

In the United States, ethical scandals occur with depressing regularity. Consider this sampling of recent events:

- the William Clinton–Monica Lewinsky debacle, which led to impeachment proceedings
- the Enron bankruptcy and resulting discovery of illegal activities
- the Abner Louima and Amadou Diallo incidents in New York
- the Ramparts scandal in Los Angeles
- the Oakland "Riders" scandal, with the city paying more than $10 million to victims of out-of-control officers
- various election irregularities by both political parties in the 2000 and 2004 elections

- the ethics code violations of numerous legislators and politicians, including Tom DeLay, Larry Craig, David Vitter, and James McGreevey.
- the Abu Ghraib prison scandal, the "secret prisons" of the CIA, and the continuing controversy over what methods constitute torture in Guantanamo and other detention facilities around the country
- allegations of sexual assaults of female soldiers by male soldiers
- the Mark Foley scandal, with allegations that Congressman Foley coerced male students who were pages for Congress into sexual liaisons
- the finding by the FBI, while enforcing a search warrant in relation to a corruption investigation, that Congressman William Jefferson had $90,000 wrapped in tinfoil in his freezer
- the conviction and sentencing to prison of Congressman Randy "Duke" Cunningham for taking bribes
- the resignation of New York Governor Elliot Spitzer and the subsequent confessions of Governor David Patterson, his successor, who admitted to infidelity and the use in his 20s of marijuana and cocaine

There is a widespread perception that the United States is at a new low in levels of ethics and morality. The reasons given for this perceived decline include the following:

1. We have eliminated many of the opportunities for the teaching of morals.
2. The community is not a cohesive force any longer.
3. The authority of religion is not as pervasive as it once was.
4. The family is weakening as a force of socialization.
5. Educators have abdicated their responsibility for moral instruction in favor of scientific neutrality.

Interestingly, as noted before, every generation seems to observe this occurrence (Menninger 1973). Whether we are less moral than in the past is debatable; however, there is no debate that we could be more moral and ethical than we are now. In most colleges in the 1800s, a course in moral philosophy was required of all graduates. This class, often taught by the college president, was designed to help college students become good citizens. The goal of college was not only to educate but also to help students attain the moral sensibility that would make them productive, worthy citizens. As it was taught, ethics involved not only the history of philosophical thought but also a system of beliefs and values and the skills to resolve moral or ethical dilemmas.

Gradually, the general field of social science has become more and more specialized. Each discipline carved out for itself an area of behavior or part of society to study, so today we have, among others, sociology, psychology, economics, history, and philosophy. The increasing empiricism of these disciplines crowded out the earlier emphasis on moral decision making. Schools affiliated with religious denominations still routinely require courses that focus on moral character, but these courses are, for the most part, missing in undergraduate curriculums. The issue of moral education in the school is examined in the Policy Box.

Most professional schools today (in law, medicine, and business) require at least one class in professional ethics. Typically, these classes present the opportunity to

| POLICY BOX | MORAL EDUCATION IN THE SCHOOLS? |

There is a growing trend among school districts to include character education or moral education in school curriculums. Among a number of packaged curriculums available for schools to distribute to teachers include those that concentrate on promoting honesty, diversity, and citizenship.

Anti-bullying curricula gained new prominence after the Columbine school shooting because of a perception that the schools were doing a poor job of protecting children from their peers' bullying. Although most people believe that this is a good thing, some resent schools taking on this role and believe that it should be a parent's prerogative. This argument grows in intensity when applied to issues such as tolerance for gay or alternative lifestyles.

Law: There are no laws at issue in this policy choice, unless the character education is faith-based, in which case the constitutionality of the curriculum might be challenged because of the First Amendment.

Policy: School district policies should reflect the will of the parents. If parents over-whelmingly disapprove of such curriculums, one assumes that districts would remove them or not begin them. But if the majority of parents want the schools to teach intoler-ance and bigotry, should school boards abide by parental wishes? It is probably also true that many parents are not aware of what is being taught in schools.

Individual ethics: Individual dilemmas may arise on the part of teachers. For instance, if there is a teaching unit on diversity that promotes the idea that everyone should be treated with equal respect, including gays, and a teacher's religious belief is that gays should be condemned, how should the teacher reconcile his or her individual beliefs with the teaching curriculum?

If you said that you think the teacher should follow the curriculum and promote a tolerant viewpoint because that's part of the job, would you also agree that teachers in Nazi Germany were correct to promote a racist viewpoint in their teachings because that was "their job?" How do you distinguish between the two situations?

examine the ethical dilemmas that individuals may encounter as members of that pro-fession and help students discover the best way to decide ethical issues. Usually the classes combine discussion and instruction. Although some class time is devoted to having students discuss their views, certainly part of the task is to train them in what has been determined to be correct behavior. The alternative, of course, would be to ignore ethics in the learning phase of an occupation and let the person encounter ethical dilemmas on the job, such as in the following examples:

1. When a prosecutor is tempted to ignore evidence to ensure an easy conviction
2. When a doctor must choose between two people who both need a heart transplant
3. When a business executive is asked to accept a bribe to award a contract.

In the rushed, pressure-filled real world, ethical decisions will be made in haste, with emotional overtones, and with peer and situational pressures heavily influencing the decision.

In the growing field of ethics instruction, businesses are hiring "ethics officers" to ensure that their workers behave honestly and ethically, and ethics centers are offering training to state and private organizations. Neil Trautman's National Ethics Institute in Mississippi and the Center for Law Enforcement Ethics in Texas are two centers that offer ethics training to law enforcement and correctional agencies. The Josephson Institute is a training center that markets to a broader range of businesses and organizations. Trautman (2008) offers the "Corruption Continuum," which details how organizations can become corrupt through

- administrative indifference toward integrity,
- ignoring obvious ethical problems, and creating a
- hypocrisy and fear dominated culture; all which lead to
- a survival of the fittest approach by individual employees.

Trautman, along with others, argues that ethical training is an essential element of addressing corruption in public agencies. Whether ethics classes are successful will depend, in large part, on whether CEOs and organizational leaders are good students. As the "In the News" box indicates, ethics classes may not do much to raise the ethical standards of employees if managers don't take them seriously.

Administrators and managers exert the strongest influence on the ethical climate of an agency, regardless of whether ethics classes are offered. If leaders are honest, ethical, and caring, there is a good chance that those who work for these managers are also ethical. If administrators and/or managers are hypocritical, untruthful, and use their positions for personal gain, workers often march in these same footsteps. If the business itself is premised on misleading the consumer and perpetrating fraud to secure higher profits, why should business leaders expect that workers would behave any differently?

IN THE NEWS | ETHICS CLASSES: SOLUTION OR SCAM?

In an editorial poking fun at the recent rise of ethics classes, Joan Ryan of the *San Francisco Chronicle* writes that Raytheon, a defense contractor, has produced a video in which the company's vice president, along with Roger Ebert, the film critic, give thumbs-up or thumbs-down to a series of behaviors. Ryan wonders if Bert and Ernie of *Sesame Street* might have done a better job. An attempt to improve the ethics of a work force is laudable, but the approach may be patronizing or even cynical, depending on the company's motivation.

Ryan points out that businesses that have ethics programs in place are eligible for reduced fines if they are found guilty of corporate wrongdoing. The behavior of leaders and the values of the company are more important determiners of employees' behaviors than whether or not they sat through a class. She says, "[T]he post-Enron era is much like the pre-Enron. Companies were cooking the books, faking transactions, lying to shareholders. The problem was about perpetuating a sham. Now so, too, is the solution."

Do you think that ethics classes will help in reducing corporate wrongdoing? Why or why not?

Source: J. Ryan , 2002: A11.

WHY BE ETHICAL?

So far, we have explored how to determine what is ethical, in Chapter 2, and in this chapter the various explanations of why people choose either ethical (and legal) behaviors or unethical (and/or illegal) behaviors. Regardless of which ethical system or set of principles the individual feels more comfortable with, everyone would do well to become more aware of the implications of day-to-day choices—sharpen his or her ethical antennae, so to speak. Small decisions become larger life positions in a slow, cumulative way.

When faced with a choice of behavior, one should at least perform the following steps:

1. *Examine all possible solutions to the problem and be aware of the direct and indirect effects of each response.* Often, when ethical issues arise, they are not recognized for what they are. The individual may limit analysis of a problem to finding a short-term solution or making a quick decision, in which case the larger issues or the ethical implications of the situation are not addressed. It becomes easy to rationalize unethical behavior in this way by explaining that it happened only once, or it was the easiest way, or there was no intention to do wrong.
2. *Determine whether any solutions would be viewed as unacceptable if they were made public, and for what reason.* If an individual would be uncomfortable with publicizing an action, chances are that it is questionable. Too often, unethical decisions are protected by a shroud of secrecy, and then the secrecy is defended by pleading institutional or agency confidentiality. On an individual level, unethical behavior is almost always hidden, and further unethical behavior may follow to cover up what has been done already. Probably the best signal that something is wrong is when a person hesitates to make it public knowledge.
3. *Reconcile the decision with one's personal set of values or ethical system.* When one has to make a difficult decision about a moral issue, although one has recourse to value systems passed on by family and advice and counsel from friends and colleagues, ultimately the decision should be one for which the individual is willing to take responsibility.

After completing a class on ethics that involved detailed explanations and applications of the ethical systems discussed in this book, an individual responded with, "Why should we?" The student was asking why anyone should be ethical or moral. There is a long version and a short version of the answer to this question. The short answer was given by another class member: "So you can sleep at night." The long version of the answer is that philosophers down through the ages have examined, debated, and analyzed this same question. The ethical systems can be seen as not only answering the question "What is good?" but also the question "Why be good?"

1. Under *ethical formalism*, the answer is that the world works better, and it is rational to do one's duty and live up to the categorical imperative.
2. Under *utilitarianism*, the answer is that it is better for everyone, including the individual, to do what benefits the majority.

3. Under *the ethics of care*, the answer is that we naturally and instinctively have the capacity to care and to be concerned about others.

Each of the other frameworks also provides answers. One dominant theme emerges from all the ethical systems—that we are connected to one another in fundamental and emotional ways. This connection is recognized in

1. the Golden Rule
2. the universalism principle under the categorical imperative
3. rule utilitarianism
4. enlightened egoism

The theme running through the ethical systems is empathy and caring for one another. The reason we should act ethically can be explained rationally (ethical formalism and utilitarianism) or intuitively (ethics of care and religion). It can also be explained by socio-biologists who would say that it is the nature of humans to care for each other and that to act contrary to our nature will cause personal discomfort of some type.

CONCLUSION

Philosophers, religious scholars, biologists, psychologists, sociologists, and criminologists have all tried to explain why people do bad things. The following three approaches were discussed in this chapter.

1. *Biological theorists* do not propose biological determinism, only that certain traits or biological characteristics may influence one's behavior. Socio-biology explores the possibility that altruism and empathy may be a feature that has evolved in humans because human groups whose members exhibited these traits were more likely to survive.

2. *Learning theorists* argue that people learn morals through rewards. This approach is relativistic in that it postulates human learning as neutral. There is no one true moral theory to discover; rather, the individual will adopt whatever moral theory has been rewarded. Social learning theory posits that humans are active participants in interpreting and adapting to the rewards around them. Bandura, especially, has offered explanations of how individuals can turn off self-regulatory mechanisms (conscience) and perform inhuman acts.

3. *Developmental theorists* propose that morality comes only at an advanced stage of emotional and social development and is linked to cognitive development. Kohlberg's theory proposes a hierarchy of moral stages, with the highest stage holding the most perfect moral principles. However, not everyone has the cognitive capacity or the proper exposure to discover these principles. According to Kohlberg, in the higher stages of moral development, ethical relativism must give way to universalism, and those who reach the highest stages have discovered the true moral principles that are absolute and exist apart from humanity.

If one believes that morals are simply what humans choose to define as such, one might be more inclined to a learning theory perspective. If one believes that morals exist naturally and humans discover their existence only through reasoning ability, one might be more inclined to accept the developmental stage theory of moral development. However, the approaches to moral development presented in this chapter are not necessarily mutually exclusive. One might agree with stage theory with the understanding that at lower stages, rewards are necessary to elicit moral behaviors (e.g., rewarding young children for sharing). One might support learning theory but also accept the notion that when we are intellectually mature, our reasoning abilities mediate simple rewards. Thus, although young children might be fooled into thinking that practicing the piano is bad because someone was punished for it in a story, no older child or adult would be taken in by such a trick, and individuals in a totalitarian society may continue to believe in democratic ideals (through reasoning) regardless of punishments they may receive for such beliefs.

Biological research indicates that moral decision making comes from both the reasoning centers of the brain and the more primitive emotional centers of the brain. Thus, people's feelings of empathy and sympathy and "doing the right thing" may be the result of evolution. This finding fits nicely with Carol Gilligan's research that empathy and caring are related to morality.

We also explored the connection between immorality and behavior, especially criminality. Some research has attempted to predict behavior from measures of morality. Also, there has been interesting research that indicates that some types of interventions can improve the moral reasoning abilities of some offenders. Whether moral reasoning will affect behavior is a different question.

Key Terms

cognitive dissonance *69*

developmental theories *71*

inductive discipline *78*

Kohlberg's moral stages *72*

modeling *68*

recognition measures *77*

reinforcement *68*

self-efficacy *69*

socio-moral reasoning programs *80*

Review Questions

1. Provide your own answer to the question, "Why do people do bad things?"
2. What are the three basic approaches to explaining human behavior? Explain each.
3. Briefly explain how biological approaches might explain antisocial behavior.
4. What are some differences between males and females noted by biological researchers?
5. Discuss learning theory as it applies to moral development. Explain modeling and reinforcement. What problems do critics see with this theory?
6. Explain Kohlberg's moral development theory. What problems do critics have with his theory?
7. How does one measure moral beliefs? What are the problems with such measurements?
8. How does Carol Gilligan disagree with Kohlberg's stage theory?
9. What are the elements necessary for teaching ethics?
10. Describe some applications of moral training in corrections.

Writing/Discussion Questions

1. Develop an essay on (or discuss) the development of morality. Who has been the greatest influence on your moral development? Why? How? Why do you think people behave in ways that hurt other people?

Have you ever done something you knew to be wrong? Why did you do it?
2. Develop an essay on (or discuss) the relationships between morality, moral/ethical teaching, and criminality. Do thieves have

the same moral beliefs as others? Do they know that stealing is wrong? Can we successfully predict which individuals will perform unethical or immoral actions?

3. Develop an essay on (or discuss) why you think the United States doesn't rank higher on the Transparency International integrity survey. (You may want to go to TI's website to read the methodology of this survey). What recent events indicate that everyone should be concerned with the development of moral reasoning and ethical behavior?

Ethical Dilemmas

Situation 1

You are a rookie police officer and are riding with a field training officer (FTO). During your shift the FTO stops at a convenience store and quickly drinks four beers in the back room of the store. He is visibly affected by the beers, and the smell of alcohol is noticeable. What should you do? What if the FTO had just written a favorable evaluation of you even though you should have received a reprimand for an improper disposition of a traffic accident?

Situation 2

You are a criminal justice student interning at a police department. One of the tasks you learn at the department is how to look up individuals' criminal histories on the computer. You are telling your friends about your experiences, and they want you to look up their names to see what, if anything, is listed for them. You are basically left alone to do your work at the police department, and it would be an easy matter to look up anyone. What would you tell your friends?

Situation 3

You are a senior getting close to graduation and have taken too many classes during your last semester. You find yourself getting behind in classes and not doing well on tests. One of the classes requires a thirty-page term paper, and you simply do not have the time to complete the paper by the due date. While you are on the Internet one day, you see that term papers can be purchased on any topic. You ordinarily would do your own work, but the time pressure of this last semester is such that you see no other way. Do you purchase the paper and turn it in as your own?

Situation 4

Your fifteen-year-old brother is visiting you at college. You are surprised by how much he drinks, and by the second day you understand that he really has a problem. When you tell him that you have to tell your parents, he freaks out and tells you that he'll run away or do something crazy if they find out, and that he will get it under control during the summer when he has time to "chill out." What do you do?

Situation 5

You are working your way through college as a jail officer. You detest the job, partly because of the inmates, and partly because of the other officers. Many of them are redneck sadists who enjoy and abuse their power. You try to stay out of the way of the most vocal ones, but one day you are on the floor when one of them proceeds to castigate a black inmate for not sweeping properly. He utters a number of racial epithets and pushes the inmate around. You can see that the inmate is tense and ready to fight. What should you do?

Suggested Readings

Gilligan, C. 1982. *In a Different Voice: Psychological Theory and Women's Development.* Cambridge, MA: Harvard University Press.

Hickey, J., and Scharf, P.1980. *Toward a Just Correctional System.* San Francisco: Jossey-Bass.

Kohlberg, L. (Ed.), 1984. *The Psychology of Moral Development.*New York: Harper & Row.

Larrabee, M. 1993. *An Ethics of Care: Feminist and Interdisciplinary Perspectives.*New York: Routledge.

Menninger, K. 1973. *Whatever Became of Sin.* New York: Hawthorne Books.

Puka, B. (Ed.). 1994. *The Great Justice Debate: Kohlberg Criticism.* New York: Garland.

Shermer, M. 2004. *The Science of Good and Evil: Why People Cheat, Gossip, Care, Share, and Follow the Golden Rule.* New York: Times Books/ Holt & Co.

Walsh, A.2002. *Biosocial Criminology: Introduction and Integration.* Cincinnati, OH: Anderson Publishing Company.

Wasserman, D., and Wachbroit, R. 2001. *Genetics and Criminal Behavior.* New York: Cambridge University Press.

THE ORIGINS AND CONCEPT OF JUSTICE

CHAPTER 4

© Ted Soqui/CORBIS

What is a just punishment for someone who has committed three felonies? Some people believe life in prison is just; others, such as these protestors in California, believe that the three strikes law, which allows for a life sentence for a third felony, violates the very essence of justice. What do you think?

CHAPTER OBJECTIVES

1. Know the definitions, concepts, and origins of justice.

2. Understand the components of justice: distributive, corrective, and commutative.

3. Be able to define procedural and substantive justice.

4. Understand the difference between the utilitarian rationale and the retributive rationale under corrective justice.

CHAPTER OUTLINE

What is justice? Harold Hall would argue that he didn't receive justice by spending twenty years in a California prison for a crime he didn't commit. In 1985, at the age of eighteen, he was arrested for a double homicide and rape. He was interrogated for 17 hours, handcuffed to a chair, and denied food and water. The police told him that they had evidence linking him to the crime. Finally he told police what he thought they wanted to hear. That confession and the perjured testimony of a jailhouse informant was enough for a jury to convict him to life in prison. After twenty years in prison Hall was finally released after an appellate court finally agreed to his pleas for a test of the DNA collected from the crime scene. The testing led to his exoneration and release (Hall, 2008).

Hall had been subjected to a lawful arrest; he had the benefit of a trial during which time he was defended by an attorney; and he had the right to appeal. Some would say that the legal system worked as it was supposed to have worked, but did he receive justice?

How is justice related to law? Professionals in the criminal justice system serve and promote the interests of law and justice, and this chapter explores these concepts. An underlying theme is that the ends of law and justice are not always the same. Although *law* is often defined as "the administration of justice," it may very well be the case that law forces consequences that many might conclude are "unjust." Legal rights might be different from moral rights, rights might be different from needs, and needs may not be protected under either the law or justice.

Definitions of justice include the following concepts:

1. fairness
2. equality
3. impartiality
4. appropriate rewards or punishments

According to Lucas (1980: 3), justice "differs from benevolence, generosity, gratitude, friendship, and compassion." Justice is not something for which we should feel grateful but, rather, something upon which we have a right to insist. Justice should not be confused with "good." Some actions may be considered good but not necessarily just. For instance, the recipients of charity, benevolence, and forgiveness do not have a right to these things; therefore, it is not an injustice to withhold them. Justice concerns rights and interests more often than needs. Although the idea of need is important in some discussions of justice, it is not the only component or even the primary one. It is important to understand that what is just and what is good are not necessarily the same.

People can be described as displaying unique combinations of generosity and selfishness, fairness, and self-interest. Some writers insist that the need for justice arises from the nature of human beings and that we are not naturally generous, open-hearted, or fair. On the one hand, if we were to behave all the time in accordance with those virtues, we would have no need for justice. On the other hand, if humans were to always act in selfish, grasping, and unfair ways, we would be unable to follow the rules and principles of justice. Therefore, we uphold and cherish the concept of justice in our society because it is the mediator between people's essential selfishness and generosity. In other words, justice is the result of a logical and rational acceptance of the concept of fairness in human relations.

Anthony Walsh (2000) presents the interesting idea that justice is a biologically adaptive trait. He uses evolutionary psychology to argue that the sense of justice is emotional rather than rational and is the result of natural selection. His argument, simplified, is that humans, similar to other animal species, have "cheaters" and "suckers." Cheaters are those who do not engage in "reciprocal altruism" (basically, cooperation). Suckers are those who are continually taken advantage of by cheaters. They are not optimally adapted for survival, and if they perish, cheaters would perish as well because they need victims to take advantage of. Thus, "grudgers" evolve as a response; they may be fooled once by cheaters, but they are outraged and demand punishment when they are victimized. This adaptation successfully ensures the continued existence of grudgers as well as cheaters. Our "moral outrage," in other words, is an evolutionary response, as is our emotional demand for justice.

David Hume, a philosopher, said that "justice does not dictate a perfect world, but one in which people live up to agreements and are treated fairly" (cited in Feinberg and Gross, 1977: 75). Galston (1980: 282) described justice as

> ...more than voluntary agreement, [but] ... less than perfect community. It allows us to retain our separate existences and our self-regard; it does not ask us to share the pleasures, pains, and sentiments of others. Justice is intelligent self-regard, modified, by the requirements of rational consistency.

ORIGINS OF THE CONCEPT OF JUSTICE

Justice originated in the Greek word *dike,* which is associated with the concept of everything staying in its assigned place or natural role (Feinberg and Gross, 1977: i). This idea is closely associated with the definitions of justice given by Plato and Aristotle. Even today, some writers describe justice as "the demand for order: everything in its proper place or relation" (Feibleman, 1985: 23).

According to Plato, justice consists of maintaining the societal status quo. Justice is one of four civic virtues, the others being wisdom, temperance, and courage (Feibleman, 1985: 173). In an ordered state everyone performs his or her role and does not interfere with others. Each person's role is the one for which the individual is best fitted by nature; thus, *natural law* is upheld. Moreover, it is in everyone's self-interest to have this ordered existence continue because it provides the means to a good life and appropriate human happiness. Plato's society is a *class system*, based on innate abilities, rather than a *caste system,* which differentiates purely by accidents of birth.

Aristotle believed that justice exists in the law and that the law is "the unwritten custom of all or the majority of men which draws a distinction between what is honorable and what is base" (Feibleman, 1985: 174). Aristotle distinguished *distributive justice* from *rectificatory justice*:

1. *Rectificatory justice*, or *commutative justice*, concerns business deals where unfair advantage or undeserved harm has occurred. Justice demands remedies or compensations to the injured party.
2. *Distributive justice* concerns what measurement should be used to allocate society's resources. Aristotle believed in the idea of proportionality along with equality.

In Aristotle's conception of justice, the lack of freedom and opportunity for some people—slaves and women, for instance—did not conflict with justice, as long as the individual was in the role in which, by nature, he or she belonged. In other words, unequal people should get unequal shares.

COMPONENTS OF JUSTICE

We still recognize these basic components of justice, and justice today can be separated into distributive, corrective, and commutative justice (Feinberg and Gross, 1977: 53):

1. **Distributive justice** is concerned with the allocation of the goods and burdens of society to its respective members. Rewards and benefits from society include wealth, education, entitlement programs, and health care. Because some people get fewer goods than others, it may be that these goods are not distributed fairly. Burdens and responsibilities must also be distributed among the members of society. For instance, decisions must be made about who should fight in war, who should take care of the elderly and infirm, who should pay taxes, and how much each should pay. The difficulties in deciding how to divide these goods and burdens and what each person deserves are the subjects of any discussion of distributive justice.
2. **Corrective justice** concerns the determination and methods of punishments. Again, the concept of *desert* emerges. In corrective justice we speak of offenders getting what they deserve, but this time the desert is punishment rather than societal goods or opportunities. The difficulty, of course, is in determining the *just desert* for a specific crime.
3. **Commutative justice** is associated with transactions and interchanges in which one person feels unfairly treated. The process of determining a fair resolution— for example, when one is cheated in a business deal or when a contract is not completed—calls into play the concepts of commutative justice. The method for determining a fair and just resolution to the conflict depends on particular concepts such as rights and interests.

Any discussion of justice includes at least three continuing themes: fairness, equality, and impartiality.

1. *Fairness.* Parents ordinarily give each child the same allowance unless differences between the children, such as age or duties, warrant different amounts. Children are sensitive to issues of fairness long before they grasp more abstract

ideas of justice. No doubt every parent has heard the plaintive cry, "It's not fair—Johnny got more than I did" or, "It's not fair—she always gets to sit in the front seat!" What children are sensing is unequal and, therefore, unfair treatment. The concept of fairness is inextricably tied to equality and impartiality.

2. *Equality.* There is a predisposition to demand equity or equal shares for all. (In contrast to the concept of equal shares is the idea of needs or deserts; in other words, we should get what we need or, alternatively, what we deserve by status, merit, or other reasons.) The concept of equality is also present in retributive justice in the belief that similar cases should be treated equally—for instance, that all individuals who commit a similar crime should be similarly punished. (Again, the alternative argument is that sometimes it serves the purpose of justice to treat similar crimes differently because of individual circumstances.) Are there ever any situations where people are truly equal? If we want to distribute opportunities equally to equals, how would we measure equality? Do we assume that everyone starts off with the same skills, backgrounds, and family circumstances, or must we not take into account individual differences, societal goals, and a host of other factors in decisions such as whether to employ affirmative action plans, individualized sentences, and receipt of social services?

3. *Impartiality.* At the core of our system of criminal justice is the theme of impartiality. Our symbol of justice represents, with her blindfold, impartiality toward special groups and, with her scales, proportionally just punishments. Impartiality implies fair and equal treatment of all without discrimination and bias. It is hard to reconcile the ideal of "blind justice" with the individualized justice of the "treatment ethic" because one can hardly look at individual circumstance if one is blind toward the particulars of the case. Indeed, most would argue, individual differences and culpabilities should be taken into consideration—if not during a finding of guilt or innocence, then at least when sentencing occurs. The blindfold may signify no special treatment for the rich or the powerful, but then it must also signify no special consideration for the young, for the misled, or for extraordinary circumstances. These issues will be addressed in Chapter 5.

DISTRIBUTIVE JUSTICE

The concept of the appropriate and just allocation of society's goods and interests is one of the central themes in all discussions of justice. According to one writer, justice always involves *rightful possession* (Galston, 1980: 117–119). The goods that one might possess include

1. economic goods (income or property)
2. opportunities for development (education or citizenship)
3. recognition (honor or status).

If there was enough of everything (goods, opportunity, status) for everyone, issues of distributive justice would not arise; it is only because there is usually a condition of scarcity that a problem arises with the allocation of goods. Two valid claims to possession are *need* and *desert*. The principles of justice involve the application of these claims to specific entitlements. Different writers have presented various proposals for deciding issues of entitlement.

Lucas (1980: 164–165) listed several different distribution theories. They involve distributions based on

1. need
2. merit
3. performance
4. ability
5. rank
6. station
7. worth
8. work
9. agreements
10. requirements of the common good
11. valuation of services
12. legal entitlement

Despite differences, all schemes include some concept of need and merit (also see Raphael, 1980: 90). In the "In the News" box it is clear that some people's concept of what one *deserves* is related to need rather than merit.

IN THE NEWS | AFTER CASH RAINS DOWN IN MIAMI, FINDERS REMAIN QUIET KEEPERS

MIAMI—Police went from door to door through one of Miami's poorest neighborhoods Thursday, asking people to admit they scooped up some of the half million dollars that spilled from a Brinks truck and, if they did, to give it back. Residents generally responded with a good laugh.

"Nobody's going to tell them," said Debbie, a resident of Overtown who, like most, would give only her first name.

"This is a once-in-a-lifetime thing," added another resident named George. "This couldn't happen to a more *deserving* [emphasis added] neighborhood."

Thousands of dollars in coins, bills, and food stamps rained down on the street Wednesday morning after an armored Brinks truck carrying $3.7 million overturned on an Interstate 95 overpass. People swarmed over the area, digging money out of the dirt and scooping it off the street, stuffing bags, boxes, and pockets before police took charge. An estimated $500,000 vanished. Thursday, police knocked on seventy-five doors urging people to turn in the money, no questions asked, before a two-day grace period ends at noon Saturday. Nobody did.

After the grace period expires, police plan to seek television news videotape to aid them in identifying money grabbers. Those caught with more than $1,000 could face grand theft charges.

Which, if any, system supports the individual's justification that he or she "deserved" the stolen money? Did people "deserve" the material possessions that were looted in New Orleans after it was flooded? What about food? Gas?

Source: Reprinted with permission of the Associated Press, 1997: A7.

The difficulty in distributing society's goods lies in deciding the weight of each of the criteria discussed above. The various theories can be categorized as egalitarian, Marxist, libertarian, or utilitarian, depending on the factors that are emphasized (Beauchamp, 1982):

1. *Egalitarian theories* start with the basic premise of equality or equal shares for all.
2. *Marxist theories* place need above desert or entitlement.
3. *Libertarian theories* promote freedom from interference by government in social and economic spheres; therefore, merit, entitlement, and productive contributions are given weight over need or equal shares.
4. *Utilitarian theories* attempt to maximize benefits for individuals and society in a mixed emphasis on entitlements and needs.

Sterba (1980) offers one system for distribution. It is displayed in Box 4.1, "Sterba's Distribution System."

How do the theories apply to the wide disparities in salaries found in the United States? For instance, a professional athlete's salary is sometimes one hundred times greater than a police officer's salary. The average CEO's salary of the Forbes' top 100 companies in 2006 was $10 million per year! As amazing as that sounds, some CEOs made much higher amounts when considering all forms of compensation (see the "In the News" box "How Much Does the Boss Make?"). Which distribution principle justifies such extreme discrepancies? Libertarian theorists would shrug at such disparity; Marxist theorists would not.

Obviously, few would agree that workers in all jobs and all professions should be paid the same amount of money. First, not many people would be willing to put up with the long hours and many years of schooling needed in some professions if there were no incentives. Second, some types of jobs demand more responsibility

---

| **BOX 4.1** | **STERBA'S DISTRIBUTION SYSTEM** |

1. *Principle of Need.* Each person is guaranteed the primary social goods that are necessary to meet the normal costs of satisfying his or her basic needs in the society in which he or she lives.
2. *Principle of Appropriation and Exchange.* Additional primary goods are to be distributed on the basis of private appropriation and voluntary agreement and exchange.
3. *Principle of Minimal Contribution.* A minimal contribution to society is required of those who are capable of contributing when social and economic resources are insufficient to provide the guaranteed minimum to everyone in society without requiring that contribution or when the incentive to contribute to society would otherwise be adversely affected, so that persons would not maximize their contribution to society.
4. *Principle of Saving.* The rate of saving for each generation should represent its fair contribution toward realizing and maintaining a society in which all the members can fully enjoy the benefit of its just institution.

Source: Adapted from Sterba (1980: 55).

IN THE NEWS | HOW MUCH DOES THE BOSS MAKE?

Average CEO salary in 2006 was $10 million a year.

CEO of Capital One	249 million
Yahoo	231 million
Cendant	140 million
KB Homes	136 million
Lehman Bros.	123 million

This included stock options and all "perks" of the job, including things such as a car and driver.

Do you think these men deserve these compensation packages? Why?

Source: DeCarlo, 2006.

---

and involve greater stress than others. However, we can readily see that some remuneration is entirely out of proportion to an objective analysis of worth.

If we are concerned primarily with performance and ability, why do we not pay individual workers in the same job category differently if one works harder than the other? Although some production jobs pay according to how much is produced (the piecework payment method), most of us are paid according to a step-grade position, earning roughly what others in the same position earn. Which is the fairer system of payment? What about people who produce less in the piecework system because they are helping their co-workers or taking more time to produce higher-quality products? Is it fair for them to earn less? If all work were paid according to production, how would one pay secretaries, teachers, or customer service workers, whose production is more difficult to measure? How would one pay police officers—by the number of arrests?

Thus far, we have discussed only salaries, but even in the workplace other goods also are distributed, such as promotions, merit increases, job postings, desirable offices, and parking places.

Marxist distribution systems propose that we pay people according to need. This sounds fair in one sense because people would get only what they need to survive at some predetermined level. In that case, a person with two children would earn more than a person with no children. In the past, this was the argument used by employers to explain why they would favor men over women in hiring, promotions, and pay increases—because men had families to support and women did not. Two arguments were used against this type of discriminatory treatment: The first was that women deserve as much pay as men if they are of equal ability and performance. The second was that women also, more often than not, have to support families. These two arguments emphasize different principles of justice. The first is based on an equal-deserts argument; the second rests on an equal-needs argument.

Just distribution of other goods in society is also problematic. There are perennial arguments over how much people should receive in entitlement programs, such as food stamps and Aid For Dependent Children (AFDC). The principle of need is the rationale we use to take from the financially solvent, through taxes, and give to those who have little or nothing. There is always some resentment over this redistribution because of the belief that some people choose not to work and take advantage of governmental "hand-outs." If cheaters were dropped from such programs, what about their children? Do they also *deserve* to be punished? What do children deserve from the state?

In the 2008 presidential election the issue of universal health care was a flash-point of controversy. While some politicians, like Hillary Clinton, believe the government should ensure universal health care (basic health care for everyone in society regardless of their ability to pay), others take positions that it is the proper role of employers and the free market to provide such coverage. The United States is compared to European countries and Canada favorably or unfavorably in its access to and quality of health care, depending on one's opinion on universal health coverage.

Another "good" that society distributes to its members is opportunity. Many people would argue that education (at least at the university level) is a privilege that should be reserved for those few who have the ability and the drive to succeed. However, the educational system in the United States is fundamentally democratic. Not only do we have guaranteed, in fact, compulsory, education at elementary and secondary levels; we also have open admission to some universities. Moreover, remedial courses are available to help those without the skills to meet college standards. Massive amounts of time and money are devoted to helping some students improve their skills and ultimately graduate from college. Might some argue that this system wastes resources? Other countries "track" students very early and identify those who have natural skills, then allow only that selected group to take advantage of state-supported higher education. Is this a more efficient use of state resources?

There is also a compelling argument that although the *ideal* of education is democratic, the *reality* is that because of unequal tax bases, school districts are incredibly unequal and distribute the opportunity of education unequally. While some school districts have swimming pools, computers in every classroom, and teachers with specialized education, other school districts make do with donated textbooks and buildings that are poorly heated and ventilated. Likewise, there are vast differences in the quality and status of higher education, with degrees from some universities worth much more than others. Who deserves to go to these better universities? If you said "those with better grades," do you also agree with the process whereby high schools are ranked by admissions committees so that a 4.0 in one high school is ranked lower than a 4.0 from another high school?

Affirmative action programs were designed to provide opportunities to groups that historically have been discriminated against—blacks, women, and Hispanics, among others. Some believe that taking affirmative steps to increase opportunities for minority groups has simply transferred unfair treatment to white males. What is acceptable to overcome previous discrimination? Unfortunately, a promise to admit (to a university or a law school) or to hire "the best person for the job" is not enough, because historical and institutionalized discrimination may take many years to overcome. For instance, some claim that underfunded schools produce students who are less qualified, and then these individuals are denied jobs based on their lack of abilities. To assume that one is eliminating discrimination by hiring on the basis of individual abilities does not solve the problem of blocked access; it merely perpetuates it in a more subtle way.

The Supreme Court has ruled against affirmative action attempts, such as race-based criteria in law school and university admissions. States are also passing legislation to bar hiring decisions, promotions, and admission to state schools based on race. The same "equal protection" argument used to pass civil rights legislation in the 1960s is now being used to dismantle these programs. What effect such decisions will have on access to the opportunity of education remains to be seen. Some predict that the progress we have seen in educational and economic success for historically blocked minority groups will be negated.

This controversy points out the extreme difficulty of determining a just distribution of goods. The fact that everyone is not equal, in terms of ability, performance, motivation, need, or any other measure, is easy enough to agree on. On the one hand, few people would argue that everyone in every position should receive the same salary, get the same education, and achieve the same status in society. On the other hand, to acknowledge inequality puts us in the position of distributing goods and other benefits on the basis of other criteria, and it is here that problems arise. When injustice occurs, we sense it on the basis of fairness. We think somehow that it is not fair that there are starving children and conspicuous wealth in the same country or the same world. We sense unfairness when people work hard yet still struggle to get along on poverty wages, while star actors or athletes make millions of dollars largely through luck or for contributions to societal welfare that seem trivial in comparison. The Policy Box addresses the question of "The Future of Affirmative Action."

John Rawls's theory of justice is perhaps the best-known current conception of justice. He elegantly combines utilitarian and rights-based concepts in his theory. Basically, he proposes an equal distribution unless a different distribution would benefit the disadvantaged. Rawls believes that any inequalities of society should be to the benefit of those who are least advantaged (Rawls, 1971: 15). He proposed the following (cited in Kaplan, 1976: 114):

1. Each person is to have an equal right to the most extensive total system of basic liberties compatible with a similar system of liberty for all.
2. Social and economic inequalities are to be arranged so that they are both reasonably expected to be to everyone's advantage, and attached to positions and offices open to all (except when inequality is to the advantage of those least well-off).

So, for instance, Rawls may argue for a purely objective hiring scoring system except when they give extra points for those who are least well off, and tax rebates that are equally distributed except if they are a bit more favorable for those in the lower income brackets. Rawls uses a heuristic device that he calls the **veil of ignorance** to explain the idea that people will develop fair principles of distribution

| POLICY BOX | THE FUTURE OF AFFIRMATIVE ACTION? |

Should members of minority groups that historically have been discriminated against receive special privileges in hiring decisions in police departments? This question is extremely controversial. One argument is that preferential hiring of minorities strengthens police departments by helping the department more closely reflect the neighborhoods it polices and increases the skill sets of the officers. Another argument is that quota systems and the pressure to hire minorities made hiring standards go down and that unfit people have been hired as police officers. Further, even those who are qualified and good candidates are stigmatized because of a perception that they were hired only because of their gender, race, or ethnicity. How should hiring decisions be made when applicants are roughly similar in education, background, and civil service test scores?

Law: Voters in Michigan passed a state constitutional amendment that eliminated affirmative action programs in public agencies. Five more states were considering such measures for their November 2008 elections (Slevin, 2008). Proponents of killing affirmative action argue that the usefulness of such programs has passed and that they should be ruled illegal because they discriminate against whites. Supreme Court decisions have struck down broad-based affirmative action programs but have held that race can be *one* factor in decisions regarding admitting students to universities or hiring. Opponents would argue that race should *never* be used in such decisions.

Policy: Agencies differ on their policies regarding affirmative action. In 2003, only about 11 percent of officers were women and 24 percent were minorities (Hickman and Reaves, 2006). Some agencies continue to aggressively recruit minorities and may have policies that favor minority and female applicants, but it may be the case that affirmative action programs are simply policy choices today and not legally mandated, and such programs actually may be the subject of discrimination suits by white men. Remember—even without affirmative action, it is still illegal *not* to hire an applicant *because* of his or her race or gender.

Individual ethics: Individual ethics arise for those who are doing the hiring and those who are hired. If individuals know that they have been hired solely because of their gender, race, or ethnicity, what should they do? Should the hiring decision makers consider these elements, even though there is no formal policy to do so? What does distributive justice dictate when the applicant is a single, black working mother who scores 10 points lower than a white male on a civil service test, but in every other way the two are similar?

only if they are ignorant of their position in society, for they just as easily may be "have-nots" as "haves" (Rawls, 1971: 12). Thus, justice and fairness are in everyone's rational self-interest because, under the veil of ignorance, one's own situation is unknown, and the best and most rational distribution is the one that is most equal to all.

The following criticisms of Rawls's theory of justice have been presented:

1. The veil of ignorance is not sufficient to counteract humanity's basic selfishness: Given the chance, people would still seek to maximize their own gain, even if doing so involves a risk (Kaplan, 1976: 199).

2. Rawls's preference toward those who are least well-off is contrary to the good of society. Rawls states that "all social values—liberty and opportunity, income and wealth and the bases of self-respect—are to be distributed equally unless an unequal distribution of any, or all, of these values is to the advantage of the least favored" (quoted in Sterba, 1980: 32). This may be ultimately dysfunctional for society, for if those who are least well-off have the advantages of society preferentially, there will be no incentive for others to excel.

3. Some also argue that Rawls is wrong to ignore desert in his distribution of goods (Galston, 1980: 3).

Let us now turn to how these theories of distributive justice relate to the ethical systems discussed in Chapter 2. The ethics of care is consistent with a Marxist theory of justice, for both emphasize need. Utilitarian theories try to maximize societal good, so some balance of need and merit would be necessary to provide the incentive to produce. Ethical formalism is concerned solely with rights; thus, issues of societal good or others' needs may not be as important as the individual's rights (however those might be defined). Rawls's theory is both utilitarian and Kantian because it demands a basic level of individual rights but also attempts to establish a preference toward those who have less, for the good of all society.

How are these concepts of distributive justice relevant to criminal justice? First, the discussion illuminates the issues regarding the appropriateness of affirmative action in the hiring and promotion of police officers and other criminal justice professionals. Should your race give you special hiring privileges? What if the profession is one such as policing, which has been historically closed to minorities? Another issue that is related to distributive justice is how much to pay police officers compared to other professions. Most people believe that police are underpaid. If so, how much is a fair salary, and how does that salary compare to others, such as elementary school teachers? The criteria you used to determine these answers should have some basis in the distribution systems discussed above.

Finally, there is a connection between distributive justice and corrective justice, which will be discussed next. If it is true that socioeconomic status predicts criminal predisposition, should we care? Is it fair that poor people tend to end up in prison and those with more resources usually receive a lesser form of punishment? Further, should we consider issues of distributive justice (i.e., what someone has by accident of birth) in any discussion of corrective justice (i.e., what people deserve when they commit a crime)? Reiman (2004), for instance, presents a comprehensive argument that places economic power as the center of lawmaking, lawbreaking, enforcement, and punishment practices. Clearly, distributive justice is an important concept in any discussion of the criminal justice system.

CORRECTIVE JUSTICE

As mentioned before, corrective justice is concerned with dispensing punishment. As with distributive justice, the concepts of equality and desert, fairness and impartiality are important. Two components of corrective justice should be differentiated.

Substantive justice involves the concept of just deserts, or how one determines a fair punishment for a particular offense, and **procedural justice** concerns the steps we must take before administering punishment.

SUBSTANTIVE JUSTICE

What is a fair punishment for the crime of murder? Many believe that the only just punishment is death because that is the only punishment of a degree equal to the harm caused by the offender. Others might say that life imprisonment is equitable and fair. One's beliefs about what is fair punishment are usually related to one's perception of the seriousness of the crime. More serious crimes deserve more serious punishments.

Since the beginning of codified law, just punishment has been perceived as punishment set in relation to the degree of harm incurred. This was a natural outcome of the early, remedial forms of justice, which provided remedies for wrongs. For instance, the response to a theft of a slave or the killing of a horse involved compensation. The only just solution was the return or replacement of the slave or horse. This remedial or compensatory system of justice contrasts with a punishment system: The first system forces the offender to provide compensation to the victim or the victim's family, and the second apportions punishment based on the degree of seriousness of the crime suffered by the victim. They both involve a measurement of the harm, but in the first case, measurement is taken to adequately compensate the victim, and in the second it is to punish the offender. In a punishment-based system, the victim is a peripheral figure. The state, rather than the victim, becomes the central figure—serving both as victim and as punisher (Karmen, 1984).

Two *philosophies* of corrective justice can be identified: retributive justice and utilitarian justice.

Retributive Justice   The concept of **retributive justice** is one of balance. The criminal must suffer pain or loss proportional to what the victim was forced to suffer. In an extreme form this retribution takes the form of *lex talionis*, a vengeance-oriented justice concerned with equal retaliation ("an eye for an eye; a tooth for a tooth"). A milder form is *lex salica*, which allows compensation; the harm can be repaired by payment or atonement (Allen and Simonsen, 1986: 4). A life for a life might be easy to measure, but most cases involve other forms of harm. In other types of victimizations, how does one determine the amount of physical or mental pain suffered by the victim, or financial loss such as lost income or future loss? And if the offender cannot pay back financial losses, how does one equate imprisonment with fines or restitution?

Historically, corporal and capital punishment were used for both property crime and violent crime. With the development of the penitentiary system in the early 1800s, punishment became equated with terms of imprisonment rather than amounts of physical pain. The greater ease of measuring out prison sentences probably contributed to the rapid acceptance of prison sentences. An offender might be sentenced to one, two, or five years, depending on the seriousness of the crime. Imprisonment had several advantages over earlier forms of punishment.

1. It was considered more humane than corporal punishment.
2. It was incapacitating (preventing offenders from further crime).
3. It allowed offenders to reflect on their crime and repent.
4. It did not elicit sympathy for the offenders from the populace.

However, a term of imprisonment is much harder to equate to a particular crime. Although one can intuitively understand the natural balance of a life for a life, $10 for $10, or even a beating for an assault, it is much harder to argue that a burglary of $100 is equal to a year in prison or that an assault is equal to a term of two years. A year in prison is hard to define. Research on prison adjustment indicates that a year means different things to different people. For some, it might be no more than mildly inconvenient; for others, it might lead to suicide or mental illness (Toch, 1977).

In addition to retribution, imprisonment was tied to the reform of the criminal offender. Reform or rehabilitation may be a laudable goal, but it has no place in a retributive scheme of justice. Retributive punishment is based on balancing the victim's harm with the offender's pain or suffering. Treatment involves no such balance; therefore, there is no retributive rationale for its existence. Philosophical support for rehabilitative treatment of criminal offenders is found in utilitarianism.

Retributive justice is not a simple equation because factors in addition to the seriousness of the crime are taken into account. For instance, *mens rea* (intent) has long been considered a necessary element in determining culpability. Those who are incapable of rational thought, such as the insane and the very young, are said to be neither morally nor legally culpable; therefore, to punish them would be an injustice under a retributive framework. Other situations might prove to involve partial responsibility—for example, the presence of compulsion, coercion, or irresistible impulse. In these cases, most people believe that justice is not compromised by a lesser amount of punishment, even though the harm to the victim is obviously the same as if the offender had acted deliberately and intentionally. In this sense, we see that the amount of punishment is not measured solely by the amount of harm to the victim but involves characteristics of the offender as well.

Just punishment may also involve considering the participation of the victim. Victim precipitation (when the victim has done something that makes the criminal act more likely) may lessen the culpability of the offender. Other factors also play a part in determining punishment, some of which would not be consistent with retributive justice. In earlier systems of justice, the status of the victim was important in determining the level of harm and, thus, the punishment. Nobles were more important than free men, who were more important than slaves. Men were more important than women. Punishment for offenders was weighted according to these designations of the worth of the victim. Although we have no formal system for weighting punishment in this way and have rejected the worth of the victim as a rationale for punishment (except in a few cases, such as assaulting a police officer), many believe that our justice system still follows this practice informally. People argue that harsher sentences are given when the victim is white than when the victim is black and when the victim is rich as opposed to poor. In a similar manner, many argue that the justice system discriminates unfairly and unjustly against characteristics of the offender. Many believe that offenders receive harsher sentences because of their race, background, or income.

Whether or not these charges are true, it is important to recognize that earlier systems of justice, including the Greek and Roman, approved of and rationalized such different treatment as perfectly fair and just. Our system of justice has rejected these discriminations even while holding on to others—specifically, intent, partial responsibility, and, to some extent, victim precipitation. It is difficult, if not impossible, for everyone to agree upon a fair and equitable measurement of punishment when one allows for exceptions, mediating factors, and partial responsibility. That is why there is so little agreement on what is fair punishment. Even when two defendants are involved in a single crime, our system of justice can support different punishments under a retributive rationale. Issues of culpability will be discussed in more detail in Chapter 5.

In Rawls's theory of justice, retributive punishment is limited in the following way (quoted in Hickey and Scharf, 1980: 168):

> [T]he liberties of a person ... may only be reduced, compared with the liberties of other people, when it is for the good of the least advantaged, considered from the "veil of ignorance" assumption of not knowing what role one will occupy.

This statement means that only when punishment can be shown to benefit the least advantaged (the victim) can it be justified; when the advantage changes (when the victim has been repaid), punishment must cease. Hickey and Scharf (1980: 169) point out that this limitation is similar to that proposed by Norval Morris:

1. We must punish only to the extent that the loss of liberty would be agreeable were one not to know whether one were to be the criminal, the victim, or a member of the general public; and
2. The loss of liberty must be justified as the minimal loss consistent with the maintenance of the same liberty among others.

In both of these propositions, the moral limit of punishment is reached when what is done to the criminal equals the extent of his or her forfeiture, as determined by the crime.

One other issue that must be addressed here is the concept of mercy. Seemingly inconsistent with any definition of retributive justice, mercy is, nevertheless, always associated with the concept. From the very beginnings of law, there has also been the element of forgiveness. Even tribal societies had special allowances and clemencies for offenders, usually granted by the king or chief. For instance, the concept of **sanctuary** allowed offenders respite from punishment as long as they were within the confines of church grounds. Benefit of clergy, dispensation, and even probation are examples of mercy by the court. However, it must be made clear that mercy is different from just deserts. If, on the one hand, because of circumstances of the crime, of the criminal, or of the victim, the offender deserves little or no punishment, then that is what he or she deserves, and it is not mercy to give a suspended sentence or probation. On the other hand, if an offender truly deserves the punishment and is instead forgiven, then the individual has been granted mercy. As the "In the News" box on Karla Faye Tucker shows, sometimes mercy is not forthcoming.

IN THE NEWS | KARLA FAYE TUCKER'S DEATH SENTENCE

In 1998, Karla Faye Tucker received worldwide attention in her bid to receive a commutation of her death sentence. A legion of supporters, including international leaders and the Pope, pleaded with Texas Governor George W. Bush to recommend that her death sentence be commuted and let her serve a life sentence instead. The major argument was that she had changed from the drug-addled young woman who had embedded a pickaxe into her victim's chest. She was now thirty-five years old and had been a leader and calming influence upon the other women on Death Row. She had spent years engaged in charitable activities in the prison. She experienced real remorse for her crime and believed that her lifetime was devoted to making up for it. Also, her childhood involved sexual and physical abuse; she was prostituted by her mother at a young age and was already addicted to alcohol by the time she was twelve. Further, she had become a true Christian. Her spirituality and, in all likelihood, true conversion to religion allowed her to face death with the attitude that it was part of a divine plan. Finally, similar murders by others did not result in the death sentence. Governor Bush refused to commute her sentence, and she was executed amid the cheers and tears of the opposing groups.

Do you think that her death sentence should have been commuted? Why? Identify the rationales that underlie the above arguments. Are the arguments based on desert or mercy?

Murphy (1985/1995) proposes that retributive emotions derive from self-respect, that it is a healthy response to an injury to feel angry, resentful, and, yes, even vengeful. However, it is also acceptable to forgive and extend mercy to one's assailant if the forgiveness extends not from a lack of self-respect but, rather, from a moral system. For instance, he points out that many religions include the concept of "turning the other cheek" and extending mercy to enemies. Mercy is appropriate when the offender is divorced in some way from his or her offense. One way to this separation is true repentance.

Murphy (1988: 10) summarizes the points of mercy as follows:

1. It is an autonomous moral virtue (separate from justice).
2. It is a virtue that tempers or "seasons" justice—something that one adds to justice.
3. It is never owed to anyone as a right or a matter of desert or justice.
4. As a moral virtue, it derives its value at least in part because it flows from love or compassion while not losing sight of the importance of justice.
5. It requires a generally retributive outlook on punishment and responsibility.

Therefore, mercy is related to justice but is not necessarily a part of it. It is connected with a change in the offender because, typically, there must be repentance before mercy is extended. Also, it is connected with the compassion, charity, or benevolence of the victim.

Other questions of mercy remain, however. Who has the right to extend mercy? At times, victims or the families of victims are upset with a sentencing judge because of the lenient sentence administered to the offender. Should victims be the only ones who have the right to give the gift of mercy?

Utilitarian Justice   We have been discussing retributive justice as a rationale for and a means to determine punishment. However, other rationales, such as **utilitarian justice**, also support punishment. Whereas the goal of a retributive framework of justice is to restore a natural balance by righting a wrong or neutralizing criminal gain with an equal amount of loss or pain, the goal of utilitarian justice is to benefit society by administering punishment to deter offenders from future crime.

Caesare Beccaria (1738–1794) and Jeremy Bentham (1748–1832) provided a utilitarian rationale for proportionality in punishment. Punishment should be based on the seriousness of the crime: The more serious the crime (or the greater the reward the crime offered the criminal), the more serious and severe the punishment should be, to deter the individual from committing the crime. A utilitarian framework of justice would determine punishment on the basis of deterrence.

Bentham's *hedonistic calculus*, for instance, is concerned with measuring the potential rewards of the crime so the amount of threatened pain could be set to deter people from committing that crime. The use of proportionality in this scheme is deterrence, not balance. In a retributive system, we measure to determine the proportional amount of punishment to right the wrong; in a utilitarian system, we measure to determine the amount of punishment needed to deter. We see that under the utilitarian framework, there is no necessity for perfect balance. In that conception one must threaten a slightly higher degree of pain or punishment than the gain or pleasure that comes from the criminal act; otherwise, there would be no deterrent value in the punishment.

In some cases, retributive notions of justice and utilitarian notions of justice may conflict. If a criminal is sure to commit more crime, the utilitarian could justify holding him in prison as a means of incapacitation, but to hold him past the time "equal" to his crime would be seen as an injustice under a retributive system. We might punish an offender more seriously than he "deserves" under a utilitarian system if it could be shown to deter many others. Deterrence is the primary determinant of justice under a utilitarian system, but desert is the only determinant of a retributive system of justice. Treatment is prevention, not deterrence *per se*, but it is also acceptable under a utilitarian justice system and irrelevant and unsupported by a retributive one. The "In the News" box explicates a Supreme Court ruling involving cocaine use that illustrates the difficulty of determining what is a just punishment for any crime.

PROCEDURAL JUSTICE

We turn now to the procedure of administering punishment—our legal system. Law includes the procedures and rules used to determine punishment or resolve disputes. It is a system of rules for human relations—the "whole field of the principles laid down, the decisions reached in accordance with them, and the procedures whereby the principles are applied to individual cases" (Raphael, 1980: 74). There can be a difference between justice and law. You might think of justice as the concept of fairness, while law is a system of rules.

The law is an imperfect system. Fuller (1969: 39) explored the weaknesses of law and described ways that the procedure of law may fail to achieve justice. Possible failures include

1. a failure to achieve rules at all, so that every decision must be made on its own
2. a failure to publicize rules
3. retroactive application of law, which abuses the concept of justice
4. the existence of contradictory rules
5. too-frequent changes in rules
6. a lack of consistency between the rules and their actual administration.

These failures weaken the law's ability to resolve disputes or control conflict in an objective and fair manner.

Some argue that because of the legal system's inability to determine what is just, justice derives not from the application of legal rules but, rather, from deciding each case on its merits without regard to rule or precedent. Early equity courts in England were developed because there was dissatisfaction with the King's (legal) courts' emphasis on rules and precedent that, in some cases, frustrated the ends of justice. Some argue that legal precedent is an unsatisfactory way of determining justice because the particularity of each case is important. However, individual, intuitive decisions are no better, for justice then becomes "unsteady" and "wavering" (Feinberg and Gross, 1977: 28–34). Some have argued that property and interest cases can be decided by legal rule but that those cases involving conflicts of human conduct cannot. Even this bifurcation is criticized, however, because the most straightforward contract disagreements may involve human action, misinterpretation, and interest (Wasserman, cited in Feinberg and Gross, 1977: 34).

We are left to assume that although a system of law is necessary for the ordered existence of society, it is not necessarily helpful in determining what is just. "Moral rights" may differ from "legal rights," and "legal interests" may not be moral. However, it should be noted that rules often specify the procedures and steps necessary in judicial decision making. If these rules and procedures are broken, we believe that an injustice has occurred.

Shakespeare's *The Merchant of Venice* (excerpted in the "Quote and Query" box) addresses many of the issues discussed in this chapter. Here the plea for mercy emphasizes the relationship between justice and mercy. Shylock's demand for the court's enforcement of his legal right (his pound of flesh) and the unwillingness of the court to deny it, despite the clear implication that it would be a tragedy,

QUOTE AND QUERY

The quality of mercy is not strained;
It droppeth as the gentle rain from heaven
Upon the place beneath. It is twice blest;
It blesseth him that gives and him that takes.

...

It is an attribute to God himself,
And earthly power doth then show likest God's
When mercy seasons justice. Therefore, Jew,
Though justice be thy plea, consider this,
That, in the course of justice, none of us
Should see salvation. We do pray for mercy,
And that same prayer doth teach us all to render
The deeds of mercy. I have spoke thus much
To mitigate the justice of thy plea,
Which if thou follow, this strict court of Venice
Must needs give sentence 'gainst the merchant there.

Shakespeare, 1969.

What is the magistrate in this passage asking Shylock to do? How do you believe mercy should "season" justice? What would be procedural justice in this case? What would be substantive justice?

---

illustrate how law sometimes has little to do with justice. Then Portia's surprise argument—that because Shylock's contract mentioned only flesh and not blood, so no blood could be spilled, and thus Shylock is denied his compensation—is a superb illustration of the law's slavish devotion to technical rules over substance. As a legal trick, this interpretation of a contract has not been improved upon yet, in fiction or in reality.

In our system of justice, **due process** exemplifies procedural justice. Our constitutional rights of due process require careful inquiry and investigation before punishment or forfeiture of any protected right can be carried out by the state. In Box 4.2, certain selected rights embodied in the Bill of Rights have been provided. Notice that the "due process" clause appears in both the Fifth and the Fourteenth amendments.

One has the right to due process whenever the government seeks to deprive an individual of protected rights of life, liberty, or property. Due process is the sequence of steps taken by the state that is designed to eliminate or at least minimize error. Procedural protections include

1. notice of charges
2. neutral hearing body
3. right of cross-examination
4. right to present evidence
5. representation by counsel
6. statement of findings
7. appeal

BOX 4.2 | THE BILL OF RIGHTS AND SELECTED AMENDMENTS

Article I. Congress shall make no law respecting an establishment of religion, or prohibiting the free exercise thereof; or abridging the freedom of speech, or of the press; or the right of the people peaceably to assemble, and to petition the Government for a redress of grievance.

Article II. A well regulated militia, being necessary to the security of a free State, the right of the people to keep and bear arms, shall not be infringed.

Article III. No Soldier shall, in time of peace be quartered in any house, without the consent of the owner, nor in time of war, but in a manner to be prescribed by law.

Article IV. The right of the people to be secure in their persons, houses, papers, and effects, against unreasonable searches and seizures, shall not be violated, and no warrants shall issue, but upon probable cause, supported by oath or affirmation, and particularly describing the place to be searched, and the persons or things to be seized.

Article V. No person shall be held to answer for a capital, or otherwise infamous crime, unless on a presentment or indictment of a Grand Jury, except in cases arising in the land or naval forces, or in the militia, when in actual service in time of war or public danger; nor shall any person be subject for the same offense to be twice put in jeopardy of life or limb; nor shall be compelled in any criminal case to be a witness against himself, nor be deprived of life, liberty, or property, without due process of law; nor shall private property be taken for public use, without just compensation.

Article VI. In all criminal prosecutions, the accused shall enjoy the right to a speedy and public trial, by an impartial jury of the State and district wherein the crime shall have been committed, which district shall have been previously ascertained by law, and to be informed of the nature and cause of the accusation; to be confronted with the witnesses against him; to have compulsory process for obtaining witnesses in his favor, and to have the assistance of counsel for his defense.

Article VII. In Suits at common law, where the value in controversy shall exceed twenty dollars, the right of trial by jury shall be preserved, and no fact tried by a jury, shall be otherwise reexamined in any Court of the United States, than according to the rules of the common law.

Article VIII. Excessive bail shall not be required, nor excessive fines imposed, nor cruel and unusual punishments inflicted.

Article IX. The enumeration in the Constitution, of certain rights, shall not be construed to deny or disparage others retained by the people.

Article X. The powers not delegated to the United States by the Constitution, nor prohibited by it to the States, are reserved to the States respectively, or to the people.

Article XIII. Section 1. Neither slavery nor involuntary servitude, except as a punishment for crime whereof the party shall have been duly convicted, shall exist within the United States, or any place subject to their jurisdiction.

Section 2. Congress shall have power to enforce this article by appropriate legislation.

Article XIV. Section 1. All persons born or naturalized to the United States, and subject to the jurisdiction thereof, are citizens of the United States and of the State wherein they reside. No State shall make or enforce any law which shall abridge the privileges or immunities of citizens of the United States; nor shall any State deprive any person of life, liberty, or property, without due process of law; nor deny to any person within its jurisdiction the equal protection of the laws....

Article XV. Section 1. The right of citizens of the United States to vote shall not be denied or abridged by the United States or by any State on account of race, color, or previous condition of servitude....

Article XIX. The right of citizens of the United States to vote shall not be denied or abridged by the United States or by any State on account of sex....

These protections do not eliminate deprivation or punishment, but they do result in more accurate and just deprivations and punishments. Thus, if due process has been violated—by use of a coerced confession, tainted evidence, or improper police procedure—an injustice has occurred. The injustice does not arise because the offender does not deserve to be punished but, rather, because the state does not deserve to do the punishing, having relied on unfair procedures.

Some point out that procedural justice is recognized only for certain groups—specifically, "all persons born or naturalized in the United States...." Many people believe that illegal aliens and noncitizens should have no rights recognized by the Constitution. This allowed practices such as the incarceration of the Cuban "Marielitos" without any form of due process at all. Some of these refugees were imprisoned for more than a decade in federal prisons without any finding of guilt, harm, or reason. Jimmy Carter, in 1993, discussed their imprisonment (quoted in Hamm, 1995: 39):

> Every nation that grossly violates human rights justifies it by claiming they are acting within their laws. The way we are doing it now is the same kind of human rights violation that we'd vehemently condemn if it was perpetrated in another country.

The Supreme Court has held that such detentions were illegal. In a 7–2 decision, the Court held, in *Clark v. Martinez*, 125 S. Ct. 716 (2005), that the government may not "indefinitely" detain illegal immigrants, even if they have been found guilty of a crime. The Court said the government could not restrain individuals past a "reasonable" amount of time. The government argued that the ruling would affect counterterrorism efforts. Several important decisions are emerging about the right of the executive branch to fashion new rules regarding due process in the "war on terror."

After 9/11, several thousand individuals who were suspected of terrorist ties were held without charges and without any procedural protections that might allow them to prove in a fair and neutral hearing that those ties did not exist. Part of the reason given for their detention was that they violated immigration laws—for instance, they overstayed their visas. Instead of deportation, however, more than a thousand individuals were incarcerated, sometimes without even notice to their families of where they were. The federal courts have had to wrestle with how to protect individual liberties balanced against the government's right to protect itself. The touchstone of this analysis is always, and always has to be, due process.

In *Hamdi v. Rumsfeld*, 542 U.S. 507, 124 S.Ct. 2633 (2004), the Supreme Court held that a U.S. citizen could not be held indefinitely as an "enemy combatant" without some form of due process. However, the decision was split between those who believed that U.S. citizens could be held and prosecuted as enemy combatants by a military court and those who distinguished U.S. citizens from noncitizens. In *Rasul v. Bush*, 542 U.S. 466, 124 S.Ct. 2686 (2004), the Supreme Court held that those being held in Guantanamo Bay were subject to the laws of the United States and deserved some form of due process. But the Court, in *Hamdan v. Rumsfeld*, 125 S.Ct. 972, 160 L.Ed.2d 910 (2005) denied *certiorari* to another Guantanamo Bay detainee who lost at the court of appeals level in his bid to have the Court recognize various protections granted to the detainees by the Geneva Convention. The Court then reversed itself.

In a second case, *Hamdan v. Rumsfeld*, 548 U.S. 557 (2006), the Supreme Court (5-3) invalidated the Military Commissions set up by the Bush administration to try the detainees. This form of due process was ruled as outside the power of the President to create because the commissions didn't conform to the Uniform Code of Military Justice or the Geneva Conventions. The Court indicated that Congress might create this hybrid form of due process and, in 2006, Congress passed the Military Commissions Act. The firestorm of controversy that resulted was because the Act basically eliminated habeas corpus for those defined as enemy combatants and it was solely within the power of the President or his designees to decide who was an enemy combatant.

In June of 2008, the Supreme Court ruled that the Congress-created Military Commissions also violated the Constitutional rights of the detainees. In *Boumediene v. Bush (No. 06-1195)*, the Court, in a 5-4 decision, held that the Military Commissions Act fell short of protecting individuals' due process rights because it eliminated habeas corpus.

Is the right to be free from governmental deprivation of liberty without some finding of guilt a **natural right** that every government must recognize for all people, or a *legal* right that can be written into existence, written out of existence, and defined in whatever way a government chooses, depending on a perceived threat? These questions depend on one's beliefs regarding natural law, individual rights, and definitions of justice.

Due process protects the individual from error and governmental abuse of power. One of the more controversial tools of due process is the **exclusionary rule**, which is supposed to ensure that the state follows the correct procedures before exacting punishment by excluding illegal evidence from the trial. There is debate as to whether the exclusionary rule is a mere legal protective device created by the Supreme Court or a natural inherent right embedded in the Constitution. The exclusionary rule has been subject to a great deal of criticism because it is perceived as a rule that lets criminals go free.

On the one hand, a utilitarian framework might support punishment even if the procedural rules were broken, for the net utility of punishment might outweigh the violation of due process. On the other hand, even a utilitarian may argue against punishment when the procedural protections have been broken if the damage to general respect for the law is greater than the deterrent utility of punishment. One of the rationales for the exclusionary rule is that it serves as a judicial "slap" to police departments and a deterrent against improper investigation procedures. This is clearly a utilitarian argument.

Under a retributive system of punishment, it would seem that justice is violated whether one is punished or not if procedural justice is violated. If we allow the offender to go free because of the error, the crime has not been balanced by punishment. If we punish the offender, we violate our system of procedural justice and protection of individual rights.

Supreme Court decisions have shown reduced support for the exclusionary rule. Exceptions have been created that some say threaten to undermine the rule itself. Three landmark cases illustrate some exceptions:

1. The *inevitable discovery exception* allows the tainted evidence if it would have been discovered without the improper procedure (*Nix v. Williams*, 104 S.Ct. 250 [1984]).
2. The *good faith exception* was recognized by the Court in a case where the law enforcement officers thought they had a legal warrant even though the warrant, and therefore their search, was actually unlawful (*United States v. Leon*, 104 S.Ct. 3405 [1984]).
3. The *pubic safety exception* was recognized in *New York v. Quarles* (104 S.Ct. 2626 [1984]). In this case, because the officer's goal was public safety and not collection of evidence, his failure to give Miranda warnings did not result in excluding the evidence he obtained by questioning a suspect without Miranda warnings.

The majority of justices displayed distinctly utilitarian reasoning in their cost/benefit arguments to support the holdings of the previously mentioned cases. It may be that the Supreme Court will become reluctant to uphold sanctions against any but the most extreme misconduct by police and use a *shocking to the conscience test* rather than a test that measures the violation to procedural rights. In this test, police behavior is evaluated against substantive rights to be free from outrageous governmental action, such as torture, forced blood samples, or surgery, or, in the case most closely associated with the test, forced regurgitation (*Rochin v. California*, 343 U.S. 165 [1952]).

We have been discussing legal procedures for determining punishment, but in some cases legal procedures may be strictly followed and injustice still occurs. For instance, it is unlikely that anyone would argue that Nelson Mandela, when he was imprisoned in South Africa, or Andre Sakharov, a Soviet dissident, received *just* punishment even though the legal procedures of their respective countries might have been scrupulously followed. These are clear examples that illustrate the difference between "procedural" justice and "substantive" justice.

CONCLUSION

In this chapter we have explored the origins and components of justice. Whereas justice is a philosophical concept concerned with rights and needs, law is the administration of justice. Justice can be further differentiated into distributive justice and corrective justice. Corrective justice is the central concern of the criminal justice system and can be further divided into substantive and procedural issues. Substantive justice is concerned with the fairness of what we do to offenders; procedural justice is concerned with the procedures that must be undertaken before punishment occurs.

Key Terms

commutative
  justice *92*

corrective justice *92*

distributive justice *92*

due process *107*

exclusionary rule *110*

justice *91*

natural right *110*

procedural justice *101*

retributive justice *101*

sanctuary *103*

substantive justice *101*

utilitarian justice *105*

veil of ignorance *98*

Review Questions

1. Explain how Plato and Aristotle associated status with justice.
2. Define rectificatory justice.
3. Describe distributive, corrective, and commutative justice.
4. Describe the various types of distributive justice.
5. Describe Sterba's system of distribution.
6. Discuss the differences between substantive justice and procedural justice.
7. How do you define mercy?
8. Define due process.
9. What is the retributive argument for punishment?
10. What is the utilitarian argument for punishment?

Writing/Discussion Questions

1. Write an essay on (or discuss) how the government should distribute societal resources such as education and health care. How would you answer the argument of a couple who did not believe they should have to pay school taxes because they have no children? What about the argument that rich school districts should share their wealth with poor districts (keeping in mind that those who pay higher taxes in that district might have moved there because of the reputation of the school)? What are the arguments for and against universal health care?

2. Write an essay on (or discuss) what the proper punishment should be for a burglary, for a murder in an armed robbery, and for a million-dollar embezzlement. If you were being punished for a crime, would you rather receive a year in prison or fifty lashes? Why do we not use corporal punishment for criminal offenders? Do you think we should? Are there situations in our justice system where victims or offenders are treated differently than others because of who they are?

3. Write an essay on (or discuss) the following cases under procedural and substantive justice:

   a. An eighty-seven-year-old man living in Chicago is exposed as a soldier who took part in killing hundreds of Jewish concentration camp victims. U.S. extradition procedures are followed to the letter, and he is extradited to Israel to stand trial. Israeli law determines that courts in Israel have jurisdiction over Nazi war crimes. Israeli legal procedure is followed without error, and he is convicted of war crimes and sentenced to death.

   b. Federal law enforcement agents determine that a citizen of another country participated in a drug cartel that sold drugs in the United States. A small group of agents goes to the foreign country, kidnaps the offender, drugs him, and brings him back to the United States to stand trial. Upon challenge, the government agents explain that, although these actions would have been unconstitutional and illegal against a citizen of the United States in this country, because they were conducted on foreign soil against a non-U.S. citizen, they were not illegal.

4. Write an essay on (or discuss) the just resolution of the following cases:

   a. In a civil dispute, one side has a strong claim and almost surely would win in court, yet because the attorney missed a filing deadline, the judge throws out the case.

   b. In a death penalty case, new evidence emerges that supports the defendant's allegations of innocence, but the evidence had been uncovered after the deadline for filing an appeal. Should the execution go forward?

c. An individual befriends an elderly person, takes care of him, and provides him comfort in his old age even at the sacrifice of personal time and expense. When the elderly person dies, however, a distant relative who had expressed the view that it wasn't her duty to take care of her relative inherits substantial assets.

Is this fair? Is this just? If the law (which typically would uphold the inheritance absent any special elements such as contract or payment for personal services) does not support any recognition of the friend's non-legal "rights" to any portion of the inheritance, what theory of justice might support it?

Ethical Dilemmas

Situation 1

Two individuals are being sentenced for the exact same crime of burglary. You are the judge. One of the individuals is a twenty-year-old who has not been in trouble before and participated only because the other individual was his friend. The second person has a history of juvenile delinquency and is now twenty-five. Would you sentence them differently? How would you justify your decision?

Situation 2

In your apartment building there lives a young man who appears to be of Middle Eastern descent. You notice that other young men often visit him and that they come and go at odd hours of the day and night. You engage in a conversation with him one day, and during the course of the conversation, he states that "the United States deserved what happened on September 11 because of their imperialistic actions across the world and their support for the oppression of the Palestinian people." You think it is your duty to report him to the local police, and they appear to be interested in your report. One day you observe him taken away in handcuffs, and you never see him again. Several weeks later his apartment is vacant, and you do not know what happened to his belongings. Would you attempt to find out what happened to him? Do you believe you should investigate further?

Situation 3

You are serving on a jury for a murder trial. The evidence presented at trial was largely circumstantial and, in your mind, equivocal. During closing, the prosecutor argued that you must find the defendant guilty because he confessed to the crime. The defense attorney immediately objected, and the judge sternly instructed you to disregard the prosecutor's statement. Although you do not know exactly what happened, you suspect that the confession was excluded because of some procedural error. Would you be able to ignore the prosecutor's statement in your deliberations? Should you? Would you tell the judge if the jury members discussed the statement and seemed to be influenced by it?

Situation 4

You are a legislator who believes absolutely and strongly that abortion is a sin. You have polled your constituents and are surprised to find that the majority do not believe that the government should legislate the private decision of a woman to have an abortion. Should you vote your conscience or the will of the majority of your constituents?

Situation 5

You are a probation officer who must prepare sentencing recommendation reports for the judge. The juvenile defendant to be sentenced in one case grew up in a desperately poor family, according to school records. He had a part-time job in a local grocery store, stocking the shelves and providing general cleanup. The store owner caught him stealing meat. Actually, this is the second time he has been caught stealing food.

The first time he shoplifted at the store, and the deferred adjudication included his commitment to work for the store owner. He explained that he was trying to help his mother, who could not provide enough food for his family. In general, failure to succeed at deferred adjudication results in a commitment to a juvenile facility. What would you recommend to the judge?

Suggested Readings

Cole, D. 1999. *No Equal Justice.* New York: Free Press.

Hamm, M. 1995. *The Abandoned Ones.* Boston: Northeastern University Press.

MacIntyre, A. 1988. *Whose Justice? Which Rationality?* Notre Dame, IN: University of Notre Dame Press.

Monique, J. 2002. *The Origins of Justice: the Evolution of Morality, Human Rights, and Law.* Philadelphia: the University of Pennsylvania Press.

Murphie, J. 1988. "Forgiveness, Mercy, and the Retributive Emotions." *Criminal Justice Ethics* 7(2): 3–15.

Rawls, J. 1971. *A Theory of Justice.* Cambridge, MA: Belknap.

Reiman, J. 1990. *Justice and Modern Moral Philosophy.* New Haven, CT: Yale University Press.

Reiman, J. 2005/2007. *The Rich Get Richer and the Poor Get Prison: Ideology, Class, and Criminal Justice.* Boston: Allyn & Bacon.

Walsh, A. 1995. *Biosociology: An Emerging Paradigm.* Trenton, NJ: Praeger.

Walsh, A. 2000. "Evolutionary Psychology and the Origins of Justice." *Justice Quarterly* 17(4): 841–864.

LAW AND THE INDIVIDUAL

Lt. Commander Charles Swift may have lost his career in the Navy because of his zealous defense of a Guantanamo Bay detainee. In his view, protection of the law and the rights that the law creates, such as habeas corpus, is the most important goal of a justice system.

© Mark Wilson/Getty Images

CHAPTER OBJECTIVES

1. Understand the paradigms of law.

2. Understand the justifications for law, including legal paternalism and legal moralism.

3. Distinguish between moral culpability and legal culpability.

4. Be familiar with the issues of culpability for juveniles, the mentally ill and mentally handicapped, white-collar criminals, and in situations of victim precipitation.

5. Be familiar with the concepts of restorative justice.

Anyone would tell you that Charles Swift was an excellent attorney. He was also an officer in the United States Navy. As the "Walking the Walk" selection illustrates, Swift's commitment to the law, and to his professional obligations, may have cost him his career in the military. Swift was the Navy lawyer who defended Salim Ahmed Hamdan and won in the Supreme Court case against the federal government, which took the position that Guantanamo detainees could be held indefinitely with no due process. Swift was also an attorney who believed that his duty was to uphold the law scrupulously, even if it wasn't politically popular.

"We are a nation of laws, not of men" is a phrase meaning that once a law is duly enacted, it applies to all of us. Once a legal right is recognized, it cannot be denied to anyone. As we discussed in Chapter 4, law can be considered the administration of justice. Civil law is the administration of commutative (or rectifactory) justice, and criminal law is the administration of corrective justice. Law recognizes and enforces the rights of the individual versus the state, and the rights of each party in conflicts between individuals.

Law can also be viewed as a tool of behavior change, especially when considering criminal law. Law can be seen as a tool of social engineering and a way of changing behavior to a desired state (Hornum and Stavish, 1978: 148). Law may influence behavior directly by prohibiting or mandating certain behavior, or indirectly by affecting social institutions such as family or education that, in turn, influence behavior (Dror, 1969: 93). Thus, law controls behavior by providing sanctions but also, perhaps even more important, by teaching people which behaviors are acceptable and which behaviors are not. People who commit crimes are assumed to have freely chosen to submit themselves to legal sanctions. Their culpability or responsibility will be assessed, which will then determine their degree of punishment. In this chapter we will discuss issues of culpability, especially with certain groups—the mentally challenged, juveniles, and white-collar criminals. We will also discuss situations wherein laws themselves are morally suspect. Finally, we present the concept of restorative justice, which can be seen as an attempt by current legal systems to better meet the needs of justice. The "Quote and Query" box indicates the historical vulnerability and culpability of some individuals.

QUOTE AND QUERY

Laws are just like spider's webs, they will hold the weak and delicate who might be caught in their meshes, but will be torn to pieces by the rich and powerful.

— **Anacharsis, 600** B.C.E.

The more mandates and laws which are enacted, the more there will be thieves and robbers.

—**Lao-Tze, 600** B.C.E.

Quoted in Roth and Roth (1989: 3).

What do these statements mean? Is it true that laws are manipulated by the powerful and oppress the weak?

WALKING THE WALK

Charles Swift is from a small town in North Carolina. He entered the United States Naval Academy in 1980 and served seven years as a surface-warfare officer. He graduated from Seattle University School of Law in 1994 and returned to active duty as a member of the Judge Advocate General's Corps (JAG). In March of 2003, he was assigned to the defense counsel's team for the Office of Military Commissions, set up to provide a unique form of due process for Guantanamo detainees. Lt. Commander Swift was assigned to defend Salim Ahmed Hamdan, a Yemeni who at one time had been Osama Bin Laden's driver.

One of the first things Swift was told in the case was that he could have access to his client only on the condition that he attempt to negotiate a guilty plea from him. When Swift decided that it was clear that there was no real due process in the so-called Military Commissions process, as it did not follow the Uniform Military Code, the Geneva Convention, or any rule of law recognized in 250 years of United States jurisprudence, he sued his chain of command, including the Commander-in-Chief, President George W. Bush. He says:

> [in most countries]...when a military officer openly opposes the president, it is called a coup. In the United States, it is called *Hamdan v. Rumsfeld*. After the Supreme Court's decision ..., the world was rightly in awe of our system. ...[W]e proved once again that we are a nation of laws and not of men.

Swift's exhaustive and fearless defense of Hamdan, a defense that basically challenged the Military Commissions as constructed by the Bush administration, resulted in the Supreme Court ruling 5–3 that the President had exceeded his power in ignoring the Geneva Convention, the Military Justice Code, and Congress in creating the tribunals. In an irony that was not lost on any observer, Swift was passed over for promotion and was forced to retire from his beloved Navy shortly after the Supreme Court decision was handed down. His superiors said they had submitted exemplary reports on his performance, but that promotions are granted for "breadth," not just "depth," and, therefore, even though he was a brilliant lawyer, he would not be rewarded with a promotion.

Because of the Navy's up-or-out promotional policies, Swift had to leave the Navy at the age of 44 and was not around for further developments, such as the Military Commissions Act of 2006, where Congress put the Military Commissions back in play by providing the legal imprimatur for them. In June 2007, the Supreme Court refused to hear two court challenges to the Congressional Act's Military Commissions but then reversed its decision. In December of 2007, arguments were heard in *Boumediene v. Bush* (06-1195) and in June of 2008, the Court issued its final ruling that the Military Commissions, without any habeas corpus protection, did not meet minimum due process requirements and were, therefore, unconstitutional.

Would Swift do it differently if he had it to do over? He says, "If we are to be a great nation, then we must be willing to be a nation bound by the rule of law in our treatment of all people." He isn't finished defending the laws of this country. He continues to oppose the Military Commissions, arguing that there was no reason for creation of the Military Commissions other than to be able to use evidence obtained by the use of torture in Guantanamo and other locations. He argues that officials knew that information obtained through the use of torture would be ruled unacceptable in a military or civilian court.

Today, Swift is a Visiting Associate Professor and Acting Director of the International Humanitarian Law Clinic at Emory University, providing legal assistance to those involved in humanitarian law, including military tribunals. He was honored with the Medal of Liberty by the American Civil Liberties Union and named by the *National Law Journal* as one of the most influential lawyers in the country.

Source: Swift, 2007; Shukovsky, 2006.

PARADIGMS OF LAW

The law serves as a written embodiment of society's ethics and morals. It is said to be declarative as well as active; it declares correct behavior and serves as a tool for enforcement. Law is both a prohibition and a promise. It cautions against certain types of behavior and warns of the consequences for ignoring the warning. **Natural law** refers to the belief that some law is inherent in the natural world and can be discovered by reason. A corollary of this thought is that some behavior is intrinsically wrong (*mala in se*). In contrast, **positive law** refers to those laws written and enforced by society. This type of law is of human construction and, therefore, fallible (Mackie, 1977: 232).

We can trace the history of law back to very early codes, such as the Code of Hammurabi (ca. 2000 B.C.E.), which mixed secular and religious proscriptions of behavior. These codes also standardized punishments and atonements for wrongdoing. Early codes of law did not differentiate between what we might call public wrongs and private wrongs. As mentioned, two different areas of law can be distinguished today: criminal law, which is punitive; and, civil law, which is reparative (or restitutive). The first punishes, whereas the second seeks to redress wrong or loss. Of the two, criminal law is more closely associated with enforcing the moral standards of society, yet it is by no means comprehensive in its coverage of behavior. Our understanding of the law's function in society is informed by more fundamental views of the world around us.

Basic paradigms aid our understanding of the function of law in society. According to Rich (1978: 1), a **paradigm** is a "fundamental image of the subject matter within a science.... It subsumes, defines, and interrelates the exemplars, theories, and methods/tools that exist within it." Essentially, a paradigm helps us organize the vast array of knowledge that we absorb every day. We see the world and interpret facts in a way that is influenced by our paradigms; e.g., if we have a paradigm that government is corrupt, everything we read and hear will be scanned for facts that fit our paradigm, and inconsistent or contrary facts will be ignored and/or forgotten.

Paradigms aren't bad or good; they are simply a function of how the human mind works. Our paradigms can shift, of course, when we are confronted with overwhelming facts that come from trusted sources or personal experiences that are contrary to our paradigm. Below are three paradigms that view law very differently.

1. The **consensus paradigm** views society as a community consisting of likeminded individuals who agree on goals that are important for ultimate survival. This view is functionalist because it sees law as an aid to the growth and/or survival of society.
2. The **conflict paradigm** views society as being made up of competing and conflicting interests. According to this view, governance is based on power; if some win, others lose, and those who hold power in society promote self-interest, not a "greater good."
3. The **pluralist paradigm** shares the perception that society is made up of competing interests; however, pluralism describes more than two basic interest groups and also recognizes that the power balance may shift when interest groups form or coalitions emerge. These power shifts occur as part of the dynamics of societal change.

THE CONSENSUS PARADIGM

According to the consensus paradigm, law serves as a tool of unification. Emile Durkheim (1858–1917) wrote that there are two types of law: the *repressive*, criminal law, which enforces universal norms, and the *restitutive*, civil law, which developed because of the division of labor in society and resulting social interests. In Durkheim's view, criminal law exists as a manifestation of consensual norms: "We must not say that an action shocks the common conscience because it is criminal, but rather that it is criminal because it shocks the common conscience" (Durkheim, 1969: 21). What this statement means is that we define an action as criminal because the majority of the populace holds the opinion that it is wrong. This "common" or "collective" conscience is referred to as **mechanical solidarity**. Each individual's moral beliefs are indistinguishable from the whole. The function of **repressive law** is the maintenance of social cohesion. Law contributes to the collective conscience by providing an example of deviance.

Although Durkheim recognized individual differences, he believed that these differences, resulting from the division of labor in society, only made the individual more dependent on society as a part of a whole. His concept of **organic solidarity** draws the analogy of individuals in society as parts of an organism—all doing different things, but as parts of a whole. Individuals exist, but they are tied inextricably to society and its common conscience. **Restitutive law** is said to mediate those differences that may come about because of the division of labor. Even here the law serves an integrative function.

The consensus view would point to evidence that people agree on, for the most part, what behaviors are wrong and the relative seriousness of different types of wrongful behavior. In criminology, the consensus view is represented by classical thinkers such as Jeremy Bentham and Cesare Beccaria, who relied on the accepted definitions of crime in their day without questioning the validity of these definitions, only their implementation. While the positivist school of criminology, which looked for the cause of crime in the individual, virtually ignored societal definitions of crime, Raffaele Garofalo (1852–1932), a legal anthropologist, believed in natural law. As defined earlier, natural law holds that certain behaviors are so inherently heinous that they go against nature; therefore, there are natural proscriptions against such behavior that transcend individual societies or time periods (Kramer, 1982: 36).

We have evidence that there is at least some consensus in people's definitions of what constitutes criminal behavior. Studies have shown that not only do individuals in Western culture tend to agree on the relative seriousness of different kinds of crime but there is substantial agreement cross-culturally as well (Nettler, 1978: 215). In the consensus paradigm:

1. *Law is representative.* It is a compilation of the do's and don'ts that we all agree on.
2. *Law reinforces social cohesion.* It emphasizes our "we-ness" by illustrating deviance.
3. *Law is value-neutral.* It resolves conflicts in an objective and neutral manner.

THE CONFLICT PARADIGM

A second paradigm of law and society is the conflict paradigm. Rather than perceiving law as representative, this perspective sees law as a tool of power holders that they use for their own purposes—to maintain and control the status quo. In the conflict paradigm, law is perceived as restrictive or repressive, rather than representative, and as an instrument of special interests.

Basically, the conflict paradigm has three parts (Sheley, 1985: 1):

1. Criminal definitions are relative.
2. Those who control major social institutions determine how crime is defined.
3. The definition of crime is fundamentally a tool of power.

Quinney (1974: 15–16) outlined the following points as making up the conflict paradigm:

1. American society is based on an advanced capitalistic society.
2. The state is organized to serve the interests of the dominant economic class.
3. Criminal law is an instrument of the state and ruling class to maintain and perpetuate the existing social and economic order.

4.   Crime control in a capitalist society is accomplished through a variety of institutions and agencies established and administered by a governmental elite.
5.   The contradictions of advanced capitalism require that the subordinate classes remain oppressed by whatever means necessary.
6.   Only with the collapse of capitalist society and the creation of a new society will there be a solution to the crime problem.

Advocates of the conflict paradigm would point to laws against only certain types of gambling or against the use of only certain types of drugs as evidence that the ruling class punishes the activities of other classes more severely than their own activities. In other words, cultural differences in behavior exist, but only the activities of certain groups (the powerless) are labeled deviant. For instance, numbers running is always illegal, yet some states have legalized horseracing, dog racing, and/or casinos. Heroin and cocaine are illegal; Valium and alcohol are not.

The federal sentencing guideline system is an example of how law treats different groups in a disparate manner. For example, more severe sanctions have existed for crack cocaine than for powder cocaine. Originating in the height of the drug war in the 1980s, the guidelines for crack and powder cocaine specify a 1:100 difference in punishments (5 grams of crack earned the same amount of prison time as 500 grams of powder cocaine). Many believe that it was not merely a coincidence that crack cocaine is more likely to be the drug of choice for minorities (crack is cheaper), whereas powder cocaine is associated with Caucasians and social elites.

Interestingly, the Supreme Court ruled in a sequence of cases that the Sentencing Commission guidelines could only be advisory for federal judges, not mandatory, because the evidence used to determine the sentence was not duly admitted at trial under rules of evidence. Then the Court upheld the right of federal judges to sentence offenders to less than the sentencing guidelines dictated without being ruled "unreasonable" even if no extraordinary circumstances existed. These cases will be discussed in Chapter 11. In November of 2007, the Sentencing Commission passed an amendment to the guidelines that reduced the disparity, and then in December of 2007 made it retroactive so that upwards of 19,500 sentenced drug offenders may have their sentences reduced by federal courts if there is a determination that they pose no risk to the public (Faherty, 2008).

Recall Jeffrey Reiman's description, presented in Chapter 1, of the difference between reporting a mining accident and a multiple murder. Despite the same result (dead victims), the mining company would probably not be prosecuted, or it would receive a minor punishment for its role in the death of the miners. For the conflict theorist this is an example of how law has been written differentially to serve the interests of the power holders.

The definition of what is criminal often excludes corporate behavior, such as price fixing, toxic waste dumping, and monopolistic trade practices, because these behaviors, although just as harmful to the public good as street crime, are engaged in by those who have the power to define criminality. The *regulation* of business, instead of the *criminalization* of harmful business practices, is seen as arising from the ability of those in powerful positions to redefine their activities to their own advantage.

The Occupational Safety Board, the Food and Drug Administration, the Federal Aeronautics Administration, and other similar governmental agencies are charged with the task of enforcing regulations governing business activities in their respective areas; however, regulatory sanctions are not as stigmatizing or painful as criminal convictions. Critics also argue that the relationships between the watchdog agencies and those they watch are frequently incestuous: Heads of business are often named to watchdog agencies, and employees of these agencies may move to the business sector they previously regulated.

In criminology, the conflict view was represented by early theorists such as Willem Bonger (1876–1940), a Marxist sociologist who explained that crime was caused by the economic power differential and that power holders labeled only others' behavior as criminal. During the 1970s a small number of criminologists attempted to redefine criminals as political prisoners, based on their views that the state used criminal definitions to control minority groups (Reasons, 1973). Labeling theorists also questioned the criminal justice system's definitions by pointing out that only some offenders are formally labeled and treated as deviant.

Conflict theory is represented by theorists such as Anthony Platt, Julia and Herman Schwendinger, Barry Krisberg, Richard Quinney, Ian Taylor, Paul Walton, Jock Young, and Walter Chambliss (Kramer, 1982: 41). The conflict theorists explain that the myth of justice and equality under the law serves to protect the interests of the ruling class, because as long as there is a perception of fairness, fundamental questions about the distribution of goods will not be raised (Krisberg, 1975). Law functions to depoliticize even the most obviously political actions of the oppressed by defining these actions as crime, but its greatest power is to hide the basic injustice of society itself. Reiman (2005/2007) presents the conflict theorist's view that the definitions of law, as well as its enforcement, are fundamentally affected by power.

It is important to understand that our paradigms of law shape our interpretation of current events. The Los Angeles riots of 1992 were sparked by the acquittal of four police officers who were videotaped beating Rodney King, a motorist who had outstanding arrest warrants for traffic violations. The riots were described by some as political action. According to this view, minorities who were frustrated by economic hopelessness and angered by the criminal justice system's oppressive and brutal treatment retaliated in like form. In this view, the riots were political statements against oppression. Alternatively, others described the same actions as blatant and simple criminality. In this perspective, violent individuals merely took advantage of the incident to exhibit their individual deviance. Conflict theorists would support the first definition, and consensus theorists would support the second.

In the aftermath of the New Orleans flooding, there was looting and general lawlessness. On the one hand, conflict theorists would see the looting and crimes of those left behind through the prism of economic hopelessness and desperation. Conflict theorists argue that the poor and African American citizens were left behind while those who had the means to do so escaped the flooding; and government bodies did not make any effort to evacuate the poor even after a general evacuation order was administered. Further, they would point to other forms of lawlessness, such as price gouging, and no-bid contracts with large profits for the contractor, as just as heinous as looting and assault.

Consensus theorists, on the other hand, would see the crimes as examples of individual deviance and point out that most people who were trapped in the city did not resort to violence. Further, some later evidence emerged that deaths did not occur disproportionately among minorities and the poor, as some had claimed (Simerman, Ott, and Mellnik, 2005).

Generally, in the conflict paradigm:

1. *Law is repressive.* It oppresses the poor and powerless by differential definitions and/or enforcement.
2. *Law is a tool of the powerful.* Those who write the laws do so in a way to promote their economic and political interests.
3. *Law is* not *value-neutral.* It is biased and bent toward the interests of the powerful.

THE PLURALIST PARADIGM

Distinct from the conflict paradigm is the *pluralist paradigm.* In this view, law is seen as arising from interest groups, but power is more complicated than the bifurcated system described by the Marxist tradition. Roscoe Pound (as cited in Quinney, 1974) defined the following as interests protected by power holders:

1. security against actions that threaten the social group
2. security of social institutions
3. security of morals
4. conservation of national resources
5. general progress
6. individual life

Power is exercised in the political order, the economic order, the religious order, the kinship order, the educational order, and the public order. Law and social control constitute the public order, and powerful interests affect the law by influencing the writing of laws and the enforcement of written laws (Quinney, 1974).

Pluralism views law as influenced by interest groups that are in flux. Some interests may be at odds with other interests, or certainly the interpretation of them may be. For instance, conservation of natural resources is a basic interest necessary to the survival of society, but it may be interpreted by lumber companies as allowing them to harvest trees in national forests as long as they replant trees or, alternatively, interpreted by conservation groups as mandating more wilderness areas. According to the pluralist paradigm, laws are written by the group whose voice is more powerful at any particular time.

Interest groups hold power, but their power may shrink or grow depending on various factors. Coalitions and shared interests may shift the balance of power. The definition of crime may change, depending on which interest groups have the power to define criminal behavior and what is currently perceived to be in the best interests of the most powerful groups. In the example of the crack versus cocaine sentencing controversy described above, conflict theory cannot explain why the 1:100 ratio has been addressed with efforts to reduce the disparity, and ongoing efforts in Congress to eliminate it entirely. A pluralist paradigm would point to the growing public sentiment that the sentencing guidelines were unfair. Diverse groups such as the National Organization of Mayors, Families Against Mandatory

POLICY BOX | ARE YOU A CITIZEN?

There is controversy across the nation regarding the proper role of local law enforcement in enforcing immigration law. Some police departments argue that it is not their role to enforce federal immigration law, and they do not ask witnesses, victims, or even suspects what their immigration status is. Other departments follow a policy that their role is to enforce the law—federal as well as state and local. Critics argue that if police officers become enforcers for Immigration and Customs Enforcement (ICE), witnesses to crimes will not come forward, victims will not receive help, and illegal immigrants will become easy prey for predators.

Law: Federal, not state or local, laws relate to immigration; therefore, local police may hold suspected offenders for federal officers to arrive. ICE is training local law enforcement on federal laws and how to investigate illegal immigration status.

Policy: Policy considerations of local law enforcement agencies are very different, with some cities declaring openly that they will not be agents for ICE, and federal officials threatening to cut off federal funds for law enforcement. A compromise policy used by some agencies is to check the immigration status of those who are arrested but not those with whom they come into contact as witnesses or victims.

Individual ethics: While immigration laws are clear, and city and local law enforcement policies may be put in place after due consideration, the individual officer is still left with the decision to ask the person who reports a crime, or the victim who was just beat up: "Are you a citizen?"

Minimums, and the American Bar Association, as well as individual federal justices and prosecutors, have all criticized the disparate sentences. In a pluralistic shifting political power struggle, the number of people who oppose the 1:100 ratio seem to be turning the tide of public opinion, and the law follows. The Policy Box addresses the role of law enforcement in immigration law, an area of law that also seems to shift in accordance with changes in public opinion and the power of interest groups.

JUSTIFICATIONS FOR LAW

The major justification for corrective (criminal) law is prevention of harm. Under the **social contract theory**, law is a contract; each individual gives up some liberties and, in return, is protected from others who have their liberties restricted as well. Thomas Hobbes's (1588–1679) claim that self-preservation (the law of the jungle) is paramount, and John Locke's (1632–1704) view that property is a natural right created the foundation for the social contract theory. According to this theory, members of society were originally engaged in a "war of all against all" where

> ...every man is an enemy to every man ... [there is] continual fear and danger of violent death; and the life of man, solitary, poor, nasty, brutish, and short. (Hobbes, 1651/1982)

BOX 5.1 | JUSTIFICATIONS FOR LAW

1. *The harm principle*: To prevent harm to persons other than the actor (laws against assault, robbery, arson and such crimes prohibit and punish harming others)
2. *The offense principle*: To prevent serious offense to persons other than the actor (for instance, public indecency or lewdness to prohibit behaviors that shock, disgust, or offend reasonable people)
3. *Legal paternalism*: To prevent harm—physical, psychological, or economic—to the actor (laws that protect the individual, such as requiring drivers to wear seat belts)

4. *Legal moralism*: To prohibit conduct that is inherently immoral (laws prohibiting gambling and other private so-called victimless crimes to protect the morals of the community)
5. *Benefit to others*: To provide, through prohibition of an action, some benefit to persons other than the actor (for instance, prohibiting toxic waste dumping that benefit the rest of us, not necessarily the offender)

Source: Feinberg, cited in Feibleman, 1985: xiii.

In this "contract" individuals give up the freedom to aggress against others in return for their own safety. According to Hobbes, each individual has chosen to "lay down this right to all things; and be contented with so much liberty against other men, as he would allow other men against himself" (from Hobbes, 1651/1982). Hobbes said that in order to avoid this war of all against all, people needed to be assured that people will not harm one another and that they will keep their agreements. This sounds like enlightened egoism, where we do things for our long-term, rather than short-term, interests.

But how much liberty should be restricted, and what behaviors should be prohibited? Rough formulas or guidelines indicate that the law should interfere as little as possible in natural liberties and should step in only when the liberty in question injures or impinges on the interests of another. There is an obvious need for law in circumstances where one individual harms another (such as murder, rape, robbery, arson, and so on); however, we next discuss in more detail two rationales for laws that do not necessarily involve direct harm to another—*legal paternalism* and *legal moralism*. Box 5.1 presents the major justifications for laws.

LEGAL PATERNALISM

Many laws can be described as examples of **legal paternalism**—laws in which the state tries to protect people from their own behavior. Examples include seat belt laws, motorcycle helmet laws, speed limits, drug laws, licensing laws, alcohol consumption and sale laws, smoking prohibitions, and laws limiting certain types of sexual behavior. The strict libertarian view would hold that the government has no business interfering in a person's decisions about these behaviors as long as they don't negatively affect others. The opposing view is that as long as a person is a member of society (and everyone is), he or she has a value to that society, and society is therefore compelled to protect the person with or without his or her cooperation.

It may also be true that there are no harmful or potentially harmful behaviors to oneself that do not also hurt others, however indirectly, so society is protecting others when it controls each individual. Speeding drivers may crash into someone else; drug addicts may commit crimes to support their habit; gamblers may neglect their families and cause expense to the state; and so on. You may remember that in Chapter 1 we limited moral judgments to behavior that influences another. The justification for paternalistic laws depends on the view that almost everything we do affects others, however indirectly.

Some believe that government can justify paternalism only with certain restrictions. These rules try to create a balance between an individual's liberty and government control (Thompson, 1980):

1. The decision-making ability of the person may be somehow impaired, by lack of knowledge or competency. Examples are child labor laws and laws that restrict the sale to and consumption of alcohol by children. In both cases there is a presumption that children do not understand the dangers of such behavior and, therefore, need protection.
2. The restriction should be as limited as possible. For example, driving-under-the-influence (DUI) laws define the point of legal intoxication as when one's ability to drive safely is impaired, not simply after any alcohol consumption at all. When mountain passes are closed, they are reopened as soon as it is relatively safe to cross them. Laws exist that ban the sale of cigarettes to minors, but cigarettes are still available to adults—who supposedly have reached a level of maturity to understand the dangers associated with smoking.
3. The laws should seek only to prevent a serious and irreversible error—a death from DUI, an accident on an icy road, and so on.

Paternalistic laws can be supported by an ethics of care. Remember that in this framework, morality is viewed as integral to a system of relationships. The individual is seen as having ties to society and to every other member of society. Relationships involve responsibilities as well as rights. We can expect the minimum level of care necessary for survival from society under the ethics of care. However, the corollary is that society can also care for us by restricting harmful behaviors. Rights are less important in this framework; therefore, to ask whether society has a right to intervene or an individual has a right to a liberty is not relevant to the discussion. Utilitarianism would also support paternalistic laws because of the net utility to society that results from protecting each of its members.

Other ethical systems may not so clearly support paternalistic laws. Individual rights are perhaps more important under ethical formalism than the other ethical systems; individuals must be treated with respect and as ends in themselves. This view results in recognizing the rights of individuals to engage in careless or even harmful behavior as long as it is consistent with the universalism principle of the categorical imperative. In other words, people may have the moral right to engage in self-destructive or careless behavior as long as they do not hurt others. Of course, the opposing argument would be that all behaviors prohibited by paternalistic laws have the potential to affect others indirectly.

LEGAL MORALISM

The law also acts as the moral agent of society, some say in areas where there is no moral agreement. This rationale is called **legal moralism**. Some sexual behaviors, gambling, drug use, pornography, and even suicide and euthanasia are defined as wrong and are prohibited. The laws against these behaviors may be based on principles of harm or paternalism, but they also exist to reinforce society's definitions of moral behavior. For example, consensual sexual behavior between adults arguably harms no one, yet the Georgia state law prohibiting sodomy was upheld by the U.S. Supreme Court in *Bowers v. Hardwick*, 106 S.Ct. 2841 (1986).

What harm was the state preventing by prohibiting this consensual behavior? The answer may be in the harm to community standards of morality. However, in *Lawrence v. Texas*, 539 U.S. 558 (2003), the Supreme Court held that Texas's law criminalizing same-sex sodomy was unconstitutional, effectively overturning Bowers. More recently, there has been a great debate over whether the law ought to recognize and legitimize same-sex marriages. The underlying justification that both sides employ is legal moralism.

Pornography (at least that involving consenting adults) that is defined as obscene is prohibited arguably because of moral standards, not harmful effect. One governmental commission concluded that pornography contributes to sex crimes (Attorney General's Commission on Pornography, 1986). There is a factual issue as to whether pornography is harmful. Yet, even if pornography does not prove to be harmful to others, legal moralism endorses the government's right to prohibit the sale and purchase of pornographic materials. Under the legal moralism rationale, pornography is prohibited simply because it is wrong. The issue has become even more complicated with the increasing use of the Internet and the ease with which individuals may obtain pornographic materials from anywhere in the world. Privacy rights conflict with the government's right to enforce morality.

One's opinion regarding the rights of individuals versus the government is greatly influenced by whether one is inclined more to the consensus view or the conflict view. If we operate under the consensus view that laws represent the majority, then legal moralism as a justification for laws would be less controversial. In our society, though, there is by no means agreement among all citizens that the government represents the people's view. Conflict theorists argue that the government has no moral authority because it does not represent the views of everyone.

It should also be noted that whether an action is moral or immoral is a different question than whether there should be laws and governmental sanctions regarding the behavior. In some cases, individuals may agree that a particular action is immoral but at the same time may not believe that the government should have any power to restrict an individual's choice. Some proponents of choice regarding abortion take great care to distinguish between pro-choice and pro-abortion. To them, one does not have to approve of abortion to believe that it is wrong for government to interfere in the private decision of the individual to use the procedure. Similarly, some who advocate decriminalization of drugs do so because of cost-effectiveness or libertarian reasons, not because they approve of drug use. As mentioned in Chapter 4, we do not have a legal system that completely overlaps our moral code, and some would argue that it would be impossible in a society as heterogeneous as ours for this to occur.

Hate-crime legislation gives us another example of a law that might be rationalized under legal moralism, although it could also be supported by a harm principle. In challenges to hate-crime legislation, appellate courts have typically drawn a line between action and speech. That is, if a person commits an act that is already a crime, such as vandalism, assault, stalking, or harassment, and does so because of an expressed hatred for the victim's membership in a protected class, then the act can be punished as a "hate crime." However, if the only act prohibited by the hate-crime legislation is speech, then the law violates the First Amendment's protection of free speech. Even though we abhor the message, we must protect the right of the person to express it, unless he or she also engages in a "legal harm." The interesting question is why we think it necessary to create a new law instead of using the existing act-based law (such as vandalism). The reason might be that the true rationale for hate crime is legal moralism: We believe it is important to enforce our moral code that hating others because of their race or sexual orientation is wrong.

Evidence indicates that hate crimes are predominantly less serious instances of harassment or vandalism but that they are not rare (Wilson and Ruback, 2003). Even the federal statistics, which probably seriously under-report such crimes, indicate that the numbers are not inconsequential. Does this show that laws are not effective in changing behavior, or does it support the need for such laws?

Some propose that only those actions that violate some universal standard of morality, as opposed to merely a conventional standard, should be criminalized. This *limited legal moralism* would prevent the situation of some groups forcing their moral code on others. Of course, this begs the question of what behaviors would meet this universal standard. Even child pornographers argue that their behavior is unfairly condemned by a conventional, rather than a universal, morality. The vast profits that are made by producing and distributing child pornography indicate that many people buy such products. Does this mean that it is simply a matter of choice and not some universal moral sense that should influence whether children should be seen as objects of sexual gratification? What would Immanuel Kant say about child pornography? What would Jeremy Bentham say about it?

In conclusion, we must allow for the possibility that some laws that are justified under legal moralism may not necessarily conform to our personal views of good and bad. Many criminal justice professionals also believe that some of the so-called gray areas of crime are not very serious, so it is not surprising that law enforcement professionals employ their discretion in enforcement. Police will ignore prostitution, for instance, until the public complains; police may routinely let petty drug offenders go rather than take the trouble to arrest; and police may let gamblers go with a warning if no publicity is attached to the arrest. Police use discretion in this way partly because these behaviors are not universally condemned. One can see, for instance, that the state loses its moral authority to condemn gambling when there is a state lottery.

CRIMINAL AND MORAL CULPABILITY

In Chapter 4 we discussed some culpability issues concerning corrective (retributive) justice. **Culpability** can be defined, for our purposes, as legal responsibility. Both terms have been analyzed in great detail in studies of law and morality. Cane (2002) takes great care, for instance, to distinguish between responsibility and liability. One might be responsible (causally) for a result but not be liable for it (under the law). Legal liability relates to the formal rules and decisions that have defined the limits of what a person will be held legally responsible for, whereas moral responsibility is a concept that derives from ethical analysis.

Positive law (human-made law) defines legal liability (or culpability), but many legal theorists subscribe to the concepts of natural law. For instance, Hart (1961: 176) argued that morality is something "to be recognized," not made by "deliberate human choice." Human-made law derives from moral truths. Thus, according to this viewpoint, legal rules stem from natural law. One moral and legal truth is that we recognize different levels of mental blameworthiness in the concept of *mens rea*. Someone who intentionally or knowingly commits an act is more blameworthy than someone who recklessly or negligently commits an act. In the latter case the individual is still responsible, but his or her culpability is moderated by a lack of intent.

In Chapter 1 we also discussed how moral culpability depends on rationality. One cannot be held accountable for one's actions morally if one is not rational, and the two groups that have historically been seen as irrational are the mentally ill and the young. We uphold this distinction in our legal system as well, but there are indications that the historical and traditional exceptions for these two groups are eroding. In addition to discussing the culpability of these groups, we look at the culpability of those who commit white collar crimes, and those who commit a crime where there is victim precipitation.

PUNISHING THE MENTALLY CHALLENGED

Miller and Radelet (1993: 2–4) discuss the long history of excusing the mentally ill, a practice that dates back to medieval times. The supporting rationales for not punishing those judged as insane are as follows:

1. Humanitarian reasons require mercy.
2. The mentally ill can't help themselves.
3. Retributive goals are not met because the mentally ill don't appreciate their suffering.
4. The mentally ill can't spiritually prepare for death, so it is cruel to execute them.
5. Deterrence is not served because others identify only with premeditated acts, not those borne of insanity.
6. They can't help in their own defense, calling into question the accuracy of guilt.

What would cause someone to kidnap an innocent woman, rape her, kill her, and mutilate her body by cutting out her vagina and eating it? For Arthur Shawcross, condemned to 250 years in prison in Rochester, New York, it may have been the sexual abuse by his mother that he endured as a child, or it may have been a cyst and scarring in the frontal lobes of his brain that was revealed in an MRI but not shared with the jury during his trial. He killed two children and served fifteen years for that crime; then, after his release, he committed gruesome rapes and killings while serving in Vietnam. After he returned home, he confessed to the grisly mutilation and murders of eleven women in Rochester, New York, but the jury found him sane (Lewis, 1998). How is this possible? It seems that the murderers who commit the most bizarre acts are those whom we are most likely to label as sane.

Probably the reason is that many believe such people must be punished for their crimes, and only by finding them sane will they be sure to be executed or serve life without parole. Or perhaps there is such revulsion and fear about their acts that we have a primitive urge to kill them. There are many examples of individuals who were not only prosecuted but were convicted and executed, arguably because of the extreme nature of their crimes rather than a sincere belief that their actions stemmed from rational thought. Several states have passed laws that create a "guilty but insane" conviction rather than the previous acquittal "by reason of insanity." Thus, these states need no legal fiction of "sanity" in order to punish. Individuals are housed in forensic facilities until (or unless) they are "cured," at which time they are transferred to penal facilities for punishment.

Dorothy Lewis (1998), a psychiatrist, examined dozens of murderers on Death Rows across the country, including Arthur Shawcross, Ted Bundy, and Mark Chapman. She described how the violent killers she has diagnosed were physically abused, deprived, and sexually brutalized as children; many had suffered severe head trauma and, in all likelihood, were brain-injured. The neurological injuries and psychiatric illnesses of these killers are evidence that they were not in control, or in some cases not even aware of their own actions at the time they committed their crimes. Yet, time after time, despite expert testimony to the contrary, juries found them sane.

Holding the mentally ill responsible for their behavior runs contrary to our conception of rational culpability. In most states, in order to find a defendant insane, the jury must find that the person did not know what he or she was doing, or did not know that it was wrong. This test, known as the **McNaughten rule**, was developed in the mid-nineteenth century. It forces psychiatrists to explain the defendant's behavior to the jury solely on the question of whether he or she knew right from wrong. Compulsion, or diminished capacity, is not recognized in this definition.

Andrea Yates was convicted in Houston, Texas, in 2002 and sentenced to forty years in prison. She was a thirty-six-year-old mother of five children, ranging in age from six months to seven years. One day when her husband was at work, she systematically took each child into the bathroom and drowned them all. Her lawyers presented evidence that she was under psychiatric care for postpartum depression, that she probably suffered from postpartum psychosis, that she had been institutionalized because of depression and suicide ideation, and that an earlier diagnosis by a doctor indicated that she should not have any more children because her syndrome seemed to be worsening with each pregnancy.

In a deep depression after the birth of her last child, she came to believe that she was a terrible mother and that some great harm would befall the children if she did not commit them to God's care. After she killed them, she called the police. Many people argue that the death penalty surely must be for someone like Andrea Yates, who killed five helpless children. Yet, is it possible to imagine that a mother who, by all accounts, was a loving mother when she wasn't suffering from depression or psychosis, could commit such a horrible act rationally?

Does one rationally kill one's children and then call the police? A small number of people proposed the ridiculous argument that she was "tired of being a mother" and killed them because she was sure she would be acquitted; however, most people struggled to resolve concepts of culpability and justice in this case. The jury members hedged their bets. They did not acquit her by reason of insanity. Therefore, they declared her sane, but they sentenced her to forty years instead of the death penalty. If she rationally and sanely killed her five children, why was she not executed? If she was not rational and insane, why did the jury not acquit her?

Upon appeal, a Texas appellate court overturned Yates's conviction because of the admission of erroneous testimony by a prosecution witness who told the jury that she had seen a *Law and Order* television episode where a woman killed her children and was acquitted. That episode did not exist at the time Yates killed her children. In 2006, in a new trial, the jury found Yates not guilty by reason of insanity and she was committed to a mental facility. She is still there (Associated Press, 2008a).

Other cases pose difficult questions concerning what we should do when individuals commit violent acts. We are only beginning to understand how brain functioning and life experiences are dynamically related to each other and how they influence behavior. Children who grow up in abusive homes and endure constant stress have reduced levels of serotonin, a brain chemical that tends to inhibit aggressive impulses. Over time, chronic stress can literally change the brain; thus, it should come as no surprise when we discover that those on Death Row have almost always endured severe abuse as children. Ironically, the law does allow some reduction of culpability under a diminished-capacity argument for "passion" crimes (e.g., killing an unfaithful spouse), arguably because the "reasonable" person might also be tempted to commit the violent act. However, most of us are clearly unable to empathize with those who do the most horrific, "unreasonable" crimes. Thus, they are often found to be "sane" and receive our most severe punishments.

Related to the issue of punishing the mentally ill is the issue of punishing the mentally handicapped. The issues of competence and culpability are the same as with the mentally ill, or a closer parallel is how the law views children. At a certain level of immaturity, one is not responsible for one's actions, and the mentally handicapped are said to have the mental capabilities of children, not adults. In *Atkins v. Virginia*, 536 U.S. 304 (2002), the Supreme Court determined that it is unconstitutional to execute the mentally handicapped. However, if juries ignore the evidence of mental retardation, they could sentence individuals to death who might not understand how they got there or perhaps even what is happening to them. Lewis (1998) related a case of a Death Row inmate whose mental impairment was so severe that it was unlikely he could have been capable of assisting in his own defense; he didn't really even know what was about to happen to him at his execution because he asked to save the piece of pecan pie from his last meal so he could have a midnight snack, evidently not understanding that after midnight he wouldn't be around to enjoy it.

The issue of intelligence, in general, has been used to explain why people commit crimes, and there is some evidence to indicate a correlation between intelligence and criminality. But cognitive psychology is extremely complicated. Many argue that our current methods of measuring intelligence are rife with problems, and we don't really even share a common understanding of what intelligence is.

Gardner (2006) is widely cited for his proposal that there are multiple centers of intelligence and that we have "multiple" intelligences, not just one. These include musical intelligence, bodily-kinesthetic intelligence (sports), logical-mathematical intelligence, linguistic intelligence, spatial intelligence, interpersonal intelligence, (ability to recognize emotions), naturalist intelligence (Darwinist), and even existential intelligence (philosophical).

The theory is supported by the fact that damage to the brain will result in decay in the skill set of these different domains. He points to how with idiot savants and those who suffer from autism, skill level can be particularized even with profound weaknesses in other areas. He also argues that intelligence is not perfectly symmetrical with performance and that performance may be influenced by values, culture, personality characteristics and family, which put different emphases on different intelligences/domains. Gardner (2006: 28) also speaks to the idea of morality as being a product of intellectual reasoning and argues that this type of performance is culture-dependent, not a basic intellectual faculty.

PUNISHING JUVENILES

Nathaniel Brazill brought a gun to school and shot a well-liked teacher in the face, killing him. Brazill was thirteen. The jury was asked to decide if he committed premeditated murder. Is a thirteen-year-old capable of "cold-blooded murder?" Throughout most of this country's history, we have excused juveniles from their crimes because of a belief that their immaturity prevented them from engaging in the calm, rational deliberation that is required for criminal (and moral) culpability. This is the same reasoning that supports laws preventing juveniles from drinking alcohol or buying cigarettes, voting, or serving in the military. Others argue that thirteen-year-olds know right from wrong and should be held accountable for their actions.

If you think that a thirteen-year-old murderer is responsible enough for his or her own behavior to serve a life sentence or even be executed, would you also agree that a thirteen-year-old is mature enough to know whether to smoke or drink? Quit school if he feels like it? Serve in the military? If you answered yes to the life sentence but no to the smoking or military question, how do you explain the contradiction? Brazill's jury found him guilty of second-degree murder, and he was sentenced to serve twenty-eight years in prison. His earliest release date will be when he is forty-one (Associated Press, 2004).

Lionel Tate was twelve years old when he killed a six-year-old by breaking her neck, imitating what he saw while watching pro wrestlers. His attorneys argued that he had not meant to hurt her and was just playing. It seems possible that he did not mean to hurt the girl, and prosecutors must have thought so, too, because they offered him a sentence of three years in a juvenile facility, one year of house arrest, and ten years of probation. However, because he was a juvenile, his mother had the power to make the decision for him and she refused the plea bargain and insisted upon going to trial. The jury found him guilty of first-degree murder, and he was sentenced to a mandatory term of life without parole (CNN.com, 2001).

Tate has become the poster child for a reexamination of how we treat juvenile offenders. Even the prosecutor in that case advocated a less harsh sentence for juveniles convicted of murder (Riddle, 2001). On January 29, 2004, after an appeal seeking a retrial, the prosecutor and defense reached a plea agreement whereby Tate pleaded guilty to second-degree murder with a sentence of three years in juvenile custody and one year of house arrest. Because he had already served that amount of time, he was released. Since then, sadly, he has been arrested for new crimes. Those who are in favor of harsher sentences for juveniles point to his new crimes as evidence that he was criminally sophisticated in the first crime; those who advocate for treating juveniles differently believe that his new arrests are evidence that if you put a 12-year-old with criminals, he will turn out to be a criminal.

In the 1990s, many states enacted new laws or changed existing laws to increase the controls and sanctions over juveniles. Some of these laws included curfew laws, parental responsibility laws, anti-gang laws, juvenile boot camps, gun laws, removing laws that seal juvenile records, and laws that allow the transfer of juveniles to adult court (Bartollas and Miller, 2001: 7). The move to treat juvenile criminals more harshly has been fueled by the Columbine and other school shootings, by the serious crimes committed by gang members, and by the pervasive view that juvenile crime is growing and that the juvenile justice system is too lenient. Juvenile offenders are increasingly being waived to and prosecuted in the adult court system, and sent to adult prisons. In 2006, Florida had 221 juveniles in adult prisons, Connecticut had 425, New York had 219, North Carolina had 188, and Texas had 162 (Sabol, Minton, and Harrison, 2008).

Part of the impetus for this harsher treatment of juveniles has been a public perception that juvenile crime is increasing and is becoming more violent. Because lawmakers respond to public pressure, public perceptions affect laws. For instance, the public perceives there is a growing risk of violence in schools; therefore, we have seen an incredible escalation of security procedures and zero-tolerance treatment of juveniles who express hostile feelings.

In some cases the zero-tolerance approach toward expressions of violence has reached extreme levels that many believe are counterproductive. A ten-year-old girl who whispered "I could kill her" after she wet her pants because her teacher refused to let her go to the bathroom was suspended; a ten-year-old who said "I oughtta murder his face" when a classmate messed up his desk was suspended; a classmate who uttered a threat after he was pushed was suspended. A nine-year-old boy who shot a wad of toilet paper and a youth in the school cafeteria line who warned his classmates that if they ate all the potatoes he would "get them" were also suspended. Many of these children now have juvenile records for such acts. In all, fifty suspensions in six weeks occurred in one school district after the county prosecutor met with school officials and told them that they had no discretion in reporting threats to authorities (Zernike, 2001).

Some parents and other observers believe that the "cure" is worse than the problem if schools are attempting to prevent violence by such draconian policies. The American Bar Association has passed a resolution condemning zero-tolerance policies that allow no discretion in defining children's acts as criminal (Zernike, 2001). Some states have been contemplating bills that would require schools to employ discretion in punishment decisions rather than continue to enforce zero-tolerance policies; however, as one legislator said, "you can't legislate common sense." (Associated Press, 2007c).

Observers note that there have been cyclical periods of repressive and treatment-oriented movements for juveniles from the beginning of our nation's court systems. What distinguishes the juvenile system from the adult legal system is that it supposedly addresses the needs of those who are abused or neglected, as well as those who have committed acts that would be crimes if committed by adults. Many juveniles, of course, fit into both groups. Until the 1970s, children who were taken into care for "their own good" were sometimes housed with adjudicated offenders. In the 1970s, this practice was ruled unconstitutional, and some due-process rights of juveniles were recognized in a series of court cases that forced the system to behave, in some ways, more like the adult system (Bartollas and Miller, 2001). However, differences were still recognized. Juveniles do not need all of the protections afforded adult criminals, supposedly, because the system's mission is to do what is best for them.

Before waiver to adult court, juveniles must be determined to be **competent**. This legal concept means that juveniles are mature enough to know what is happening, to be able to judge the consequences of the decisions they make, and be able to assist in their defense. This determination expects that juveniles understand right from wrong, but it does not require that juveniles understand why they did what they did, or that they be able to control their actions.

Although some states require that juveniles have counsel or parents present when being interrogated by police, other states have no such requirement, or the juvenile is allowed to waive that right (Bartollas and Miller, 2001: 74). Advocates for juveniles argue that they are simply unable to protect their own interests and are vulnerable to manipulation and intimidation by police officers. The danger can be illustrated by the 1989 Central Park jogger rape case. Many years later, the juveniles who pled guilty were exonerated by the confession of a serial rapist and by DNA evidence that linked him alone to the crime. Lawyers for the boys (now men) had argued that their confessions were coerced by police through threats of the death penalty. Adults have been known to confess to crimes they did not commit, so it is not difficult to understand why fourteen-year-olds might be manipulated into confessing. Even though the prosecutor's office declined to retry this case and the young men won their freedom, they all served prison time for this conviction (Schanberg, 2002).

Many believe that juvenile crime is becoming increasingly violent and that kids are literally "getting away with murder." This perception has been nurtured by the media's attention to a few notorious cases, the emphasis on gang activity in both fiction and news, and the idea that juvenile crime is increasing. According to the Uniform Crime Reports (2006), however, between 1997 and 2006, arrests of juveniles for murder decreased 42 percent, for rape 30 percent, for robbery 35 percent, and for property crime 44 percent.

Observers also have serious concerns that the juvenile justice system discriminates on the basis of race. Black and other minority youth are much more likely than whites to be formally processed and end up in juvenile or adult facilities. Poor children are also more likely to be taken into the system. This is partly because of lack of family support. Juveniles with families who are willing and able to work with justice officials are more likely to be referred to community programs than to be institutionalized.

There are no easy answers for what to do with intractable juveniles. In some cases, youths sent to juvenile institutions are raped and abused by other youths. In Texas in 2007, there was a horrific scandal involving two administrators of a remote juvenile facility who evidently targeted boys, coerced sex from them, and then blocked their release. These administrators continued to sexually victimize the juveniles in the facility even after the staff complained and even after a Texas Ranger came to investigate. It would be two years before the story broke in the newspaper, and the resulting scandal led to the indictments of the two perpetrators, the resignation or retirement of several officials who arguably ignored the situation, and a complete restructuring of the agency (Moreno, 2007). The prosecutor who didn't prosecute, even though he was handed the case by a Texas Ranger, was reelected.

Juveniles who are abused in detention facilities may become more violent, and many will be sent, after a more serious crime, to adult facilities, where they once again become prey for adult predators. It is highly doubtful that they will emerge as anything but bitter and damaged. Hate and rage are often the only emotions that young offenders are familiar with.

Only recently has the United States joined the majority of nations in banning the execution of juveniles. In 2004, fifty-nine individuals were executed who committed their crime before the age of eighteen, but then, in *Roper v. Simmons*, 543 U.S. 551 (2005), the Supreme Court, in a 5-4 decision, held that the Eighth and Fourteenth Amendments barred the execution of anyone who committed the crime before the age of eighteen. At the time, twenty states allowed the execution of offenders who committed their crimes when they were sixteen or seventeen. (Lane, 2005: A1).

PUNISHING WHITE-COLLAR CRIMINALS

Thus far, we have brought up issues of the moral and legal culpability of those who, because of mental impairment or youth, may not be fully responsible for their actions. What about white-collar criminals? Are they as guilty as street criminals?

In 2001 the public discovered that the Firestone tires installed on the Ford Explorer were vulnerable to blowing out in high temperatures at a high rate of speed, causing rollovers. More than 100 fatal accidents were tied to tire blowouts. When this fact came to light, the media also reported that both the tire company and Ford Motor Company knew about the tires' weakness and continued to use the tires on new Explorers. Angry consumers were even more enraged when they discovered that Ford had voluntarily replaced the tires and stopped using them on Ford vehicles sold overseas, but not in the United States. Ford eventually replaced

13 million tires at a reputed cost of $3 billion. A costly lesson, surely. But the financial loss was less costly than going to prison for knowingly exposing an unsuspecting public to a preventable risk.

Should Ford executives who knew of the test results have been held *criminally* culpable for their decision to continue to sell vehicles with the faulty tires? The case was similar to the infamous Ford Pinto case back in the 1970s, when it was discovered that there had been corporate knowledge that the gas tank was vulnerable to explosions, but a decision been made that it was less costly to defend wrongful-death suits than it would be to reengineer the automobile. Ford executives were charged with negligent manslaughter, but they were ultimately acquitted of criminal wrongdoing.

The difficulty in attaching criminal culpability to corporate criminals is that it is usually unclear who has responsibility for the decision that might form the offense. Thus, in a decision to continue marketing an unsafe product, no one person emerges as the clear culprit and everyone has an excuse as to why it was not his or her responsibility to do anything. There are legitimate questions of responsibility and guilt in cases of corporate misdoings. Obviously, decisions regarding whether or not to put a safety device in a car or a warning on a cigarette package are not the same as taking a gun into a convenience store and shooting a clerk in the course of a robbery. But if we accept as fact that some robbers end up killing their victim unintentionally, is the corporate criminal any less morally culpable when participating in actions where deaths are weighed against profits and factored into the bottom line?

Fraud and other forms of white-collar crime are easier to prosecute. The Enron executives who knew that their accounting practices were fraudulent and engaged in them to hide corporate losses and to obtain high bonuses for themselves were no different from criminals who use stolen credit cards or run a "scam" on an elderly victim. Other white-collar criminals have also been prosecuted, and some have received long sentences, as cited by Farrell (2005):

1. WorldCom: CEO Bernie Ebbers, convicted of masterminding an $11 billion accounting fraud scheme, received a twenty-five-year sentence.
2. Adelphia Communications: CEOs Jon Rigas and Tim Rigas, convicted of theft, received, respectively, fifteen and twenty years.
3. Tyco: CEO Dennis Kozlowski and CFO Mark Swartz were convicted of grand larceny.
4. ImClone Systems: CEO Sam Waksal, convicted of insider trading, received an eighty-seven-month sentence.
5. Martha Stewart: convicted of obstruction and perjury and received a three-month sentence and house arrest.

In other cases, white-collar defendants were either acquitted or the prosecution was dropped (Farrell, 2005):

1. HealthSouth: CEO Richard Scrushy was acquitted of a $2.7 billion fraud even though the government had already received fifteen guilty pleas in the same case.
2. Kmart: Two indictments against company executives for accounting fraud were withdrawn.

3. Arthur Andersen: A judge threw out the conviction against the company, holding that the jury instructions were faulty.
4. Qwest: Two mid-level executives were acquitted of criminal charges in relation to accounting fraud even though the government had already secured guilty pleas from two other executives.

What is a just sentence for someone who engages in price fixing, insider trading, gouging, or other forms of corporate crime? What is a fair punishment for someone who dumps toxic waste because it is too expensive to dispose of properly and a community suffers high rates of cancer because of it? It may be harder for prosecutors to secure convictions in these cases because there is a perception that they are less "guilty" than so-called street criminals. A sentence of prison seems somehow more punitive for them than for street muggers. Should that make a difference in the determination of punishment? If we do take into consideration that prison is a harsher sentence for an upper-class executive, is that not somehow punishing the poor burglar for being poor?

VICTIM PRECIPITATION

The concept that the offender is always purely guilty and the victim is always purely innocent is not completely accurate in reality. Sometimes there is random chance in who ends up in a pool of blood and who is left standing. Both parties may be equally culpable in starting and participating in the events that led to the injury or death. **Victim precipitation** refers to the victim's role in the criminal event, and indicates that the victim played a crucial part in setting the crime in motion. Some people fear that an analysis of the victim's actions has the potential to blame the victim rather than the offender for the crime. Others argue that it is naïve to ignore the victim's role.

In certain situations the victim must share some of the responsibility for the crime. For instance, when someone starts a bar fight and ends up the victim, that is a victim-precipitated crime. When a victim engages in careless or dangerous behavior, events are set in motion that lead to a crime. This does not mean that individuals who go out late at night deserve to be robbed or that women who are out alone drinking deserve to be raped.

Victim precipitation refers to situations in which, for instance, batterers taunt their victims to shoot them—and they do. In this case, the batterer is ostensibly the victim because he has been shot, but an examination of his conduct would reveal that the so-called offender is also a victim and that the batterer's own behavior largely contributed to his victimization. In these situations the victim actually participates in the criminal event. We might allow for partial culpability; for the responsibility for the crime must be shared by the offender and the victim.

The point is that the media and the justice system seem to conspire to paint a picture where there are purely innocent victims and purely evil offenders. The real world doesn't work that way. It is the case with some crimes, but sometimes, the offender is also a victim and the victim is not without fault. This does not mean that justice cannot be served, but it does mean that there are often no simple answers.

IMMORAL LAWS AND THE MORAL PERSON

In the discussion of legal moralism, we looked at laws that prohibit behaviors that are judged as immoral, at least by some part of the population. Here, we will look at laws and governmental edicts that are themselves immoral. Examples might include the laws of the Spanish Inquisition in the 1200s that resulted in large numbers of people being tortured and killed for having dissenting religious beliefs, and the Nuremberg laws of Nazi Germany stripping Jewish citizens of their citizenship and later laws requiring Jews to give themselves up to be transported to concentration camps and often death. Examples in the United States might include the internment laws during World War II that forced U.S. citizens of Japanese descent to give up land and property and be confined in internment camps until the end of the war, and the segregationist laws that once forced blacks to use different doors and water fountains than whites.

These laws are now thought of as immoral, but they were not at the time. The most common example of immoral laws are those that deprive certain groups of liberty or treat some groups differently, giving them either more or fewer rights and privileges than other groups. Boss (2001) has described unjust laws as having the following characteristics:

1.   They are degrading to humans.
2.   They are discriminatory against certain groups.
3.   They are enacted by unrepresentative authorities.
4.   They are unjustly applied.

Most ethical systems would condemn such laws, and an objective ethical analysis would probably prevent the passage of such laws in the first place. The example of Japanese American internment can be used to illustrate how one might use the ethical systems to judge a specific law. The religious ethical framework would probably not provide moral support for the action because it runs contrary to some basic Christian principles, such as, "Do unto others as you would have them do unto you." Ethical formalism could not be used to support this law because it runs counter to the categorical imperative that each person must be treated as an end rather than as a means, and to the universalism principle. The principle of forfeiture could not justify the action because these were innocent individuals, many of whom were fiercely loyal to the United States. The only ethical framework that might be used to support the morality of this law is utilitarianism. We must be able to show that the total utility derived from internment outweighed the negative effect it had on the Japanese Americans who lost their land and liberty. Did it save the country from a Japanese invasion? Did it allow other Americans to sleep better at night? Did the benefits outweigh the harm to Japanese Americans?

Are there any laws today that might be considered immoral? After 9/11, there was some discussion of deporting all those of Middle Eastern origin, regardless of their immigration status. This idea was rejected, perhaps partly because moral hindsight has shown that the Japanese internment was a flawed response to the fear created by World War II. However, thousands of Middle Easterners were required to register, and many were detained for expired visas and other immigration irregularities. The detainees in Guantanamo have been held for years without

BOX 5.2 | CIVIL DISOBEDIENCE

1. It must be nonviolent in form and actuality.
2. No other means of remedying the evil should be available.
3. Those who resort to civil disobedience must accept the legal sanctions and punishments imposed by law.
4. A major moral issue must be at stake.
5. When intelligent men [sic] of good will differ on complex moral issues, discussion is more appropriate than action.
6. There must be some reason for the time, place, and target selected.
7. One should adhere to "historical time."

Source: Hook, quoted in Fink (1977: 126–127).

any due process, in violation, many argue, of the Geneva Convention. Unfortunately, fear makes actions seem reasonable that, in retrospect, may not be legally or morally justifiable.

In other countries the legal climate has allowed torture and death squads to be used. If you lived in a South African country and knew of assassinations by government police and nighttime kidnappings and disappearances, would you follow a law requiring you to turn in political subversives? If you were living in a troubled country in Europe, such as Bosnia, would you support a law that dispossessed members of a rival faction of their property? These issues are at the heart of our next discussion. Can one be a moral person while enforcing or obeying an immoral law?

Martin Luther King, Jr., Mahatma Gandhi, and Henry David Thoreau agreed with St. Augustine that "an unjust law is no law at all." There is a well-known story about Thoreau, jailed for nonpayment of what he considered unfair taxes. When asked by a friend, "What are you doing in jail?" Thoreau responded, "What are you doing out of jail?" The point of the story is that if a law is wrong, a moral person is honor-bound to disobey that law. Box 5.2 addresses civil disobedience. If moral people were to disobey laws, what would happen to the stability of society?

Another story concerns Socrates. About to be punished for the crime of teaching radical ideas to youth, he had the opportunity to escape and was begged by his friends to leave the country, yet he willingly accepted his death by hemlock because of a fundamental respect for the laws of his country. This position supports the notion that one should never place one's own moral code above the duly enacted laws of the land. One should change the laws, if believed to be wrong, through the process of legislation and appeal, not by committing unlawful acts, because the latter is dangerous to the stability of society.

If we agree with the proposition that an unjust law is no law at all, we may set up a situation in which all citizens follow or disobey laws at will, depending on their own conscience. If one holds a relativist view of morality—specifically the

QUOTE AND QUERY

Under a government which imprisons any unjustly, the true place for a just man is also a prison....

Thoreau, quoted in Fink, 1977: 109

[T]here are two types of laws[:] just and unjust. I would be the first to advocate obeying just laws. One has not only a legal but a moral responsibility to obey just laws. Conversely, one has a moral responsibility to disobey unjust laws.

Martin Luther King, Jr., quoted in Barry, 1985: ii

Do you believe that a just person has a moral obligation to disobey an unjust law?

belief that one can intuit morals and decide morality on an individual basis—two people holding different moral positions could both be right even though one position might be inconsistent with the law. An absolutist view holds that there is only one universal truth, which would mean that if one knew a law to be wrong based on this universal truth, that person would be morally obliged to disobey the law. Evidently, either position could support civil disobedience.

The "Quote and Query" box presents quotes on just and unjust laws, by Henry David Thoreau and Martin Luther King.

Civil disobedience is the voluntary disobedience of established laws based on one's moral beliefs. Rawls (1971) defined it as a public, nonviolent, conscientious, yet political act contrary to law and usually done with the aim of bringing about a change in the law or policies of the government. Many great social thinkers and leaders have advocated breaking certain laws thought to be wrong. Philosophers believe that the moral person follows a higher law of behavior that usually, but not necessarily, conforms to human law. However, it is an exceptional person who willfully and publicly disobeys laws that he or she believes to be wrong. Psychological experiments show us that it is difficult for individuals to resist authority, even when they know that they are being asked to do something that is wrong.

The Milgram experiments are often used to show how easily one can command blind obedience to authority. In these experiments, subjects were told to administer shocks to individuals hooked up to electrical equipment as part of a learning experiment (Milgram, 1963). Unbeknownst to the subjects, the "victims" were really associates of the experimenter and faked painful reactions only when the subjects thought they were administering shocks. In one instance, the subject and the "victim" were separated, and the subject heard only cries of pain and exclamations of distress, then silence, indicating that the "victim" was unconscious. Even when the subjects thought they were harming the "victims," they continued to administer shocks because the experimenter directed them to do so and reminded them of their duty (Milgram, 1963).

Although it is always with caution that one applies laboratory results to the real world, history shows that individual submission to authority, even immoral authority, is not uncommon. Those who turned in Jewish neighbors to Nazis and those who participated in massacres of Native Americans in this country were only following the law or instructions from a superior authority. To determine what laws are unjust, Martin Luther King, Jr. used the following guidelines:

> A just law is one that is consistent with morality. An unjust law is any that degrades human personality or compels a minority to obey something the majority does not adhere to or is a law that the minority had no part in making. (quoted in Barry, 1985: 3)

To explore this issue further, one could refer to the two paradigms of conflict and consensus. The consensus view of society would probably provide a stronger argument for the position of following laws whether one agrees with them or not. In contrast, the conflict and pluralist perspectives hold that laws may be tools of power and are not necessarily the embodiment of the will of the people; therefore, individuals may legitimately disagree with immoral laws and have a duty to disobey them. From another perspective, Kohlberg might propose that only individuals who have reached higher stages of morality would think to challenge conventional definitions of right and wrong.

There is a widespread belief that law is synonymous with morality and that as long as one remains inside the law, one can be considered a moral person. Callahan (1982: 64) points out the following:

> We live in a society where the borderline between law and ethics often becomes blurred. For many, morality is simply doing that which the law requires; a fear of punishment is the only motivation for behavior in some minimally acceptable way.

Obviously, Callahan is concerned with the false perception of law as a total representation of morals. Most of us struggle to achieve goodness using the definitions of the society we live in; very few reach beyond accepted definitions to meet a higher standard of morality. Luckily, most of us have little need to do so—or do we? The "Quote and Query" box is a chilling reminder of what happens when good citizens remain silent in the face of evil.

QUOTE AND QUERY

What there was, from the start, was the great silence, which appears in every civilized country that passively accepts the inevitability of violence, and then the fear that suddenly befalls it. That silence which can transform any nation into an accomplice. The silence which existed in Germany, when even many well-intentioned individuals assumed that everything would return to normal once Hitler finished with the Communists and Jews. Or when the Russians assumed that everything would return to normal once Stalin eliminated the Trotskyites. Initially, this was the conviction in Argentina. Then came fear. And after the fear, indifference. "Nothing happens to someone who stays out of politics." Such silence begins in the channels of communication. Certain political leaders, institutions, and priests attempt to denounce what is happening, but are unable to establish contact with the population. The silence begins with a strong odor. People sniff the suicides, but it eludes them. The silence finds another ally: solitude. People fear suicides as they fear madmen. And the person who wants to fight senses his solitude and is frightened.

Jacobo Timerman, 1981: 51

Why do people keep quiet when they see others being oppressed or mistreated?

Source: Reprinted with permission of Alfred A. Knopf, Inc.

Remember that civil disobedience occurs when the individual truly believes the law to be wrong and therefore believes that the enforcement of it or obedience to it would also be wrong. We are not referring to chronic lawbreaking because of immediate rewards. Indeed, most criminals have a fairly conventional sense of morality. They agree with the laws, even though they break them. Even those gray-area laws that involve disagreement over the "wrongness" of the behavior are not proper grounds for disobedience unless one believes that the government is immorally oppressing certain people.

Thus far, we have been focusing on the culpability of the offender. Laws are written as proscriptions directed toward behaviors that are deemed to be harmful. Some people may be less culpable than others because of either their age or mental illness. Another situation entirely is one in which an individual may be morally culpable for obeying a law when that law is immoral. Now we will shift the focus to the victim.

VICTIMS' RIGHTS

In ancient codes of law, the focus was on compensating the victim. This focus changed to the state and punishment in English common law around the time of the Magna Carta (1215). Eventually, two systems of law developed—one to deal with private wrongs (civil law) and one to deal with public wrongs (criminal law). The two may overlap. For instance, a rape victim may sue her attacker in civil court concomitantly with a state prosecution. And to cite a well-known example involving both systems, the family of Nicole Simpson sued O. J. Simpson for wrongful death after he was acquitted in a criminal trial of her murder.

This does not create double jeopardy. Because rules of evidence and standards of proof are different, a person may be acquitted in a criminal trial and still be held responsible civilly. The legal theory of the state as opponent is that the harm done in any crime is done only incidentally to an individual. The more important harm is the crime against the state, even though it is the individual victim who is injured.

Victimology has emerged as a separate discipline in criminology, which may help to provide a better balance between state harm and individual harm. Victims' rights bills, for example, provide various protections and rights to victims of crime. Although it is popular for politicians to campaign with a pro-victim, crime-control agenda, their message usually panders to the voting public's fears rather than shedding light on a complex social problem where there are at times no distinct lines between victims and offenders. The media also contributes to public fear and to the stereotype of the white middle-class victim and the lower-class minority criminal.

Actually, minority groups and the poor are much more likely than the middle class to be victimized. Most victims and offenders come from the same neighborhood. Criminals are often victims of past or current crimes themselves. Moreover, there are many more victims than those defined as such by the system. Customers of inner-city supermarkets that charge higher prices because they know their customers do not have transportation to shop competitively are victims of economic exploitation. There are victims of retail credit schemes in which furniture rental stores rent and repossess a single piece of furniture several times for multiple profits. There are victims of employers who pay less than minimum wage or suddenly do not pay at all because they know the employees will not protest—either because they are illegal aliens or because they desperately need the job. Finally, there are victims of slum landlords, who must pay rent or be evicted even though the apartment has a multitude of health and safety hazards. These victims are rarely considered part of the "crime problem."

MEDIA'S PORTRAYAL OF VICTIMS

The media might be most responsible for creating a false perception of crime. Whereas violence occupies up to three-quarters of all television news time, it is a small percentage of actual crime (Elias, 1986: 43). The constant barrage of murders, rapes, and robberies in television drama contributes to the public's general fear of crime, as does the local news media's sensationalistic treatment of such crimes even while ignoring more pervasive social problems. An individual is more likely to die of pneumonia, cancer, heart disease, household fires, auto crashes, or suicide than of homicide (Elias, 1986: 43). The "In the News" box offers a further look at the media's role.

This is not to say that violent crime is not a problem, but there is disproportionate emphasis on violence relative to other types of victimization, and a tendency to present every criminal event as a case of pure innocence versus pure evil. More recently, there has been recognition of the tendency of the news media to focus on disappearances of young, pretty white women. The story is carried by all major news sources as if it were a movie, with the original disappearance as a

---

IN THE NEWS | MEDIA ETHICS

In 1997 two news stories raised questions of media ethics. In one case, the terrible sexual abuse and murder of a child in a prominent family in Colorado created a media frenzy before police were able to identify any suspects. One tabloid published crime-scene photos of the body, shocking even some hardened newspaper professionals by the insensitivity and gratuitousness of the graphic nature of the photos, not to mention the issue of how the photos were obtained. Should crime scene photos of murders be published?

Should those who provided them be prosecuted?
In a Dallas case, two prominent athletes were accused of raping a young woman at gunpoint. The police department immediately held a news conference, and papers across the country and world reported the allegations, along with the past legal troubles of one of the athletes. The woman then recanted, and police and prosecutors charged her with providing a false report. Then some members of the media proposed that they were "victims" of her false allegations, also claiming that the police department was at fault for having a news conference that they were bound to report. The athletes and their lawyers demanded that the media report the recantation with the same enthusiasm that the initial allegations were reported.
Should the police hold news conferences when their only evidence is a victim's allegation? Should the media withhold the accused party's name in a rape charge as they do the rape victim's name, at least until there is an indictment?

mystery, the search as the drama, and the resolution the climax—either in a successful return or with the arrest and conviction of an offender. Examples of white women as victims include the highly publicized cases of Laci Peterson, Chandra Levy, and Lori Hacking. Conversely, young black women such as Tamika Huston, who disappeared in Spartanburg, South Carolina, garner little if any interest from the national news agencies, even when families repeatedly ask for help in the search efforts. The trouble with this pattern of coverage is that other disappearances—of men, of minority women, of homeless people—are ignored. There is a perception that primarily racism is responsible for the uneven coverage, and it is a charge that is hard to refute (Mankiewicz, 2005).

Most crime victims suffer relatively small losses but also receive virtually no help from the system. Police do not respond at all to many burglary calls because there are so many calls and so little the police can do about them. Assault calls may be handled informally and cavalierly when the combatants are acquaintances or relatives. Victims rarely have much to do with the system unless a suspect is arrested—a rare occurrence in many categories of crime. When there is a prosecution, the victim might feel used by the system because the goal is to get a conviction, not to provide aid or compensation. The prosecutor is more interested in how the jury will perceive the victim than how much the victim lost or suffered from the crime.

After a "rediscovery" of victims' rights, many states enacted victims' rights bills that enumerate various rights that victims have under the law. These rights may include the following:

- Being present at trial (circumventing procedural rules that exclude victim witnesses from the courtroom during other testimony)
- Being notified of any hearing dates and plea-bargain arrangements
- Submitting a victim-impact statement to be considered during the sentencing decision
- Being treated courteously and compassionately by all law enforcement and justice system personnel

Some of these bills have created victim-witness programs in police departments or prosecutors' offices that attend to the needs of victim witnesses. Duties of program personnel might include keeping victims informed of their case, providing information, accompanying victims to court, and helping them fill out victim-compensation forms.

Victim-compensation programs have also been created in many states. These programs provide compensation for certain types of crime when the victim is without insurance or other means of reimbursement. Funding comes either through court costs paid into a general fund by all criminal offenders or through the state's general funds. Usually, only violent crimes and not property crimes are targeted by such programs. However, they can provide help with expenses such as lost wages, hospital and doctor bills, and even burial expenses, whether or not the offender is arrested. Restitution programs are much more common today than they have been, and these programs target property victims as well as victims of violent crime. Still, restitution programs help only victims of criminals who are caught, and that, unfortunately, is not likely for crimes such as burglary or larceny.

Victims have a right to be treated fairly by the system. All people should be afforded the same level of service and treatment, regardless of who they are. The "bag lady" should receive the same care as the mayor if both are mugged. Victims should also receive equal treatment in any punishment decision. The amount of punishment inflicted on an offender should not be based on the economic or social status of the victim, any more than it should be based on the economic or social status of the offender.

Other issues are not so simple. For instance, should the victim have an equal say in the amount of punishment? What if the prosecutor believes that a plea bargain of probation is sufficient punishment, considering the crime and the costs of a trial, but the victim demands imprisonment? Should a burglary victim have the right to veto a plea bargain? What about an assault victim? Some argue that we have gone too far in catering to victims' rights and that the system is now oriented toward victim satisfaction rather than justice (Stickels, 2003).

We spoke of mercy before. Would not some argue that the state does not have the power to grant mercy, only the victim? These questions also relate to the decision to parole. Many states now have procedures whereby the victim or the victim's family has the right to address the parole board when the criminal's parole date comes up. Should these victims have the right to veto parole when the board would have otherwise paroled the criminal? We characterize the victim's feelings of vengeance as personal revenge and the state's as retribution or justice, with the implication that one is bad and the other is good.

Victims who "take the law into their own hands" become criminals themselves. But why is the state's determination of sufficient punishment any better than the victim's? Supposedly, it is because the state has the power to objectively and rationally determine the correct measurement, but if other variables, such as goals of efficiency and convenience, are at work, where is the objective measurement of punishment? Favoritism, bribery, and incompetence may also affect outcomes. Obviously, in these cases neither the victim nor the offender receives justice.

Some mistrust the current interest in victims' rights and believe that this movement is really a cynical manipulation of victim witnesses to advance the goal of making them better witnesses for the state. Also, because the definition of the victim continues to be narrow and limited to stereotypes, obfuscation about who are victims continues. This serves to blind those most at risk to the realities of their own victimization and to protect those who victimize in ways other than street crimes, such as white-collar and social crimes (Elias, 1986).

RESTORATIVE JUSTICE

Our current system of law and justice is oriented completely to the offender. What would a system be like if the emphasis were on the victim's rights, needs, and compensation? In a system with a primary emphasis on the victim rather than the offender, money would be spent on victim services rather than prisons. It would be victims who would receive job skills training, not offenders. Some of the money that now goes to law enforcement and corrections would be channeled to compensation programs for victims of personal and property crimes. Victims would be helped even if their offenders were not caught. The major goal would not be punishment, but service. Offenders would be peripheral figures; they would be required to pay restitution to victims, and punishment would occur only if they did not fulfill their obligation to their victims. Could such a system work? Would such a system provide better justice?

Although the restorative justice movement does not propose quite this level of radical restructuring, it does dramatically redesign the justice system and offers a new alternative to retributive justice. **Restorative justice** is a term used to describe a number of programs that seek to move compensation back to center stage in the justice system, instead of retribution. A similar philosophy has been called "peacemaking justice" by Braswell and Gold (2002). Programs that require the offender to confront the victim and provide compensation, and programs that place the victim in the middle of the process of deciding what to do about the offender, can be categorized under the restorative justice rubric. The propositions of the movement are as follows (Van Ness and Strong, 1997):

1. Justice requires restoring victims, offenders, and communities who have been injured by crime.
2. Victims, offenders, and communities should have the opportunity to be a fully active part of the justice process.
3. Government should restore order, but the community should establish peace.

The roots of restorative justice can be found as far back as Roman and Grecian law. Both were based on repayment to victims. Recall that Aristotle's "rectificatory justice" was concerned with ill-gotten gains in contract and business relationships that had to be remedied.

In the 1970s, a trend toward "community justice" was part of the larger movement of community empowerment and development. Community justice boards or local justice committees were created as part of the justice system (Schweigert, 2002). This model actually comes from earlier examples of tribal justice, such as the Maori tribal council of New Zealand, which involves members of the families of both the victims and the offenders. The model uses reintegrative shaming, and responsibility for the crime is shared by the offender's family. Another example is the Skokomish Community Peacemaking Panel. Tribal peacemakers are selected from community members, and an adversarial system is specifically rejected in favor of one that seeks to solve the issue rather than simply to assess punishment (Schweigert, 2002). The "Quote and Query" box gives one perspective on why alternatives to the rule of law are so appealing to many people.

Hallmarks of community justice models include the following (Schweigert, 2002: 25):

1. The process of justice employs local leadership, is informal, and invites participation from community members.
2. The goal is to repair the harm done to a community member by another community member in a way that will restore the health of the community relationship.
3. The authority of the justice is through the customs and traditions accepted by all members.

QUOTE AND QUERY

I have by degrees given up my faith in the rule of law. It is not only that the relatively absolute power we give lawgivers and law enforcers tends to corrupt these power holders absolutely. It is that imposing a pre-existing law or rule on someone literally amounts to letting one's prejudices override one's capacity to hear the many and various explanations and desires parties have.

Pepinsky, 1999: 64

What does Pepinsky mean when he argues that the law allows people to let their prejudices override their capacity to hear explanations?

In community or restorative justice models, crime is viewed as a natural human error that should be dealt with by the community. Offenders remain a part of the community. Some make distinctions between restorative justice and community justice models.

> Restorative justice is a philosophical approach to correctional intervention, in which crime is seen as a conflict between individuals and their community whereby the party that causes the injury incurs an obligation to make things right—whenever and however possible.... Community justice is similar to restorative justice but with a stronger emphasis on prevention. Community justice involves a partnership between the justice system and community organizations to control crime and social disorder. (Carey, 2005: 5)

More generally, however, community and restorative justice can be distinguished from retributive justice in fundamental ways. Carey (2005: 25) details the differences between retributive justice and restorative justice:

1. In retributive justice the question is, "Who did it?" while in restorative justice the question is, "What is the harm?"
2. In retributive justice the question is, "Which laws were broken?" while in restorative justice the question is, "What needs to be done to repair the harm?"
3. In retributive justice the question is, "What should the punishment be?" while in restorative justice, the question is, "Who is responsible for this repair?"

Types of restorative justice programs include victim–offender mediation (or victim–offender reconciliation programs), whereby victims and offenders get together so the victim can make it clear to the offender what harm has occurred and they can decide together how to make it right. Reparative boards have community members (rather than justice officials) decide what should happen after a crime has been committed and an offender identified. Family group conferencing and circle sentencing include family members and other interested parties in the decision on what should happen to an offender (Braithwaite, 2002). It has been found that victims are more satisfied in restorative justice programs than with traditional sentencing (79 percent compared to 57 percent). Offenders were also more likely to successfully satisfy their restitution orders in such programs (Braithwaite, 2002: 71).

"Community reparative boards" are more common with youthful offenders. They are also called youth panels, neighborhood boards, or community diversion boards, and they have been in use since the 1920s. These boards reemerged in the mid-1990s, especially in Vermont. The goals are (Braithwaite, 2002: 73):

1. Promote citizen ownership of process.
2. Provide opportunity for victims and community members to confront offenders in a constructive manner.
3. Provide an opportunity for the offender to take personal responsibility.
4. Generate meaningful community-based responses to crime and reduce dependence on formal justice processing.

"Family group conferencing" comes from the Maori tribal model and was made a part of national legislation in New Zealand in 1989. The Wagga Wagga model in Southern Australia employs police to set up family conferences of offenders, victims, families, and interested or involved others to resolve the problem. The goals of this type of program are as follows (Braithwaite, 2002: 76):

1. Provide an opportunity for the victim to be directly involved in the decisions of sanctions
2. Increase the offender's awareness of the human impact of his/her behavior and give an opportunity for the offender to take responsibility for it
3. Engage the collective responsibility of the offender's support system
4. Allow both offender and victim to reconnect to key community support systems

"Circle sentencing," a similar model, comes from the Navajos in North America. Everyone involved directly in a criminal offense sits in a circle and gets a turn to speak. The entire circle decides what should be done. The goal is not to respond only to the current offense but also to heal the community. The goals of this type of sentencing are the following (Braithwaite, 2002: 77):

1. Promote healing.
2. Provide the offender an opportunity to make amends.
3. Empower victims, community members, families, and offenders.
4. Address underlying causes of criminal behavior.
5. Build a sense of community and promote and share community values.

There are potential problems with, and some criticisms of, these types of programs (Braithwaite, 2002; Dzur and Wertheimer, 2002). For instance, victims may feel pressured to forgive before they are ready. Less due process may be given to offenders because the goal is not to punish; thus, issues of guilt or innocence may be unresolved. However, restorative justice seems to offer a possible mediation between legal culpability and justice for everyone. Legal sanctions may not resolve the problems of the victim or change the offender. Restorative justice attempts to do both.

CONCLUSION

Paradigms of law help us understand that there are different perceptions regarding the function of law in society. While some view law as enforcing the will of the majority, others see law as a tool of oppression by those in power. The justification for law is primarily prevention of harm, including paternalistic laws that seek to protect individuals from themselves, and laws that enforce society's morals. One's paradigm influences one's views on the moral authority of the government to enforce such laws.

Ultimately, law defines who is legally, if not morally, culpable. Certain groups have special issues of culpability, such as the mentally ill, juveniles, white-collar criminals, and those whose

crimes may be the result of victim precipitation. Civil disobedience refers to instances in which a moral person must disobey law. Finally, the trend toward victims' rights could focus solely on retribution or could move toward a restorative justice approach that carries the potential of leaving the victim more fully compensated than retributive justice models.

Key Terms

civil disobedience *140*

competent *134*

conflict paradigm *119*

consensus
   paradigm *119*

culpability *129*

legal moralism *127*

legal paternalism *125*

McNaughten rule *130*

mechanical
   solidarity *119*

natural law *118*

organic solidarity *119*

paradigm *118*

pluralist paradigm *119*

positive law *118*

repressive law *119*

restitutive law *120*

restorative justice *146*

social contract
   theory *124*

victim
   precipitation *137*

victim-compensation
   programs *144*

victimology *142*

Review Questions

1. Explain how people distinguish between law and justice.
2. Discuss the three paradigms of law. How is pluralism differentiated from conflict theory?
3. Discuss the major justifications for law.
4. Discuss some laws justified by legal paternalism. Provide the rationale for such laws, as well as opposing arguments.
5. Discuss some types of laws that are justified by legal moralism. What are the major arguments for and against such laws?

6. What is the McNaughten rule?
7. What are some recent laws passed to control crime by juveniles?
8. Define and give examples of civil disobedience. What are the principles?
9. What are victims' bills of rights? Explain victim precipitation.
10. Describe restorative justice.

Writing/Discussion Questions

1. Write an essay on (or discuss) how the conflict and consensus paradigms would interpret the following: decriminalization of marijuana for medical purposes, stem-cell research, passage of hate-crime legislation, prohibiting the use of race in admissions procedures in universities and in competi-

tions for state scholarships, and laws prohibiting racial profiling in police stops.
2. Write an essay on (or discuss) the legitimate functions of law in society. Do you agree with laws that prohibit gambling? Drinking while driving? Under-age drinking? Prostitution? Liquor violations? Drugs? Helmet

laws for bicycles or motorcycles? Leash laws? Seat belts? Smoking in public places? Can you think of any paternalistic laws not mentioned above? Analyze pornography, gambling, homosexuality, and drug use under the ethical systems discussed in Chapter 2. What other laws have limited Americans' (or certain groups') freedoms? Can they be justified under any ethical rationale?

3. Write an essay on (or discuss) whether civil disobedience is ever justified. Discuss war protesters, anti-abortion activists who burn down clinics, protestors who are arrested for trespassing, and so on. If you believe that civil disobedience might be justified, when and in what circumstances would it be acceptable?

4. Write an essay on (or discuss) punishment of the mentally ill and juveniles. What are the legal arguments? What are the moral arguments?

Ethical Dilemmas

Situation 1

You ride a motorcycle, and you think it is much more enjoyable to ride without a helmet. You also believe that your vision and hearing are better without a helmet. Your state has just passed a helmet law, and you have already received two warnings. What will you do? What if your child were riding on the motorcycle? Do you think your position would be any different if you had any previous accidents and had been hurt?

Situation 2

You are asked to enforce a law that you believe to be wrong. In this situation, you are supposed to protect a member of the Ku Klux Klan during a speech when your feelings are contrary to the views expressed by this individual and you don't believe that he should have the right to speak. What would you do? What would you do if you were told to deliberately perform your job in such a way as to ensure that the speaker will be injured by a hostile crowd?

Situation 3

You are a district attorney prosecuting a burglary case. The defendant is willing to plead guilty in return for a sentence of probation, and you believe that this is a fair punishment because your evidence may not support a conviction. However, the victims are upset and want to see the offender receive prison time. They insist that you try the case. What should you do?

Situation 4

You are a prosecutor with the unwelcome task of prosecuting a twelve-year-old for a particularly brutal assault. You personally believe that the child basically went along with his older brother in the assault, and you think that he should have been left in the juvenile system. However, the juvenile court judge waived him to the adult system, and the media and the victim's family are demanding that he be tried as an adult. You have to decide whether to try him for attempted murder, assault, or some lesser crime. You could deny the waiver and send the case back to juvenile court. What will you do? How do you determine your duty? Is it to the victims, to society, or to your own conscience?

Situation 5

You are a juvenile prosecutor excited about the beginning of a new restorative justice program in your community. You truly believe that it will be a huge benefit for offenders and victims alike because it uses victim–offender mediation and circle sentencing in response to the juvenile's crime. The problem is that in the first case that has been referred to the program, you believe that there is not enough evidence to justify prosecution. There is no eyewitness to the burglary, and the offender has confessed, retracted, and then confessed again. You believe that the evidence is equivocal and that he could be guilty or innocent. It is too close to call. On the one hand, you cringe at the possibility that an innocent person is going to be considered guilty without due process. On the other hand, you believe that circle sentencing may result in needed intervention for this youth, for if he didn't commit this burglary, he certainly has been involved in other crimes. What would you do?

Suggested Readings

Bedau, H. 1969. *Civil Disobedience: Theory and Practice*. New York: Pegasus.

Boss, J. 2001. *Ethics for Life*, 2d ed. Mountain View, CA: Mayfield Publishing.

Cane, P. 2002. *Responsibility in Law and Morality*. Portland, OR: Oxford Press.

Crank, J. 2003. *Imagining Justice*. Cincinnati, OH: Anderson Publishing Company.

Feinberg, J., and Coleman, J. 2007. *Philosophy of Law*. Belmont, CA: Wadsworth.

Kramer, M. 2004. *Where Law and Morality Meet*. New York: Oxford University Press.

Lewis, D. 1998. *Guilty by Reason of Insanity*. New York: Ivy.

Perry, J. 2002. *Repairing Communities Through Restorative Justice*. Lanham, MD: American Correctional Association.

Van Ness, D., and Heetderks Strong, K. 1997. *Restoring Justice*. Cincinnati, OH: Anderson.

ETHICS AND THE CRIMINAL JUSTICE PROFESSIONAL

Police officers are sworn to uphold the law and serve the public. Sometimes the formal oath, which emphasizes the values of duty, protection, and service, is threatened by the pressures of controlling crime in our communities.

© David Gard/CORBIS

CHAPTER OBJECTIVES

1. Become familiar with the ways that paradigms and ideologies shape our beliefs about crime and how to control criminals.

2. Understand how policy makers moderate the law and how criminal justice professionals implement policy.

3. Become familiar with some of the issues faced by criminal justice professionals.

4. Learn the elements of good, ethical leadership.

5. Become familiar with the reasons for and elements of ethics training.

In 2007 Bernard Kerik saw his illustrious career crash and burn. At one point in 2006, he was President Bush's pick to head the Department of Homeland Security. In November of 2007, he was indicted by a federal Grand Jury on corruption and tax evasion charges. When he was the New York City corrections commissioner (1996–2000) and, later, the police commissioner (2000–2001), he evidently accepted illegal gifts from individuals who sought his favor. One of the gifts was a remodeling of his New York City apartment that was valued at more than $165,000. He pled guilty to violating New York City ethics charges and, later, also pled guilty to the federal charges (*Washington Post*, 2007).

Kerik was the administrative head and policy maker of the largest municipal law enforcement agency in this country. He was supposed to be the ethical leader for the more than 35,000 police officers under his authority. When someone of Kerik's stature not only commits unethical acts but actually breaks the law, we realize that the legitimacy and reputation of agencies of justice are always vulnerable, because they are composed of humans with all our human weaknesses.

In the preceding chapters we have discussed the concepts of morality, ethics, justice, and law. If law is the administration of justice, policy making is the administration of law. The final and most important link in the chain of justice is the criminal justice professional.

POLICY MAKING IN CRIMINAL JUSTICE

Professionals in criminal justice are called upon to enforce laws and also to implement policies. Policies can be formal or informal. Formal policy making is undertaken by the executive and legislative branches of the government, as well as by agencies in the criminal justice system. **Policies** can be considered the guidelines for action that dictate the priority of goals or objectives. They have tremendous influence on people's lives. For instance, the policy of *zero tolerance* in the war on drugs has meant that many individuals have become entangled in the criminal justice system who may not have been except for the policy. If one thinks of laws as the skeletal system of justice, policies can be considered as the muscular system— they influence the way that the laws are enforced.

There are also informal policies, which sometimes usurp or subvert formal policies. While a mayor may preach crime control, a police department may informally make it clear to its officers that they should ignore crimes in the red-light district. An informal policy may come from management or develop among front-line workers. Policies may be related to views of justice or may stem from self-interest.

The development of policies may have more to do with belief systems than with empirical reality. Next we present a discussion of liberalism and conservatism. Although these descriptions are stereotypical, they are so powerful in our thought processes that a great deal of meaning is transmitted by the use of the terms. The label of *liberal* or *conservative* communicates definitional elements that, if not universally agreed upon, at least provide the beginning of a dialogue.

IDEOLOGIES OF LIBERALISM AND CONSERVATISM

An **ideology** is "a set of general and abstract beliefs or assumptions about the correct or proper state of things, particularly with respect to the moral order and political arrangements, which serve to shape one's positions on specific issues" (Hornum and Stavish, 1978: 143). Two opposing ideologies that have great influence on one's thoughts about social issues, including crime and criminals, are the liberal view and the conservative view. Both the liberal perspective and the conservative perspective operate primarily under the consensus paradigm described in Chapter 5, in that they accept the basic definitions of crime as given by law.

The Liberal Perspective   The liberal perspective explains criminal behavior and deviance through reference to psychological, social, or biological causation. Because individuals are seen as being influenced by factors outside of their control, they are not completely culpable for their crimes. Rather, explanations are developed to explain behavior, including psychological, sociological, and other definitions of why behavior occurs.

In policing, the liberal perspective is manifested by attempts of police departments to make themselves more accessible to the community. Innovations such as neighborhood or community policing, team policing, and youth groups attempt to help the police understand and empathize with certain groups with which they come into contact. The liberal ideology would endorse the use of police officers as a positive social control tool. Their provision of services to the community not only provides direct services but also is seen as influencing pro-social values.

For instance, school safety officers teach bicycle safety tips and also relay the message that the police officer is a friend and that the child should look up to him or her as a role model. "Storefront" police stations transmit the message that the police are a part of the community, and neighborhood policing allows police officers to become involved in non-crime issues in the community, creating and cementing relational ties to the community that is being policed.

In courts, the liberal perspective is seen in *individualized justice*—the preference to consider the offender rather than the offense. This would involve the acceptance of reasons or rationales for unlawful behavior. For instance, the burglar who had lost his job and had bills to pay, the enraged wife who killed her husband because he left her for another woman, and the ghetto youth whose father turned him on to drugs—all would have their individual backgrounds considered in decisions regarding responsibility and punishment. The liberal perspective perceives that law cannot easily label and set punishment for wrongdoing because human behavior is complex, not categorical. Thus, the courts, and their human representatives in the legal system, must use discretion to administer individual justice.

In corrections, the liberal ideology supports most correctional programming. Attempts to make criminals more like us, by vocational training, education, and social skills training, are based on the idea that the criminal could change given a different environment, different influences, or solutions to problems such as illiteracy or addiction. Correctional programs may target underlying problems that lead to criminal choices, including

1. biological problems (e.g., addiction),
2. social problems (e.g., negative role models), and
3. psychological problems (e.g., weak ego state).

These programs are based on the assumption that if the problem is corrected, the criminal will no longer commit crime.

The liberal perspective may identify as unethical any treatment of the offender by the system that does not take individual factors into account. For instance, it would be considered unethical to

1. ignore the fact that an individual was coerced into an illegal action,
2. ignore a prisoner's need for special attention or medical care,
3. prosecute a very young offender in the same way that one would prosecute a more culpable older offender, and
4. ignore evidence that an individual was mentally ill when committing an offense.

Basically, the liberal perspective is concerned when the law tries to uphold some unrealistic standard of objective justice, for that is not possible.

The Conservative Perspective   The conservative perspective, in general, agrees with the liberal perspective that the legal code is a true representation of society's morals and values, but differs in the perception of the offender. Rather than being influenced by forces beyond their control, offenders are seen as persons who freely choose actions and must be held accountable for them. Public safety is paramount, and victims deserve more care and attention than offenders. Thus, if some technical rules are violated in order to get an offender off the street, that is an acceptable cost for protecting innocent victims.

The conservative perspective views the police as enforcers of society's morality, and any attempts to weaken that role are to be resisted. Court restrictions against police power or police actions should be limited because criminals must be caught and punished in whatever way is most effective. Police are seen as becoming "soft" or bureaucratized in recent years, and there may be a wistful element in the popularity of fictional characters such as Dirty Harry, who bypass due process to get criminals off the streets.

In the conservative perspective, judges are judged on the length of the sentences they hand down and criticized if they appear too "soft." Conservatives believe the death penalty is justified and is not used often enough. Criminals are believed to have too many rights and victims none.

Under the conservative perspective, correctional facilities should not be too comfortable, and old-fashioned punishments, such as chain gangs and rock piles, are seen as appropriate and worthy. Although prisons should satisfy basic needs, anything beyond what is absolutely necessary for survival is considered a luxury and decreases the effectiveness of prison as a deterrent.

The conservative concern for ethics involves criminal justice practitioners who may use their powers of discretion too freely. For the conservative, it would be considered unethical

1. to let criminals off because of courtroom deals or because of some error in the proceedings;
2. for police to ignore wrongdoing when it is done by informants, especially if it is someone who will continue the behavior; and
3. for criminal justice practitioners to give special privileges to criminals because of status or money—for instance, to give special favors to mobsters in prison.

Whenever the system is less than objective in handing out punishment, the conservatives' concern for ethics is aroused, and that would also include disparate sentencing based on offender characteristics. For instance, if two defendants had committed the same crime, it would be considered wrong for one defendant to get fewer years in prison than the other because of different circumstances.

Smith (1982: 137) uses the terms *right* and *left* instead of our terms *conservative* and *liberal*, and presents additional definitional elements of the two ideologies. For the right, the paramount value is order—an ordered society based on a pervasive and binding morality. The paramount danger is disorder—social, moral, and political. For the left, the paramount value is justice—a just society based on a fair and equitable distribution of power, wealth, prestige, and privilege. The paramount evil is injustice. The left's concern for justice includes distributive justice, and that is why offenders' backgrounds are considered in the equation.

Although Smith (1982) and others associate the liberal (or left) viewpoint with due process, the liberal ideology does not necessarily, or even logically, imply a due-process position. Recall that due process is concerned with procedural justice, the steps taken to ensure that individual liberty is protected against state power. The liberal support of treatment implies that one may go beyond what even conservative, retributive ends would dictate. Further, the liberal perspective does not distrust state power; rather, it embraces the power of the state to do good.

The liberal is ends-oriented; therefore, the means may be considered less important—a position that is contrary to due process, which is all about the means employed, and whether each step in the process was completed correctly. Thus, a due-process perspective may be a separate ideology, one that is concerned with means more than ends, and rights more than results. A due-process advocate, as opposed to a liberal, would believe that a homeless alcoholic schizophrenic has a right to his or her affliction and lifestyle unless these pose a danger to self or others. A liberal would believe that the state could and should respond to the ills of the individual, even if the individual doesn't seem to know what is good for him or her.

Of course, these descriptions are simplistic. Most people do not want to be labeled as conservative or liberal, probably because such labeling denies the presence of more complicated views of humanity and human relationships. Despite the obvious generalizations apparent in these characterizations, however, they can be detected in news coverage and political speeches and are useful in order to understand the development of policy. People's positions on topics are fairly predictable once the person is identified as a conservative or a liberal, including topics such as: immigration reform, affirmative action, death penalty, decriminalization of drugs, universal health care, restorative justice, and zero-tolerance policies. It should also be noted, however, that sometimes the individual does not conform to predictions. For instance, the late William Buckley was an avowed conservative, but he favored some degree of decriminalization of drugs, labeling the war on drugs as an abject failure.

One's ideology may affect one's beliefs regarding public policies and also may affect one's behavior and actions and what one considers unethical behavior. If one's ideology affects how one conducts research, for instance, by ignoring or slanting contrary findings, that is a problem. If one's ideology affects how one receives research, as a policy maker, by ignoring contrary research and supporting public policy that is contrary to what research indicates is effective or acceptable, that is also a problem. The ethical researcher, public policy maker, and public servant should be careful not to let their ideology eclipse evidence in their decision making.

Braswell and Whitehead (1999) urge putting aside liberal and conservative viewpoints in favor of a different approach and point to dangerous practices when presenting research from one point of view or the other. They explain the liberal approach as represented by those who present prison research in a light that denies the possibility that prisons do have an effect on crime or that prisons might actually help offenders. The conservative approach is represented by those who view prisons as a management issue with no recognition or concern for the social, racial, and economic factors that so obviously play a part in the way prisons are used in society today.

Conservatives point to research showing that the public favors incarceration and the death penalty. Liberals point to research showing that when the public is offered alternatives, the answers change. Both sides are dishonest, even if unconsciously, in presenting research that is less than the truth, unbalanced, and biased. Braswell and Whitehead (1999) argue for **wholesight**—using the heart as well as the head to understand and present research findings.

MYTHS AND REALITY IN CRIMINAL JUSTICE

What we believe about crime and criminals is partially influenced by our ideology, as described above, but it is also influenced by what we know about crime—or what we think we know. Several excellent sources have debunked some of the more standard myths and truisms in criminal justice. Walker (1985/2005) was one of the first to address fundamental beliefs that influence criminal justice policy. For example, the belief that more police patrols would reduce crime has little, if any, empirical support. He also addressed fundamental beliefs that support liberal ideology. For example, the belief that education reduces crime is refuted by some studies that show no effect. Some of Walker's findings and use of empirical evidence may be criticized, but the approach of a skeptic is necessary if we want to avoid complacency and policy making influenced by unsupported truisms.

Others have continued this inquiry. For instance, Kappeler, Blumberg, and Potter (2000/2005) present a series of what they call myths that influence criminal justice policy:

• the myth of crime waves
• the myth of large numbers of child abductions by strangers
• the myth of the drug crisis
• the myth of equal justice
• the myth of the utility of punishment
• the myth of a lenient criminal justice system

Bohm (1996) also discusses myths, such as that

1. crime is a bad social problem,
2. the criminal justice system enforces all laws,
3. crime is primarily violent, and
4. crime is increasing.

He examines the influence of myths on criminal justice policy and explains their function.

1. Myths offer identities (good guy, bad guy).
2. Myths aid comprehension by creating order out of the bombardment of information we receive today.
3. Myths help to form common bonds and reinforce a sense of community.

Space does not allow more comprehensive discussion of these identified myths and the evidence the authors use to declare something as a myth as opposed to an evidence-based conclusion. The important point is that what *we think we know* affects what policies we support. These sources show us that what we think we know is not necessarily accurate. If our beliefs about what should be done with criminals are based on the myth that the system is lenient and/or the myth that crime is increasing, we are operating under faulty assumptions.

How do these myths develop? The media and the government are obvious participants in creating and perpetuating false perceptions, but social science bears a great deal of responsibility as well.

CRIMINAL JUSTICE RESEARCHERS—PARTICIPANTS IN MYTH MAKING?

The argument that social science cannot be truly objective has been discussed in a variety of venues (Roberg, 1981). A social scientist is influenced by his or her value system, ideology, and perception of reality. Which questions to ask may be more important than the answers one finds. Individual perceptions will always somewhat influence the research process; however, if hypothesis construction and methodology are tainted by special interest groups or political agendas, one must question any results that emerge from such research. The "In the News" box, concerning the looting and violence in New Orleans following the hurricane and flood, illustrates how people's beliefs are affected by what they perceive as facts, but what we think we know may not necessarily be true. We tend to accept what we are told

---

IN THE NEWS | LOOTING—FACT OR FICTION?

Many individuals were horrified by video of New Orleans residents looting businesses and residences following Hurricane Katrina. Some video even showed police officers carting away goods. Then certain experts argued that stories of widespread looting were exaggerated. Several experts who were interviewed argued that there was no hard evidence and that it was "victim blaming" to focus on looting when there were only a few isolated cases; they said that widespread looting and violence did not happen in New Orleans. They even argued that the rapes and murders that were said to have happened in the Superdome did not occur.

These positions taken by experts were received with skepticism, but later news stories indicated that it may be the case that the "bodies stacked up" in the Superdome were exaggerations and falsehoods that were then spread by the national news media. Evidently, there was one known homicide at the Convention Center and only one substantiated attempted rape. Of course, some argue that rapes may not all be reported. The true number of incidents may never be known.

Why do you think that stories of the looting and violence after Hurricane Katrina were exaggerated? Did journalists and public policy makers violate their ethics by reporting rumors before they were substantiated? What might have been the effects of such rumors?

Sources: Shea, 2005: H1, H4; B; Thevenot and Russell, 2005: A1, A7.

---

by the media and, especially, social or medical science research, but the veracity of such findings may be questionable.

One study of criminal justice researchers' experiences with ethical dilemmas found that the most common ethical dilemma was perceived pressure to study a certain topic, issue, or question, and/or pressure to influence the findings (Longmire, 1983). Research findings may be less than accurate because of laziness, incompetence, or political pressure. Exposés in the medical research field have called into question what we think we know about things such as heart disease and stem-cell research, and the scientific arguments over global warming and even intelligent design versus evolution show us that even the most esteemed scientists can disagree vehemently on what we think we know. Unethical researchers in criminal justice may also affect what we think we know about crime and criminals.

In addition to outside pressures that influence the selection of a research question or prompt improper influence over, improper use of, or outright falsification of research findings, other dilemmas in research include

1. protection of subject confidentiality;
2. negative effects of the research on the subject (the Milgram experiment and the Zimbardo experiment are the two best-known examples of research that had tremendously negative effects on subjects) and issues of privacy for subjects;
3. deception of subjects in terms of what they will experience or the true focus of the research;
4. obtaining informed voluntary consent;
5. withholding benefits or services to subjects for the purpose of research; and
6. use of research findings—either through misinterpretation or overreaching—to justify otherwise illegal or unethical treatment.

There has been concern over the perceived influence exerted by government officials over scientific findings. The Bush Administration has been accused of attempting to influence or suppress scientific findings concerning global warming and the effects of oil exploration in the Alaska wilderness areas. In criminal justice, concern was raised in 2005 when Lawrence Greenfield, director of the Bureau of Justice Statistics since 2001, was asked to step down when he refused to delete certain findings from a press release on a governmental study of racial profiling. The Bureau of Justice Statistics (BJS) is a little-known division of the U.S. Department of Justice that compiles and distributes statistical reports on victims, offenders, and correctional populations. According to news reports, Greenfield was asked not to include the finding that although blacks were not stopped disproportionately, blacks were more than twice as likely to be searched, and they were more likely to be targets of force. After refusing to delete these references, no press release was issued and the report appeared on the agency's website without notice. He was demoted and moved to another agency (Lichtblau, 2005; Hickman, 2009).

Many also saw an ominous trend when Congress planned to cut the budget of the Bureau of Justice Statistics. Criminal justice researchers use BJS reports almost exclusively when their research requires national statistics. Government officials made the decision to cut the budget in favor of awarding contracts to do statistical analysis to private/public contract vendors (such as private research foundations). Many criminal justice researchers were concerned that such vendors would be influenced by their desire to obtain more contracts and so would not be objective purveyors of facts. Further, because the contract vendors are a less stable source, the possibility of comparing longitudinal data would be compromised. Funding was eventually restored to the agency, and its budget has been fairly stable at about 35 million dollars for the last several years.

The interactions among ideology, knowledge acquisition, and policy formation are complicated. Policies may originate in ideology and then become supported by research, or research may influence a shift in ideology. The danger is that individual decision making may be subverted by myths and that individual ethics may be the victim of misguided ideologies. Ethical obligations require researchers to be eternally vigilant in preventing their research from being co-opted by political or other ideology. Objectivity is the hallmark of science, even if there is no such thing as perfect objectivity. See the Policy Box for a discussion of how social science research sometimes has real effects on the way the criminal justice system operates.

BALANCING LAW AND JUSTICE

The passing of a law by legislators is only the first step in social control. For the law to be effective, it must be enforced by law enforcement, and violators prosecuted and punished. We know that policy making affects the passage of laws, as well as their implementation. We also know that the discretion in each step of the criminal justice system creates a situation in which written laws do not necessarily represent the reality of enforcement. Police departments create prostitution crackdowns, traffic ticket "blizzards," drug sweeps, and pornography raids in more or less cyclical patterns, sometimes in response to political pressure, sometimes not. The enforcement is, for the most part, independent of legislative intent. In

 **DOMESTIC VIOLENCE: ARREST OR NOT?**

The widespread policy of mandatory arrest in domestic violence calls is directly related to the Minneapolis Study, which found that arrest was the only intervention that reduced future violence. The trouble with the policy is that when the research was replicated in several other cities, the findings were different: The mandatory arrests made the situation worse in some circumstances and had no effect in some areas. The replication studies have earned much less press than the original studies, so law enforcement continues to justify the mandatory arrest policy by research findings that are in question.

Law: Although there are obviously laws against assault and domestic violence, as with all laws, there is a great deal of discretion in how and whether to implement such laws in every case.

Policy: The decision to have, in effect, a zero-tolerance policy for domestic violence and to make an arrest in almost all circumstances has resulted in what seems to be an unintended effect—that of more arrests of women for domestic violence. Thus, a policy that was supposed to be put in place to assist victims of domestic violence (perceived to be largely women) has actually created a situation in which they are more likely to be arrested.

Individual ethics: Individual officers who might have ignored domestic violence can no longer do so, but officers who might have tried alternatives to arrest now have an ethical dilemma as to whether to ignore departmental policy or abide by it, even if they believe that arrest is unwarranted.

this sense, police are *de facto* definers of the law because they are the agents of implementation.

If we see laws as an "ought" in societal definitions of misbehavior, enforcement policies must be viewed as the "is" of what is tolerated and what is not. A few old laws are routinely ignored and forgotten, especially in the area of private behavior. One might ask why such laws are not thrown out as irrelevant to the times in which we live. The reason they continue to exist is that no politician is going to champion removal of "ought" laws because it would seem that he or she was in favor of the behavior that the law defines as immoral. Therefore, some states still have laws against private sexual behavior, "blue" laws restricting business activity or the sale of liquor, and so on. Some argue that to have laws that are ignored endangers the credibility of the entire legal system.

Studies generally agree that most corruption and graft come from **gray areas of crimes** such as prostitution, gambling, and drugs. It is easy to explain the emergence of unethical behavior by criminal justice professionals in these areas because such crimes do not have the same moral sentiments behind them as do "serious crimes" such as murder and child molestation. Many police officers who would have no problem letting a prostitute go free will risk their lives to catch a child killer. Part of this discretionary enforcement comes from a personal perception of the immorality of the behavior and also a perception of society's tolerance or intolerance for such behavior.

Individual officers often administer what has been called **street justice.** For instance, when a store owner has a legal right to prosecute a shoplifter but the shoplifter is eighty-seven years old, poor, and shoplifting food so she can eat, the police officer might try to convince the store owner not to prosecute, in an attempt to soften the harshness of the law. Prosecutors may "lose" evidence in a subjective judgment that a criminal defendant doesn't have to be prosecuted. Alternatively, police may stringently enforce the law against those they consider jerks, and prosecutors may ask for continuances to keep a defendant in jail, knowing that the case will ultimately be dismissed. The potential problem with street justice and *de facto* justice is that once law is ignored in favor of the application of subjective justice, individual definitions of what is "fair" and "just" may be arbitrary and capricious.

Spader (1984) discusses discretion and the rule of law as a *golden zigzag* between fundamental values (see Box 6.1, "Spader's Rule of Law Versus Rule of Man"). In this discussion, discretion has positive and negative elements, as does

---

BOX 6.1 °	**SPADER'S RULE OF LAW VERSUS RULE OF MAN**

Rule of Law	Rule of Man
(Positives)	*(Positives)*
equal protection	individualization
evenhandedness	flexibility
due process	mercy
fairness	compassion
rationality	equity
notice	creativity
visibility	adaptability
predictability	informality
centralized limits on power	efficiency
universality	
(Negatives)	*(Negatives)*
inflexibility	disparity
harshness	inconsistency
rigidity	arbitrary and capricious abuse
mandatory legalism	uncertainty
technicalities	invisibility
red tape	uncontrolled provincialism
blind formalism	
inefficiency	

Source: Adapted from Spader, 1984: 379–394.

the Rule of Law. On the Rule of Law side, one sees that when laws are followed objectively, one can expect rational decision making, predictability, and evenhandedness; the laws are applied to everyone regardless of whom the victim or the offender is and regardless of the circumstances. For instance, traffic tickets would be given to everyone who commits traffic violations of any kind. The negative of an absolute Rule of Law is that some circumstances might call for relaxing the application of law (e.g., when the traffic offense was not serious, it was the first offense, and/or there was a good reason for the offense).

Spader's Rule of Man accepts that *discretion* would allow for equitable decision making. Sometimes the offender would deserve the ticket, and sometimes the offender would not. The legal agent on the Rule of Man side has the ability to individualize the decision based on the people involved and the circumstances. Unfortunately, the negative element of this power is that sometimes discretion is used inappropriately, with disparate, arbitrary and capricious decisions.

The ideal is to use discretion wisely in pursuit of ethical goals. Criminal justice professionals can be seen as mediating the harshness and inflexibility of law in the application of street justice. However, the same discretion that allows them to perform benevolent acts allows them to act in arbitrary and oppressive ways as well.

The moral commitment that professionals have toward the laws they are supposed to uphold influences their actions. Soldiers are more loyal when they believe in the morality of the war. Police are more determined when they believe in the laws they are enforcing. Prosecutors and defense attorneys are more committed to due process when they believe in it. Correctional officials are less likely to allow prisoners to corrupt them when they have a strong sense of their goals. And all criminal justice professionals are more likely to operate in an ethical manner when they believe in the validity and justness of the system that employs them.

THE CRIMINAL JUSTICE PROFESSIONAL

For the criminal justice professional who must uphold and enforce the law, this discussion of morality, justice, and law is not just academic. Line officers often face questions of individual morality versus obedience and loyalty to one's superiors or the organization.

The My Lai incident in Vietnam has almost passed out of this nation's consciousness, but at the time, there was great debate over whether soldiers should follow their superiors' orders blindly or make an independent assessment of the morality of the action. In this case, several officers were prosecuted by a military court for killing women and children in a village during the Vietnam war without any evidence that they were a threat to the unit's safety. The officers' defense was that their superiors gave the orders to take the village without regard to whether the inhabitants were civilians or guerrillas. The rationale was that often there wasn't time to establish whether a civilian was friendly or not and that, in any event, civilians often carried grenades and otherwise harmed U.S. troops. There was heated public discussion in support of and against the soldiers' actions.

Movies such as *Platoon* provide dramatic fictional accounts of other actions ordered by officers and the dilemmas of soldiers who knew that such actions were unethical and illegal. Is an individual excused from moral culpability when following

IN THE NEWS | WINTER SOLDIERS: PATRIOTS OR LIARS?

On March 13–16, 2008, several hundred veterans who served in Iraq or Afghanistan met in Silver Spring, Maryland, to record testimony about atrocities and war crimes they observed or heard about during their tour of duty. The event was called the "Winter Soldier hearings"—referring to similar hearings during the Vietnam era about atrocities committed by soldiers in Vietnam. The name "Winter Soldiers" comes from a Thomas Paine poem about "winter soldiers" whose patriotism stands firm in the darkest moments, as opposed to fair-weather soldiers whose patriotism withers away in times of trouble. Ironically, their patriotism is exactly what is at issue in the current discussion, as well as the patriotism of those earlier soldiers in 1971. The most famous of the winter soldiers of the 1970s is John Kerry, and some say that his actions in that earlier testimony and the Swift Boat Veterans' public opposition to his testimony cost him the presidential election.

The winter soldiers' testimony included statements from veterans who recounted shooting at unarmed civilians and other acts that could be described as war crimes. Those who testified described a pervasive culture of the military that denoted *all* Iraqis as the enemy, with the use of derogatory terms such as "sand nigger," "towelhead," and "haji" for all Iraqis.

The most interesting aspect of the Winter Soldier hearings, however, was the almost complete lack of coverage by major media outlets. There were no stories in *The New York Times* or the *Washington Post*, and only a few of the major city newspapers covered the event. It was covered by alternative news sources such as *Democracy Now!* and foreign news sources. In the United States, conservative news organization such as the *National Review* also covered the event, but the tone was critical and writers argued that these veterans, like the earlier veterans, either would not or could not support their accusations with hard evidence.

According to one source, those in the earlier hearings who did supply information to Army and Navy intelligence did not have their stories substantiated. The conclusion drawn by critics is that the earlier soldiers were liars who sought to harm the country's efforts in that war. They also take the position that the current winter soldiers are liars, exaggerators, or erroneously assume that the bad things that happen in wartime are always war crimes.

Conversely, the American Civil Liberties Union released nearly 10,000 pages of court martial summaries and military reports obtained through freedom-of-information demands that indicate a pattern of civilian killings, including killings of detainees in custody. Attorneys with the ACLU allege that there are many more incidents than the public knows in which soldiers broke rules of engagement. So what is the truth? Perhaps, to paraphrase Jack Nicholson's character in the movie *A Few Good Men*, "we can't handle the truth."

Why do you think the Winter Soldiers event was not covered by the major newspapers?

Sources: Owens, 2008; Nicosia, 2008; Fletcher, 2008; Lenz, 2007: A1. A4.

---

orders, or should one disobey orders that one believes to be illegal or immoral? The "In the News" box indicates that the Iraq war has brought new charges and counter-charges of wartime atrocities.

In the Abu Ghraib prison scandal, soldiers argued that they were only following orders when they abused the detainees. Joseph Darby (profiled in the "Walking the Walk" box in Chapter 2) was so distressed by the pictures showing various types of abuse that he turned them in to the Army's CID, and the resulting investigation led to indictments and resignations. Some, however, blamed Darby and held the position that he should not have exposed what the other soldiers had been doing. Some condemned Darby as a traitor to his country, and he and his family received death threats and were not able to return to their hometown to live because of the town's hostility to him.

A soldier's dilemma is not all that different from a police officer's dilemma in that both organizations place a great emphasis on chain of command and loyalty. It is possible that police officers may receive orders that they know to be illegal and/or unethical from their Field Training Officer (FTO) or other supervisor. Does the police officer (or any other criminal justice professional) have the duty to use personal moral judgment, or is obedience to superiors mandatory? In these circumstances one has to depend on the law rather than the chain of command. If the action is clearly illegal, there will be no legitimate defense if the individual officer goes along with the offense; he or she is as guilty as any other officer who engages in the act.

The Nuremberg war trials held individuals personally accountable when they committed war crimes (defined as actions that violated the Geneva Conventions), whether they were or were not following orders. If the action is not against the law but is against policy, departmental sanctions may be applied. If the action is not against the law and not against departmental policy, it is a much grayer area as to which, if any, ethical system would support going against one's superior. The stronger ethical position in this case may be to follow appropriate grievance procedures if something seems to be wrong. The "In the News" box relates the Abu Ghraib case involving Lynndie England, one of the soldiers in Abu Ghraib who argued she was only following orders.

Individuals each face moral choices in the course of their careers. Some of these choices are easy to make, but some of the hardest decisions involve going against

---

IN THE NEWS | LYNNDIE ENGLAND AND ABU GHRAIB

Was Lynndie England a willing participant in the abuses documented at the Abu Ghraib prison in Iraq, or was she a mentally challenged young woman who was under the power of her lover, Charles Graner? It depends on whether you listen to the prosecutor or to the defense attorney in her trial for conspiracy, maltreating detainees, and committing an indecent act. She had pled guilty in May 2005, but the judge refused to accept the plea, holding that it was inconsistent with the evidence because she and her witnesses argued that they did nothing wrong. She then pled not guilty but was convicted of numerous counts of mistreating prisoners and was sentenced to three years in prison.

Source: Toohey, 2005: B1, B3; Cloud, 2005b: A1, A4.

Update

Lynndie England was released in March, 2007 after serving 17 months. She lives in West Virginia with her family and son. The child's father was Charles Graner, the soldier and ex-prison guard who was perceived to be the ringleader of the abuse. He is serving a 10-year prison sentence.

Whose responsibility is it when soldiers mistreat prisoners in a military prison? How far up in the command structure should the culpability lie?

Source: Moore, 2008.

superiors or colleagues. Even if the behavior is obviously illegal, it is difficult to challenge authority. **Whistleblowers** are those who risk their career to expose wrongdoing in their organization. Of course, some may have purely egocentric reasons for exposing wrongdoing, but many whistleblowers do so because their principles and individual ethical system will not allow them to stand quiet when others in the organization are committing unethical and/or illegal acts. Box 6.2 gives some examples of whistleblowers.

For criminal justice practitioners, ethical dilemmas often arise from the exercise of discretion and the use of power. The types of issues that might give rise to ethical dilemmas include

1. the limits of the state's right to control the individual,
2. the ethical use of force, and
3. the appropriate use of discretion.

| BOX 6.2 | BLOWING THE WHISTLE ON WRONGDOING |

Many people risk their careers, their livelihood, and even, in some cases, their safety, by coming forward when they believe their organization and/or superiors are committing unethical or illegal acts. Often, despite whistleblower laws that protect individuals who work in governmental agencies from retaliation, the individual pays a heavy price.

Mathew Zipoli: Zipoli was a police officer at the Lawrence Livermore National Laboratory. He contacted federal officials in 2001 to report safety and security lapses at the nuclear weapons facility. Although a federal investigation confirmed Zipoli's allegations, he was fired by the University of California, which ran the lab. He ultimately received a $175,000 settlement but had to give up his job and agree to a permanent ban on employment there.

Donna Trueblood: Trueblood told state and federal environmental officials that her employer, a waste incineration plant, was not handling toxic chemicals correctly. Although Trueblood received a settlement that was sealed by the court, she also had to agree to a lifetime employment ban there.

Coleen Rowley: Rowley, an FBI agent, wrote a widely publicized memorandum to FBI Head Robert Mueller, describing in detail how the agency had mishandled information concerning alleged terrorist Zacarias Moussaoui. She was named as one of the "Persons of the Year" by *Time* magazine in 2002, retired from the FBI in 2004, and ran an unsuccessful campaign for Congress in 2006.

Babek Pasdar: Pasdar was a computer security analyst who discovered a mysterious "Quantico circuit" in a major telecommunications company that he was hired to review for security problems. The circuit was a transmission conduit for all information that flowed through the company; anyone with access could peek into citizens' phone and e-mail transmissions. He was told to leave the circuit alone, and his urgent advice that it at least should have a log to determine who accessed it resulted in his being pulled from the project.

Richard Conrad: Conrad was a Navy officer who warned the Navy that proper repair procedures were not being followed in the Navy aviation base in San Diego. In return for his persistent reporting to his superiors that the Navy was endangering pilots by not following current procedures, he was isolated, his work duties were drastically curtailed, and he was forced to accept an early retirement. Then, after an Inspector General Report, the Navy awarded Conrad a commendation.

Sources: Whistleblowers Australia, 2007. Also see the Government Accountability Project website: www.whistleblower.org/template/index.cfm.

Although professionals and practitioners may get bogged down with day-to-day problems and bureaucratic agendas may cause them to lose sight of larger goals, foremost in their minds should always be the true scope and meaning of the power inherent in the criminal justice system. It is people who make a *justice* system *just* or *corrupt*.

To protect the citizenry from misuse and abuse of power, personnel in the criminal justice system must have a strong professional identity. There is continuing debate over whether police officers can be described as professionals, and there is even more debate over whether correctional officers can be described as such. These arguments miss a central point: Whether one calls the men and women who wear these uniforms professionals, practitioners, or some other term, they have immense power over other people's lives. This power must be recognized for what it is and held as a sacred trust.

Criminal justice professionals are public servants and, as such, should aspire to a higher standard of behavior. They have a duty to the citizenry they serve, but even more than that, they must possess the moral and ethical sense to prevent the power inherent in their positions from being used for tyranny. Education isn't enough. Learning a body of knowledge and acquiring essential skills do not give individuals the moral sense necessary to use those skills wisely. Witness the recurring scandals involving lawyers and business professionals. A highly educated group is not necessarily free from corruption.

Criminal justice practitioners find themselves faced with a wide spectrum of ethical choices including

1. balancing friendship against institutional integrity—that is, when friends and colleagues engage in inappropriate or illegal behavior or rule breaking;
2. balancing client (offender) needs against bureaucratic efficiency and institutional goals; and
3. balancing personal goals or biases that conflict with fair and impartial treatment of the public and the clients served; the inappropriate use of discretion occurs when the professional uses unethical criteria to resolve decisions.

Most people in the criminal justice field (or, indeed, any profession) have basically good character. However, it can be argued that in some situations even those who have formed habits of honesty, truthfulness, and integrity are sincerely perplexed as to the correct course of behavior. These situations arise because the behavior choice seems so innocuous or trivial (e.g., whether to accept free coffee) or so difficult (e.g., a partner or friend wants you to cover up something she did wrong). In these instances, where basically good people have trouble deciding what to do, the ethical systems might help them analyze their choices.

It must also be accepted that in some dilemmas there are going to be costs involved in making the right decision. For instance, an officer who knows it is his duty to provide evidence against his brother-in-law who is a major drug dealer may lose his wife's and children's love. There is no assurance that "doing the right thing" will not come at a high cost. The ethical person may not necessarily be honored; some have been heavily sanctioned. However, those who do not expose wrongdoing and/or go along with it in an effort not to "rock the boat" often find that their long-term peace of mind pays the price for their silence. One of the most important elements in individuals making the right decisions when faced with ethical dilemmas is how much support the organization provides for doing the right thing. Next we look generally at how organizations, and especially leaders, can contribute to a climate that encourages ethical behavior.

LEADERSHIP, TRAINING, AND THE ETHICAL ORGANIZATION

In any organization there are those who will almost always make ethical choices, those who will usually make unethical ones, and those who can be influenced one way or the other. The best course of action is to identify those in the second group and encourage them to find other employment or at least remove them from temptation. Then organizational leaders must create an atmosphere for the third group that encourages ethical decision making. This can be done by promoting ethical administrators, rewarding morally courageous behavior, and providing clear and powerful organizational policies that emphasize worthwhile goals and honest means.

Howard Gardner's work on multiple intelligences was reviewed in Chapter 5. In more recent work (Gardner, 2007), he discusses the Good Works Foundation, a private foundation that does research and advises businesses on how to achieve excellence through ethical practices and principles. In his work he argues that in order to meet future challenges, companies and organizations will have to recognize responsibilities to the greater community. Workers will need the following five types of cognitive capabilities:

1. the "disciplined mind": the ability to focus and learn a field of study;
2. the "synthesizing mind": the ability to integrate diverse ideas into a coherent whole;
3. the "creating mind": the ability to recognize and solve problems;
4. the "respectful mind": the ability to form and maintain good relationships with other people; and
5. the "ethical mind": the ability to fulfill one's responsibilities as a citizen and to identify with fellow human beings.

Basically, Gardner argues, much like Aristotle, that to be an excellent person or organization, there is an essential element of ethics that must be a part of the beliefs, values, and principles of the organization (or individual's self-definition). For an organization to be excellent and succeed in the future, individuals in the organization must be more than intelligent and educated; they must be ethical.

An ethical organization must have ethical administrators and managers. They are responsible not only for their personal conduct but also for the actions of those they supervise. In other countries and cultures this responsibility seems to be more pronounced than in the United States. For instance, after the onset of the Falkland War, Lord Carrington, the foreign minister in Great Britain, resigned. He did so because the situation happened on "his watch." Even though he did nothing that was personally blameworthy, was not negligent in his duties, and in all respects performed his job competently, he held himself personally responsible because he failed to know of, and, therefore, warn of or prepare for, the threat that Argentina presented.

Contrast this with the attitude of the captain of the *Exxon Valdez*, responsible for the largest oil spill in history, who professed innocence because he wasn't the one on the bridge at the time of the incident; or Daryl Gates, the Los Angeles police chief who, even after the Christopher Commission described a widespread management lapse, insisted that the problem of brutal officers was an individual problem and not one for which he should be held responsible. Military commanders of the Abu Ghraib prison argued that they didn't know about or didn't sanction the abuse that went on in the prison, yet if commanders don't know what is happening, who is supposed to know?

So few seem to be willing to take responsibility for their actions that when someone does say, "I did it, I'm responsible, and I'm sorry," it comes as a refreshing surprise. Recall the response of Scott Waddle, profiled in the "Walking the Walk" box in Chapter 1, commander of the submarine that killed several Japanese citizens. He did not attempt to displace or share the blame for the incident and actually traveled to Japan to seek forgiveness. This response is, unfortunately, all too rare. As the "In the News" box indicates, more often than not executives caught in ethical scandals attempt to divert blame.

What does it mean to be an ethical leader? Obviously, one first has to be sure that one is not personally engaged in unethical and corrupt behaviors. Unfortunately, in many recent examples, leaders cannot pass even this first test. In addition, one has to take responsibility for the larger role responsibilities of a leader position. One of

---

IN THE NEWS | SCANDALS IN PUBLIC AND PRIVATE AGENCIES

Hewlett Packard Spy Scandal: The so-called boardroom spying scandal erupted in 2006, when it was discovered that detectives hired by officials at Hewlett Packard investigated who was leaking confidential information by spying on board members. This included using pretexting—using the target's social security number to convince telephone companies to release the telephone records of the person. The head of H-P, Patricia Dunn, resigned, and she and other top officials, as well as the detectives, faced state and federal charges of identity theft, fraud, and wiretapping. State charges were ultimately dismissed, but federal charges may still be pending.

Chicago's Hired Truck Scandal: State and federal investigations began in 2002 and are ongoing into a corruption scheme in city government. The core of the corrupt activities lies in the hiring practices of city officials who would allocate jobs and contracts to those who would pay kickbacks and/or would campaign for the political figures who approved the position or contract. The resulting investigations concerned how high up the corrupt scheme went, some arguing that even Mayor Richard Daley was involved.

"Top Cop" Indicted: As noted at the beginning of this chapter, Bernard Kerik was New York City's police commissioner in 2000–2001, a close aide to Rudolph Giuliani, and chosen by President George Bush to head the Department of Homeland Security in 2006. Instead of taking that position, he was indicted for charges that could have resulted in a prison sentence of 142 years. The charges concerned omissions of financial dealings with those who had business with the City. Among the charges were Kerik's acceptance of $165,000 in renovations from a company that wanted city contracts, and not reporting a $28,000 loan as required by city law and when he was vetted by White House investigators. In 2006 Kerik pled guilty to two misdemeanors and was ordered to pay $221,000 in fines, but, in return, the state dropped all other charges and Kerik is currently running a security consulting business.

Sources: Associated Press. 2007a Von Bergen, 2006: A1, A13; Hays, 2006.

QUOTE AND QUERY

In its waning months, the 109th Congress ... is a symbol of utter corruption. Over the past two years, the congressional scandals have traversed the universe from the gross to the grandiose to the grotesque: visits from call girls, gifts of Rolls Royces and fancy commodes, sweetheart deals for contractors, high-paying lobbyist jobs for underachieving children, free vacations for members and their families.... If the page scandal captures the raw depravity that is the 109th Congress, the proposed solution captures its raw audacity. Faced with the abuse of children, some lawmakers have called for the removal of the children.

Turley, 2006.

This quote is from an editorial written in response to the scandal of Mark Foley, who had exchanged explicit e-mails with Congressional pages and engaged in sexual relations with at least two of them after they turned 18. The resulting investigation revealed that other members of Congress might have engaged in inappropriate relationships with the pages as well and that those in leadership positions knew about the possibility of wrongdoing much sooner than any official action was taken.

Why should those youth who have a desire to serve as a Congressional page lose that opportunity because a few congressmen couldn't leave them alone? Whose responsibility is it to police its members?

the most distressing aspects of public scandals involving public officials is the discovery that their wrongdoing was often well known to those who should have done something about it, the topic of the "Quote and Query" box.

Standards applied to public administrators can be helpful to this discussion. The American Society for Public Administration (1979) promulgated standards that can be applied to all administrators who aspire to be good leaders. The standards include the following:

1. *Responsibility and accountability*: Measures of quality service delivery should be developed and implemented to enable the administrator to identify strengths and weaknesses.
2. *Commitment*: Leaders should be dedicated and enthusiastic about the role of the organization, as well as have a commitment to the law, codes, regulations, and professional standards of behavior.
3. *Responsiveness*: Leaders should be sensitive to changing circumstances and evolving demands and needs of the public. Good leadership exhibits flexibility in the face of social change.
4. *Knowledge and skills*: Technology is dynamic, and leadership must keep abreast of better ways of accomplishing its mission, as well as possess the understanding to interpret data that are relevant to the mission of the organization. Training—both upon entry and in-service—is a necessity in order to have an effective workforce.
5. *Conflicts of interest*: Since there will always be conflicts, the administrator should be sensitive to them, especially when personal needs conflict with organizational needs.

6. *Professional ethics*: Administrators should practice self-reflection and continually check their decision making against some ethical standard.

Administrators and managers do not necessarily ensure that an organization will be free from corruption merely by not engaging in corrupt practices themselves; they must take affirmative steps to encourage ethical actions. Issues that could be examined in a discussion of ethical leadership include the practice of recruitment, training, discipline and reward structures, and evaluation of performance.

Souryal (1992: 307) offers advice to leaders who would like to advance ethical decision making and emphasizes the importance of organizational support for ethical actions. Ethical leaders should do the following:

1. Create an environment that is conducive to dignified treatment on the job.
2. Increase ethical awareness among the ranks through formal and informal socialization.
3. Avoid deception and manipulation in the way officers are assigned, rewarded, or promoted.
4. Allow for openness and the free flow of unclassified information.
5. Foster a sense of shared values and incorporate such values in the subculture of the agency.
6. Demonstrate an obligation to honesty, fairness, and decency by example.
7. Discuss the issue of corruption publicly, expose corrupt behavior, and reward ethical behavior.

Metz (1990) offers a similar set of advice. He proposes that ethical administrators follow these steps:

1. Establish realistic goals and objectives.
2. Provide ethical leadership (meaning set a moral tone by actions).
3. Establish formal written codes of ethics.
4. Provide a whistleblowing mechanism.
5. Discipline violators of ethical standards.
6. Train all personnel in ethics.

When top leaders take responsibility for their subordinates' behavior, they will lead and administer with greater awareness, interaction, and responsibility. Because of this responsibility, a supervisor or administrator must be concerned with how the workplace treats the worker, how the worker views the mission, and how the public views the organization. Concern for one's public image may be shared by ethical leaders and egoistic bureaucrats, but the first group has a sincere desire to understand the public's complaints and respond to them, and the second group is concerned solely with protecting the image of the organization—a stand that may mean punishing whistleblowers rather than appreciating them for bringing problems out in the open.

A strong ethical leader would have a personal relationship with subordinates—without showing favoritism. This personal relationship is the building block of modeling, identification, and persuasive authority. Strong leadership involves caring and commitment to the organization. A strong leader is someone who is connected with others but also has a larger vision, if you will, of goals and mission.

Delattre (1989b) discusses a realistic idealist—and it's possible that he would also be content with the term an *idealistic realist*. What he is referring to is the capacity for good leaders to understand social realities but to avoid cynicism in the face of such social realities. For instance, in the use of force, a realistic idealist would understand that force is necessary at times but would attempt every alternative means to protect all human life, including the offender's life. Leaders must never lose sight of the organizational mission; for public servants, the mission is public service.

Souryal also describes ethical leaders as those with "a mental state that is characterized by vision, enlightened reasoning, and moral responsibility" (1992: 186). Good leaders must recognize and relay the idea that public service applies to all, not just a favored few. Criminals are also part of the public that the criminal justice system serves. This means that they deserve the same civility, protections, and services as the rest of us unless such is prohibited by law or unless personal safety is threatened. When the protections represented by our Bill of Rights and democratic process become reserved for certain groups, the rights of all are threatened.

TEACHING ETHICS IN CRIMINAL JUSTICE

Many believe that it is much more effective to present moral or ethical questions to new members of a profession before these individuals are faced with "real-life" dilemmas. Of course, what often happens is that once students leave this setting, they are usually told to forget what they've learned. This happens often in police and correctional academies, where cadets are taught "the book," and then learn "the street" when they are paired with an older officer. This also happens when lawyers realize that the high ideals of justice they learned in law school have little to do with the bargaining and bureaucratic law of the courthouse.

People respond to the discrepancies between official and subcultural ethics in a number of ways: They may ignore, participate in, or confront activities of their peers that they think are wrong. It is difficult to ignore actions that run contrary to one's own value system, but often employees establish complicated rationalizations to explain why it is not their business that others around them steal, perform less than adequately, or conduct illicit business during working hours. People often do not believe it is right to confront the immoral behavior of others even when their own behavior is consistent with accepted standards of morality. Individuals are sometimes confronted with the choice of saying nothing and allowing corruption to continue, or expose wrongdoing and risk censure. Individuals in criminal justice agencies have, perhaps, more temptations placed in front of them than the average worker. The "In the News" box shows what can happen when individuals cannot withstand these temptations.

For those who are interested in changing unethical behavior in an organization, the primary target might be new recruits, as those who have been engaging in unethical activities for some time have built up comprehensive rationales for their behavior. On the one hand, socio-moral reasoning opportunities could exist in classroom settings, such as academies. Learning theorists, on the other hand, might say that the most effective way to change the ethics of a profession is to make sure that behavior changes. According to learning theory principles, if one was sure to be punished for accepting bribes, lying, or performing other unethical behaviors, the subcultural supports for such behaviors and the moral apologia for

IN THE NEWS | CORRUPTION AT THE BORDER

One of the inescapable facts of policing the border is that there are border agents who can be bought to look the other way and allow guns, drugs, or illegal aliens across. In 2006 alone more than 600 criminal investigations were opened of U.S. immigration officials accused of corruption-related charges. In 2006, nine officers were arrested or sentenced for charges such as bribery and smuggling. Texas cases include: David Duque (bribery and selling identification documents), Lizandro Martinez (allowing drugs to pass through his inspection lane; money laundering), Fabian Solis (smuggling undocumented migrants for money), Juan Alfredo Alvarez (bribery; drug conspiracy), and Aldo Manuel Erives (allowed drugs and immigrants through checkpoint). Officers who give in to the temptation to accept money in return for looking the other way could earn as much as $60,000 in a single shift—the equivalent of a year's salary.

One of the more troubling aspects of these examples of corruption is that some of the agents, such as Martinez, had more than a dozen misconduct complaints before being arrested and were still allowed to work in the agency. Michael Maxwell, who was the head of internal affairs at the U.S. Citizenship and Immigration Services (USCIS), resigned in frustration and sought whistleblower protection after his complaints to Congress about what he believed to be rampant corruption in the agency went unheeded. The Department of Homeland Security's Office of Inspector General and the Office of Professional Responsibility at Immigration and Customs Enforcement (ICE) investigate corruption complaints. The two agencies have only 309 investigators to follow up on complaints for 72,000 immigration employees.

Why do you think that Michael Maxwell's warning went unheeded by superiors?

Source: Arrillaga, 2006: A13.

---

them would disappear. But only pure behaviorists would conclude that mere monitoring and application of consistent rewards and punishments would result in an ethical work force. Others believe that although monitoring might result in a work force that performs in an ethical manner, in order for ethical behavior to continue without monitoring, and for people to believe in principles of right and wrong, they must internalize an ethical system.

According to Sherman (1982: 17–18), the following elements are necessary for any ethics program relating to criminal justice:

1. Stimulating the "moral imagination" by posing difficult moral dilemmas.
2. Encouraging the recognition of ethical issues and larger questions instead of more immediate issues such as efficiency and goals.
3. Helping to develop analytical skills and the tools of ethical analysis.
4. Eliciting a sense of moral obligation and personal responsibility to show why ethics should be taken seriously.
5. Tolerating and resisting disagreement and ambiguity.
6. Understanding the morality of coercion, which is intrinsic to criminal justice.
7. Integrating technical and moral competence, especially recognizing the difference between what we are capable of doing and what we should do.
8. Becoming familiar with the full range of moral issues in criminology and criminal justice in the study of criminal justice ethics.

Issues that could be discussed in ethics training courses might include the following:

1. The definitions of justice and crime
2. The appropriate use of force
3. The relative importance of due process over efficiency
4. The ethical use of technology to control the populace
5. The variables used to determine responsibility and punishment
6. The right of society to treat (or punish)
7. The limits that should be placed on treatment (or punishment)

A wealth of excellent material has been published over the last several years, so the student or interested reader should be able to find sources that explore the issues above, as well as others. The Suggested Readings at the end of each chapter provide a good beginning for anyone interested in this body of literature.

Avoiding Cynicism and Burnout

Two of the greatest dangers in criminal justice are cynicism and burnout. Cynical leadership, cynical instructors, and overwhelming evidence that we live in an imperfect world create the all-too-common occurrence of workers who are cynical, who are burned out, and who have abandoned the ideals that led them to the profession in the first place. As mentioned before, ethical leaders should be able to transmit a vision and be committed to the mission of the organization, but many administrators and managers exhibit only pessimistic cynicism over the potential for change, the worth of humanity, and the importance of doing what is right.

How does one avoid cynicism and **burnout**? First, adopt realistic goals before entering the profession. A police officer cannot expect to save the world, and a treatment professional should not expect to find success with every client. A more realistic career goal might be a resolution to do one's best and to always follow the law.

The second element in avoiding burnout and cynicism is to find and nurture a network of mentors and colleagues that promote ethical values. Cynical people are contagious, and cynicism breeds rationalizations for committing unethical behavior—from leaving work early or falsifying overtime records to violating the rights of suspects or defendants. In every department that has a corruption scandal, however, there are also those who have managed to avoid participating in such activity.

The third element is to seek self-fulfillment and personal enrichment. This could be by gaining higher education, reading self-help books, attending church, joining interest clubs, participating in charitable activities, volunteering to coach community sport teams, or becoming involved in the PTA. Note that these activities all have the element of communication and interaction with others. Such activities promote connectedness with the community at large and counteract the negativity that pervades the criminal justice field. Unfortunately, criminal justice professionals see humanity at its worst, and there is a great need to see the best of the human spirit as well.

CONCLUSION

Professional ethics is merely an application of moral systems to a particular set of questions or a specific environment. The basis of all professional ethical codes is the same: To be a good professional, one must be a good person. Many of the ethical choices one will make throughout the course of a career are easy: No one has to tell a police officer that bribery is wrong, or correctional officers that hitting a shackled and helpless inmate is wrong. These actions occur because individuals have chosen to take the path of least resistance, pursue personal interests over organizational values, or succumb to emotions such as fear and anger.

For those choices that are truly difficult, people of good will, using rationality and sensitivity, can apply any ethical system and come up with an ethical solution. It may not be one that everyone will agree upon, but it will allow the individual to make the decision public and will allow the person to be satisfied that his or her choice is based on ethics rather than egoism.

The first five chapters in this text addressed issues including morality, ethics, justice, and law in the abstract. This chapter focused on criminal justice professionals and how these concepts can be applied to them. Issues faced by the criminal justice professional involve a broad array of ethical questions, and it is important to recognize them for what they are. Further, what people do is sometimes influenced by what they think they know, so criminal justice researchers must also monitor their practices and be careful to avoid letting bias and political or financial pressure influence their research.

Law and policy are set by politicians and administrators, and they must make sure that they are objective in their evaluation of research and information that is used to help them make decisions. Informal policies are always the discretion of the line staff. How staff members perform their job determines whether justice is a reality or an illusion. The greatest protection against corruption of power is a belief in and commitment to the democratic process and all it entails. If one desires a career in criminal justice, one must ask these questions:

Do I believe in the Constitution?
Do I believe in the Bill of Rights?
Do I truly believe in the sanctity and natural right of due process?

If the individual views these as impediments, nuisances, or irrelevant, that person should not be a public servant. In the chapters to follow, we examine in greater detail the issues that criminal justice professionals face.

Key Terms

burnout *175*	ideology *155*	street justice *163*	wholesight *158*
gray areas of crimes *162*	policies *154*	whistleblowers *167*	

Review Questions

1. Distinguish between the ideologies of conservatism and liberalism in areas such as rights of the accused and corrections.
2. Why is the liberal perspective not associated with due process?
3. How do social scientists contribute to the mythology of crime and criminal justice?
4. Explain Spader's rule of law versus rule of man.
5. What are some of the issues that criminal justice professionals face?
6. What are some standards that can be applied to good leadership?
7. What advice do Souryal and Metz offer to those who desire to be good leaders?

8. What necessary elements did Sherman identify for teaching ethics in criminal justice?

9. How does one avoid cynicism and burnout?

Writing/Discussion Questions

1. Write an essay on (or discuss) a governmental policy (it can be drugs, poverty, illegal immigration, or any other) and the facts or evidence used to support such a policy. Present examples of conservative and liberal views on the policy. How does each group use facts or evidence to support its position? Try to uncover specifics that either are in dispute or are used in a biased manner to bolster a position.

2. Write an essay on (or discuss) how "crime myths" have supported crime policies. Provide examples.

3. Write an essay on (or discuss) how the media constructs reality. Use one news story to show how different media outlets (e.g., the liberal MSNBC and the conservative FOX news shows) present the same story.

4. Write an essay on (or discuss) your own principles for creating an ethical organization.

Ethical Dilemmas

Situation 1

You are a prosecutor trying your first case. You are thrilled with how well it is going. Every objection you make is upheld, and every objection the defense makes is overruled. The judge shakes her head affirmatively every time you make a point and scowls and makes disparaging comments about and to the defense attorney. As the trial proceeds, you begin to see that it is going so well not because of your legal expertise but, rather, because the judge is obviously and seriously biased against the defense. You do not know if she simply does not like the defense attorney or she does this in all the trials, but you do know that she is making it extremely difficult for the jury to ignore her and, thus, is violating the due process rights of the accused. Should you be grateful for your good luck and accept an easy conviction or make a stand against the judge's actions?

Situation 2

You are a police officer assigned to the juvenile division. For the most part you enjoy your job and believe that you have sometimes even made a difference when the juvenile has listened to you and stayed out of trouble (at least as far as you knew). One day you are told repeatedly by your captain to pick up a juvenile, even though you don't think there is any probable cause to do so. This is the third time you have been ordered to pick him up and bring him into the station. You discover that the detectives are trying to get the juvenile to become an informant because he is related to a suspected drug dealer. Should you participate in the attempt to intimidate him or refuse to do so?

Situation 3

You are an undercover officer involved in a drug sting at a local high school. You are told by your drug task force supervisor to get the evidence "at any cost" even if you have to use drugs or sex to gain the trust of dealers. You are told that if you don't bring in a conviction on this case, the task force will be disbanded, and you believe that it has been effective in helping to get drugs off the street. You are at a party with the suspects and everyone uses drugs and then offers some to you. What should you do?

Situation 4

As a member of the mayor's task force on juvenile crime, you have the opportunity to set crime policy for the next decade. What principles, programs, or objectives would you emphasize and advocate for in the coming discussions?

Situation 5

Your partner has been on the force twenty-five years, and you value her opinion greatly. However, you have noticed that she has become progressively more lethargic and unenthusiastic about the job. When dispatch asks for available cars, she won't let you respond. When you see accidents on the highway, she instructs you to go around the block so that you won't have to stop. Even when you receive calls, she tells you to advise dispatch that you are otherwise occupied. You believe that she has just gotten burned out and isn't performing up to the standard that you know she is capable of. What, if anything, would you do about it?

Suggested Readings

Albanese, J. 2006. *Professional Ethics in Criminal Justice: Being Ethical When No One is Looking*. Boston: Allyn & Bacon.

Braswell, M., McCarthy, B., and McCarthy, B. 2007. *Justice, Crime and Ethics*. Cincinnati, OH: Anderson Publishing Company.

Gardner, H., Csikszentmihalyi, M., and Damon, W. 2002. *Good Work: When Excellence and Ethics Meet*. New York: Basic Books.

Kappeler, V., Blumberg, M., and Potter, G. 2005. *The Mythology of Crime and Justice*. Prospect Heights, IL: Waveland.

Lersch, K. (Ed.). 2002a. *Policing and Misconduct*. Upper Saddle River, NJ: Prentice-Hall.

Souryal, S. 1992/2004. *Ethics in Criminal Justice: In Search of the Truth*. Cincinnati, OH: Anderson Publishing Company.

Walker, S. 2005. *Sense and Nonsense About Crime and Drugs: A Policy Guide*. Belmont, CA: Wadsworth.

THE POLICE ROLE IN SOCIETY: CRIME FIGHTER OR PUBLIC SERVANT?

CHAPTER 7

© Mario Tama/Getty Images

New police officers are socialized to the informal norms and value systems of the profession. The informal "subculture" of policing may be breaking down today, but police officers continue to value loyalty to other officers.

CHAPTER OBJECTIVES

1. Understand the role of law enforcement in a democracy, including the use of authority, power, force, and persuasion.

2. Become familiar with the differences between the formal ethics of law enforcement and the values of the police subculture.

3. Understand the extent of discretion and its creation of opportunities for unethical decision making.

4. Become familiar with the issue of racial profiling, why it is an ethical issue, and the methodological problems presented when attempting to establish its prevalence.

Even though the incident happened two decades ago, the video of the Rodney King beating is indelibly imprinted on the psyche of the American public. In this one violent encounter, many of the elements discussed in this chapter are reflected.

1. The "signification" of some citizens as criminal and deserving of the harshest application of police power
2. The P.O.P.O. ("pissing off a police officer") doctrine that describes how affronts to police authority (in the King case, refusing to stop) often end in unethical uses of force
3. The quick resort to violence in a department that encouraged aggressive "crime control"
4. The subcultural and organizational support and/or tolerance for such violence (evidenced by the computer messages that joked about it afterward)
5. The initial easy acceptance of police and media definitions that justified such violence against some types of citizens (specifically, early reports indicating that Rodney King was a criminal and drug user, with the implication that he deserved what happened to him)
6. The presence of societal divisions based on race and socioeconomic circumstance that shaped the perception of the justice system

Arguably, the Simi Valley jury acquitted the officers because white, middle-class citizens must (and do) see their police force as good; therefore, they couldn't believe that the "good guys" could be bad. The verdict for the plaintiff in the Los Angeles County civil trial was also predictable because juries in inner cities are less apt to believe police and more apt to believe that police can and do mistreat citizens.

The O. J. Simpson trial in 1994 was as much a trial of police credibility as it was the guilt or innocence of the defendant. It indicated in a dramatic way what happens when doubt replaces trust in police performance, and when police testimony is received with suspicion rather than trust.

The credibility of L.A.P.D. officers was under attack again after the Ramparts Division scandal, in which an anti-gang squad evidently "ran amok" until one of its members confessed and implicated all the others. The highly publicized findings that some officers manufactured evidence, planted guns on suspects, and lied on the witness stand inflicted a grievous harm to the credibility of all L.A.P.D. officers.

Other cities are not exempt. The Amadou Diallo case in New York City was moved to Albany, arguably so the police officer defendants who shot an unarmed Diallo in 1999 could obtain a fair trial. They were acquitted, and many minorities perceived the acquittal as part of a consistent pattern of oppression and brutality by police officers, who, more often than not, are not punished. Officers who are prosecuted for inappropriate use of force do seem to often receive the benefit of the doubt by juries and civilian review boards, even when their department has fired them. For instance, in 1996, several off-duty Indianapolis police officers were evidently intoxicated after a sports game and were prosecuted for public intoxication and threat with a firearm. Despite a great deal of publicity and witnesses, the trial ended in a hung jury (Chermak, McGarrell, and Gruenewald, 2006). Another example of officers being acquitted is offered in the "Walking the Walk" box in Chapter 9, which describes the "Oakland Riders."

Every few years a major city seems to undergo a scandal involving an individual or a group of police officers whose misconduct tarnishes the department. Many more local stories never enter the national newscasts. The Internet and the ubiquitous video recorder have created a situation in which members of the public who might never have encounters with police can see for themselves problematic incidents of police conduct. One has only to Google "police misconduct" or "police brutality" or use the search terms in Youtube.com to see dozens of videos where the use of Tasers, batons, restraints, and other forms of force raise legal and ethical questions. Two further examples appear in the "In the News" feature.

IN THE NEWS | POLICE POWER ABUSED?

Hope Steffey: Steffey is an Ohio woman who was injured in a fight, and when police responded to a 911 call, she ended up allegedly being slammed to the ground by the responding officer and then stripped naked by several sheriff's deputies and left for six hours in a cell. The video of her being stripped by officers was seen by millions after it was obtained by her lawyer, as part of the civil suit against the officials responsible and shared with major news outlets. See Video at http://www.wkyc.com/news/news_article.aspx?storyid=82866.

S.A.P.D officers sued: San Antonio police officers were being sued in federal court over an alleged body-cavity search conducted on an African American man (on a city street) who was detained on suspicion of selling marijuana. Following this incident in 2007, about a dozen men and women claimed that they were strip-searched by officers in a bar. The latter incident led to the suspension of four officers. S.A.P.D was embarrassed further by several officers who allegedly paid an 18-year-old woman for sex while they were on duty and in their patrol cars.

While some people would see these uses of force as abuses of power, others see them as legitimate responses to suspects. Which position is supported by utilitarianism? Ethical formalism?

Source: McDonald, 2007.

Some of these videos provide excellent tools to understand the extremely difficult decisions police are faced with when confronted with drunk, unruly, uncooperative, and/or physically combative individuals. The comments posted to such videos also illustrate clearly the two extreme camps of opinions. Some believe that police power should have no restraints and that those who defy police or commit a crime, no matter how small, somehow deserve whatever happens to them. The opposing camp believes that police officers are all fascist instruments of state power who look for ways to abuse and oppress citizens. Obviously, the use of police power and the role of police in society cannot be understood by such simplistic paradigms.

CRIME FIGHTER OR PUBLIC SERVANT?

As we discuss issues of law enforcement ethics, we must keep in mind that the majority of officers are honest and ethical and spend their careers simply trying to do a good job. These men and women usually do not appear in newspapers or on the evening news, but they pay the price for the few who do, through decreased public confidence and even public scorn. In Chapter 8, we explore a variety of ways in which individual officers abuse their position. In Chapter 9, after looking at corruption as a means to the end of crime control, we look at what some believe to be the institutionalized tolerance of corruption in some departments. What are the perceptions, world views, and values that shape and influence such tolerance for fellow officers' misconduct? Even more troubling is when officers who do expose wrongdoing are isolated and ridiculed or receive even worse forms of peer sanctions. Why do some police—who supposedly are the law's agents—ignore and subvert the law when fellow officers are involved?

Harsh scrutiny is often directed at police actions, and officers think they are treated unfairly by the public and the media. However, there is an important reason for such scrutiny: The police represent the "thin blue line" between disorder and order, between the "war of all against all" and lawful order. No other criminal justice professional comes under as much constant and public scrutiny—but no other criminal justice professional wields as much discretion in so many situations. The scrutiny is understandable when one realizes that the police are power personified. They have the choice to arrest or not to arrest, to mediate or to charge, and in decisions to use deadly force, they even hold the power of life and death. The "Quote and Query" box points out the awesome power of police. Authority, force, and discretion are elements inherent in the role of a law enforcement officer.

QUOTE AND QUERY

The police officer, in one split second, without the benefit of law school or judicial roles or legal appeals, acting as judge, jury and executioner may accomplish the same final result [as the death penalty].

Murphy and Moran, 1981: 91.

Can you think of any other professional who holds the power of life and death?

CRIME CONTROL

We will approach law enforcement with an underlying premise that what drives individual decisions on the part of law enforcement officers and society's reactions to them are derived from a perception of their mission. If one views police as *crime control agents*, these presumptions follow:

1. Criminals are the "enemy," and fundamentally different from "good" people.
2. Police are the "army" that fights the enemy, using any means necessary to control, capture, and punish them.
3. "Good" people accept and understand that police are in a "war" and must be allowed deference in their decision making because they—not us—are the experts and only they "know the enemy."

If one views police as **public servants**, other presumptions follow:

1. Criminals are not a distinct group; they shop, pay taxes, have kids and parents, and often are one's next-door neighbor.
2. Police have limited ability to affect crime rates one way or the other because crime is a complex social phenomenon, and the history of law enforcement originates in order maintenance, not crime control.
3. Police as "public servants" serve *all* people, including criminals and, therefore, should not make quick judgments about an individual's worthiness to receive their services.

Police perception of their role as crime fighters will lead to certain decisions in their use of force, their definition of duty, their use of deception and coercion, and other areas. Public perception of the police role as crime fighters leads to a willingness to accept certain definitions and justifications of behavior: that drug addicts are crazed, that individuals beaten must have deserved it, that all defendants must be guilty, and so on.

Typically, those who have a crime control outlook show public outrage only when police accidentally violate the rights of the "good" guys instead of the "bad" guys: when a white person is the target of police brutality, when the victim of deadly force turns out to be a middle-class insurance agent, or when the evening news shows police officers hitting someone who doesn't look like a criminal. In these cases the easy rationalization that people get what they deserve comes into question.

Alternatively, a perception of the police role as public servant implies a much more restrictive view of the use of force and police power. The utilitarian "end (of crime control) justifies the means" decision-making approach is rejected in favor of an approach that is more protective of due process and equal protection. This would be a rights-based conception of social control. Law enforcement, above all, protects the rights of every citizen and—only in this way—escapes the taint of its historical role as a tool of oppression for the powerful.

This discussion is obviously based on Herbert Packer's (1968) model of law enforcement. He described a crime control orientation as operating under the following principles:

1. Repression of criminal conduct is the most important function.
2. Failure of law enforcement means the breakdown of order.

3. Criminal process is the positive guarantor of social freedom.
4. Efficiency is a top priority.
5. Emphasis is on speed and finality.
6. A conveyor belt is the model for the system.
7. There is a presumption of guilt.

The due-process model, in contrast, operates on these principles:

1. There is a possibility of error.
2. Finality is not a priority.
3. There is insistence on prevention and elimination of mistakes.
4. Efficiency is rejected if it involves shortcuts.
5. Protection of process is as important as protection of innocents.
6. The coercive power of the state is always subject to abuse.

The addition to Packer's original model that is proposed here is that, besides the emphasis on rights in the second model, law enforcement is perceived as "owned" by all people, so the public-servant role is foremost and police must respond to all constituencies, including groups that may be less supportive than white middle-class communities. These two models are better understood if we take a brief look at the history of law enforcement in the United States.

Kappeler, Sluder, and Alpert (1984/1994) have discussed the early origins of law enforcement as a model of service. Police were involved in social service activities: They ran soup kitchens, provided lodging for indigents, and spurred moral reform movements against cigarettes and alcohol. Of course, early law enforcement personnel were also involved in social control and employed utilitarian violence—that is, they acted as the force for power holders in society and were union busters and political-machine enforcers. Such force was frequently used against immigrants and the poor (Alpert and Dunham, 2004).

Early police departments also were marred by frequent graft and other forms of corruption. Crank (2003), for instance, discusses how police were involved in local political machines. They stuffed ballot boxes and coerced votes. Their graft was widely tolerated because of their meager salaries. In the 1950s, the Kefauver Committee revealed that police in cities such as Philadelphia and New York City overlooked prostitution, gambling, and other forms of vice in exchange for $3,000 to $4,000 a month per precinct (Fogelson, 1977: 172).

The move toward police "professionalism," starting in the 1920s, was spurred by several factors, one of which was to improve the image of police as *objective* enforcers of the law rather than enforcers for whomever happened to be in power. In effect, there was a real or perceived shift of police loyalty from political bosses to the law itself (Kappeler et al., 1994: 49; Fogelson, 1977). Part of this transformation involved the idea that police were crime fighters—professional soldiers in the war on crime—a concept that implies objectivity, professional expertise, and specialized training. This role deemphasized the social service role and ultimately led to policing characterized by detachment from the community being policed instead of integration in that community. In this new role, police were proactive rather than simply reactive to public demands (Payne, 2002; Crank and Caldero, 2000/2005).

Even though the professional crime fighter role of the police officer has been well established for more than sixty years, we can see the legacy of both the early political enforcer role and the public service role. The political enforcer role is present when law enforcement is involved in responding to strikes, labor disputes, or public protests. Today, law enforcement is not engaged in strike busting; however, some might argue that the role still involves using power against those who oppose the status quo.

For instance, in December 1999, massive protests against the World Trade Organization set off riots in Seattle. Police were both praised for their restraint and criticized for excessive violence in their use of rubber bullets, tear gas, and concussion grenades to disperse large groups of protesters and bystanders. In 2004, New York City police were widely criticized for mass arrests of those who wanted to protest in front of the Republican National Convention. Although 1,800 were arrested and held in makeshift detention facilities until the convention was over, 90 percent of the arrests led to dismissals. Critics argue that police utilized their power not for the enforcement of the law but, rather, to restrain the freedom to exercise political beliefs (Dwyer, 2005).

In May 2007, L.A.P.D. used rubber bullets and batons against what was described as a peaceful demonstration in support of illegal immigrants in MacArthur Park. Although the police resort to force was prompted by the actions of the demonstrators, Chief Bratton ended up sanctioning the commanders in charge that day, indicating that the police use of force was inappropriate and against policy, if not illegal (Steptoe 2007).

COMMUNITY POLICING

The other historical role of police is that of public service. It is represented most clearly by community policing. The early role of social service is resurrected in the **community policing** movement, which involves having officers develop closer relationships with community leaders to help them solve some of the social problems that are believed to be associated with the development of disorder and lead to crime. Police officers may be involved in cleaning up parks, getting the city to raze abandoned houses, cleaning up graffiti, helping to start youth programs, having community meetings to listen to what citizens think are the problems of the community, and so on. The elements of community policing include the following (National Institute of Justice, 1992: 3):

1. A move away from a position of anonymity to direct engagement with the community, which will give officers more information about neighborhood problems.
2. Freeing the officer from emergency response to engage in proactive crime prevention.
3. More visible operations that increase police accountability.
4. Decentralized operations that lead to greater familiarity with specific neighborhoods.
5. Encouraging officers to see citizens as partners.

6. Moving decision making and discretion downward to patrol officers who know the neighborhood best.
7. Encouraging citizens to take more initiative in preventing and solving crimes.

Patrol officers' resistance to community policing models may make sense if one views neighborhood policing as trading in the "crime fighter" role for a much less esteemed "social worker" role. However, even those who resisted the community policing model admitted that the role of law enforcement has always included community relations and community service—what some have called "order maintenance."

Schafer (2002) describes the history and philosophy of community policing with a focus on its potential for corruption, although he notes the absence of evidence to indicate that community policing efforts are associated with more police corruption than traditional service delivery. Schafer (2002: 200) identifies the following elements in community policing efforts:

1. A different philosophy and structure of policing
2. A problem-oriented approach to policing
3. Working with the community
4. Developing trust with the community
5. Creativity and innovation
6. A broader focus than just crime control
7. A geographic focus on one neighborhood or community

Schafer (2002) then presents some potential issues for community policing strategies as they relate to corruption. Gratuities may be more of an issue for officers who are expected to create and maintain close ties to the community. Gratuities then may create the slippery-slope slide into more serious forms of misconduct. Officers may be exposed to wider corruption among city employees, such as building inspectors, and, by such exposure, have a harder time withstanding minor transgressions themselves.

In addition to those issues, close relationships with the community blur the lines between good and bad people, and the police officer's discretion regarding when to enforce the law is compromised by personal relationships. Finally, increased freedom and autonomy and decreased supervision provide more opportunities for misconduct.

Schafer (2002) also notes that because community policing seems to lessen cynicism and burnout and reduces the anonymity of individual police officers, it may act as an insulator against misconduct. Further, because officers share a closer relationship with community members, the possibility of brutality may be decreased. However, there are no data to indicate that this is the case.

While some aspects of the community policing approach have been institutionalized, observers note that 9/11 has led to a retrenchment in policing and a return to more traditional crime-fighting elements (Murray, 2005, Brown, 2007). Murray (2005) argues, for instance, that traditional policing relies on a central command structure with rigid lines of authority, discourages initiative, rewards an authoritarian style of leadership, enforces a punitive and rule-based discipline for police officers, and is distanced from the community it serves. This style of policing is directly at odds with community policing and has regained some traction since 2001.

Because one might argue that aspects of the police culture never fully fit with the community policing approach, it is not hard to understand why the threat of terrorism might have derailed the success and acceptance of community policing. Problem-solving policing and zero tolerance for community disorder seem to have remained as current elements of law enforcement management; however, community–police partnerships and police as troubleshooters for purely social problems may be a trend that has come and gone.

It is important to understand that both the crime fighter role and the public servant role have the potential and capacity for wrongdoing. The professional crime fighter may trample rights in the interest of efficiency in catching criminals, and community police officers may be too eager to do the bidding of community members in controlling those who upset the "order" of the community (by over-enforcement of noise ordinances or loitering laws). The point cannot be overemphasized that police officers have powers unlike any other group. Now we will examine police power more carefully.

AUTHORITY AND POWER

Klockars (1984) describes police control as consisting of the following elements: authority, power, persuasion, and force.

1. **Authority** is the unquestionable entitlement to be obeyed that comes from fulfilling a specific role. Neither persuasion nor force is needed to achieve domination when one possesses authority. Police officers are usually obeyed simply when they tell a citizen to do something. We do what they tell us because of their uniform. A teacher has a type of authority in the classroom, and parents have authority over their own children (but not over other people's children).

2. **Power** is similar to authority in that it is inherent in the role and the individual merely draws upon it, but it is different from authority in that power implies that there might be resistance to overcome. It also implies that if there is resistance, it will be crushed. Power is the means to achieve domination. The baton, the handcuffs, and the power of arrest symbolize police power.

3. **Persuasion** may also be used in response to resistance but seeks to overcome it "by mobilizing signs, symbols, words, and arguments that induce in the mind of the person persuaded the belief that he or she ought to comply" (Klockars, 1984: 530). Although those who have power don't have to use persuasion, they often do, to avoid the use of force.

4. **Force** is different from the previous three means of control in that it is physical, whereas the other three are exercised through mental domination and control. When force is used, "the will of the person coerced is irrelevant" (Klockars, 1984: 532). Police show their ability to use force when they use their arrest power, or when they physically restrain and subdue an individual. Force is ultimately behind every position of authority.

Police exercise these four different types of domination, from unquestioned authority to physical force. Why does law enforcement have the right to employ these types of control? "We give it to them" is the easy answer. Police power is a governmental right invested in federal, state, and local law enforcement agencies.

It means that these organizations, unlike almost any other except perhaps the military, have the right to control citizens' movements to the point of using physical and even deadly force to do so.

Cohen and Feldberg (1991) developed a careful analysis of, and justification for, police power and proposed that it stems from the **social contract**. As discussed in Chapter 5, Thomas Hobbes (1588–1679) and John Locke (1632–1704) created the concept of the social contract to explain why people have given up liberties in civilized societies. According to this theory, each citizen gives up complete liberty in return for societal protection against others. Complete freedom is given up in return for guaranteed protection. Police power is part of this *quid pro quo*: We give the police these powers in order to protect us, but we also recognize that their power can be used against us.

This general idea has corollary principles. First, each of us should be able to feel protected. If not, we are not gaining anything from the social contract and may decide to renegotiate the contract by regaining some of the liberties given up. For instance, vigilante movements arise when the populace thinks that formal agents of social control do not protect them, and isolationist groups "opt out" of most traditional societal controls because they believe that they can create a better society.

Second, because the deprivations of freedoms are limited to those necessary to ensure protection against others, police power should be circumscribed to the minimal necessary to meet the goals of protection. If police exceed this threshold, the public rightly objects.

Third, police ethics are inextricably linked to their purpose. If the social contract is the basis of their power, it is also the basis of their ethics. Cohen and Feldberg (1991) propose five ethical standards that can be derived from the social contract:

1. fair access
2. public trust
3. safety and security
4. teamwork
5. objectivity

Delattre (1989b) approaches police authority and power from a slightly different point of view. He asserts that police, as public servants, need those qualities that one desires in any public servant. He quotes James Madison, who stated that essential to any public servant are these characteristics:

- wisdom
- good character
- balanced perception
- integrity

Only if the person entrusted with public power has these qualities can we be assured that there will be no abuse of such authority and power: "Granting authority without expecting public servants to live up to it would be unfair to everyone they are expected to serve" (Delattre, 1989b: 79). In this proposition the right to authority lies in the character of the person. If one has those virtues necessary to be a public servant, one has the right to use the authority invested in the role; if one does not have those virtues, one should not be in that position to begin with.

Is it simply a matter of individual character, or can the organization train officers to use their authority and power ethically and wisely? How can the organization maximize the possibility of ethical action and minimize any abuses in the exercise of the four types of control? Formal codes of ethics for police agencies attempt to provide such guidance.

FORMAL ETHICS FOR POLICE OFFICERS

A value system or a code of ethics to educate and guide the behavior of those who work within an organization is common, and some organizations have both. An organizational value system identifies the mission and the important objectives of the organization. Just as individual values influence one's ethics, an organizational value system influences the ethics of the organization's members. For example, if a person's highest value is wealth, integrity may be sacrificed to achieve it. In a similar way, if the value system of an organization promotes profits over all else, customer satisfaction and quality may be sacrificed. A police department with a value system emphasizing crime control may allocate resources differently than one with a value system promoting community-oriented policing. Officers in these two departments may be rewarded differently, and the formal culture of the agency will encourage different behavior patterns.

A code of ethics is more specific to the behavior of the individual officer. A professional code of ethics addresses the unique issues and discretionary practices of that profession. Davis (1991) explains that there are three distinct kinds of codes:

1. an aspiration or ideal describing the perfect professional
2. principles or guidelines that relate to the value system of the organization
3. mandatory rules of conduct that can serve as the basis of discipline.

THE LAW ENFORCEMENT CODE OF ETHICS

The code of ethics promulgated by the International Association of Chiefs of Police (IACP) is the first kind of code in that it describes a "perfect" officer. The IACP promulgated the Law Enforcement Code of Ethics and the Canons of Police Ethics (see the inside covers), and many departments have used these or adapted them to their own situations. More recently, the IACP has endorsed the Oath of Honor (displayed in the "Quote and Query" box). This Oath, developed by a committee of the IACP, is offered as a shortened version encapsulating the contents of the Code of Ethics.

Even though codes of ethics have been widely adopted, there is some question as to their relevance to individual police officers (Felkenes, 1984; Johnson and Copus, 1981: 59–65). One argument is that the original IACP Code of Ethics specifies such perfect behavior that it is irrelevant to the realities of most officers. The wide disparity between the code and actual behavior is detrimental to the validity and credibility of the code. For instance, Davis, referring to the code provision,

"I will never act officiously or permit personal feelings, prejudices, animosities or friendships to influence my decisions," writes that "any officer who takes this mandatory language seriously will quickly learn that he cannot do what the code seems to require. He will then either have to quit the force or consign its mandates to Code Heaven" (Davis, 1991: 18). Others argue that the code is vague, confusing, and impractical (Felkenes, 1984: 212).

The opposing argument is that the code is valuable specifically because it provides an ideal for officers to aspire to. The code is a goal to work toward, not a descriptive average of existing behavior. It would be hard to be proud of a professional code that would instruct an officer

- to be unbiased and objective *unless* there were extenuating personal reasons
- to be courageous *unless* personal danger were involved
- to be honest in thought and deed *unless* to do so went against personal interest.

Because the code describes the highest standard of policing, all officers can improve because no officer is perfect. However, Davis (1991) contends that an **aspirational code** cannot be used to judge or discipline behavior that falls short of it. This comment is no doubt true; departmental policies and rulebooks, which are more objective and enforceable, better serve discipline systems. A code is far more valuable as a motivator than as a discipline device, a symbol rather than a stick. The more recent Oath is offered as a short, direct statement of what law enforcement should aspire to. It should (according to the creators) be printed on the back of service cards that police carry, framed and on the wall, and recited at every academy graduation.

The International Chiefs of Police code or other codes of ethics for law enforcement have at least four major themes:

1. The principle of justice or *fairness* is the single most dominant theme in the law enforcement code. Police officers must uphold the law regardless of the offender's identity. They must not single out special groups for different

treatment. Police officers must not use their authority and power to take advantage, either for personal profit or professional goals. They must avoid gratuities because these give the appearance of special treatment.

2. A second theme is that of *service*. Police officers exist to serve the community, and their role appropriately and essentially concerns this idea. Public service involves checking on the elderly, helping victims, and, in the community service model, taking a broad approach to service by helping the community deal with problems such as broken street lights and dilapidated buildings.

3. Still another theme is the *importance of the law*. Police are protectors of the Constitution and must not go beyond it or substitute rules of their own. Because the law is so important, police not only must be concerned with lawbreakers, but also their own behavior must be totally within the bounds set for them by the law. In investigation, capture, and collection of evidence, their conduct must conform to the dictates of law.

4. The final theme is one of *personal conduct*. Police, at all times, must uphold a standard of behavior consistent with their public position. This involves a higher standard of behavior in their professional and personal lives than that expected from the general public. "Conduct unbecoming" is one of the most often cited discipline infractions and can include everything from committing a crime to having an affair or being drunk in public. (Bossard, 1981: 31)

Interestingly, the emphasis on service, justice for all groups, and higher standards for police behavior is consistent with the *public servant paradigm* more so than the *crime fighter paradigm*. This may be why the code is perceived as vague and confusing, for the code promotes a public servant ideal, but police are, for the most part, socialized and rewarded for actions consistent with the crime fighter role.

Why are professional ethics important to law enforcement? First of all, ethics contribute to the image of law enforcement as a profession. Sykes (1989) writes that a profession includes the following:

- a body of specialized, internationally recognized knowledge
- a pre-professional education and continuing education
- legal autonomy to exercise discretionary judgment
- lateral movement
- authorized self-regulation.

According to some authors, because law enforcement is missing certain of these elements, it cannot be defined as a profession.

Whether or not officers have "legal autonomy to exercise discretionary judgment" is perhaps the most important debate in this discussion. One argument is that officers have much less discretion to make decisions than is thought because they must abide by the law. Others point out that officers are allowed the latitude to decide whether to write tickets and whether to handle neighbor disputes with formal arrest or informal threat. Sykes (1989) argues that because law enforcement is an example of a classic bureaucratic organization, with rules, supervisors, and many lines of authority, these reduce discretion, so the elements necessary to meet a definition of a profession are missing. An alternative argument is that the nature of law enforcement involves problem solving: Every situation is unique and must be handled differently, and "cookbook" approaches to law enforcement rarely work. These characteristics support the concept of the field as a profession.

One might also suspect that the discussion holds more interest for academics than for officers on the street. Whatever one calls the job, it requires a certain set of skills and some amount of discretion. Officers make decisions regarding the calls they respond to in very different ways. Ideally, a set of ethics will help the officer make these decisions in a lawful, humane, and fair manner.

A code of ethics also helps engender self-respect in individual officers; pride comes from knowing that one has conducted oneself in a proper and appropriate manner. Further, a code of ethics contributes to mutual respect among police officers and helps in the development of an *esprit de corps* and common goals. Agreement on methods, means, and aims is important to these feelings. As with any profession, an agreed-upon code of ethics is a unifying element. A code can help define law enforcement as a profession, for it indicates a willingness to uphold certain standards of behavior and promotes the goal of public service, an essential element of any profession.

THE POLICE SUBCULTURE

Research on police culture, which began as early as the 1970s, described an occupational culture that was at odds with the formal ethics and values of the police organization. Some early research indicated that police officers were significantly different from others in their values and characteristics. For instance, some research has found police officers to be generally cynical, isolated, alienated, defensive, distrustful, dogmatic, and authoritarian, and as having a poor self-image (Johnson and Copus, 1981: 52). While not all research replicates these findings, cynicism and authoritarianism are two traits that seem to characterize police officers, although it is not clear whether individuals are changed by the environment, or those with such traits are attracted to policing.

Scheingold (1984) described the factors that lead to the extreme nature of the police subculture:

- Police typically form a homogenous social group.
- They have a uniquely stressful work environment.
- They participate in a basically closed social system.

Historically, police in the United States have come from the white middle and lower classes; they have been similar racially, culturally, and economically. Because of these similarities, police consider themselves to be more similar to one another than to the public they encounter as a part of their job. Homogeneous social groups lead to **group think**, the tendency for everyone to agree with the group values or beliefs, arguably because those who don't will be ostracized.

Police are further set apart by their work life. The job of a police officer entails a great deal of stress caused by danger and unpleasant experiences. This results in the perception that police are special and different from everyone else. Police also have unusual working hours and experience some degree of social stigma; thus, their social life tends to be largely involved with other police officers. This leads to closed viewpoints and legitimization of subcultural values (Scheingold, 1984: 97–100).

THEMES AND VALUE SYSTEMS

Van Maanen (1978) discussed how police operate with stereotypes of the people with whom they come into contact. The individual who does not recognize police authority is "the asshole." Other names for this type of person include: creep, animal, mope, rough, jerk-off, clown, wise-guy. The idea is the same—that some individuals are troublemakers, not necessarily because they have broken the law but, rather, because they do not recognize police authority (1978: 227). Others have identified the same concept in terms such as: bad guy, punk, idiot, knucklehead, terrorist, predator (Herbert, 1996). Herbert further points out the problem whereby officers are so quick to identify these types of individuals as threats to safety that they may overgeneralize and identify, for instance, everyone living in a neighborhood in the same way.

Van Maanen (1978: 226) observed that "certain classes in society—for example, the young, the black, the militant, the homosexual—are … 'fixed' by the police as a sort of permanent asshole grouping." He argued that the professionalism movement of law enforcement might widen the distance between the police and the community they served, and further allow them to be "moral entrepreneurs" who were even more likely to define some groups as "bad" simply because they did not conform to some preconceived standards of behavior (1978: 236).

Sherman (1982: 10–19) also has described some common themes running through police attitudes and values of the police culture. First, loyalty to colleagues is essential; second, the public, or most of it, is the enemy (echoing, to some extent, van Maanen's research). Further, Sherman explained that police use their discretion in a way that takes into account who the victim and offender are (attitude, class, and race impact decisions of how to enforce the law). Disrespect for the authority of police (P.O.P.O.,"pissing off a police officer") is especially important in how police choose to deal with situations. Further, Sherman argued that police officers believe in the use of force for those who deserve it. The "Quote and Query" box illustrates this

QUOTE AND QUERY

Some guys need a beating. In the street or the back of the precinct, there's a guy who needs a beating. And you got to do it. If you don't do it, the next situation that a cop runs into this character, it's going to be bad. It's hard for people to understand or believe that. But the fact of the matter is, if this guy runs into a cop, gets into a fistfight and really beats the shit out of him, he believes he can beat up all cops, if you arrest him without working him out. He's got to know that the next time he does this, he's going to get his ass kicked in. So I have no problem with that. Neither did any cop I've ever known have any problem with that. As long as you don't do it in public, as long as the guy really needs it, and as long as you don't carry it too far....

M. Baker, 1985: 286.

What part of the formal code justifies this principle? Which element of the "informal code" justifies it? Do you believe that "some guys need a beating?"

Source: Reprinted with permission of Simon & Schuster from *Cops: Their Lives in Their Own Words* by Mark Baker. Copyright © 1985 by Mark Baker.

concept. Other elements described by Sherman include disparagement of due process as a barrier to doing the job and the value of deception and lying, even on the witness stand, if it means getting a bad guy. Finally, Sherman described a priority of "real" policing (crime control) over "garbage calls" (social service) (Sherman, 1982: 10–19).

Scheingold (1984: 100–104) has emphasized three dominant characteristics of the police subculture:

1. *Cynicism.* Police view all citizens with suspicion. Everyone represents a possible problem, but especially those who fit a type, specifically, van Maanen's "asshole." Recruits learn this way of looking at others from older officers. **Cynicism** spills over to their relations with everyone, for they have found that friends expect favors and special treatment, and police routinely witness negative behavior from almost all citizens. Their work life leads them to the conclusion that all people are weak, corrupt, and/or dangerous.

2. *Use of force.* The police subculture embraces force for all situations wherein a threat is perceived. Threats may be interpreted as threats against the officer's authority rather than the physical person, so anyone with an "attitude problem" is thought to deserve a lesson in humility. Force is both expressive and instrumental. It is a clear symbol of the police officer's authority and legitimate dominance in any interaction with the public, and it is also believed to be the most effective method of control. It cuts across all social and economic barriers and is the most effective tool for keeping people in line and getting them to do what is required without argument.

3. *Police as victims.* This refers to the perception that police are victims of public misunderstanding and scorn, of low wages and vindictive administrators. This feeling of victimization sets police apart from others and rationalizes a different set of rules for them.

In a more recent discussion of the police culture, Herbert (1996) discusses six "normative orders" of policing:

1. law
2. bureaucratic control
3. adventure/machismo
4. safety
5. competence
6. morality

The last concept, morality, is related to the idea that police draw on moral definitions to justify their actions. Herbert's observational study allowed him to draw on field experiences to present examples whereby officers would continually be told and express the view that they were the "good guys" against the "evil out there."

Crank (1998) discussed a number of "themes" of policing. These themes are not values *per se* but, rather, elements of police work and/or shared perceptions of police officers:

- coercive territorial control
- force
- illicit coercion
- importance of guns

- suspicion
- danger
- uncertainty
- "maintaining the edge"
- solidarity
- masculinity
- excitement and crime

Crank argued that police learn how to be criminals from expertise gained through policing.

Zhao, He, and Lovrich (1998) examined police officers' values compared to those of the general population. They described a value as an "enduring belief that a specific mode of conduct or end-state of existence is personally or socially preferable" (1998: 23) and reported that individuals' values (specifically, freedom and equality) have been shown to affect their political preferences. They found that police exhibited similar value preferences across time (comparing 1961 to 1997) and across place (comparing Tacoma, Washington, to Spokane, Washington). In their study they found that police rated equality significantly lower than did the general public and, in general, were more conservative than the general public in their viewpoint. Crank and Caldero (2000/2005) also have discussed the values of police, reporting on other research showing that police officers place less emphasis on independence and more emphasis on obedience.

THE COP CODE

Part of any culture is socialization in what is appropriate behavior. In a subculture, approved behaviors may be contrary to formal codes of conduct. Many authors present versions of the informal "code of conduct" that new officers are taught through informal socialization. Muir (1977: 191) described some elements of the informal police code:

You cover your men: don't let any officer take a job alone.

Keep a cool head.

Don't backdoor it (a prohibition against certain gratuities).

Reuss-Ianni (1983: 14) presented an inclusive list:

Watch out for your partner first and then the rest of the guys working that tour.

Don't give up another cop.

Show balls.

Be aggressive when you have to, but don't be too eager.

Don't get involved in anything in another guy's sector.

Hold up your end of the work.

If you get caught off base, don't implicate anybody else.

Make sure the other guys know if another cop is dangerous or 'crazy.'

Don't trust a new guy until you have checked him out.

Don't tell anybody else more than they have to know.

Don't talk too much or too little.

Don't leave work for the next tour.

The informal code also specified conduct indicating that management was not to be trusted. Those code rules that are specific toward management included these (Reuss-Ianni, 1983: 14):

Protect your ass.

Don't make waves.

Don't give them too much activity.

Keep out of the way of any boss from outside your precinct.

Don't look for favors just for yourself.

Don't take on the patrol sergeant by yourself

Know your bosses.

Don't do the bosses' work for them.

Don't trust bosses to look out for your interest

A DIFFERENT CULTURE?

What is obvious is that the police culture in its values and informal code of behavior, as described above, is different from the formal principles as espoused by management. Some principles of the informal code directly contradict the formal Code of Ethics as presented by the International Chiefs of Police.

Scheingold (1984: 97) described the police subculture as no more than an extreme of the dominant U.S. culture and argued that it closely resembles a conservative political perspective. In other words, we all agree with certain elements of the police value system and, if the general public is less extreme in its views, it is only because we have not had a steady diet of dealing with crime and criminal behavior as have the police. Furthermore, citizens are not too upset when the civil rights of "criminal types" are violated, only when police misbehavior is directed at "good" people.

The subculture and the values described above may be breaking down in police departments today. Several factors contribute to the possible weakening of the subculture:

1. *Increasing diversity* of police recruits has eliminated the social homogeneity of the work force. Many diverse groups are now represented in police departments, including African Americans, Hispanics, women, and the college-educated. These different groups bring elements of their own cultural backgrounds and value systems into the police environment.

2. *Police unions*, with their increasing power, formalize relationships between the line staff and the administration. Subcultural methods for coping with

perceived administrative unfairness are giving way to more formal rather than informal means of balancing different objectives of management and line staff.

3. *Civil litigation* has increased the risk of covering for another officer. Although police officers may lie to Internal Affairs or even on a witness stand to save a fellow officer from sanctions, they may be less likely to do so when large monetary damages may be leveled against them because of negligence and perjury.

One might add that many of the authors who described the police culture did so in the 1970s and 1980s, when the Supreme Court recognized due process protections that were groundbreaking. Older police who didn't have to give Miranda warnings or obtain search warrants were understandably slow to be socialized to the new order. Today's recruit officers were born after the Miranda warning was institutionalized as a standard arrest element and have never known a time when police did not need a search warrant. Today's recruit is also more likely to have been exposed to community policing and its tenets of community–police partnership and other progressive police practices through television, education, or other means.

It is also no doubt the case that the subculture of police varies from department to department. Size, regional differences, and management may influence the strength of the subculture.

In a more recent but incomplete measurement of police subculture, Paoline, Myers, and Worden (2000) found that the police subculture is by no means monolithic. Using responses from officers in a survey research project, they were able to measure seven outlooks that they believe were associated with the informal subculture described in the literature:

1. orientation to law enforcement
2. orientation to order maintenance
3. orientation to community policing
4. aggressiveness
5. selectivity
6. distrust of citizens
7. perceptions of citizen cooperation

They found substantial variation among the officers and differences in their cultural views. Further, no factors emerged as strong predictors of officers' values. There were weak and inconsistent associations between sex and cultural values. There were some expected associations between race and cultural values, with minority officers having more positive orientations than white officers toward order maintenance and community policing concepts; however, the associations were not strong. The association between aggressive patrol and race was stronger, with minority officers displaying less support than white officers for aggressive patrol. In general, most of the associations were of small magnitude. The authors conclude, on the one hand, that the police culture may be less uniform and less powerful than other researchers have portrayed. They admit, on the other hand, that their measures did not directly or comprehensively measure the aspects of the police culture as described.

Research continues to support the idea that there is a police culture, albeit one that is more fragmented and weaker than in earlier decades (Murray, 2005; Conti, 2006). Academy training of recruits, for instance, is reported to pay formal attention to community policing and public service elements, but the informal message of instructors and the academy experience tends to promote the "warrior" role that can lead to ends-based policing (Conti and Nolan, 2005; Quinn, 2005). The support for force—the premise that everyone is in van Maanen's typology an "asshole" until proven otherwise—and some of the other values may have given way, but one value that seems to continue is loyalty to other officers, even those officers who don't deserve it.

In a survey sponsored by the National Institute of Justice, police respondents indicated that support for the use of force was still modestly present (about a quarter agreed or strongly agreed that sometimes illegal force was acceptable), but a much larger percentage (67 percent) agreed that someone who reported another officer's misconduct would be ostracized and 50 percent disagreed that police officers would always report serious criminal violations of other officers (Weisburd and Greenspan, 2000: 2, 5).

Thus, it is probably still safe to say that the police, like any occupational group, maintains some type of informal subterranean value system that guides and provides a rationale for decision making. This value system may be more influential than the police rulebook or code of ethics.

DISCRETION, DUTY, AND DISCRIMINATION

Discretion can be defined as having the authority to choose between two or more courses of behavior. Law enforcement professionals have a great deal of discretion regarding when to enforce a law, how to enforce it, how to handle disputes, when to use force, and so on. Every day is filled with decisions—some minor, some major.

Duty can be defined as the responsibilities that are attached to a specific role. In the case of police officers, myriad duties are attached to their role; however, there is a great deal of individual variation in how officers perceive their duty. Discretion allows officers to choose different courses of action, depending on how they perceive their duty.

Discrimination occurs when discretion allows a decision maker to treat a group or individual different from others for no justifiable reason.

DISCRETION

Discretion is by no means limited to law enforcement. In subsequent chapters we will see that discretion is an important element in the role of other criminal justice practitioners and plays a part in the creation of ethical dilemmas for them as well. Discretion in criminal justice has been attacked as contributing to injustice. McAnany (1981) chronicles disillusionment with discretion, citing works such as Davis's *Discretionary Justice* (1973) and the American Friends Service Committee's *Struggle for Justice* (1971). An argument might be made that solutions that attempt to establish guidelines for discretion are unsatisfactory because the suggested rules and standards either limit decision making to mechanistic applications of given rules or provide only rhetorical ideals with little or no enforcement capability. Cohen (1983; 1985) described discretion as balancing justice for the individual against justice for the group and pointed out that full enforcement would be unfair to individuals at times. Even courts have seemed to support police discretion over full enforcement (Williams, 1984: 26). The goal is for criminal justice professionals to use their discretion ethically.

Discretion is a necessary element in law enforcement, but the need for discretion also leads to greater dependence on individual ethical codes in place of rules and laws. Patrol officers are the most visible members of the police force and have a duty to patrol, monitor, and intervene in matters of crime, conflict, accident, and welfare. Investigators are concerned primarily with collecting evidence to be used in court. The ethical decisions that these two groups encounter are sometimes different. Patrol officers may have to make decisions relevant to defining crime and initiating the formal legal process. Undercover officers must make decisions regarding informants, deception, and target selection. Managers and administrators have discretion in their decision-making role over their subordinates (Bossard, 1981: 25; Cohen, 1985). We should also note that because most police departments in the United States are small, many officers fulfill two or more functions, so their discretion crosses the boundaries designated above.

Patrol officers possess a great deal of discretion in defining criminal behavior and deciding what to do about it. When police stop people for minor traffic violations, they can write tickets or give warnings. When they pick up teenagers for drinking or other delinquent acts, they can bring in the teens for formal processing or take them home. After stopping a fight on the street, they can arrest both parties or allow the combatants to work out their problems. In many day-to-day decisions, police hold a great deal of decision-making power over people's lives because of their power to decide when to enforce the law.

One early study found that police do not make arrests in 43 percent of all felony cases and 52 percent of all misdemeanor cases (Williams, 1984: 4). The amount of discretion and how it is used depend on the style of policing that is characteristic of a certain area. Wilson (1976) described the styles as follows.

1. The *legalistic* style of policing is described as the least amenable to discretionary enforcement.
2. The *watchman* style describes police who define situations as threatening or serious depending on the groups or individuals involved, and act accordingly.
3. The *caretaker* style treats citizens differently, depending on their relative power and position in society.

Brown (1981: 224) described four types of police officers, each with a different application of discretion:

1. *Old-style crime fighters* are concerned only with action that might be considered crime control.
2. *Clean-beat officers* seek to control all behavior in their jurisdiction.
3. *Service-style officers* emphasize public order and peace officer tasks.
4. *Professional-style officers* are the epitome of bureaucratic, by-the-book policing.

Muir (1977: 145) described these four types:

1. The *professional*, who balances coercion with compassion.
2. The *reciprocating officer*, who allows citizens to solve problems and may engage in deals to keep the peace.
3. The *enforcer*, who uses coercion exclusively.
4. The *avoider*, who either cannot handle the power he or she must use or fears it and so avoids situations where he or she may be challenged.

Each of these descriptions is obviously more detailed than our binary description of the crime control versus public servant model. However, all of these descriptions illustrate that different beliefs about their mission and their role in society will affect officers' decisions. The nature of policing necessarily involves some discretion. However, this opens the door for unethical decisions. The power to make a decision regarding arrest creates the power to make that decision using unethical criteria, such as not arresting someone in return for a bribe (Brown, 1981: 160).

The Commission on Accreditation for Law Enforcement Agencies (CALEA) promulgates standards, one of which states that law enforcement agencies should have "[a] written directive [that] defines the authority, guidelines, and circumstances where sworn personnel may exercise alternatives to arrest..." (Commission on Accreditation for Law Enforcement Agencies, 1994). Besides standard directives, perhaps another effective way to encourage using discretion in an ethical manner is to delineate ethical versus unethical criteria for decision making. For example, the decision to ticket a motorist stopped for speeding or to let the driver go with a warning can be made using ethical criteria, which might include the number of miles over the speed limit, the amount of danger posed by the speeding (school zone or open road?), the excuse used (emergency or late to work?), and probably others. Unethical criteria might include sexual attraction (or not), the identity of the motorist (fellow police officer, political figure, entertainment figure), the race of the motorist, the offer of a bribe, and so on.

Other factors are less clear: Is the fact of a quota an ethical or an unethical criterion? What about attitude? Many officers explain that a person might get a ticket, even for a minor violation, if the driver displays a hostile or unrepentant attitude. Is this merely an egoistic use of power on the part of an officer or a utilitarian use of the ticket as a tool for social learning? After all, if the individual does not display any remorse, there is no assurance that the person won't commit the same violation as soon as the officer is out of sight.

Above the Law?   Many officers defend the use of professional courtesy to other officers stopped for speeding. Justifications for different treatment are diverse and creative. For instance, some honest justifications are purely egoistic: "If I do it for him, he will do it for me one day." Other justifications are under the guise of utilitarianism: "It's best for all of us not to get tickets, and the public isn't hurt because we're trained to drive faster." There is even a website called CopsWritingCops.com where officers can post their complaints about particular officers or departments when they or their family members are given a ticket. In other websites where police officers post comments, the issue of professional courtesy (for officers and their family members) is a hot-button topic that generates strong emotions on both sides.

If the officer would let another person go with a warning in the same situation, it is not an unethical use of discretion. However, if *every other person* would have received a ticket but the officer did not issue one *only because* the motorist was a fellow officer, that is a violation of the code of ethics ("enforce the law ... without fear or favor"). It is a violation of deontological universalism as well as utilitarianism: Under deontological ethics, it is the officer's duty to enforce the law against everyone, including officers. Under utilitarianism, the fact that the speeding officer can cause an accident means that the utility for society is greater if the ticket is issued, for it might make the officer slow down and, by doing that, accidents can be avoided.

Recall that not giving an officer a ticket when a citizen motorist would not have received a ticket either is not an unethical use of discretion. It is an unfair use of discretion when the speed or driving conditions would have warranted a ticket to anyone else, but professional courtesy forestalled issuing a ticket because the motorist was another officer. In the "Quote and Query" box, an officer, upset over receiving a ticket in another state, illustrates how entrenched the practice is in the culture of policing. Officers, such as the one quoted here, who seem to think of this so-called professional courtesy as a job "perk" similar to medical professionals who receive free medical care from colleagues or cooks and restaurant workers who receive free dinners from other restaurants, simply do not understand the ideals of public service, nor do they fully understand their extremely important role in the administration of law and justice.

One troubling aspect of professional courtesy for traffic offenses is that the practice has a tendency to bleed over into other forms of misconduct. Officers who are stopped for driving while intoxicated are sometimes driven home rather than arrested, but this application of discretion is highly unlikely to be afforded to any other citizen. In some cases of domestic violence, victims of police officer-husbands or boyfriends describe how the responding officers do nothing or take their complaints more lightly than they would if the alleged perpetrator were not a police officer.

The idea that officers are "above the law" is insidious. Officers who believe that they should not have to follow the same laws they enforce against others may

QUOTE AND QUERY

I .... am presently in my 44th year of law enforcement as a narcotics detective. I have never in all those years issued a citation to another police officer or member of there [sic] family. When conducting training classes at the ... Police academy, between 1964–1985 we trained officers in the proper way to treat our brothers in law enforcement.

Excerpt from posted entry on www:CopsWritingCops, 2008.

What is the likelihood that in all those years of not writing tickets to officers, every single case was a situation where a citizen-motorist would also not have received the ticket? Why do you think officers are upset when they get a speeding ticket? (Note: Since April 2008, when this quote was excerpted, the website has evidently been closed to non-registered readers.)

be more prone to other forms of abuse of authority as well. It should also be noted that many officers think that they are held to a higher standard of behavior than the public. Officers point out that a domestic violence, DUI, or any other arrest may cost them their job, which may not be the case for others. The argument against this position is that one who is tasked with enforcing the law should not engage in unlawful behavior.

Discretion and Dilemmas Discretion also comes into play when the officer is faced with situations that have no good solutions. Many officers agonize over family disturbance calls where there are allegations of abuse, or when one family member wants the police to remove another family member. Other calls involve elderly persons who want police to do something about the "hoodlums" in the neighborhood, homeless people with young children who are turned away from full shelters, and victims of crime who are left without sufficient resources with which to survive. These types of "messy" social service calls are probably much more common than the exciting crime control calls that characterize cop shows on television. In all cases, there are no good solutions to the misery and problems of the citizenry. In response to each of these calls, officers must decide what course of action to take and can decide to do nothing at all. We revisit this issue under the concept of duty, discussed next.

Most ethical dilemmas that police officers face derive from their powers of discretion. These ethical dilemmas are part and parcel of the job. Muir describes moral dilemmas of the police officer as frequent and unavoidable, not academic, always unpopular with some groups, usually resolved quickly, dealt with alone, and involving complex criteria (Muir, 1977: 211).

DUTY

How would one characterize the duties of a police officer? Is enforcing the law the only duty an officer has? It has been clearly established that most of police work has been *order maintenance*. Police are called into situations that do not involve crime control and are often termed "social-work calls." Many police officers do not believe that these are legitimate calls for their time and either give them superficial attention or do not respond at all. Brown calls the skill that police develop in avoiding these calls *engineering* (Brown, 1981: 142).

Police may respond to a domestic dispute and find a wife who is not seriously injured, but is bruised, upset, and without money or resources to help herself or her children. The officer may ascertain that departmental policy or law does not dictate any action and that the woman is afraid to press charges, so the officer can leave with a clear conscience that official duties have been completed. However, the officer could take the woman to a shelter or otherwise help her get out of a bad situation. What is the ethical choice? It is difficult to determine the extent of the officer's responsibility in cases where there is no offender to arrest or law to enforce.

Law enforcement's response to domestic violence calls historically has been noninterference, with the perception that domestic violence was not a crime control matter unless it involved injury amounting to felony assault, so women who were battered received different treatment depending on whether their batterer was their intimate partner or a stranger and whether the crime was determined to be a felony or a misdemeanor. This situation is personified most dramatically by *Thurman v. City of Torrington*, 595 F. Supp. 1521 (D. Conn. 1984), which involved a woman who was beaten, stomped, and stabbed by her ex-husband on the front steps of her mother's house while a police officer sat in a car and watched.

Obviously, few cases are as dramatic as *Thurman*. Also, there are many other complicating factors in domestic violence, so how to intervene is not always a simple matter. Nevertheless, it must be recognized that part of the problem was a perception on the part of police that domestic violence was somehow different from stranger violence, and deserving of less intervention. A crime control approach supports such discrimination; a public service model probably would not.

Mandatory arrest policies were supposed to protect victims of domestic violence by forcing police to take action by arresting the perpetrator. However, what seems to have happened is a greater likelihood that both victim and offender will be arrested when there is any evidence that both received injuries, no matter how minor. Police officers may simply refuse to sort out what happened. Thus, a crime control response (mandatory arrest policies) may have resulted in worse consequences for the victims it was supposed to help.

The formal Code of Ethics gives no clear guidelines on how much consideration police should give to a citizen in distress. The caretaker style of policing found in small cities and suburbs, where police departments are community oriented, emphasizes service and encourages police assistance to victims or citizens who need it. However, Matthews and Marshall (1981) discuss the lack of departmental support for any action beyond the minimal obligations of duty. Officers who become personally involved or commit the resources of the department beyond the necessary requirements are sometimes not rewarded, and are viewed as troublemakers. Structural support for this ethical action does not exist. Officers who attempt to do what they believe is right are often on their own, risking formal or informal censure.

Referring again to our two paradigms of police as crime fighters or public servants, it is apparent that the deemphasis on service and, indeed, sanctions for performing some service functions are attributable to the police and public view of police as crime fighters first and foremost. The approach of neighborhood or community policing changes these parameters considerably and renews the historical emphasis on peacekeeping and community integration functions, yet community policing never caught the imagination of a majority of officers, even while enjoying support and promotion from national organizations such as the Department of Justice. Today, because federal support has been, for the most part, withdrawn, we suspect that this model will continue to decline in popularity.

In situations involving questions of duty, three questions are:

1. What must police do under the law?
2. What does departmental policy dictate?
3. What do individual ethics dictate?

An altruistic, involved style of interaction in which the police officer would be compelled to help the victims in any way possible is supported by the ethics of care, the ethics of virtue, utilitarianism, religious ethics, and ethical formalism. But a more self-protective standard, in which the actions mandated would be only those necessary to maintain a self-image consistent with the police role as crime fighter, might also be justified using utilitarianism or ethical formalism.

If police were to become personally involved in every case and go out of their way to help all victims, they would exhaust their emotional reserves in a short time. As a matter of psychological survival, police must develop an emotional barrier between themselves and the victims they encounter. It is virtually impossible to observe suffering on a consistent basis if one does not protect oneself in such a way. Unfortunately, the result is often perceived as callousness, and because of the extreme personal resources needed to remain sensitive to individual pain, emotional deadening may result in unethical behavior toward individual victims.

Duty and Dilemmas   When asked to share ethical dilemmas, police officers often raise the concept of duty. Officers are faced with the choice of responding to certain situations or not, leading to tempting opportunities to ignore duty. In many less serious calls for service, the officer's duty is to serve the pubic, but shirking that duty does not seem to be an egregious lapse of ethics. These mundane, some might say trivial, decisions are faced by all officers, and their repeated decisions in such situations form the fabric of their moral character.

Officers must decide how much to get involved in any particular incident. Their legal duty is usually to take a report, and many officers think that taking a report is also the extent of their moral duty, even when the victim or citizen is in need. Some officers do not consider "social work" their problem, but other officers do. These instances show clear differences between role conceptions of crime fighter or public servant.

Another issue of duty is raised by the nature of police work and how easy it is for officers to abuse their freedoms. Officers may report that they are on a call when in reality they are doing nothing or are performing personal tasks such as shopping or standing in line at the post office. Some officers have been known to attend college classes during duty hours while informing the dispatcher that they are out on a call. Officers may turn in overtime slips for surveillance when they actually were at home. They may misrepresent the times they started and finished the day. Finally, the way in which court appearances can be used to increase one's monthly salary is part of the socialization of every rookie.

That these actions are wrong is not in question, and it is also true that they are not qualitatively different from the minor and not-so-minor egoistic actions of those in other occupations and professions: Office workers leave early or call in sick to go to a ball game. Salespeople call in to say that they are out making sales calls when they actually are heading home for a quiet afternoon nap. Businesspeople declare imaginary expenses on travel vouchers. Police officers, like all employees, rationalize these behaviors in a variety of ways, such as by pointing out their low pay or that they sometimes do "police work" when off duty. The general acceptance of such behavior leads to an environment where each individual sets personal limits on the extent to which he or she will deviate from formal ethics. Even those who stop at minor transgressions must cover their actions by lying, which adds another layer of deception.

IN THE NEWS | FOLLOWING ORDERS

A New York City police officer refused a direct order to arrest a homeless man who was found sleeping in a private garage. The officer disagreed with the zero-tolerance policy that has been enforced against the homeless, involving sealing off all the places where they might find shelter and arresting those who are left on the street. The officer was suspended for thirty days, and his career doesn't look promising. Raymond Kelley, the police commissioner, had this to say about the officer's decision: "You have to be able to follow the directions of a supervisor. Being a police officer is not for everybody. And perhaps this officer feels he's not suited for the job."

An Austin, Texas, police rookie (Ramon Perez) filed a civil lawsuit against the department when he was fired for not following his Field Training Officer's orders to use his Taser on a non-compliant citizen. The man was suspected of domestic abuse, and he kept walking after Perez ordered him to stop. His FTO pushed the man and then struggled with him, ordering Perez to use his Taser. Perez argued that the man's age and apparent health condition, as well as his lack of serious resistance, indicated that there was no need for the Taser, and the two officers were able to handcuff him and put him in the police car without any greater use of force. However, Perez was transferred to the night shift and then ordered to report to the police psychologist. The psychologist's report indicated that Perez was unfit for duty because his moral and religious beliefs impaired his ability to follow orders. He was fired; hence, the civil suit. Ironically, Perez was awarded a humanitarian award by his fellow cadets when he graduated from the police academy, for his "compassion, integrity, and leadership."

Do you think these officers should have obeyed the orders they disagreed with? Do you believe they should have been punished?

Source: J. Getlin, 2002: A8; Smith, 2006.

An additional issue to consider is how an officer should resolve the dilemma when his or her own values conflict with a direct order. We have previously discussed the concept of civil disobedience—the act of resisting an immoral law. Do police have a duty to enforce laws or orders they do not agree with, or do they have a larger duty to perform in a way that is consistent with their own moral code? The "In the News" box illustrates two situations in which an officer took a moral stand and paid a price.

How officers use their discretion, whether that be to file a report or not, to answer a call or not, to stop and investigate or not, to avoid a traffic accident or not, is just as relevant to an evaluation of ethics as racial profiling (discussed later in this chapter), or the decision to accept a gratuity or report the use of excessive force—issues that will be dealt with in Chapter 8.

DISCRIMINATION

When individuals have discretion, individual prejudices and perceptions of groups such as women, minorities, and homosexuals can influence their decision making. Officers' views of the world affect the way they do their job. If this view includes prejudicial attitudes toward groups, it may be that action is affected and those groups may not receive the same protections as "good" citizens. The point is not that police officers are more prejudiced than the rest of us; it is that their special position creates the possibility that their prejudices could cause a citizen to receive less protection from the law than other citizens would. Essentially, when police act on personal prejudices while performing their jobs, they discriminate either in the allocation of services or enforcement of the law. Discrimination often takes the form of either enforcing the law differentially or withholding the protections and benefits of the law (Kappeler, Sluder, and Alpert, 1994: 175).

As has been discussed before, officers form viewpoints regarding certain groups of people, and these viewpoints affect officers' behaviors and decision making. The "assholes" in Van Maanen's typology, by whatever name, comprise one group that may be the target of discrimination because police may behave differently once a citizen is labeled as such. Other groups that may be treated differently are gays and the poor, and obviously there is the longstanding, pervasive—some may say endemic—issue of discrimination toward minorities, especially African Americans.

Sexual Orientation   Kappeler, Sluder, and Alpert (1994: 176–184) discuss the case of Konerak Sinthasomphone—one of Jeffrey Dahmer's victims—as an example of police bias and discriminatory treatment of homosexuals and racial minorities. Sinthasomphone was the Laotian boy who was found wandering the streets, incoherent, naked, and bleeding from the rectum. He had escaped from Dahmer's apartment after he had been drugged, tortured, and sexually abused. Two African American women called the police. When the police arrived, the women tried to tell them that Sinthasomphone was an injured boy and that Dahmer was the one who hurt him. Despite the women's attempts, police officers on the scene helped Dahmer take Sinthasomphone back to his apartment and waved away emergency medical technicians who were starting to examine him. If they had examined him, they would have discovered the holes that Dahmer had already drilled into his skull and the acid that he had poured into the holes. Dismissing the incident as a "homosexual thing," the officers left Sinthasomphone with Dahmer, who strangled him shortly after they left.

This case is not about a simple mistake in judgment on the part of police officers. Their conduct represents a pattern of enforcement that allots police protection based on membership in certain categorical groups. If the Laotian boy had been white, if he had been a she, if Dahmer had been a minority member instead of a Caucasian, if the two women who requested assistance had not been African American, we might have seen a different response. Even more telling was that even though the police chief suspended the officers involved, they were supported by the police union and were ultimately reinstated with back pay. No further sanctions were taken against them. See Box 7.1, "Dimensions of Police Discrimination," for other examples of how discrimination can occur in law enforcement.

Race   There is a pervasive sense among minority groups in the United States that law enforcement is fundamentally racist (Cole, 1999; Walker, Spohn, and DeLone, 2000). Some argue that this perception is based in reality. Crank (1998) is one researcher who argues that racial bias is "endemic" in police departments. However, it should be strongly emphasized that the charge of racism is not limited to law enforcement but, rather, has been leveled against the whole legal system. The system of laws and punishment, the courts that administer the laws, and the

BOX 7.1 | DIMENSIONS OF POLICE DISCRIMINATION

Administrators/Managers

Internal

- Refusing to place female officers in "dangerous" assignments
- Placing minority employees in undesirable assignments
- Making promotion decisions on the basis of race/ethnicity or other factors not related to the ability to perform the job
- Refusing to commend officers for exceptional performance on the basis of factors such as race/ethnicity, gender, age
- Segregating in assignments by assigning only African American officers to work together as partners or Caucasian officers to work together as partners
- Failing to take corrective action when subordinates discriminate against co-workers

External

- Making selection decisions on the basis of factors such as race/ethnicity, gender, political, or religious affiliation
- Refusing to respond to complaints by minority citizens or neighborhoods populated predominantly by minorities
- Using police resources and personnel to harass certain segments of the community (e.g., businesses, community groups)
- By practice or custom, failing to provide police services to minority segments of the community (e.g., homosexuals, ethnic groups, religious groups)
- Failing to take corrective action when officers discriminate against citizens

Officers

Internal

- Intimidating minority officers by threatening not to back them up on calls
- Making racist or sexist comments in the presence of minority officers
- Writing graffiti or posting offensive pictures on lockers belonging to minority officers
- Engaging in sexual harassment

External

- Not trying to solve crimes when minorities are victims
- Harassing youths, college students, or other groups
- Hassling businesses frequented by minorities
- Not responding to, or purposefully delaying responding to, calls in minority neighborhoods
- Using racial slurs or derogatory language when dealing with Hispanic citizens

Source: Kappeler, Sluder, and Alpert, 1994: 173. Reprinted by permission of Waveland Press, Inc. All rights reserved.

corrections system that makes decisions regarding the liberties of those convicted have all been described as agencies that systematically and pervasively discriminate against minority groups. Police, in this view, are just one element in systematic, even institutional, racism.

Studies show that civil rights complaints against police are correlated positively to the percentage of minorities in the population, as well as the income differential of the jurisdiction (Holmes, 2000). Some studies report that lower-class African Americans have significantly more negative interactions with police. More than twice as many report disrespectful language or swearing by police officers (Weitzer, 1999). Interestingly, some studies indicate that middle-class African Americans

WALKING THE WALK

Anthony Bouza was a Spanish immigrant who entered police work for economic security. He obtained a bachelor's degree and a master's degree during 12 years of night school in New York while working as a police officer in the Bronx. He initiated early police–community contacts that pre-dated community policing and was a vocal critic of social inequality.

In 1976 he quit before he was fired after making some ill-advised comments that the middle and upper class only wanted the police to make the problems of the lower class invisible. He was asked to be Chief of Police in Minneapolis, where he continued to make waves. During the 1980s his officers sometimes arrested his wife, an activist who was an ardent opponent of the military. He butted heads frequently with city council, but his most vocal opponents were his officers, who did not like his position that he owed his loyalty to the citizens of Minneapolis, not his fellow police officers, and so did they. He voluntarily stepped down in 1989 and went on to run unsuccessfully for governor of Minnesota.

Bouza is not a perfect man. He may be described as "full of himself." He may be criticized for having a flip and indiscreet tongue. But one thing that most people, even his critics, will admit is that he acts as he believes and he believes in the values of public service and integrity.

Source: Bouza, 2001.

express more negative attitudes than do lower-class African Americans. One speculation for this finding is that those who live in bad neighborhoods and experience the danger and inconvenience of prevalent criminality allow police more latitude to control those who "have it coming to them" (Weitzer, 1999: 838).

In their review of the literature, Weitzer and Tuch (2002) found no consensus, and, although some studies report that disadvantaged blacks have more negative views of police, others report that high-status blacks express more dissatisfaction, and still other studies report that class is not a factor. In their study using a telephone survey of more than 2,000 respondents, Weitzer and Tuch found that age, income, sex, and education all influenced attitudes toward police. The "Walking the Walk" box is the story of one man who spent his career attempting to make police agencies more responsive to all segments of the community.

Studies have indicated that African Americans and Hispanics are most supportive of police reforms such as racial diversification of police departments, enhanced mechanisms of accountability, and community policing. Not surprisingly, minorities who lived in metropolitan areas, had less education and less income, were younger, and reported more bad experiences with the police, perceived more police misconduct, and exhibited the highest endorsement of police reforms (Weitzer and Tuch, 2000). Reisig and Parks (2000) found that areas of concentrated disadvantage showed the least satisfaction with police but that race was still a predictor, even when controlling for neighborhood.

The Project on Policing studies utilized 240 hours of observations of encounters with 3,130 suspects in Indianapolis and St. Petersburg in 1996–1997. In this study, trained observers noted characteristics of these encounters, and the results were used to examine things such as police officers' use of force and disrespect. The authors provide a careful review of prior studies and note that police behavior toward citizens is influenced by disrespectful or resistant behavior, intoxication, or mental illness. In other words, the results tend to point to aspects of demeanor rather than race or class. But recall that studies that ask people about their experiences with police tend to show significant differences between blacks and whites in their perceptions about whether or not they believe they have experienced disrespect from police officers (Mastrofski, Reisig, and McCluskey, 2002, citing Wesley Skogan; but see also Weitzer, 1999).

Those authors point to Donald Black's theory that individuals will treat people worse if there is great social distance and the recipient is of lower status. According to this idea, the actor engages in "moralism," whereby the lower-status target can become even more vulnerable by resisting, in some way, the authority of the actor. In these cases the authority figures may feel "morally justified" in their aggression toward the target (Mastrofski, Reisig, and McCluskey, 2002). Arguably, this explains why there may be more police violence in socially disadvantaged neighborhoods, especially when the citizen disrespects the police officer's authority, either verbally or by physically resisting.

Researchers noted that suspects were disrespectful toward police in 15 percent of encounters, while police were *initially* disrespectful toward suspects in only 5 percent of encounters. The elements that were related to suspect disrespect toward police included heightened emotion, number of bystanders, presence of intoxicants, being mentally impaired, and being in a disadvantaged neighborhood (Reisig, McCluskey, Mastrofski, and Terrill, 2004; Mastrofski, Reisig, and McCluskey, 2002: 534).

The researchers, citing other studies indicating that minorities consistently rated police respect and civility at lower rates than whites did, and that satisfaction with police was rated lower among minorities, examined the relationship between race and police civility. Contrary to other studies and popular opinion, these researchers found that minority suspects experienced less "disrespect" than white citizens. The difference was more pronounced in St. Petersburg, arguably because a new police chief made race relations a priority in his administration (Mastrofski, Reisig, and McCluskey, 2002). This research controlled for other factors, such as resistance. Only in the presence of large crowds when the minority suspects were disrespectful did they have a higher risk than whites of being shown disrespect.

Other findings indicated that age, sex, and wealth influenced whether or not the citizen would experience disrespect, controlling for their behavior (Mastrofski, Reisig, and McCluskey, 2002). The authors pointed out that although the presence of researcher-observers may have affected the officers' treatment of citizens, it seems unlikely because the observers saw extreme cases where officers used excessive force. Further, race did seem to be a predictor in the use of verbal and physical coercion by officers observed in the encounters (Terrill, 2001; Terrill, Paoline, and Manning, 2003).

Mastrofski, Reisig, and McCluskey (2002) also suggest the possibility that minority members may experience more disrespect if the frequency of encounters for them is greater than for whites. That is what actually happened, because blacks in both cities appeared in the pool of encounters at roughly one-and-one-half times their percentage in the general population. In other words, even though when

IN THE NEWS | THE SHAME OF TULIA, TEXAS

Tulia, Texas, has gained an international reputation—but it is not a cause for pride for Texans. In this small Texas town, the local police department hired an investigator to gather evidence for arresting drug dealers. This investigator, who, it turned out, had been fired by other law enforcement agencies and had outstanding misdemeanor warrants against him in another county, collected his evidence, which resulted in 46 indictments. In 1999, 43 people were arrested.

No drugs or weapons were found during the surprise arrests, but all who were charged were found guilty. What makes this an issue? The reason is that almost all 43 persons arrested were blacks, and the few whites who were arrested were married to or dating blacks. The arrests were a substantial percentage (about 10 percent) of the small total of blacks in the town.

White juries who accepted the investigator's word that those arrested had sold him drugs, even though there was little evidence beyond his word, handed down the convictions. In some cases, the investigator could not even recognize the person charged as the one who sold drugs to him. In at least one case, defense witnesses placed the accused in another state when the so-called sale was supposed to have occurred. Even though the charges were all sales worth less than $200, the sentences averaged 90 years.

The NAACP and out-of-state lawyers mounted a campaign to overturn these convictions, without much help from the Texas Attorney General's office or the Department of Justice. They were successful in getting a district court judge to recommend to the Texas Court of Criminal Appeals that all convictions be overturned. Legislation was written and signed by Governor Rick Perry that resulted in the immediate release of those incarcerated on the perjured testimony of this undercover officer. Tom Coleman, the undercover officer, was convicted of perjury, and the prosecutor is one of the few prosecutors ever to be formally sanctioned by the Bar Association.

Why do you think it took out-of-state journalists and lawyers to take up the cause of those wrongly accused in Tulia?

Sources: Talvi, 2002; Herbert, 2002; Robinson, 2003; Hockstader, 2003; Herbert, 2003.

---

stopped, blacks were no more likely than whites to receive disrespect, they were stopped one-and-one-half times as often as their population percentage would have predicted. Thus, the rate of blacks receiving disrespect was higher than that of whites (Mastrofski, Reisig, and McCluskey, 2002: 543).

The "In the News" box offers an egregious case of police misconduct that seems to be related to racial discrimination. Although one officer is largely responsible for this travesty of justice, it should not be forgotten that the system itself failed those who were innocent of wrongdoing.

Racial Profiling   Racial profiling occurs when a police officer uses a "profile" as reasonable suspicion to stop a driver (although it can also be used to refer to stops of pedestrians). The so-called profile is based on race. When a young, black man is seen, for instance, driving a newer-model, expensive car, police officers suspect that the vehicle is stolen and/or that the man is holding drugs. A "pretext stop" refers to the practice of police officers to use some minor traffic offense to stop the individual and, in the course of the traffic stop, look for other evidence of wrongdoing, specifically by a search, usually a consent search. In general, minorities are targeted because of a belief that they are more likely to be criminal.

Racial profiling began when federal agents developed a profile of drug smugglers to assist border patrol and custom agents in airports. The list of indicators included behavior as well as demographic indices, including race. The concept was developed for highway drivers by state patrol officers who were attempting to stem the flow of drugs up through the interstates in Florida, Georgia, Texas, and other southern states. Bob Vogel, a Florida Highway Patrol officer, became famous nationally for his profile-based stops and their supposed success in uncovering drug smugglers (Harris, 2004). Crank (2003: 242) reported that in Volusia County, Florida, 70 percent of stops and 80 percent of searches after stops were directed toward African Americans or Latinos, though these groups made up only 5 percent of drivers.

In 1999 President Bill Clinton condemned the practice, and congressional hearings were held to investigate how widespread the practice was. Most people object to racial profiling. In their telephone attitude survey of 2,006 respondents in 1999, Weitzer and Tuch (2002: 441) discovered that only 6 percent of blacks and only 16 percent of whites were in favor of stops based on race. The result of federal attention was that many states passed legislation requiring police departments to collect demographic information on police stops to determine whether racial profiling was an issue.

Smith and Alpert (2002) have reviewed the methodological problems involved in analyzing the extent of racial profiling, especially as it relates to the use of social science in courtrooms. They point out that about half of the available studies were done by law enforcement agencies using their own data and personnel. The other half of the studies were by outside researchers using the agencies' data. For instance, one study by the New York Attorney General's office found that although blacks represent only about 26 percent of the New York City population, 51 percent of all stops by N.Y.P.D. officers are of blacks (as represented by "field interrogation cards") (Smith and Alpert, 2002: 675).

Smith and Alpert (2002) also reviewed the court cases dealing with police practices that use race in decision making. In cases such as *United States v. Martinez-Fuerte*, 425 U.S. 931 (1976), the U.S. Supreme Court has basically legitimated the use of race as a criterion in profiles (although lower courts are not in agreement when race seems to be the sole or primary reason for the stop). Further, pretext stops have been accepted by the court in *Wren v. United States*, 517 U.S. 806 (1996), in effect allowing the police to use their discretion to enforce minor laws as a tool to implement race-based stops.

Engel, Calnon, and Bernard (2002) reviewed all of the racial profiling studies conducted up to the time of their study and examined the various methods used by researchers. They point out the problems with measurement:

1. Determining the base rate is difficult because one might use the percentage of nonwhites in the population, the percentage of nonwhite drivers, the percentage of nonwhite drivers who engage in traffic offenses, or some other denominator. Most of the earlier studies used percentage-of-population figures, but other researchers are highly critical of this rough approximation of the base rate. Although some argue that perhaps young black drivers engage in traffic offenses differentially to other population groups and that is why they appear disproportionately in police stops, others point out that blacks are less likely

than whites to be automobile drivers, which would make the disproportional stops even more disproportional to the true population that was driving.

2. Interpreting the data is also mentioned as a problem. Numbers are typically collected without any theoretical framework, and they are often collected by the agencies themselves. Newspapers have published results of their analysis of department-collected numbers (obtained via freedom-of-information acts) using questionable methodology and then reach the conclusion that the police department is racist without exploring any race-neutral alternative hypothesis.

3. No exploration of the connection between attitudes and behavior accompanies most racial profiling studies. Researchers have not asked the question of why officers stop black drivers or pedestrians differentially. Do police officers who stop blacks exhibit more racist attitudes than the general population or not?

4. Although it may not explain the initial stop, suspects' demeanor may explain why blacks are more likely to be searched. Racial profiling studies typically do not include measures of the suspects' demeanor even though another body of research concerning police–citizen stops and interactions (including use of force) has identified the important role of a suspect's demeanor in police decision making.

5. Police departments may be implicitly encouraging racial profiling or not by reward structures and training. Most studies place the decision making solely within the purview of the individual officer, but it is important to note organizational influences on such behavior, especially because studies show that black officers are just as likely as white officers to stop blacks in disproportionate numbers.

A utilitarian argument for racial profiling would be that the "end" of drug interdiction justifies the "means" of harassing and inconveniencing the group. However, it appears that the end is not well served. The "hit rate" for finding drugs is lower for African Americans than it is for other racial groups (Cole and Lamberth, 2001). Harris (2004) proposes the idea that when officers use race in decision making, they become less effective, not more effective, because they do not concentrate on what is important for investigation—behavior, not demographics.

An ethical formalist system would probably not support profile searches because this approach is treating those individuals as a means, and it is probably contrary to the universalism principle unless everyone would agree that they should be stopped in the same manner. Because most of us would object to numerous stops every week by police who have no reason to be suspicious other than the color of our skin, it violates the first part of the categorical imperative. The Policy Box discusses racial profiling.

In response to public scrutiny, police departments began collecting statistics on the race of those who were stopped and which stops ended with searches. Interestingly, at least one city discovered that the percentage of searches has gone down dramatically since such statistics have been routinely collected. In Austin, Texas, it was reported that the number of traffic stops between 2004 to 2005 went up from 177, 741 to 183, 201, while the number of consent searches decreased by 78.5 percent (from 804 to 173). Policies put in place after a critical report of the city's search practices required that officers document the reason for their search and get

POLICY BOX	RACIAL PROFILING

Widespread public opinion condemns racial profiling. Departmental policies have seen some changes over the last several years in their endorsement of such practices.

Law: Many states now have laws mandating that police collect demographic information on stops. Case law is somewhat contradictory, but it seems clear that the courts will not allow police stops based solely on race, although race can be one element that makes up reasonable suspicion. Generally, searches must be based on probable cause unless consent is given. Border searches are different, with different legal parameters.

Policy: After federal and public scrutiny, most police departments created formal policies that discourage and/or prohibit stops based solely on race. However, informal policies in departments still must support such stops because studies continue to show disproportionate stops of minorities. But it seems to be the case that such policies vary by city; thus, some departments are more successful than others in effecting formal policies.

Ethics: An individual officer has a duty to prevent crime. If he or she believes that an individual is likely to be a criminal, based on race, formal policies are going to conflict with individual ethics and the perception of duty. Some argue that police officers' informal policies will not change until they are educated as to the evidence that stops and searches of blacks are less likely to result in a discovery of contraband than stops based on more sophisticated, behavioral-based criteria. As long as police officers believe that racial profiling is effective policing, formal policies that prohibit it will be contrary to their individual ethics and perception of duty.

written consent from the motorist. While the traffic stops roughly paralleled each race/ethnicity's percent of the population, there were still differences in the likelihood of stops ending in searches, with 10 percent of blacks, 7.8 percent of Hispanics and 3 percent of whites being asked to consent to search.

Some might argue that this is evidence that police officers are not providing as much proactive policing as they did before; however, it should be noted that even with the drastic reduction in stops and searches, 92–95 percent of them still ended with no contraband being found (Plohetski, 2006). Other research indicates that new controls on consent searches for contraband at the border also reduced racial disparities and increased the percentage of searches that resulted in a discovery of contraband (reported in Walker, 2007).

African Americans are not the only minorities who suffer from differential enforcement patterns. Perhaps some of the most egregious cases of discriminatory law enforcement occur on this nation's southern borders. Crank (2003) and Huspek, Martinez, and Jiminez (2001) discuss the excessive force that is used against Latinos in controlling the flow of illegal aliens across the border. It was reported to researchers that Immigration and Naturalization Service (INS) officers routinely violated the human rights of aliens and deported them before they could report actions of officers.

According to Huspek, Martinez, and Jiminez (2001: 185), there are "substantial numbers" of brutal or harassing incidents on the border by INS officers toward legal and illegal residents. In their study of incidents over a three-year period, they found that such abuses are a routine occurrence and that they have a pattern and an identifiable logic. Of the 204 persons who participated in their study, 43 percent reported seeing physical brutality and 12 percent reported being victimized by sexual or physical abuse (2001: 187).

Many of those reporting incidents were legal residents of the United States, though of Mexican origin. Their passports were thrown away and official documents torn up, and they were told that they should go back to Mexico. They then had to wait in Mexico until family members could replace the documents and help them get back across the border. White citizens have been threatened when they questioned the actions of INS agents (2001: 193).

Huspek, Martinez, and Jiminez (2001: 185) argue that border agents act this way because they are encouraged by the "rhetoric of fear" and tacit acceptance of any means necessary to reduce or discourage illegal immigration. In the Policy Box in Chapter 5, the practice of local law enforcement enforcing immigration laws was discussed. It is possible that as illegal immigration becomes a more central political issue, local law enforcement agencies will be pressured to use "any means" to help enforce immigration laws, and that this will lead to racial profiling of Latinos. Would the Supreme Court uphold the use of a racial profile for illegal immigrants? Could police officers implement stops based only on the individual's apparent ethnicity? Besides the legal answers to these questions, what are the ethical answers?

After 9/11, those who looked like they were Middle Eastern were subject to increased scrutiny before they boarded airliners. In some cases, individuals were denied entry to airplanes when other passengers complained that they would not fly with the men who looked like they might be suicide bombers. In general, airline security now conducts random searches (along with more targeted searches), and many people object that it is wasteful to search "a little old lady from Kansas" in an effort to be "politically correct." Others argue that everyone should be subject to the same scrutiny because the risk is so high and people might have something slipped into their luggage without their knowledge.

Applying a utilitarian argument again for this type of racial profiling, does the end (preventing terrorist bombings) justify actions that a less serious end (drug interdiction) would not? Is it acceptable to more thoroughly search all Middle Eastern individuals because the risk is higher and the number of them smaller than the number of African Americans (thereby reducing the "disutility" of the actions)? Many people who objected to racial profiling when the targets were African Americans and the "end" was drug interdiction do not object when the targets are Middle Eastern and the "end" is to prevent a terrorist attack. Has the argument changed, requiring different answers, or would the same arguments apply?

CRIME FIGHTER *AND* PUBLIC SERVANT?

Police hear mixed messages from the public regarding certain types of crime. They are asked to enforce laws against gambling, pornography, and prostitution, but not too stringently. They are expected to enforce laws against drunk driving but also to be tolerant of individuals who aren't really "criminal." They are expected to uphold laws regarding assault unless it is a family or interpersonal dispute that the disputants want to settle privately. In other words, we want the police to enforce the law unless they enforce it against us.

We also ask the police to take care of social problems such as the homeless, even if they have to step outside the law to do so. Extra-legal means are acceptable as long as they are not used against us. Citizens who want police to move the transients out of a park or get the crack dealers off the corner aren't concerned with the fact that the police might not have the legal authority to do so. If a little "informal" justice is needed to accomplish the task, that is fine with some people, as long as it is used against those we don't like.

When we accept and encourage such extra-legal power in some situations, we shouldn't be surprised when it is used in other situations as well. The police role as enforcer in a pluralistic society is problematic. The justification for police power is that police represent the public: "The police officer can only validly use coercive force when he or she in fact represents the body politic" (Malloy, 1982: 12). But if the police do not represent all groups, their authority is seen as oppressive. It should be no surprise that police were seen as an invading army in the ghettos of the 1960s. They were not seen as representing the interests of the people who were the target of their force. The Los Angeles riots after acquittal of the officers who were charged with beating Rodney King illustrate the tension between minority communities and police departments. More recent disturbances have occurred in other cities, sparked by perceived police abuses.

Police take their cue from the community they serve. If they serve a community that emphasizes crime control over individual rights or other public service, we will see the results of that message in the way laws are enforced. An example of a crime control approach is William Bratton's **zero-tolerance policy**, implemented when he was police chief of New York City in the 1990s. Police officers were instructed to take an aggressive stance against street people and minor criminals, especially those who roamed the downtown Manhattan business area and subway system.

The dramatic decline in crime enjoyed by New York City was touted as the result of the zero-tolerance policy. When the little criminals are arrested, so goes the theory, the big crimes don't happen. It was true that frequently the minor offenders arrested had outstanding warrants for more serious crimes. From 1993 to 1997, felony complaints dropped by 44.3 percent. Murder and non-negligent homicide dropped 62 percent, forcible rape dropped 12.4 percent, robbery dropped 48 percent, and burglary rates dropped 45 percent (Greene, 1999: 176). However, critics argued that New York's success might have had something to do with the 40-percent increase in sworn officers that also occurred during this time. Further, the decline of crime was felt all over the country, not just in New York City. For instance, in San Diego, without an increase in sworn officers, the crime rate declined by almost as much as New York's (Greene, 1999).

The problematic issue regarding zero tolerance is the effect it had on police–community relations. Citizen complaints against New York City police went up 75 percent in the four-year period between 1995 and 1999 (Greene, 1999: 176). Even downtown merchants, who were thrilled with the effects of the crackdown when the Times Square area was described as "safe for tourists" again, were now feeling the effects of the pervasive police influence. Some complained that police were harassing them by enforcing trivial ordinances (such as placement and size of window signs or sidewalk sales). Some New Yorkers complained that the crackdown had altered what made New York what it was, such as sidewalk vendors hawking everything from hotdogs to sunglasses. The most serious charge was that the aggressive policing policies of zero tolerance led to some police officers employing an "anything goes" philosophy, and contributed to extreme cases such as the Abner Louima assault (1997) and the Amadou Diallo shooting (1999), even though Bratton was gone by the time these incidents occurred, as his tenure in New York City lasted only from 1994 to 1996.

William Bratton next became the chief of Los Angeles, in 2002, a city that had experienced serious tension between the minority community and the police department. By most accounts, Bratton has been successful in achieving his goal of reducing crime. Between 2002 and 2007 Los Angeles experienced a 31 percent decrease in serious crimes and a 44 percent decrease in homicides. Further, civil lawsuits against the department declined. Bratton has been successful in wresting the money from the city council to hire hundreds of new police officers and was applauded for taking swift action against officers in the "May Day Melee" in 2007, when officers fired on demonstrators with rubber bullets (Steptoe, 2007).

Bratton was sworn in for a second five-year term in 2007, the first chief since the 1980s to survive to a second term (Buntin, 2007). His management tools, including Compstat, a computerized crime-counting method that emphasizes accountability of middle managers, may be the key to improving the efficiency of police organizations. One could argue that accountability, as long as it covers the *means* as well as the *ends* of law enforcement, is the key to an efficient and ethical police department.

Whereas the formal code of ethics emphasizes the public servant role of law enforcement, the informal subculture emphasizes the crime fighter role. The public, too, probably expects the police to live up to the crime fighter role but also expects more. The public expects the police to be problem solvers and supermen (and superwomen). From noisy neighbors to incest, we expect the police to have the answers to our problems—to be the one-stop shop for solving problems. The surprising thing is that the police do so well at this impossible task.

The Gallup Poll has measured respect for police since 1965. In a 2005 poll, 56 percent of Americans indicated that they had "great" respect for police. This is down from about 70 percent in the 1960s, but when those who answered with "some" respect is added, 89 percent of the population has some or a great deal of respect for police (Gallup Poll, 2005).

Interestingly, at least one study found that while extensive media coverage of a police scandal influenced the public's belief about the guilt of the officers involved, it did not seem to affect the general perceptions of respect for the agency by the public (Chermak, McGarrell, and Gruenewald 2005). Another study found that public attitudes about police misconduct are separate and distinct from their attitudes about police effectiveness. The most influential factors on public attitudes about police misconduct were personal experiences of self, family and friends, neighborhood characteristics, and media coverage, while public attitudes of police effectiveness were influenced by other factors (Miller and Davis, 2007).

Public perceptions of police misconduct have been linked to the public's trust in the police and the recognition of police as agents of legal and moral authority (Tyler, 1990; Tyler and Wakslak 2004). Public attitudes toward police misconduct/police legitimacy have even been linked to violent crime (Kane, 2005). Therefore, it is important for police departments to set and maintain high standards of conduct not only for their own professional pride but also because it seems that police ethics impact public safety in a more general sense. Police officers who ignore the law evidently give others the green light to do so as well.

CONCLUSION

In this chapter we have explored the formal and informal culture of law enforcement officers. The police subculture is no longer monolithic but still seems to be contrary to formal codes of ethics in some respects. We looked at reasons for the lack of consistency between the formal code and the informal subculture. When discussing a range of issues, including how police use their discretion, the types of dilemmas they face, and the inconsistency between the formal code and the informal subculture, the mission and role of police as crime fighters or public servants is a pervasive theme.

Key Terms

aspirational code *190*

authority *187*

community policing *185*

cynicism *194*

discretion *198*

discrimination *198*

duty *198*

force *187*

group think *192*

persuasion *187*

power *187*

public servants *183*

social contract *188*

zero-tolerance policy *215*

Review Questions

1. Explain the public servant role and the crime fighter role and why the two roles may be inconsistent.
2. What potential ethical issues arise with community policing? Why might community policing act as an "insulator" against unethical behavior?
3. What are Klockars' descriptions of police authority, power, persuasion, and force.
4. Explain how the social contract is the source of police power, and explain the elements or characteristics of policing that logically flow from such power.

5. Describe the elements of the formal code of ethics, and contrast them with the values of the police subculture.
6. Present the criticisms leveled against the use of any code of ethics for police officers.
7. What are Sherman's police "values"?
8. Explain why some people think the police subculture is breaking down.
9. Describe Wilson and Brown's typologies of police, and explain how each might use discretion.
10. Evaluate the research on racial profiling. What methodological problems exist? What do most studies show?

Writing/Discussion Questions

1. Write an essay on (or discuss) discretion in policing. In this essay, define discretion, give examples, and discuss unethical and ethical criteria for the use of discretion. Find newspaper articles illustrating police use of

discretion. Analyze the officer's use of discretion in relation to the ethical systems described in earlier chapters.
2. Write an essay on (or discuss) community policing and whether it is likely to reduce or

to encourage unethical actions by police officers. Utilize current research to illustrate whether or not community policing is growing or declining in popularity.
3. Write an essay on (or discuss) racial profiling. Review current cases of racial profiling. Discuss whether racial profiling should be used to deter or prevent terrorism. Discuss whether racial profiling should be used to deter or prevent illegal immigration.
4. Write an essay on (or discuss) the two perceptions of the police officer—crime fighter or public servant. Consider various police practices and innovations as supporting one or the other role.

Ethical Dilemmas

Situation 1

As a patrol officer, you are only doing your job when you stop a car for running a red light. Unfortunately, the driver of the car happens to be the mayor. You ticket her anyway, but the next morning you get called into the captain's office and told in no uncertain terms that you screwed up, because of an informal policy extending "courtesy" to city politicians. Several nights later you observe the mayor's car weaving erratically across lanes and speeding. What would you do? What if the driver were a fellow police officer? What if the driver were a high school friend?

Situation 2

There is a well-known minor criminal in your district. Everyone is aware that he is engaged in a variety of crimes, including burglary, fencing, and drug dealing. However, you have been unable to make a case against him. Now he is the victim of a crime—he has been assaulted and robbed at gunpoint. How would you treat his case?

Situation 3

You are completing an internship with a local police agency. The officers you ride with are great and let you come along on everything they do. One day the officer you are riding with takes you along on a drug raid. You are invited to come in when the house is secure, and you observe six young men sitting on two sofas in the living room. The officers are ransacking the house and asking the young men where they have hidden the drugs. Four of the youth are black and two are white. One of the officers walks behind the sofa where the blacks are sitting and slaps each one hard on the side of the head as he walks past. He ignores the two white boys sitting on the other sofa. You are shocked by his actions, but you know that if you say anything, your chance of being hired by this agency will be very small. You desperately want a good recommendation from the officers you ride with. What would you do?

Situation 4

You are a police officer in New Orleans. During the flood following Hurricane Katrina, you are ordered to patrol a section of the downtown area to prevent looting. The water is waist high in some places, and the stores and shops in this section of blocks are, for the most part, inundated with floodwater. You come upon one shop where the plate-glass window has been broken, and about a dozen people are coming out of the shop with clothing in their arms. You suspect that the shop's contents will be written off anyway by the owners, and covered by insurance. Should that make a difference in your decision? What if the store were in an area of the city that wasn't flooded and the contents were not ruined?

What if the people said they were desperate and didn't have any clothes because their belongings were under water? What if the items being taken were televisions and other electronics?

Situation 5

You are a rookie on traffic patrol. You watch as a young black man drives past you in a brand-new silver Porsche. You estimate the car's value at around $40,000, yet the neighborhood you are patrolling in is characterized by low-income housing, cheap apartments, and tiny houses on the lowest end of the housing spectrum. You follow him and observe that he forgets to signal when he changes lanes. Ordinarily you wouldn't waste your time on something so minor. What would you do?

Suggested Readings

Barker, T. 2006 *Police Ethics: Crisis in Law Enforcement*. Springfield, IL: Charles C Thomas, Publisher.

Barker, T., and Carter, D. 1993. *Police Deviance*. Cincinnati, OH: Anderson Publishing Company.

Bouza, A. 2001. *Police Unbound: Corruption, Abuse, and Heroism by the Boys in Blue*. Amherst, NY: Prometheus.

Cole, D. 1999. *No Equal Justice*. New York: Free Press.

Delattre, E. 2005. *Character and Cops: Ethics in Policing*, 5th ed. Washington, DC: AEI Press.

Dunham, R., and Alpert, G. 2005. *Critical Issues in Policing*, 4th ed. Prospect Heights, IL: Waveland.

Heffernan, W., and Stroup, T. 1985. *Police Ethics: Hard Choices in Law Enforcement*. New York: John Jay Press.

Kappeler, V., Sluder, R. and Alpert, G. 1998. *Forces of Deviance: Understanding the Dark Side of Policing*. Prospect Heights, IL: Waveland.

Kleinig, J. 1996. *The Ethics of Policing*. Cambridge: Cambridge University Press.

Kleinig, J. (Ed.). 1996. *Handled with Discretion*. Lanham: MD: Rowman & Littlefield.

Lersch, K. 2002. *Policing and Misconduct*. Upper Saddle River, NJ: Prentice-Hall.

Manning, P. 1997. *Policework*, 2d Ed. Prospect Heights, IL: Waveland.

Perez, D., and Moore, J. 2002. *Police Ethics: A Matter of Character*. Cincinnati, OH: Copperhouse/ Atomic Dog Publishing.

Walker, S., Spohn, C., and DeLone, M. 2000. *The Color of Justice*. Belmont, CA: Wadsworth.

CORRUPTION AND THE "CODE"

Allegations of police brutality often serve as a trigger for community unrest, as did the police shooting of Sean Bell in November 2006, who was killed by police officers on the morning of his wedding day. The discretion to use fatal force is an awesome power and responsibility.

CHAPTER OBJECTIVES

1. Become aware of the range of law enforcement deviance.

2. Understand the arguments that support and criticize the practice of gratuities.

3. Become familiar with the prevalence of and explanations for the use of excessive force by police officers.

4. Become familiar with the types and range of law enforcement deviance in other countries.

5. Understand the various explanations offered for law enforcement deviance.

Frank Serpico is arguably the most famous police officer in the United States even though he hasn't worked in law enforcement since 1972. After serving in Korea, he became a New York City police officer in 1959. His pride in wearing the uniform quickly dissipated when he realized that his partner was picking up "pad" money—payments by store owners to ensure that the cops would be there in case of trouble but also ignore minor violations of store owners and their customers. The "pad" was widespread in the department at the time, and Serpico quickly became known as the cop who didn't want the money, earning him the distrust of those who did.

Eventually, over 12 years, he rose to the rank of detective. When he discovered that corruption was rampant in the divisions he worked in, he began talking to police supervisors about the wrongdoing, but to no avail. It seemed that no matter whom he talked to, nothing was done and he continued to get the runaround. Finally, in 1970–1971, he and David Durk, a fellow officer, went to *The New York Times* and participated in an expose of police corruption.

The series of stories led to Mayor John Lindsay convening the Knapp Commission, which conducted a wide-ranging investigation of police corruption. Serpico and Durk continued to work even though rumors that they were the "rats" were widespread and there was a real danger that corrupt police officers would retaliate against them. Before he had a chance to testify, Serpico was shot at point-blank range in the face in a drug bust while his fellow officers stood behind him. The shooting was suspected of being a set-up, especially since the "officer down" call never was issued; however, no officer was investigated or charged with any wrongdoing in relation to the shooting.

Serpico survived and went on to testify before the Knapp Commission. He received a Medal of Honor from the police department but retired and left the United States for 10 years. He returned in the early 1980s and continues to speak out against police corruption and supports whistleblowers, whom he calls "lamplighters" instead—referring to Paul Revere's famous ride. "Doing the right thing" evidently continues to be his life's work. (See his official website, at http://www.frankserpico.com/).

One of the sad facts is that the name Serpico continues to elicit two different reactions. For some, he represents the epitome of an honest and brave man who stood against corruption at great risk to self. For others, he represents a "rat," a man who turned his back on his friends, and to be called a "Serpico" is an insult in some police departments. Corruption continues today in the New York City police department and other departments across the country, although the pervasiveness of corruption is probably much less than it was when Serpico was an officer. So, too, continues the idea that loyalty comes before honesty. The "blue curtain of secrecy" is one of the topics of Chapter 9.

The vast majority of police officers are honest and strive to be ethical in all they do; however, it is a sad fact that examples of corruption and graft in law enforcement agencies are not difficult to find. Since the very beginnings of organized police departments, various investigative bodies have documented cases of corruption (Barker and Carter, 1994; Murphy and Moran, 1981: 87). Fyfe and Kane (2006), for instance, provide a long list of commissions and task forces that investigated police corruption scandals in a number of cities, including the Chicago Police Committee (in 1931), the Knapp Commission (New York City in 1972), the Kolts Commission (Los Angeles County in 1992), the Mollen Commission (New York City in 1993), the Philadelphia Police Study Task Force (in 1987), the Christopher Commission (Los Angeles in 1996), the New Orleans Mayor's Advisory Committee (in 1993), the Royal Commission (Sydney, Australia, in 1997), and the St. Clair Commission (Boston, in 1992), to name only a few. Cities also pay out large sums of money for settlements and in response to losing cases in court when police officers and their departments are sued for excessive force and other forms of misconduct.

Even though there is a large body of literature on police corruption, few studies have attempted to measure the extent and prevalence of police officer misconduct. An obvious barrier to discovery is getting police officers to admit to wrongdoing. One early study reported that, by officers' own accounts, 39 percent of their number engaged in brutality, 22 percent perjured themselves, 31 percent had sex on duty, 8 percent drank on duty, and 39 percent slept on duty (Barker and Carter, 1994). Barker (1983) reported that between 9 and 31 percent of officers who had been employed for eleven months or less reported observing corrupt practices.

In a sample of narcotics officers, Stevens (1999) reported that 63 percent said they had very often heard of narcotics officers' using more force than necessary to make an arrest, 26 percent had often heard of other officers personally consuming and/or selling drugs, and 82 percent had very often heard of other narcotics officers violating the civil rights of suspects. These numbers must be interpreted carefully in that they do not mean that large numbers of officers were corrupt, only that a fairly large number of officers had heard of some case of corruption "very often."

Fyfe and Kane (2006) studied police officers in New York City who were terminated for cause and found that only 2 percent of officers in the 22 years under study (1975–1996) were terminated for misconduct. We will review this study in detail in the coming paragraphs, as it is helpful to understand the factors associated with officers who are investigated and found to have committed misconduct serious enough to warrant termination. The number of officers who come to the attention of supervisors and are officially sanctioned by termination is probably quite a bit lower than the numbers who commit corrupt acts. Official investigations and findings do not necessarily reflect the true prevalence of such behaviors, but it is no doubt true that only a small number of officers engage in serious corruption.

Unfortunately, the perception that police are corrupt is widespread in some cities. In one older New York City poll, 93 percent of those polled believed that police were "corrupt" (Kraus, 1994). Moore (1997) reported, interestingly, that the public still has a high opinion of police even though the majority also believes that the police are dishonest. National opinion polls show that more people have a high respect for police officers' integrity and ethics today than in decades past. In 1977, 37 percent of the public rated police integrity and ethics as high or very high and 12 percent as low or very low. By 1997, the percentage of those who rated police high or very high went up to 49 percent and those who rated police low or very low was 10 percent. By 2007, 53 percent of the public rated police integrity as high or very high and only 9 percent of the population rated this factor as low or very low (Sourcebook of Criminal Justice, 2007).

Most misdeeds of police officers are only marginally different from the unethical behaviors of other professions. For instance, some doctors prescribe unneeded surgery or experiment with unknown drugs, some businesspeople cheat on their expense accounts, lawyers sometimes overcharge clients, and contract bidders and purchase agents offer and accept bribes. It is an unfortunate fact of life that people in any profession or occupation will find ways to exploit their position for personal gain. This is not to excuse these actions but, rather, to show that police are no more deviant than other professional groups. In all of these occupational areas, most people attempt to uphold the profession's code of ethics and their own personal moral code. However, a few exploit their position and exhibit extremely unethical behaviors.

TYPES OF CORRUPTION

Corruption has been described as "acting on opportunities, created by virtue of one's authority, for personal gain at the expense of the public one is authorized to serve" (Cohen, 1986: 23). There is a huge body of literature on police corruption, only some of which is touched on in this chapter. As we said, trying to establish the prevalence of corruption is exceedingly difficult, but so, too, is trying to agree upon a definitive description of what constitutes corruption.

In 1973 the Knapp Commission detailed its findings of corruption in the New York City Police Department. The terms **grass eaters** and **meat eaters** were used to describe New York City police officers who took advantage of their position to engage in corrupt practices. Accepting bribes, gratuities, and unsolicited protection money was the extent of the corruption engaged in by *grass eaters*, who were fairly passive in their deviant practices. *Meat eaters* participated in shakedowns, "shopped" at burglary scenes, and engaged in more active deviant practices. The Mollen Commission, which investigated New York City Police Department corruption twenty years later (1993), concluded that meat eaters were engaged in a qualitatively different kind of corruption in more recent times. Beyond just cooperating with criminals, the corrupt cops were active criminals themselves, selling drugs, robbing drug dealers, and operating burglary rings.

The distinction between passive and active corruption is a helpful one. Another way to identify and categorize police corruption is offered by Barker and Carter (1994), who propose that police abuse of authority comes in three different areas:

1. Physical abuse—excessive force, physical harassment
2. Psychological abuse—disrespect, harassment, ridicule, excessive stops, intimidation
3. Legal abuse—unlawful searches or seizures, manufacturing evidence

In another source, Barker (2002) lists the types of police corruption as including corruption of authority (gratuities), kickbacks, opportunistic theft, shakedowns, protection of illegal activities, fixes (quashing tickets), direct criminal activities, and internal payoffs.

Fyfe and Kane (2006) also provide a detailed discussion of the types of police corruption. They argue that it is important to note that in some situations when police officers commit crimes, it is not truly police corruption in that the crimes are committed off-duty and have no relationship to their job. In effect, they are criminals who happen to be cops but being cops has no relationship to their criminality. However, they might have learned how to commit the crime, obtained criminal contacts, or developed criminal values through their job, so, in a sense, it might be considered job-related corruption. The point is that it is difficult to draw a line between police corruption (acts intrinsically tied to the job) and criminals who happen to be police officers. Fyfe and Kane (2006) go through a detailed explanation of the types of police misconduct discussed in the literature.

Police crime. These are situations where police officers violate criminal statutes. On the one hand, police might engage in crimes that have nothing to do with their position (e.g., commit burglaries or insurance fraud while off-duty). On the other hand, their ability to commit the crime might be entirely related to their position (e.g., stealing drugs from an evidence locker or identity theft using information obtained by writing tickets).

Police corruption. These are offenses where the officer uses his or her position, by act or omission, to obtain improper financial benefit. For instance, police may take bribes either to not do their job (write a ticket), or to do their job (provide police protection). Note that these acts may overlap with police crime because some police corruption violates criminal statutes as well (e.g., extortion and bribery). Police officers may commit acts for personal profit of either a non-criminal or a criminal nature related to their employment. An example of a non-criminal form of police corruption would be to violate the department's extra-job policy or to take gratuities. An example of criminal corruption would be to take a bribe.

The key element of this type of corruption is personal gain. Examples offered by Fyfe and Kane of "unambiguous" police corruption would be an officer who steals from a drug seizure (an individual "event") or a group of officers who repeatedly extort or accept money from criminals (an "arrangement"). However, it is not clear how these activities are distinct from police crimes as defined above.

Abuse of power. These are actions where officers physically injure or offend a citizen's sense of dignity. Physical abuse can be divided into "brutality," which occurs when officers inflict physical abuse on persons to teach them a lesson; and, unnecessary force, which occurs when police officers make mistakes that lead them to have to resort to force that would not have been necessary had they followed proper procedures. Psychological abuse ranges from deception in interrogation to intimidation on the street. Legal abuse involves various forms of wrongdoing designed to convict wrongdoers, including perjury, planting evidence, and hiding exculpatory evidence. Another type of abuse of power involves off-duty misconduct, (e.g., driving while intoxicated or physical assaults, with the expectation that the wrongdoing will be covered up by fellow officers).

In their own classification of police misconduct, Fyfe and Kane (2006: 37–38) offer the following typology:

1. Profit-motivated crimes (all offenses except those that are drug-related with the goal of profit)
2. Off-duty crimes against persons (all assaultive, non-profit-related crimes off-duty)
3. Off-duty public-order crimes (not including drugs, and most commonly DWI [driving while intoxicated] and disorderly conduct)
4. Drugs (all crimes related to possession, sale, conspiracy, and failing departmental drug tests)
5. On-duty abuse (use of excessive force, psychological abuse, or discrimination)
6. Obstruction of justice (conspiracy, perjury, official misconduct, and all other offenses with the goal of obstructing justice)
7. Administrative/failure to perform (violating one or more departmental rules, policies, and procedures)
8. Conduct-related probationary failures (simple failure to meet expectations)

An important distinction that should be made is between crimes and ethical transgressions. It is an insult to law enforcement officers when certain actions, such as stealing from a burglary scene or taking money from a drug dealer to guard a shipment of drugs, are discussed as if they were ethical dilemmas in the same category as whether to avoid responding to a fender-bender call or whether an officer should call in sick so he can go fishing. Stealing, robbing, and conspiring to sell drugs are crimes. The officers who engage in such acts are criminals who are quite distinct from officers who commit ethical lapses akin to other workers who do so within the parameters of their particular professions or jobs. The "In the News" box recounts the widely publicized case of a Chicago police officer who committed criminal assault.

GRATUITIES

Gratuities are items of value received by an individual because of his or her role or position rather than because of a personal relationship with the giver. The widespread practices of free coffee in convenience stores, half-price or free meals in restaurants, and half-price dry cleaning are examples of gratuities. Frequently, businesspeople offer gratuities, such as half-price meals, as a token of sincere appreciation for the police officers' work. Although the formal code of ethics prohibits accepting gratuities, many officers believe there is nothing wrong with

---

IN THE NEWS | **OFFICER ABBATE AND THE CHICAGO POLICE DEPARTMENT**

In February of 2007, Officer Abbate of the Chicago Police Department was caught on a tavern's security video brutally attacking the female bartender after she refused to give him another drink because he appeared to be intoxicated. He cornered her behind the bar and threw her to the floor, kicking her, pummeling her, and pulling her hair. To make matters worse, she and the bar owner were evidently intimidated and threatened by Abbate and other officers in an attempt to keep them quiet about the attack. The video, aired worldwide through the news media and Youtube.com along with another beating in another bar by other off-duty officers, has resulted in drastic changes in the Chicago police department. (See the video at http://cbs2chicago.com/topstories/Chicago. Police.Anthony.2.335957.html)

The mayor appointed a new superintendent, and there have been changes in the Independent Police Review Authority that should move cases through more quickly and eliminate the multi-year backlog that existed, 21 of 25 police district commanders have been replaced, and there is a new bureau of professional standards. The new superintendent has also issued a new mission statement of values emphasizing public service and professionalism.

Source: ChicagoTribune.com. 2008.

---

businesses giving "freebies" to police officers. They see these as small rewards indeed for the difficulties they endure in police work.

What do others think? Prenzler (1995: 21) collected 398 responses from patrons of sporting clubs in Brisbane, Queensland (Australia), concerning their attitude toward police gratuities. Only 4 percent of this group expressed unqualified support, 55 percent believed that police should not accept gratuities, and 35 percent indicated that doing so was acceptable only under certain circumstances. However, when presented with hypothetical examples, two-thirds of respondents agreed that it was acceptable for police to take coffee, and about one-quarter approved of Christmas gifts. The majority of them were still opposed to large gifts and regular gifts, and 76 percent were opposed to *regular* free coffee, cold drinks, or discounted meals when on duty.

Few of Prenzler's respondents agreed with the commonly used arguments for acceptance of gratuities:

- that they build community relations (15 percent)
- that they give businesses police protection (8 percent)
- that every occupation has its perks (6 percent)
- that they compensate police for poor pay (6 percent)

It is unknown whether these responses from Australia are similar to what would be gathered in the United States. In criminal justice classrooms it is common to find fairly strong support for minor gratuities, but this may not be true if one were to poll other groups. Lord and Bjerregaard (2003) found that students initially ranked gratuities as a minor ethical issue but, after taking a criminal justice ethics class, ranked accepting gratuities as a more serious ethical transgression.

One author writes that gratuities "erode public confidence in law enforcement and undermine our quest for professionalism" (Stefanic, 1981: 63). How do gratuities undermine public confidence? Cohen (1986: 26) believes that gratuities are dangerous because what might start without intent on the part of the officer may become a patterned expectation; it is the taking in an official capacity that is wrong, for the social contract is violated when citizens give up their liberty to exploit only to be exploited, in turn, by the enforcement agency that prevents them from engaging in similar behavior. To push this argument to the extreme, some might argue that there are similarities between someone coming into an inner-city store and demanding "protection money" (to avoid torching and vandalism) and a police officer coming into the store expecting liquor or other goods (if the store owner believes that he will receive a lower level of protection if he doesn't provide them). How does the store owner know that his silent alarm will receive the same speed of response if he is not grateful and generous to police officers?

Offering a different view, Kania (1988: 37). writes that police "should be encouraged to accept freely offered minor gratuities and . . . such gratuities should be perceived as the building blocks of positive social relationships between our police and the public." He rejects the two major arguments against gratuities:

1. the slippery slope argument—that taking gratuities leads to future, more serious, deviance
2. the unjust enrichment argument—that the only honest remuneration for police officers is the paycheck

Kania proposes that gratuities actually help cement relations between the police department and the public. Officers who stay and drink coffee with store owners and businesspeople are better informed than officers who don't, according to Kania. A gift, freely given, ties the giver and receiver together in a bond of social reciprocity. This should not be viewed negatively but, rather, as part of a community-oriented policing concept. Kania also points out that those who offer gratuities tend to be more frequent users of police services, which justifies more payment than the average citizen.

The only problem, according to Kania, is when the intent of the giver is to give in exchange for some future service, not as reward for past services rendered. Another problematic situation would be when the intent of the taker is not to receive unsolicited but appreciated gifts but, rather, to use the position of police officer to extort goods from business owners. Finally, if the giver were to expect special treatment and the officer has the intent to perform the special service, that would be an unethical exchange as well. Box 8.1 presents a more detailed explanation of Kania's position.

Another issue that Kania alludes to but doesn't clearly articulate is that a pattern of gratuities changes what would have been a formal relationship into a personal, informal one. This moves the storekeeper–giver into a role that is more similar to a friend, relative, or fellow officer, in which case personal loyalty issues are involved when the law has to be administered. In the same way that an officer encounters an ethical dilemma when a best friend is stopped for speeding, the officer who stops a store owner who has been providing him or her with free coffee for the past year may also experience divided loyalties. They have become, if not friends, at least personally involved with each other to the extent that formal duty becomes complicated by the personal relationship.

BOX 8.1	RELATIONSHIP OF GIVER AND POLICE

Name	Giver's Perception	Police Perception
Ethical		
True reward	gratitude for contribution or heroic deed	accepted with acknowledgment of significance
True gift	expression of gratitude for pattern of police service	accepted without further obligation
True gratuity	expression of wish that legitimate police services will be continued	accepted in spirit of continuing reciprocal obligation
Unethical Only for Police		
Uncalled debt	expression of wish that legitimate police services will be continued	accepted in credit for future legal, quasi-legal, or illegal favors
Ethical Only for Police		
Bad investment	offered to receive future legal advantages, secure favors, gain special status	accepted in spirit of continuing reciprocal obligation
Unethical and Illegal		
An understanding	offered to receive future legal advantages, secure favors, gain special status	accepted as credit for future legal, quasi-legal, or illegal favors
A bribe	offered to exempt illegal actions or omissions from police action	accepted to overlook or ignore ongoing illegal activities
An arrangement	offered to exempt ongoing illegal actions or omissions from police action	accepted to overlook or ignore ongoing illegal activities
A shakedown	paid unwillingly to secure protection from police enforcement action	demanded to overlook or ignore present or future illegal activities

Source: Adapted from R. Kania, 1988. Used with permission of the publisher.

Kania revisited this issue when he was asked to respond to two critics of his fifteen-year-old article. The critics (Ruiz and Bono 2004; Coleman 2004a, 2004b) argue against gratuities for the following reasons:

1. Police are professionals, and professionals don't take gratuities.
2. Gratuities are incipient corruptors because people expect different treatment.
3. Gratuities are an abuse of authority and create a sense of entitlement.
4. Gratuities add up to substantial amounts of money and can constitute as high as 30 percent of an officer's income.
5. Gratuities can be the beginning of more serious forms of corruption.

6. Gratuities are contrary to democratic ideals because they are a type of fee-for-service of public functions.
7. Gratuities create a public perception that police are corrupt.

Kania (2004) continues to argue that gratuities, if freely offered and received with no strings attached, are ethical. He argues the following:

1. Other professionals accept gratuities.
2. There is nothing wrong with more frequent users of police services "paying" extra.
3. "No gratuity" rules are tools of playing "gotcha" that erode morale.
4. Educators and academics tend to distort the seriousness of gratuities.

Where should one draw the line between harmless rewards and inappropriate gifts? Is a discount on a meal OK, but not a free meal? Is a meal OK, but not any other item, such as groceries or tires or car stereos? Do the store or restaurant owners expect anything for their money, such as more frequent patrols or over-looking sales of alcohol to under-age juveniles? Should they expect different treatment from officers than the treatment given to those who do not offer gratuities? Suppose that an officer is told by a convenience store owner that she can help her-self to anything in the store—free coffee, candy, cigarettes, chips, magazines, and such. In the same conversation, the store owner asks the officer for her personal pager number "in case something happens and I need to get in contact with you." Is this a gift, or is it an exchange? Should the officer accept the free merchandise?

Many merchants give free or discount food to officers because they like to have police around, especially late at night. The question then becomes the one asked frequently by citizens: Why are two or three police cars always at a certain restau-rant? Police argue that they deserve to take their breaks wherever they want within their patrol area. If it happens that they choose the same place, that shouldn't be a concern of the public. However, an impression of unequal protection occurs when officers make a habit of eating at certain restaurants or congregating at certain con-venience stores. Free meals or even coffee may influence the pattern of police patrol and, thus, may be wrong because some citizens are not receiving equal protection.

What happens when all surrounding businesses give gratuities to officers and a new business moves in? Do officers come to expect special favors? Do merchants feel pressured to offer them? Many nightclubs allow off-duty officers to enter with-out paying cover charges. Does this lead to resentment and a feeling of discrimina-tion by paying customers? Does it lead to the officers thinking that they are special and different from everyone else? Other examples of gratuities are when police accept movie tickets, tickets to ball games and other events, free dry cleaning, and free or discounted merchandise.

The extent of gratuities varies from city to city. In cities where rules against gratuities are loosely enforced, "dragging the sack" may be developed to an art form by some police officers, who go out of their way to collect free meals and other gifts. One story is told of a large Midwestern city where officers from various divisions were upset because the merchants in some areas provided Christmas gifts, such as liquor, food, cigarettes, and other merchandise, whereas merchants in other divisions either gave nothing or gave less attractive gifts. The commander, finally tired of the bickering, ordered that no individual officer could receive any gifts and instead sent a patrol car to all the merchants in every district. Laden with all the things the merchants would have given to individual officers, the patrol car returned, and the commander parceled out the gifts to the whole department based on rank and seniority.

Ruiz and Bono (2004) presented other instances of gratuities. In a southern city, a restaurant owner who had been giving free meals to officers stopped doing so. Officers then engaged in a ticket-writing campaign, targeting his customers who double-parked. After several weeks of this, the restaurant owner changed his mind and began giving free meals to officers again. Those authors also mentioned a type of contest whereby officers competed to see how many free bottles of liquor they could collect; the winning team collected fifty bottles from the bars and businesses in one district on a single shift. "The blue discount suit," according to the authors, was a term that indicated how officers felt about gratuities. Some other terms described businesses that offered free or discounted goods; these establishments were said to "show love" or give "pop"—hence the saying, "If you got no pop, you got no cop."

Officers in some departments are known for their skill in soliciting free food and liquor for after-hours parties. In the same vein, officers also solicit merchants for free food and beverages for charity events sponsored by police, such as youth softball leagues. The first situation is similar to individual officers receiving gratuities, but the second situation is harder to criticize. Officers bring up the seeming hypocrisy of a departmental prohibition against individual officers accepting gratuities, yet at the same time there may be an administrative policy of actively soliciting and receiving donations from merchants for departmental events, such as pastries, coffee, or more expensive catering items.

It might be instructive to look at other occupations. Do judges or college professors receive any types of gratuities? Obviously, an attempt to give these professionals gifts would be perceived as an attempt to influence their decisions in matters involving the gift giver. Professional ethics always discourages gifts or gratuities when the profession involves discretionary judgments about a clientele. Professors cannot receive gifts from students and expect to maintain the appearance of neutrality.

Judges are usually careful to avoid the appearance that they have received anything of value from the participants in any proceeding. If there is any chance of a conflict of interest, if the judge is compromised by a relationship with or knowledge of the participants, he or she is supposed to pass the case on to a neutral colleague. A revelation that a gift from either side was accepted by the judge would probably result in a mistrial, a successful appeal, and the judge being sanctioned by the commission on judicial conduct.

It is also true that the system of electing judges is heavily criticized, using terms such as "justice for sale," because judges typically rely on attorneys for campaign contributions and these same attorneys practice in the judges' courts. The suspicion is that judges can't help but be favorably disposed to attorneys who contributed large sums of money to their campaigns.

The receipt of gifts or campaign contributions by politicians is a frequent news item because of the belief that such gifts are buying votes or influence. When members of Congress receive large sums of money from special-interest groups, when companies routinely distribute complimentary gifts to members of Congress, or when a lobbyist takes politicians on an expensive "fact-finding junket," there is the appearance of impropriety. Although politicians would argue that these gifts do no harm and are only tokens of esteem, there is a strong suspicion that such practices are not in the public interest because the politicians who receive gifts will be influenced. That is the reason that conflict-of-interest laws exist. While bribery laws punish taking or receiving something of value in return for a specific act of omission or commission related to one's office, conflict-of-interest laws punish merely taking something of value prohibited by the law when one holds a public office, with no necessity to show that a specific vote or decision was directly influenced by receipt of the valued items or services.

On the one hand, conflict-of-interest laws take, as a given, the reality that one's discretion is compromised after receiving things of value. On the other hand, it does not seem unusual or particularly unethical for a doctor, a lawyer, a mechanic, or a mail carrier to receive gifts from grateful clients. Whether gifts are unethical relates to whether one's occupation or profession involves judgments that affect the gift givers. The police obviously have discretionary authority and make judgments that affect store owners and other gift givers. This may explain why some think it is wrong for police to accept gifts or favors. It also explains why so many people do not see anything wrong with some types of gratuities, for police officers in most situations are not making decisions that affect the giver and, instead, are simply providing a service, such as responding to a burglary, or disturbance call.

An important distinction that might aid the discussion is the difference between a *gift* and a *gratuity*. A gift is something that is clearly given with no strings attached. An example might be when a citizen pays for a police officer's meal without telling the officer; when the officer gets ready to pay, the bill is already taken care of. Many officers have had this experience. In this case, because the police officer did not know of the reward (because the gift giver did not make the gift known), no judgment can be affected.

The ethical systems from Chapter 2 can be used to examine the ethics of gratuities. Religious ethics is not much help, as no clear guidelines can be gleaned from religious proscriptions of behavior. Ethical formalism is more useful because the categorical imperative, when applied to gratuities, would indicate that we must be comfortable with a universal law allowing all businesses to give all police officers certain favors or gratuities, such as free meals, free merchandise, or special consideration. However, such a blanket endorsement of this behavior would probably not be desirable.

The second principle of ethical formalism indicates that each should treat every other with respect as an individual and not as a means to an end. In this regard, we would have to condemn gratuities in cases where the giver or receiver had improper motives according to Kania's typology. If the business owner was expecting anything in return, he would be using the police officer as a means to his own end and thus would be violating the second principle of ethical formalism. This also explains why some gifts seem acceptable. When something is given freely and accepted without strings, there is no "using" of others; therefore, it might be considered an innocent, honorable act by both parties.

If utilitarian ethics were used, one would have to weigh the relative good or utility of the interaction. On one hand, harmless gratuities may create good feelings in the community toward the officers and among the officers toward the community (Kania's "cementing the bonds" argument). On the other hand, gratuities often lead to perceptions of unfairness by shopkeepers who feel discriminated against, by police who think they deserve rewards and don't get them, and so on. Thus, the overall negative results of gratuities, even "harmless" ones, might lead a utilitarian to conclude that gratuities are unethical.

There would be some differences in the argument if one were to apply act utilitarianism versus rule utilitarianism. Act utilitarianism would be more likely to allow some gratuities and not others. Each individual act would be judged on its own merits. A cup of coffee or a meal from a well-meaning citizen or a store owner to a police officer who was unlikely to take advantage of the generosity would be acceptable, but gratuities given with the intent to elicit special favors would not. Rule utilitarianism would look to the long-term utility of the rule created by the precedent of the action. From this perspective, even the most innocuous of gratuities may be deemed unethical because of the precedent set by the rule and the long-term disutility for society of that type of behavior.

An ethics of care approach would be concerned with the content of the relationship. If the relationship between the giver and the receiver was already established, an exchange between the two would not be seen as harmful. If there was no relationship—that is, if the store owner gave the gratuity to anyone in a blue uniform—there may be cause for concern. A preexisting relationship would create ties between the two parties so that one would want to help the other with or without the exchange. Kania's theory of social networking is appropriate to apply here. If there is no existing relationship, the gratuity may indicate an exchange relationship that is based on rights and duties, not care. Does the gift or gratuity turn it into an exchange relationship? Officers can usually recite stories of store owners who gave gifts with an expressed purpose of good will, only to remind the officers of their generosity at the point where a judgment was made against them, such as a traffic ticket or a parking violation. In this situation, the type of relationship isn't clear until "the bill is due."

Macintyre and Prenzler (1999) conducted a survey of officers to see if they would be influenced by gratuities. They asked officers what they would do if a café owner who gave them free coffee and meals was stopped for a traffic violation. The researchers found that supervisory officers were more likely than rookies to give a ticket. Although only 15 percent would not write the ticket and would continue to go back for meals, an additional 41 percent would also not write the ticket but would give the owner a warning and not go back for free meals. The remaining officers would write the owner a ticket. Another study evaluated police coverage in a medium-sized U.S. city, taking into account whether or not the businesses gave gratuities, food quality, cost, convenience, and location and found that gratuities increased coverage (Deleon-Granados and Wells, 1998). These studies indicate that gratuities do influence officers' decisions both in how they patrol and what they might do when they have to make a decision about a giver of gratuities. More research is needed to see if these findings would be replicated.

The ethics of virtue would be concerned with the individual qualities or virtues of the officer. A virtuous officer could take free coffee and not let it affect his or her judgment. According to this perspective, no gift or gratuity would affect the judgment of the virtuous officer. However, if the officer does not possess those qualities of virtue, such as honesty, integrity, and fairness, even free coffee may lead to special treatment. Further, these officers would seek out gifts and gratuities and abuse their authority by pursuing them.

An egoistic framework provides easy justification for the taking or giving of gratuities. It obviously makes police officers feel good to receive such favors, especially if they think that they deserve them or that the favors are a measure of esteem or appreciation. Even if the person giving the gift had ulterior motives, the police officer could accept the gift and be ethically justified in doing so under the egoistic ethical framework if the officer gained more from the transaction than he or she lost. In other words, if one would not get into trouble, could keep a positive self-image intact, and obtain the gratuity at the same time, then one would be justified in doing so, and it would be a moral action. However, let us not forget that the egoistic ethical system is discounted by a majority of philosophers.

ON-DUTY USE OF DRUGS AND ALCOHOL

Carter (1999) discussed the extent of on-duty drug use, citing previous research that found up to 20 percent of officers in one city used marijuana and other drugs while on duty. That seems to be a high figure because in other surveys about 8 percent of employees reported drug use and only 3 percent of all workers in a "protective services" category reported drug use. In a more recent survey, protective service employees were the least likely to report any drug use (Mieczkowski, 2002: 168).

It could also be that the decrease seen in the use of drugs by the general population is reflected in police officer samples. As well, the sources are not exactly comparable. Thus, it is impossible to determine which source is more accurate. However, certain circumstances are present in law enforcement that, perhaps, create more opportunities for drug use. Elements of police work (especially undercover work) that can lead to drug use include the following:

- exposure to a criminal element
- relative freedom from supervision
- uncontrolled availability of contraband

Carter (1999: 316) also discussed the phenomenon of police officers who go undercover and become socialized to the drug culture. They may adapt norms conducive to drug taking. Further, they may think they need to use drugs to maintain their cover. They are also able to rationalize stealing drugs from sellers; e.g. "It should not be a crime to steal something that is contraband in the first place." Drug use by officers creates the potential for even more serious misbehavior, such as stealing evidence, being blackmailed to perform other unethical or illegal actions, and being tempted to steal from drug users instead of arresting them. This, of course, is in addition to the obvious problem of compromising one's decision-making abilities by being under the influence of any drug while on duty.

The use of drug tests during the hiring process is longstanding, but periodic and/ or random drug testing of employed officers is a more recent policy. Many police officers, as is true of many other types of employees, are now subject to drug testing.

Employees in the protective services sector are the most likely to undergo drug testing in the workplace. While about 60 percent of protective service workers say that their workplace engages in random drug testing, only 14 percent of other professionals have the same experience (reported in Mieczkowski, 2002: 172). Generally, courts have upheld the right of law enforcement agencies to employ drug testing, applying the balancing test between a compelling governmental interest and individual privacy rights. The list of compelling-interest elements served by drug testing includes the following, as reported by Mieczkowski (2002: 179):

1. public safety
2. public trust
3. potential for official corruption
4. official credibility
5. worker morale
6. worker safety

Officers have some due process rights, however, and they must be notified of the policies and procedures involved in the agency's drug testing, have access to the findings, and have available some sort of appeal process before sanctions are taken (Mieczkowski, 2002: 179). In Fyfe and Kane's (2006) study of police officers terminated for cause in New York City, the most common reason for termination was a failed drug test.

Alcohol use is more socially acceptable than drug use, but it has also been cited as a problem. In one survey it was found that about 8 percent of those in protective services occupations (which include police officers) reported heavy alcohol use. This compared to 12 percent of construction workers and 4 percent of sales workers (Mieczkowski, 2002: 179). Barker and Carter (1994) indicated that 8 percent of officers reported drinking alcohol on duty. The problems of drinking on duty do not involve the vulnerability to corruption that drug use does, but there are obvious problems, and officers who are aware of another's on-duty intoxication are faced with an ethical dilemma of whether or not to take official action. Officers may choose to informally isolate themselves from drinking officers by refusing to partner with them or avoid working calls with them. According to one officer, however, partners of alcoholic officers do not report the partner to supervisors. He learned early in his career after doing this that it was not the thing to do:

> When I showed up for work the next night, nobody would talk to me. I was treated like an invisible stinking turd for the whole month. My new shoes and leather gloves disappeared from my locker. Even officers on the other shifts shunned me (Quinn, 2005: 34).

GRAFT

Graft is the exploitation of one's role by accepting bribes or protection money. Graft also occurs when officers receive kickbacks from tow truck drivers, defense attorneys, or bail bond companies for recommending them.

In Klockars, Ivković, and Haberfeld's (2004) international comparison of officers' views regarding hypotheticals drawn to illustrate various forms of corruption, officers in the United States rated bribery as the second most serious offense. Only

IN THE NEWS | ABUSE OF POWER

Police Chief Luis Collazo was suspended in the small town of Seguin, Texas, when reports surfaced that he was using his office to secure special treatment for himself and others. Allegedly, he ordered an officer to release a man wanted on federal charges, interfered with the arrest of another man accused of assault, and told an officer he would not support charges of yet another man who had assaulted the officer. Allegedly, Collazo routinely ordered Municipal Court employees to dismiss parking and traffic tickets, called a female officer an "Amazon lesbian," made sexually inappropriate remarks to other female officers, and allowed an employee to use city equipment to build a house for his mother-in-law on city time. A senior officer was also suspended while similar allegations were investigated. The investigation began with the complaints of officers in the department. It was cut short when Collazo resigned and stated that he would not seek another job in law enforcement.

In a nearby county the sheriff and county commissioner were indicted on public corruption charges after an investigation uncovered a variety of misuses of their office. The county commissioner was accused of using inmate labor to install electric wiring and complete other projects at his home, as well as using taxpayer funds to buy the supplies and pay a deputy to oversee the inmates. The sheriff was accused of using inmate labor and funds to build barbeque pits, which he then sold for a profit, accepting a truck paid for by a suspected drug dealer, and having inmates take down a county fence and put it up on his property. Both men pled guilty. The sheriff received a sentence of 90 days in jail and 10 years of probation plus restitution, and the county commissioner was ordered to pay restitution and resign from his position. The county judge said of the sheriff, "I think [he] is a good guy that made a mistake."

Why would the resignation of Collazo end the investigation if there is probable cause that laws have been broken? Is there less corruption in small towns and rural areas, or is there just less serious corruption by "nice guys who made a mistake?"

Sources: Bloom, 2008a, b, c.

---

theft from a crime scene was rated as more serious. Officers in Austria, Finland, Japan, the Netherlands, Sweden, and the United Kingdom rated bribery as more serious than did U.S. officers.

While police officers in small and medium-sized departments might argue that most of the misconduct described in this chapter does not happen in their department, examples of graft do appear in smaller communities. A small-town police chief has a great deal of power that is largely unnoticed and unquestioned until a blatant misuse of power brings it to the public's attention. As the "In The News" box illustrates, even small towns sometimes have scandals.

SEXUAL MISCONDUCT

It is a sad reality that a few police officers use their position of authority to extort sex from female citizens (there doesn't seem to be the parallel situation of female police officers extorting sex from male victims). Sexual harassment of female police officers is also a problem in some departments. Finally, officers may engage in other types of sexual misconduct for which they may be sanctioned.

Amnesty International has documented widespread mistreatment of women by police across the world. Egregious cases in the United States include rapes by officers on duty and by jailers in police lock-ups, and a few instances where the sexual misconduct of police officers was widespread and protected by departmental supervisors, such as in Walkill, New York. In that town the twenty-five-member police department evidently engaged in numerous instances of sexual intimidation of citizens before being investigated by the state police and sued in a federal civil rights lawsuit (reported in McGurrin and Kappeler, 2002: 133).

Kraska and Kappeler (1995) looked at a sample of 124 cases of police sexual misconduct, including 37 sexual assaults by on-duty officers. These authors challenged earlier studies indicating that sexual misconduct of officers occurred most often when women traded sexual favors for lenient treatment and that it was the victim who initiated the trade. This study's authors concluded that norms in a police department that ignored or condoned the exchange of sex for favored treatment opened the door to officers who used more aggressive tactics to coerce sex from citizens. Kraska and Kappeler (1995: 93) propose a continuum of sexual invasion that ranges from some type of invasion of privacy to sexual assault. This range of behavior includes the following:

1. viewing a victim's photos or videos for prurient purposes
2. field strip searches
3. custodial strip searches
4. illegal detentions
5. deception to gain sex
6. provision of services for sex
7. sexual harassment
8. sexual contact
9. sexual assault
10. rape

Sapp's (1994) inventory of sexual misconduct includes the following:

1. nonsexual contacts that are sexually motivated (non-valid traffic stops)
2. voyeurism (e.g., patrolling lovers' lanes to watch sexual activity)
3. contact with crime victims (excessive call-backs that are not necessary for investigative purposes)
4. contact with offenders (sexual demands or inappropriate frisks)
5. contacts with juvenile offenders (sexual harassment and sexual contact)
6. sexual shakedowns (demanding sex from prostitutes or the homeless)
7. citizen-initiated sexual contact (an officer is approached by a citizen because of his officer status)

In the "In the News" box an officer engaged in sexual misconduct that would be an example of number four in Sapp's typology or number six in Kraska and Kappeler's typology.

Even the most innocuous of contacts between female citizens and officers—whereby an officer might ask a woman he has stopped for a date—involve issues of power and coercion. In a study by Kraska and Kappeler (1995: 104), police described how they routinely went "bimbo hunting," which involved sexual harassment of

IN THE NEWS | SEXUAL MISCONDUCT

Austin, Texas, April 2008: The Austin Police Chief fired an officer after an investigation that showed he had paid a woman for sex with crack cocaine, Vicodin, and Xanax, obtained in some instances from the trunk of his police car. He accepted phone calls from the woman after she was sent to jail on a probation violation, he provided information to her from her offense report, and he solicited fellow officers to change their testimony to internal affairs investigators.

What crimes did this officer commit? Do you think he should be prosecuted for any of these crimes?

Source: Plohetski, 2008, 2008: B1, B5.

women out drinking (Kraska and Kappeler, 1995: 104). Prostitutes and homeless women are extremely vulnerable populations to sexual extortion by police officers, but studies indicate that middle-class citizens have also been subject to intimidation and outright assault. Most victims are under age thirty (McGurrin and Kappeler, 2002). The defense of officers is usually that, if sex occurred, it was consensual. The problem is that when officers acting in their official capacity meet women (as victims, witnesses, defendants, or suspects), the power differential makes consent extremely problematic.

McGurrin and Kappeler (2002) reported on a study of official records of sexual misconduct by police officers that uncovered hundreds of instances of sexual assault, rape, and even murder by police officers in and out of uniform. Rape charges commonly are downgraded to a conviction of "official oppression" in a plea agreement. Also, some officers who had criminal records for sexual offenses simply moved and obtained law enforcement positions in other jurisdictions.

In their own study of newspaper articles concerning sexual misconduct, McGurrin and Kappeler (2002: 134) uncovered more than two dozen cases where the officers had been disciplined for sexual misconduct prior to the case that was reported in the news article. They also found that of the cases taken up by the justice system, about half of the alleged offenders did not receive any punishment. Only a third received jail or prison time. A department may be aware of an officer's pattern of sexual harassment and do nothing about it. This obvious lapse of supervision is unfair to the public and also costs money. Kraska and Kappeler (1995) reported that police lost 69 percent of the civil rights suits brought by the victim of sexual misconduct.

Two newspaper reports of sexual abuse by a police officer in 2007 (Bloom, 2007) illustrate two different types of sexual abuse. In the first case, a police officer was arrested and charged with indecency with a child after he was accused of fondling a child after the officer consumed large quantities of alcohol at a party. In the second case, a sheriff's deputy was found guilty and sentenced to two years of probation and fined for "improper sexual activity with a person in custody" based on an incident in which he ordered a college co-ed to expose herself and groped her breasts, threatening her with a DWI arrest. In this case the county settled a civil lawsuit by the victim.

In the first case the fact that the alleged perpetrator was a police officer is immaterial and unrelated to the offense; but in the second case, the deputy used his position to victimize a citizen that he was entrusted to "protect and serve." Because police officers are in a position to stop women late at night, events like this are incredible blows to a department's reputation. Unfortunately, the relatively few cases of sexual abuse by police officers have led to the popular advice for women who drive late at night to "drive slowly with parking lights on to a well-illuminated location with people around" before stopping for flashing lights. Ethical officers should understand and accept this response from motorists who have come to fear potential victimization by officers.

Sexual harassment of fellow officers is also a problem. In one research study, 70 percent of female officers reported being sexually harassed by other police officers (Kraska and Kappeler, 1995: 92). It may be that the culture of policing is particularly problematic for sexual harassment. It has been described as a "macho" or "locker room" culture even though women have been integrated into patrol since the early 1970s. Female officers do not encounter the virulent harassment and hostility that was present in the 1970s when patrol forces were first integrated, but some remnants of that culture remain. More research is needed to update older studies of the prevalence of sexual harassment.

Sexual harassment is a violation of policy and against the law, and it is also unethical. None of the ethical systems from Chapter 2 would support coercing co-workers for sex or creating a hostile work environment. Perpetrators' defense may be that it is innocent "kidding" or honest infatuation, but universalism provides a good check on this type of behavior. Would the perpetrator want his daughter or sister to be subjected to the behavior?

There have been other cases where officers may receive administrative punishments for "conduct unbecoming to an officer" related to their sexual activity or other off-duty conduct. For instance, in a few cases officers have posed nude, participated in sexually explicit videos, or, in one case, an officer posted nude pictures of his wife on the internet. In the cases where these officers have been fired, courts have generally upheld the department's right to fire, although the First Amendment rights of officers is still an unsettled area of law.

In other cases, officers who have affairs with supervisors, co-workers, or wives of co-workers sometimes get sanctioned for "conduct unbecoming" (Martinelli, 2007). The fact of the matter is that officers are held to a higher standard of behavior, and even when no laws are broken, the behavior may be unethical in that it brings discredit or embarrassment to the department and makes it harder for fellow officers to keep the respect of the citizenry. For instance, in the case of the officer who posted nude pictures of his wife, a female officer in that town testified at the disciplinary hearing that citizens familiar with the website urged her to take off her clothes when she entered a bar to break up a fight (Egelko, 2007).

CRIMINAL COPS

There are instances where the transgressions that officers engage in go beyond ethics and enter the realm of crime and criminal conspiracies. The "Buddy Boys" in New York were able to operate almost openly in a precinct rife with lesser forms of corruption. Ultimately, 13 officers in a precinct of only a little over 200 were indicted for crimes ranging from drug use to drug sales and armed robbery.

The Buddy Boys graduated from stealing cash and drugs from drug dealers during official arrests to planned thefts where, sometimes on duty, they would target crack houses or apartments and break in and steal drugs, cash, and other valuables.

In at least one such instance, customers came to buy drugs and the officers obliged by selling drugs through the door. The officers had relatively nothing to fear from their victims because the individuals targeted were minority drug dealers. The victims could hardly report a robbery, and if other police in the precinct had any idea about what was going on, they evidently did little to investigate. The situation was finally exposed when internal affairs investigators caught two of the individual officers accepting protection money and forced them to wear "wires" to help gather evidence on the others. Ultimately, the police commissioner transferred all officers in the precinct to other divisions (Kappeler, Sluder, and Alpert, 1984/1994).

Michael Dowd, another New York City police officer, testified to the Mollen Commission in 1993 that he and other officers accepted money for protecting illegal drug operations, used drugs and alcohol while on duty, robbed crime victims and drug dealers of money and drugs, and even robbed corpses of their valuables (Kappeler, Sluder, and Alpert, 1994: 201–202). The "In the News" box describes another case of criminal cops.

New York City has experienced police scandals with depressing regularity. Widescale investigations and exposés occurred in 1894, 1913, 1932 (the Wickersham Commission), 1949 (the Kefauver Commission), 1972 (the Knapp Commission), and 1993 (the Mollen Commission). New York City is definitely not alone. The "Miami River Rats" committed armed robberies of drug deals, collecting cash and drugs. These robberies by a small group of police officers eventually led to at least one homicide (Dorschner, 1989; see also Rothlein, 1999; Crank and Caldero,

---

IN THE NEWS | MAFIA COPS

Louis Eppolito and Stephen Caracappa were New York City police officers. They were indicted in September of 2005 for a range of crimes, including murder, said to have been committed while they were police officers on the payroll of the Luchese crime family. Prosecutors allege that the two officers received thousands of dollars a month for being "hit men" for the mob. They both had retired from the N.Y.P.D. to Las Vegas, where they were arrested. Ironically, Eppolito wrote a book called *Mafia Cop: The Story of an Honest Cop Whose Family Was the Mob*, detailing his upbringing in the Gambino crime family and subsequent career as a police officer.

Eppolito and Caracappa were identified as mob informants as far back as 1994 by a Mafia member who turned state's evidence, yet the two retired without ever having come up on charges. Eventually they were convicted of a wide range of racketeering and other charges in federal court in 2006, but the judge threw out most of the convictions, saying that the statute of limitations on the racketeering charges had expired. They have been in a federal detention center while the case is on appeal.

How could these two police officers engage in acts of kidnapping, murder, and informing on drug raids and other police investigations without ever drawing the attention of internal affairs?

Sources: Feurer and Rashbaum, 2005, from http://www.ipsn.org/indictments/caracappa_indictment/blodd_ties_2_officers.htm. Also see Breslin, 2008.

2000: 162). A New Orleans police officer is in a federal prison today because he used a police radio to order a hit on a woman who was going to testify against him and others in a corruption trial. He was being monitored by federal agents who decoded the thinly disguised assassination attempt (Human Rights Watch, 1998).

Many other large cities have their own historical cycles of corruption and exposure (Kappeler, Sluder, and Alpert, 1994: 197). In 1998, forty-four Cleveland cops were indicted for providing protection for cocaine shipments. Chicago has also had its share of corruption scandals. In 1996, seven Chicago cops were indicted for conspiracy to commit robbery and extortion for shaking down undercover agents they thought were drug dealers (Crank and Caldero, 2000). In 2001, a former chief of detectives pled guilty to running a jewel-theft ring for more than a decade. This detective used police computers to follow the path of traveling jewelry sales representatives to target them (Fountain, 2001). Other Chicago police officers have been accused of shaking down Polish immigrants and robbing suspected drug dealers (who turned out to be FBI agents). This group of officers evidently joined forces with a street gang to control the cocaine trade. Brutality charges and other corruption charges have also been leveled against Chicago officers (Babwin, 2001).

Drugs are the root of several different kinds of deviance. The range of behaviors where drugs are involved include using drugs on duty, buying drugs, selling drugs, providing protection to drug dealers, robbing drug dealers, stealing from drug dealers, and using drugs to pay informants. The large amounts of money in the drug trade and the perception that this is "just drug money" lead to some officers' stealing evidence or robbing drug dealers. In 1998 the General Accounting Office conducted a study for U.S. Representative Charles Rangel that collected academic and other findings to explore the extent and range of corruption in law enforcement related to drugs. Clearly, the large amount of money in the drug trade is a powerful corruptor (General Accounting Office, 1998). The "In the News" box describes a drug trafficking case involving Boston police officers.

IN THE NEWS | BOSTON'S DRUG COPS

A trio of Boston police officers was prosecuted and convicted in 2008 of being involved in drug trafficking. The ringleader, Roberto Pulido, evidently recruited the others to help him provide counter-surveillance and protection to undercover FBI agents posing as drug dealers. The officers were arrested in Miami in 2006 after they accepted payment for their services. Pulido was also implicated in an identity theft scam where he sold the identities of individuals he stopped for traffic violations to be used for fraud, and he also sold illegal steroids. He evidently framed a former business partner by planting guns and drugs in his car and then having him arrested.

There are reports that the officers have implicated other Boston police officers, officials, and private citizens. The Boston police commissioner was evidently so shaken by the scandal that he posted a Youtube.com video so all Boston police officers would be made aware that he believed that the department as a whole was not corrupt and that he would investigate and severely punish any officer who was involved.

Sources: Vaznis, J., 2008; WBZtv.com. 2007; United States Attorney's Office, 2008; Sullivan, Murphy, and Smalley, 2006.

Carter (1999: 321) concludes that some mechanisms can be used to control drug corruption:

- leadership by the chief
- management and supervision
- supervisory training
- organizational control and information management
- internal auditing of the use of informants
- internal affairs
- drug enforcement units having audit controls
- periodic turnover of staff
- better evidence handling
- early warning systems
- better training and discipline

Several books, such as *Serpico* (Maas, 1973) and *Prince of the City* (Daley, 1984), detail the pervasiveness of corruption and criminality and the relative ease with which individual officers may develop rationales to justify greater and greater infractions. For instance, the main character in *Prince of the City* progresses from relatively minor rule-breaking to fairly serious infractions and unethical conduct, such as supplying drugs to an addicted informant, without having to make major decisions regarding his morality. It is only when the totality of his actions becomes apparent that he realizes the extent of his deviance.

We have examined a range of corruption, from the arguably trivial (gratuities) to criminal acts that include murder. There is a legitimate argument that the officers who engage in minor rule breaking or some types of unethical behaviors that are not criminal should not be in the same discussion as "criminal cops" whose pattern of wrongdoing and criminality is much more serious. The opposing argument is that the minor transgressions lead to an environment in which the truly rogue cops feel free to engage in criminality because of the minor transgressions of everyone, leading to a situation where all officers engage in a conspiracy of silence.

EXCESSIVE FORCE

Police have an uncontested right to use force when necessary to apprehend and/or subdue a suspect of a crime. When their use of force exceeds that which is necessary to accomplish their lawful purpose, or when their purpose is not lawful apprehension or self-defense but, rather, personal retaliation or coercion, it is defined as **excessive force** and is unethical and illegal. The ultimate example of excessive force is the *unjustified* use of lethal force.

The Supreme Court has defined legal force as that force which is objectively reasonable (*Graham v. Connor*, 490 U.S. 386 [1989]). What is reasonable, however, is still subject to controversy. Police departments' use-of-force policies specify when force may be used, when it may not be used, and the proper level of force to be used given certain circumstances. Most departments utilize a continuum-of-force approach that allows proportional force to the suspect's resistance, with increasing levels of force by the officer in direct response to escalating resistance of the suspect (Walker, 2007).

Probably the most well known use of force was that by Los Angeles police against Rodney King revealed by the amateur video taken by a bystander. This can still be seen on YouTube.com even though the event occurred in 1991. It is an example of force used for instrumental or expressive ends, depending on one's perception. In watching the video, King clearly continued to try to rise and the officers continued to taze, kick, and hit him with their batons. Some argue that the officers continued to hit him because he continued to resist; others argue that he continued to resist because he was disoriented and was trying to escape the injuries being inflicted upon him.

This case represents a situation in which policy, law, and ethics present different answers to this question: "Did the officers do anything wrong?" The legal question of unlawful use of force is contingent on whether the Los Angeles Police Department's use-of-force policy was legal and whether the officers conformed to departmental policy. The policy stated that the officers could use escalating and proportional force to a suspect's "offensive" behavior.

The reason that two use-of-force experts—one for the prosecution and one for the defense—disagreed was that the policy, like many other policies in policing, depends on the ethical use of discretion. The defense's use-of-force expert analyzed the video and identified offensive movements in his every attempt to rise and in every arm movement. The prosecution expert (who wrote the departmental policy) testified that a suspect lying on the ground is not in a position to present offensive movements to officers; therefore, any use of force once the suspect is down is excessive. The point is that if an officer perceives offensiveness in any movement of a suspect, the policy justifies his or her use of force.

One can see that, despite evidence that police departments' use-of-force policies have reduced the incidence of improper use of force by officers, these policies still leave a great deal of discretion. In many cases, an officer's ethics will become as powerful as his or her training and understanding of the policy itself. If an officer gets shot at, the policy obviously would justify use of force, but if the officer decides that he or she is safe enough behind his or her patrol car to talk the suspect out of shooting again and into giving up the weapon, the use-of-force policy would support that nonviolent response as well. If an officer is hit in the face by a drunk, the policy would support use of force because the drunk obviously performed an offensive action; however, the officer who accepts that the drunk is irrational, allows for it, and simply puts the person in the back of the patrol car (in effect, giving him a "free punch") is also supported by the policy. In other words, the policy can be used to justify all but the most blatant abuse of police power, or not, depending on the interpretation of the individual officer.

Thus, in the Rodney King incident, an initial act of passing a police vehicle and leading officers in a high-speed chase (although the actual speed of such chase was subject to dispute) led to the involvement of twelve police cars, one helicopter, and up to twenty-seven officers. The incident resulted in King being struck at least fifty-six times, with eleven skull fractures, a broken cheekbone, a fractured eye socket, a broken ankle, missing teeth, kidney damage, external burns, and permanent brain damage (Kappeler, Sluder, and Alpert, 1994: 146).

After the incident, officers justified their actions by the explanation that King was on the drug PCP (he was not, and, in fact, his alcohol level was .075), impervious to pain, and wild. These claims were repeated in the newspapers and can be interpreted as the attempt to fit the use of force into a pattern that the public could understand and accept. This use of force probably was prosecuted (unsuccessfully) in this case only because of the existence and widespread dissemination of the videotape. In other circumstances it would hardly have rated a small newspaper article. The media typically become interested in police use of force when the victim cannot be fit into the stereotype of the "dangerous criminal"—when he is a middle-class insurance agent (as in the Miami case that sparked riots), Andrew Young's son (in an incident involving the Washington, D.C., police), or a high-school athlete who would have been on his way to Yale on an academic/athletic scholarship.

In a 2005 case in Austin, Texas, an event that was similar to the Rodney King case occurred with similar results. Ramon Hernandez was involved in a minor car accident and ran from the scene. After being tackled and brought to the ground, three police officers surrounded him and, when he continued to try to get up, one held his foot to Hernandez' neck and another administered many blows to his back. Hernandez argued that his face was being pressed into an anthill and that he was only struggling to move away from that. The officers argued that he had earlier tried to wrest one's gun away and Hernandez was, and continued to be, physically combative. The officers were acquitted of official oppression charges, and they also won a federal civil lawsuit against them by Hernandez (Kreytak, 2008).

Similar to the Rodney King case, individuals can look at the tape of the incident (http://www.statesman.com/news/mplayer/m/2949) and see either a legitimate use of force that conforms to the continuum-of-force policy (meeting resistance with force) or a gratuitous application of force that was not necessary to subdue the suspect. Legally, it appears that the officers did nothing wrong, at least according to the juries who decided the criminal and federal civil cases. As for policy, one officer was fired, one resigned, and one received a 70-day suspension, so it seems that their superiors did find that they violated the department's policy on the use of force.

After the verdicts, the officers stated that they believed they engaged in a proper use of force exactly in the way they were taught. If they did nothing wrong, why were they punished? If they believed that they were acting according to training and policy, who is wrong? Perhaps the answer lies in our understanding of discretion. Just because you *can* do something, doesn't mean you *should*.

The most common layman's explanations for excessive force is that force is the only thing "these people" understand or that "officers are only human" and consequently get mad or frightened or angry, just like anyone else would in that situation. Another comment that seems to be fairly prevalent among individuals who respond to these events is that the person "deserved it" because of his or her commission of a crime or because he or she ran away from police. The weakness of such arguments is obvious. Even if the only thing "these people" understand is force, it removes the differences that we like to think exist between us and "them." If other people get angry and use force, it is called assault and battery, and they are arrested and prosecuted. Finally, punishment comes after a finding of guilt in a court of law, not by law enforcement officers, and does not ever involve the infliction of corporal punishment, which has been ruled as violating the Eighth Amendment.

Although reasonable people may disagree about the Hernandez case, or even the Rodney King case, the Abner Louima case involved, without question, clearly illegal force. N.Y.P.D officer Justin Volpe's assault on Abner Louima shocked the nation and led to a prison sentence for Volpe. The truly amazing thing about this criminal act is that it occurred in a police station with at least one officer reportedly assisting but with a whole squad room just outside the door. Volpe brutally sodomized Louima with a broken broom handle, requiring several operations to repair the damage. According to Volpe's testimony, Louima was brought up to the squad room and taken into the bathroom for the purpose of beating him, and the broken handle was put in the bathroom for that purpose. This evidently didn't raise any red flags to officers at the booking desk or other officers. How could this have happened in a police station? The fact that Louima was a minority, the fact that Volpe believed he had been hit in the head by Louima, and the fact that the blue curtain of secrecy is still intact in many police departments seem to be insufficient to answer this question.

How do victims of excessive force come to the attention of police? Often it is by challenging police authority—passing a patrol car, asking questions, challenging the stop, or intervening in the arrest of another (Kappeler, Sluder, and Alpert, 1994: 159). In Klockars's (1984) description of types of police power (authority, power, persuasion, and force) described in Chapter 7, force is brought into play when one's authority is challenged. Thus, individuals who question or refuse to recognize police authority become vulnerable to the use of force. Such use of force may be perfectly legal. Officers have the right to tackle a fleeing suspect or hit back when they are defending themselves. Illegal or excessive force occurs when the officer goes beyond what is necessary to effect a lawful arrest or has no lawful reason to use force at all. For instance, gratuitous violence in response to verbal insults is excessive force, as is beating a suspect who is handcuffed and helpless. The "Quote and Query" box is one police account illustrating excessive force.

QUOTE AND QUERY

I saw one guy arrested once for speeding, and the police officer lost his temper. Of course, this highway patrolman brought it on himself because he was badmouthing the guy. Finally—he's a man, too—the guy lost his temper and spit on the highway patrolman. Right on the side of a U.S. highway on a Sunday afternoon, the highway patrolman wrestled the guy down, took a handful of hair and held his head down in the dirt and started packing the guy's mouth full of sand. The guy was choking and spitting and this patrolman was shoving sand in his mouth. "I'll teach you to spit at a trooper, boy." Those were his exact words. I'm standing in the background, watching the cars go by, slowing down to stare at this event. It looked bad.

Do you think anyone "deserves" to be beaten by police officers?

Baker, 1985: 139–140.

Source: Reprinted with the permission of Simon & Schuster. Copyright © 1985 by Mark Baker.

CULTURE OF FORCE

The use of force in response to perceived challenges to police authority is highly resistant to change, even in the presence of public scrutiny and management pressure. Even with the notoriety of the Rodney King episode and the extreme public reaction to the spectacle of police use of force, several incidents involving other officers' abusive behavior toward motorists occurred shortly thereafter. This pattern might be so ingrained in some police department cultures that it remains relatively unaffected.

The Los Angeles Police Department (L.A.P.D.), at least in the past, seems to have had the type of culture that tolerated, perhaps even encouraged, a high level of violence. The Christopher Commission reported that L.A.P.D. management was responsible, to some extent, for the brutality exhibited by the Rodney King incident in that there was an apparent failure to punish or control those who had repeated citizen complaints of violence (Rothlein, 1999). Further, there was a culture that encouraged the use of force, coupled with an ineffective citizen complaint system, with no civilian oversight. In other words, leadership did not exist to actively discourage the excessive use of force.

Skolnick and Fyfe (1993), too, have discussed the culture of L.A.P.D. as one where the use of violence was tolerated, even encouraged. This has resulted in civil rights cases. Breaking up departments into elite units seems to encourage "swashbuckling behavior." Skolnick and Fyfe (1993: 191) described one case where an L.A.P.D. elite squad, acting on a tip, totally destroyed a citizen's home, including breaking toilets, ripping sofas, and spray-painting "L.A.P.D. Rules!" on the wall of the house (1993: 191). These specialized units create their own culture, even within the subculture of the larger department, and sometimes this subculture promotes violence. L.A.P.D. officials under the leadership of William Bratton may be changing the culture of the department successfully today.

The Human Rights Watch (1998) identified serious problems in Atlanta, Boston, Chicago, Detroit, Indianapolis, Los Angeles, Minneapolis, New Orleans, New York, Philadelphia, Portland, Providence, San Francisco, and Washington, D.C. The report cited police leadership and the "blue wall of secrecy" as serious barriers to reducing police violence. According to this report, the mechanisms for handling police offenders ensure that violence will continue. In most cases where a citizen alleges excessive force, there is no discipline and the case is closed as unfounded. If there is a civil suit and the plaintiff wins, the city pays, and, again, the officer may not even be disciplined. One study is cited concerning the fate of police officers named in 100 civil lawsuits between 1986 and 1991 in twenty-two states in which juries awarded payments of $100,000 or more. It was found that only eight of these officers were disciplined (Human Rights Watch, 1998: 82; see also Payne, 2002). More recently, Detroit reportedly paid out in excess of $45 million for police officer misconduct between 2002 and 2005 (Associated Press, 2005).

Amnesty International is another human rights organization that looks at official oppression all around the world and has long been a critic of the U.S. justice and corrections system. Amnesty International alleges that police use Taser or stun guns in hundreds of cases in which their use is unjustified and "routinely" inflict injury, pain, and death. Its investigation uncovered the fact that the Tasers were

IN THE NEWS | TASER USED IN TRAFFIC STOP

In Austin, Texas, a police officer used a Taser on a Black motorist on his way to a Thanksgiving dinner with his mother because the driver did not produce his license when requested. The incident was caught on the officer's patrol camera, and the police chief made an unprecedented decision to release the tape and use it for training purposes. The officer was suspended, and members of the police officer union apologized to the public at large for the actions of this one officer. (You can view the tape at http://www. statesman.com/news/mplayer/news/32386).

Source: Plohetski, 2007.

used on unarmed suspects 80 percent of the time and for verbal noncompliance in 36 percent of the cases. Tasers allegedly have been used on "unruly schoolchildren," the "mentally disturbed or intoxicated," and those who do not comply immediately with police commands. There were seventy Taser-related deaths in four years (Dart, 2004), but it should also be noted that Tasers seem to be associated with a decrease in the number of deaths of suspects, a decrease in the number of injuries to suspects, and a decrease in the number of injuries to officers (Dart, 2004: A14). Further, manufacturers allege that Tasers are safe in the vast majority of cases and are potentially lethal only when there is some underlying medical condition.

The "In the News" box gives an account of one incident where an officer used a Taser on an uncooperative motorist.

RESEARCH ON EXCESSIVE FORCE

All information regarding police use of force is controlled by police, including the number of incidents, the taking of reports, and the amount of information recorded. The ability to access this information is limited, even in cases dealing with a challenge to the officer's use of force. The official version of any event is that force was necessary because of dangerous, offensive actions. This interpretation is often supported by other police, and there is usually little evidence to the contrary (unless there is a videotape). The victim is often an unsavory character who would be a poor choice for sympathy, and supporting witnesses may have their credibility questioned. Thus, it is difficult to determine the true number of incidents of excessive force. Researchers address the questions in four ways:

1. They use official documents, such as police incident reports.
2. They ask police officers about their actions or the actions of their peers regarding excessive force.
3. They use civil rights complaints or public opinion surveys to ask people what their experiences have been.
4. They use observers in police cars to record interactions between police and citizens, including instances of excessive force.

In general, there is quite a lot of research, but it is on use of force rather than excessive force specifically. One perhaps can assume that officers who are identified as using force, or factors associated with the use of force, also are related to the use of excessive force, but research usually does not specifically prove that connection. Further, some findings are inconsistent; however, a few generalizations can be made:

1. Force seems to be present in a small percentage of the total encounters between police and citizens.
2. A small percentage of officers seem to be responsible for a disproportionate percentage of the force incidents.
3. Some studies do find an association between force and race or socioeconomic status, but other factors, such as demeanor, seem to be even more influential.

Number of Incidents   Research indicates that few encounters actually end in the use of force, much less, excessive force. Worden and Catlin (2002) offer studies showing that use of force is present in between 1.3 and 2.5 percent of all encounters. Garner, Maxwell, and Heraux (2002) found in their study that use of force ranged from 12.7 percent of encounters in one city to 22.9 percent of encounters in another city. Alpert and Dunham (2004) review the research as well and point to studies showing that officers used force in an estimated 53 percent of vehicle pursuits. Further, 47 percent of the surveyed suspects who fled from police reported that force was used (in contrast to the official number of 17 percent).

In addition, Alpert and Dunham (2004: 47) reported on a national survey of law enforcement agencies that found that the rate of use-of-force events varied by region, with the highest in the South (90 incidents per 100,000), followed by the Northeast (72), the Midwest (68) and the West (50) (Terrill, 2005). In a study based on participant observations of police–citizen encounters, Alpert and Dunham (2004: 47) reported that officers did not use the level of force that they were legally and (by policy) entitled to use in the majority of encounters, based on the resistance of the suspect.

In documenting the perceptions of the use of excessive or unnecessary force, Alpert and Dunham (2004) reported on research where officers estimated that 13 percent of vehicle pursuits ended in excessive use of force. In addition, Weisburd and Greenspan (2000) asked officers about use of force, and 22 percent of the respondents said that police officers in their department "sometimes," "often," or "always" used *more force than necessary* when making an arrest. Further, 15 percent of the respondents indicated that their fellow officers "sometimes," "often," or "always" responded to verbal abuse with physical force. However, 97 percent thought that extreme uses of unnecessary force were extremely rare.

Recall that in Barker and Carter's (1994) study, officers reported that 39 percent of their peers engaged in brutality. A Gallup Poll finding indicated that 20 percent of respondents said they knew someone who had been abused by police, but the percentage increased to 30 percent of minority respondents (reported in Alpert and Dunham, 2004: 36).

Disproportional Use of Force by a Small Number of Officers   Some officers seem to get involved in use-of-force situations repeatedly, whereas others, even in similar patrol neighborhoods, rarely get involved in such altercations. Thus, even if every use of force meets the guidelines of departmental policy, there are lingering questions as to why some officers seem to need to resort to force more often than others and why some interpret actions more often as offensive.

According to Souryal (1992: 242), the report by the Independent Commission of the Los Angeles Police Department in 1991 revealed that the top 5 percent of officers ranked by number of reports of the use of force accounted for more than 20 percent of all reports, and that of approximately 1,800 officers who had been reported for excessive use of force between 1986 and 1990, most had only one or two allegations but forty-four had six or more, sixteen had eight or more, and one had sixteen allegations.

Worden and Catlin (2002) reported on a number of studies documenting the presence of differential use of force by officers in police departments. A small number of officers seem to be disproportionately involved in use-of-force incidents and, arguably, are more likely to also engage in excessive force. Further, some evidence seems to indicate that these officers may be identifiable by certain psychological traits:

- lack of empathy
- antisocial and paranoid tendencies
- proclivity toward abusive behavior
- inability to learn from experience
- tendency not to take responsibility for their actions
- cynicism
- strong identification with the police subculture

Other risk factors include age of the officer (being young and impressionable may increase the risk of using improper force) and being involved in a traumatic event (thus, use of force would be a type of post-traumatic stress behavior) (reported in Worden and Catlin, 2002: 101). Terrill, Paoline, and Manning (2003) found that officers who identified more strongly with the police culture were more likely to use force and that differences between individuals were more predictive than differences in departments' management strategies or formal cultures of departments.

Race and Other Factors Nelson (2000) chronicled a long list of personal stories of harassment, brutality, illegal arrests, and coerced confessions by police toward minority members, especially African Americans. Her conclusion was that in the minority community, at least, there are reasons to fear police. Holmes (2000) found that the number of civil rights complaints filed (which were mostly claims of excessive force) was only weakly affected by the percentage of blacks in the population in small cities. However, there was a significant association between race and number of civil rights complaints in cities with a population exceeding 150,000, and there was also a stronger association between the number of complaints filed and the percentage of Hispanics in the city's population (Garner, Maxwell, and Heraux, 2002; Smith and Holmes, 2003).

Alpert and Dunham (2004) developed the statistic of a "force factor" in their study of Miami-Dade use-of-force incidents to determine when the force used by the officer exceeded the level of resistance by the subject and then evaluated factors such as age, gender, and race of the suspect and officer. They found that female officers used significantly less force in response to resistance, and the longer an officer was employed, the more force was used in relation to the suspect's resistance. As to race, there were few significant relationships, but the highest force factors occurred with Hispanic officers to Hispanic suspects. Black and Hispanic officers who arrested Black suspects also employed higher levels of force. They found that Black and Anglo officers arresting Anglo suspects used lower levels of force in relation to level of resistance than other ethnic matches (2004: 159).

Race does seem to be associated with the use of force. However, only a few studies have controlled for other factors, such as those discussed next, to determine if race continues to be a significant factor when measuring other factors. The other issue, of course, is that most studies (except those that use civil rights complaints) are measuring use of force, not excessive force.

Several researchers have tried to determine what factors are associated with police use of force (Garner, Maxwell, and Heraux, 2002; Alpert and MacDonald, 2001; Terrill and Mastrofsky, 2002; Alpert and Dunham, 2004). They conclude that the following (not in order of rank and not necessarily with consistent findings) have been associated with a greater likelihood that the police officer will use force:

- suspect's race
- suspect's manner toward police (disrespectful demeanor)
- general agitation or emotionality of suspect
- suspect's mental illness
- intoxication of suspect
- number of citizens present (positive association)
- number of police officers present (positive association)
- possession of a weapon by the suspect (or belief that there is a weapon)
- knowledge that suspect had committed other crimes (especially, violent crimes)
- suspect's use of force
- gang involvement
- suspect being male
- officer being male
- age of officer (younger)
- officer having prior injuries
- encounter involving a car chase
- race of officer (but the association is for Hispanics, not African Americans)
- socioeconomic status of suspect

Alpert and MacDonald (2001) found that agencies that required supervisors to fill out use-of-force forms had lower levels of use of force than did agencies that allowed officers to fill out their own forms. It should be noted that these factors are associated with the use of force, not necessarily excessive force.

DEADLY FORCE

Nothing is more divisive in a minority community than a police shooting that appears to be unjustified. Cities are quite different in their shooting policies and in their rates of civilian deaths. There can also be quite a change within one city. The District of Columbia, for instance, went from thirty-two police shootings (with twelve deaths) in 1998 to only seventeen in 2001 (with three deaths) (C. Murphy, 2002). The D.C. police department was under a court monitor, which might have had something to do with the fairly dramatic decline in shootings.

POLICY BOX | **SHOOTING-REVIEW BOARDS**

All departments have some mechanism for reviewing an officer's use of a firearm. A shooting-review board would require the officer to appear before a hearing made up of fellow officers and supervisors. The review board would not only evaluate whether the case was justified but also review elements of the shooting to see if any improvements could be made in training to assist officers.

Law: It is unlawful to shoot unless the officer is in fear of his or her life or the offender poses a threat to others. However, that law covers a wide spectrum of situations. If the officer's shooting was found to be unjustified, he or she could be held on a range of charges up to murder, but usually some form of voluntary manslaughter. The department may be legally liable if training was found to be insufficient.

Policy: No police department wants to endanger citizens' lives with police officers who shoot unnecessarily; therefore, policies are in place and officers are trained to use their weapon as a last resort. However, informal policies regarding shooting evidently vary quite a bit from department to department.

Ethics: Officers who would be asked to participate in this review board may have an ethical dilemma in that they might think that they would be showing some form of disloyalty to their fellow police officer to appear as a board member. The individual who used his or her weapon has an ethical duty to tell the truth. The board members have a duty to decide against the officer if, in their collective judgment, they decide that it was not a "good" shooting. It is possible that an officer may have committed no crime but also did not follow departmental policy and ethics in decisions leading up to the need to shoot.

Skolnick and Fyfe (1993: 235) and Chevigny (1995) describe New York City's shooting policy and argue that the policy may be instrumental in why the N.Y.P.D. has such a low shooting rate. There is an automatic investigation every time shots are fired. The investigation is conducted by the Firearms Discharge Review Board, with multiple layers of report writing and investigation before the officer is cleared. The authors also noted that N.Y.P.D. officers showed a lower rate of being shot than in other cities, so the stringent policy has not seemed to affect their safety.

Even New York, however, has had its share of deaths that have raised tensions. Amadou Diallo allegedly resembled a rapist, and when he ignored police orders to show his hands and continued to unlock an apartment building door to go inside, he was shot at forty-one times by officers in the Special Crimes Unit of N.Y.P.D. The case threatened to spark riots in the city, especially when the police officers' trial was moved to Albany and the officers were acquitted. The Policy Box examines the use of shooting-review boards.

SUMMARY

The use of excessive force is probably not as pervasive in the United States today as it was even two decades ago. However, it is hard to know what occurs because the data are not readily available and individual victims often do not come forward or, if they do, are not taken seriously. Use-of-force policies have been found to reduce the use of force, especially when policies require supervisors to write a report on every use of force (Walker, 2007).

A few officers in every department seem to be truly abusers of power, but the other officers and an organizational culture protect these officers from sanctions. The more common ethical issue concerning the use of force is that of the officer who observes an unlawful use of force by another officer. This issue is addressed in Chapter 9.

A WORLDWIDE PROBLEM

Police corruption does not occur just in the United States. Across the world there are instances of many different types of corruption. *Baksheesh*, a euphemism for graft, is endemic in many developing countries. Officials, including law enforcement officers, expect *baksheesh* to do the job they are supposed to do; alternatively, they extort money in exchange for not doing their job. "It's just the way it is" is the explanation for why such corruption exists. In all countries, corruption includes the following:

- corruption of authority
- kickbacks
- opportunistic theft
- shakedowns
- protection of illegal activity
- internal payoffs
- excessive force

Tim Prenzler and his colleagues tracked and analyzed police corruption in Australia. In Queensland, the Fitzgerald (1989) Inquiry found a network of vertical corruption reaching to the commissioner, and widespread misconduct including fabrication of evidence, assaults on suspects, and bribery related to gambling and prostitution. The scandal eventually resulted in legislation pertaining to freedom of information and whistleblower protection. In addition, an independent watchdog agency—the Criminal Justice Commission—was created (Prenzler, Harrison, and Ede, 1996: 5; Prenzler and Ransley, 2002; Fitzgerald, 1989). The Wood Commission Report exposed corruption in the New South Wales Police Department in 1997 (Wood, 1997), including instances of fabrication of evidence, theft, armed robberies, sale of drug evidence, sale of information, and a protection racket (Prenzler, Harrison, and Ede, 1996).

Every country has had notable scandals. Police scandals have emerged when suspects die or are severely injured in police custody (Austria, Canada, Great Britain, Pakistan, South Africa), when police use illegal means to catch suspects (Canada, Great Britain, Ireland), or when investigations seem to be compromised by police relationships with the suspect (Belgium). Often police are implicated in bribery scandals (France, Pakistan, Russia) and having "slush funds" (Japan). Drug scandals also have arisen in other countries where police are accused of accepting bribes and conspire with smugglers or dealers (Netherlands, Mexico)

It was reported that 284 police commanders in Mexico were purged from the top ranks of the federal police force in 2007 in an effort to combat the influence of drug cartel leaders on law enforcement. The commanders were replaced with members of an elite squad that had been trained and tested. In 2007 more than 1,000 civilians and 178 police officers and 19 soldiers have been killed in drug-related shootings. Traffickers often employ police officers as the shooters.

Source: McKinley, 2007.

(Edelbacher and Ivković, 2004; Neyroud and Beckley, 2001; Alain, 2004; Mores, 2002, Barker, 2002; Westmorland, 2004; Fielding, 2003; D. Johnson, 2004; Chattha and Ivković, 2004; Associated Press, 2008b). The "In the News" box gives an example of corruption in Mexico.

MEASURES OF CORRUPTION

Transparency International (2008) charts corruption worldwide, ranking ninety-one countries. This agency defines corruption as abuse of public office (including police) for private gain (e.g., bribe taking). The countries with the highest scores for honesty include Finland, Denmark, New Zealand, and Sweden. Some of the poorest countries, including Azerbaijan, Bolivia, Kenya, Uganda, and Bangladesh, produced very low scores. The United States, to many people's surprise, perhaps, does not rate as highly as a number of other countries.

Finland is a country that evidently has a very low level of police corruption (Puonti, Vuorinen, and Ivković, 2004). It has received the highest or one of the highest rankings by Transparency International for the last several years. According to official records, the country had only twenty-three cases of official corruption in the 1990s, and only one of these cases involved a police officer (Laitinen, 2004). Only about 10 percent of all citizen complaints about officials are about law enforcement officers (Laitinen, 2002).

Surveys indicate that Finnish people trust their police more than any other professional group, including court officials and church officials (Laitinen, 2004). This phenomenon may be attributed to the culture of open and accountable government. Finland's police force is highly educated as well and can be described as endorsing a public service model of policing. There are strong proscriptions against most of the types of corruption that have been described in this chapter, even gratuities. Laitinen (2004) illustrates that gratuities, in general, are frowned on by a joke in which gratuities are described as the difference between a "cold sandwich and a warm beer," which is acceptable, and a "warm sandwich and a cold beer," which is a gratuity. Although there certainly are cases of corrupt police officers in Finland, the police there do seem to have a strong ethical code that minimizes the level of corruption.

Croatia, in contrast, has been known as having fairly corrupt police. In 2000, only 46 percent of the respondents had confidence in the police, according to public opinion polls. However, Croatia's police may be becoming less corrupt—or at least the perception is that they are. In 2000, Croatia's ranking in the Transparency

International survey went up to 51st place, and in 2001 it went up to 47th place (Ivković and Klockars, 2004). It would be instructive to examine countries that seem to have minimal levels of corruption and then contrast them with other countries to see what elements contribute to the relatively higher levels of ethics.

One interesting study that has compared the police of different countries was conducted by Klockars, Ivković, and Haberfeld (2004). In this study, samples of police officers from fourteen countries rated the seriousness of eleven hypothetical situations ranging from gratuities to "shopping" at a crime scene. They also indicated what level of discipline would be administered to the transgressions. This second measure reflected the officers' perception of the degree of seriousness that management staff would assign to the incidents.

There were great differences in the rankings of some of the hypotheticals. For instance, the excessive-force situation was ranked as the third most serious in Hungary but the least serious in Pakistan, and ranked seventh in seriousness by police in the United States. Although most countries ranked bribery very high, Croatia and Hungary did not. Theft from a found wallet was ranked high in all countries except South Africa.

Countries also differed in their pattern of rankings. Some countries ranked all situations relatively high, whereas other countries ranked all or almost all situations relatively low. For instance, Finland ranked all but three situations in the 4+ range (the scores went up to 5), but South African police ranked only one situation in the 4+ range. However, Pakistani police also ranked all but two situations highly, indicating perhaps that they answered the survey in the way they thought they were supposed to. An important finding of the research was that the officers' beliefs seemed to be influenced by what discipline they perceived would be forthcoming for each incident (Klockars, Ivkovic', and Haberfeld, 2004). Thus, management has an opportunity to shape officers' beliefs by its responses to deviant behavior. Whether beliefs, in turn, influence behavior is another question. Now we will look at some explanations of deviance.

EXPLANATIONS OF DEVIANCE

Explanations of corruption can be described as

- individual
- institutional (or organizational)
- systemic (or societal)

Individual explanations, such as the *rotten apple* argument (discussed below), assume that the individual officer has deviant inclinations before he or she even enters the police department and merely exploits the position. Sloppy recruiting and the development of a police personality are other individual explanations of deviance. Institutional (or organizational) explanations point to organizational problems (low managerial visibility, low public visibility, and peer-group secrecy, among others). Institutional explanations also include looking at the police role in the criminal justice system (as the front-line interface with criminals), the tension between the use of discretion and bureaucraticism, and the role of commanders in spreading corruption. A systemic (or societal) explanation of police deviance focuses on the relationship between the police and the public (Johnston, 1995).

INDIVIDUAL EXPLANATIONS

The most common explanation of police officer corruption is the **rotten-apple argument**—that the officer alone is deviant and that it was simply a mistake to hire him or her. This argument has been extended to describe *rotten bushels*—groups of officers banding together to commit deviant acts. The point of this argument is that nothing is wrong with the barrel, that deviance is individual, not endemic.

Sherman (1982) explained that deviant officers go through what he called a "moral career" as they pass through various stages of rationalization to more serious misdeeds in a graduated and systematic way. Once an individual is able to get past the first "moral crisis," it becomes less difficult to rationalize new and more unethical behaviors. The previous behaviors serve as an underpinning to a different ethical standard, for one must explain and justify one's own behaviors to preserve psychological well-being (Sherman, 1982).

When one accepts gradations of behavior, the line between right and wrong can more easily be moved farther and farther away from an absolute standard of morality. Many believe, for instance, that gratuities are only the first step in a spiral downward: "For police, the passage from free coffee at the all night diner and Christmas gifts to participation in drug-dealing and organized burglary is normally a slow if steady one" (Malloy, 1982: 33). Malloy described a passage from "perks" to "shopping" to premeditated theft (1982: 36).

Others dispute the view that after the first cup of coffee, every police officer inevitably ends up performing more serious ethical violations. Many police officers have clear personal guidelines on what is acceptable and not acceptable. Whereas many, perhaps even the majority of, police see nothing wrong with accepting minor gratuities, few police would accept outright cash, and fewer still would condone thefts and bribes. The problematic element is that the gradations between what is acceptable or not can vary from officer to officer and department to department.

Sherman also believes in the importance of a signification factor, or labeling an individual action that is acceptable under a personal rationale (Sherman, 1985a: 253). Police routinely deal with the seamier side of society—not only drug addicts and muggers but also middle-class people who are involved in dishonesty and corruption. The constant displays of lying, hiding, cheating, and theft create cynicism, and this, in turn, may develop into a vulnerability to temptation because officers may redefine them as acceptable behaviors.

Following are some rationales that police might easily use to justify unethical behavior (Murphy and Moran, 1981: 93):

1. The public thinks every cop is a crook—so why try to be honest?
2. The money is out there; if I don't take it, someone else will.
3. I'm only taking what's rightfully mine; if the city paid me a decent wage, I wouldn't have to get it on my own.

4. I can use it because it's for a good cause—my son needs an operation, or dental work, or tuition for medical school, or a new bicycle. . . .

Other research has looked at correlates of police misconduct; in other words, are some individuals more likely to succumb to the temptations of police work? Fyfe and Kane (2006), in their study of New York City police officers who were terminated for misconduct, analyzed correlates that might influence misconduct. In the discussion below, their review of the literature and their findings are used to discuss possible predictors.

Gender   In journalistic accounts of police corruption and in common thought; there is a perception that female police officers are less likely to be involved in corrupt activities. No women have been involved in the largest scandals in recent memory. Some academic research has indicated that women engage in less aggressive policing and receive fewer citizen complaints. However, measurements of police-culture attitudes by other researchers indicate that women are not significantly different from male officers in their values and beliefs. Fyfe and Kane found that women in their sample were more likely than male officers to be terminated during their probation. They also found that, although male officers were more likely to be terminated for bribery, there was no difference in all other profit-oriented misconduct. Male officers were more likely than female officers to be terminated for brutality and other forms of non-profit-oriented abuses, but women were more likely to be terminated for non-line-of-duty criminal conduct (e.g., drug crimes) and administrative rulebreaking. Thus women may be just as prone to certain types of corruption as male officers, although the researchers were cautious in this finding because of the small numbers and because the relationship seemed to wash out when conducting multivariate analysis.

Age   Prior research on age indicates that, although younger officers (younger than 22) have fewer instances of prior bad behavior, they are more likely to be terminated during probationary periods than officers who were older when they were hired. Other research indicates that age has no relationship to use of force. In Fyfe and Kane's New York City study, those under 22 years of age when appointed were more likely to be terminated during probation but no more likely than older officers to be terminated for any form of misconduct after probation.

Education   College-educated officers receive fewer citizen complaints; however, researchers wonder if this finding isn't confounded by assignments because educated officers are also more likely to be promoted off the street into supervisory or detective positions. Although some research indicates that there is a relationship with higher education and less misconduct, other research finds no relationship. In the New York City study, those with more years of education upon hire were less likely to be terminated for misconduct.

Race   Prior research indicates that blacks were more likely than whites to be disciplined for misconduct. A possible explanation might be differential rule enforcement or differential assignments and vulnerability to situations where use of force, for instance, was necessary. Research seems to support the notion that differential assignments have something to do with black officers' greater use of force. Fyfe and Kane's study found that blacks, but not other minorities, were more likely to be terminated during probation, and terminated for misconduct, including non-line-of-duty criminal conduct, drug test failures, and administrative rulebreaking.

Military Experience, Performance in the Academy, and Background Characteristics   Research indicates that prior bad conduct predicts future bad conduct. If someone has received unfavorable job evaluations or been dishonorably discharged from the military, they are more likely to commit police misconduct as well. Other indicators of misconduct seem to be poor performance in the academy and other forms of misconduct, such as misdemeanors or other arrest histories. In Fyfe and Kane's study, those who had prior negative employment histories, dishonorable discharges, and/or did poorly in the academy were more likely to be terminated for misconduct.

In sum, according to this one study of terminations for misconduct, factors associated with high risk include: being black or (to a lesser extent) Latino, prior citizen complaints, prior criminal history, history of a public-order offense, and prior employment disciplinary history. Non-individual factors included being assigned to posts with low supervision and high citizen contact. Length of service, higher education and older age at appointment were negatively related to misconduct (Fyfe and Kane, 2006: xxvi–xxviii). These findings must be viewed with caution, however, as they are only from one department, they utilize only official reports of misconduct, and they do not control for other variables.

ORGANIZATIONAL EXPLANATIONS

The Miami River scandal involved officers committing armed robberies of drug dealers. Some argue that it was caused by the rapid hiring of minorities during an affirmative action drive without proper background checks; disaffection by white, mid-level supervisors who basically did not do their job of supervision, who were, instead, merely counting the days to retirement; ethnic divisions in the department; and the pervasive influence of politics in the department, which disrupted internal discipline mechanisms (Dorschner, 1989). These concepts are largely organizational explanations of police corruption. Another example of the effects of rapid hiring is the finding that of the 1,000 new officers hired by Washington, D.C., in the early 1990s as a result of political pressure, nearly a quarter have been fired because of their involvement in various acts of misconduct or crime (reported in Lersch, 2002b: 77).

Murphy and Caplan (1989) argue that there are situational elements that "breed corruption," including lax community standards over certain types of behavior (gambling, prostitution), hesitation of the chief to enforce rules and discipline officers, tolerance by fellow officers, unguided police discretion and incompetence, and lack of support from prosecutors and the courts (or corruption at that stage of the system as well). Most of these explanations fall into an organizational category as well.

Crank and Caldero's (2000/2005) "noble-cause" explanation of some types of deviance (described more fully in Chapter 9), whereby officers lie or commit other unethical acts to catch criminals, is an organizational explanation, as is any description of deviance that includes the aspect of subcultural support. Whenever deviance is explained as being supported by the organizational culture—whether that be the "formal culture" or the "informal culture"—it falls into this category.

Gilmartin and Harris (1998) also have discussed why some officers become compromised and argue that it is because the law enforcement organization does not adequately train them to understand and respond to the ethical dilemmas that they will face. They coined the term the "continuum of compromise" to illustrate what happens to the officer. The first element is a "perceived sense of victimization," which refers to what happens when officers enter the profession with naïve ideas about what the job will be like. Citizen disrespect, bureaucratic barriers, and the justice system's realities sometimes makes officers cynical, feeling that no one cares and that they are needlessly exposed to danger. Cynicism leads to distrust of the administration and the citizenry. At that point, the officer is alienated and more prone to corruption.

When officers feel victimized, they are more likely to rationalize acts of omission. For instance, they may choose not to stop at a traffic accident or not to stop when they see a drug buy. Officers rationalize by saying, "You will never get in trouble for the stop you don't make." Officers may also commit acts that violate administrative rules, such as carrying unauthorized equipment or otherwise breaking small rules. Officers rationalize these acts by saying that the rules aren't important or they know better than administrators how to get the job done. Officers may then proceed to criminal acts, such as throwing away evidence, falsifying overtime records, and so on. Because these acts could get them fired, they add a layer of deceit to their initial wrongdoing when they have to lie about it.

Gilmartin and Harris (1998) also talk about the officers' sense of entitlement and how that can lead to corruption. There is a sense that the rules don't apply to them because they are different from the citizenry they police. This leads to the "blue curtain of secrecy," discussed more fully in Chapter 9, when officers believe it is more ethical to cover up for other cops than it is to tell the truth.

Neil Trautman (2008) has also discussed how organizational leaders contribute to the unethical actions of their employees. In his "corruption continuum" he argues that organizations create unethical employees through the following steps:

1. An atmosphere of administrative indifference toward integrity: There is no ethics training and internal politics, and hidden agendas and unfairness are the organizational culture. Indifference is also apparent in the quality of recruitment and hiring, unfair promotions or discipline, allowing disgruntled field officers to influence recruits, and supervisors' treating employees with a lack of respect.
2. Ignoring obvious ethical problems: Supervisors ignore problem employees and, in the worst cases, engage in active cover-ups rather than try to rectify the problem.
3. Hypocrisy and fear-dominated culture: After years of indifference and ignoring problem individuals, employees come to fear saying anything. They believe that there are always hidden agendas and it is better to be a survivor than a whistle-blower. Morale is low because no one wants to work in such an environment.

4. Survival of the fittest: Employees will do whatever it takes to survive in the organization and honest employees fear the dishonest, cover-ups are the standard method of response when scandals threaten, and there is no hope of things getting better.

Trautman's (2008) solutions include better background investigations, a high-quality field training officer (FTO) program, fighting political interference, consistent and fair accountability, effective ethics training, positive leadership models, not letting a culture of victimization begin (referring to Gilmartin and Harris's continuum), and implementing an effective employee intervention process.

Finally, in Fyfe and Kane's (2006: xxiv) study of police misconduct in New York City, they found that instances of termination for misconduct for all groups (Black, White, and Latino officers and male and female officers) went down as the department became more diverse. They argue for more diverse police departments with mechanisms in place to check unethical behavior, such as drug tests, supervisor reports on all use of force incidents, and integrity testing.

SOCIETAL EXPLANATIONS

Rationalizations used by some police when they take bribes or protection money from prostitutes or drug dealers are made easier by the public's tolerant stance toward certain areas of vice; e.g., to accept protection money from a prostitute may be rationalized by the relative lack of concern that the public shows for this type of lawbreaking. The same argument could be made about gambling or even drugs. We often formally expect the police to enforce laws while we informally encourage them to ignore the same laws.

Signification occurs here as well. Although gambling carries connotations of the mob and organized crime, we typically don't think of church bingo or the friendly football pool down at Joe's Bar. If police were to enforce gambling laws against the stereotypical criminal, the public would support the action, but if the enforcement were to take place against "upstanding citizens," there would be an outraged response. "Police Arrest Grandma Bingo Players!" would be the headline.

Fyfe and Kane (2006) present an interesting societal explanation of why profit-motivated corruption seems to occur more often in large Northeastern cities, and abuse of authority (specifically in the use of force) occurs more often in Western "newer" cities. They argue that the older cities are characterized by the "watchman" style of policing that performs differential policing depending on the sector of the community. Police enforce laws that are perceived as inapplicable and undesirable to ethnic enclaves. Members of these ethnic communities do not trust government, and thriving underground economies are present. Lack of investment in the laws on the part of the community leads to kickbacks, protection rackets, bribery, and other forms of graft by the police who do not care if the "gray area" laws are enforced or not in these communities.

Western cities, by contrast, were settled by homogeneous groups that arrived around the same time. Policing was perceived to be all about keeping undesirables under control; therefore, use of force was tolerated and even expected, while profit-oriented corruption was harshly punished. The "legalistic" style of policing characterized, until recently, cities such as Los Angeles, Denver, Seattle, and others.

If police are expected to make a distinction between "good" people and "bad" people, and "good" people should be excused, ignored, or, at worst, scolded for their involvement, but "bad" people should be investigated, caught, and punished, it should come as no surprise that they sometimes take extra-legal liberties with those they think are "bad" people. It should also come as no surprise that if the public doesn't want full enforcement of the laws, especially if it impacts them, some officers may decide that a hypocritical public won't mind a few gambling operations, or a certain number of prostitutes plying their trade, or even a few drug dealers, so they might as well accept protection money.

As long as the public supports certain types of illegal activities by patronage, it is no surprise that some police officers are able to rationalize non-enforcement. Also, as long as the public relays a message that crime control, especially against "bad" people, is more important than individual liberties and rights, we should not be surprised when police act on that message.

CONCLUSION

In this chapter we reviewed the range of deviant behaviors in law enforcement. There are types of deviance that are purely for self-interest, and then there is deviance that stems from "noble-cause" corruption—which will be discussed in Chapter 9. One of the most serious forms of deviance is the use of excessive force. An important factor that seems to be associated with excessive force is a challenge to police authority. Race also seems to be a factor. It was also noted that police scandals have occurred in all countries around the world but that there are apparent differences in the relative levels of corruption among police in different countries. Reasons for law-enforcement deviance can be categorized into individual explanations, organizational explanations, and societal explanations.

Key Terms

baksheesh 252

graft 235

gratuities 226

rotten-apple argument 255

excessive force 242

grass eaters 224

meat eaters 224

Review Questions

1. List and describe various forms of law-enforcement deviance.
2. What are Barker and Carter's types of abuse?
3. What are grass eaters and meat eaters?
4. What are the arguments for and against the acceptance of gratuities?
5. What is the continuum of sexual misconduct?
6. Discuss the research concerning use of force. What factors seem to be associated with the use of force?
7. Provide examples of law enforcement corruption in other countries.
8. What are the individual explanations of police officer deviance?
9. What are the organizational explanations of police officer deviance?
10. What are the societal explanations for police officer deviance?

Writing/Discussion Questions

1. Write an essay on (or discuss) gratuities. Prove a persuasive argument as to whether or not gratuities should be acceptable. If you are arguing that they are ethical and should be acceptable, discuss what limits, if any, should be placed upon them.

2. Write an essay on (or discuss) the potential disciplinary sanctions that should be taken against officers who commit legal, policy, and/or ethical transgressions. What is the rationale for the administration of punishment? Which acts warrant more severe sanctions? What should be done with an officer who has a drinking or drug problem? Taking a bribe? Stealing from a crime scene? Hitting a hand-cuffed suspect? Having checks bounce? Being disrespectful to a member of a minority group? Sexually harassing a co-worker?

3. Write an essay on (or discuss) the explanations of police deviance that seem to make the most sense. Does this explanation explain all forms of deviance? Explain how an officer faced with a choice of behaviors could use the ethical systems to determine the right course of action (e.g., being offered a bribe, wanting to ask a motorist for a date, wanting to hit a verbally abusive suspect who was finally handcuffed and subdued after a struggle). Do the ethical systems help at all? Explain why or why not.

4. Write an essay on (or discuss) what explanation best explains excessive force. If you could be a change agent in a police department, describe the changes or procedures you would institute that you believe would reduce the incidence of excessive force.

Ethical Dilemmas

Situation 1

You are a rookie police officer on your first patrol. The older, experienced officer tells you that the restaurant on the corner likes to have you guys around, so it gives free meals. Your partner orders steak, potatoes, and all the trimmings. What are you going to do? What if it were just coffee at a convenience store? What if the owner refused to take your money at the cash register?

Situation 2

You are a rookie police officer who responds to a call for officer assistance. Arriving at the scene, you see a ring of officers surrounding a suspect who is down on his knees. You don't know what happened before you arrived, but you see a sergeant use a Taser on the suspect, and you see two or three officers step in and take turns hitting the suspect with their nightsticks about the head and shoulders. This goes on for several minutes as you stand in the back of the circle. No one says anything that would indicate that this is not appropriate behavior. What would you do? What would you do later when asked to testify that you observed the suspect make "threatening" gestures to the officers involved?

Situation 3

You (a female police officer) have been working in a small-town police department for about six months. During that time you have been dealing with a fellow police officer who persists in making comments about how pretty you are, how you don't look like a police officer, how you shouldn't be dealing with the "garbage" out on the streets, and so on. He has asked you out more than a dozen times even though you have told him every time that you are not interested and that you want him to stop asking you out and to stop making comments. Although he hasn't made any derogatory or offensive comments, his constant attention is beginning to make you not want to go to work. You have a romantic partner, and you are definitely not interested in your fellow officer. You have mentioned it to your FTO, who is a type of father figure, but he likes the guy and tells you that you should be flattered. You want to file a sexual harassment charge against him but hesitate because, although you do feel harassed, you don't feel especially threatened; further, you know that you would encounter negative reactions from the other officers in the department who like the guy. What should you do?

Situation 4

You and your partner have been working together for more than five years. He has seen you through the serious illness of your young child, and you have been there for him during his divorce. After the divorce, though, you have become increasingly anxious about him. He is obviously not taking care of his health, he drinks too much, and he has been consistently late to roll call. Now you can smell alcohol on his breath during the day and suspect that the ever-present cup of coffee he carries has more than a little whiskey in it. You've tried talking to him several times, but he just gets angry and tells you to mind your own business. Today, when you both responded to an accident scene, a witness drew you aside and said, "Aren't you going to do something about him?" pointing to your partner. Unfortunately, you knew what she meant, for he was literally swaying, trying to keep his balance in the hot sun. To make matters worse, he insists on driving. What would you do?

Situation 5

You are a waitress (or waiter) in an all-night diner and are not too happy about pulling the midnight shift. Every evening, luckily, police officers drift in for their coffee breaks. You have been told that the diner does not offer gratuities and that you are not to give free coffee or meals to anyone, including police officers. But it's 2:00 A.M., and there are a lot of scary people out there. You figure that the pot of coffee might cost only a couple of bucks, so it's worth it to keep officers coming in. You suspect that the owner of the diner wouldn't be happy (because he doesn't like police), but he's not here, so you fall into the habit of giving all the officers free coffee. Then it escalates to free pie (it was going to be thrown out anyway), and now when no one is around, you'll let the officers go without paying for their meal. Do you see a problem with your actions? Who should make the decision—the owner or the employee who is on site? If you were to stop giving free coffee and pie, do you think the officers would stop coming in?

Suggested Readings

Alpert, G. and Dunham, R. 2004. *Understanding Police Use of Force*. New York: Cambridge University Press.

Barker, T. 2006. *Police Ethics: Crisis in Law Enforcement*, 2d Ed. Springfield, IL: Charles C Thomas.

Barker, T., and Carter, D. 1991. *Police Deviance*. Cincinnati, OH: Anderson.

Dunham, R., and Alpert, G. 2004. *Critical Issues in Policing*, 2d Ed. Prospect Heights, IL: Waveland.

Bouza, A. 2001. *Police Unbound: Corruption, Abuse, and Heroism by the Boys in Blue*. Amherst, NY: Prometheus.

Einstein, S., and Amir, M. 2003. *Police Corruption: Paradigms, Models and Concepts: Challenges for Developing Countries*. Huntsville, TX: Office of

International Criminal Justice (OICJ), Sam Houston State University.

Einstein, S., and Amir, M. 2004. *Police Corruption: Challenges for Developed Countries: Comparative Issues and Commissions of Inquiry*. Huntsville, TX: Office of International Criminal Justice (OICJ), Sam Houston State University.

Heffernan, W., and Stroup, T. 1985. *Police Ethics: Hard Choices in Law Enforcement*. New York: John Jay Press.

Hickman, M., Piquero, A. and Greene, J. 2003. *Police Integrity and Ethics*. Belmont, CA: Wadsworth Publishing.

Human Rights Watch. 1998. *Shielded from Justice: Police Brutality and Accountability in the United States*. Available from http://www.hrw.org

Kappeler, V., Sluder, R., and Alpert, G. 1994. *Forces of Deviance: Understanding the Dark Side of Policing*. Prospect Heights, IL: Waveland.

Klockars, C., Ivković, S., and Haberfeld, M. (Eds.). *The Contours of Police Integrity*, pp. 130–160. Thousand Oaks, CA: Sage.

Lersch, K. 2002. *Policing and Misconduct*. Upper Saddle River, NJ: Prentice-Hall.

Nelson, J. (Ed.). 2000. *Police Brutality*. New York: Norton.

Prenzler, T., and Ransley, J. 2002. *Police Reform: Building Integrity*. Sydney, Australia: Hawkins.

Skolnick, J. and Fyfe, J. 1993. *Above the Law: Police and the Excessive Use of Force*. New York: Free Press.

INVESTIGATIVE METHODS, NOBLE-CAUSE, AND REDUCING POLICE CORRUPTION

Frank Serpico spoke out against police corruption as a young police officer in the late 1960s and early 1970s, most notably in front of the Knapp Commission in 1971 (left). Thirty years later, Serpico continues his fight against the blue curtain of secrecy and crooked cops, here testifying at a New York City Council meeting discussing legislation to establish an independent commission to monitor police corruption.

CHAPTER OBJECTIVES

1. Understand the concept of noble-cause corruption.

2. Understand the ethical issues involved in investigation and interrogation.

3. Distinguish between physical and mental coercion, and understand the arguments for and against these methods of interrogation.

4. Become familiar with the ethical justifications for and arguments against whistleblowing versus loyalty to coworkers.

5. Be able to describe an effective, ethical leader.

6. Understand the methods employed to reduce or minimize corruption among police officers.

CHAPTER OUTLINE

The selection of Joseph Pistone as an undercover agent to infiltrate the Mafia made sense. He was Sicilian and grew up on the mean streets where Mafia "wiseguys" drove the big cars and had the most money. After he had been with the FBI for seven years, he was selected to work undercover in 1976 to bust a truck hijacking ring. His success in that role led his FBI supervisors to decide that he would make a good small-time jewel thief in order to get close to Mafia members. He became Donnie Brasco. His six years as Donnie Brasco meant that he lived the life of the "wannabe wiseguy," with his visits to his wife and daughter, who were moved to another state, limited to every three or four months for a day or so. Eventually he got close to some of the most powerful organized crime figures in New York.

When his Mafia friends decided that he had to be "made"—an honor that meant he would be a full member of the family, but only after he completed a hit on someone they targeted—the FBI decided to pull him out. Brasco's information led to 200 indictments, 100 convictions, and a $500,000 contract on his head. Later, the FBI convinced organized crime figures to rescind the contract, but Brasco continued to travel and live in a way that protects his identity. A movie based on his book about the experience, called *Donnie Brasco*, was a hit in the late 1990s (Pistone, 1987; Pistone and Brandt, 2007).

This chapter covers the methods of law enforcement, including undercover work, that may raise ethical issues. The central question of this chapter is: "What means are acceptable to catch a criminal?" The answer may depend on whether you subscribe to a crime control model or a public servant model of law enforcement, and whether you subscribe to utilitarianism or ethical formalism.

NOBLE-CAUSE CORRUPTION

Klockars (1983) presented us with the question of whether one could still be a good person if bad means were used to arrive at a good end. In the "Dirty Harry problem" (with due credit to Clint Eastwood), Klockars asked whether it was ethically acceptable for a police officer to inflict pain on a suspect in order to acquire

IN THE NEWS | OFFICER ESCAPES INDICTMENT

After an internal investigation, it was concluded that an officer lied in a police report about the reason he stopped and searched the car of a suspect he arrested for drug possession. In the police report he stated that he had seen a crack pipe but told investigators that he had lied. He also stated in the report that the suspect's companion "ground her foot" in the dirt in an attempt to destroy evidence, but his patrol-car camera does not show her doing what he said she did. Although this officer was fired for lying, the Grand Jury refused to issue an indictment for false swearing.

Source: Plohetski, 2008.

---

information that would save an innocent victim. We will explore that question more carefully in the discussion of interrogation later in the chapter, but we use it now to begin our discussion of what has been called **noble-cause corruption**. The argument of those who discuss noble-cause corruption is that officers sometimes (maybe even frequently) employ unethical, perhaps even illegal, means to catch criminals because they believe it is right to do so.

This is an example of the utilitarian viewpoint—that "the end justifies the means." Crank and Caldero (2000/2005), for instance, argue that practices such as testilying (lying to get a warrant or a conviction) and coercion are not caused by selfishness but, rather, by *ends-oriented thinking*. In the "In the News" box, one officer employed ends-oriented thinking to secure a conviction when he found contraband following a potentially illegal search.

The noble cause of police officers is "a profound moral commitment to make the world a safer place to live" (Crank and Caldero, 2000: 9). Officers will do what it takes to get an offender off the street, even if it is a "magic pencil"—that is, to make up facts on an affidavit to justify a warrant or to establish probable cause for arrests. Arguably, they are inclined to behave this way because we hire those who have values that support such actions and train and socialize them to internalize these values even more deeply, and then put them in situations where their values dictate doing whatever it takes to "make the world safe" (2000: 88).

Further, police are not the only actors who subscribe to noble-cause values. Crime-lab investigators and prosecutors also engage in shortcuts and magic pencils in order to convict the perceived guilty. Prosecutors have been known to suppress evidence and allow perjured testimony, so it is not only police officers who feel compelled to break the law in order to further the noble cause of crime control (Crank and Caldero, 2000: 134).

How pervasive is this tendency? Studies show that about 60 percent of rookies support mild lies to achieve a conviction (Crank and Caldero, 2000: 157). Recall from Chapter 8 that the officers surveyed by Barker and Carter (1991) reported that about a quarter of the officers perjured themselves. In *dropsy* testimony, officers report that a drug suspect dropped the drugs and ran. This is convenient because it puts the drugs in plain sight and justifies the subsequent arrest. The trouble is that dropsy testimony rose exponentially after the Supreme Court ruled that street pat-downs for evidence required probable cause. How many officers "fudge the truth" about how they found the drugs is unknown. What is known is that many of those who commit perjury do so out of a sincere desire to get the criminal convicted.

Other authors argue vehemently that noble-cause corruption is a dangerous concept because it gives credence to illegal behavior on the part of officers. Alderson (1998: 68), for instance, protests that

> ...noble-cause corruption ... is a euphemism for perjury, which is a serious crime.... In ethical police terms justice is not divisible in this way into means and ends, and the peddlers of this perversion of justice are guilty of the immorality of the totalitarian police state, and their views stand to be roundly condemned.

However, it may be that Alderson misunderstands those who present the noble-cause concepts. Crank and Caldero (2000), for instance, do not seem to be supporting the rationale; rather, they argue that "noble cause" is the underlying reason for much of officers' unethical behaviors, so efforts to control corruption must take cognizance of this motivation in order to be effective. If selfishness and personal gain are not the motives for misdeeds, then monitoring and punishments may not work.

The culture of police is not supportive of egoistic criminality, but it is supportive of "catching the criminal—whatever it takes." If we want to change this attitude, we must address it directly. Further, Crank and Caldero seem to argue that such an attitude must change because we are increasingly living in a world where pluralism is the reality and the values of the police organization may not be reflective of the citizenry they police. As multiculturalism becomes the dominant reality, police must learn to adapt and accommodate the needs and priorities of different groups.

In an exploration that tries to measure noble-cause values and their relationship to crime, researchers defined noble cause as a utilitarian value of approving of illegal means to convict criminals. In a small sample of sheriffs' deputies, the researchers found that there were wide variations in support for noble-cause statements and that adherence to noble cause did not seem to be related to a perception of level of crime (Crank, Flaherty and Giacomazzi, 2007). More research has to be done to validate the concept of noble cause and to test hypotheses regarding its relationship to factors such as perception of crime as a problem and willingness to commit testilying and other forms of misconduct.

The following discussion explores some of the law enforcement practices used to investigate and prosecute criminals. These methods can be evaluated under legal standards—e.g., whether or not police action reaches the definition of entrapment as provided by the courts—but they can also be evaluated under ethical standards and systems. We absolutely do not mean to say that all these activities are examples of noble-cause corruption. However, understanding the concept of noble cause makes it clear that the following methods can sometimes slide into noble-cause misconduct—for instance, when undercover officers go too far to maintain their cover, when interrogation methods cross the line, and when police officers protect their informant at the cost of justice for his or her victims. The underlying questions are invariably the same:

1. Is a practice or an act legal?
2. Is a practice or an act allowed under the departmental policy or standards of behavior?
3. Is a practice or an act ethical? (This may be different from legal!)

In order to answer the last question, we have to consider a final question.

4.   Is the practice or act justified under any ethical system, or, is act utilitarianism the only ethical system that supports it?

INVESTIGATION

The goal of investigative law enforcement is to collect evidence in order to identify and successfully prosecute the criminal. Different issues are involved in *reactive* investigations versus *proactive* investigations. In reactive investigations a crime has already occurred and the police sift through clues to determine the perpetrator. When police and other investigators develop an early prejudice concerning whom they believe is the guilty party, they look at evidence less objectively and are tempted to engage in noble-cause corruption in order to convict. This can take the form of ignoring witnesses or evidence or even manufacturing evidence to shore up a case against an individual.

Rossmo (2008) brings together descriptions of several investigations that failed because of the human tendency to ignore evidence that does not fit preconceived notions. In these cases the true criminal was not discovered and others were suspected, and sometimes charged and convicted, because police officers did not follow proper protocol in the collection and interpretation of evidence. Protocol is necessary to avoid errors in judgment when a criminal investigator who "knows" someone is guilty happens to be wrong. Good investigators do not let their assumptions influence their investigations because assumptions jeopardize effectiveness. Unfortunately, one can find examples, as Rossmo has, where, evidently, proper investigative methods were discarded because of police officers who thought they knew who committed the crime.

This tendency to slant the evidence is not limited to police investigators. Several news outlets reported charges that FBI lab examiners had compromised cases by completing shoddy work and misrepresenting their findings (Sniffen, 1997). The motivation of examiners was evidently to support police theories regarding the guilty party. In effect, they were not objective scientists but, rather, co-conspirators with police. This led to overstating their findings on the witness stand and covering up tests that were done improperly. A whistleblower exposed these practices and was suspended for his efforts. Ultimately, thirteen examiners were implicated, although only two were ever formally censured (Serrano and Ostrow, 2000).

The Houston crime lab has been a target of investigation. Lab practices and possible perjury by examiners have forced the district attorney's office to reexamine more than 100 cases. Similar charges have been leveled at the Fort Worth crime lab (Axtman, 2003). In the Houston case the police lab was eventually shut down in 2002 because of shoddy practices. An independent investigation by the Justice Department discovered that untrained workers were conducting DNA analysis, there was evidence of contamination from a leaky roof, "drylabbing" (making up scientific results) was being done, and there was no quality control. More than 2,000 cases required review because of potentially tainted testimony from the police lab. Two men have had their sentences overturned or been granted new trials because of the findings concerning the lab (Hays, 2005).

Other labs across the country have also been the subject of news reports. Joyce Gilchrist was the supervisor of the forensic lab for the Oklahoma City police department. She came under scrutiny for shoddy practices and alleged misstatement of the evidence while testifying. After several convicted individuals were exonerated, her testimony came under scrutiny and the Oklahoma attorney general suspended executions while the cases could be reexamined (Luscombe, 2001). Sometimes the criticism has been simple incompetence and shoddy work practices, but in other allegations it appears that the lab examiners are engaged in "noble-cause" corruption by working with police departments to arrive at desired results.

The problem is that once investigators decide who the guilty party is, they may ignore evidence that doesn't fit with their idea of who did it and how it was done. It is human nature to "complete the puzzle"—to see things that conform to one's way of looking at the world. Good police work doesn't close the door to contrary evidence, but human nature does. Utilitarian ends-oriented thinkers may be more likely to ignore contrary evidence or overstate existing evidence if they believe they have the "guilty" party. Ethical formalism, however, emphasizes duties, not the end result, so those whose ethical values lean toward ethical formalism may be less likely to slide into the types of behaviors that have put these forensic professionals under scrutiny.

PROACTIVE INVESTIGATIONS

In proactive police investigations, police officers initiate investigations rather than simply respond to crimes. Drug distribution networks, pornography rings, and fences of stolen property all tend to be investigated using methods that involve undercover work and informants. This is because such crimes often do not result in victims coming forward or crimes being reported. It may be that deception is a necessary element in this type of investigation.

According to one author, "Deception is considered by police—and courts as well—to be as natural to detecting as pouncing is to a cat" (Skolnick, 1982: 40). Offenses involving drugs, vice, and stolen property are covert activities that are not easily detected. Klockars (1984) discussed "blue lies and police placebos." In his description of the types of lies that police routinely use, he differentiated *placebos* as being in the best interest of those being lied to—for example, lying to the mentally ill that police will take care of laser beams from Mars, lying to people that police will keep an eye out for them, or not telling a person how a loved one was killed. The motive is benign, and the effect relatively harmless. *Blue lies* are those used to control the person or to make the job easier in situations where force could be used. For example, to make an arrest easier, an officer will lie about where the suspect is being taken, or to get someone out on the street to be arrested, the officer will say that she only wants to talk.

Barker and Carter (1991, 1994) proposed a typology of lies differentiating accepted lies, tolerated lies, and deviant lies. *Accepted lies* are those used during undercover investigations, sting operations, and so on. Accepted lies must meet the following standards:

1. They must be in furtherance of a legitimate organizational purpose.
2. There must be a clear relationship between the need to deceive and the accomplishment of an organizational purpose.
3. The nature of the deception must be one wherein officers and the management structure acknowledge that deception will better serve the public interest than the truth.

Tolerated lies, according to Barker and Carter, are those that are "necessary evils," such as lying about selective enforcement. Police may routinely profess to enforce certain laws (such as prostitution) while, in reality, they use a selective manner of enforcement. Lies during interrogation or threats to troublemakers that they will be arrested if they don't cease their troublemaking are also tolerated lies.

Deviant lies are those used in the courtroom to make a case or to cover up wrongdoing. However, one might argue with Barker and Carter that, in a few documented instances, the lies of rogue divisions to make a case seemed to become prevalent enough to be categorized as tolerated lies rather than deviant lies.

Targets of Investigation   In proactive investigations, the central question is who the police target and why. Selection of targets on any basis other than reasonable suspicion is a questionable use of discretion. Members of Congress convicted of bribery in the Abscam operation in 1980 alleged improper conduct in the FBI's selection of targets. Marion Barry, ex-mayor of the District of Columbia, alleged that he was "set up" because of his race after he was videotaped using drugs with a girlfriend in a hotel room in 1990. Representative William Jefferson was targeted by an FBI sting in 2005. As part of that sting, he was offered and accepted money to bribe the Nigerian president to give lucrative contracts to a technology company that he was connected with. When an FBI team searched his home, they found $90,000 wrapped in tinfoil and hidden in his freezer. Jefferson maintains that he was entrapped and that he was conducting his own investigation. Voters in Louisiana reelected him in 2007 even though he was under federal indictment for bribery and a range of other crimes (Foxnews.com,2007).

How targets are selected is a serious question. Arguably, the selection should be based on reasonable suspicion. However, Sherman (1985b) reported that "tips" are notoriously inaccurate as a reason to focus on a certain person. To the targets of an FBI sting, it may appear that they have been unfairly targeted and, especially when targets are political figures, the charge of improper target selection is easy to make.

Police operations that provide opportunities for crime change the police role from one of discovering who has committed a crime to one of discovering who might commit a crime if given a chance. For instance:

- A fake deer placed by the side of the road is used to entice overly eager hunters, who are then arrested for violating hunting laws.
- Police officer decoys are dressed as drunks and pretend to pass out on sidewalks with money sticking out of their pockets.

- Undercover officers, posing as criminals, entice doctors to prescribe unneeded medications that are controlled substances, such as Percoset and Oxycontin.
- Police undertake various stings in which they set up fencing operations to buy stolen goods.

Are only bad people tempted? If taken too far, this role expansion is arguably dangerous, undesirable, and inconsistent with the social-contract basis of policing because police are, in effect, creating crime. The opposing argument is that crimes would occur regardless of whether police set up the opportunity and that the good of catching criminals outweighs the negative possibility that some people might not have committed that particular crime at that time if the police had not presented the opportunity. Both of these arguments exist under a utilitarian framework. So even when using the same ethical system, a particular action may be judged as ethical or unethical.

Other types of stings are designed to catch those who have already committed crimes, and thus are, arguably, less problematic. Creative scams include sending party invitations or prize announcements to those with outstanding warrants to get them to come to a certain location, or staging a murder in a high-crime neighborhood and then arresting those (with outstanding warrants) who come out to see what is happening. The utility of such stings is undeniable. The only argument against them is that the government deception appears unseemly. It is also possible that such actions may undermine public confidence in the police when they are telling the truth.

Entrapment   In legal terms, entrapment occurs when an otherwise innocent person commits an illegal act because of police encouragement or enticement. Two approaches have been used to determine whether entrapment has occurred. The *subjective approach* looks at the defendant's background, character, and predisposition toward crime. The *objective approach* examines the government's participation and whether it has exceeded accepted legal standards. For instance, if the state provided an "essential element" that made the crime possible, or if there was extensive and coercive pressure on the defendant to engage in the actions, a court might rule that entrapment had occurred (Klotter and Pollock, 2007). See the "In the News" box for a description of one such case.

Stitt and James (1985) criticize the subjective test for the following reasons:

1. It allows the police to entrap people with criminal records who might not otherwise have been tempted.
2. It allows hearsay and rumor to establish predisposition.
3. It forces the individual charged to admit factual guilt, which may stigmatize him or her.
4. It provides a free rein for police discretion in choice of targets.
5. It degrades the criminal justice system by allowing the police to use misrepresentation and deceit.

Supporters say that the subjective test allows police to go after those who are most likely to harm society. The objective test would punish the police and let the criminal go free, forcing police to perjure themselves to save a case (Stitt and James, 1985: 133–136).

| IN THE NEWS | A CASE OF ENTRAPMENT? |

When police raided an X-rated materials mail-order house, they found Keith Jacobsen's name and address, as well as the information that he had ordered two magazines, *Bare Boys I* and *Bare Boys II*, neither of which had been determined to be obscene material by any court. The police created a fictitious company called "The American Hedonist Society" and sent Jacobson a membership application and questionnaire. He joined and indicated an interest in pre-teen sexual material.

In other mailings over the course of three years, the government represented itself as "Midlands Data Research," "Hartland Institute for a New Tomorrow," and Carl Long, an individual interested in erotic material. Finally, a mailing from the government posing as the "Far Eastern Trading Company, Ltd." resulted in an order from Jacobson for *Boys Who Love*. He was arrested by federal agents after he accepted receipt of the order.

Do you think federal law enforcement should be soliciting people to buy pornography?

Source: Dix, 1991: 12–13 .

Legal standards, as we have discussed earlier, are often useful guidelines for determining ethical standards, but they are not the same thing as ethical standards. For instance, one might disagree with legal standards as being too restrictive if one believes that police should be able to do anything necessary to trap criminals. Alternatively, legal guidelines may not be sufficient to eliminate what some consider to be unethical behavior. For example, do you agree that an undercover officer should pose as a client in a methadone clinic and pretend to befriend other clients, then ask them to "hook him up" with a drug dealer? If they do it, they will be guilty of a crime. What if the undercover officer targeted someone for eleven months, continually begging and pleading with the target to sell him drugs, until finally, simply to get rid of him, the target did so and was promptly arrested? Does this violate the subjective test of entrapment? (Remember that a methadone client would be considered predisposed to drug crimes.) Is this an ethical use of police resources?

POLICE DECEPTION AND THE MEDIA

Journalists who unwittingly assist police by believing and publishing false stories criticize the use of deception by police. There are a number of ethical issues in the relationship between the police and the media. Should the police intentionally lie to the media for a valuable end? Examples are lying about the stage of an investigation or about the travel path of a public figure for security reasons. In the 2002 Washington, D.C., sniper case, the media and the police had an extremely close relationship, and the police were especially sensitive to media issues (e.g., how the media could be used to encourage tips) but also how the story might create public panic. Some believed that the media were fed "red herrings," such as the importance of the white van, to divert the snipers' suspicions regarding how the police investigation was going.

Should the media have complete power to publish or report crime activities regardless of the negative effect on the level of public fear or the possibility of receiving an unbiased trial? Should the media become so involved in hostage situations that they become the news rather than just the reporters of news? The situation involving David Koresh and his cult of Branch Davidians in Waco, Texas, in the spring of 1993 raised a number of questions concerning the relationship between the police and the media. In that instance, the media were banished to a distance far from the cult compound. Is this an acceptable use of police power, or does it infringe on the public's right to know? Could police have ethically used the media to deceive Koresh into giving up by feeding the media false information in response to his stated wish for a sign? Should the media have been better informed during the course of the final assault?

THE USE OF UNDERCOVER OFFICERS

Undercover officers, such as Joseph Pistone (Donnie Brasco), described at the beginning of the chapter, may pretend to be drug dealers, prostitutes, johns, crime bosses, friends, and—perhaps—lovers in order to collect evidence of crime. They have to observe or even participate in illegal activities to protect their cover. Undercover work is said to be a difficult role for individual officers, who may play the part so well that they lose their previous identity. Marx (1985a: 109) cited examples of officers who became addicted to drugs or alcohol and destroyed their marriages or careers because of undercover assignments. He noted a disturbing belief system among undercover officers that the laws don't apply to them or that they are exempt from the law because of their assignment. It has been found that undercover officers possess high levels of neuroticism and low levels of impulse control, and that there are adverse psychological effects from the experience of being undercover (Mieczkowski, 2002: 162).

Conlon (2004), a Harvard-educated New York City police officer, described how undercover officers entered a no-man's land in the department, where they were treated almost more like informants than fellow cops. Those who were successful at setting up buys were treated like "star performers," and some developed "prima donna" attitudes. In general, they were treated and they behaved in a way that made it hard for them to maintain relationships with other police, not to mention probable issues with their families.

Policemen routinely pretend they are johns, and policewomen dress up as prostitutes. Community members who live in neighborhoods plagued with street prostitution may applaud any police efforts to clean up their streets. But do we want our police officers to engage in this type of activity? An important element of this debate is the type of relationship involved in the police deception. The two extremes of intimacy are, at one extreme, a brief buy–bust incident wherein the officer pretends to be a drug pusher and buys from a street dealer, and moments later an arrest is made. At the other extreme is a situation in which an undercover officer pretends to be romantically involved with a target of an investigation to maintain his or her cover.

The second situation violates our sense of privacy to a much greater extent. In one case a private detective (not a police detective) engaged in this type of relationship over a period of months and even agreed to an engagement of marriage with the suspect in order to get a confession on tape (Schoeman, 1986: 21). In another case a police officer acted as a friend to a target of an investigation, to the extent of looking after his child and living in his house for six months. The purpose of the investigation was to get evidence on the man so the topless bar he owned could be shut down. Eventually the officer found some white powder on a desk in the home that tested positive for cocaine, and a conviction was secured. The Supreme Court denied a writ of certiorari in this case (*United States v. Baldwin*, 621 F.2d 251 [1980]), letting the decision stand.

More recently it was reported that New York City undercover officers, a year before the 2004 Republican convention, began to infiltrate activist groups that they believed might be a problem during the convention. Officers attended meetings, made friends, signed petitions, and then reported on the activities to supervisors. In the records of the N.Y.P.D.'s "Intelligence Squad" are hundreds of reports on people who had no clear criminal plan, including church groups, anti-war organizations, and anti-Bush groups. Reports were evidently shared with police departments in other cities. Whether the prior undercover investigations had any relationships to the mass arrests that occurred during the convention is not clear (Dwyer, 2007).

Undercover operations during the anti-war activist era of the 1960s and early 1970s led to strict controls on police powers to engage in undercover investigations absent probable cause that a group was planning to commit a crime. Covert government surveillance of groups antagonistic to government policy is considered to be a threat to democracy by civil liberty experts. Obviously, there is a proper role for law enforcement in preventing threats to public safety, but the need to investigate threats while, at the same time, respect the privacy rights of citizens who, in a democracy, are free to oppose governmental policies must be carefully balanced.

Many people do not see anything wrong with deceiving a criminal who is ultimately convicted, but what about others who are involved? In the case described above, what does one say to the child who found out that a trusted friend had been living a lie? What about those in perfectly legal, non-violent protest groups who thought that the undercover officer was a trusted friend? One of the reasons that some disagree with deceptive practices that use personal relationships is that they betray trust, an essential element of social life.

As Schoeman (1985: 144) explains, intimate relationships are different from public exchanges and should be protected:

> Intimacy involves bringing another person within one's soul or being, not for any independently personal or instrumental objective, but for the sake of the other person or for the sake of the bond and attachment between the persons..... There is an expression of vulnerability and unenforceable trust within intimate relationships not present in business or social relationships.... Exploitation of trust and intimacy is also degrading to all persons who have respect for intimate relationships. Intimate relationships involve potential transformations of moral duties. Morally, an intimate relationship may take precedence over a concern for social well-beinggenerally.

Note that Schoeman is probably arguing from an ethics-of-care position. In this ethical system, the relationship of two people is more important than rights, duties, or laws. There is no forfeiture of rights in the ethics-of-care position; thus, one can't say that the suspect deserves to be deceived. The harm to the relationship goes in both directions. In cases where a personal relationship has developed, if the target is hurt by the deception, so, too, is the deceiver. In the "Quote and Query" box, the

QUOTE AND QUERY

They were just looking at me. I couldn't even look these guys in the eyes. Here's guys I hung out with, guys I broke bread with. I really came to like some of them. And they liked me, trusted me. One guy comes up to me and says, "How could you do this, Ben? You're my friend. How could you do this?" He was sixty some years old. He was like anybody's grandfather, a nice guy, but he dealt in stolen securities. That's what we locked him up for. He put a heavy guilt trip on me. I couldn't look at him. I had to put my head down....

Undercover is a very strange way to do police work, because you identify with them, the bad guys. It's a strange feeling to be trusted by someone and then betray them.

Baker, 1985: 139–140

Do you think you would be able to befriend suspects and become close to them in order to obtain incriminating evidence? Do you think that doing so is wrong? What if your target was another police officer?

Source: Reprinted with the permission of Simon & Schuster, from *Cops: Their Lives in Their Own Works*. Copyright © 1985 by Mark Baker.

---

experience clearly was painful for the officer, regardless of the fact that the people he would testify against were criminals.

Schoeman (1985:140) goes on to suggest some guidelines to be used when police interact with others in a deceptive manner. First, he believes that no interaction should go on longer than twenty-four hours without a warrant with probable cause. During this twenty-four-hour period, the officer may not enter any private area, even if invited, unless it is specifically to undertake some illegal activity. Second, although an undercover officer may deceptively engage in business and social relationships during the course of an investigation, he or she may not engage in intimate relationships. Finally, any evidence obtained in violation of the first two principles should be excluded from criminal trials against the targets.

Police would obviously criticize these suggestions by raising the following objections:

1. If there is probable cause, an arrest is possible, so why engage in a dangerous undercover operation?
2. Almost all undercover operations last more than twenty-fourhours.
3. Requiring a warrant is often unworkable, given how undercover operations develop.

The question remains: How can police best minimize the harm, yet still obtain some utility from the action? This balancing is characteristic of utilitarian ethics. Do police engage in investigative deception because it is the best way to investigate drug sales, prostitution, organized crime, or illegal alien smuggling, or because it is simply the easiest way? Is it necessary in undercover work, especially in the area of vice, to employ deception and techniques that might slide into entrapment? If the goal of police is purely crime control, there is a greater inclination to use utilitarian rationales to justify deception as a means to an end. If the goal of police is public service with an emphasis on due process, such activities are arguably harder to justify.

Marx (1985a: 106–107) proposed that before engaging in undercover operations, police investigators should ask the following questions:

1. How serious is the crime being investigated?
2. How clear is the definition of the crime—that is, would the target know that what he or she is doing is clearly illegal?
3. Are there any alternatives to deceptive practices?
4. Is the undercover operation consistent with the spirit as well as the letter of the law?
5. Is it public knowledge that the police may engage in such practices, and is the decision to do so a result of democratic decision making?
6. Is the goal prosecution, as opposed to general intelligence gathering or harassment?
7. Is there a likelihood that the crime would occur regardless of the government's involvement?
8. Are there reasonable grounds to suspect the target?
9. Will the practice prevent a serious crime from occurring?

THE USE OF INFORMANTS

Informants are individuals who are not police officers but assist police by providing information about criminal activity, acting as buyers in drug sales or otherwise "setting up" a criminal act so police may gather evidence against the target. Informants perform such services for a reward: for money, to get charges dropped or reduced, or—in some documented cases—for drugs supplied by an officer. They may inform on former associates to get back at them for real or perceived wrongs, or they may cooperate with police to get rid of criminal rivals. Informants typically are not middle-class, upstanding-citizens. South (2001) lists reasons that informants cooperate: money, revenge, dementia, kicks, attention, repentance, and coercion.

Informants have been, or are probably engaged in, criminal activities themselves. Police use informants who often continue to commit crime while helping police. In some instances the police handlers protect the informant from prosecution (Scheingold, 1984: 122). In one case that is reputed to be the basis for the 2006 movie *The Departed*, it came to light that the FBI protected two mob informers even after they had committed murders. John Connolly, an FBI agent, was convicted of obstruction of justice, and is serving a ten-year prison sentence for protecting two organized crime figures who were implicated in eighteen murders, during the time they worked for the FBI. Connolly has also been indicted by a Florida grand jury for murder. Allegedly, he tipped off the criminals about a man who was informing on them and about to give testimony to a grand jury. They had him killed as a result. That trial was due to start in September of 2008 (Lush, 2007).

Other agents have admitted that they "bend the rules" in order to keep information sources. The "In the News" box shows that some FBI agents evidently believed that the "end" of convicting some criminals justified the "means" of letting four innocent men languish in prison. Critics argue that FBI agents should not make decisions regarding which crimes are more or less important (Donn, 2003: A16).

IN THE NEWS | RELEASED AFTER THIRTY YEARS

For thirty years Peter Limone and Joe Salvati were imprisoned for murder. Limone ended up on Death Row for the murder. Salvati got a life sentence. Two other men convicted of the same murder died in prison. For thirty years the wives of Limone and Salvati waited for them and raised their children. Their pleas of innocence were disbelieved until evidence came to light that they were framed by the mob hitmen who had committed the murder. They were finally exonerated when secret FBI files were released showing that FBI agents knew that one of the witnesses had lied in order to protect the real killer. Since he and the real killer were informants for the FBI, the agents kept the truth from the prosecutors and the framed men ended up spending decades—and for two of them, the rest of their lives—in prison for crimes they didn't commit.

In a lawsuit, the federal government presented an incredible argument that the FBI agents had no duty to share the truth with the prosecutors, even if innocent men would go to the electric chair. The judge did not agree and awarded the largest settlement on record to the four families. They will split a $100 million dollar settlement, unless the judgment is overturned on appeal.

Source: Lavoie, 2007: A19, 21; Belluck, 2007: A13.

The federal witness protection program has provided new identities for some witnesses *after* they have accumulated bad debts or otherwise victimized an unwary public. The rationale for informant protection is that greater benefit is derived from using them to catch other criminals than their punishment would bring. This also extends to overlooking any minor crime they engage in during the period of time they provide information, or afterward if that is part of the deal (Marx, 1985a: 109). However, the ethical soundness of this judgment may be seriously questioned.

One of the problems in using informants is that it presents temptations for police to slide into unethical acts as a result of the relationship with them. Officers may develop friendships with professional criminals that compromise their judgment; officers may pay informants with tips or drugs and violate the law themselves; officers may protect informants when other law enforcement officials pursue them for other crimes; and officers may unknowingly allow the informant to use them by directing law-enforcement investigations to criminal rivals. Some police officers develop close working relationships with informants, whereas others maintain that you can't trust them no matter how long you've known them.

One of the biggest problems with informants is that their reliability is highly questionable. Their rewards, whatever those might be, are contingent upon delivering some evidence of crime to law enforcement. In some cases this evidence may be purely manufactured. In Dallas an informant was used to buy drugs from suspected drug dealers, who were then arrested and convicted using his testimony. When the supposed cocaine that he allegedly bought from those arrested was tested, it turned out to be powdered plasterboard. In several cases involving the same informant, there was no evidence at all that the drug buy had taken place. Defendants, in the meantime, had spent months in jail protesting their innocence before charges were dropped. Police and prosecutors concluded that this informant had lied and used the cocaine substitute to get innocent men arrested. Why? He had been paid for

IN THE NEWS | WIDESPREAD CORRUPTION IN ATLANTA

Prosecutors in Atlanta allege that the police department has a problem with widespread corruption in that officers routinely lie to obtain search warrants. The situation was brought to light by an incident in which the officers lied to get a search warrant for a woman's home. They received a tip from an informant but did not bother to send someone to buy the drugs there. Instead, they said they had done so in an affidavit for a search warrant.

In the ensuing raid, the 88-year-old female homeowner was killed in a hail of bullets, and when the officers did not find any drugs in her house, to justify the raid, they planted marijuana and heroin and falsely claimed they found the drugs. They also demanded that one of their informants lie about buying drugs from her at the house.

Two of the three officers eventually confessed and pled guilty to involuntary manslaughter and violating the dead woman's civil rights. The incident and subsequent scandal led to a wide-ranging review of criminal cases where officers might have employed similar tactics. The third officer's defense is that he was following his training (by lying on legal documents). The Atlanta chief of police said that his officers were not trained to lie.

Is this an example of noble-cause corruption or something else? Officers who start with noble-cause corruption may end up committing purely egoistic acts to cover their own misconduct.

Source: Dewan and Goodman. 2007: A18.

every "buy" and had earned $200,000 before his lies were finally discovered (Curry, 2002).

Sometimes officers are tempted to manufacture informants. When writing affidavits for search warrants, officers may use information supplied by a "confidential informant" without having to name the informant. All the officer has to do is to state that the informant has given good information in the past and that it would be dangerous to reveal his or her identity. This boilerplate language is routinely accepted, so information is used to establish probable cause that cannot be verified or challenged. Barker and Carter (1991) argues that some officers are tempted to use imaginary confidential informants to allow the use of otherwise illegally obtained or simply manufactured evidence. They report on a tragic case in which an officer made up evidence from a so-called informant in order to get a search warrant. In the search, an officer was killed and the lie was exposed. The "In the News" box relates a more recent case where something similar occurred.

Some officers openly admit that they could not do their job without informants. However, there are other arguments that the perceived value of informants is overstated. In a British study the Home Office concluded that informants were cost-effective. But other analysts argued that the study did not factor in other issues, such as tolerating continued crime (by informants) and informants who create crime in order to report it (Dunningham and Norris, 1999).

South (2001) summarizes the ethical issues with using informants as follows:

1. Getting too close and/or engaging in love affairs with informants
2. Overestimating the veracity of the information
3. Being a pawn of the informant who is taking advantage of the system for money or other reasons

4. Creating crimes by letting the informant entrap people who would not otherwise have committed the crime
5. Engaging in unethical or illegal behaviors for the informant, such as providing drugs
6. Letting the informant invade one's personal life
7. Using coercion and intimidation to get the informant to cooperate

There are disturbing questions that one might ask about using informants. It may be true that narcotics investigations are difficult, if not impossible, without the use of informants. If so, guidelines and standards are needed to govern the use of informants. The Commission on Accreditation for Law Enforcement Agencies (CALEA) has developed such standards.

JUSTIFICATIONS FOR UNDERCOVER OPERATIONS

There are arguments both for and against the use of undercover operations and informants (see Box 9.1). Marx (1985b, 1991) argues that undercover operations might actually create more crime. They may also lead to unintended crime and danger. For instance, Marx mentioned situations where decoys have been attacked, undercover officers have been robbed, undercover officers have been killed by other officers who mistook them for criminals, and policewomen acting as prostitutes have been attacked.

Undercover operations have been criticized for the following reasons (Marx, 1992: 17–18):

1. They may generate a market for the purchase or sale of illegal goods and services.
2. They may generate the idea for the crime.
3. They may generate the motive.
4. They may provide a missing resource.
5. They may entail coercion or intimidation of a person otherwise not predisposed to commit the offense.
6. They may generate a covert opportunity structure for illegal actions on the part of the undercover agent or informant.
7. They may lead to retaliatory violence against informers.
8. They may stimulate a variety of crimes on the part of those who are not targets of the undercover operation (for example, impersonation of a police officer, crimes committed against undercover officers).

Ethical systems may or may not support undercover operations. The **principle of double effect** holds that when one does an action to achieve a good end and an inevitable but unintended effect is negative, the action might be justified. We might justify police action in this way if the unethical consequence, such as the deception of an innocent, was not the intended consequence of the action and the goal was an ethical one. However, deceiving the suspect could not be justified under the principle of double effect because that is an intended effect, not an unintended effect.

Religious ethics would probably condemn many kinds of police actions because of the deceptions involved. Ethical formalism would probably also condemn such

| BOX 9.1 | JUSTIFICATIONS FOR AND ARGUMENTS AGAINST UNDERCOVER WORK |

For

1. Citizens grant to government the right to use means that they individually forsake.
2. Undercover work is ethical when its targets are persons who freely choose to commit crimes that they know may call forth deceptive police practices.
3. Undercover work is ethical when used for a good and important end.
4. Undercover work is ethical when there are reasonably specific grounds to suspect that a serious crime is planned or has been carried out.
5. Undercover work is ethical when it is directed against persons whom there are reasonable grounds to suspect.
6. When citizens use questionable means, government agents are justified in using equivalent means.
7. Special risks justify special precautions.
8. Undercover work is ethical when it is the best means.
9. The law should be enforced equally.
10. The guilty should be convicted.
11. An investigation should be as unobtrusive and noncoercive as possible.
12. Undercover work is ethical when it is undertaken with the intention of eventually being made public and literally judged in court.
13. Undercover work is ethical when it is carried out by persons of upright character in accountable organizations.

Against

1. Truth telling is moral; lying is immoral.
2. The government should not make deals with criminals.
3. The government should neither participate in nor be a party to crime, nor break laws in order to enforce them.
4. The government, through its actions, should reduce, not increase crime.
5. The government should not create an intention to commit a crime that is impossible to carry out.
6. The government should neither tempt the weak, nor offer temptation indiscriminately, nor offer unrealistically attractive temptations.
7. No harm should be done to the innocent.
8. The sanctity of private places should be respected.
9. The sanctity of intimate relations should be respected.
10. The right to freedom of expression and action should be respected.
11. The government should not do by stealth what it is prohibited from doing openly.

actions because the actions could not be justified under the categorical imperative because innocent people would be used. Egoism might or might not justify such actions, depending on the officer involved and what his or her maximum gain and loss was determined to be.

Utilitarian ethics would justify police deception and deceptive techniques using the argument that catching criminals provides greater benefit to society than allowing them to go free by refusing to engage in such practices. Act utilitarianism would probably support deceptive practices, but rule utilitarianism might not, because the actions, although beneficial under certain circumstances, might in the long run undermine and threaten our system of law. Under act utilitarianism, one would measure the harm of the criminal activity against the methods used to control it. Deceptive practices, then, might be justified in the case of drug offenses but not for business misdeeds, or for finding a murderer but not for trapping a prostitute, and so on.

The difficulty of this line of reasoning, of course, is to agree on a standard of seriousness. I might decide that drugs are serious enough to justify otherwise unethical practices, but you might not. Pornography and prostitution may be serious enough to some to justify unethical practices, but to others only murder or violent crime would justify the practices.

Cohen (1991) proposed a test to determine the ethical justification for police practices. His focus is the use of coercive power to stop and search, but we might apply the same test to analyze undercover or other deceptive practices:

1. The end must be justified as a good—for instance, conviction of a serious criminal rather than general intelligence gathering.
2. The means must be a plausible way to achieve the end—for example, choosing a target with no reasonable suspicion is not a plausible way to reduce any type of crime.
3. There must be no better alternative means to achieve the same end—no less intrusive means or methods of collecting evidence exist.
4. The means must not undermine some other equal or greater end—if the method results in loss of trust or faith in the legal system, it fails the test.

Many people see nothing wrong—certainly nothing illegal—in using any methods necessary to catch criminals. But we are concerned with methods in use before individuals are found guilty. Can an innocent person, such as you, be entrapped into crime? Perhaps not, but are we comfortable in a society where the person who offers you drugs or sex or a cheap way to hook into cable television turns out to be an undercover police officer? Are we content to assume that our telephone may be tapped or our best friend could be reporting our conversations to someone else? When we encounter police behavior in these areas, the practices often have been used to catch a person who, we realize after the fact, had engaged in wrongdoing, so we believe that police officers are justified in performing in slightly unethical ways. What protectors of due process and critics of police investigation practices help us to remember is that those practices, if not curbed, may be used just as easily on the innocent as on the guilty.

Clearly, norms support police deception during the investigative phase. If their norms support deception during investigation, it is not surprising that some officers protect themselves with deception when their methods are legally questioned. One of the problems with deceptive practices is that they may lead to more deception to cover up illegal methods. For instance, Skolnick (1982) argued that weak or nonexistent standards during the investigation phase of policing lead directly to lying on the witness stand because that is sometimes the only way an officer can save his or her case.

These investigative techniques are unlikely to be eliminated. Perhaps they should not be, as they are effective in catching a number of people who should be punished. Even if one has doubts about the ethics of these practices, it is entirely possible that there is no other way to accomplish the goal of crime control. However one decides these difficult questions, there are no easy answers. Also, we must realize that for us these questions are academic, but for thousands of police officers they are very real.

INTERROGATION

Deception often takes a different form in the interrogation phase of a case. Several court cases document the use of mental coercion, through either threat or promise. The *father confessor approach* (a sympathetic paternal figure for the defendant to confide to) or *Mutt and Jeff partners* (a "nice guy" and a seemingly brutal, threatening officer) are other ways to induce confessions and/or obtain information (Kamisar, LeFave, and Israel, 1980: 54).

Skolnick and Leo (1992) have presented a typology of deceptive interrogation techniques. The following is a brief summary of their descriptions of these practices:

- Calling the questioning an interview rather than an interrogation by questioning in a noncustodial setting and telling the suspect that he [or she] is free to leave, thus eliminating the need for Miranda warnings
- Presenting Miranda warnings in a way designed to negate their effect, by mumbling or by using a tone suggesting that the offender had better not exercise the rights delineated or that they are unnecessary
- Misrepresenting the nature or seriousness of the offense by, for instance, not telling the suspect that the victim has died
- Using manipulative appeals to conscience through role playing or other means
- Misrepresenting the moral seriousness of the offense—for instance, by pretending that the rape victim "deserved" to be raped, in order to get a confession
- Using promises of lesser sentences or nonprosecution beyond the power of the police to offer
- Misrepresenting identity by pretending to be lawyers or priests
- Using fabricated evidence such as polygraph results or fingerprint findings that don't really exist

Skolnick (1982) wrote that because physical means of coercion are no longer used—the infamous "third degree"—mental deception is the only means left for police officers to gain information or confessions from suspects. How does one get a killer to admit to where she left the murder weapon? If police are imaginative, they may be able to get the defendant to confess by encouraging her to think about what would happen if children were to find the gun. Or police might discover the location of a body by convincing the killer after he had refused to talk to police that the victim deserves a Christian burial (see *Brewer v. Williams*, 430 U.S. 387 [1977]). In *Brewer v. Williams*, the Supreme Court ruled that police unconstitutionally infringed on the defendant's right to counsel because the conversation constituted an interrogation without counsel, after counsel had been appointed. However, other cases that involved deceptive conversations *before* counsel has been appointed have been approved by the Supreme Court.

Whether police have a legal right to deceive a suspect is not the same question as whether the deception is ethical and, if so, the limits of such deception. Skolnick's argument is that deception is used because physical coercion cannot be used. It is true, of course, that the use of physical force to obtain a conviction is illegal. Most countries have eliminated torture and formally condemn the practice. Unfortunately, some countries still endorse physical coercion as acceptable police practice. Amnesty International has documented abuses in Chile, Argentina, and many other countries around the world. It is important to note that often in these situations police are used as the means of control by the dominant political power. Therefore, they operate not under the law, as the code of ethics dictates, but above the law. Codes of ethics, adopted by many police departments that have recognized the danger of police power being misused, are clear in directing police to abide by the law and not allow themselves to be used by political parties or those in power (Bossard, 1981).

Legal proscriptions against torture come not from an ethical rationale but, rather, from a legal rationale based on the belief that torture renders a confession unreliable. Tortured victims might confess to stop their suffering; thus, the court would not get truthful information. Many would argue that whatever information is gained from an individual who is physically coerced into confessing or giving information is not worth the sacrifice of moral standards even if the information is truthful. Human rights treaties signed by the majority of free countries condemn such practices, regardless of the reason for the interrogation. In Chapter 15 we will discuss the use of torture in the context of Guantanamo and counter-terrorismefforts.

Klockars (1983) described the inevitability of certain unethical or immoral police behaviors as the **Dirty Harry problem**, after the movie character who did not let the law get in his way when pursuing criminals. In Klockars' view, using immoral means to reach a desired moral end is an irresolvable problem because there are situations where one knows the "dirty act" will result in a good end, there are no other means to achieve the good end, and the "dirty act" will not be in vain. Klockars' example of this type of problem, taken from the movie, is a situation where a captured criminal refuses to tell the location of a kidnapped victim. Because the victim is sure to die without help, the police officer (played by Clint Eastwood) tortures the criminal by stepping on his injured leg until he admits the location.

Obviously, this is an immoral act, but Klockars' point is that is the situation has no solution. If the police officer would behave in a professional manner, the victim would be sure to die. If the officer would behave in an immoral manner, there is a chance he could save a life. This is a dominant theme in detective and police fiction. Klockars' conclusion is that by engaging in "dirty" means for good ends, the officer has tainted his innocence and must be punished, for there is always a danger that dirty means will be redefined as neutral or even good by those who use them. Police may lose their sense of moral proportion if the action is not punished, even though the individual police officer involved may have no other way out of the moral dilemma.

Delattre (1989a) also discussed the use of coercive power. He disagreed with Klockars that the officer must inevitably be tainted in the Dirty Harry situation. Delattre pointed out that choosing physical coercion, regardless of temptation, leads to perjury and lying about the activity and perhaps other tactics to ensure that the offender does not go free because of the illegal behavior of the police officer. However, Delattre (1989:211) also excused the actions of those who succumb to temptation in extreme situations and perform an illegal act:

> Such an act may be unjustifiable by an unconditional principle, but it also may be excusable.... Still less does it follow that those who commit such acts are bad, that their character is besmirched, or that their honor is tainted.

However, one might argue that if officers commit an illegal and unethical act, it is hard for their character not to be affected or their honor tainted. To understand an action (in this case an act that results from anger or frustration) is not to excuse it. Delattre presents a virtue-based ethical system and evidently believes that an officer can have all the virtues of a good officer and still commit a bad action—in this case, the illegal use of force. His point that one act of violence does not necessarily mean that the officer is unethical in other ways is well taken. Indeed, we usually reserve the terms *ethical* and *unethical* for actions rather than persons. The reaction of the officer to his or her mistake is the true test of character. Does the officer cover up and/or ask his or her partner to cover up the action? Does the officer lie to protect himself or herself? Or does the officer admit wrongdoing and accept the consequences?

Klockars' underlying point is more subtle: We all are guilty in a sense by expecting certain ones among us to do the dirty work and then condemning them for their actions. In times of war or other threats, the populace often wants results without wanting to know tactics. What percentage of the population cared that the CIA attempted to assassinate Fidel Castro or that the Attorney General's office during the Kennedy years used questionable tactics and violated the due-process rights of Cosa Nostra members targeted in the campaign against organized crime? How many of us truly want to know about the clandestine operations of Special Forces in Afghanistan or Iraq?

Klockars points out the position of those who perform despicable acts that benefit the rest of us; we are comfortable in our ignorance and comfortable in our judgments as long as we don't have to look too closely at our own role in the events. In effect, police (and other law enforcement) become our *sin eaters* of early folklore; they are the shady characters on the fringe of society who absorb evil so the rest of us may remain pure. Shunned and avoided, these persons and their value are taken for granted.

It is certainly much easier to justify mental coercion than physical coercion and intimidation, but their justifications are the same: They are an effective and perhaps necessary means to get needed information from a resisting subject. The criticism against them is the same. Mental coercion may also result in false confessions. Several convictions have been overturned because new evidence proves that those convicted were innocent, yet they confessed. Why would someone confess to a crime he or she didn't commit?

A suspect might confess because he is a fourteen-year-old juvenile who was mentally overpowered by police using pressure who fed him information from the crime. This is alleged to have happened in the Central Park jogger "wilding" case. In 1990, five Black and Hispanic youths were convicted of the beating and rape of a female stockbroker. It appears that they may have been innocent. Matias Reyes confessed, stating that he acted alone in the crime. DNA evidence supports his contention that he raped the victim (Tanner, 2002; Getlin, 2002b). Evidently, the youths were intimidated by police interrogators into confessing to the crime.

Allegedly, a similar scenario occurred in an Austin, Texas, case where two men were found guilty and sentenced to death for a robbery/murder. One of them confessed and implicated the other. Then, twelve years later, another man wrote to the district attorney offering his confession. DNA evidence confirmed his guilt. The convicted man who confessed alleges that he did so because the police officer who interrogated him threatened that if he did not confess, Mexican police would arrest his mother and they could not guarantee her safety. They also told him that he would receive the death penalty if he didn't confess (Hafetz, 2002).

Keith Longtin said that he was held by Prince George police detectives for 38 hours after his wife was raped and stabbed to death. He alleges that during the 38 hours he was held, police officers would not let him leave, they accompanied him to the bathroom, they would not let him call an attorney, and they continually questioned him (employing different teams of interrogators) for 38 hours. Finally, they said that he told them what happened, but he remembers it as them telling him what happened to her and asking him to speculate about how the murder occurred.

Detectives allege that he confessed. Longtin alleged that he never did. A sex crimes investigator noticed the similarity between the attack and other rapes in the area, and after the rape suspect was arrested, a DNA test proved that this man killed Longtin's wife. Longtin was freed after 8 months in jail, and all charges were dropped. Longtin's case and four other homicide confessions that were thrown out because other evidence proved they were false confessions led to a federal monitor for this law enforcement agency (Witt, 2001).

Although such events sound like something from television drama rather than reality, they do happen. In 2001, Illinois Governor Ryan commuted the death sentences of everyone on Death Row because of suspicion that more innocent men may be in danger of being executed. Thirteen death penalty cases were overturned when evidence indicated that the convicted might be innocent or, at the very least, did not receive due process. Five of those thirteen were from Chicago, and evidence indicated that the convictions were obtained through coerced confessions and manufactured evidence by the Chicago police investigators (Babwin, 2001).

LOYALTY AND WHISTLEBLOWING

Even though we have concentrated, in this and the last chapter, on officers who may have engaged in misconduct, it bears repeating that the vast majority of police strive to do their job professionally and hold themselves to high standards of behavior. A problematic situation for even these officers, however, is what to do about fellow officers who do commit wrongs. One of the most difficult ethical dilemmas that officers confront is being faced with the wrongdoing of another officer. Informing or testifying against one's peers has always been perceived negatively by any group, whether that group be lawyers, doctors, students, prisoners, or police officers. Although the **code of silence** is present in other occupations and groups as well, in policing it can be understood as a type of noble-cause corruption.

QUOTE AND QUERY

The problem is that the atmosphere does not yet exist in which honest police officers can act without fear of ridicule or reprisal from fellow officers....

Frank Serpico, Knapp Commission, 1971, as reported in Hentoff, 1999

Cops don't tell on cops.... [I]f a cop decided to tell on me, his career's ruined. ... [H]e's going to be labeled as a rat.

Police officer testimony in Mollen Commission, 1992, as reported in Walker, 2001

I saw that happening to men all around me; men who could have been good officers; men of decent impulse, men of ideas, but men who were without decent leadership, men who were told in a hundred ways every day, go along, forget about the law, don't make waves and shut up. ...

So your report has to tell us about the district attorneys and the courts and the bar; and the mayor and the governor and what they have done, and what they have failed to do, and how great a measure of responsibility they also bear. Otherwise, if you suggest or allow others to suggest that the responsibility belongs only to the police, then for the patrolmen on the beat and in the radio cars, this commission will be just another part of the swindle.

David Durk, 1972, cited in Menninger, 1973

How would you create an atmosphere in a police department wherein officers would feel more comfortable reporting the misdoings/criminality of other officers? Or would you even want to?

The books *Serpico* (Maas, 1973) and *Prince of the City* (Daley, 1984) describe two examples of police officers who chose to challenge the "blue curtain" of secrecy and testify against their fellow officers in corruption hearings. In the "Quote and Query" box, Serpico's statement to the Knapp Commission illustrates the problem of police loyalty when officers are willing to cover up corruption. The later statement indicates that nothing much had changed in the decades between the Knapp Commission and the Mollen Commission. David Durk's statement to the Knapp Commission (cited in Menninger, 1973) is eloquent in his plea for the Commission to understand that the problem was not only with the police department.

The police subculture described in Chapter 7 has been identified as the source of the particularly strong pattern of protecting co-workers who commit unethical acts in law enforcement. This practice in policing has been called the **blue curtain of secrecy**. It should be noted that research indicates that this practice may be breaking down. Barker (2002), for instance, reported on some research indicating that minorities and women have led to a less homogenous force and a weaker subcultural norm of covering up wrongdoing, as evidenced by the proliferation of complaints against fellow officers. For instance, Barker notes that there were more than thirty cases in Los Angeles where officers were the primary witnesses against other officers. Another survey (Rothwell and Baldwin, 2007) found that police respondents were more likely to report misdemeanors and felonies of their fellow officers than were civilian employee-respondents in other agencies. An additional factor that was substantially related to reporting was whether or not the agency had a mandatory reporting policy.

Quinn (2005) describes many cases in his career when he stood up to unethical and illegal police practices such as using excessive force, accepting gratuities, and engaging in other misconduct. He describes how reporting such actions to supervisors led to threats and retaliation, but that the illegal or unethical behavior also did not continue to happen in his presence. He argues that good officers are sucked into the corrupt cover-ups because of the nature of policing. Every officer does something wrong, and the most common mistake, perhaps, is using too much force. When an officer has just experienced a life-threatening event, such as a high-speed chase, a foot chase, or a fight for his weapon, the adrenalin "hijacks" reason, according to Quinn, and some officers overreact. When co-workers cover for the officer, the officer who made the mistake is indebted and trapped in a situation where the officer thinks he or she must do the same. Even if the offending officer would have told the truth about his or her mistake, the officer who covered up has lied and, therefore, it is almost impossible to "sacrifice" that loyal officer by churlishly telling the truth and calling him or her a liar.

Thus, officers are still more likely to "not see" something and not come forward when someone in their midst is engaged in some forms of wrongdoing. It is even likely that the rank and file will ostracize and sanction the officer who does so. In their large attitude survey of police officers, Weisburd and Greenspan (2000) discovered that, although 80 percent of police officers did not think that the "code of silence" was essential for police trust and good policing, fully two-thirds reported that a whistleblower would encounter sanctions. Further, more than half agreed that it was not unusual for police to ignore improper conduct on the part of other officers and 61 percent indicated that police officers do not always report even the most serious violations/crimes of other officers.

Another study found that police officers were more likely to report wrongdoing of other officers if it involved acquisition of goods or money (except for gratuities) rather than excessive force or "bending" rules. In this study, even though almost all respondents thought that stealing from a burglary scene was very serious, about a quarter thought that their colleagues would not report it (Westmarland, 2005).

Special problems are involved when police officers protect one another. One of the greatest harms of cover-ups is the damage inflicted on a police officer's credibility. Sykes (1996) described a civil case wherein a jury awarded $15.9 million in damages after a case of police brutality. Jurors simply did not believe the police version of the events, and a videotape supported the plaintiff's allegations that excessive force was used. The "cost" of police cover-ups eventually becomes public distrust of police testimony. The O. J. Simpson trial has become the classic example of what happens when a jury loses confidence in police testimony. Prosecutors ordinarily can rely on a jury to take police testimony as fact and even believe police testimony over non-police witnesses. When police testimony is given no greater weight than any other witness—indeed, when jury members believe that police are prone to lie on the stand—the justice system itself is at risk. Most of the time, however, in most cities, in most cases where police officers are accused of crimes, jurors still believe them—even when they are accused by another officer. In the "Walking the Walk" box, one officer stood alone against several of his fellow officers.

WALKING THE WALK

THE OAKLAND "RIDERS" AND KEITH BATT

In the movie *Training Day*, a new recruit is "schooled" in the methods of a veteran, decorated cop that included brutalizing suspects, planting drugs, and generally committing crimes to catch the criminals. In a real-life version of *Training Day*, Keith Batt earned a criminal justice degree at California State University at Sacramento and fulfilled his life's dream by being hired by the Oakland Police Department. He graduated at the top of his recruit class and became an Oakland police officer in 1999.

Batt was assigned to Clarence Mabanag as his field training officer. Almost from the first day, Batt says he was told to falsify offense reports and to use force on suspects. Batt did as he was told for two-and-a-half weeks, including hitting a suspect and lying on an offense report, because, he said, he knew that he would be retaliated against if he did not. Then he decided that he could not continue to be a police officer if it meant violating the law he was sworn to uphold. He quit the Oakland force and turned in his FTO and the other officers to internal affairs.

Mabanag and other officers, including Matt Hornug, Jude Siapno, and Frank (Choker) Vazquez, were known as the "Riders." According to testimony, they patrolled their western, poverty-stricken district of Oakland with an iron fist and used excessive force, planted drugs, and intimidated witnesses as the means to keep the peace. Partly as a result of Keith Batt's report, all four officers were fired and charged with a range of offenses including obstruction of justice, conspiracy to obstruct justice, filing false police reports, assault and battery, kidnapping, and false imprisonment. Even before these charges, the four had records of misconduct. The department had paid $200,000 to settle suits involving Siapno and Mabanag, and other lawsuits existed against Vazguez and Hornug.

Not everyone believes the foursome's culpability or applauds Keith Batt's decision to testify against them. According to one fellow officer at the time, "These guys are awesome cops, they never did anything to anybody who was innocent, just pukes, criminals, see? They just got a little too intense and went over the line." Even residents had mixed feelings, with some arguing that it took a tough cop to police a tough street. As one resident said, "The only thing the bad people understand is force...." Sometimes, however, their activities evidently were not limited to just drug dealers and other criminals. One witness testified that he called police to report a stolen stereo and when his dog wouldn't stop barking and Mabanag threatened to shoot the dog, his angry response resulted in Mabanag's choking him and ordering Batt to lie on the offense report to cover the use of force.

In the course of the ensuing scandal, Oakland paid out 11 million dollars to settle civil suits from 119 victims of police officers (including the Riders) and ended up under a court-ordered federal consent decree. Hornug, Mabanag, and Siapno were prosecuted in two lengthy trials between 2000 and 2005. Vasquez is a fugitive of justice, believed to be in Mexico. Perhaps he should have waited to have his day in court, too, as all three escaped guilty verdicts. Hornug was acquitted of all charges, and the jury deadlocked in two trials on Mabanag and Siapno. The police chief has refused to reinstate them, and they have sued for back pay and reinstatement.

The fired officers and their attorneys say that the deadlocked jurors exonerated them. The prosecutor is convinced of their guilt but decided not to seek a third trial because he believed that he could not get a jury to convict them. Batt has been honored as a courageous whistleblower that stood up to the "blue curtain of secrecy" but also has been vilified as a "liar" who feared a negative evaluation. Today, he is a respected police officer in Pleasanton, California, who received an award for "Ethical Courage." But Clarence Mubanag is also a police officer in a different department in southern California that hired him after the deadlocked jury verdict. Litigation continues.

Sources: Institute for Law Enforcement Administration. 2008; Lee, 2004; Zamora, Lee, and van Derbeke, 2003; Bay City News, 2007.

TELEOLOGICAL ARGUMENTS

Recall that teleological rationales are those arguing that the end justifies the means. Egoism may support not coming forward because it may not be in one's best interest: We don't want to get involved; we don't want to face the scorn of others; we don't think it is our job to come forward when there are others who are supposed to look out for and punish wrongdoing; we don't want to alienate peers who committed wrongs by reporting them. These are all egoistic reasons for not coming forward.

There are also utilitarian reasons to keep quiet about observed wrongdoing. For instance, some activities that are labeled corrupt may actually further the ends of justice, and adhering to regulations would undermine detection and enforcement. Also, the loss of a skilled police officer, even though that officer may be moderately corrupt, is a loss to society. One may believe that the harm to the police department in exposing the deviance of one officer is greater than the harm to society created by what that officer is doing, or that there is greater utility in stopping the officer without making the issue public.

There are also teleological arguments for coming forward. Egoism may dictate that an individual has to come forward to protect himself from being accused of wrongdoing. The police officer may also endure such a crisis of conscience or fear of being punished that she can attain peace of mind only by "coming clean."

Utilitarian arguments for coming forward are offered as well. The harm that comes from letting the individual carry on his misdeeds or not forcing the individual to a public punishment may be greater than the harm that would come from the scandal of public exposure. This is especially true if one is forced to either tell the truth or lie; in this case, the harm to police credibility must be taken into account.

DEONTOLOGICAL ARGUMENTS

Deontological arguments can also be used to support not exposing other officers, or for coming forward. Arguments against exposing other officers include the idea that discretion and secrecy are obligations that one assumes by joining a police force, and that it would be unjust to subject an otherwise good and heroic police officer to the punishment of exposure. Arguments for coming forward are much stronger, including the argument that a police officer has a sworn duty to uphold the law. Also, one cannot remain silent in one situation unless one could approve of silence in all situations (Kant's categorical imperative), and one must do one's duty, which involves telling the truth when under an oath (Wren, 1985: 32–33).

It should be noted that, in general, deontological ethics support whistleblowing because it is a higher duty to uphold the law than it is to defend one's fellow officers. This argument also depends on whether the primary role of officers is as crime fighter or as public servant. If one perceives oneself as primarily a crime fighter, the duty to the law becomes subservient to the duty to fight crime; however if one primarily sees one's duty to be a public servant sworn to uphold the law, then crimefighting is subservient to the law and the legal process.

LOYALTY

The previous arguments are what Wren (1985) calls external moral arguments, which he contrasts with internal arguments, such as loyalty. When one considers whether to come forward to expose the wrongdoing of others, external moral philosophies, such as the utilitarian "it is best for everyone" rationale, are rarely articulated. What often is the prime motivator for truth-telling is personal integrity. Yet, the individual often feels great anguish and self-doubt over turning in or testifying against friends and colleagues, and that is understandable because "a person's character is defined by his commitments, the more basic of which reveal to a person what his life is all about and give him a reason for going on" (Wren, 1985: 35). Loyalty is a difficult concept that others have written about extensively; it can be a vehicle of both ethical and unethical behavior (Fletcher, 1993).

Loyalty in police work is explained in that police depend on one another, sometimes in life-or-death situations. Loyalty to one's fellows is part of the *esprit de corps* of policing and is an essential element of a healthy department. Ewin (1990) writes that something is wrong if a police officer doesn't feel loyalty to fellow officers. Loyalty is a personal relationship, not a judgment. Therefore, loyalty is uncalculating. We do not extend loyalty in a rational way or based on contingencies. Loyalty to groups or persons is emotional, grounded in affection rather than reflection.

Loyalty refers to a preference for one group over another (Ewin, 1990:13). Loyalty always involves some exclusion: One is loyal to X rather than to Y, so Y is thus excluded. At times the reverse can also be true: If a group of people is excluded (whether or not they are properly excluded), they can feel a common cause in response to what they see as oppression, which can result in the growth of loyalty among them. That loyalty, provoked by a dislike and perhaps distrust of the other group, is likely to be marked by behavior that ignores legitimate interests and concerns of the other group.

The application to policing is obvious. If police officers feel isolated from the community, their loyalty is to other police officers and not to the community at large. If they feel oppressed by and distrust the police administration, they draw together against the "common enemy." To address abuses of loyalty, one would not want to attack the loyalty itself because it is necessary for the health of the organization. Rather, one would want to extend the loyalty beyond other officers to the department and to the community. Permeability rather than isolation promotes community loyalty, just as the movement toward professionalism promotes loyalty to the principles of ethical policing rather than to individuals in a particular department.

Wren (1985) believes that police departments can resolve the dilemma of the individual officer who knows of wrongdoing by making the consequences more palatable—that is, by having a fair system of investigation and punishment, by instituting helping programs for those with alcohol and drug problems, and by using more moderate punishments than dismissal or public exposure for other sorts of misbehavior. This is consistent with the ethics of care, which is concerned with needs and relationships.

Delattre (1989a) handled the problem differently but came to somewhat similar conclusions. He turned to Aristotle to support the idea that when a friend becomes a scoundrel, the moral individual cannot stand by and do nothing. Rather, one has a moral duty to bring the wrongdoing to the friend's attention and urge him or her to change. If the friend will not, then he or she is more scoundrel than friend, and the individual's duty shifts to those who might be victimized by the officer's behavior. We see here not the ethics of care but, rather, a combination of virtue-based and deontological duty-basedethics.

Souryal (1996b, 1999b) discussed loyalty to superiors or to fellow police as misplaced. He argued that there are different kinds of loyalty: personal loyalty, institutional loyalty, and integrated loyalty (which relates to the ideal values of the profession). Loyalty to superiors is traced back to *divine right*—the idea that persons are indistinguishable from their office (1996b: 48). Today, however, we are governed by laws, not kings, and such loyalty should be properly placed in our laws and our values rather than an individual. Souryal (1996b) noted that personal loyalties often lead to unethical actions and that loyalty to values or organizations is more appropriate. One might argue that even loyalty to a police organization may be misplaced if it leads to lying to protect the organization against scandal.

SANCTIONS AGAINST WHISTLEBLOWERS

The informal practice of punishing individuals who come forward is an especially distressing aspect of loyalty. Individual police officers are ostracized and become the target of a wide variety of retaliatory gestures after "ratting" on another officer. Reports include having equipment stolen, threats made to the officer and his family members, interfering with radio calls and thereby jeopardizing her safety, scrawling the word rat on his locker, putting cheese or dead rats in her locker, vandalizing his patrol car, or destroying her uniform.

As distressing as these acts are, the more incomprehensible reaction is that of administrators. Administrators sometimes tell the accused officer who informed on them, or support the retaliation against the officer who came forward implicitly or explicitly. Instead of rewarding officers who expose wrongdoing, administrators sometimes punish them by administrative sanctions, transfers to less desirable positions, or reduced performance reports. More than forty Los Angeles police officers filed a class action suit against such administrative sanctions for whistleblowers (Johnson, 2005). This retaliation is not just true of law enforcement agencies. Sanctions against whistleblowers are so common that most states and the federal

QUOTE AND QUERY

...Two nights later I was walking through the courthouse, in uniform. One of the officers I had accused of assault grabbed me by the front of my jacket and pushed me into a corner. With his face touching mine he whispered ..., "If you ever snitch us off again I will kill you." Then he walked away. [The incident occurred after Officer Quinn had reported to the deputy chief and his lieutenant that a prostitute in his district had been beaten up by a police officer.]

Quinn, 2005: 41

Why do you think police officers have similar ("don't snitch") subcultural prohibitions as criminals?

government now have laws designed to protect whistleblowers. The "Quote and Query" box is one account of what happened to a whistleblower.

A typical example of retaliation was reported in a San Antonio, Texas, newspaper concerning an officer in the San Antonio Police Department who arrested a sergeant for driving while intoxicated. Even though the officer had averaged fewer than two complaints a year during his eleven years at the police department, after he arrested the sergeant, he received nine complaints, resulting in a total of eighty-six days of suspension. He also encountered hang-up calls on his unlisted home telephone, his belongings were stolen, his car was towed away from the police parking lot twice, officers refused to sit next to him, and officers did not respond to his requests for back-up. Witnesses also reported that they overheard officers discussing what other forms of retaliation to take against him. The sergeant who was arrested for drunken driving was released before being taken to a magistrate, contrary to departmental policy, and received no disciplinary sanctions (Casey, 1996).

REDUCING POLICE CORRUPTION

Chapter 6 included a discussion of leadership and ethics training and presented general principles of how ethical leadership and good training can improve the level of integrity in an organization. Here we explore these issues again, but with a specific focus on law enforcement. Although the need for ethical leaders and training is obviously similar between law enforcement and other agencies in criminal justice, there are unique and prevalent temptations in law enforcement. The risk of police misconduct has also resulted in a wider range of initiatives and responses in law enforcement that merit consideration.

Malloy (1982: 37–40) has offered some possible solutions to police corruption:

- Increase the salary of police.
- Eliminate unenforceable laws.
- Establish civilian review boards.
- Improve training.

Metz (1990) suggested several ways that police administrators can encourage ethical conduct among officers:

- Set realistic goals and objectives for the department.
- Provide ethical leadership.
- Provide a written code of ethics.
- Provide a whistleblowing procedure that ensures fair treatment of all parties.
- Provide training in law enforcement ethics.

How does one minimize or eliminate existing corruption in a police department? Because so much of police work is unpredictable and involves such a wide range of situations, it is impossible to fashion rules for all possible occurrences. What should take the place of extensive rules are strong ethical standards. However, the internalization of these standards by individual police officers is at best tenuous; the informal police subculture is the most obvious threat to the internalization of ethical standards.

EDUCATION AND TRAINING

Education has been promoted as a necessary element to improve the ethics of policing; however, education itself is certainly not a panacea. Many of the unethical officers described in this book have been college graduates. Fyfe and Kane (2006) did find a correlation between education and reduced risk of terminations for cause in the New York Police Department; however, it is by no means clear that education by itself increases the ethics of police officers.

Ethics training in the academy, and in in-service courses, is common and is recommended for all police departments today. Reuss-Ianni (1983) described how, after the Knapp Commission uncovered wide-ranging corruption in the New York Police Department, ethical awareness workshops were begun. Unfortunately, they have not stopped the periodic corruption scandals that have occurred since that time.

The International Chiefs of Police (2008), after conducting a two-year study of ethics training, presented its findings. Among them, in 1997 (when the survey was done) about 80 percent of responding agencies said they committed resources to ethics instruction. Most of the courses were lecture (78 percent), followed by readings and discussion (67 percent), videotapes (53 percent), and video scenarios (49 percent). Other methods (role playing, computers, or games) were used less often. Most (70 percent) reported that the course was four hours or less.

In terms of content, 81 percent discussed gratuities, 76 percent discussed conflicts of interest, 90 percent discussed abuse of force, 80 percent discussed abuse of authority, 69 percent discussed corruption, and 71 percent discussed off-duty ethics. The IACP (2008) found that the amount of time devoted to ethics topics did not match how important respondents indicated the topics were. Interestingly, only about a third of the agencies utilized an ethics criterion for probationary officer evaluations.

The major recommendations of the IACP based on this study were to provide job-specific training on ethics and to differentiate training for recruits, in-service, and management, as well as other units. Another recommendation was that ethics training begin with recruits and be an integral part of the departments' structure and policies. The IACP also recommended enhancing content, and using appropriate learning styles. A final recommendation was that departments concentrate more on field training officer ethics (IACP, 2008).

Moran (2005) described several models of police ethics training, including a view of ethics as a "shield" to protect officers from trouble, as a programmed element in the officer's training "hardwire," as a mission or crusade, or as a "command from on high," along with the sanctions for disobeying. He explained most ethical training as presenting the "slippery slope" argument—i.e. don't do the little stuff, because you may slide into doing more serious acts of misconduct. The second most common approach in training is to warn recruits against the elements of the police culture that lead to transgressions.

Delattre (1989a) and Delaney (1990) have emphasized the importance of character. In Chapter 2 we discussed the ethics of virtue, which answers the question "How does one live a good life?" with "Developing and forming good habits of character." Delattre and Delaney apply this approach to police ethics. If a person has a bad character, ethical analysis is irrelevant because that individual will continue to behave in conformance with his or her traits of avarice, deceptiveness, cowardice, and so on. An individual who has good character possesses those virtues that are necessary for moral and ethical decision making. Training may help by reinforcing appropriate values, but one's character is already formed. What are the virtues necessary to be a good police officer? Delattre proposes justice, courage, temperance, and compassion. Delaney suggests sagacity, sincerity, and persistence.

This approach would seem to negate the relevance of any attempts to improve the ethics of officers, for character is fairly well formed by adulthood. Yet, we might say that ethics training at this point serves to delineate those situations that might not be recognized as questions of ethics. Also, discussions of such dilemmas point out egoistic rationalizations for unethical behavior, making them harder to use by those who would try. Other training options may concentrate on only one ethical system, such as utilitarianism, or involve a more balanced treatment of other ethical systems. All must resolve the issues of relativism versus absolutism, duty versus personal needs, and minor transgressions versus major transgressions.

Martinelli (2000) offers a different training model. He proposes a course that is grounded in the actual discipline cases of each law enforcement agency. He argues that some of the law enforcement code provisions are ambiguous to officers and require explanations—such as keeping one's private life "unsullied." Officers may not realize that they can receive departmental sanctions for their behavior in their private life. Further, case law indicates that if some attempts are not made to instruct officers in appropriate behaviors, and if agencies and city councils continue to rubber-stamp the violation of civil rights that some officers commit, the agencies themselves will be held responsible. For instance, if there is a pattern of abuse in a discipline record and the officer then commits another violation, the city and police department will probably lose a resulting civil suit.

INTEGRITY TESTING

Integrity testing is a "set-up" in which a police officer is placed in a position where he or she might be tempted to break a rule or a law and monitored to see what he or she will do. New York City has used integrity testing since the late 1970s, after the Knapp Commission exposed widespread corruption. Field associates were recruited straight from academies to investigate suspected officers (Reuss-Ianni, 1983: 80).

An example of integrity testing is as follows: An officer responds to a report of an open door to an apartment, and when he checks it out, he sees money in plain sight. The scene is being monitored to see if he takes the cash. Another test is "found" wallet is turned in to see if officers would take money out of the wallet (Marx, 1991). It is reported that almost 30 percent of officers have failed this type of honesty test (Prenzler and Ronken, 2001a: 322).

After the Mollen Commission in the mid-1990s, the integrity testing program was expanded. Prenzler and Ronken (2001a: 322) report that such "integrity tests" may be getting better results today. Of 355 tests involving 762 officers, no criminal failures were reported, and only 45 procedural failures were reported. See the Policy Box for a discussion of the policy of integrity testing.

Prenzler and Ronken (2001a) discuss integrity testing in police departments in Australia and around the world. They point out that the London Metropolitan Police instituted random integrity testing in 1998. In their study of Australia, they discovered that only two reporting police agencies used *targeted* integrity testing

---

POLICY BOX | **USE OF INTEGRITY TESTING**

As indicated in this chapter, New York City and some other cities have used integrity testing of officers. Most police officers are strongly against the practice.

Law: There is no law that prevents a police department from setting up "stings" of its own officers. On the one hand, case law that defines entrapment would apply to police as well in criminal charges but would be irrelevant to administrative sanctions. On the other hand, civil service and police unions may create contractual rights for officers.

Policy: Some police departments have a range of policies that make it clear that unethical behavior will not be tolerated. There is a difference between formal and informal policies, however, and in some police departments officers believe that investigations and sanctions are directed only to those officers without "juice" and that some officers who have friends in high places are immune from being targeted or from being punished. If true, that situation leads to informal policies in internal affairs where certain officers are protected from scrutiny. Management is distrusted, and behavioral practices of officers are adjusted to avoid detection rather than to avoid unethical behavior.

Ethics: The officers who are used in integrity test "stings" may have an ethical dilemma in that they are lying to a fellow officer. Usually, new recruits are used for this reason so the officers do not know them by sight. The undercover officer may eventually have to testify against the targeted officer, and that may lead to ostracism and other sanctions by peers. It may be an ethical issue for members of management to use young officers in this manner because they probably can do little to protect these officers from peer sanctions. If management targets certain officers unfairly for stings or ignores the wrongdoing of some officers, that, of course, is an issue as well. The major ethical issue is that of the officer who is faced with the opportunity to commit a wrongful act.

IN THE NEWS | INTEGRITY TESTS FOR POLICE

Baltimore police engage in random sting operations. New Orleans police stage car wrecks, leave money in abandoned cars, and set up fake drug buys. New York has undercover operators ask police officers for directions to see how polite they are. These are all integrity tests of officers. Some departments use such tests only when an officer is already under suspicion, but others engage in random testing.

A Baltimore police officer was caught in a sting where a bag of cocaine was left on a park bench and then an anonymous tip was placed with the police dispatcher. The officer who responded did bring in the bag but falsely stated that he saw a burglary suspect place it on the bench, and then used the lie to justify arresting the suspect. He was suspended and is facing charges of perjury.

Is this a type of noble-cause corruption? Explain why or why not.

Source: O'Hagan, 2000: B1.

---

and none used *random* integrity testing. In New South Wales, integrity testing resulted in 37 percent failing; only 27 percent passed, and the rest were referred for further investigation or discontinued (2001a: 327).

Needless to say, most police officers have highly negative attitudes about integrity testing. Spokesmen argue that "testing raises serious issues regarding privacy, deception, entrapment, provocation and the legal rights of individuals" (Prenzler and Ronken, 2001a: 323–324). There is a widespread belief that testing is unfair, overly intrusive, wasteful of resources, and detrimental to morale. One study of opinions of police managers found that the majority agreed that targeted integrity testing had a place in the investigation of wrongdoing but that random testing was ill-advised (Prenzler, 2006).

It is interesting to compare integrity testing with undercover operations. The planted wallet is similar to the buy–bust operation, and the use of field associates is similar to undercover operations. Officers despise the idea that an officer who pretends to be a friend may instead be someone who is trying to obtain evidence that they are doing wrong. The argument for undercover work is that if officers aren't doing anything wrong, they have nothing to fear. However, field associates create a sense of betrayal and lack of trust, regardless of whether someone is involved in wrongdoing. This same argument, of course, is used to criticize undercover operations. Specifically, critics argue that the use of undercover operations may undermine the fabric of social relations by reducing the level of trust. After reading the "In the News" box, think about whether you believe that these efforts are a good idea or a bad idea.

INTERNAL AFFAIRS

In the **internal affairs model,** the police investigate themselves and use an internal discipline system. This is widely seen as ineffective. Citizens are discouraged from reporting, police are seen as ineffective, and the approach seems to be ineffective in discouraging corruption or misconduct. In one Toronto study, 70 percent of those who filed complaints were not confident with the process, and only 14 percent thought their complaint was handled fairly (Prenzler and Ronken, 2001b:

180). There is no research that evaluates the actual effectiveness of internal affair models (Walker, 2007).

Some departments have "beefed up" their internal anti-corruption units. These units, especially in other countries, now undertake a mission of not only investigation and punishment but also deterrence and prevention. Such units may undertake integrity testing, promote awareness, improve selection and screening procedures, develop performance standards, and in other ways "police" the police to minimize corruption (Moran, 2005). This may represent the future of internal anti-corruption models.

CIVILIAN REVIEW/COMPLAINT BOARDS

There is a continuing belief that some police departments have proven that they are incapable of internal policing and that what is needed is some outside oversight. Civilian review boards have been created in several cities to monitor and review the investigation and discipline of officers who have complaints filed against them. Many models exist for the idea of civilian review, and no one model has been reported to be more effective or better than any other. Prenzler and Ronken (2001b) argue that it is difficult to analyze the success of such bodies because a high level of complaints may mean that there is greater trust in the process, not necessarily an increase in misconduct.

In the **civilian review/complaint model**, an independent civilian agency audits complaints and investigations. The board may also respond to appeals and act in an advisory role in investigations. Police still investigate and conduct the discipline proceeding. The Police Complaints Authority in the United Kingdom is one example of this model. Other models may involve an external board, but without any powers of subpoena or oversight (Prenzler and Ronken, 2001b).

Walker (2001) reviewed the range of civilian review models but did not find that any one model seemed to be better than any other. Worrall (2002) found that cities with civilian review procedures received more citizen complaints. This was a consequence of having a process that made it easier for citizens to complain rather than more incidents of police misconduct. Prenzler and Ronken (2001b) reported that external review models have about the same substantiation rate as do internal affairs models—about 10 percent of all complaints filed. The major criticism of such models centers on the idea that they are not truly independent, for police still conduct the investigations and sometimes even sit on the board. Prenzler (2000) argues that the "capture" theory is operative in civilian review models. This occurs when the regulatory or investigative body is "co-opted" by the investigated agency through informal relationships.

EARLY WARNING OR AUDIT SYSTEMS

Barker (2002) describes the evidence indicating that a small percentage of officers often accounts for a disproportionate number of abuse or corruption complaints. This problem was first recognized as far back as the 1970s (Walker and Alpert, 2002). Therefore, the practice of identifying these officers through some form of early warning system seems logical. The officers who were prone to use force were the first targets of early warning systems. It seemed clear that a small percentage of officers was responsible for a disproportionate share of excessive-force complaints. Then the practice spread to officers who garnered a disproportionate share of any type of citizen complaint.

Early warning systems have been used in New Orleans, Portland (Oregon), and Pittsburgh (Barker, 2002). The early warning systems look at number of complaints, use-of-force reports, use-of-weapon reports, reprimands, or other indicators to identify officers. Intervention may include more supervision, additional training, and/or counseling. In one city's program, the officer's supervisor is alerted that the system has tagged the officer; then the supervisor may counsel the officer, engage in other responses, or do nothing (Walker and Alpert, 2002: 225).

In Miami's early warning system, officers identified by the early warning system may be subject to the following (Walker and Alpert, 2002: 224):

1. reassignment
2. retraining
3. transfer
4. referral to an employee assistance program
5. fitness for duty evaluation
6. dismissal

These programs have been endorsed by the National Institute of Justice and have been incorporated into several consent decrees between cities and federal courts to avert civil rights litigation. By 1999, about 27 percent of all police agencies had early warning systems in place (reported in Walker and Alpert, 2002: 220).

Walker (2007) reports that early warning systems are different in the elements they count and where they set the threshold of concern. The systems also have different objectives: Some departments use them to provide assistance and additional training, others utilize them for punishment, and still others use them to target high achievers. The "In the News" box describes a computer-assisted early warning system.

IN THE NEWS | COMPUTERS IDENTIFY ROGUE COPS

The Los Angeles police department began using a 35-million-dollar computer system that tracks citizen complaints and other indicators to alert supervisors to officers who may be engaging in misconduct. The system is in response to a consent decree with the U.S. Justice Department, in which the department promised to improve oversight of rogue officers. The system tracks complaints, pursuits, lawsuits, uses of force, and other indicators to identify patterns of misconduct. Those who exhibit unusual patterns of action are flagged and supervisors are notified. Police union leaders argue that the system could create a situation where "good cops" hesitate to take action, creating the potential for harm.

Do you think that the police union leaders have a legitimate complaint against the system? Why or why not?

Source: Marquez, 2005: A15.

One cannot simply count the number of incidents or complaints, because the officer's shift and duty, length of service, types of calls responded to, and other factors affect the number of complaints (Walker and Alpert, 2002: 223). Further, the programs are only as effective as the interventions that are triggered by the identification of a problem. Walker and Alpert note that such systems are as much of a reflection of management as of individual officers. Supervisors are put on notice that they may have a problem officer and, thus, are more responsible if nothing is done and the officer engages in serious forms of misconduct.

Other Methods

Hunter (1999) proposed several means to minimize or reduce misconduct among police:

- decertification of officers who commit serious misconduct
- community policing programs
- college
- enhanced discipline
- civilian review
- better training

In his survey of police officers in Florida, Hunter found that officers believed that strict and fair discipline was the best response and deterrent to misconduct. The officers also identified

- clear policies
- superior performance of supervisors
- peer review boards

It was clear that, according to officers, leadership had everything to do with an ethical police force; 95 percent believed that supervisors should be moral examples, and 70 percent that unethical supervisors contributed to the problem. However, less than half (42 percent) agreed with the idea of a citizen review board.

Mores (2002) also discussed a range of methods to deter corruption, including the following:

- proper recruitment
- economic incentives
- community-oriented policing
- greater accountability
- rotation of assignments
- the use of informants
- the use of surveillance techniques
- prosecution of offenders

Prenzler and Ransley (2002) presented the most exhaustive list, also found in the 1997 Wood Report, written after an investigation of widespread corruption in the New South Wales (Australia) police department. Their list of "Methods to Reduce Police Corruption" is reproduced in Box 9.2.

| BOX 9.2 | METHODS TO REDUCE POLICE CORRUPTION |

Internal affairs units
Independent civilian oversight agencies
Overt recording devices (videocameras in cars)
Covert high technology surveillance
Targeted integrity testing
Randomized integrity testing
Drug and alcohol testing
Quality assurance test (customer service monitors)
Internal informants
Complaints profiling
Supervisor accountability
Integrity reviews
Mandatory reporting
Whistleblower protection
Compulsory rotation in corruption-prone sections

Asset and financial reviews
Surveys of police
Surveys of public
Personnel diversification
Comprehensive ethics training
Inquisitorial methods (fact-finding rather than due-process emphasis)
Complaint resolution
Monitoring and regulation of police procedures (of informants)
Decriminalizing vice
Risk analysis (to see what areas are vulnerable to corruption)

Source: Wood, 1997.

ETHICAL LEADERSHIP

Crank (1998: 187) and others have noted that there is a pervasive sense among rank-and-file police that administrators are not to be trusted: "Officers protect each other, not only against the public, but against police administrators frequently seen to be capricious and out of touch." The classic work in this regard is Reuss-Ianni's (1983) study of a New York City precinct in the late 1970s. She described the "two cultures" of policing—street cops and management cops. She observed that law enforcement managers were classic bureaucrats who made decisions based on modern management principles. This contrasted with the street-cop sub-culture, which still had remnants of quasi-familial relationships in which "loyalties and commitments took precedence over the rule book" (1983: 4). The result of this conflict between the two value systems was alienation of the street cop.

Despite the gulf between management and line staff, most people agree that employee behavior is influenced more directly by the behavior of superiors than by the stated directives or ethics of the organization. Executives engaged in price fixing and overcharging should not be surprised that their employees steal company supplies or time. Managers cannot espouse ethical ideals, act unethically, and then expect employees to act ethically. Thus, regardless of formal ethical codes, police are influenced by the standards of behavior they observe in their superiors. One might note that most large-scale police corruption that has been exposed has implicated very-high-level officials. Alternatively, police departments that have remained relatively free of corruption have administrators who practice ethical behavior on a day-to-daybasis.

Research reveals that close supervision, especially by mid-level managers such as sergeants, reduces the use of force and incidents of misconduct by officers

(Walker, 2007). Other research indicates that role modeling seems to be significant in limiting unethical conduct of an interpersonal nature (sexual harassment, discrimination, bullying), while strictness in supervision seems to be more important in controlling the misuse of resources, fraud, and other forms of financial corruption.

A third component of leadership was described as openness and refers to leaders encouraging subordinates to talk to them about ethical dilemmas. This was associated with fewer violations in a number of areas, especially in favoritism and discrimination. Interestingly, this study of more than 6,000 police officers found that strictness had no effect on reducing the gratuitous use of violence but that role modeling and openness did. This seems to support a police culture explanation of excessive force (Huberts, Kaptein and Lasthuizen, 2007).

Administrators face their own unique ethical dilemmas. Budget allocations, the use of drug testing, affirmative action, sexual harassment, and decisions about corrupt officers all present ethical dilemmas for administrators and supervisors. For instance, some supervisors face problems when they are promoted from the ranks and have friends who become their subordinates. Such friends may expect special consideration, leaving the supervisor to decide how to respond. Supervisors also report ethical dilemmas about how they should allocate resources, such as a new patrol car or overtime. Should seniority take precedence over competence? Should friendship take precedence over seniority?

Another issue is what should be done with officers who have drug or alcohol problems. If the administrator decides to counsel or suggest treatment without any change in duty status and the officer endangers the life of someone or actually harms a citizen or other officer because of the problem, is the administrator to blame? In many situations where police leaders must make decisions, lives, property, or liberty can be at stake. It is extremely important for supervisors and administrators to understand the impact that their decisions and their behavior have on everyone in the organization.

Even if leaders are not directly involved in corruption, encouraging or participating in the harassment and ostracism directed at those who expose wrongdoers supports an organizational culture that punishes whistleblowers. In some departments there is a perception that favored cliques are not punished for behaviors for which others would receive punishment. This climate destroys the trust in police leadership that is essential to ensure good communication from the rank and file.

It seems that management is just as likely as peer officers to cover up wrongdoing of officers. Only when the scandal cannot be contained does management "throw officers to the wolves." Unless there is a scandal, corruption is swept under the rug and individual offending officers may receive little or no discipline. For instance, Crank and Caldero (2000: 114) reported that in 100 civil lawsuits in 22 states between 1986 and 1991, the awards paid out by cities and police departments totaled $92 million, but of the 185 officers involved, only 8 were disciplined. In fact, 17 were promoted. It may be that noble-cause corruption is ignored by management and self-interest corruption is identified and sanctioned, but that does not seem to be the case when exploring case studies such as in New York and Los Angeles. What starts out, perhaps, as noble-cause corruption seems to lead to a perception that one is above the law, and self-interest corruption soon follows. See Box 9.3, "A Tale of Two Cities."

BOX 9.3	A TALE OF TWO CITIES

New York

The Investigator

Sgt. John Tromboli was stymied in his attempt to investigate and expose the actions of Michael Dowd, an obviously crooked cop whose lifestyle far exceeded a cop's pay. For five years Tromboli had been trying to get enough evidence on Dowd to file charges but was routinely turned down by his superiors for extra resources and for permission for wiretaps and other means of investigation. Tromboli believed that his superiors were trying to shut down his investigation. Dowd was finally arrested by Suffolk County police when he was videotaped conducting narcotics transactions in uniform and in a police car. Internal Affairs routinely did not share information with the prosecutor's office on crooked cops. Instead, information on corrupt officers would be hidden in a "tickler file" that was never made public.

The Scandal

The Mollen Commission in New York was formed in 1992 by Mayor David Dinkins to investigate allegations of corruption. The practices of Dowd and a number of other officers were exposed, including drug dealing, theft from corpses, robberies of drug dealers, setting up rival drug dealers for arrest and prosecution, protection rackets, and other misconduct. In the highly publicized hearings, officers were pressured to testify against others, and indictments and punishments were handed down. The hearings prompted Judge Mollen to comment that the Knapp Commission found that officers were in league with criminals but that, today, officers have become the criminals themselves.

Los Angeles

The Investigator

Detective Russell Poole, a Robbery–Homicide Division investigator, uncovered a pattern of complaints of violence by the anti-gang task force in the Ramparts Division when investigating an alleged beating of a gang member in a police squad room. He concluded that a number of the officers in the division were "vigilante cops" and requested that the investigation proceed further, but Chief Parks ordered him to limit his investigation solely to the Jimenez beating.

His superiors replaced a forty-page report he had prepared for the prosecutor's office with a two-page report that did not give any information about the possibility that there might be a pattern of corruption on the part of Ramparts officers. A year later the Ramparts scandal exploded. Poole quit the force.

The Scandal

The Ramparts scandal refers to the public disclosure of a wide range of corrupt activities by an anti-gang unit task force in the Ramparts Division of the L.A.P.D.(C.R.A.S.H.—Community Resources Against Street Hoodlums). Investigators from the prosecutor's office discovered the pattern of corruption when they made a deal with Rafael Perez, a Ramparts officer who had stolen cocaine from the evidence room. The scandal eventually led to dozens of criminal cases being voided because the prosecutor's office could not depend on the truthfulness of officers' testimony. Evidence indicated that between 1995 and 1998 the officers lied, planted evidence, beat suspects, and shot unarmed suspects. Officers also evidently held parties to celebrate shooting, gave out plaques when one killed a gang member, and spread ketchup at a crime scene to imitate blood.

Hundreds of cases had to be reviewed by the staff in the prosecutor's office to evaluate whether there was a possibility of manufactured evidence. At least one gang member's conviction was overturned when Rafael Perez, the officer who implicated all the others, confessed under oath that they had shot the man and then planted a gun on

(Continued)

him and testified that he had shot at them first. The suspect has been released from prison but is paralyzed and in a wheelchair.

Some evidence indicates at least ninety-nine people were framed by Ramparts officers. Prosecutors were also quoted in the paper as saying, "You can't trust the L.A.P.D.anymore." Mayor Richard Riordan reported to the press that the city would have to use $100 million of tobacco settlements to cover anticipated lawsuits. Eleven officers were fired, and forty convictions were overturned.

The L.A.P.D. responded with an internal management audit that admitted to a lapse of supervision and oversight. The report concluded that the corruption was caused by a few individuals whose wrongdoing had a "contagion effect." This report (conducted just eight years after the Christopher Commission presented a scathing commentary concerning the management and ethos of L.A.P.D) recommended an outside civilian oversight committee. However, the issue might be out of the department's hands at this point because the L.A.P.D came under a court monitor.

Why were police investigators blocked in their effort to uncover corruption? In what ways is the pattern of corruption similar in New York and Los Angeles? Do you see any differences?

Sources: Rothlein, 1999; Glover and Lait, 2000; Lait and Glover, 2000; Jablon, 2000; Sterngold, 2000; Deutsch, 2001; Golab, 2000.

CONCLUSION

We began these three chapters on law enforcement with the image of the use of force on Rodney King by the Los Angeles police and close with this same image. Some of us remember images from the 1960s, wherein law enforcement officers appeared on newscasts beating and using attack dogs against peaceful civil rights demonstrators. One might argue that those negative images of the 1960s led to greater professionalism, better training, and racial and sexual integration of police departments in the 1970s and 1980s.

The Rodney King incident and the resulting scrutiny have led to a groundswell of attention to "police ethics," including a national outcry against racial profiling and discriminatory enforcement. Today we face the greatest challenge to law enforcement in recent memory with the threat of terrorism. The enemy is more fearsome, the stakes are higher, and the fear is stronger. Thus, noble-cause corruption has a new cause that is even more noble than drug interdiction or simple crime fighting.

Although the drug war has been eclipsed by the war on terrorism, the question of whether it is ethical to achieve a good end through bad acts is still with us. Some argue that the question has changed; others argue that the answer has changed. It seems clear that how one resolves the dilemmas involved in counter-terrorism has everything to do with whether law enforcement officers are seen fundamentally as crime fighters or as public servants. We will revisit this important issue in the last chapter of this book.

Key Terms

blue curtain of
  secrecy *287*
civilian review/
  complaint model *298*

code of silence *286*
Dirty Harry
  problem *284*
informants *277*

integrity
  testing *295*
internal affairs
  model *297*

noble-cause
  corruption *267*
principle of double
  effect *280*

Review Questions

1. Explain the term *noble-cause corruption*.
2. Describe Barker and Carter's typology of lies.
3. Define entrapment using the legal test. Discuss whether you believe that the legal test is the same as an ethical test of entrapment.
4. List the questions posed by Marx that police should use before engaging in undercover operations.
5. What are the ethical problems in using informants?
6. Discuss the justifications and criticisms of undercover operations as offered by Marx.
7. What is the Dirty Harry problem?
8. Discuss the teleological and deontological arguments for and against whistleblowing.
9. Discuss the possible efforts to reduce or eliminate various forms of police misbehavior.
10. Discuss the rights-based concept of policing versus a utilitarian crime control model, and explain how each would resolve questions of the use of deception and invasive investigative techniques.

Writing/Discussion Questions

1. Write an essay on (or discuss) whether you think it is ever right for a police officer to do any of the following: lie on the witness stand, plant evidence, hide lab evidence, or ignore witnesses who want to give exculpatory evidence. Is it ever right for an undercover police officer to do any of the following to maintain his or her cover: lie to an innocent, engage in a sexual relationship, use drugs, injure someone, or allow a crime to take place?
2. Write an essay on (or discuss) appropriate tools in interrogation. For this essay you should review important court cases and research typical police practices. Should interrogations be videotaped? Should attorneys always be present? Should juveniles ever be interrogated without their parents? Should deception be used? If so, what kinds?
3. Write an essay on (or discuss) the best methods to reduce noble-cause corruption among officers. Are they the same methods as those that should be used to reduce egoistic corruption for pecuniary gain? Explain why or why not. Also explain why you think the selected methods would work.

Ethical Dilemmas

Situation 1

You are a police officer testifying about a particular crime. It is a case where you honestly don't know whether or not the suspect is guilty. While on the witness stand, you answer all the prosecutor's and the defense attorney's questions. You complete your testimony and exit the courtroom, knowing that you have specific knowledge that may help the defense attorney's case. You have answered all questions truthfully, but the specific question needed to help the defense was not asked. What should you do?

Situation 2

You are an undercover officer, and during training your instructors have taught you how to avoid using drugs while maintaining your cover. Once out on the street, you are told by co-workers that such training is unrealistic and that if you want to stay undercover, you will eventually have to use drugs. What would you do?

Situation 3

You are a male suspect in a murder case. You were drunk the night of the homicide and did meet and dance with the victim, a young college girl. You admit that you had a lot to drink but are 99-percent sure that you didn't see her except in the bar. The trouble is that you drank way too much and passed out in someone's apartment close to the bar rather than drive home. The girl was found in an apartment in the same complex. Police are telling you that they have forensic evidence that ties you to the murder. They say that they have her blood on your clothes and that it is your DNA in the sperm found in her body. They have been interrogating you now for several hours, and you are beginning to doubt your memory. You are also told that if you plead guilty, you would probably get voluntary manslaughter and might get probation, but if you insist on your innocence, you will be charged with first-degree murder and face the death penalty. What would you do?

[Obviously, this situation shifts our focus from the criminal justice professional's dilemma. If you decided earlier that the police tactic of lying about forensic evidence is ethical, this hypothetical illustrates what might happen when innocent suspects are lied to (assuming you are innocent!).]

Situation 4

There is an officer in your division known as a "rat" because he testified against his partner in a criminal trial and a civil suit. The partner evidently hit a handcuffed suspect in the head several times in anger, and the man sustained brain injuries and is now a paraplegic. Although none of the officers you know supports the excessive use of force, they are also appalled that this officer did not back up his partner's testimony that the suspect continued to struggle, in an attempt to justify his use of force. After all, punishing the officer wasn't going to make the victim any better. Now no one will ride with this guy, and no one responds to his calls for back-ups. There have been incidents such as a dead rat being found in his locker, and the extra uniform in his locker was set on fire.

One day you are parking your car and see your buddies in the employee parking lot moving away from his car; they admit they just slashed his tires. Each officer is being called into the captain's office to state whether he or she knows anything about this latest incident. Your turn is coming. What are you going to do? What are you going to do if the officers ask you to call his home and threaten harm to his children in order to "teach him a lesson."

Situation 5

You are a police officer testifying in a drug case. You have already testified that you engaged in a buy–bust operation, and the defendant was identified by an undercover officer as the one who sold him a small quantity of drugs. You testified that you chased the suspect down an alley and apprehended him. Immediately before you caught up with him, he threw down a number of glassine envelopes filled with what turned out to be cocaine. The prosecutor finished his direct examination, and now the defense attorney has begun cross-examining you. He asked if you had the suspect in your sight the entire time between when you identified him as the one who sold to the undercover officer and when you put the handcuffs on him. Your arrest report didn't mention it, but for a couple of seconds you slipped as you went around the corner of the alley and fell down. During that short time the suspect had proceeded a considerable distance down the alley.

You do not think there was anyone else around, and you are as sure as you possibly can be that it was your suspect who dropped the bags, but you know that if you testify to this incident truthfully, the defense attorney might be able to argue successfully that the bags were not dropped by the suspect and get him acquitted of the much more serious possession-with-intent-to-distribute charge. What should you do?

Situation 6

You are a federal agent and have been investigating a major drug ring for a long time. One of your informants is fairly highly placed within this ring and has been providing you with good information. You were able to "turn" him because he faces a murder charge: There is probable cause that he shot and killed a co-worker during an argument about five years ago, before he became involved in the drug ring. You have been holding the murder charge over his head to get him to cooperate and have been able, with the help of the U.S. District Attorney's office, to keep the local prosecutor from filing charges and arresting him. The local prosecutor is upset because the family wants some resolution in the case. You believe that the information he is able to provide you will result in charges of major drug sales and racketeering against several of the top smugglers, putting a dent in the drug trade for your region. At the same time, you understand that you are constantly risking the possibility that he may escape prosecution by leaving the country and that you are blocking the justice that the family of the murdered victim deserves. What would you do?

Suggested Readings

Alderson, J. 1998. *Principled Policing: Protecting the Public with Integrity*. Winchester, MA: Waterside.

Conlon, E. 2004. *Blue Blood*. New York: Riverhead.

Crank, J. 2004. *Understanding Police Culture*. Cincinnati, OH: Anderson Publishing Company.

Crank, J., and Caldero, M. M. 2004. *Police Ethics: The Corruption of Noble Cause*. Cincinnati, OH: Anderson Publishing Company.

Einstein, S., and Amir, M. 2001. *Policing, Security and Democracy: Special Aspects of Democratic Policing*. Huntsville, TX: Office of International Criminal Justice (OICJ), Sam Houston State University.

Haberfeld, M. 2006. *Police Leadership*. Upper Saddle River, NJ: Prentice-Hall.

Klockars, C., and Mastrofski, S. 1991. *Thinking About Police*. New York: McGraw-Hill.

Lynch, G. (Ed.). 1999. *Human Dignity and the Police: Ethics and Integrity in Police Work*. Springfield, IL: Charles C Thomas.

Prenzler, T., and Ransley, J. 2002. *Police Reform: Building Integrity*. Sydney, Australia: Hawkins.

Quinn, M. 2005. *The Police Code of Silence: Walking with the Devil*. Minneapolis: Quinn and Associates.

Rossmo, K. 2008. *Criminal Investigative Failures*. Boca Raton, FL: Taylor & Francis.

Walker, S. 2007. *Police Accountability: Current Issues and Research Needs*. Paper presented at National Institute of Justice, Policing Research Workshop: Planning for the Future, Washington, DC, November 28–29, 2006. Available through National Institute of Justice, Washington D.C.

Wozencraft, K. 1990. *Rush*. New York: Random House.

ETHICS AND LEGAL PROFESSIONALS

CHAPTER 10

© Harry Lynch/Newscom

The ethical duty of prosecutors is to pursue justice, but sometimes this goal is subverted. Mike Nifong, the prosecutor who ignored and covered up evidence to continue his prosecution of Duke University lacrosse team members in 2006 on rape charges, serves as an example of a prosecutor who forgot his duty.

CHAPTER OBJECTIVES

1. Become familiar with the source of legal ethics.

2. Understand the concept of an attorney as a moral agent or as a legal agent.

3. Learn the variety of ethical issues faced by defense attorneys.

4. Learn the variety of ethical issues faced by prosecutors.

CHAPTER OUTLINE

Imagine that you have been arrested for a crime you did not commit. You don't know how it happened, but somehow police have decided that you acted with another person to commit a murder and they have arrested you. You are facing a potential death sentence and, as much as you hope and believe that the justice system will sort out the truth, you are frightened of what might happen to you. The police do not seem to want to hear that you don't know the suspect who has implicated you, and you don't know the victim; it seems the police only want a confession from you. The more you try to explain how you couldn't have done it, the more they twist your words and make it seem like you did do it. After hours of questioning, you finally realize that you'd better get a lawyer. You now realize that this lawyer, whoever he or she might be, could be the most important person in your life.

Do people end up in prison for crimes they did not commit? The fact is that they do. Joyce Ann Brown and James Curtis Giles are two examples. Both of these individuals were accused of crimes that were committed by someone with the same name. James Curtis Giles was finally exonerated of a gang rape after spending 10 years in prison and 14 years as a registered sex offender. DNA analysis showed that there was no physical evidence linking him to rape, and there was evidence of another perpetrator. In 1982, a man who pleaded guilty to the rape said he did it with a James Giles and Michael Brown. James Curtis Giles lived 15 miles away from the victim and did not match her description of the attacker. He also had an alibi. Investigators ignored another man with same name who lived across the street from the victim and had been arrested with Brown on other charges. Despite this information, the wrong Giles was convicted (Garay, 2007).

A similar pattern of mistaken identity occurred when Joyce Ann Brown was arrested and convicted for a murder she did not commit. The real perpetrator shared the same name as Brown, who was imprisoned for 9 years before she was exonerated (Brown and Gaines, 1990). Each of these cases represents a grievous mistake that should have been corrected by the due process protections provided in the criminal justice system but was not. One of the strongest protections in place to protect against errors is the right to counsel.

FIRST, LET'S KILL ALL THE LAWYERS...

Public perceptions of lawyers indicate that the public has little confidence in their ability to live up to ideals of equity, fairness, and justice. In 2006, respondents in a Gallup Poll rated their level of trust in the integrity of attorneys. Only about 18 percent rated attorneys as "high" or "very" high. Only a few professions were rated lower than lawyers, including stockbrokers, senators, congressmen, HMO managers, car salesmen and advertising executives (Gallup Poll, 2006).

In the 1980s the law scandal was the savings and loan fiasco, in which the greed and corruption of those in the banking industry were ably assisted by the industry's attorneys, and the taxpayers picked up the bill for the bankrupt institutions and outstanding loans. The scandal of the 1990s was the Bill Clinton–Monica Lewinsky investigation, with opinions mixed as to which set of lawyers was more embarrassing—those who could coach the President that oral sex wasn't technically "sexual relations" or the special prosecutor, Kenneth Starr, and his assistants, who spent millions of dollars in an investigation that centered on semen stains and the definition of sex. The new century brought us the debacle of WorldCom and Enron, and, again, lawyers played a central role, along with business executives and accountants.

Most recently, we have the situation of the White House counsel parsing the definition of torture in secret memoranda, the politicization of the Justice Department, and hundreds of individuals being released from prison by Innocence Projects nationwide because of egregious errors and/or unethical behaviors on the part of police, prosecutors, defense attorneys, and judges.

Apparently, even lawyers don't think much of their profession. In a 2006 poll about 60 percent of those in the practice of law for 6–9 years were dissatisfied with their career, although the percentage went down to 40 percent for those practicing more than 10 years. Overall, only about 55 percent of attorneys were satisfied with their career. Only about a third of lawyers practicing 6–9 years would recommend law as a profession to young people; and 44 percent of all lawyers would recommend it as a career (S. Ward, 2007).

The perception of the lawyer as an amoral "hired gun" is in sharp contrast to the ideal of the lawyer as an officer of the court, sworn to uphold the ideals of justice declared sacrosanct under our system of law. Interestingly, but perhaps not surprisingly, our government is made up predominantly of lawyers: A large percentage of elected officials are lawyers, and twenty-three of forty-one presidents have been lawyers (Glendon, 1994: 12). Our nation's leaders and historical heroes have just as likely been lawyers (Abraham Lincoln, for example) as military generals, and our nation's consciousness is permeated with the belief in law and legal vindication.

On the one hand, the public tends to agree with a stereotype of lawyers as amoral, motivated by money, and with no conscience or concern for morality. On the other hand, the first response to any perception of wrong is to find a legal advocate and sue, with the belief that a lawyer will right any wrong and solve any problem.

Throughout history the ethics of those associated with the legal process has been suspect. Plato and Aristotle condemned advocates because of their ability to make the truth appear false and the guilty appear innocent. This early distrust

QUOTE AND QUERY

Lawyers are upset. They have discovered what they believe to be an alarming new trend: People don't like them. The American Bar Association recently appointed a special panel to investigate the legal profession's bad image. The California State Bar has commissioned a survey to find out why so many people dislike lawyers....We wish to reassure lawyers. This wave of anti-lawyer feeling is nothing new. People have always hated you.

Roth and Roth, 1989: i

This passage is humorous, but the underlying problem is not. Why do people have such low opinions of lawyers?

continued throughout history. Early colonial lawyers were distrusted and even punished for practicing law. For many years, lawyers could not charge a fee for their services because the mercenary aspect of the profession was condemned (Papke, 1986: 32). Gradually, lawyers and the profession itself were accepted, but suspicion and controversy continued in the area of fees and qualifications. Partly to counteract public antipathy, lawyers formed their own organization, the American Bar Association (ABA), in 1878. Shortly afterward, this professional organization established the first ethical guidelines for lawyers. The "Quote and Query" box puts the problem in a humorous light.

Perhaps the best explanation for the longstanding distrust of lawyers is that they typically represent trouble. People don't require a lawyer unless they believe that a wrong has been done to them or that they need to be defended. The ability of lawyers to argue either side raises a level of distrust. We would prefer a passionate advocate rather than a paid advocate. We will explore basic perceptions that influence a lawyer's advocacy in our criminal justice system. Finally, let us not forget the full context of the quote, "First, let's kill all the lawyers . . .," widely used as a stab at attorneys. In Shakespeare's *Henry IV*, *Part II*, the statement is from a despot who, before making a grab for power, argues that the first thing he must do is kill all the lawyers, for it is lawyers who are the guardians of law. However, the reason the existing power holders in the play were vulnerable to an overthrow in the first place was that they were using the law to oppress the powerless. And so it is today. The law can be either a tool of oppression or a sword of justice, with lawyers and judges as the ones who wield its power.

ETHICAL ISSUES FOR LEGAL PROFESSIONALS

A profession, as defined in Chapter 6, involves a specialized body of knowledge, commitment to the social good, the ability to regulate itself, and high social status (Davis and Elliston, 1986: 13). The presence of ethical standards is essential to the definition of a profession. More important, membership in a profession implies a special set of rules, different from those applied to everyone else. Often these rules dictate a higher standard of behavior, but they may also involve greater privileges or the right to act in a different way from everyone else by virtue of that membership.

Formal ethical standards for lawyers and judges were originally promulgated by the American Bar Association in the Model Code of Professional Responsibility. The original Canons, adapted from the Alabama Bar Association Code of 1887, were adopted by the ABA in 1908 and have been revised frequently since then. In 1983, the ABA switched its endorsement of the Model Code as the general guide for ethical behavior to the Model Rules of Professional Responsibility. The Model Rules continue to be revised periodically, responding to changing sensibilities and emerging issues. Today's Model Rules cover many aspects of the lawyer's profession, including areas such as client–lawyer relationships, the lawyer as counselor, the lawyer as advocate, transactions with others, public service, and maintaining the integrity of the profession. Box 10.1 presents the table of contents for the latest edition of the Model Rules.

In the commentary to the Model Rules, it is clear that they are provided to help attorneys resolve ethical dilemmas; however, the Rules rarely solve a problem definitively and professional discretion is always needed. Overall, the rules require that attorneys zealously protect and pursue a client's interest within the boundaries of the rules while maintaining a professional and civil demeanor toward everyone involved in the legal process.

In addition to the Model Rules, there is also the American Law Institute's Restatement of the Law Governing Lawyers (Martyn, Fox, and Wendel, 2008). Developed in 2000, the Restatement provides guidelines and commentary covering most of the same issues that the Model Rules cover. Some of the Sections of the Restatement are:

- Admission to Practice Law
- A Lawyer's Duty of Supervision
- A Lawyer's Duties to a Prospective Client
- Client–Lawyer Contracts
- Duty of Care to a Client
- A Lawyer's Duty to Safeguard Confidential Client Information
- Using or Disclosing Information to Prevent Death or Serious Bodily Harm
- Client Crime or Fraud
- Falsifying or Destroying Evidence

The Restatement has eight chapters and 135 different sections. In addition to these national guidelines, state bar associations have their own sets of rules that are used for disciplinary purposes. Finally, it should be noted that the Model Rules and the Restatement cover the practice of law generally; thus, most of the commentary and elements relate to civil practice. In this chapter, which concentrates exclusively on criminal defense attorneys and prosecutors, we will be referring to the Criminal Justice Standards, as promulgated by the American Bar Association. These Standards offer guidelines and commentary directed specifically to the practice of criminal law. Ethical issues in criminal law may involve courtroom behavior, perjury, conflicts of interest, use of the media, investigation efforts, use of immunity, discovery and the sharing of evidence, relationships with opposing attorneys, and plea bargaining.

To enforce rules of ethics, the ABA has a standing committee on ethical responsibility to offer formal and informal opinions when charges of impropriety

BOX 10.1 | MODEL RULES OF PROFESSIONAL CONDUCT

Client-Lawyer Relationship

1.1 Competence
1.2 Scope of Representation and Allocation of Authority Between Client and Lawyer
1.3 Diligence
1.4 Communication
1.5 Fees
1.6 Confidentiality of Information
1.7 Conflict of Interest: Current Clients
1.8 Conflict of Interest: Current Clients: Specific Rules
1.9 Duties to Former Clients
1.10 Imputation of Conflicts of Interest: General Rule
1.11 Special Conflicts of Interest for Former and Current Government Officers and Employees
1.12 Former Judge, Arbitrator, Mediator, or other Third-Party Neutral
1.13 Organization as Client
1.14 Client with Diminished Capacity
1.15 Safekeeping Property
1.16 Declining or Terminating Representation
1.17 Sale of Law Practice
1.18 Duties to Prospective Client

Counselor

2.1 Advisor
2.2 Deleted
2.3 Evaluation for Use by Third Persons
2.4 Lawyer Serving as Third-Party Neutral

Advocate

3.1 Meritorious Claims and Contentions
3.2 Expediting Litigation
3.3 Candor Toward the Tribunal
3.4 Fairness to Opposing Party and Counsel
3.5 Impartiality and Decorum of the Tribunal
3.6 Trial Publicity
3.7 Lawyer as Witness
3.8 Special Responsibilities of a Prosecutor
3.9 Advocate in Nonadjudicative Proceedings

Transactions With Persons Other Than Clients

4.1 Truthfulness in Statements to Others
4.2 Communication with Person Represented by Counsel
4.3 Dealing with Unrepresented Persons
4.4 Respect for Rights of Third Persons

Law Firms and Associations

5.1 Responsibilities of Partners, Managers, and Supervisory Lawyers
5.2 Responsibilities of a Subordinate Lawyer
5.3 Responsibilities Regarding Nonlawyer Assistants
5.4 Professional Independence of a Lawyer
5.5 Unauthorized Practice of law; Multijurisdictional practice of law
5.6 Restrictions of Right to Practice
5.7 Responsibilities Regarding Law-Related Services

Public Service

6.1 Voluntary Pro Bono Public Service
6.2 Accepting Appointments
6.3 Membership in Legal Services Organizations
6.4 Law Reform Activities Affecting Client Interests
6.5 Nonprofit and Court-Annexed Limited Legal-Service Programs

Information About Legal Services

7.1 Communications Concerning a Lawyer's Services
7.2 Advertising
7.3 Direct Contact with Prospective Clients
7.4 Communication of Fields of Practice and Specialization
7.5 Firm Names and Letterheads
7.6 Political Contributions to Obtain Government Legal Engagements or Appointments by Judges

Maintaining the Integrity of the Profession

8.1 Bar Admission and Disciplinary Matters
8.2 Judicial and Legal Officials
8.3 Reporting Professional Misconduct
8.4 Misconduct
8.5 Disciplinary Authority: Choice of Law

Source: Martyn, Fox, and Wendel, 2008.

have been made. Also, each state bar association has the power to sanction offending attorneys by private or public censure or to recommend a court suspend their privilege to practice law. Thus, the rules enforced by the state bar have essentially the power of law behind them. The bar associations also have the power to grant entry into the profession because one must ordinarily belong to the bar association of a particular state to practice law there. Bar associations judge competence by testing the applicant's knowledge, and they also judge moral worthiness by background checks of individuals. The purpose of these restrictive admission procedures is to protect the public image of the legal profession by rejecting unscrupulous or dishonest individuals or those unfit to practice for other reasons. However, many believe that if bar associations were serious about protecting the profession, they would also continue to monitor the behavior and moral standing of current members with the same care they seem to take in the initial decision regarding entry (Elliston, 1986: 53).

Disciplinary committees investigate a practicing attorney only when a complaint is lodged against him or her. The investigative bodies have been described as decentralized, informal, and secret. They do little for dissatisfied clients because most client complaints involve incompetence and/or lack of attention; these charges are vague and ill-defined (Marks, Raymond, and Cathcart, 1986: 72). The "In the News" box chronicles the reasons for disbarring one lawyer.

Many bar disciplinary committees are hopelessly understaffed and overburdened with complaints. Complaints may take years to investigate, and in the meantime, if prospective clients call, they will be told only that the attorney is in good standing and has no substantiated complaints. A study of attorney discipline by an organization for legal reform reported that only 3 percent of investigations by state disciplinary committees result in public sanctions and only 1 percent end in disbarment (*San Antonio Express News*, 2002).

While individuals with complaints against their lawyers in the civil arena receive little satisfaction, criminal defendants are arguably even less likely to have anyone care or rectify incompetence or unethical behavior on the part of their attorney. "You get what you pay for" may be true to an extent, but even that phrase does not truly represent the possibility of a family mortgaging its home, signing over

---

IN THE NEWS | A LAWYER DISBARRED

A lawyer in New York was disbarred for incompetent defense and other actions. Among the charges was a case where he accepted $20,000 to conduct an immigration deportation appeal but then did nothing and did not file the appeal. The client was deported, and the lawyer refused requests from the family to give back any of the money. The lawyer also refused to return clients' bail money after it was returned by the court.

In another case, this lawyer had a criminal client sign a deposit fee agreement stating that the $10,000 deposit was non-refundable regardless of how much time was spent on the case. The defendant signed the deposit agreement, and immediately afterward the attorney was disqualified from representing the client because he was also representing a co-conspirator; however, he refused to return any of the deposit money.

How would the attorney justify these acts under any ethical system?

Source: Lin, 2006.

cars, and emptying its bank account for an attorney who promises to represent a family member against a criminal charge and then finding that the attorney will not answer calls, doesn't appear in court, or is unprepared and forgets to file necessary motions.

Law schools have been criticized for being singularly uninterested in fostering any type of moral conscience in graduating students. Law schools purport to be in the practice of reshaping law students so that when they emerge "thinking like a lawyer," they have mastered a type of thinking that is concerned with detail and logical analysis. Others argue this is done at the expense of being sensitive to morality and larger social issues (Spence, 1989). Stover (1989) writes how public interest values decline during law school. The reason for this decline seemingly has to do with the low value placed on public-interest issues by the law school curriculum, which also treats ethical and normative concerns as irrelevant or trivial compared to the "bar courses" such as contract law and torts.

Even though all law schools today require professional-responsibility courses, sometimes these courses do not promote morality and ethics. Instead, instructors relate stories (humorous and otherwise) of how to get around ethical and legal mandates. For instance, law students are taught that in the discovery phase of a lawsuit, the legal rule that requires an attorney to turn over documents requested by the other side (that are not otherwise privileged) can be circumvented by burying important documents in 600 boxes of paperwork. Rather than being taught to abide by the spirit and principle of the ethical guidelines, sometimes these are presented as obstacles to be overcome.

Ethical issues have received more attention in recent years, and most law schools now have a variety of public service clinics where students help the poor, elderly, immigrants, and/or criminal clients. Bar exams now have a special section devoted to the Model Rules and the state's own professional responsibility code, but these tests are often hyper-technical, testing the minutiae of the rules rather than the spirit of practicing law ethically and honestly. Most states also require continuing legal education credit hours in the area of ethics. However, similar to our earlier discussion of police officers, classroom ethics training that encourages one set of behaviors is often contradicted and disparaged by the professional subculture. If this is the case, such training might not be very effective.

THE ATTORNEY–CLIENT RELATIONSHIP

Model Rules 1.1 through 1.18 cover the special relationship between attorney and client. Many lawyers believe that loyalty to the client is paramount to their duties as a professional. This loyalty surpasses and eclipses individual and private decision making, and the special relationship said to exist between lawyer and client justifies decisions that otherwise might be deemed morally unacceptable. The various relationships proposed between lawyers and clients are described below.

1. *Legal agent.* An extreme position is that the attorney is no more than the *legal agent* of the client. The lawyer is neither immoral nor moral, but merely a legal tool. This position is represented by the statement, "I am a lawyer, first and foremost."

2. *Special relationship.* A more moderate position is that the loyalty to the client presents a *special relationship* between client and lawyer, similar to that between mother and child or with a trusted friend. This protected relationship justifies fewer actions than the legal agent relationship. The lawyer is expected to dissuade the client from taking unethical or immoral actions, but loyalty would preclude putting anyone's interests above the client's.

3. *Moral agent.* The third position is that the lawyer is a *moral agent* who has to adhere to his or her own moral code. The client's interests come first only as long as they do not conflict with the lawyer's morality and ethical code. If there is a conflict, the lawyer follows his or her conscience.

Some critics of the legal agent approach reject perspectives that discount the lawyer's responsibility as an individual to make his or her own moral decisions. In this view, lawyers should be the legal *and* moral agents of their clients rather than merely legal agents. Their personal responsibility to avoid wrongdoing precludes involving themselves in their clients' wrongdoing (Postema, 1986: 168). This position is represented by the statement, "I am a person first, a lawyer second."

LEGAL AGENT VERSUS MORAL AGENT?

Elliott Cohen (1991), an advocate of the moral agent position, believes that being a purely legal advocate is inconsistent with being a morally good person in several ways. For instance, the virtue of justice would be inconsistent with a zealous advocate who would maximize the chance of his or her client's winning, regardless of the fairness of the outcome.

A pure legal agent would sacrifice values of truthfulness, moral courage, benevolence, trustworthiness, and moral autonomy in furtherance of his or her client's interests. Only if the attorney is a moral agent as well as a legal advocate can there be any possibility of the attorney maintaining individual morality. E. Cohen (1991: 135–136) suggests some principles for attorneys to follow to be considered moral:

1. Treat others as ends in themselves and not as mere means to winning cases.
2. Treat clients and other professional relations who are relatively similar in a similar fashion.
3. Do not deliberately engage in behavior that is apt to deceive the court as to the truth.
4. Be willing, if necessary, to make reasonable personal sacrifices—of time, money, popularity, and so on—for what you justifiably believe to be a morally good cause.
5. Do not give money to, or accept money from, clients for wrongful purposes or in wrongful amounts.
6. Avoid harming others in the process of representing your client.
7. Be loyal to your clients, and do not betray their confidences.
8. Make your own moral decisions to the best of your ability, and act consistently upon them.

The rationale for these principles seems to be an amalgamation of ethical formalism, utilitarianism, and other ethical frameworks. Some of the principles may seem impossible to uphold and be subject to bitter criticism on the part of practicing attorneys. For instance, how does one avoid harming others when one is an advocate for one side in a contest? There are losers and winners in civil contests as well as in criminal law, and lawyers must recognize their responsibility when the loser is harmed in financial or emotional ways.

Cohen's position has been attacked as naïve and wrong on several counts. Memory and Rose (2002: 29) argued against Cohen's proposed principle that a lawyer "may refuse to aid or participate in conduct that he sincerely believes, after careful reflection on the relevant facts, to be unjust or otherwise morally wrong notwithstanding his obligation to seek the lawful objectives of his client." They believe that lawyers can be effective and morally good at the same time and argue that rules in place already prevent unscrupulous acts. For instance, Model Rule 3.3 prohibits lying. It states that lawyers may not make false statements of material facts or law, cannot fail to disclose a material fact to a tribunal when disclosure is necessary to avoid assisting a criminal or fraudulent act by the client, cannot fail to disclose legal authority that is directly adverse to one's client's interest, or cannot offer evidence that one knows to be false. According to the authors, this rule and others prevent attorneys from sacrificing truth even when zealously pursuing clients' interests.

Further, Memory and Rose (2002) argue that decisions regarding justice and morality are so subjective that it is impossible for them to be judged after the fact. Moreover, the Model Rules prevent most cases of abuse by lawyers. They argue that if lawyers were to act as moral agents, the result would be the loss of the clients' trust in lawyers, for the lawyer would be able to substitute his or her individual morality for the clients.

In a rebuttal article, Elliott Cohen (2002: 39) used the ethics of care as the rationale for his continued defense of the moral agent idea:

> [M]orality concerns concrete interpersonal relationships that can be understood only by people who have compassion and empathy for the predicaments of other people.... Morally virtuous lawyers (moral agents) possess such affective aspects of emotional development, but it is precisely such a dimension that must be lacking from the pure legal advocate who must get used to working injury upon others without having any strong feelings of guilt, sorrow, or regret.

In general, Cohen (1991) and Memory and Rose (2002) seem to be in agreement that the Rules should prevent the most egregious misconduct of lawyers. Their disagreement comes from the value they place on rules versus individual responsibility for more ambiguous moral judgments.

Chapter 6 made the point that rules have never been able to substitute for moral decision making on the part of individual actors. This is more consistent with Cohen's position than that of Memory and Rose. Cohen's argument is essentially that training and socialization into the "culture of law" create the legal agent role and encourage a type of "noble-cause corruption" similar to that of police officers, as discussed in Chapter 9. In the legal profession the "noble cause" is winning a case (at all costs). In a culture that supports "ends" thinking (winning) over "means," rules are no more likely to control misconduct by lawyers than they do some police officers. The "Quote and Query" box gives examples of legal agent and moral agent statements.

QUOTE AND QUERY

About half the practice of a decent lawyer consists in telling would-be clients that they are damned fools and should stop.

Reported in Glendon, 1994: 76

You're an attorney. It's your duty to lie, conceal and distort everything, and slander everybody.

Giradeaux, 1949: Act Two

Which of these statements represents a legal agent statement? Which represents a moral agent statement?

Research indicates that the position taken by attorneys depends partially on whom they represent. On the one hand, public defenders take a more authoritarian role and seem to support the attorney as a "guru" who tells the client what to do; attorneys for corporations, on the other hand, are apt to follow a more client-centered approach (Mather, 2003).

In an interesting application of Carol Gilligan's ethics-of-care approach, Vogelstein (2003) argues that attorneys' rules are concerned with rights, not care. Thus, attorneys must sacrifice third parties if they are to follow the rules and protect their clients' interests. This, she argues, contributes to the negative perception of attorneys. She proposes a type of moral agent approach in which the attorney must take into consideration the needs of others, as well as of the clients. Of course, others, such as Memory and Rose, who argued against Cohen's propositions, would strongly disagree. It should be noted that the rules show glimmers of the moral agent idea. For instance, Rule 2.1 states that "a lawyer may refer not only to law but to other considerations such as moral, economic, social and political factors...." in making decisions. This indicates that the Rules do encourage attorneys to look to the ethical systems to resolve problems. Again, though, the rules are not much help when the client and the attorney strongly disagree over what is the right thing to do.

A HIGHER STANDARD OF BEHAVIOR?

In Chapter 7 we discussed the concept of police officers, as public servants, being held to a higher standard of conduct than those they serve. This same principle applies to attorneys. The Model Code of Professional Responsibility for lawyers dictates that they should be "temperate and dignified" and "refrain from all illegal and morally reprehensible conduct." The Model Rules expect that "a lawyer's conduct should conform to the requirements of the law, both in professional service to clients and in the lawyer's business and personal affairs." These prescriptions are similar to those found in the Law Enforcement Code of Ethics. Both groups of professionals are expected to uphold a higher standard of behavior than the general public. These professionals have chosen to work within the legal system and help to enforce the law; thus, it is not unreasonable, perhaps, to expect that they provide a model of behavior for the rest of us.

IN THE NEWS | A LEWD LAWYER

A trial judge held a lawyer in contempt and sentenced him to 90 days in jail for making gestures simulating masturbation during a plea-taking in the courtroom. Evidently, the lawyer made the gestures while looking at the female judge and rolling his eyes. It wasn't clear exactly what message he was trying to convey, but he was frustrated with the plea process going on and angry at the prosecutor. The lawyer said the gesture was directed at the prosecutor, not the judge. The appellate judge held that he "tarnished the dignity of the judicial process" and upheld the original judge's order of 90 days. The sentence was appealed.

Does it make a difference whether the gestures were directed at the judge or at the prosecutor? Why would a professional engage in this kind of conduct in a court of law?

Source: Kreytak, 2008: B1, B6.

Some allege that instead of a *higher* standard, lawyers (like some police officers) allow themselves a *double* standard. Lying is lying unless it is done by a lawyer, and then it is just doing one's duty, or a "misstatement of fact." In a highly critical overview of the legal profession, Glendon (1994) proposed that the legal profession has changed in dramatic ways, not all of which have been for the better. Although the practice of law was once governed by rules of ethics and etiquette and lawyers acted like gentlemen (literally, because the profession was, for the most part, closed to women, minorities, and the lower class), it has become open to those excluded groups in the last twenty-five years. At the same time, law practice has become a world of "no rules" or, more accurately, only one rule: "Winning is everything." The "In the News" box gives a case of one lawyer who might agree.

ETHICAL ISSUES FOR DEFENSE ATTORNEYS

The role of the defense attorney is to protect the due-process rights of the defendant. Due process is supposed to minimize mistakes in judicial proceedings that might result in deprivation of life, liberty, or property. Due-process rights, including notice, neutral fact finders, cross-examination, and presentation of evidence and witnesses, are supposed to minimize the risk of error. The defense attorney is there during the important steps of the process to ensure that these rights are protected. For instance, during interrogation to make sure no coercion is used, at lineup to make sure it is fair and unbiased, and during trial to ensure adequate cross-examination and presentation of evidence. This pure role of advocate is contradictory to the reality that the defense attorney must, if he or she is to work with the other actors in the court system, accommodate their needs as well as those of clients.

In fiction, defense attorneys seem to be presented as either fearless crusaders who always manage to defend innocent clients (usually against unethical prosecutors) or as sleazy deal makers who are either too burned out or too selfish to care about their clients. The reality, of course, fits neither of these portrayals. Kittel (1990) finds that the majority of defense attorneys would not change their career given an opportunity to do so, and that most chose their career because they were interested in the trial work it offered or for public policy reasons. These findings are contrary to the common myth that criminal defense attorneys enter the field because they were not successful at more lucrative fields of law.

Many defense attorneys started out as prosecutors. This sometimes causes problems when they have trouble making the transition from "good guy battling evil" to the more subtle role of defender of due process. If the attorney cannot make the transition from prosecution to defense and feel comfortable in the role, it is difficult to offer a zealous defense (R. Cohen, 2001).

As mentioned earlier, the system tends to operate under a presumption of guilt. Indeed, defense attorneys are often in the position of defending clients they know are guilty. The rationale for defending a guilty person is that any person deserves due process before a finding of guilt and punishment. Before punishment is imposed, a fair procedure ensures that the punishment is appropriate. Due process involves a set of fact-finding procedures, and the defense attorney's role is to make sure that these procedures are followed. If defense attorneys are doing their job, we can be more sure that when a defendant is duly convicted and sentenced, the result is a just one. If they are not doing their job, we have no system of justice, and none of us is safe from wrongful prosecution and the awesome power of the state to investigate, prosecute, and punish. In the "In the News" box, one lawyer decided that justice demanded that he subvert the role of the defense attorney. What is the attorney's responsibility to the client when he or she knows the client is guilty of a horrible crime?

In 1991–1992 the American Bar Association promulgated its Standards for Criminal Justice. Chapter 4, "The Defense Function" covers a multitude of issues, such as these:

- Function of defense counsel
- Punctuality
- Public statements
- Duty to the administration of justice
- Access and the lawyer–client relationship
- Duty to investigate
- Control and direction of litigation
- Plea bargaining
- Trial conduct
- Appeal

IN THE NEWS | A LACK OF ADVOCACY

"I decided that Mr. Tucker deserved to die, and I would not do anything to prevent his execution."

This statement was made by defense attorney David Smith of Greensboro, North Carolina, who accepted a capital appeal case and then admitted that he "sabotaged" the appeal of his client because he believed the man deserved execution. The attorney went through a moral crisis afterward and confessed to the state bar what he did.

You are on a state bar disciplinary committee. Would you vote to disbar Smith?

Source: Rimer, 2000.

These standards are much more specific than the Law Enforcement Code of Ethics. Instead of being aspirational, the standards are specific guidelines for behavior. We will explore only a few of the many different ethical issues that confront defense attorneys in their representation of clients. (The Criminal Justice Standards from the American Bar Association's website can be accessed at www.abanet.org/crimjust/standards/home.html.)

RESPONSIBILITY TO THE CLIENT

> The basic duty defense counsel owes to the administration of justice and as an officer of the court is to serve as the accused's counselor and advocate with courage and devotion and to render effective, quality representation (Standard 4-1.2(b)).

Defense attorneys are always in the position of balancing the rights of the individual client against overall effectiveness. Extreme attempts to protect these rights will reduce the defense attorney's effectiveness for other clients. Furthermore, defense attorneys must balance the needs and problems of the client against their ethical responsibilities to the system and the profession.

A lawyer is supposed to provide legal assistance to clients without regard for personal preference or interest. A lawyer is not allowed to withdraw from a case simply because he or she no longer wishes to represent the client. A lawyer will be allowed to withdraw in these situations:

- if the legal action is for harassment or malicious purposes,
- if continued employment will result in violation of a disciplinary rule,
- if discharged by a client, or
- if a mental or physical condition renders effective counsel impossible.

In other cases a judge *may* grant permission to withdraw when the client insists on illegal or unethical actions, is uncooperative and does not follow the attorney's advice, or otherwise makes effective counsel difficult. In general, judges are loath to allow a defendant to proceed with a *pro se* defense (defending oneself) because of the risk that the conviction will be overturned on appeal. Nor are judges likely to allow withdrawal if it will delay ongoing proceedings.

Legal ethics mandate that people with unpopular causes and individuals who are obviously guilty still deserve counsel, and that it is the ethical duty of an attorney to provide such counsel.

Many people are firmly convinced that the quality of legal representation is directly related to how much money the defendant can pay. When people can make bail and hire private attorneys, do they receive a better defense? Research, unfortunately, supports the proposition that those who can afford private attorneys receive "better" representation (Martinez and Pollock, 2008). However, a private attorney, appointed by the court and paid with state funds, may not be better than a public defender. A Harvard study found, in reviewing federal criminal cases between 1997 and 2001, that lawyers who were appointed to represent indigent clients were less qualified than federal public defenders, took longer to resolve cases, with worse results for clients, including sentences that were, on average, eight months longer (Liptak, 2007). The private-appointed attorneys also cost the public

$61 million dollars more than the public defenders. Evidently, these findings were due to inexperience, as public defenders practiced federal criminal law fulltime. In the federal system, roughly three-fourths of all defendants are represented by publicly funded attorneys, about half are public defenders and the other half are appointed (Liptak, 2007).

Do defense attorneys exert more effort for clients who pay well than they do for court-appointed clients? Obviously, professional ethics would dictate equal consideration, but individual values also affect behavior. If an attorney was confident that his or her court-appointed clients would receive at least adequate representation, could one not justify a more zealous defense for a paying client? Where adequate representation is vaguely and poorly defined, this question is problematic.

CONFIDENTIALITY

> Defense counsel should not reveal information relating to representation of a client unless the client consents after consultation, except for disclosures that are impliedly authorized in order to carry out the representation and except that defense counsel may reveal such information to the extent he or she reasonably believes necessary to prevent the client from committing a criminal act that defense counsel believes is likely to result in imminent death or substantial bodily harm (Standard 4-3.7(d)).

The **attorney–client privilege** refers to the inability of authorities to compel an attorney (through subpoena or threat of contempt) to disclose confidential information regarding his or her client. The ethical duty of confidentiality prohibits an attorney from disclosing to any person, or using for one's own gain, information about one's client obtained through the attorney–client relationship.

Confidentiality is inherent in the fiduciary relationship between the client and the attorney, but more important is that the client must be able to expect and receive the full and complete assistance of his or her lawyer. If a client feels compelled to withhold negative and incriminatory information, he or she will not be able to receive the best defense; thus, the lawyer must be perceived as a completely confidential agent of the client. Parallels to the attorney–client relationship are relationships between husband and wife and between priest and penitent. In these cases the relationship creates a legal entity that approximates a single interest rather than two interests, so a break in confidentiality would violate the Fifth Amendment protection against self-incrimination (Schoeman, 1982: 260).

The only situations wherein a lawyer can ethically reveal confidences of a client are these:

- when the client consents
- when disclosure is required by law or court order
- when one needs to defend oneself or employees against an accusation of wrongful conduct
- to prevent reasonably certain death or substantial bodily harm
- to prevent the client from committing a crime or fraud that is reasonably certain to result in substantial injury to the financial interests or property of another and the lawyer's services have been used to accomplish that end

- to prevent, mitigate, or rectify substantial injury to the financial interest or property of another that is reasonably certain to result or has resulted from the client's commission of a crime or fraud when the lawyer's services have been used

One of the most debated portions has been the part of this rule that specifies what type of crime can be used to support divulging the confidences of a client. The Model Code (used before the Model Rules) allowed disclosure to prevent *any* crime. An earlier version of the Model Rules dictated that an attorney could ethically violate a client's confidence only to prevent a future crime involving imminent death or grievous bodily harm. Many state bar associations refused to adopt the restrictive rule, or have enlarged it to include any crime. The current version allows for financial crimes if there is substantial injury, but it also protects a lawyer who divulges confidences to mitigate or rectify a financial crime. The Enron and World-Com cases no doubt influenced the committee that updated this rule. Proponents of enlarging the scope of the rule argued that such a rule would have prevented Enron lawyers from participating in the scheme to defraud stockholders by hiding the true level of debt.

Neither the restricted rule nor the inclusive rule regarding disclosing a client's future crime applied to the Garrow incident (described in the "Walking the Walk" box), so the lawyers felt ethically bound to withhold the location of two bodies from the family of the victims. Do the ethical systems support keeping the client's confidences in a situation such as the one faced by Armani when defending Robert Garrow? The rule seems to be justified by utilitarianism because society benefits in the long run from the presence of attorney–client confidence. Therefore, this confidence should be sacrificed only when it endangers a life (which would be a greater loss than the benefit of client–attorney trust) (Harris 1986). Religious ethics might condemn the attorneys' actions because withholding the location of the bodies was a form of deception. In the Catholic religion, however, a similar ethical dilemma might arise if someone were to confess to a priest. In that case the priest could not betray that confession no matter what the circumstances.

No easy answers to the dilemma are forthcoming using ethical formalism. First of all, under the categorical imperative, the lawyers' actions must be such that we would be willing for all others to engage in similar behavior under like circumstances. Could one will that it become universal law for attorneys to keep such information secret? What if you were the parents who did not know the whereabouts of their daughter, or even if she was alive or dead? It is hard to imagine that they would be willing to agree with this universal law. If you were the criminal, however, you would not want a lawyer to betray confidences that would hurt your case. If you were a lawyer, you would want a rule encouraging a client to be truthful so you would be able to provide an adequate defense. Ethical formalism is also concerned with duty; it is obvious that the duty of an attorney is always to protect the interests of his or her client. On the other hand, we might differentiate circumstances of future crimes and circumstances of past crimes because, one might argue, one has a greater duty to protect life than to protect confidences.

The ethics of care would be concerned with the needs of both the client and the parents in the case described. It would perhaps resolve the issue in a less absolutist

WALKING THE WALK

FRANK ARMANI AND ROBERT GARROW

Frank Armani may be one of the most revered and, also, hated lawyers in the past century. In 1973, Armani was asked to represent Robert Garrow, accused of attempted murder and murder. Garrow, who had already served eight years in prison for rape, was identified as the man who tied up four college students and brutally stabbed one to death, although, luckily the other three got away. Because of the similarity of the attacks, Garrow was also suspected of being responsible for another murder of a young man. The man's companion was missing, and authorities were desperate to either find her alive or find her body. One other young woman was also missing, and Garrow was suspected of being responsible for her disappearance as well.

Armani took the case because he had previously represented Garrow on a minor charge. Armani brought in Francis Belge, a criminal defense attorney. During their questioning of Garrow, he confessed to the murders of the two missing women and told the lawyers where the bodies were hidden. The two confirmed that the bodies were where Garrow said they were, and they even took pictures. In one location the girl's head was 10 feet away from her torso and Belge moved the head closer to the body before he took the picture. In the other case the body was in an abandoned mine shaft and the lawyers lowered each other down to take pictures.

The two believed that attorney–client confidentiality prevented them from revealing the location of the bodies or even that Garrow had confessed to being involved. They did, however, imply to the District Attorney that Garrow might reveal the location in a plea agreement. They were trying to get the prosecutor to agree to an insanity plea with commitment to a mental hospital. The prosecutor refused the deal and before the case could come to trial for the first murder, the two girls' bodies were found. Garrow was the prime suspect.

In the small town where the trial was held, the two attorneys were shunned, vilified, and threatened. Both of the missing girls' families had pleaded with the attorneys to tell them if their daughters were alive or dead, and the families had no doubt that the attorneys knew more than they would reveal. Their suspicions became clear because after Garrow was convicted, Armani and Belge admitted in a press interview that they had known about the bodies all along.

The enraged prosecutor charged Belge with the crime of "failure to give a proper burial" and threatened both with obstruction of justice. The criminal charges were dropped, as were the state ethics charges, but both attorneys endured threats and the virtual loss of their law practices. One newspaper editorial at the time called Armani "a malignant cancer on the society that fostered him" and "less than useless to the human race." Belge left the practice of law entirely, and Armani was forced to build up his practices again after most of his clients left him. His marriage almost failed, and he flirted with alcoholism and suffered two heart attacks during the long ordeal.

When asked why he kept the murderer's secrets, Armani explained that civil rights are for the worst of us because, only then, are they there for the best of us. Eventually he was recognized for his ethical courage, but many still disagree on his stand that the client's confidentiality rights are more important than "common decency." One thing that no one can dispute, however, is that he paid a high price for his ethical principles.

Sources: Zitrin and Langford, 1999. Hansen, 2007: 28–29.

fashion than the other rationales. For instance, when discussing this case in a college classroom, many students immediately decide that they would call in the location of the bodies anonymously, thereby relieving the parents' anxiety and also protecting, to some extent, the confidential communication. However, this compromise is unsupported by an absolute view of confidentiality because it endangers the client (perhaps he would not even be charged with the crimes if the bodies were never found), but it does protect the relationship of the attorney and the client and still meets the needs of the parents.

It should be noted that the rule of confidentiality does not apply to physical evidence. Anything that is discoverable in the possession of a client is equally discoverable if in the possession of an attorney. Therefore, an attorney must hand over files or other incriminating evidence subject to a valid search warrant, motion, or subpoena. If the attorney is merely told where these items may be found, he or she is not obliged to tell the authorities where they are. For instance, if a client tells an attorney that a murder weapon is in a certain location, the attorney cannot divulge that information to authorities. However, if the client drops a murder weapon in the attorney's lap, the lawyer runs the risk of being charged with a felony if it is hidden or withheld from the police. If the attorney is told where a murder weapon is and goes to check, that information is still protected; however, if the attorney takes the weapon back to his or her office or moves it in any way, then the attorney may be subjected to felony charges of obstruction of justice or evidence tampering. Belge was charged in the above case because he moved the body, although he was never convicted.

A defense attorney's ethics may also be compromised when a client insists on taking the stand to commit perjury. Model Rule 3.3 specifically forbids the lawyer from allowing perjury to take place; if it happens before the attorney realizes the intent of the client, the defense must not use or refer to the perjured testimony (Freedman, 1986; Kleinig, 1986). The quandary is that if the attorney shows his or her disbelief or discredits the client, this behavior violates the ethical mandate of a zealous defense, and to inform the court of the perjury violates the ethical rule of confidentiality.

Pellicotti (1990) explains that an attorney should first try to dissuade the client from committing perjury. If the client persists in plans to lie, the attorney then has an ethical duty to withdraw from the case, and there is some authority that the attorney should disclose the client's plan to the court. Withdrawal is problematic because it will usually jeopardize a case, and disclosure is even more problematic because, arguably, it will affect the judgment of the hearing judge. An attorney may refuse to call witnesses who plan to lie, but if the defendant's testimony will be perjured, it is, arguably, a violation of his or her rights for the attorney not to allow the defendant to take the stand.

In *Nix v. Whiteside* (475 U.S. 157, 89 L.Ed.2d 123 [1986]), the Supreme Court held that it did not violate the defendant's Sixth Amendment right to counsel for the attorney to refuse to help the defendant commit perjury. In this murder case the defendant told his lawyer that he had not seen a gun in the victim's hand. At a later point he told his attorney that if he didn't testify that he saw a gun, he would be "dead" (lose the case). The attorney told him that if he were to testify falsely, he would have to impeach him and would seek to withdraw from the case. The defendant testified truthfully, was found guilty, and then appealed based on ineffective counsel. The court found that the right to effective counsel did not include the right to an attorney who would suborn perjury.

Pellicotti (1990) describes the *passive* role and the *active* role of an attorney with a client who commits perjury. In the passive role the attorney asks no questions during direct examination that would elicit untruthful answers and may make a statement that the client is taking the stand against the advice of an attorney. The attorney does not refer to perjured testimony during summation or any arguments. The active role allows for the attorney to disclose to the court the fact of the perjured testimony. There is no great weight of authority to commend either approach, leaving attorneys with a difficult ethical dilemma. The best defense of some attorneys is not to know about the lie in the first place.

If the attorney is not sure that the client would be committing perjury, there is no legal duty to disclose. The weight of authority indicates that the attorney with doubts should proceed with the testimony; any disclosure of such doubts is improper and unethical. Thus, some attorneys tell a client, "Before you say anything, I need to tell you that I cannot participate in perjury, and if I know for a fact that you plan to lie, I cannot put you on the stand," or they ask the client, "What do I need to know that is damaging to this case?" rather than ask if the client is guilty of the crime. Further, many attorneys argue that all defendants lie about everything and they can't be believed anyway. If this is true, some attorneys may conclude that there are always doubts, and this allows an easy justification for allowing the defendant to say anything on the stand.

CONFLICTS OF INTEREST

> Defense counsel should not permit his or her professional judgment or obligations to be affected by his or her own political, business, property, or personal interests (Standard 4-3.5(a)).

This standard and Model Rules 1.7, 1.8, 1.10 and 1.11 cover conflicts of interest. Attorneys are supposed to avoid any conflicts of interest when defending clients. For instance; an attorney may not represent a client who owns a company that is a rival to one in which the attorney has an interest. The attorney also must not represent two clients who have opposing interests—for instance, co-defendants in a criminal case—for one often will testify against the other. The attorney would find it impossible in such a situation to represent each individual fairly. Disciplinary rules even prohibit two lawyers from a single firm from representing clients with conflicting interests.

Although attorneys may not ethically accept clients with conflicting interests, there is no guidance on the more abstract problem that all criminal clients in a caseload have conflicting interests if their cases are looked upon as part of a workload rather than considered separately. Many defense attorneys make a living by taking cases from people with very modest means or taking court-appointed cases with the fee set by the court. The defense attorney then becomes a "fast-food lawyer," depending on volume and speed to make a profit. What happens here, of course, is that quality may get sacrificed along the way. When lawyers pick up clients in the hallways of courtrooms and from bail company referrals, the goal is to arrange bail, get a plea bargain, and move on to the next case. Rarely do these cases even come to trial.

The vast majority of cases in the criminal justice system are settled by a **plea bargain**, an exchange of a guilty plea for a reduced charge or sentence. The defense attorney's goal in plea bargaining is to get the best possible deal for the client— probation or the shortest prison sentence that the prosecutor is willing to give for a guilty plea. The defense attorney is aware that he or she cannot aggressively push every case without endangering the ongoing relationship with the prosecutor. A courtroom appearance may be an isolated event for the client, but for the defense attorney and prosecutor it is an ongoing, weekly ritual; only the names of the defendants change. Because of the nature of the continuing relationship, the defense attorney must weigh present needs against future gains. If the defense becomes known as unwilling to "play ball," reduced effectiveness may hurt future clients.

Another conflict of interest may arise if the attorney desires to represent the client's interests in selling literary or media rights. Standard 4–3.4 specifically forbids entering into such an agreement before the case is complete. The temptations are obvious: If the attorney hopes to acquire financial rewards from a share of profits, his or her professional judgment on how best to defend the client may be clouded. It is debatable whether putting off signing such an agreement until the case is complete removes the possibility of unethical decisions. In the O. J. Simpson murder trial, it appears that every major player wrote a book about the trial. One wonders if trial tactics and speeches aren't evaluated, at least subconsciously, on how they will appear in a later first-person narrative or movie screenplay. The potential for biased judgments is obvious. For instance, if an attorney has a client who has committed a particularly spectacular crime, there is the potential for celebrity status only if the case comes to trial, so a plea bargain—even if it is in the best interest of the client—may be considered less carefully by the attorney.

ZEALOUS DEFENSE

> Defense counsel, in common with all members of the bar, is subject to standards of conduct stated in statutes, rules, decisions of courts, and codes, canons, or other standards of professional conduct. Defense counsel has no duty to execute any directive of the accused which does not comport with law or such standards. Defense counsel is the professional representative of the accused, not the accused's alter ego (Standard 4-1.2(e)).

Few would challenge the idea that all people deserve to have their due-process rights protected. However, what many people find unsettling is the zeal with which some defense attorneys approach the courtroom contest. How diligent should the defense be in protecting the defendant's rights? A conflict may arise between providing an effective defense and maintaining professional ethics and individual morality. Lawyers should represent clients zealously within the bounds of the law, but the law is sometimes vague and difficult to determine.

Ethical standards and rules forbid some actions. The lawyer may not:

- engage in motions or actions to intentionally and maliciously harm others, knowingly advance unwarranted claims or defenses,
- conceal or fail to disclose that which he or she is required by law to reveal,

- knowingly use perjured testimony or false evidence,
- knowingly make a false statement of law or fact,
- participate in the creation or preservation of evidence when he or she knows or it is obvious that the evidence is false,
- counsel the client in conduct that is illegal, or
- engage in other illegal conduct.

The attorney is also expected to maintain a professional and courteous relationship with the opposing attorneys, litigants, and witnesses and to refrain from disparaging statements or badgering conduct. The defense attorney must not intimidate or otherwise influence the jury or trier of fact or use the media for these same purposes.

Despite these ethical rules, practices such as withholding evidence, manufacturing evidence, witness badgering, and defamation of victims' characters are sometimes used as tactics in the defense arsenal. For instance, the practice of bringing out the sexual history of rape victims is done purely to paint her as a victim who deserved or asked for her rape. Even though rape-shield laws prohibit exposés of sexual history solely to discredit the reputation of the victim-witness, attorneys still attempt to bring in such evidence. Destroying the credibility of honest witnesses is considered good advocacy, at least for defense attorneys. For instance, if a witness accurately testifies to what he or she saw, a good attorney may still cast doubt in the jurors' minds by bringing out evidence of the use of eyeglasses, mistakes of judgment, and other facts that tend to obfuscate and undercut the credibility of the witness. Attorneys will do this even when they know that the witness is telling the truth. A zealous defense demands questioning the credibility of all prosecution witnesses.

In a very few cases, defense attorneys go to extreme lengths to change the course of testimony, such as bribing witnesses, allowing their client to intimidate a witness, or instructing their client to destroy physical evidence or to manufacture an alibi and then commit perjury. Chapter 9 addresses noble-cause corruption on the part of law enforcement officers. This type of motivation may also affect the behavior of attorneys when they believe that their client is innocent, or for other reasons that they believe are more important than the rules of their profession.

Most ethical conflicts arise over more subtle questions of how far one should go to provide a zealous defense. It is sometimes difficult to determine when a defense attorney's treatment of a witness is badgering as opposed to energetic cross-examination, or when exploring a witness's background is character assassination as opposed to a careful examination of credibility. Some attorneys focus attacks on opposing counsel. For example, female attorneys report that opposing male attorneys attempt to infantilize, patronize, or sexualize them in front of the judge and jury, as a tactic to destroy their credibility. Young attorneys encounter treatment by opposing counsel, with comments such as, "What my young colleague here has evidently not learned yet…", designed to persuade the jury that the older attorney is wiser, more honest, or more mature than the younger attorney. Personal attacks on credibility and more subtle attempts to influence juries' perceptions of opposing counsel may also be leveled—such as talking during opposing counsel's opening or closing, rolling one's eyes in response to a statement or question, and making other verbal or physical gestures indicating disbelief, amusement, or disdain. These tactics are obviously not in the same category as bribing witnesses or manufacturing evidence, but are they ethical?

Defense attorneys may sacrifice integrity or friendships for the sake of a case. In one trial a defense attorney and a prosecutor were getting ready for a trial in a bar-room murder case. The prosecutor had only one eyewitness to the shooting—the bartender. None of the others in the bar were willing to testify that they saw anything. The prosecutor had other circumstantial evidence of the defendant's guilt, but the eyewitness was crucial. Unfortunately, the bartender had a ten-year-old murder conviction—a fact that would reduce his credibility in the jury's eyes. This fact could be brought out by the defense under the rules of evidence; however, the prosecutor could petition the court to have the fact suppressed and have a good chance of succeeding because it bore no relevance to the case and would be prejudicial. In this instance, however, the prosecutor had forgotten to file the appropriate motion.

Just before the trial was about to start, she asked the defense attorney if he was going to bring out this fact on his cross-examination of the bartender. If he planned to do so, the prosecutor would have asked for a continuance and filed a motion to have it suppressed, or at least brought it out on direct to reduce its impact. He told her specifically and clearly that he had no intention of using that information or questioning the witness about it because it was so long ago and irrelevant to the case.

When the direct examination of this witness was over and the defense attorney started his cross-examination, his very first question was, "Isn't it true that you were convicted of murder in 19--?" Although the prosecutor may have committed an error in judgment by trusting the defense attorney, the defense attorney deliberately misled the prosecutor as to his intentions. He lied.

When asked about his actions, the defense attorney explained that it "just slipped out" and complained that the prosecutor took these things "too seriously." This is an example of a lie used for short-term gain, an egoistic rationalization, and a view of due process as a game, for when an opponent is offended by the lie, she is taking things "too seriously." In this case the defense attorney may have lost more than he gained by the trick. A conviction was achieved in spite of the witness's background, and the attorney found that previously cooperative prosecutors were suddenly unwilling to agree to continuances, closed their files to him even though it was generally an "open file" office, and in other ways treated him as untrustworthy—which indeed he was—but was his action unethical or was he ethically and zealously defending his client?

Jury Consultants   A recent innovation in trial tactics is the development of "scientific" jury selection. Attorneys often contend that a trial has already been won or lost once they have selected the jury. Whether or not this is true, attorneys are becoming increasingly sophisticated in their methods of choosing which members of a jury panel would make good jurors. A good juror for a defense attorney (or prosecutor) is not someone who is unbiased and fair but, rather, someone who is predisposed to be sympathetic to that attorney's case. Jury experts are psychologists, communication specialists, or other professionals, who sit with the attorney and, through a combination of nonverbal and verbal clues, identify those jury panel members who are predisposed to believe the case presented by the attorney. Some allege that jury consultants can help to stack juries with the least sophisticated or most educated group, or any other type of group desired by the attorney.

Some lawyers, such as the famed "Racehorse" Haynes of Houston, have used methods such as surveying a large sample of the population in the community where the case is to be tried to discover what certain demographic groups think about issues relevant to the case so these findings can be used when the jury is selected. Another method uses a **shadow jury**—a panel of people selected by the defense attorney to represent the actual jury that sits through the trial and provides feedback to the attorney on the evidence being presented during the trial. This allows the attorney to adjust his or her trial tactics in response.

Attorneys have always used intuition and less sophisticated means to decide which jury members to exclude, but the more modern tactics are questioned by some as too contrary to the basic idea that a trial is supposed to start with an unbiased jury (Smith and Meyer, 1987). Consultants provide services such as

- preparing witnesses
- assisting with mock trials
- developing desirable juror profiles
- conducting phone surveys on public attitudes about a case
- analyzing "shadow juries"
- giving advice on effective posture, clothing choice, and tone of voice

One powerful tactic is to use "focus groups" to find out opinions about a case. Consultants work on an estimated 6,000 trials a year, mostly civil cases. The American Society of Trial Consultants, a professional organization, has more than 400 members, who charge around $150 an hour (Gavzer, 1997).

Ethical Analysis of Zealous Defense   Can our ethical systems help to determine what actions are ethically justified in defending a client zealously? Utilitarianism and egoism would probably allow a wider range of actions, depending on the particular interests or rewards represented by the case. Ethical formalism and religion might restrict the actions of a defense attorney to those allowed by a strict interpretation of the Model Rules.

Aronson (1977: 59–63) discusses two methods for resolving ethical dilemmas. The first is called the **situational model**, wherein lawyers weigh the priorities and decide each case on the specific factors present. This is similar to our explanation of situational ethics. On the one hand, client confidentiality may be sacrificed when others' interests are at stake, but, on the other hand, be paramount in other cases. The **systems model** utilizes a more absolute or legalistic model in that behavior would always be considered wrong or right depending on the ethical rule guiding the definition. Obviously, these two systems of decision making bear a great deal of resemblance to the situational and absolutist ethical models discussed in Chapter 2. As a pure advocate, the defense attorney's duty is to pursue a client's interest. As long as the attorney does not run afoul of the law or ethical mandates, the client's defense is the sole objective.

ETHICAL ISSUES FOR PROSECUTORS

Prosecutors do not serve an individual client; rather, their client is the system or society itself. Pursuit of justice rather than pursuit of the best interest of the client characterizes the aims of prosecutors. As the second line of decision makers in the system, prosecutors have extremely broad powers of discretion. The prosecutor acts like a strainer; he or she collects some cases for formal prosecution while eliminating a great many others.

Prosecuting every case is impossible. Resources are limited, and some cases' evidence is weak, making it unlikely to win a conviction. Early diversion of such cases saves taxpayers money and saves individuals trouble and expense.

Typically, a state's code of criminal procedure provides standards for prosecutors. In addition, the state may have a Code of Professional Responsibility that specifically mentions prosecutors' duties. There are also National Prosecution Standards promulgated by the National District Attorneys Association. Model Rule 3.8 covers the duties of a prosecutor. Finally, Chapter 3 of the ABA Standards for Criminal Justice covers the prosecution function. (You can access these standards by going to http://www.abanet.org/crimjust/standards/pfunc_toc.html.) These cover topics similar to those for defense attorneys, but they also make special note of the unique role of the prosecutor as a representative of the court system and the state. In 2008 the American Bar Association added a new Standard called Prosecutorial Investigations. The Table of Contents for this Standard is presented in Box 10.2.

USE OF DISCRETION

A prosecutor should not institute ... criminal charges ... not supported by probable cause (Standard 3–3.9(a)).

The prosecutor must seek justice, not merely a conviction. Toward this end, prosecutors must share evidence, exercise restraint in the use of their power, represent the public interest, and give the accused the benefit of reasonable doubt. Disciplinary rules are more specific. They forbid the prosecutor from pursuing charges when there is no probable cause and mandate timely disclosure to defense counsel of evidence, especially exculpatory evidence or evidence that might mitigate guilt or reduce the punishment. Despite these ideals of prosecutorial duty, an unstated influence over prosecutorial discretion is that prosecutors want to and must (to be considered successful) win. A decision to prosecute is influenced by political and public pressures, the chance for conviction, the severity of the crime, a "gut" feeling of guilt or innocence, prison overcrowding, and the weight of evidence. The prosecutorial role is to seek justice, but justice doesn't mean the same thing to everyone and certainly does not mean prosecuting everyone to the fullest extent of the law. Whether to charge is one of the most important decisions of the criminal justice process. The decision should be fair, neutral, and accomplished with due process, but this is an ideal that is sometimes supplanted by other considerations. Prosecutors don't usually use their charging power for intimidation or harassment, but other factors may be involved in the decision to charge. For instance, a prosecutor might have a particular interest in a type of crime such as child abuse or drugs and pursues these cases more intensely.

BOX 10.2 | ABA STANDARDS FOR CRIMINAL JUSTICE

Prosecutorial Investigations

PREAMBLE
Part 1: General Standards
Standard 1.1 The Function of These Standards
Standard 1.2 General Principles
Standard 1.3 Working With Police and Other Law Enforcement Agents
Standard 1.4 Victims, Potential Witnesses, and Targets During the Investigative Process
Standard 1.5 Contacts with the Public During the Investigative Process

Part 2: Standards for Specific Investigative Functions of the Prosecutor
Standard 2.1 The Decision to Initiate or to Continue an Investigation
Standard 2.2 Selecting Investigative Techniques
Standard 2.3 Use of Undercover Law Enforcement Agents and Undercover Operations
Standard 2.4 Use of Confidential Informants
Standard 2.5 Cooperation Agreements and Cooperating Individuals and Organizational Witnesses
Standard 2.6 The Decision to Arrest During a Continuing Criminal Investigation
Standard 2.7 Use of Subpoenas
Standard 2.8 Search Warrants
Standard 2.9 Use of the Investigative Powers of the Grand Jury
Standard 2.10 Technologically-Assisted Physical Surveillance
Standard 2.11 Consensual Interception, Transmission and Recording of Communications
Standard 2.12 Non-Consensual Electronic Surveillance

Standard 2.13 Conducting Parallel Civil and Criminal Investigations
Standard 2.14 Terminating the Investigation, Retention of Evidence and Post-Investigation Analysis
Standard 2.15 Guidance and Training for Line Prosecutors
Standard 2.16 Special Prosecutors, Independent Counsel and Special Prosecution Units
Standard 2.17 Use of Information, Money, or Resources Provided by Non-Governmental Sources
Standard 2.18 Use of Sensitive, Classified or Other Information Implicating Investigative Privileges

Part 3: Prosecutor's Role in Resolving Investigation Problems
Standard 3.1 Prosecutor's Role in Addressing Suspected Law Enforcement Misconduct
Standard 3.2 Prosecutor's Role in Addressing Suspected Judicial Misconduct
Standard 3.3 Prosecutor's Role in Addressing Suspected Misconduct by Defense Counsel
Standard 3.4 Prosecutor's Role in Addressing Suspected Misconduct by Witnesses, Informants or Jurors
Standard 3.5 Illegally Obtained Evidence
Standard 3.6 Responding to Political Pressure and Consideration of the Impact of Criminal Investigations on the Political Process
Standard 3.7 Review and Oversight of Criminal Investigations by Government Agencies and Officials

Source: American Bar Association. 2008. Accessed via website on 5/26/2008 from http://www.abanet.org/crimjust/standards/pinvestigate .html.

The Genarlow Wilson case presents a difficult issue of how prosecutorial discretion is sometimes used (McCaffrey, 2007; ESPN News Service, 2007). Wilson was a 17-year-old high-school athlete on his way to a college scholarship. Instead, he ended up in prison because of a party in which several teenagers, including Wilson, engaged in consensual sex. One of the girls involved was 15. The evidence was incontrovertible—a videotape clearly showing Wilson with the underage girl. The prosecutor charged him with rape, and a jury convicted him, which meant a mandatory 10-year prison sentence. The uproar resulted in the legislature changing the law to make sex between teenagers a misdemeanor, but the law could not be retroactively applied to Wilson. He spent two years in prison before the Georgia Supreme Court released him on the grounds that the punishment was cruel and unusual. The prosecutor decided to charge Wilson rather than use his discretion and decide not to charge, and he also filed an appeal against the first appellate decision to reduce Wilson's sentence to 12 months. In cases such as these, the prosecutor's beliefs about what is considered justice are extremely important.

Other considerations that affect the decision to charge include pressure from law enforcement—for instance, when a bargain is struck for a lesser charge in return for testimony or information that could lead to further convictions. There is also the pressure of public opinion. Prosecutors might pursue cases that they otherwise would have dropped if there is a great deal of public interest in the case. Victims who have mental impairments may not make the best witnesses and there may be less chance of getting a conviction. In one such case, five women with developmental disabilities had been raped and terrorized by the owner of a licensed home where they lived. The prosecutor declined to pursue charges under the rationale that "any woman with a developmental disability would have zero credibility in court." Only when the licensing authority secured additional testimony, revoked the license of the owner, and publicly exposed the situation did the prosecutor press charges (Hook, 2001).

Prosecutors in state capitals often have "public integrity" units that prosecute wrongdoing on the part of public officials. On the one hand, prosecutors might charge at election time for political purposes; on the other hand, they might be falsely accused of such political considerations when they do charge politicians with public-integrity violations.

A special case of discretion and charging is the decision to pursue a capital homicide conviction. Prosecutors have the power to decide whether to seek the death penalty or a prison term. Clearly, the decision to seek the death penalty is not made uniformly across jurisdictions. One of the biggest considerations is cost. Because capital trials are extremely expensive, counties that have bigger budgets are more likely to seek the death penalty; they have the resources and staff to handle the cases (Hall, 2002). Obviously, these considerations have nothing to do with justice, and it should cause concern that a criterion other than severity of the crime or future risk affects whether an offender ultimately receives the death penalty.

To give immunity to one defendant accused of a brutal crime to gain testimony against others is efficient, but is it consistent with justice? Not to charge people because they contribute to judicial campaigns or are relatives of powerful politicians is obviously an unethical use of discretion. In some situations, prosecutors do not charge because of an outpouring of public sympathy or support for the accused, perhaps because of the type of crime or identity of the victim. Prosecutors who do not charge in these cases may attribute the reason to lack of evidence or the unlikelihood of obtaining a conviction, but their political popularity probably also has something to do with their decision.

Various studies have attempted to describe prosecutors' decision making; one cites office policy as an important influence (Jacoby, Mellon, and Smith, 1980):

1. *Legal sufficiency* is an office policy that weeds out those cases in which the evidence is not strong enough to support further action.
2. *System efficiency* is an office policy with goals of efficiency and accountability; all decisions are made with these goals in mind, so many cases result in dismissals.
3. *Defendant rehabilitation* emphasizes diversion and other rehabilitation tools rather than punitive goals.
4. *Trial sufficiency* is an office policy that encourages a charge that can be sustained through trial.

Another study looked at the prosecutor as operating in an exchange system. The relationship between the prosecutor and the police was described as one of give-and-take. Prosecutors balance police needs or wishes against their own vulnerability. The prosecutor makes personal judgments about which police officers can be trusted. Exchange also takes place between the prosecutor's office and the courts. When the jails become overcrowded, prosecutors recommend deferred adjudication and probation; when dockets back up, prosecutors drop charges. Finally, exchange takes place between defense attorneys and prosecutors, especially because many defense attorneys have previously served as prosecutors and may be personally familiar with the procedures and even personalities in the prosecutor's office (Cole, 1970).

On one hand, discretion is considered essential to the prosecutorial function of promoting individualized justice and softening the impersonal effects of the law. On the other hand, the presence of discretion is the reason that the legal system is considered unfair and biased toward certain groups of people or individuals. Even though we would not want to eliminate prosecutorial discretion, it could be guided by regulations or internal guidelines. For instance, an office policy might include a procedure for providing written reasons for dropping charges, and this procedure would respond to charges of unbridled discretion.

One writer argues that the ethics of virtue can help determine ethical decisions for prosecutors. Cassidy (2006) presents three ethical issues:

1. When is it proper for a prosecutor to offer charging or sentencing concessions to an accomplice in order to secure the accomplice's testimony against a co-defendant?
2. When, if ever, may a prosecutor impeach a defense witness who the prosecutor believes has testified truthfully?
3. How should a prosecutor react at trial when opposing counsel appears to be advocating ineffectively on behalf of his client?

Then Cassidy describes Aristotle's ethics of virtue, as well as the thinking of St. Thomas Aquinas and Alastair MacIntyre, a modern virtue theorist. Basically, as we learned in Chapter 2, the ethics of virtue proposes that the ethical person is the virtuous person and the virtuous person is the person who behaves in a way consistent with the virtues. Aristotle classified virtues into moral virtues and intellectual virtues. His moral virtues include temperance, courage, industriousness, generosity, pride, good temper, truthfulness, friendliness, modesty, justice, and pleasantness;

and the intellectual virtues include understanding, science, theoretical wisdom (philosophy), craft and practical wisdom. St. Thomas Aquinas added theological virtues of faith, hope, and charity. Alasdair MacIntyre defined the most important virtues as justice, courage, honesty, and prudence. Cassidy argues that virtue ethics are different from absolute rule-based ethics and that each person must have sensitivity to the "salient features of [particular] situations" (2006: 637).

Turning to the ethical dilemmas, Cassidy explains that neither Model Rule 3.8 nor the Standards gives prosecutors much guidance in any of the cases, and so they must apply the virtues. In the situation of offering a deal to a co-conspirator, he argues that the virtue of courage would require the prosecutor to have the courage to refuse to deal if justice demanded it. The virtue of honesty would mean that the prosecutor must make sure that the suspect was not lying and, also, make sure that he or she was not more culpable than the person he or she was testifying against. The prosecutor must disclose the agreement to the defense and the court so the veracity of the testimony can be challenged. The virtue of justice or fairness would mean that the prosecutor should not give the most punishment to those who are least involved.

In the second ethical dilemma, the prosecutor must decide whether to try to impeach a witness who is telling the truth. Cassidy (2006) argues that the Rules allow defense attorneys the right to impeach prosecution witnesses even if they are telling the truth, but there is no mandate that prosecutors should do so, as they are supposed to be seeking justice, not pursuing the best interest of their client. He offers Standard 3-5.7(b), which states:

> The prosecutor's belief that the witness is telling the truth does not preclude cross-examination, but may affect the method and scope of cross-examination. A prosecutor should not use the power of cross examination to discredit or undermine a witness if the prosecutor knows the witness is testifying truthfully.

Cassidy (2006) argues that the virtues of honesty and courage require a prosecutor to forgo cross-examination if he or she knows that the truth has been told. Regarding the last ethical dilemma involving an incompetent defense attorney, he points to Model Rule 8.3, which requires that attorneys report incompetent colleagues to bar authorities, but also admits that the "snitch" rule is widely ignored by all attorneys. Further, it would be difficult to distinguish incompetence from trial tactics in some cases. The virtues that apply are justice and honesty, and if the attorney's actions seem to be offending the system of justice, it is the prosecutor's duty to bring it to the attention of the judge.

Admitting that the virtues of courage, honesty, and prudence are only slightly more abstract than the concept of justice, Cassidy (2006) urges prosecutors' offices to seek employees who already exhibit character that displays virtue. Qualifications for hiring should include evidence that the individual is honest and sensitive to others. Further, those working in a prosecutor's office should be rewarded for virtuous behaviour over and above simply winning cases.

CONFLICTS OF INTEREST

> A prosecutor should avoid a conflict of interest with respect to his or her official duties (Standard 3.1-3(a)).

Part-time prosecutors present a host of ethical issues. A Bureau of Justice Statistics bulletin (1992) reported that 47 percent of prosecutors held their jobs as a part-time occupation (Dawson, 1992: 1). Obviously, this poses the possibility of a conflict of interest. It may happen that a part-time prosecutor has a private practice, and there may be situations where the duty to a private client runs counter to the duty of the prosecutor to the public. In some cases a client may become a defendant, necessitating the prosecutor to hire a special prosecutor. Even when there are no direct conflicts of interest, the pressure of time inevitably poses a conflict. The division of time between the private practice, where income is generated by the number of cases and hours billed, and prosecuting cases, where income is fixed no matter how many hours are spent, may result in a less energetic prosecutorial function than one might wish.

It is well-known that the prosecutor's job is a good stepping-stone to politics, and many use it as such. In these cases one has to wonder whether cases are taken on the basis of merit or on their ability to place the prosecutor in the public eye and help his or her career. Populous counties have many assistant district attorneys (ADAs), perhaps hundreds, and only the district attorney is elected. Many ADAs work in the prosecutor's office for a number of years and then move into the private sector. The reason has largely to do with money. Assistant district attorneys make an average of $40,000 to $60,000 a year, but in private practice they could make much more than that (R. Cohen, 2001). The question then becomes: Does the career plan to enter private practice as a litigator affect their prosecutorial decision making to try cases?

Asset Forfeiture   The RICO statute has increasingly been used for its **asset forfeiture** provision, a tool to confiscate property and money associated with organized criminal activity. Once this tactic was approved by the courts, a veritable flood of prosecutions began that were designed, it seems, primarily to obtain cash, boats, houses, and other property of drug dealers. Making decisions based on the potential for what can be confiscated rather than the culpability of offenders is a real and dangerous development in this type of prosecution.

The origins of civil forfeiture were in the Comprehensive Drug Abuse and Control Act of 1970 and the Organized Crime Control Act of 1970. Both of these laws allowed mechanisms for the government to seize assets gained through illegal means. Eventually the types of assets vulnerable to seizure were expanded, including assets *intended* to be used as well as those gained by or used in illegal activities. All of the states have passed similar asset forfeiture laws. The "take" from asset forfeiture increased from $27.2 million in 1985 to $874 million in 1992 (Jenson and Gerber, 1996). Between the early 1990s and the early 2000s, the total amount of federal forfeiture proceeds shared with state and local law enforcement was $2.5 billion! (Hartman, 2001).

There are a number of problematic issues with asset forfeiture. The exclusionary rule does not apply to civil forfeiture proceedings, so some allege that police are now pursuing assets instead of criminals, because in a civil proceeding the defendant does not receive legal aid. A civil forfeiture hearing can take place without any criminal prosecution and without the alleged criminal being present. Unlike a criminal trial, in asset forfeiture it had been the case that the government had only to show probable cause, and then the burden of proof shifted to the individual to prove his or her innocence. This changed when President Bill Clinton signed into law the Civil Asset Forfeiture Reform Act, which shifted the burden of proof from the claimant to the government (Worral, 2001). Now at least the presumption of innocence has been put back into place.

Perhaps one of the most troubling aspects of civil forfeiture is that third parties are often those most hurt by the loss. For example, the spouse or parents of a suspected drug dealer may lose their home. In one of the most widely publicized forfeiture cases, a man solicited a prostitute; the state instituted proceedings and was successful in seizing the car he was driving when he solicited the prostitute—which was, in fact, his wife's car! This case received so much press because the Supreme Court ruled that no constitutional violation occurred with the forfeiture, even though his wife had nothing to do with the criminal activity. Another case that received a great deal of media attention was that of a man who lost his expensive motorboat when one marijuana cigarette was found on it. These and other uses of asset forfeiture have spurred reforms and court decisions that are curtailing its use to some extent. However, asset forfeiture clearly has become an almost indispensable source of revenue for law enforcement and the courts (Worral, 2001).

PLEA BARGAINING

> A prosecutor should not knowingly make false statements or representations as to fact or law in the course of plea discussions with defense counsel or the accused (Standard 3–4.1(c)).

As discussed earlier, there are serious ethical concerns over the practice of plea bargaining. In jurisdictions that have determinate sentencing, plea bargaining has become "charge bargaining" instead of sentence bargaining. Most conclude that plea bargaining, even if not exactly "right," is certainly efficient and probably inevitable. Should we measure the morality of an action by its efficiency? This efficiency argument is similar to the argument used to defend some deceptive investigative practices of police. If the goals of the system are crime control or bureaucratic efficiency, plea bargaining makes sense. If the goals of the system are the protection of individual rights and the protection of due process, plea bargaining is much harder to justify. Obviously, plea bargaining would fail under the categorical imperative, for the individual is treated as a means in the argument that plea bargaining is good for the system. See the Policy Box for a critique of plea bargaining.

Arguments given in defense of plea bargaining include the heavy caseloads, limited resources, legislative over-criminalization, individualized justice, and legal problems of cases (legal errors that would result in mistrials or dropped charges if the client didn't plead) (Knudten, 1978: 275). If we concede that plea bargaining can be justified, there are remaining ethical problems concerning specific practices relating to it. Only 36 percent of chief prosecutors reported that explicit criteria for plea bargains were in place in 1990 (Bureau of Justice Statistics, 1992). Guidelines providing a range of years for certain types of charges would help individual prosecutors maintain some level of consistency in a particular jurisdiction. Unfortunately, no more current

POLICY BOX | **PLEA BARGAINING**

The practice of exchanging a reduced charge or a reduced sentence for a guilty plea is widespread. Although some disagree with the practice and say it leads to innocent people pleading guilty and a reduction in the integrity of the system, most argue that the system couldn't work without the practice. Also, proponents argue that it is ethical to give the offender something in exchange for not putting the state to the expense of a trial.

Law: U.S. Supreme Court opinions have legitimated the use of plea bargaining. They have held that prosecutors and judges must abide by the agreements made and that defendants cannot turn around and claim afterward that the exchange was unfair.

Policy: Different prosecutors' offices handle plea bargaining differently. Some have guidelines, and others leave it to the prosecutor's discretion. In general, there are informal office policies so that some offices give more generous offers than other jurisdictions do. Plea bargaining is something that is covered in the training of new prosecutors.

Ethics: Prosecutors' ethical issues with plea bargaining include whether or not to over-charge to get someone to plead or to lie about how much evidence there is. Defense attorneys' ethical issues include the extent to which they will try to convince individuals to plead if they swear they are innocent. Judges have ethical issues as well, in that they do not have to accept a plea in a case where they do not believe evidence is sufficient to uphold the verdict.

statistics are available, but popular accounts indicate that plea bargaining is prevalent across the United States.

Should prosecutors overcharge—that is, charge at a higher degree of severity or press more charges than could possibly be sustained by evidence—so they can bargain down? Should prosecutors mislead defense attorneys about the amount of evidence or the kind of evidence they have or about the sentence they can offer to obtain a guilty plea? Gershman (1991) documents instances of prosecutors engaged in false promises, fraud, misrepresentation of conditions, deals without benefit of counsel, package deals, and threats during plea bargaining. Critics contend that prosecutors hold all the cards in plea bargaining.

MEDIA RELATIONS

The prosecutor has an important relationship with the press. The media can be enemy or friend, depending on how charismatic or forthcoming the prosecutor is in interviews. Sometimes cases are said to be "tried in the media," with the defense attorney and the prosecutor staging verbal sparring matches for public consumption. Prosecutors may react to cases and judges' decisions in the media, criticizing the decision or the sentence and, in the process, denigrating the dignity of the system. More often, the defense attempts to sway the press to a sympathetic view of the offense, which is easier to accomplish during prosecutorial silence.

ABA Model Rule 3.6(b) is a prohibition against out-of-court statements that a reasonable person should expect would have a substantial likelihood of materially prejudicing a proceeding. Defense attorneys might be expected to make statements to exonerate their client and disparage the state's case, but prosecutors' statements have a greater ring of authority. The rule specifies that no statements should be given involving any of the following topics:

- The character, credibility, reputation, or criminal record of a party, suspect, or witness
- The identity of a witness
- The expected testimony of a party or witness
- The performance or results of any test or examination
- The refusal of any party to submit to such tests or examinations
- The identity or nature of physical evidence
- Inadmissible information
- The possibility of a guilty plea
- The existence or contents of a confession or an admission
- The defendant's refusal to make a statement
- An opinion about the guilt or innocence of the defendant or suspect
- A statement that the defendant has been charged with a crime unless it is in the context that a charge does not mean the party is guilty

The following facts may be disclosed:

- The general nature of the claim or charge
- Any information in a public record
- The fact that the matter is being investigated and the scope of the investigation
- The schedule of litigation
- A request for assistance in obtaining information
- A warning of danger
- The identity, residence, occupation, and family status of the accused
- Information to enable the accused's capture (if at large)
- The fact, time, and place of arrest
- The identity of investigating and arresting officers

The case of the Duke Lacrosse players accused of rape resulted in the prosecutor (Mike Nifong) being disbarred. In this high-profile 2007 case, a stripper alleged that she was raped by members of the lacrosse team after she was hired to perform at a party for them. Very early in the case the district attorney made several public statements indicating that the athletes were guilty, that just because they were white and rich and the alleged victim was black and poor, they weren't going to get away with the crime, and so on. No doubt the fact that the district attorney was in a hotly contested election had something to do with his decision to make such public statements so early in the case.

As the investigation progressed, the victim's story changed in substantive ways about who raped her and when it took place. Furthermore, no physical evidence substantiated her story. Despite this, the district attorney continued to make comments to the media that the players were guilty. Later, the alibi of one defendant was substantiated by an ATM camera showing that he was somewhere else when the rape was supposed to have taken place. Still Nifong did not drop the charges and in fact instructed a lab technician to drop a sentence from his report indicating that the semen found on the alleged victim contained the DNA of several unknown males, but not the accused men's.

Eventually, the State Attorney General sent in a special prosecutor to handle the case, and this prosecutor promptly dropped the charges against the accused college athletes. Nifong was publicly sanctioned and, in an unusually harsh punishment, was disbarred from the practice of law. Ethical experts argue that Nifong's actions were egregious. The case is a good example of why public expressions of guilt are strictly prohibited: The prosecutor gets locked into a position that is difficult to back out of. After Nifong had committed himself to the conclusion that the college men were guilty, he found himself under intense pressure to pursue the case, even in the face of contradictory evidence (Jeffrey, 2007).

Another prosecutor in the news was U.S. Attorney Johnny Sutton, in the Southern District of Texas, when he pursued charges against two border agents after they shot a suspected drug smuggler. The agents, Jose Compean and Ignacio Ramos, are serving more than 10 years in prison for shooting the unarmed man, violating their use-of-force policies, and the law by trying to cover up the shooting.

During the trial and after the conviction, there was an outpouring of anger that the prosecutor was "supporting the enemy" rather than our own agents, especially for pursuing the charge of "use of a firearm in the course of another crime," which was the basis for the mandatory 10-year sentence under federal sentencing law. Sutton's position in pursuing charges was that the agents had broken the law, and no one is above the law.

During Michael Mukasey's confirmation hearings as U.S. Attorney General in October of 2007, several legislators urged him to commit to an investigation of the case and Sutton's decision to prosecute (Moscoso, 2007). Although it might have been more politically popular to drop or reduce the charges against the border agents in the face of public and political pressure, the prosecutor in this case chose to endure public antipathy in his decision to pursue prosecution. Most decisions do not generate public controversy, but each decision to prosecute begins with a prosecutor choosing whether and how to pursue charges against suspected offenders.

EXPERT WITNESSES

A prosecutor who engages an expert for an opinion should respect the independence of the expert and should not seek to dictate the formation of the expert's opinion on the subject (Standard 3–3.3(a)).

Expert witnesses, who can receive a fee, are often accused of compromising their integrity for money or notoriety. The use of expert witnesses has risen in recent years. Psychiatrists often testify as to the mental competency or legal insanity of an accused. Criminologists and other social scientists may be asked to testify on topics such as victimization in prison, statistical evidence of sentencing discrimination, the effectiveness of predictive instruments for prison riots and other disturbances, risk assessment for individual offenders, mental health services in prison, patterns of criminality, the battered-woman syndrome, and so on (see Anderson and Winfree, 1987). Expert testimony is allowed as evidence in trials when it is based on principles generally accepted in the scientific community. Judges apply this standard, and they can accept or bar such evidence from being offered to the jury.

When experts are honest in their presentation as to the limitations and potential bias of the material, no ethical issues arise. However, expert witnesses may testify in a realm beyond fact or make testimony appear factual when some questions are not clearly answerable. Because of the **halo effect**—essentially, when a person with expertise or status in one area is given deference in all areas—an expert witness may endow a statement or conclusion with more legitimacy than it warrants. When expert witnesses take the stand, they run the risk of having their credibility attacked by the opposing side. Credibility is obviously much easier to attack when a witness has attempted to present theory or supposition as fact or conclusion, either for ideological reasons or because of pressure from zealous attorneys. Those who always appear on one side or the other may also lose their credibility. For instance, a doctor who is used often by prosecutors in one jurisdiction during capital-sentencing hearings has become known as "Dr. Death" because he always determines that the defendant poses a future risk to society—one of the necessary elements for the death penalty. Although this doctor is well-known by reputation to prosecutors and defense attorneys alike, juries would not be expected to know of his predilection for finding future risk and would take his testimony at face value unless the defense attorney brings out this information during cross-examination. Because much of expert testimony concerns scientific principles that are incomprehensible to laypeople, the potential for being misled by an expert witness is magnified.

***CSI* and the Courts**   For many years, forensic experts have testified regarding factual issues of evidence ranging from ballistics to blood spatter. Television shows such as *CSI* contribute to the mystique of crime-scene investigators as scientific Sherlock Holmes who use physics, chemistry, and biology to catch criminals. However, the reality is that some of this "expert" testimony has been called *junk science* (McRoberts, Mills, and Possley, 2004).

As mentioned in Chapter 9, the FBI and several police departments have had their labs come under fire for shoddy practices or biased analyses. The Houston police crime lab has been investigated and was even closed down for a period of time, and several defendants have been exonerated by retests of the DNA evidence that convicted them. Criticism of the lab included poorly trained technicians, lax procedures, shoddy records, overstated testimony, and the inability to do certain tasks such as separate DNA from mixed samples. Thousands of cases were eventually reviewed, but because Harris County has sent more defendants to Death Row than any other county in Texas, some of those convicted through tainted evidence may have been executed (Liptak, 2003; Axtman, 2003).

The highly respected Virginia state crime lab has also been investigated after outside experts hired by the defense called into question the DNA analysis that sent a man to Death Row. This case is one of several dozen Death Row cases around the country that are being reviewed because of potentially faulty, biased, or perjured lab analyst testimony (Possley, Mills, and McRoberts, 2004). Two other lab scandals—in Oklahoma and in West Virginia—have led to millions of dollars in settlements for those falsely incarcerated, and forced reviews of hundreds of cases. In Montana there was a petition to the state supreme court to undertake independent testing of hundreds of cases handled by a lab examiner who was responsible for three false convictions based on faulty hair analysis (Possley, Mills, and McRoberts, 2004).

Even when mismanagement, shoddy practices, and untrained staff aren't the issue, many areas of the so-called science of **criminalistics** seem to be more in the nature of art than science. Criminalists have been defined as professionals who are involved in the "scientific discipline directed to the recognition, identification, individualization, and evaluation of physical evidence by the application of the natural sciences to law–science matters" (Lindquist, 1994: 59). Questions have been raised about the reliability of virtually all areas of this science:

1. *Hair analysis.* A Justice Department study of 240 crime labs found hair-comparison error rates ranging from 28 percent to 68 percent. Hair-comparison testimony is so suspect that it is outlawed in Michigan and Illinois (Hall, 2002). In Montana a chief lab analyst collected more than 5,000 hair samples and claimed a statistical analysis that could identify a person's hair from the sample with an error rate of 1 in 1,000. A panel of experts disagreed, and convictions based on this analyst's testimony have been overturned (Possley, Mills, and McRoberts, 2004).

2. *Arson investigation.* Arson "science" started when arson investigators used their experience with thousands of fires, confessions of suspects, and crude experiments to identify burn patterns and accelerants. "Facts" such as "fires started with accelerants burn hotter" have been disproved. So-called "pour patterns" that have been used as proof of arson have now been associated with a natural phenomenon called "flashover," which occurs when smoke and gas in a room build to a point where the entire room explodes in flames, consuming everything. The flashover effect also calls into question the traditional belief that if the floor showed burning, it was arson because heat rises and the floor shouldn't show burning unless an accelerant is used (Posseley, 2004).

   Part of the reason that older theories of arson are not supported by current experimentation is that the presence of synthetics has changed the composition of fires, so what arson investigators observed thirty years ago no longer has any relevance to today's fires. Synthetics burn hotter and are highly combustible; thus, fires are more likely to be mislabeled as arson (Possley, 2004).

   In a Texas case, a man may have been executed in 2004 based on faulty arson "science." The Innocence Project commissioned a panel to study some of the arson "facts" that were presented in the case, and the study proved that many were not supported. For instance, glass cracking in a spidery fashion may not prove that it is a hotter fire caused by an accelerant; it is just as likely to be caused by water sprayed by firefighters. There also was no way to prove that the fire has multiple origins. Fire investigators are still testifying in court based on science that is called by some "a hodgepodge of old wives tales" (Tanner, 2006).

3. *Ballistics testing.* Recently there have been questions as to the accuracy of the chemical composition tests the FBI labs use to match bullets. This method has been used in thousands of cases to tie suspects to the bullet retrieved at the crime scene. The theory is that the chemical composition of bullets in a single production batch is similar and that bullets from a single batch are different

from those from other batches. Bullets owned by the suspect are compared to the crime-scene bullet, and the expert testifies as to whether the crime-scene bullet came from the suspect's box of remaining bullets.

Independent scientific studies by the National Research Council challenged the method because tests indicated a large margin of error; chemical compositions between batches are more similar than believed, and the chemical composition within a batch can vary quite a bit depending on a number of factors. These findings indicated that ballistics experts from the FBI lab and other labs have testified in a way that greatly overstated the importance of the chemical matches (Piller and Mejia, 2003; Piller, 2003). Although the FBI stopped comparative bullet lead analysis in 2004 in response to these findings, FBI lab experts were allowed to testify in cases that had already been analyzed through 2005. Also, the FBI has been criticized for not releasing a list of cases in which the testimony of lab examiners was given on the faulty science so the case could be reviewed to see if an innocent person was convicted on the basis of the results (Post, 2005).

Frederick Whitehurts, the FBI lab examiner who went public with criticism of FBI lab practices and won a whistleblower lawsuit after he was demoted and sanctioned, is now the executive director of an independent organization called the Forensic Justice Project, which collects and disseminates information about controversial forensic science (Post, 2005). In 2007, the FBI was criticized in investigative reports by the television show *60 Minutes* and by the *Washington Post* for continuing to withhold the names of about 2,500 defendants who were convicted partially based on the results of the faulty testing. In response, the FBI stated that it thought that public announcements of the faulty tests should have been notice enough to these individuals to pursue any appropriate appeals. In November of 2007, the FBI spokesperson finally agreed that the FBI would send letters to the prosecutors in these cases to notify them that the testimony was based on faulty science. Unfortunately for many of these defendants, it may come too late to file an appeal (Solomon, 2007b).

In one New Jersey case, the state Supreme Court threw out a murder conviction that had been based on the testimony of an FBI ballistics expert using the faulty testing method (Post, 2005). In a North Carolina case, a former state Supreme Court chief justice took up the case of Lee Wayne Hunt, who has been in prison for 22 years for a shooting based on FBI testimony on comparative lead analysis and the testimony of a co-defendant. Recently the co-defendant's attorney came forward and said the man confessed to him that he had lied about Hunt's involvement in return for a plea deal. The attorney came forward only because his former client had died (J. Solomon, 2007a). Arguably, Hunt may not have been convicted but for the ballistics testimony that supported the co-defendant's perjury.

4. *DNA testing.* DNA testing also has been called into question (Anderson, 1989). The use of DNA evidence has risen dramatically in recent years. Based on the scientific principle that no two individuals possess the same DNA (deoxyribonucleic acid), a DNA "fingerprint" is analyzed from organic matter such as semen, blood, hair, or skin. Whereas a blood test can identify an individual only as being a member of a group (e.g., all those with blood type A positive), DNA testing can determine, with a small margin of error, whether

two samples come from the same individual. This has been described as the greatest breakthrough in scientific evidence since fingerprinting, but there are problems with its use. Careless laboratory procedures render results useless, and there are no enforced guidelines or criteria for forensic laboratories conducting DNA tests.

Labs often have only a small amount of organic matter to extract DNA. They use a procedure whereby the incomplete DNA strand is replicated using computer-simulation models. This procedure allows a DNA analysis of the tiniest speck of blood or skin, but critics argue that it opens a door to a margin of error that is unacceptable. Without vigorous investigation and examination of lab results from the opposing counsel, incorrect DNA test results or poorly interpreted results may be entered as evidence and used to determine guilt or innocence.

5. *Fingerprint analysis.* Most citizens assume that fingerprint analysis is infallible, that all criminals' fingerprints are accessible through computer- matching technology, and that fingerprint technicians can retrieve fingerprints from almost any surface and can use partials to make a match. Unfortunately, the reality is far from what is seen on television. There have been attempts to undertake a comprehensive analysis of how much of a partial print is necessary to have a reliable match—an objective that is resisted by professional fingerprint examiners. Most fingerprints are partials and smudged. Some studies show that about a quarter of matches are false positives.

In 2006, the federal government settled a suit for $2 million dollars after three FBI fingerprint examiners mistakenly identified the fingerprint related to a terrorist bombing in Madrid, Spain as belonging to an Oregon lawyer. European fingerprint analysts discovered the error (CBS/AP, 2006). Standards do not exist for determining how many points of comparison are necessary to declare a match (Mills and McRoberts, 2004).

6. *Bite mark comparison.* There is no accurate way to measure the reliability of bite mark comparisons, yet forensic dentists have given testimony that resulted in convictions of several innocent defendants. Evidently, the experts sometimes can't even agree if an injury is a bite mark at all. One study indicated that identifications were flawed in two-thirds of the cases. Even their own organization cautions that analysts should not use the term "match," because the technique is not exact enough, but many do. Contrary to popular belief, a bite mark is not just like a fingerprint. Teeth change over time, and the condition of the skin or other substance holding the bite mark changes the indentation patterns of teeth (McRoberts and Mills, 2004).

The use of expert witnesses can present ethical problems when the witness is used in a dishonest fashion. Obviously, to pay an expert for his or her time is not unethical, but to shop for experts until finding one who benefits the case may be unethical, for the credibility of the witness is suspect. Another difficulty arises when either side obtains an expert who develops a conclusion or a set of findings that would help the other side. Ethical rules do not prohibit an attorney in a civil matter or criminal defense attorneys from merely disregarding the information and not giving notice to the opponent that there is information that could benefit his or her case. However, prosecutors operate under a special set of ethics because their goal is justice, not pure advocacy. Any exculpatory information is supposed to be shared with the defense; this obviously includes test results and may also include expert witness findings.

Still another problem is when prosecutors intentionally use scientific evidence that they know to be false. There are proven instances where prosecutors put on the stand so-called experts that they knew were unqualified and/or their expertise was without merit (Gershman, 2003). Prosecutors may bolster a witness's credentials or allow him or her to make gratuitous and unsupported claims on the witness stand, such as to state "unequivocally" that the fingerprint, or hair, or lip print was the defendant's.

In their closing arguments, prosecutors may overstate the expert's testimony so "is consistent with" becomes "matched" (Gershman, 2003: 36). In some egregious cases, prosecutors have simply lied about physical evidence, such as stating that the red substance on a victim's underpants was blood when, in fact, it was paint (Gershman, 2003: 36).

ZEALOUS PROSECUTION

The duty of the prosecutor is to seek justice, not merely to convict (Standard 3-1.2(c)).

Just as the defense attorney is at times overly zealous in defense of clients, prosecutors may be overly ambitious in order to attain a conviction. The prosecutor, in preparing a case, is putting together a puzzle, and each fact or bit of evidence is a piece of that puzzle. Any piece of evidence that doesn't fit the puzzle is sometimes conveniently ignored. The problem is that this type of evidence may be exculpatory, and the prosecutor has a duty to provide it to the defense.

Both defense attorneys and prosecutors sometimes engage in tactics such as using witnesses with less than credible reasons for testifying, preparing witnesses (both in appearance and testimony), and "shopping" for experts. Witnesses are not supposed to be paid, but their expenses can be reimbursed, and often this is incentive enough for witnesses to say what they think the prosecutor wants to hear. A tool in the prosecutor's arsenal that the defense attorney does not have is that prosecutors can make deals to reduce charges in return for favorable testimony. Many offenders are in prison because of co-defendant testimony against them that was "bought" by a reduced charge or sentence. These practices are not illegal, but whether they are ethical or not is a different question.

Prosecutors want to win, and there are few checks or monitors on their behavior (Elliott and Weiser, 2004). Noble-cause corruption is when prosecutors do "anything it takes" to win a case. This can take the form of persistent references to illegal evidence, leading witnesses, nondisclosure of evidence to the defense, appeals to emotions, games and tricks, and so on. One prosecutor admitted that early in his career he sometimes made faces at the defendant while his back was to the jury and the defense attorney wasn't looking. The jury saw the defendant glowering and looking angry for no discernible reason, which led to a negative perception of his sanity, temper, or both. Of course, the defense attorney may engage in the same type of actions, so the contest becomes who has better "tricks" rather than who has the better case.

PROSECUTORIAL MISCONDUCT

When prosecutors forget that their mission is to protect due process, not obtain a conviction at all costs, misconduct can occur. The types of misconduct range from minor lapses of ethical rules to commission of criminal acts (such as hiding evidence). Following are some of the possible rules that are violated when prosecutors forget their mission.

Communications with Defendants   When a criminal defendant is represented by an attorney, the prosecutor should not attempt any communication with the defendant outside the presence of the defense attorney. The attorney's presence is designed to eliminate the possibility of improper or intimidating behavior, illegal deals, and improper interrogation or plea-bargain offers.

Ex Parte Communications with the Judge   Prosecutors and judges work together daily. There is a prohibition on attorneys and judges discussing a case outside the presence of the other attorney, but because of working conditions, this is much more likely to apply to prosecutors than to defense attorneys. The reason for the rule is fairness. It is not fair for the judge to hear one side without the other side there to defend its point of view. This rule applies to casual conversations as well as more formal interchanges or offerings of information.

Duty to Correct False Testimony   Similar to a defense attorney's quandary when a witness commits perjury, a prosecutor must also take steps to avoid allowing false testimony to stand. The prosecutor's role is the easier one because there are no conflicting duties to protect a client; therefore, when a prosecution witness perjures himself or herself, the prosecutor has an affirmative duty to bring it to the attention of the court. The prosecutor in the Tulia case, mentioned in Chapter 9, knew that the police officer on the stand had lied about his past, yet he did not disclose that information and allowed the perjury to stand. He was sanctioned by the Texas bar and almost lost his law license. Many believe that he should have, considering his role in the convictions.

Failure to Disclose Evidence   Perhaps the most common charge leveled against prosecutors, failure to disclose evidence, stems from a duty to reveal exculpatory evidence to the defense (if the defense files a "Brady motion" requesting such evidence). Because the rule indicates that only evidence that is "likely to lead to a different outcome" is subject to this discovery requirement, some prosecutors who withhold evidence argue that "It wasn't important" or "I didn't believe it." These rationalizations ignore a basic difference between the role of the prosecutor and the role of the defense attorney. Whereas the defense attorney's only mission is the defense of his or her client, the prosecutor's role is to seek justice. This means that all evidence should be brought forward and shared so "truth shall prevail."

Examples   Examples of prosecutorial misconduct typically involve ignoring the procedural protections of due process. When prosecutors are too zealous in their attempts to obtain a conviction, their role as officer of the court is ignored and they become judge and jury. A *Chicago Tribune* investigation found that since 1963, 381 defendants across the country have had a homicide conviction thrown out because prosecutors concealed exculpatory evidence or presented evidence they knew to be false. Of the 381 defendants, 67 had been sentenced to death and were exonerated by DNA evidence or independent investigations. Nearly 30 of the 67 on Death Row were freed, but they served between 5 and 26 years before their convictions were reversed (Armstrong and Possley, 2002). The prosecutorial misconduct included the following (Armstrong and Possley, 2002):

- Concealed evidence that discredited their star witnesses, pointed to other suspects, or supported defendants' claim of self-defense
- Suppressed evidence that the murder occurred when the defendant had an alibi, or where the murder occurred
- Depicted red paint as blood
- Portrayed hog blood as human
- Suppressed statements of eyewitnesses that offenders were white when prosecuting two black men
- Received a knife from a crime scene from police but hid it, and when defendant argued that he killed after he had been stabbed with the knife, the prosecutor challenged the defense because of the absence of a knife
- Hid a victim's gun when the defendant argued self-defense
- Hid an iron pipe the victim had used to attack the defendant
- Hid blood-spatter expert's report that supported the defendant's version of events
- Withheld evidence suggesting that a police informant had framed the defendant
- Concealed evidence indicating that their chief witness was the killer, not the defendant

Sanctions   Despite the highly publicized disbarment of Mike Nifong in the Duke lacrosse case, there are few controls on the behavior of prosecutors in the courtroom. Voters have some control over who becomes a prosecutor, but once in office, most prosecutors stay in the good graces of a voting public unless there is a major scandal or an energetic competitor. In cities, most of the work is conducted by assistant prosecutors, who are hired rather than elected. Misconduct in the courtroom is sometimes orally sanctioned by trial judges. Perhaps an appellate decision may overturn a conviction, but prosecutors are rarely punished even when cases are overturned.

Gershman (1991) writes that prosecutors misbehave because it works and they can get away with it. Because misconduct is scrutinized only when the defense attorney makes an objection and then files an appeal (and even then the appellate court may rule that it was a harmless error), there is a great deal of incentive to use improper tactics in the courtroom. The main reason that prosecutors engage in misconduct is that they want to win and there is very little chance of their being punished.

The Supreme Court has ruled that prosecutors cannot be subject to civil suits against them even in cases of egregious rulebreaking. The most important fact

IN THE NEWS | PROSECUTOR MISCONDUCT

A prosecutor released a videotape of teenagers having sex in response to an open-records request without blurring the faces of the alleged victims or suspects. The prosecutor said that the law required him to release the tape; critics argue that he released the tape to discredit the suspect's case that he should not have been charged because it was consensual sex between teenagers. Some argue that the prosecutor's action in releasing the tape could even be defined as distributing child pornography.

Source: McCaffrey, 2007: A6.

The California Supreme Court held that prosecutors should not intentionally tell different juries that two defendants each were the primary responsible party for the same crime. A prosecutor first argued in one case that the defendant was the person who killed the victim in a murder case after obtaining a first-degree murder conviction, he then argued in the second trial to a different jury that the second defendant was the primary killer and obtained a second first-degree murder conviction. Both defendants were sentenced to death. The higher court held that the prosecutor should pursue only one theory of how the crime was committed.

Source: Dolan, 2005.

A former federal prosecutor and a State Department security officer were indicted on charges that they lied during the trial of a suspected terrorist. The two were charged with conspiracy, obstruction of justice, and making false statements in connection with the 2003 prosecution of Karim Koubriti and others who were suspected of being members of a sleeper cell. The convictions were overturned because of gross prosecutorial misconduct.

It is alleged that Richard Covertino, the prosecutor charged, presented false information at a sentencing hearing in order to get a favorable sentence for an informant and failed to turn over exculpatory evidence to the defense. Covertino alleges that he was the target of a smear campaign because of his whistleblower lawsuit against the government. In the subsequent trial both men were acquitted of all charges.

Source: Eggen, 2006: A03; Hsu, S. 2007: A03.

A government aviation lawyer working with the prosecutors of the Zacarias Moussaoui trial was admonished by the trial judge for improperly coaching witnesses. Moussaoui was alleged to have been involved in the 9/11 attack, and government officials sought to try him for the World Trade Tower deaths, arguing that his knowledge could have prevented the attack from happening. The prosecution was seriously damaged when the judge refused to allow testimony of aviation officials after it was discovered that the lawyer Carla Martin had shared trial transcripts with the witnesses and tried to shape their testimony to help the prosecution's case.

Source: Markon and Dwyer, 2006: A01.

The Court of Criminal Appeals granted an appeal by a convicted murderer based on an allegation that prosecutors made a deal with a jailhouse informant. In the case, the convicted man alleges that the informant was promised a favorable sentence in which he would be sent to a federal prison instead of state prison in return for his testimony that the convicted man confessed to him while they were cellmates in jail. During the trial, when asked by the defense attorney if anything had been promised to him for his testimony, the informant committed perjury by answering that he had not been promised anything. It is alleged that prosecutors allowed the perjury to take place, knowing that he was lying.

Source: Lindell, 2007: B1, B5.

How might prosecutors justify the actions above using either their professional rules and/or the ethical systems?

uncovered in the *Chicago Tribune* investigation was that not one of the prosecutors was convicted of a crime, and none was even disbarred. Some became judges or district attorneys, and one became a congressman! (Armstrong and Possley, 2002).

CONCLUSION

In this chapter we examined the source of legal ethics and the reasons that the public seems to have such a poor opinion of the ethics of legal professionals. One might expect that the public's respect and trust for legal professionals, as guardians of the justice system, would be high, but that is not the case. Part of the reason is the ability to take "either side" in a controversy. Also, the advocacy role that attorneys embrace at times justifies "means" that appear to be, and even may be, ethically questionable.

There are crucial differences in the duties and ethical responsibilities of defense attorneys and prosecutors. The prosecutor's goal is justice, which should imply an objective pursuit of the truth; however, we know that in a few cases the only goal seems to be winning.

Key Terms

asset forfeiture *337*	criminalistics *343*	plea bargain *328*	situational model *331*
attorney–client privilege *323*	halo effect *342*	shadow jury *331*	systems model *331*

Review Questions

1. What do polls show regarding the public's attitude toward attorneys?
2. Where do rules of behavior for attorneys come from, and how are they enforced?
3. Describe the moral-agent, legal-agent, and special-relationship views of the attorney–client relationship.
4. What is Cohen's position regarding the lawyer's role? How do Memory and Rose criticize this position?
5. Explain the confidentiality rules of defense attorneys, and some situations where they may be able to disclose confidential information.
6. Compare the potential conflicts of interest of defense attorney and those of prosecutors.
7. Compare the potential zealous defense issues of defense attorneys and those of prosecutors.
8. Discuss what jury consultants do and why they have been criticized.
9. Discuss the various forms of forensic testimony and why they have been criticized.
10. List and describe the kinds of misconduct engaged in by prosecutors.

Writing/Discussion Questions

1. Write an essay on (or discuss) the proper role of defense attorneys regarding their clients.

Should attorneys pursue the wishes of their clients even if they think it is not in the clients' best interest? What if it would hurt a third party (but not be illegal)? Do you think that attorneys should maintain confidentiality if their clients are involved in ongoing criminal activity that is not inherently dangerous?

2. Write an essay on (or discuss) what your decision would be if you were on a disciplinary committee evaluating the following case: A prosecutor was working with police in a standoff between a triple murderer and police. When the murderer demanded to talk to a public defender, the police did not want to have a public defender get involved, so the prosecutor pretended to be one. He spoke with the suspect on the telephone and lied about his name and being a public defender. The man then surrendered to police. The prosecutor was sanctioned by the state bar for misrepresentation and was put on probation and required to take twenty hours of continuing legal education in ethics, pass the Multistate Professional Responsibility Examination, and be supervised by another attorney (Tarnoff, 2001). In your essay, describe what you think should have occurred, and why.

3. Write an essay on (or discuss) the legality/ethics of the following actions of a prosecutor:

- Announcing a suspect of a drive-by shooting to the media so the offender is in danger from the rival gang members, and then offering protective custody only if the man will plead guilty.
- Authorizing the arrest of a ten-year-old boy who confessed to a crime, even though there was no serious possibility that he was guilty, in order to pressure a relative to confess.
- Authorizing the arrest of one brother for drugs, even though the prosecutor knows the charge would be thrown out (but the young man would lose a scholarship to college), in order to have leverage so that he would give evidence against his brother.

Ethical Dilemmas

Situation 1

Your first big case is a multiple murder. As defense attorney for Sy Kopath, you have come to the realization that he really did break into a couple's home and torture and kill them in the course of robbing them of jewelry and other valuables. He has even confessed to you that he did it. However, you are also aware that the police did not read him his Miranda warning and that he was coerced into giving a confession without your presence. What should you do? Would your answer be different if you believed that he was innocent or didn't know for sure?

Situation 2

You are completing an internship at a defense attorney's office during your senior year in college. After graduation you plan to enter law school and pursue a career as an attorney, although you have not yet decided what type of law to practice. Your duties as an intern are to assist the private practitioner you work for in a variety of tasks, including interviewing clients and witnesses, organizing case files, running errands, and photocopying. A case that you are helping with involves a defendant charged with armed robbery. One day while you are at the office, the defendant comes in and gives you a package for the attorney. In it you find a gun. You believe, but do not know for a fact, that the gun is the one used in the armed robbery. When the attorney returns, he instructs you to return the package to the defendant. What should you do? What should the attorney do?

Situation 3

You are an attorney and are aware of a colleague who could be considered grossly incompetent. He drinks and often appears in court intoxicated. He ignores his cases and does not file appropriate motions before deadlines expire. Any person who is unlucky enough to have him as a court-appointed attorney usually ends up with a conviction and a heavy sentence because he does not seem to care what happens to his clients and rarely advises going to trial. When he does take a case to trial, he is unprepared and unprofessional in the courtroom. You hear many complaints from defendants about his demeanor, competence, and ethics. Everyone—defense attorneys, prosecutors, and judges alike—knows this person and his failings, yet nothing is done. Should you do something? If so, what?

Situation 4

You are a prosecutor in a jurisdiction that does not use the grand jury system. An elderly man has administered a lethal dose of sleeping tablets to his wife, who was suffering from Alzheimer's disease. He calmly turned himself in to the police department, and the case is on the front page of the paper. It is entirely up to you whether to charge him with murder. What would you do? What criteria did you use to arrive at your decision?

Situation 5

You are a deputy prosecutor and have to decide whether to charge a defendant with possession and sale of a controlled substance. You know you have a good case because the guy sold drugs to students at the local junior high school, and many of the kids are willing to testify. The police are pressuring you to make a deal because he has promised to inform on other dealers in the area if you don't prosecute. What should you do?

Suggested Readings

Gershman, B. 1990. *Prosecutorial Misconduct*. New York: Clark Boardman.

Gershman, B. 2003. "The Use and Misuse of Forensic Evidence." *Oklahoma City University Law Review* 28: 17–45.

Glendon, M. 1994. *A Nation Under Lawyers*. New York: Farrar, Straus and Giroux.

McRoberts, F., and Mills, S. 2004. "From the Start, a Faulty Science." *Chicago Tribune*—Online Edition. Retrieved October 19, 2004, from http://www.chicagotribune.com/news/specials/chi-0410190150oct19,1,2959538,print.story

McRoberts, F., Mills, S., and Possley, M. 2004. "Forensics Under the Microscope." *Chicago Tribune*—Online Edition. Retrieved October 19, 2004, from http://www.chicagotribune.com/news/specials/chi-0410170393oct17,1,7219383,print.story

Radelet, M., Bedau, H., and Putnam, C. 1992. *In Spite of Innocence*. Boston: Northeastern University Press.

Rhode, D. 2001. *In the Interests of Justice: Reforming the Legal Profession*. New Haven, CT: Oxford University Press.

Simon, W. 1998. *The Practice of Justice: A Theory of Lawyer's Ethics*. Boston: Harvard University Press.

Spence, G. 1989. *With Justice for None*. New York: Penguin.

Zitrin, R., and Langford, C. 1999. *The Moral Compass of the American Lawyer*. New York: Ballantine.

JUSTICE AND JUDICIAL ETHICS |

The Innocence Project has helped free hundreds of inmates across the country. In Dallas, Texas, Innocence Project attorneys Gary Udashen and John Stickels watch Patrick Waller react to the news that he is free after serving 15 years in prison for a crime he did not commit.

© Tony Gutierrez/AP/Wide World Photos

CHAPTER OBJECTIVES

1. Understand the various perceptions of judicial processing.

2. Understand the responsibilities and challenges of judges in the criminal justice system.

3. Become familiar with the criticisms of the justice system, including those alleging that it perpetuates racism and social inequities.

4. Understand the concepts associated with judicial activism or constructionism. Be aware of current issues in regard to these concepts.

CHAPTER OUTLINE

Clarence Brandley was a high school janitor in a small Texas town near Houston. In 1980 a young woman on a visiting girls' volleyball team disappeared while her team was practicing. The school was empty except for five janitors and the volleyball team. A search uncovered the girl's body in the school auditorium; it was later determined that she had been raped and strangled. Clarence Brandley and another janitor found the body and were the first to be interrogated by police. Brandley was black; the other janitor was white. The police officer who interrogated them reportedly said, "One of you two is going to hang for this." Then he said to Brandley, "Since you're the nigger, you're elected." Police and prosecutors then evidently began a concerted effort to get Brandley convicted, in the following ways:

- Evidence that might have been helpful to the defense was "lost." (Caucasian hairs near the girl's vagina were never tested and compared to those of the other janitors.)
- Witnesses were coerced into sticking to stories that implicated Brandley. (One of the janitors reported that he had been threatened with jail if he didn't promote the story supporting Brandley's guilt.)
- Witnesses who came forward with contrary evidence were ignored and sent away. (The father-in-law of one of the janitors who later became a prime suspect told the prosecutor that this man had told him where the girl's clothes would be found two days before police actually found them.)
- Defense attorneys were not told of witnesses. (A woman came to the prosecutor after the second trial and stated that her common-law husband had confessed a murder to her and ran away the same night the girl's body had been found. This woman's husband had worked as a janitor at the school, had been fired a month previous to the murder, but had also been seen at the school the day of the murder.)

What defense attorneys eventually discovered was that in all probability this man and another janitor had abducted and murdered the girl. The other janitors had seen the girl with these two men (not Brandley) but had lied during the two trials. Here are the words of an appellate judge who ruled on the motion for a new trial:

> In the thirty years that this court has presided over matters in the judicial system, no case has presented a more shocking scenario of the effects of racial prejudice...and public officials who for whatever motives lost sight of what is right and just.... The court unequivocally concludes that the color of Clarence Brandley's skin was a substantial factor which pervaded all aspects of the State's capital prosecution against him. (quoted in Radelet, Bedau, and Putnam, 1992: 134)

Even after this finding, it took another *two years* for the Texas Court of Criminal Appeals to rule that Brandley deserved a new trial. He served nine years on Death Row before his defense attorneys finally obtained his freedom. At one point he was just six days away from execution (Davies, 1991).

Because of the Clarence Brandley case and many others, some people refer to the criminal justice system as the criminal *injustice* system. They have a perception that practices in this nation's courtrooms do not necessarily conform to the ideals of justice. As mentioned in previous chapters, justice is a goal that is not necessarily synonymous with law and a legal system may not always achieve moral justice. The basic elements of a justice system are an impartial fact-finding process and a fair and equitable resolution. No person is more important in this process than the person wearing the judicial robe. In this chapter we will examine the role of the judge. First, though, it is important to identify various perceptions of the judicial process.

PERCEPTIONS OF JUDICIAL PROCESSING

The ideal of the justice system is that two advocates of equal ability will engage in a pursuit of truth, guided by a neutral judge. The truth is supposed to emerge from the contest. Actual practices in our justice system may be quite different. Various descriptions profess to offer a more realistic picture of the system. One approach is to look at judicial processing as a game, with "hidden agendas" (covert motivations and goals). The adversarial system pits the defense attorney against the prosecutor, and the judge may be considered the umpire in this contest. The judge makes sure that "the rules of the game" are followed and, unless there is a jury, decides who wins the contest.

Does the "best" opponent always win? If a powerful and rich defendant is able to hire the best criminal lawyer in the country, complete with several assistants and investigators, the prosecutor (who is typically overworked and understaffed) may be overwhelmed. Of course, this is the exception. More commonly a defendant must rely on an overworked and probably inexperienced public defender or an attorney who can make criminal law profitable only by high caseloads and quick turnover. In these instances the defense is outmatched by a prosecutor in a public office with greater access to evidence and investigative assistance. Heffernan and Kleinig (2000) discuss how poverty affects a wide range of judicial processing decisions. It is hard to refute the notion that one's socioeconomic status affects one's experience in the justice system.

A variation of game theory is offered by Blumberg (1969), who refers to the practice of law as a *confidence game* because the prosecutor and the defense attorney conspire to appear as something they are not—adversaries in a do-or-die situation. What is more commonly the case is that the prosecutor and the defense attorney will still be working together when the client is gone. Defense attorneys, despite the ideal of every client being the most important priority, have large caseloads. It is possible that the defense attorney may spend more time on cases when clients can pay, but if the client has no money, the attorney may try to hasten a case to a rapid conclusion even if the accused says he or she is innocent.

Attorneys may display adversarial performances in the courtroom, but the "show" lasts only as long as the jury is in the room, and sometimes not even then.

Defense attorneys, prosecutors, and judges work together every day and often socialize together; they may even be married to each other. Many defense attorneys are ex-prosecutors. In some respects this is helpful to their clients because the defense attorneys know how the prosecutor's office works and what a reasonable plea offer would be. But one must also assume that the prosecutorial experience of these attorneys has shaped their perceptions of clients and what would be considered fair punishment. Judges also have social relationships with defense attorneys and prosecutors. The courtroom actually is often a network of social and personal relationships, all of which are a subtext to the formal interactions seen in a trial or courtroom proceeding.

Other authors, too, have used the analogy of a confidence game to describe the interaction among prosecutors, defense attorneys, and clients. For example, Scheingold (1984: 155) writes the following:

> [T]he practice of defense law is all too often a "confidence game" in which the lawyers are "double agents" who give the appearance of assiduous defense of their clients but whose real loyalty is to the criminal courts. The defendant, from this perspective, is only an episode in the attorney's enduring relationships with the prosecutors and judges whose goodwill is essential to a successful career in the defense bar.

Another perspective describes our courts as administering **bureaucratic justice**. Each case is seen as only one of many for the professionals who work in the system, and the actors merely follow the rules and walk through the steps. The goal of the system—namely, bureaucratic efficiency—becomes more important than the original goal of justice. Also, because each case is part of a workload, decision making takes on more complications. For instance, a defense lawyer may be less inclined to fight hard for a "loser" client if the lawyer wants a favor for another client later in the week. The prosecutor may decide not to charge a guilty person in order to get him or her to testify against someone else. In this sense, each case is not tried and judged separately but is linked to other cases and processed as part of a workload.

The bureaucratic system of justice is seen as developing procedures and policies that, although not intentionally discriminatory, may contribute to a perception of unfairness. For instance, a major element in bureaucratic justice is the presumption of guilt, whereas the ideal of our justice system is a presumption of innocence. District attorneys, judges, and even defense attorneys approach each case presuming guilt and place a priority on achieving the most expeditious resolution of the case. This is the basic rationale behind plea bargaining, whether it is recognized or not: The defendant is presumed to be guilty, and the negotiation is to achieve a guilty plea while bargaining for the best possible sentence. The lowest possible sentence is the goal of the defense, whereas the highest possible sentence is the goal of the prosecutor. Plea bargaining is consistent with the bureaucratic justice system because it is the most efficient way of getting maximum punishment for minimum work.

Descriptions of bureaucratic justice such as the following (Scheingold, 1984: 158) allow for the tempering of efficiency with other values and priorities:

> [T]he coercive thrust of the presumption of guilt is softened somewhat by the operational morality of fairness that leads the participants to make certain that defendants get neither more nor less than is coming to them—that defendants, in other words, get their due.

Scheingold is referring to the practices of judges, prosecutors, and defense attorneys who adapt to the changing rules of the system to maintain their personal standards of justice. This is exemplified by a judge who determines that an individual offender is a threat to society and so overlooks procedural errors during trial to make sure that he or she ends up in prison. Or a person who is legally guilty might get a break from the prosecutor because it is determined that he is a decent guy who made a mistake. Moreover, in almost all cases there may be general consensus on both sides about what is fair punishment for any given offender. Defense attorneys who argue for unrealistically low sentences do so in a desultory and uncommitted fashion, knowing that the prosecutor would not and could not offer such a sentence. Prosecutors put up little argument when defense attorneys ask for sentences that fit office guidelines.

Instead of describing the justice system as one that practices the presumption of innocence and takes careful steps to determine guilt, what may be more realistic is to view it as a system wherein all participants assume guilt, take standard, routine steps to arrive at the punishment phase, and operate under a value system that allocates punishment and mercy to offenders according to an informal consensus of fairness. It should be noted that there has been increased influence from victims in this process so that today what is "fair" may also be determined by the victim's wishes. Prosecutors may not agree to a plea bargain if the victim actively opposes it. Only in cases where the victim does not take an active part does the bureaucratic system operate unfettered (Stickels, 2003).

One other perception of the criminal justice system is that of Samuel Walker's (1985) **wedding-cake illustration,** based on a model proposed by Lawrence Friedman and Robert Percival. In this scheme, the largest portion of criminal cases form the bottom layers of the cake and the few "serious" cases form the top layer. The top layer is represented most dramatically by cases such as the murder trial of O. J. Simpson. In this highly publicized case the defendant had an extremely skilled (and highly paid) team of attorneys as well as trial consultants, investigators, and public relations specialists. Los Angeles County paid millions to keep up with its own team of attorneys, experts, and investigators. The criminal processing and trial proceeded with admirable speed. Each side worked incredibly hard and used an arsenal of tactics (which were then critiqued by armchair experts each evening). The case has been used in law school evidence classes because of the wealth of material present in pretrial discovery, exclusionary motions, jury selection, and the like. The bottom of the cake is represented by the tens of thousands of cases that are processed every year in which defendants may meet with an attorney only once or twice for a few minutes immediately before agreeing to a plea arrangement.

Because the public is exposed only to the top of the wedding cake, people develop a highly distorted perception of the system. The U.S. public may be disgusted with the multitude of evidentiary rules and the Byzantine process of the trial itself. However, these concerns may be valid for only a small portion of criminal cases. In the vast majority of cases, there is no trial at all and the process is more of an assembly line. What happens to individuals is largely determined by the courtroom work group (composed of all the actors in the court process, including defense attorneys, prosecutors, and judges).

BOX 11.1	**RULES OF THE JUSTICE GAME**

Rule I: Almost all criminal defendants are, in fact, guilty.

Rule II: All criminal defense lawyers, prosecutors, and judges understand and believe Rule I.

Rule III: It is easier to convict guilty defendants by violating the Constitution than by complying with it, and in some cases it is impossible to convict guilty defendants without violating the Constitution.

Rule IV: Almost all police lie about whether they violated the Constitution in order to convict guilty defendants.

Rule V: All prosecutors, judges, and defense attorneys are aware of Rule IV.

Rule VI: Many prosecutors implicitly encourage police to lie about whether they violated the Constitution in order to convict guilty defendants.

Rule VII: All judges are aware of Rule VI.

Rule VIII: Most trial judges pretend to believe police officers who they know are lying.

Rule IX: All appellate judges are aware of Rule VIII, yet many pretend to believe the trial judges who pretend to believe the lying police officers.

Rule X: Most judges disbelieve defendants about whether their constitutional rights have been violated, even if they are telling the truth.

Rule XI: Most judges and prosecutors would not knowingly convict a defendant whom they believe to be innocent of the crime charged (or a closely related crime).

Rule XII: Rule XI does not apply to members of organized crime, drug dealers, career criminals, or potential informers.

Rule XIII: Nobody really wants justice.

Source: Dershowitz, 1982: xxi.

According to Walker's wedding-cake analysis, the courtroom work group is believed to share definitions of seriousness and operate as a unit to keep the dynamics of the courtroom static despite changes that are forced upon it. Changes in the justice system that have occurred over time, such as the exclusionary rule, determinate sentencing, and other changes, have had surprisingly little impact on court outcomes because of a shared perception of serious crime and appropriate punishment. The vast majority of crime is considered trivial, and the processing of these cases involves little energy or attention from system actors (Walker, 1985).

Dershowitz's view of the criminal justice system (see Box 11.1) is obviously, as Dershowitz admits himself, an exaggeration, but he does touch on some aspects of the system that many people do agree with, such as a widespread perception of guilt and a general view that case processing is routine for everyone except the individual at risk of conviction. The major ethical problem with this view (if it does represent reality) is that innocence, truth, and due process are perceived as inconvenient and expendable.

ETHICAL ISSUES FOR JUDGES

Perhaps the best-known symbol of justice is the judge in a black robe. Judges are expected to be impartial, knowledgeable, and authoritative. They guide the prosecutor, defense attorney, and all the other actors in the trial process from beginning to end, helping to maintain the integrity of the proceeding. This is the ideal, but judges are human, with human failings.

ETHICAL GUIDELINES

To help guide judges in their duties, the Model Code of Judicial Conduct was developed by the American Bar Association. The latest revision was undertaken beginning in 2003, with the final document submitted to the membership in 2007. This code identifies the ethical considerations unique to judges. It is organized into four Canons, which are overriding principles of ethical behavior, and under each Canon there are more specific rules. The four Canons of the Code are as follows (ABA, 2007):

1. "A judge shall uphold and promote the independence, integrity, and impartiality of the judiciary, and shall avoid impropriety and the appearance of impropriety."
2. "A judge shall perform the duties of judicial office impartially, competently, and diligently."
3. "A judge shall conduct the judge's personal and extrajudicial activities to minimize the risk of conflict with the obligations of judicial office."
4. "A judge or candidate for judicial office shall not engage in political or campaign activity that is inconsistent with the independence, integrity, or impartiality of the judiciary."

The primary theme of judicial ethics is impartiality. If we trust the judge to give objective rulings, we must be confident that his or her objectivity isn't marred by any type of bias. Judges should not let their personal prejudices influence their decisions. To avoid this possibility, the ABA's code specifies that each judge should try to avoid all appearance of bias as well as actual bias. Judges must be careful to avoid financial involvements or personal relationships that may threaten their objectivity. We expect judges, like police officers and prosecutors, to conform to higher standards of behavior than the rest of us. Therefore, any hint of scandal in their private lives also calls into question their professional ethics. The obvious rationale is that judges who have less than admirable personal values cannot judge others objectively and that judges who are less than honest in their financial dealings do not have a right to sit in judgment of others.

There are a number of problematic issues in the perceived objectivity of judges. For instance, in states where judges are elected, the judges must solicit campaign contributions. These monies are obtained most often from attorneys, and it is not at all unusual for judges to accept money from attorneys who practice before them. In fact, quite often the judge's campaign manager is a practicing attorney. Does this not provide at least the appearance of impropriety? This situation is exacerbated in jurisdictions that use court appointments as the method for indigent representation. In these jurisdictions judges hand out appointments to the same attorneys who give money back in the form of campaign contributions or have other ties to the judge. Obviously, the appearance, if not the actuality, of bias is present in these situations.

The practice of awarding indigent cases to one's friends or for reasons other than qualifications may not only be unethical but also may have serious consequences for the defendant. The Texas Bar Association (2002) reported major problems in the system of appointing attorneys for indigent defendants. The bar association's investigation found that some lawyers who received appointments had been disciplined by the state bar and there was no system for monitoring the quality of the representation. In 2006 a major newspaper ran a series of reports after an investigation of the system of appointing lawyers for capital habeas corpus appeals for Death Row inmates. The investigation found that some lawyers turned in ridiculously short appeals that did not cover even the most obvious points, and/or were poorly written (Lindell, 2006a; 2006b; 2006c).

In one egregious case, an attorney turned in a brief in 2003 that was basically copied from one letter from the inmate, complete with nonsensical arguments, grammatical lapses, and misspelled words. For this, the attorney billed the state for about $23,000, claiming 220 hours of work. In another writ, the attorney copied facts that were from another case and didn't apply to the case under appeal (Lindell, 2006a; 2006b). The system of appointing lawyers for habeas corpus petitions, a highly technical area of appellate law, has no mechanism for evaluating the competence of attorneys in Texas, even though the brief is extremely important because if issues are not brought up by this appeal, the defendant may lose the right to ever bring them up (Lindell, 2007c).

When habeas corpus appellate attorneys are competent, they may literally save the lives of innocent men and women. Several individuals have been exonerated based on the work of their appellate lawyers. In some cases these lawyers are from well-to-do law firms and do the work on a pro bono basis; in one case the law firm estimated that it spent $3 million dollars in defending an individual on Death Row. In most circumstances, however, when the lawyer must bill the state, he or she can charge the state only $100 an hour, capped at $25,000 (which is less than half of what they could earn in private legal work). This amount of money is the total that can be spent on investigating every aspect of a case, paying psychologists, paying investigators, and paying all other costs associated with filing the writ (Lindell, 2007b).

Partially in response to the investigative report, the Texas Court of Criminal Appeals, which maintains the list of attorneys who are chosen for habeas corpus writs, "weeded out" the list in 2006 and reported that it had removed attorneys who had performed extremely incompetently. In June of 2007, a bill to establish an office of "Capital Writs" that would be staffed with fulltime public defenders well versed in habeas corpus law for the appeals of Death Row inmates was derailed by a legislator using parliamentary procedures who argued that the public did not want to fund an "anti-death penalty" organization (disregarding the fact that the public is already paying a great deal of money for appointed lawyers who are not doing a competent job). Supporters are planning to reintroduce the bill in the 2009 legislative session, but the sequence of events indicates the sometimes political nature of the judicial process (Lindell, 2007b).

USE OF DISCRETION

As we have learned in several previous chapters, discretion refers to the authority to make a choice between two or more actions. Judges' discretion occurs in two major areas: interpretation of the law and sentencing.

Interpretation of Law and Rules   As previously noted, judges are like the umpire in an athletic contest; they apply the rules and interpret them. Although rules of law are established in Rules of Criminal Procedure and case law, there is still a great deal of discretion in the interpretation of a rule—what is reasonable, what is probative, what is prejudicial, and so on. A judge assesses the legality of evidence and makes rulings on the various objections raised by both the prosecutors and the defense attorneys. A judge also writes the extremely important instructions to the jury. These are crucial because they set up the legal questions and definitions of the case. They may have an occasion to make a decision to exclude a confession or a piece of evidence because of the way it was obtained, and by so doing, allow the guilty to go free.

One of the clearest examples of judicial discretion is in the application of the **exclusionary rule**, which basically states that when the evidence has been obtained illegally, it must be excluded from use at trial. The exclusionary rule has generated a storm of controversy because it can result in a guilty party avoiding punishment because of an error committed by the police. The basis for the exclusionary rule is the right to due process. The ideals of justice reject a conviction based on tainted evidence even if obtained against a guilty party. A more practical argument for the exclusionary rule is that if we want police officers to behave in a legal manner, we must have heavy sanctions against illegalities. Arguably, if convictions are lost because of illegal collection of evidence, police will reform their behavior. Actual practice provides little support for this argument, though. Cases lost on appeal are so far removed from the day-to-day decision making of the police that they have little effect on police behavior.

Ever since its inception, there has been a swirl of controversy around the exclusionary rule, even among justices on the Supreme Court. Some have argued that the criminal should not go free because of an error on the part of a police officer. Others argue that to utilize illegally obtained evidence would be contradictory to fundamental due process rights. In the succeeding years since the cases, such as *Mapp v. Ohio*, 367 U.S. 643 (1961), that recognized the rule, several exceptions to the exclusionary rule have been recognized. Judges can now rule that the illegally obtained evidence be allowed because of public safety 467 U.S. 649 [1984]), good faith (*U.S. v. Leon*, 468 U.S. 897 [1984]), or inevitable-discovery exceptions (*Nix v. Williams* 467 U.S. 431 [1984]).

One could examine each of these decisions on the basis of law, but ethics also helps us understand judicial reasoning—specifically, utilitarian ethics. The public safety exception, for instance, basically recognizes that if the police officer questioned the suspect for information to protect public safety, not for the gathering of evidence, the absence of the Miranda warning should not bar the use of any incriminating confession of the suspect. The "end" of public safety is more important than the "end" of ensuring that the suspects know their rights by giving them the Miranda warning before questioning them.

Excluding tainted evidence disregards short-term effects for more abstract principles—specifically, the protection of due process. Do the ethical frameworks justify the decision of a judge to allow a guilty person to go free because of "tainted" evidence?

- Religious ethics doesn't give us much help unless we decide that this ethical system would support vengeance and thus would permit the judge to ignore the exclusionary rule in order to punish a criminal. However, religious ethics might also support letting the criminal go free to answer to an ultimate higher authority, for human judgment was imperfect in this case.

- Egoism would support the decision to let a criminal go free or not, depending on the effect it would have on the judge's well-being.

- Ethical formalism's emphasis on duty over "ends" would dictate that judges must apply the law even in difficult cases. The rule itself seems to be supported by the categorical imperative, because one would probably not want a universal rule accepting tainted evidence, despite the possibility of further crime or harm to individuals.

- Act utilitarianism would support ignoring the exclusionary rule if the crime was especially serious or if there was a good chance the offender would not be retried successfully. The utility derived from ignoring the rule would outweigh the good. However, rule utilitarianism does support the exclusionary rule, for the long-term effect of allowing illegal police behavior would be more serious than letting one criminal go free.

In addition to applying the exclusionary rule, the judge is called upon to decide various questions of evidence and procedure throughout a trial. Of course, the judge is guided by the law and legal precedent, but in most cases each decision involves a substantial element of subjectivity. For instance, a defendant may file a pre-trial petition for a change of venue. This means that the defendant is arguing that public notoriety and a biased jury pool would make it impossible to have a fair trial in the location where the charges were filed. It is up to the judge, however, to decide if that indeed is true or whether, despite pre-trial publicity, the defendant will be assured of a fair trial. If judges are biased either toward or against the prosecution or defense, they have the power to make it difficult for either side through their pattern of rulings on objections, and evidence admitted. Even a personal dislike of either lawyer may be picked up by jury members, and it does affect their attitude toward that side's case.

Another situation that calls for a judge to make a discretionary decision is the determination that there has been an "unambiguous" request for an attorney. If a suspect asks for an attorney during an interrogation, questioning by police is supposed to stop. However, in actual cases, what constitutes an "unambiguous" request is sometimes controversial, and judges sometimes make after-the-fact decisions that seem contrary to common sense. In one case, a 16-year-old was being questioned by police, and he told police that he wanted to speak to his mother because he didn't know how to get a lawyer and maybe she could get him one. Police officers told him he could not speak to his mother, and the interrogation continued. The judge and the appellate judges determined that the statement that he wanted his mother to get him an attorney did *not* constitute a request for an attorney (*In the Matter of H.V.*, Texas State Supreme Court, 06-005).

Despite the belief that simply applying the rules will lead to the right conclusion or decision, the reality is that judges and justices are simply human, and real biases influence their decision making. The suspicion that some appellate court judges decide where they want to end up and make up the argument to get there is one that is hard to deny after a careful reading of some case decisions.

At times, appellate decision making seems to reflect a complete absence of "equity" thinking (basic fairness) in place of hyper-technical application of rules. Petitions that are denied because a deadline was missed or appeals denied because they were not drawn up in the correct fashion are examples of this application of discretion.

In one case in Texas, the Chief Justice of the Court of Criminal Appeals refused to accept an appeal on a Death Row case because the lawyers had filed it after 5 P.M.. This was despite the fact that several justices were working late that night in case of late filings, and the attorneys had asked for permission to file it late because they were having computer problems. Sharon Keller, the Chief Justice, refused to accept the request, and the prisoner was executed. The basis of the appeal was that the method of execution (lethal injection) was cruel and unusual, and the Supreme Court of the United States, only a week later, accepted a writ of certiorari on this very issue, indicating that there was a good chance that the appeal would have resulted in at least a hearing on the merits. In fact, two days later a second appeal by a different inmate was granted, while in the case where the appeal was denied for being 30 minutes late, the man was executed. This hyper-technical application of rules was considered so wrong that nineteen attorneys filed an ethics complaint against Keller for her actions, alleging that she violated the bar association rules that judges preserve the integrity of the judiciary and act in ways that promote public confidence, and a rule that requires judges to allow interested parties to be heard according to law (Lindell, 2007c).

An attorney's ethical lapse in performing his or her duties is sometimes compounded by judges' adhering to the "letter" rather than the spirit of the law. An example is the case of Johnny Conner, who was convicted of robbery. His trial attorney neglected to bring forward evidence in which the witnesses described the robber as "sprinting" away from the scene, but Conner had nerve damage in his leg and could only limp. The appellate attorney brought up the issue on appeal, but he neglected to attach any medical evidence, so the appellate judges refused to consider it as new evidence. The Attorney General of Texas later argued that, regardless of the factuality of the evidence, it should not be allowed in the federal appeal because it was not admitted in the state appeal (Lindell, 2006c).

In another case a federal appeals court refused to hear the appeal of a condemned man based on his mental retardation because his lawyer filed the appeal one day late. The Supreme Court had already ruled that executing someone with mental retardation was cruel and unusual, but in an appeal to the Fifth Circuit Court of Appeals, the justices ruled that the appeal did not have to be heard because of the late filing. A huge outpouring of criticism of the court focused on the distinct possibility that a man would be executed even though the Supreme Court had ruled that it would be unconstitutional because of his mental retardation. In an unusual about-face, the Fifth Circuit conducted a re-hearing and changed its opinion (Liptak, 2005b).

Judges may simply apply black-and-white rules, or they may attempt to enact the "spirit of justice." At times, however, even those who believe that their job is simply to apply the rules find that there are no bright-line rules or that they are difficult to interpret in specific cases.

Sentencing   The second area of judicial discretion is in sentencing. Judges have an awesome responsibility in sentencing offenders and, yet, receive little training to guide their discretion. It is also true that judges' decisions are scrutinized by public watchdog groups and appellate-level courts. One wonders if judges actually aren't overly influenced in their sentencing by the current clamor for strict punishments, but if judges are supposed to enact community sentiment, perhaps it is proper for them to reflect its influence. Does justice dictate a certain punishment for a certain type of offender, or does the definition of what is just depend on community opinion of the crime, the criminal, and the time?

Evidence indicates that judges' decisions are actually based on personal standards, for no consistency seems to appear between the decisions of individual judges in the same community. One study found that two judges in Louisiana had remarkably different records on numbers of convictions. The two also differed in their patterns of sentencing (Pinkele and Louthan, 1985). Hofer, Blackwell, and Ruback (1999) point out that most of the disparity in sentencing in the federal system before the advent of the sentencing guidelines occurred because of different patterns exhibited by individual judges. They cite studies that found, for instance, that judges' sentences were influenced by whether they had been prosecutors and by their religion.

The other extreme is when judges have *no* discretion in sentencing. **Federal Sentencing Guidelines** were written by Congress requiring the judge to impose a specific sentence unless there was a proven mitigating or aggravating factor in the case. The Sentencing Guidelines did reduce disparity among federal judges (Hofer, Blackwell, and Ruback, 1999); however, the guidelines received a great deal of criticism because of the draconian sentences applied to drug crimes. Racial bias was alleged in that the sentence for crack cocaine crimes was 100 times longer than sentences for powder cocaine crimes, even though these two drugs are chemically exactly the same. The argument supporting this disparity was that crack cocaine was more associated with other crimes and more addictive; however, there was a widespread belief that the disparity was simply racist. African Americans are much more likely to be convicted of crack crimes, and white Americans are more likely to be convicted for powder cocaine (Hofer et al., 1999). Some federal judges, such as Lawrence Irving in 1991, and others, have been so appalled by the length of drug sentences as required by the Sentencing Guidelines that they have refused to sentence offenders. Some have even quit, refusing to impose the mandated sentences, which they considered to be ridiculously long and overly punitive in certain cases (Tonry, 2005: 43).

The U.S. Supreme Court in January of 2005, in a case that challenged the constitutionality of the mandatory nature of the Federal Sentencing Guidelines, ruled that the defendant's Sixth Amendment rights were violated if the judges used elements to increase the sentence without first proving such elements in a court of law. The Court ruled that, in general, guidelines should be advisory rather than mandatory. However, it also ruled that this finding would not be retroactive, so all the thousands of individuals who have already been sentenced under what are now considered to be unconstitutional procedures cannot appeal their sentences on the basis of the ruling (*United States v. Booker*, 125 S.Ct. 1006 [2005]).

In a 2007 case, the Supreme Court held that federal judges could sentence defendants to less than the sentence specified by the Federal Sentencing Guidelines and that the test or standard used did not have to be "extraordinary" but could be "reasonable." What this case meant was that the Supreme Court was basically upholding the discretion of federal judges to sentence as they saw fit in criminal trials without being bound by the Guidelines. In the first case (*Kimbrough v. United States*, December 10, 2007, 06-6330), the Court dealt with a case concerning a sentencing for crack cocaine and the judge ruled that the sentence should be lower (closer to the sentence for powder cocaine). However, in a second case (*Gall v. United States*, December 10, 2007, 06-7949), the Supreme Court extended its rationale to other non-drug criminal cases so federal judges can now sentence as they see fit as long as their sentencing is "reasonable." The standard to be used is an abuse of discretion test rather than extraordinary circumstances (Barnes, 2007). (See the Policy Box for a discussion of Federal Sentencing Guidelines.)

JUDICIAL MISCONDUCT

Examples of judicial misconduct are fairly rare. Operation Greylord, in Chicago, took place in the 1980s. As a result of an FBI investigation, 92 people were indicted, including 17 judges, 48 lawyers, 10 deputy sheriffs, 8 police officers, 8 court officials, and a member of the Illinois legislature; and 31 attorneys and 8 judges were convicted of bribery. Judges accepted bribes to "fix" cases—to rule in favor of the attorney offering the bribe. Not unlike law enforcement's "blue curtain of secrecy," not one attorney came forward to expose this system of corruption, even though what was occurring was fairly well-known (Weber, 1987: 60).

Thankfully, such cases are extremely rare. Judges, for the most part, are like police officers and prosecutors. They strive to fulfill their role with integrity and honesty, taking care to protect the appearance and reality of justice. In some cases, however, neutrality is questioned when judges voice strong opinions on issues or cases. Talking to the media used to be rare, but now some judges have seemed to decide that it is acceptable to express their views, take a stand, and act as advocate. Many question this role for judges. In some cases, judges have been asked to **recuse** themselves—to step down and allow another judge to take over the trial—because they have indicated to news media that they already had opinions on a case before it was concluded.

Even Justice Antonin Scalia of the Supreme Court has been the target of such a request. In 2006, Justice Scalia, in a public speech, opined that giving full due process rights to detainees in Guantanamo was "crazy" and also made remarks referring to his son, who was serving in Iraq at the time. Several groups demanded that the Justice recuse himself from the case of *Hamdan v. Rumsfeld*, 126 S. Ct. 2749 (2006) because the case was about that very subject (what, if any, due process rights in American courts the detainees deserved). Justice Scalia did not recuse

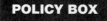 **POLICY BOX** | ### SENTENCING GUIDELINES

There has been widespread controversy concerning the Federal Sentencing Guidelines. They emerged in the 1970s and early 1980s in response to criticism that indeterminate sentencing created disparity. Guidelines were originally created by collecting the sentencing of all the judges in a jurisdiction and averaging their sentences, then presenting the average sentence to the judges, who would determine whether or not they could agree to that number. Then these guidelines would be available for all to use, but the judges would not be required to do so if they believed that a particular individual deserved more or less of a sentence. However, in some applications of sentencing guidelines, such as the Federal Sentencing Guidelines, the sentences were established by a legislative body (in this case, Congress and the Federal Sentencing Commission), and they were mandatory. Judges did not set these sentences and could not deviate from them (until recently).

Law: Supreme Court cases in 2005 ruled that the imposition of sentences using state or federal guidelines was unconstitutional when guidelines were applied using evidence that was not proven in court. For instance, the Federal Sentencing Guidelines require a longer sentence when a firearm is used in the crime, but these facts did not have to be proven in court before being used to find the mandated sentence. The Supreme Court ruled that in these cases the Guidelines were only advisory because to do otherwise would be to violate due process. The Supreme Court justices also decided cases in 2007 that gave federal judges the power to sentence outside Guideline range when it was reasonable to do so. Despite threats to rewrite the law to circumvent the Supreme Court rulings, Congress finally addressed the 100-to-1 ratio of crack-to-powder cocaine sentencing in 2008 and allowed federal judges to sentence outside the Guidelines as long as they were reasonable in drug and other cases.

Policy: After the Supreme Court held that the Federal Guidelines were unconstitutional, some circuits stopped using them, some continued to use them on a voluntary basis, and some used them but allowed individual judges to follow their conscience in individual cases. This was a situation in which individual federal judges were placed in a position where they once again had discretion. Some chose to use it, and others did not.

Ethics: The Federal Sentencing Guidelines have always been controversial in that many federal judges believe the sentences are too harsh for some drug offenders, and the judges have chafed at the lack of discretion allowed in sentencing. Several federal judges resigned because of their ethical objections to the Guidelines. When a federal judge believed that justice was not served by the sentence mandated by the Guideline, he or she had an ethical dilemma. Members of Congress also had an ethical issue in whether to support or oppose the disparity between sentencing for crack cocaine and powder cocaine offenses. This indeed may be a situation in which courageous federal justices, by choosing to take a stand, even giving up their lifetime appointments, forced a change in the law and allowed greater discretion for federal judges to sentence as they see fit, given the circumstances of the crime.

himself, and Hamdan did win his case, with the Supreme Court holding that detainees deserved some due process and that the Military Commissions that were created at the time were not sufficient. Scalia was in the dissent, however, so, arguably, one might conclude that he had already made up his mind before the case was decided (Lane, 2006).

In the 2007 Model Code of Judicial Conduct, one of the areas most debated was how judges should comport themselves in terms of public speaking and political engagement. The ideal, of course, is that judges should not have any preconceived ideas of who is right or wrong in any controversy they will rule on, but the reality is that judges do not live in a vacuum and, of course, have opinions, values, and beliefs regarding the issues of our times. Should they or should they not be allowed to speak of these issues?

Some question judges' motives in allowing cameras in the courtroom. Some argue that judges, as well as defense attorneys, prosecutors, and witnesses, become too interested in their appearance in the media rather than the interests of justice. There seems to be real concern that judges and lawyers play to the camera, perhaps to the detriment of swift resolution of the case. In general, judges who are more concerned with their public image than maintaining the judicial integrity of their office may make biased decisions. Judges who must be reelected to maintain their positions may be more vulnerable to worrying about their public image.

Another potential ethical issue is the objectivity of judges vis a vis their relationships with other actors in the courtroom. Can judges put aside personal friendships, dislikes, romantic relationships, and the like in their rulings? Judges' relationships with the lawyers or other parties in a court case raise suspicion of bias.

Courtroom decorum is established by the judge, and if judges display an irreverent or self-aggrandizing attitude or flaunt the law, their behavior degrades the entire judicial process. Some judges seem to be overly influenced by their power—as was the case of one district court judge who instructed courtroom workers to address him as "God." Most courtroom gossip includes the idiosyncrasies of some judges, such as the judge who was reputed to keep a gun under his robes and point it at tardy attorneys; the judge who arrested citizens in the hallway outside his courtroom for "creating a public disturbance" because they were talking too loud while he was holding court; the judge who ordered a woman arrested for contempt when she wrote a scathing letter to a newspaper regarding his competence; the judge who sentenced a man to probation for killing his wife (excusing such behavior in open court with a statement indicating that the nagging victim deserved it); and the judge who signed an order of execution with a smiley face. These individuals illustrate that putting on a black robe doesn't necessarily give one the wisdom of Solomon. The "In the News" box indicates that some judges may benefit from a refresher course in justice.

Other forms of unethical behavior are less blatant. Judges have a duty to conclude judicial processing with reasonable punctuality. However, there are widespread delays in processing, partly because of the lack of energy with which some judges pursue their dockets. In the same jurisdiction, and with a balanced assignment of cases, one judge may have only a couple dozen pending cases and another judge to have literally hundreds. Some judges routinely allow numerous continuances, set

IN THE NEWS | JUDICIAL MISCONDUCT

News reports indicated that there were many complaints about immigration judges who evidently did not perform their judicial role with the degree of objectivity and care that they should have. In Boston, a judge was suspended for a year because he referred to himself as Tarzan when hearing a case involving a Ugandan woman named Jane. Another judge deported a man without bothering to check to see that his tax records and birth certificate were authentic (they were). Attorney General Alberto Gonzales wrote a strongly worded memo to all federal immigration judges at the time insisting that they abide by rules of professional decorum.

Source: Simmons, 2006.

It was reported that 128 complaints were filed against Utah judges to the Judicial Conduct Commission in 2005. Two high-profile cases involved one judge who was arrested on drug charges and another who was charged with violating the law for not deciding juvenile cases by deadlines set by law. Members of the Utah Judicial Conduct Commission argue that Utah judges have fewer misconduct charges than other states, where judges have been disciplined for DUI, sexual harassment, and "using a sexual device while on the bench."

Source: Fattah, 2005.

---

trial dates far into the future, start the docket call at 10:00 A.M., conclude the day's work at 3:00 P.M., and in other ways take a desultory approach to swift justice.

We must be careful not to paint with too broad a brush. Only a few judges are involved in the most egregious examples of unethical behavior, such as taking bribes or trampling the due-process rights of defendants, just as only a small percentage of police officers, defense attorneys, and prosecutors commit extreme behaviors. Most judges are ethical and take great care to live up to the obligations of their role. However, as with the other criminal justice professionals, sometimes there are systemic biases and subtle ways in which the principles of justice and due process are subverted. It cannot be ignored that the justice system is assailed as violative of the rights of defendants, especially minorities.

JUSTICE ON TRIAL?

One of the reasons that many people distrust our justice system is that there seems to be a small—but steady—stream of cases in which prosecutors, along with police, deliberately ignore evidence, destroy exculpatory evidence, lie about evidence, or do not share exculpatory evidence with the defense. Radelet, Bedau, and Putnam (1992) gathered together dozens of capital cases where innocent defendants were convicted of crimes they did not commit. Some were sentenced to death. False convictions occurred because of incompetent defense counsel and unethical and illegal practices on the part of prosecutors and police, but also because judges, who are supposed to ensure that the process is fair, evidently did not do their job.

Scott Christianson (2004) described forty-two cases where innocent people were convicted. The errors occurred largely through the actions of police, prosecutors, and judges who neglected their duty to be objective officers of the court and traded neutrality for an individual "ends"-based approach to their duties. Eyewitness perjury (sanctioned by the prosecutor), ineffective counsel, the use of false confessions, police misconduct, fabrication of evidence, and misuse of forensics were the reasons that these innocent people were convicted. Their stories are chilling reminders that innocent people can end up in prison.

The Delma Banks case illustrates the problem: Banks was convicted based on the testimony of a police informant and a long-time drug offender who was promised a shorter sentence and coached to provide details of the crime scene. Neither of these facts was brought out at trial. Further, the jury pool was race-coded by prosecutors, and all African American jurors were excluded. Reanalysis of forensics indicated that the victim was killed when Banks was out of town. Lawyers for Banks were denied a clemency hearing from the State Board of Pardons and Paroles despite the new evidence and that the transcript of the coaching was deliberately withheld from the defense for close to nineteen years and finally surrendered only when ordered by a federal district judge. The reason the Board denied the petition? It was filed one week late (Pasztor, 2003a, 2003b). The U.S. Supreme Court issued a writ of certiorari and granted a stay of execution, and, evidently refusing to ignore the distinct possibility that an innocent man was to be executed, overturned the verdict and remanded the case for a new trial (Pasztor, 2003b; *Banks v. Dretke*, 540 U.S. 668 [2004]). Others have been executed, and only afterward did evidence or perpetrators' confessions exonerate the accused and expose the prosecution's misconduct that led to the miscarriage of justice (Radelet, Bedau, and Putnam, 1992).

Whereas some of the cases described by Radelet, Bedau, and Putnam involved pure and extreme racial prejudice, probably a more prevalent factor in false convictions is a more subtle form of racism. Many in the criminal justice system tend to prejudge the guilt of the accused, especially if they are black men. There is a pervasive stereotypical belief that all defendants are guilty and most defendants are black. This thought pattern shapes and distorts decision making on the part of prosecutors who sift and use evidence in a way that will support their predetermined beliefs.

When police or prosecutors allow their biases and prejudices to influence their decision making, evidence is lost or ignored, witnesses are discounted and disbelieved, tests aren't conducted, and true perpetrators literally "get away with murder" if there is a convenient suspect who looks guilty. When judges allow their biases to affect their rulings, the misconduct of the prosecutor and police is exacerbated. This is an ever-present and pervasive reality in our justice system and probably accounts for why there is such a divergence in the perceptions of blacks and whites regarding the fairness of the system. For instance, in a Gallup Poll, 71 percent of whites said murder charges against O. J. Simpson were probably or definitely true, but only 28 percent of blacks agreed (reported in Mitchell and Banks, 1996: B1). Is this a reflection of a different way of measuring evidence or a different perception of trust in law enforcement and legal professionals' ability to collect and interpret evidence? Is the lack of trust warranted? Unfortunately, the answer to that question is probably yes.

In a study conducted by the Columbia Law School, 68 percent of all death verdicts handed down between 1973 and 1995 were reversed because of serious errors. Between 1993 and 2002, ninety Death Row inmates were exonerated of the crimes of which they were accused. The errors involved defense lawyers' incompetence, and also police and prosecutors suppressing exculpatory evidence or engaging in other types of professional misconduct. Almost 10 percent of the cases sent back for retrial resulted in not-guilty verdicts. The study concluded that the high rate of errors occurred because of the indiscriminate use of the death penalty and factors such as race, politics, and poorly performing law enforcement systems (Columbia Law School, 2002). In this study, 328 cases over the last 15 years in which the individuals were exonerated (usually by DNA) were examined. The study authors allege that there may be thousands of innocent people in prison. Most of the cases that reach national attention are homicide and rape cases, so less serious cases, which may also suffer from the errors of mistaken eyewitness testimony, evidence withholding, and other misconduct, go undiscovered.

Prosecutors have objected to the study's methodology, arguing that the study counted cases where the evidence was weak but the defendant might still be guilty. Further, they argue that the number of exonerations is quite small compared to the number of convictions. The study found 199 exonerations of murder suspects and 120 exonerations of rape suspects. It appeared that rape suspects who were mistakenly identified by victims were disproportionately black. There have also been 125 cases identified where the mistaken verdict depended upon false confessions, usually of the mentally ill, the mentally retarded, and juveniles (Liptak, 2004; Columbia Law School, 2002). The Columbia study led to a growing storm of controversy concerning the prevalence and causes of innocent defendants being convicted.

In 2008, the Innocence Projects announced that 200 people have been exonerated by DNA evidence as a result of their efforts. The **Innocence Projects** consist of an affiliation of groups of lawyers in many states that identify cases where people may have been falsely convicted and there is DNA evidence still on file that could be used to prove or disprove their protestations of innocence. These organizations have been pivotal in getting the wrongly accused off Death Row and freed from prison. (To read more about the project, you can visit their website: http://www. innocenceproject.org/).

A typical case is one from Dallas County, Texas, in which a man was sentenced to life in prison in 1981 for rape. After an Innocence Project tested the DNA evidence, the man was cleared of the rape. He was the fifteenth inmate from Dallas County to be freed by DNA evidence since 2001, and the thirtieth wrongfully convicted inmate exonerated in Texas, the highest number of any state. The man had been convicted partially based on an eyewitness who picked him from a photo lineup, but experts report that eyewitness testimony is notoriously unreliable. Partially as a response to this case, the district attorney in Dallas County began a program where law students, supervised by Innocence Project lawyers, are reviewing about 450 cases in which convicts have requested DNA testing (Associated Press, 2008c).

Another study reviewed different sources to estimate wrongful convictions and concluded that the range was 1 percent to 15 percent, depending on which sources were used (inmate reports illustrated the higher figure) (Poveda, 2001). Even at the lower range, however, the number of innocent people imprisoned is substantial, given that close to two million are incarcerated in prisons and jails. The "Quote and Query" box presents two questions. How one might answer them depends on one's perceptions of the costs involved in wrongful convictions.

QUOTE AND QUERY

"Is it better for 100,000 guilty men to walk free rather than have one innocent man convicted? The cost–benefit policy answer is no."

(prosecutor)

"No rate of preventable errors that destroy people's lives and destroy the lives of those close to them is acceptable."

(law professor)

Liptak, 2004: 3.

Which of these statements represents ethical formalism? Which statement represents utilitarian thinking?

In an interesting study that compared a group of those who were released from prison based on exonerations and those who were executed, the authors found that there may have been at least a dozen possible executions of innocents (Harmon and Lofquist, 2005: 592). In the cases where the defendant was executed, they found that it was more likely that there were no allegations of perjury, there were multiple types of evidence, the defendant had prior felony records, and the attorneys were public defenders. The study revealed, for instance, that inmates were 9 times more likely to be released if they had a private attorney at trial (although there was no difference in the type of attorney at the appellate level). Inmates were 27 times more likely to be released when there were allegations of perjury (Harmon and Lofquist, 2005:511).

Some of the reasons for false convictions include the following (Schehr and Sears, 2005):

- mistaken eyewitness testimony
- perjury by informants
- police and prosecutorial misconduct
- false confessions
- "junk science"
- ineffective assistance of counsel
- racial bias
- **confirmatory bias** (when a specific suspect has been fixated upon and other possibilities are ignored)

One of the most often cited reasons for false convictions (in addition to eyewitness testimony) is ineffective assistance of counsel. The legal standard for what constitutes ineffective counsel is set quite high—so high that in the case of Calvin Burdine, whose lawyer slept through parts of his trial, the appellate court said that if a lawyer wasn't sleeping during a *crucial* part of the trial, it wasn't ineffective counsel. Other behaviors reported of lawyers in capital and other cases include the following (Schehr and Sears, 2005):

- attorneys use of heroin and cocaine during trial
- attorneys letting the defendant wear the same clothes described by the victim
- attorneys admitting that they didn't know the law or facts of the case

- attorneys not being able to name a single death penalty case holding
- attorneys drinking heavily each day of the trial and being arrested for a .27 blood alcohol level.

What cannot be ignored is that for every case there was a judge who did nothing to prevent the conviction even though these actions must have been obvious and harmful to the defendant's case.

Race seems to be a part of this phenomenon. As mentioned previously, wrongly accused rape suspects are disproportionately black. Further, race plays a part in the confirmatory bias mentioned above in that there is a stereotype that blacks are more likely to be criminals. Racial bias in wrongful convictions has been attributed to individual factors and structural factors. Structural factors include systemic bias against minorities in all institutions of society (political, economic, and social) that leads to different opportunities and treatment. Individual factors include these (Schehr and Sears, 2005):

- racism
- higher error rate in cross-racial identification
- stereotyping
- lack of resources of defendant

While the number of Innocence Projects is growing and the groups have been successful in identifying cases and prevailing in court, they can't be the only solution to the problem of false convictions. Unfortunately, most of these projects are under-resourced and overwhelmed. Some argue that what is needed is a model such as Great Britain's Criminal Cases Review Commission, which is a governmental agency rather than a volunteer and/or private organization. Others (Schehr and Weathered, 2004) question the efficacy of Britain's model, arguing that

- it is subordinate to the Court of Appeal and thus deferential to it.
- it relies on untrained caseworkers to review cases.
- it relies on petitioners to raise claims.
- it is understaffed and pays too little attention to each case.

Others argue that the Innocence Projects can serve an important purpose but that they must be better funded and not left to the vagaries of budget cuts.

The state of Texas executes the most people and also has freed the most offenders. Cases such as Clarence Brandley, James Curtis Giles, and Joyce Ann Brown, discussed previously, create real doubt that only guilty parties are executed. Randall Dale Adams, another freed inmate, was the subject of the documentary *The Thin Blue Line*. He was convicted in 1976 of killing a Dallas police officer who stopped a car driven by David Harris. Harris said Adams was the gunman. Adams said he wasn't even in the car. The state relied on an eyewitness who had picked someone else out of a lineup along with Harris, a sixteen-year-old with a long juvenile record. Harris eventually confessed that he killed the officer alone, but Adams spent years in prison and on Death Row (Hall, 2002).

Another case that might be added to the list of innocents is that of Cameron Todd Willingham. In what may be a tragic miscarriage of justice, he was put to death in February 2004. Willingham was convicted in the arson deaths of his three daughters. The arson evidence upon which he was convicted has since been repudiated, and four national arson experts claim that there was no evidence of arson, much less that Willingham used arson to kill his daughters. Despite their report and Willingham's pleadings of innocence, the State Board of Pardons and Paroles and the appellate courts did not stop the execution (Mills, 2005).

Ordinarily, state appellate courts that lean too far in either a liberal or conservative direction would be adjusted by appellate decisions. It is also true, however, that the Federal Circuit Courts have their own reputations for being either too conservative or too liberal, or in the case of the Fifth Circuit, "insolent." The Fifth Circuit court has been admonished by the U.S. Supreme Court because of what some call its "insolence" in ignoring the holdings of Supreme Court decisions to rehearings.

In the case of Thomas Miller-El, the Supreme Court ruled in favor of the defendant's appeal based on systematic exclusion of black jurors in Dallas County and remanded the case to the Fifth Circuit. The judges on the Fifth Circuit then used (some say plagiarized) a dissent by Clarence Thomas to deny relief. The case was appealed to the Supreme Court again, and it once again granted relief and rebuked the court, ordering the Fifth Circuit to apply its legal reasoning (Liptak and Blumenthal, 2004; *Miller-El v. Dretke*, 125 St. Ct. 2317 [2005]).

Legal scholars argue that the defiance displayed by the Fifth Circuit is extremely troubling because the U.S. Supreme Court takes only about eighty cases a year, and usually only those cases that represent a conflict between lower appellate courts. There is no room in the system to "fix" appellate decisions that defy precedent and Supreme Court rulings. One issue with the Fifth Circuit has been jury instructions that were ruled unconstitutional in 2001 but were still being used in cases that were upheld by the circuit court. In effect, the Fifth Circuit has been ignoring the Supreme Court ruling. Some of the individuals whose appeals were denied have already been executed (Liptak and Blumenthal, 2004).

The ideal, or vision, of our justice system is that it is fair, unbiased, and, through the application of due process, arrives at the truth before finding guilt and assessing punishment. The reality is that the law is administered by humans with human failings and that errors and misconduct result in innocent people being convicted, incarcerated, and sometimes executed. There is also a pervasive theme of racism in these miscarriages of justice. This indicates that something else is at work besides individuals not performing their duties and that what is wrong is more fundamental than simply bad or unethical decision making.

JUDICIAL INDEPENDENCE AND THE CONSTITUTION

Recall that discretion is the ability to make a decision and that discretion exists at each stage of the criminal justice system. Professionals at each stage have the opportunity to use their discretion wisely and ethically, or, alternatively, they may use their discretion unethically. In the courts, prosecutors have discretion to pursue prosecution or not, defense attorneys have discretion to accept or refuse cases and choose trial tactics, and judges have discretion to make rulings on evidence and other trial procedures, as well as decide on convictions and sentences.

One view of law is that it is neutral and objective and that formal and absolute rules of law are used in decision making (Pinkele and Louthan, 1985: 9). However, the reality is that lawmakers, law enforcers, and lawgivers are invested with a great deal of discretion in making and interpreting the law. Far from being absolute or objective, the law is a dynamic, ever-changing symbol of political will. If we accept that discretion is an operating reality in the justice system, we must ask in what ways legal professionals use this discretion. If individual value systems replace absolute rules or laws, the resulting decisions may be ethical or unethical. For instance, a judge may base a decision on fairness, or the judge may base the decision on prejudicial beliefs (e.g., that blacks are more criminal and deserve longer sentences, or that women are not dangerous and should get probation).

There may be many other situations where one's biases and prejudices are not so easily identified. Judges' rulings on evidentiary matters are supposed to be based on rules of evidence, but sometimes there is room for interpretation and individual discretion. While most judges use this discretion appropriately and make decisions in a best effort to conform to the spirit of the evidentiary rule, other judges use arbitrary or unfair criteria, such as personal dislike of an attorney, disagreement with a rule, or a desire for one side or the other to win the case.

Defense attorneys and prosecutors have a great deal of discretion in the decisions they must make. Prosecutors must decide whether to charge and what to charge. They must decide trial strategy and what to offer in a plea bargain, but, arguably, it is the judge who shapes the system and protects or ignores its principles. Discretionary decisions at the trial level can be reexamined through the process of appeal. Appeals are part of due process in that they serve as a check on the decision making of trial judges. Supposedly, any gross errors will be corrected and any extremely unethical actions will result in a new trial. However, petitions for review must be accepted by appellate courts that accept only a few that are filed. Even if they accept a case for review, there is seldom enough new evidence or a serious enough error to grant a new trial.

In this text we address the ethical issues in the *implementation*, rather than the *creation*, of law. As you learned in political science or government classes, the creation of law is political. Laws are written by federal and state representatives who supposedly enact the public will. One might think that once a law is created, its implementation would be fairly straightforward, but it should be clear by now that this is not the case. An appellate court can change over time and be influenced by political shifts in power. Far from being static, the implementation of law reflects political realities, in direct contrast to the ideal of judicial independence that is the cornerstone of our system of government.

If the judiciary is not independent of political powers, this calls into question the very existence of the checks and balances upon which this country's government is constructed. For instance, many Democrats suspected that the composition of the Supreme Court had a great deal to do with its decision in the case challenging the Florida vote after the Bush–Gore election. Whether or not the allegations are true, it should be obvious that the strength of the justice system rests on the independence of its judiciary.

In 2005, several leaders in Congress publicly chastised the federal judiciary because they did not like the decisions that the judges had been handing down,

QUOTE AND QUERY

"[T]he time will come for the men responsible for this to answer for their behavior.... [I want to] look at an arrogant, out-of-control, unaccountable judiciary that thumbed their nose at Congress and the president."

Tom DeLay, U.S. House of Representatives majority leader, speaking in response to the Terry Schiavo case, May 2005, as quoted in Allen, 2005

Attempts to intimidate judges into deciding pending cases in a particular way with threats of impeachment or investigation, as has been the recent practice of some members of Congress, have no place in a functioning democracy.

American Judicature, 2005

Do you think that members of Congress should be sanctioned for threatening impeachment when they don't like the decisions of federal judges? If not, who does serve as oversight for judges who are appointed for life?

---

and then, in turn, were criticized by others who argued that the essence of separation of powers is that federal judges are not influenced, intimidated, or ordered by legislative leaders to enact anyone's political agenda. The "Quote and Query" box illustrates the controversy.

The political uproar over the firings of eight federal prosecutors in 2007 may have seemed overblown to some people. After all, why shouldn't the Administration be able to hire and fire at will? However, what was at stake was the very essence of the separation of powers that is the greatest strength of our system of government. Traditionally, when a new President comes into office, he engages in a process whereby those affiliated with the old Administration are removed and new employees are placed into those positions. That has been done in all sectors of executive government, including the Justice Department, by Democrat and Republican administrations alike, with very little criticism. What happened in 2007, however, was that, apparently, in the middle of the term of office, there was a "hit list" of federal prosecutors who were removed not for incompetence or poor performance but, rather, because aides from the White House relayed a message to Justice officials that these individuals should be replaced with others who were more loyal to the Bush Administration.

Observers noted that the prosecutors targeted for firing were those who either pursued prosecutions against Republicans or were too slow to respond to pressure to pursue prosecutions against Democrats. In effect, the firings were politically motivated, not a "cleaning house" at the beginning of a term of office. When Attorney General Alberto Gonzales responded to the Congressional inquiry in an unsatisfactory way (saying more than seventy times that he couldn't remember), he ultimately had to resign because of the scandal (Carr and Herman, 2007).

If the justice system, including prosecutors and judges, is a pawn or an agent of political power, due process is a sham and the very essence of democracy is threatened. The importance of due process is that even criminals and enemies of the state are given due-process rights that protect them from errors in the deprivation of life, liberty, and property. If due process is reserved only for those who are not enemies of the state, all are threatened because anyone may become an "enemy." If for some reason state power would become despotic, it would be likely to label as enemies anyone favoring open government and democracy. What this illustrates is that the law (and the nature of its protections) is more important than the state and, indeed, is even more important than threats to the state. Those who are more influenced by political allegiance than allegiance to due process and civil liberties create a weak link in the mantle of protection against despotic state power.

The U.S. Supreme Court, as the ultimate authority of law in this country, decides constitutionality, and these interpretations are far from neutral, despite the myth of objective decision making. This is the reason that the selection of Supreme Court justices (as well as all federal judges) is such a hard-fought political contest. Ideological positions do make a difference, and no one is fooled that a black robe removes bias. The latest confirmation of John Roberts as Chief Justice illustrates this. Opponents sought to obtain information about his belief systems concerning social and legal issues such as abortion and civil rights. Roberts took the stand that he could not comment on cases in advance and that he would be guided by legal precedent. This is a legitimate stand, but one that few are comforted by because precedent has not stopped the court from overturning decisions in the past.

JUDICIAL ACTIVISM

Judges can strive to be objective, but their individual beliefs, background, politics, and even friendships no doubt influence, to a greater or lesser extent, their decision making. There are also more fundamental perceptions at work. Our law derives from the Constitution. Two basic philosophies regarding how to apply Constitutional principles are at work in the legal arena. The first group might be called **strict constructionists** because they argue that the Constitution should be implemented as written and if any changes are to take place in rights, responsibilities, or liberties, the changes should take place through the political system (Congress).

The extreme view of this position is that if a right isn't in the Constitution; it doesn't exist. So, for instance, the right to be free from state interference in the decision to abort one's fetus does not exist in the Constitution; therefore, it doesn't exist and cannot be created except through the actions of duly elected representatives. Strict constructionists argue that just because something *should* be a right doesn't mean that one can decide the framers meant for it to be a right. Judges should not create law.

Interpretationists (or activists) have a looser reading of the Constitution and read into it rights that the framers might have recognized or that should be recognized because of "evolving standards." They argue that the Constitution is meant to be a living document and that the language of the framers was intentionally written as to accommodate interpretation based on changing times and circumstances. Concepts such as due process, for instance, from the Fifth and Fourteenth Amendments, are flexible so they can be used to address new questions and new concerns. Interpretationists place less emphasis on precedent, minimize procedural

Quote and Query

When we are dealing with words that also are a constituent act, like the Constitution of the United States, we must realize that they have called into life a being the development of which could not have been foreseen completely by the most gifted of its begetters.

Oliver Wendell Holmes, Jr., as quoted in Wolfe, 1991:36

Why should we not look just in the "four corners" of the document according to Oliver Wendell Holmes?

---

obstacles (such as standing, ripeness and federalism), and offer less deference to other political decision makers (e.g., they use the strict scrutiny test rather than the rational relationship test when evaluating governmental actions). When the Court was in its most activist phase (the Warren Court), it delivered broad opinions that have had dramatic effects on the political and legal landscape (Wolfe, 1991).

Critics of judicial activism point out that just because judicial activists have been promoters of civil liberties and socially progressive causes, such as integration and free speech, there is no absolute necessity that activism could or would always champion such individual rights. Activism could, for instance, be just as likely to recognize greater rights of the state to restrict individual liberties (Wolfe, 1991).

In the opposing view, proponents of activism argue that the federal government itself has not been content to stay within the boundaries of its enumerated powers as specified in the Constitution, and that proliferation of the federal government's reach into all areas of criminal and civil law through the expansive interpretation of the Commerce Clause requires greater judicial checks. Furthermore, there are limits to judicial power, including impeachment, confirmation, Congressional definition of appellate powers, and the power to override a Supreme Court opinion through a Constitutional amendment (Wolfe, 1991). The "Quote and Query" box gives a view of the Constitution by one jurist.

The Warren Court was called activist or liberal because it recognized a whole range of civil liberties and due-process rights for groups that had been historically disenfranchised. The source of such rights was found in an expansive reading of the Constitution and based on the idea of "fundamental liberties"—those freedoms and protections that the framers would have recognized if they had been asked. Central to this view is the idea of **natural rights**. Recall that the natural law ethical system holds that there are natural laws of ethics that humans may or may not discover. Several of the authors of the Bill of Rights were natural law theorists; thus, taken out of the context of their time, they would probably recognize that humans have the following rights:

- to be free
- to be treated equal to other groups
- to be able to make decisions about personal matters without governmental interference
- to be free from torture and punishments that degrade the human spirit
- to have some protections against state power

In addition, there may be recognition that humans also have rights:

- to basic necessities to survive
- to avail themselves of opportunities to better themselves

The first set of rights leads to less government; the second set leads to more government. That is why the political terms *conservative* and *liberal* are not strictly comparable to "strict constructionist" and "interpretationist" and why there is such confusion when these terms are being used to describe judicial and political appointees and elected officials. "Liberals" argue that if the Warren Court hadn't interpreted the Constitution to recognize civil rights, blacks would still be eating at separate lunch counters. Constructionists argue that if interpretationists had their way, government and the courts would be involved in every decision from birth to death.

The Supreme Court's "activism" has been intimately tied to who has been on the bench. The era of activism occurred because of a shift in the membership of the Court. *Brown v. Board of Education*, 347 U.S. 483 (1954), which held that "separate but equal" schools were unconstitutional, is considered to be a fundamental shift in social equality or an overreaching decision that had no legal support, depending on whether one is a strict constructionist or interpretationist (Wolfe, 1991). The Supreme Court has moved back to a constructionist stance, because of the confirmations of John Roberts, Samuel Alito, Clarence Thomas, and Antonin Scalia, who are constructionists. In recent holdings, the Court has upheld federal anti-abortion laws, cut back on free-speech rights of public school students, strictly enforced procedural requirements for bringing and appealing cases, and limited school districts' ability to use racially conscious measures to achieve or preserve integration.

One can predict case decisions based on the Justices' ideological positions, with Scalia, Alito, Thomas, and Roberts almost always voting in a block and usually winning in 5–4 decisions when Justice Anthony Kennedy provides the swing vote. What is interesting is that Justices John Paul Stevens (appointed by Gerald Ford) and Justice David Souter (appointed by George H.W. Bush) of the so-called liberal Justices of today were not considered activist or liberal when they were appointed but have moved in that direction compared to the extremely constructionist justices that have been appointed since then (Greenhouse, 2007).

One thing is clear: A judge is human and carries baggage of personal, political, and social bias. Judges no doubt strive for objectivity, and we attempt to protect their independence, but individual ethics clearly are important considerations in any discussion of judicial discretion. The law is subject to interpretation; thus, individual ethics plays a part in the use of the powers given to the judiciary.

CONCLUSION

The use of discretion in the criminal justice system is pervasive, and decision makers are influenced by their individual values, ethics, and ideologies. This is also true for judges, who are the final arbiters and interpreters of the law.

Thus, it is crucial that these professionals remember and believe in the basic tenets of due process and be ever vigilant against the influence of prejudice or bias in the application of law toward the pursuit of justice. One cannot simply argue that the discussions concerning laws outlawing certain types of abortion, the exclusionary rule, integration, drug and pornography laws, and so on are *only* legal issues. They are also ethical issues, and ethical dilemmas for the judges who are called upon to enforce and interpret the law.

Key Terms

bureaucratic justice *356*

confirmatory bias *371*

exclusionary rule *361*

Federal Sentencing Guidelines *364*

Innocence Projects *370*

interpretationists *376*

natural rights *377*

recuse *365*

strict constructionists *376*

wedding-cake illustration *357*

Review Questions

1. Describe the models of court processing.
2. What are Alan Dershowitz's rules regarding the reality of the justice system?
3. What are the two areas of judicial discretion described? Give examples.
4. What are the areas covered by the Code of Judicial Conduct? Give examples of each.
5. Describe at least three issues related to a judge's ethical obligations.
6. Discuss the number of innocents who may be imprisoned. What are the sources for the estimates? What are the criticisms of the sources?
7. What factors have been identified as contributing to false convictions?
8. What are some examples of ineffective counsel?
9. What is the evidence to indicate a pervasive pattern of racial bias in the system?
10. Describe the positions of strict constructionists and interpretationists (or activists).

Writing/Discussion Questions

1. Write an essay on (or discuss), using ethical and moral criteria, courtroom practices: the use of videotaped testimony, allowing television cameras into the courtroom and jury room, victim statements during sentencing, preventive detention, neighborhood justice centers, the use of a waiver to adult court for violent juvenile offenders, and any others that have been in the news recently.
2. Write an essay on (or discuss) the ethical dilemmas of the characters after watching a movie that presents a legal dilemma (e.g., *Criminal Law, Penalty Phase, Presumed Innocent, The Witness*). Use one or more of the ethical frameworks provided in Chapter 2.
3. Write an essay on (or discuss) judicial activism. Present the arguments on both sides of the question as to whether judges should interpret or simply apply the Constitution. Provide more current examples (the current Supreme Court docket) and predict how Justices will decide. If one can predict the decisions of the Justices on the Supreme Court, where does that leave the idea that no case is prejudged?

Ethical Dilemmas

Situation 1

You are a judge who must sentence two defendants. One insisted on a jury trial and, through his defense attorney, dragged the case on for months with delays and motions. He was finally convicted by a jury. The other individual was his co-defendant, and he pleaded guilty. Apparently, they were equally responsible for the burglary. How will you sentence them?

Situation 2

You are a member of a jury. The jury is hearing a child molestation case in which the defendant is accused of a series of molestations in his neighborhood. You have been advised by the judge not to discuss the case with anyone outside the courtroom, and especially not to anyone on either side of the case. Going down in the elevator after the fourth day of the trial, you overhear the prosecutor talking to one of the police officer witnesses. They are discussing that the man has a previous arrest for child molestation but that it has not been allowed in by the judge as being too prejudicial to the jury. You were fairly sure that the guy was guilty before, but now you definitely believe he is guilty. You also know that if you tell the judge what you have heard, it will probably result in a mistrial. What would you do?

Situation 3

You are a court administrator and really like Judge Sonyer, your boss. He is pleasant, punctual, and hardworking. One day you hear him talking to the prosecutor in chambers. He is talking about the defendant in a trial that is about to start, and you hear him say that the son-of-a-bitch is "as guilty as sin." You happen to be in law school and know that, first, the prosecutor and judge should not be talking about the case without the presence of the defense attorney and, second, that the judge has expressed a pre-existing bias. The judge's statement is even more problematic because this is a bench trial and he is the sole determiner of guilt or innocence. What would you do?

Situation 4

You are a federal judge and are about to start a federal racketeering trial that is quite complicated. Prosecutors allege that certain lobbyists funneled money into political campaigns by "washing" it through individual employees of a couple of large corporations. Still, the evidence seems equivocal—at least what you've seen so far. You get a call from one of your state's U.S. senators (who is not implicated in the case, although members of his party are), and the conversation is innocuous and pleasant enough until the senator brings up the case and jocularly pressures you to agree with him that it is a "tempest in a teapot." Then he mentions that a higher, appellate-level judgeship will be opening soon and that he is sure you would like his support on it. The message is not subtle. What would you do?

Situation 5

You are a federal judge faced with a drug defendant. The Federal Sentencing Guidelines dictate that you sentence this individual to five years in prison. You believe that the sentence is arbitrary and not responsive to the defendant's individual circumstances. You think the individual deserves probation, community service, and drug counseling. What would you do?

Suggested Readings

Christianson, S. 2004. *Innocent: Inside Wrongful Conviction Cases*. New York: New York University Press.

Dwyer, J., Neufeld, P., and Scheck, B. 2001. *Actual Innocence: When Justice Goes Wrong and How to Make It Right*. New York: Signet.

Grisham, J. 2007. *The Innocent Man*. New York City: Dell Publishers.

Radelet, M., Bedau, H., and Putnam, C. 1992. *In Spite of Innocence*. Boston: Northeastern University Press.

Spence, G. 1989. *With Justice for None*. New York: Penguin.

Wolfe, C. 1991. *Judicial Activism*. Pacific Grove, CA: Brooks/Cole Publishing.

The Ethics of Punishment and Corrections

Is capital punishment just or unjust? This controversy has raged on in this country for decades. Public support for the death penalty swings back and forth, indicating the difficulty of ever resolving the legal and ethical questions surrounding it.

CHAPTER OBJECTIVES

1. Understand the definitions of punishment and treatment and their rationales.

2. Learn how the ethical frameworks justify punishment.

3. Become familiar with the arguments for and against capital punishment.

4. Understand the role that discretion, authority, and power play in corrections.

5. Explore the ethical issues involved with the privatization of corrections.

CHAPTER OUTLINE

Imagine that you are arrested and convicted of a drug crime. Because of harsh drug laws in your state, you are sent to prison for three years. Nothing in your background prepares you for the experience. Your family and friends are horrified; you are terrified. Jail was bad enough, but this is a small county and only six other women were housed there who, despite constant verbal taunting, were relatively harmless. Now, however, you arrive at the state women's facility. The whole process, from the long bus ride to the prison, to the humiliating public shower and delousing, to the body-cavity search, to the yelling of the correctional officer in charge that "all you crack ho's better get moving" has been confusing, overwhelming, and soul-destroying.

Once you finally are settled in your cell, your cellmate tells you that a woman can do certain things for the guards in this prison to make the time pass easier. Further, she says, if you catch the eye of a certain guard, you won't have any choice in the matter because he doesn't like to be refused. You think she is exaggerating. After all, things like that don't happen in real life, only in the movies. You are wrong. By the end of your first six months in prison, the person you used to be and why you are being punished are distant memories.

Once someone has been found guilty of a criminal offense, the type of punishment must be determined. Punishments range from a suspended sentence to death. Sometimes punishment includes treatment, at least in name. During incarceration the wrongdoer may be required to participate in treatment programs or self-help groups such as Alcoholics Anonymous. Probationers may be required to go to drug-treatment programs; they may even be required to get their GED or obtain some type of job training. In addition to formal punishments, there are extra-legal, informal punishments that should not exist but, unfortunately, do exist. Inmates are raped and beaten, more often by other inmates, but sometimes by guards. Their property is destroyed. They get sick or injured and receive no treatment. Prisoner advocates maintain that these events should never be part of the formal punishment of prison, but others believe that the prisoner "shouldn't do the crime if he (or she) can't do the time."

According to one author (Leiser, 1986: 198), five elements are essential to the definition of **punishment**:

1. There are at least two persons—one who inflicts the punishment and one who is punished.
2. The person who inflicts the punishment causes a certain harm to the person who is being punished.
3. The person who inflicts the punishment has been authorized, under a system of rules or laws, to harm the person who is punished in this particular way.
4. The person who is being punished has been judged by a representative of that authority to have done what he or she is forbidden to do or failed to do what he or she is required to do by some relevant rule or law.
5. The harm that is inflicted upon the person who is being punished is specifically for the act or omission mentioned in Condition 4.

We also need to define **treatment**. According to correctional terminology, treatment may be anything used to induce behavioral change. The goal is to eliminate dysfunctional or deviant behavior and to encourage productive and normal behavior patterns. In prison, treatment includes diagnosis, classification, therapy, education, religious activity, vocational training, and self-helpgroups.

The infliction of punishment and even treatment is usually limited by some rationale or guideline. For instance, von Hirsch (1976: 5) presents the following restrictive guidelines:

1. The liberty of each individual is to be protected as long as it is consistent with the liberty of others.
2. The state is obligated to observe strict parsimony in intervening in criminals' lives.
3. The state must justify each intrusion.
4. The requirements of justice ought to constrain the pursuit of crime prevention (that is, deterrence and rehabilitation).

In this chapter we will first explore the various rationales for punishment, briefly discuss capital punishment in particular, and discuss private corrections. In Chapter 13 we will examine ethical issues related to institutional corrections. In Chapter 14 we will discuss ethical issues relevant to community corrections and also discuss the concept of restorative justice.

RATIONALES FOR PUNISHMENT AND CORRECTIONS

Does society have the right to punish or correct miscreants? If it does, where does that right come from? The rationale for punishment and corrections comes from the social contract. In the same way that the social contract forms the basis for police power, it also provides a rationale for further control in the form of punishment and corrections. Recall that according to this theory, we avoid social chaos by giving the state the power to control us. In this way we protect ourselves from being victimized by others by giving up our liberty to aggress against others. If we do step outside the bounds, the state has the right to control and punish us for our transgressions. Concurrently, the state is limited in the amount of control it can exert over individuals. To be consistent with the social contract, the state should exert its power only to accomplish the purpose of protection; any further interventions in civil liberties are unwarranted.

Corrections pursues a mixture of goals, including retribution, reform, incapacitation, deterrence, and rehabilitation. The longstanding argument between proponents of punishment and proponents of treatment reveals a system without a clear mandate or rationale for action. Garland (1990) writes that the state's goal of punishment is problematic because it is marked with inconsistencies between the intent and the implementation. The moral contradictions are that it seeks to uphold freedom by means of its deprivation, and it punishes private violence by inflicting state violence. Can treatment and punishment occur at the same time? Some argue that because punishment has the goal of inflicting pain on an individual, it is fundamentally incompatible with the goal of treatment. This question is much different from whether or not treatment does exist in prison or is effective.

One of the most problematic issues in justifying what we do in the name of punishment is that what we do to offenders changes over time (and place). If what is considered to be appropriate punishment changes, how can any particular punishment be considered to be just under some form of universalism or natural law theory? In other words, in earlier centuries we might have hung a pickpocket. Was that just, or is it just today to incarcerate the person? Is it just to incarcerate drug users today when in times past (or, perhaps, in future times) they would not be imprisoned at all? Prisoners in different prisons have vastly different sentences. How can the worst prison be fair if it is just chance whether a prisoners ends up there or in a prison with better living conditions?

Since the emergence of penitentiaries in this country, we can see recurring cycles of emphasis. Reform is replaced with retribution and then swings back again. In our current punitive cycle we have virtually abandoned rehabilitation as a goal. Can a punishment system in which the definition of "just" punishment is relative and changes with time ever be considered an ethical or moral one? We simply do not seem to agree on what an individual offender deserves; therefore, specific punishments for similar crimes vary according to time, place, persons involved, and other factors.

An important question to ask is: "Whom are we punishing?" Studies show that only a small minority of individuals who commit crimes end up in prison; furthermore, we may assume that those numbers are not representative of the larger population. Those in our jails and prisons are there not only because they committed crimes but also because they are poor, members of a minority group, or powerless. Certain types of criminals tend to avoid the more punitive sanctions of the corrections system. For instance, businesses routinely bilk consumers out of billions of dollars annually and chalk up the punitive fines imposed to operating expenses; property offenders in prison cost us far less, but we punish them more severely.

Streams and land are routinely polluted by industrial waste but, again, punitive fines are the typical sanctions, and these cannot begin to restore what has been taken away in the flagrant pursuit of financial profit. Such costs are typically passed on to the consumers, so taxpayers suffer the crime and then also pay the fine.

Seldom do we see executives responsible for company policy go to prison. White-collar criminals routinely receive fines, probation, or short stays in halfway houses, whereas so-called street criminals receive prison sentences. In the Enron and WorldCom scandals there were some very public arrests and promises of prosecutions, but in the subsequent years few of the initial actors served prison time.

Long ago, criminals were viewed as sinners with no ability to change their behavior, so punishment and incapacitation were seen as the only logical ways to respond to crime. Jeremy Bentham (1748–1833) and Cesare Beccaria (1738–1794) viewed the criminal as rational and as having free will and, therefore, saw the threat of punishment as a deterrent. Neoclassicists such as Adolphe Quetelet (1796–1894) and Andre Guerry (1802–1866) recognized that insane persons and juveniles could not be held entirely responsible for their actions and, therefore, believed that they should not be punished. Those who were insane and the young were treated differently because they were considered to be moral infants, not possessing the sense to refrain from wrongdoing.

In the 1800s, the positivist school looked for differences between criminals and non-criminals. This search for differences eventually, in the 1960s and 1970s, led to the short-lived rehabilitative era and the **treatment ethic**—the idea that all criminal acts were symptoms of an underlying pathology. The treatment programs created in the last hundred years or so operate under the assumption that we can do something to offenders to reduce their criminal activity. That "something" may involve

- treating a psychological problem, such as a sociopathic or paranoid personality
- addressing social problems, such as alcoholism or addiction
- resolving more pragmatic problems, such as chronic unemployment, with vocational training and job placement.

Obviously, the perception of the criminal influences the rationale for correction and punishment.

The two major justifications for punishment and treatment are **retribution** and **prevention**. The retributive rationale postulates that punishment is an end in itself, whereas the prevention approach views punishment as a means rather than an end and embraces other responses to crime. The retributive rationale is probably more consistent with a view of the criminal as rational, and the prevention rationale, with certain exceptions, is more consistent with the view of the criminal as somehow less responsible for his or her behavior, both morally and legally.

RETRIBUTION

As mentioned before, the social contract provides the rationale for punishment. Members of society implicitly agree to society's rules and right to punish. One criticism of the social contract theory is that it is completely contingent on a consensus perspective of society. That is, members of society are assumed to share the same goals, beliefs, and power. All people benefit from the social contract because they get to keep what they've got, with the assumption that what they've got is fairly equally distributed.

Conversely, those who adhere to the conflict perspective view society as being made up of a number of conflicting groups; when one wins, the other loses, because their interests can never be the same. Under conflict theory there is less reason for some people to agree to the social contract. Those who do not benefit from the opportunities of society receive no advantage from their agreement not to aggress against others; thus, they may not agree to or be individually bound by the state's right to punish. Conflict theorists, then, would not subscribe necessarily to the social contract rationale for punishment.

The retributive rationale for punishment is consistent with the social contract theory. Simply stated, the retributive rationale is that the individual offender must be punished because he or she deserves it. Mackie (1982: 4) describes three specific types of retribution:

1. *Negative retribution* dictates that one who is not guilty must not be punished for a crime.
2. *Positive retribution* demands that one who is guilty ought to be punished.
3. *Permissive retribution* allows that one who is guilty *may* be punished.

This formulation states that retribution may support punishment but may also limit it. There are limits as to who may be punished (only those who commit crimes) and restrictions on the amount of punishment (only that sufficient to balance the wrong). Further, this formulation implies that punishment need not be administered in all cases. The exceptions, although not discussed by Mackie, may involve the concepts of mercy or diminished responsibility.

Our system of justice was created to take the place of private vengeance. We do not allow victims to seek their own revenge but, rather, replace *hot vengeance* with *cool justice*, dispassionate in its determination and distribution. The social contract supports the notion that it is intrinsically right for the state, rather than the victim's family, to execute a killer. The state has taken over the necessary task of punishment to ensure the survival of society by preventing private vengeance. Intentionally inflicting pain on another is an evil, but not if it meets the definitional elements of retributive punishment.

Another retributivist justification for punishment is that it is the only way the individual can achieve salvation. Thus, we owe the offender punishment because only through suffering can atonement occur, and only through atonement or **expiation** can the offender achieve a state of grace. Some would strongly object to this interpretation of religious ethics and argue that Christianity, while supportive of just punishment, does not necessarily support suffering as the only way to achieve a state of grace: There must be repentance, and there is also room for forgiveness.

One other view consistent with retribution is that punishment balances the advantage gained by a wrongdoer. The criminal act distorts the balance and parity of social relationships, and only a punishment or similar deprivation can restore the natural balance that existed before the criminal act. As discussed in Chapter 4, there

IN THE NEWS | **NO MERCY!**

Carla Faye Tucker was executed by the state of Texas in 1998. Her crime was a gruesome double murder. Many people across the world, including the Pope, argued that she should be spared the death penalty because (a) she was a born-again Christian, (b) she was truly repentant, (c) she committed her crime in a drug- and alcohol-induced haze, and (d) she was an abused child whose mother introduced her to prostitution at the age of twelve.

Do you believe that the Board of Pardons and Paroles and Governor George W. Bush should have commuted her sentence to life in prison? If not, for what sort of person should the power of commutation be reserved?

is always the possibility of mercy in any justice and punishment system. But mercy is not automatic, as the "In the News" box illustrates.

The question of whether to punish the crime or the criminal is longstanding and important in any discussion of retributive punishment. Jeremy Bentham believed that each criminal offense deserves a measure of punishment calculated to balance the potential pleasure or profit of the criminal offense. However, the neo-classicists allowed some characteristics of the offender (being young or insane) to influence the punishment decision. This debate continues today with those who argue for determinate sentencing over indeterminate sentencing.

Determinate sentencing punishes the offense, with the length of the sentence determined by the seriousness of the crime. **Indeterminate sentencing** was created so the offenders' punishment could be adjusted to how quickly they reformed. In most states, judges have a great deal of discretion so they can tailor the punishment to fit the individual offender. A young offender might get a second chance because he has the potential to change; a woman might receive probation instead of prison because she has an infant to take care of; a habitual criminal might be the unhappy recipient of an increased sentence because he is considered unsalvageable. Arguably, this type of individualized justice is inconsistent with a retributive rationale because punishment is based on *who* the criminal is rather than on *what* the crime was.

What is an appropriate amount of punishment? This is a difficult question even for the retributivist. The difference between a year in prison and two years in prison is measurable only by the number of days on the calendar, not by how it is experienced by different people. Should this be considered during sentencing? Punishment of any kind affects individuals differently. For instance, a whipping may be worse than death for someone with a low tolerance for pain, better than prison for someone with a great need for freedom, and perhaps even pleasurable for someone who enjoys physical pain. Prison may be experienced as an inconvenience for some, and such a traumatic experience for others that it may induce suicide. Our current system of justice seldom recognizes these individual vulnerabilities or sensitivities to various punishments.

Sentencing studies routinely show little or no agreement regarding the type or amount of punishment appropriate for a wrongdoer. Disparity in sentencing is such a problem that many reforms have been aimed at reducing or even eliminating judges' discretion, such as determinate sentencing and sentencing guidelines. Yet, when legislators take on the task themselves by setting determinate sentences, their decisions are arrived at by obscure methods, probably more influenced by political pressure and compromise than by the need for the application of fair and equitable standards.

The justice model and the just deserts model, developed in the late 1970s and early 1980s, led the way to the current punitive era. Basically, the **justice model** holds that individuals are rational and that, even though free will may not exist perfectly, the concept must serve as a basis for the criminal law. Punishment is to be used for retribution, not deterrence, treatment, or any other purpose. Finally, prisoners should be seen as volitional, responsible humans, not as patients (Fogel, 1975).

The justice model came about partly as a backlash to the abuses of discretion that characterized the rehabilitative era of the 1970s. It promoted a degree of predictability and equality in sentencing by reverting to earlier retributive goals of punishment and restricted the state's right to use treatment as a criterion for release.

The **just deserts model**, appearing about the same time as the justice model, was also retributive and based punishment on "commensurate deserts" (von Hirsch, 1976: xxvi). As the spokesperson for this view, von Hirsch (1985: 138) disagreed with combining retributive and deterrent or incapacitative goals. Crimes should be weighed in seriousness, according to von Hirsch, based on their recidivism potential. Offenders who commit similar crimes should be punished equally, but the rank ordering of crimes is determined by recidivistic potential. This system, categorical incapacitation, combines deserts and prevention but in a way that, according to von Hirsch, is not unjust to the individual offender. Von Hirsch continued to champion the retributive rationale for punishment well into the 1990s, despite what he called the **new rehabilitationists**, who advocate treatment (von Hirsch, 1985: 150; von Hirsch and Maher, 1992).

Garland (1990) offered a different view, proposing that the emphasis of society should be on socializing and educating citizens. The punishment that was still necessary for those who broke the law should be viewed as morally expressive rather than instrumental and should be retributive rather than attempt prevention goals. Feeney (2005) continues this idea that sentencing should be purely retributive, and be "morally significant" in that it expresses condemnation of the behavior. Both of these writers are similar to the earlier just deserts theorists in that they believe punishment should be retributive rather than serve the goals of deterrence.

The early writing of von Hirsch and the other just deserts theorists supported and, perhaps, served as a justification for the increasing punitiveness of the justice system in this country. Certainly, today, rehabilitation seems to be merely a footnote in the goals and mission of corrections. Our current time has been described as the era of **penal harm**; this refers to the idea that the system intentionally inflicts pain on offenders during their imprisonment, because merely depriving them of liberty is not considered sufficiently painful (Clear, 1996; Cullen, 1995).

No one doubts that we have become more punitive in sentencing and that offenders are serving more time in prison. Any current book on prisons will illustrate the tremendous increase in incarceration rates (see, e.g.,Pollock, 2004). The interested reader can also go to government sources, such as the Bureau of Justice Statistics, to see how imprisonment patterns have changed over the years. From

IN THE NEWS | NO MERCY! PART 2

Jackie Lee Thompson killed his girlfriend in 1969, when they were both fifteen. He was sentenced to life in prison. During the next thirty-five years he learned carpentry, masonry, plumbing, welding, mechanics, and electric wiring. He earned a high school diploma and an associate's degree. He displayed exemplary behavior. He earned the support of a prison official who offered him a job and place to stay. Even the victim's father asked the parole board to release him. The parole board refused. "We can forgive him …why can't you?" asked the victim's father.

What factors should be considered in deciding when someone should be paroled? If the facts that the offender was fifteen, the victim's family wanted the release, and exemplary prison behavior aren't the criteria, what are the criteria?

Source: Liptak, 2005: A7.

---

about 150 per 100,000 in the 1980s, we now incarcerate almost five times as many per 100,000 (BJS, 2006). In the current era, there seems to be very little room for mercy or redemption, as the "In the News" box illustrates.

PREVENTION

Three common justifications or rationales for punishment can all be subsumed under a general heading of "prevention." Prevention assumes that something should be done to the offender to prevent future criminal activity. There are three possible methods of prevention:

1. deterrence
2. incapacitation
3. treatment

Each of these goals is based on certain assumptions that must be considered in addition to the relevant moral questions. For instance, it is a factual question as to whether people can be deterred from crime, but it is a moral question as to what we should do to an individual to ensure deterrence.

Deterrence   There are two types of deterrence. **Specific deterrence** is what is done to offenders to prevent them from deciding to commit another offense. **General deterrence** is what is done to an offender to prevent others from deciding to engage in wrongful behavior. The first teaches through punishment; the second teaches by example.

Our right to deter an individual offender is rooted in the same rationale used to support retribution. By virtue of membership in society, individuals submit themselves to society's controls. If we think that someone's actions are damaging, we will try various means to persuade him or her to cease that activity. The implicit assumption of a deterrence philosophy is that in the absence of controls, society would revert to a jungle-like, dangerous "war of all against all"; we need the police and official punishments to keep us in line. Under this rationale, the true nature of humankind is perceived to be predatory and held in check only by external controls. Deterrence advocates support deterrence as a justification of punishment.

QUOTE AND QUERY

1. Those who violate others' rights deserve punishment.

2. However, there is a countervailing moral obligation not to deliberately add to the amount of human suffering, and punishment creates suffering.

3. Deterrence results in preventing more misery than it creates, thereby justifying punishment.

Adapted from von Hirsch, 1976: 54

Is this utilitarian thinking or ethical formalism? Explain your answer.

The "Quote and Query" box enumerates the key points of view in this justification for punishment.

The rationale of specific deterrence depends on the effectiveness of punishment in deterring future behavior. Unfortunately, it is difficult to find any studies that show that anything we do to the offender, whether under the heading of punishment or treatment, has any predictable effect on subsequent behavior. Arguments are set forth that punishment doesn't deter because it is inconsistent, uncertain, and slow. If punishment were to be applied more consistently and more swiftly, the argument goes, we would see a deterrent effect.

The support for general deterrence is even more problematic. First, it becomes much harder to justify even if there is evidence. If we know that a term of imprisonment will not deter an offender but can deter others, can it still be justified? A clear example of this situation is the so-called passion murderer who probably does not need specific deterrence because the chance of killing again is slim. However, he or she is usually given a long sentence to make it clear that killing will not be tolerated. (There is, of course, also a good retributive rationale for the long sentence.) Under deterrence theory the offender is only a tool to teach a lesson to the rest of us. The sociologist Emile Durkheim believed that the value of criminals is in establishing the parameters of acceptable behavior. Their punishment helps the rest of us define what is "good."

If one's goal is purely general deterrence, there does not necessarily have to be an original crime. Consider a futuristic society wherein the evening news routinely shows or describes the punishments received by a variety of criminals. The crime—or the punishment, for that matter—does not have to be real to be effective. If punishing innocent people for crimes they *might* do were just as effective as punishing criminal offenders, this action might satisfy the ends of deterrence but would obviously not be acceptable under any system of ethics—except perhaps act utilitarianism. The movie *Minority Report* presented a somewhat related ethical issue in that it portrayed a future where the government knew ahead of time when individuals would commit a crime and punished them for what they were going to do. The idea of punishing an individual for reasons other than their own acts seems wrong because it violates the retributive justification of punishment.

Incapacitation   Another purpose of punishment is to prevent further crime through **incapacitation**. Strictly speaking, incapacitation does not fit the classical definition of punishment, for the purpose is not to inflict pain but only to hold an offender until there is no risk of further crime. The major issue concerning incapacitation is prediction. Unfortunately, our ability to predict is no better for incapacitative purposes than it is for deterrence purposes. Two possible mistakes are: releasing an offender who commits further crimes, and not releasing an offender who would not commit further crimes.

Carrying the goal of incapacitation to its logical conclusion, one would not have to commit a crime at all to be declared potentially dangerous and subject to incapacitation. We now incarcerate career criminals, not for their last offense but for what they might do in the future. We justify habitual-felon laws by the prediction that these criminals will continue to commit crimes. Some argue that a small group of offenders commit a disproportionate share of crime and that those individuals can be identified by predictive elements such as prior convictions, prior incarcerations, juvenile convictions and detentions, use of heroin or barbiturates, and lack of employment (Greenwood, 1982). Selective incapacitation is a policy of incarcerating these individuals for longer periods of time than other criminals. More recent studies, however, have indicated that our ability to predict who would commit further crime is actually poor, with an error rate of 48 percent! (Auerhahn, 1999). Obviously, there are grave ethical issues in using these predictive devices to increase sentences when the error rate is so high.

Three-strikes laws are a type of selective incapacitation. These laws are defended under an incapacitative rationale because it is argued that these individuals are more likely to commit future crimes so they should be held for long periods of time. More than half of all states now have some type of three-strikes or habitual-offender laws, but only a few states, such as California, have used their laws to any great extent (King and Mauer, 2001).

Critics argue that for both practical and ethical reasons, the California three-strikes sentence is bad policy. It incarcerates those who are past their crime-prone-age years; it incarcerates nonviolent offenders for long periods of time; and it is so expensive that it draws resources away from other social needs, such as schools. Further, it is unfairly disproportionate to the crime. Some offenders have committed fairly minor third felonies and then received twenty-five years to life in prison (King and Mauer, 2001; Zimring, Hawkins, and Kamin, 2001). Another troubling aspect of three-strikes laws is that African Americans tend to be disproportionately affected (Cole, 1999).

The U.S. Supreme Court ruled in March 2003 that California's three-strikes law was not grossly disproportionate and deferred to the state's authority in setting punishments (*Lockyer v. Andrade*, 538 U.S. 63 [2003] and *Ewing v. California*, 538 U.S. 11 [2003]). Clearly, if three-strikes laws are changed, it will be through state courts ruling that the long sentences violate state constitutional rights or state legislatures changing the law. In the Policy Box, the law, policy, and ethics of the three-strikes movement are untangled.

Treatment   If we can find justification for the right to punish, can we also find justification for treatment? Treatment is considered to be beneficial to the individual offender as well as to society. This is a very different approach from the moral rejection implicit in retributive punishment. Treatment implies acceptance rather than rejection, support rather than hatred. However, the control over the individual is just as great as with punishment; some people would say it is even greater.

POLICY BOX | **THREE STRIKES**

Many states have three-strikes legislation, yet the majority of the public is probably not aware that this is not a new type of sentencing but has been around for a long time. The basic assumption is that the second or third felony is more serious than the first felony and/or that punishment must be made harsher because it did not deter the first time. The first is a deontological rationale; the second is a utilitarian rationale. Opponents argue that it is contrary to our justice system in that it punishes the offenders twice for the same offense.

Law: With the rulings by the Supreme Court, it is clear that no federal constitutional right is violated by a state habitual-criminal sentencing law. State courts could interpret state constitutional rights to be broader, and legislatures, of course, can change the law if the public pressures them to do so.

Policy: There is great disparity between jurisdictions in how prosecutors apply habitual sentencing laws. Some jurisdictions account for the majority of three-strikes offenders in the system, while others use it hardly at all. Thus, whether or not an offender receives a life sentence may depend, partially, on the county or state in which the crime was committed. As long as prosecutors have discretion in whether or not to charge under three-strikes statutes, such disparity will continue. Some argue also that three-strikes and habitual-offender laws are used disproportionately against minorities.

Ethics: Although prosecutors have discretion in whether or not to charge offenders under three-strikes statutes, there are ethical and unethical criteria for such decisions. Ethical criteria would be the danger posed to the public based on the felonies the offender has committed, whereas unethical criteria would include political pressure or the race of the offender.

What is treatment? We sometimes consider anything experienced after the point of sentencing to be treatment, including education, prison discipline, and religious services. Can treatment be experimental? Must it be effective to be considered treatment? A court was obliged to define treatment in *Knecht v. Gillman*, 488 F.2d 1136 (1973). Inmates challenged the state's right to use apomorphine, a drug that induces extreme nausea and a feeling of imminent death, as a form of aversive conditioning. In its holding the court stated that calling something "treatment" did not remove it from Eighth Amendment scrutiny. In other words, merely labeling some infliction of pain as treatment would not necessarily render it immune from legal challenge. Treatment was further defined as that which constitutes accepted and standard practice and which could reasonably result in a "cure."

The Supreme Court has also ruled on whether prison officials could administer antipsychotic drugs against the will of the prisoner. Despite arguments that even prisoners had an inherent right to be free from such intrusive control, the court held, in *Washington v. Harper*, 494 U.S. 210 (1990), that an inmate's right to refuse such medication did not outweigh the state's need to administer it if there was a showing that the inmate posed a security risk.

What we think needs to be cured is another issue. Recall the discussion of whether our society could be characterized by consensus or conflict. Treating a deviant may be justifiable if one believes that society is basically homogeneous in its values and beliefs, but viewed from a conflict perspective, treatment may look more like brainwashing and a coercive use of power. Civil libertarians would point out that it is no accident that political dissidents in totalitarian states are often handled as if they have mental problems and are treated with mind-altering drugs and other brainwashing regimens. The greater intrusiveness inherent in treating the mind is sometimes considered worse than punishment.

According to some experts, treatment can be effective only if it is voluntary; others disagree. It is true that much of the treatment that inmates and other correctional clients participate in is either implicitly or directly coerced. Providing treatment for those who want it is one thing; requiring those who are resistant to participate in psychotherapy, group therapy, or religious activities is quite another. It is not justifiable under a retributivist ethical system. Is it consistent with a prevention perspective? The answer is yes, as long as the results support the intervention.

The evaluation literature on rehabilitative treatment programs could fill a room. We now have more than forty years of evaluations, as well as dozens of meta-analyses, and a number of sources that reviewed the research (see, for instance, Pollock, 2004; Palmer, 1994). It is simply not true that "nothing works," as was widely believed through the 1980s and 1990s. However, what works is more complicated than one program for all offenders. One interesting finding that comes from evaluation research is that, evidently, sometimes a program works because of the staff characteristics, not the modality of the program. Thus, we can see again that the individual ethics and performance of public servants (treatment professionals in corrections) have a great deal to do with how well the system (in this case, treatment) works.

ETHICAL FRAMEWORKS FOR CORRECTIONS

The various rationales for punishment just described are well established, and can be found in corrections textbooks. The ethical systems that were introduced in Chapter 2 are discussed less commonly in corrections texts, but they form the underlying philosophical rationale for the goals or missions of retribution and prevention (including deterrence, incapacitation, and treatment).

UTILITARIANISM

The principle of utilitarianism is often used to support the last three rationales of punishment: deterrence, incapacitation, and treatment. According to utilitarianism, punishing or treating the criminal offender benefits society, and this benefit outweighs the negative effect on the individual offender. It is a teleological argument because the morality of the punishment is determined by the consequences derived—reduced crime. Jeremy Bentham was the major proponent of the utilitarian theory of punishment and established basic guidelines for its use.

Bentham believed that punishment works when it is applied rationally to rational people, but is not acceptable when the person did not make a rational decision

| BOX 12.1 | BENTHAM'S RULES OF PUNISHMENT |

1. The value of the punishment must not be less, in any case, than what is sufficient to outweigh that of the profit of the offense.
2. The greater the mischief of the offense, the greater is the expense it may be worthwhile to be at, in the way of punishment.
3. When two offenses come in competition, the punishment for the greater offense must be sufficient to induce a man to prefer the less.
4. The punishment should be adjusted in such manner to each particular offense, that for every part of the mischief there may be a motive to restrain the offender from giving birth to it.
5. The punishment ought in no case to be more than what is necessary to bring it into conformity with the rules here given.
6. That the quantity of punishment actually inflicted on each individual offender may correspond to the quantity intended for similar offenders in general, the several circumstances influencing sensibility ought always to be taken into the account.
7. That the value of the punishment may outweigh the profit of the offense, it must be increased in point of magnitude, in proportion as it falls short in point of certainty.
8. Punishment must be further increased in point of magnitude, in proportion as it falls short of proximity.
9. When the act is conclusively indicative of a habit, such an increase must be given to the punishment as may enable it to outweigh the profit, not only of the individual offense, but of such other like offenses as are likely to have been committed with impunity by the same offender.
10. When a punishment, which in point of quality is particularly well calculated to answer its intention, cannot exist in less than a certain quantity, it may sometimes be of issue, for the sake of employing it, to stretch a little beyond that quantity which, on other accounts, would be strictly necessary.
11. In particular, this may be the case where the punishment proposed is of such a nature as to be particularly well calculated to answer the purpose of a moral lesson.
12. In adjusting the quantum of punishment, the circumstances by which all punishment may be rendered unprofitable ought to be attended to.
13. Among provisions designated to perfect the proportion between punishments and offenses, if any occur which by their own particular good effects would not make up for the harm they would do by adding to the intricacy of the code, they should be omitted.

Source: Bentham, 1843/1970.

to commit the crime, such as when the law forbidding the action was passed after the act occurred, the law was unknown, the person was acting under compulsion, or the person was an infant, insane, or intoxicated (Bentham, 1970; also see Beccaria, 1977). The utility of the punishment would be lost in these cases; therefore, punishment could not be justified (Borchert and Stewart, 1986: 317). "Bentham's Rules of Punishment" are described in Box 12.1.

All of Bentham's rules ensure that punishments are acceptable to the utilitarian framework. The basic formula provides that the utility of punishment to society outweighs the negative of the punishment itself. Utilitarian theory also supports treatment and incapacitation if these can be shown to benefit society. If, for instance, treatment and punishment were to have equal amounts of utility for society, treatment would be the more ethical choice because it has a less negative

IN THE NEWS | IT'S JUST A "JOKE"

According to Dale Payne, black prisoners in the Texas prison system are subjected to a pattern of taunts, beatings, and other abuse. The last straw was when a correctional officer shocked the prisoner with a cattle prod as a "joke." The prisoner filed a lawsuit against the officer and the corrections system, acting as his own attorney. Although the officer was suspended for two days without pay, he since has been promoted to sergeant. The suit was dismissed by a federal appeals court but was reinstated by the Fifth Circuit, which held that the infliction of pain induced by the cattle prod may be found by a jury to be malicious and unnecessary.

Source: Ward, 2007.

effect on the individual. Likewise, if incapacitation and punishment would be equally effective in protecting and providing utility to society, the choice with the least negative utility would be the ethical one.

If it can be shown that imprisonment, for instance, results in a greater disutility than utility for the individual and society, it cannot be justified under utilitarianism. To take a simple example: Let us assume that an offender committed a theft of $500 and was sentenced to a year in jail. The year in jail may cost us around $18,000. Utilitarians might argue, on the one hand, that we prevented a number of other crimes by this offender that would exceed $18,000. On the other hand, it could be argued that the offender lost his legitimate job and, once released, may engage in crimes that he would not have committed otherwise, thereby increasing the total cost to society. From this simple example one can see that the utilitarian calculation of the benefits of punishment is very complicated because we need to predict what might happen in the future.

Some argue that the harms inherent in imprisonment in either jail or prison are so extreme (such as what is described in the "In the News" box) that they must be counterbalanced by rehabilitative programs in order to result in a greater good (Kleinig, 2001b). It is certainly true that minor offenders should not be incarcerated because the harm caused by incarceration far exceeds the harm they caused to a victim or society. It is also problematic when drug users are incarcerated because it is hard to identify the harm caused to others by their actions, especially as weighed against the harms that they may endure in this nation's jails and prisons, such as beatings, economic exploitation, rapes, and gratuitous abuse by correctional officers.

ETHICAL FORMALISM

Contrast the utilitarian views toward punishment with Kant's views. Ethical formalism clearly supports a retributive view of punishment. It is deontological because it is concerned not with the consequences of the punishment or treatment, only its inherent morality. It would support the idea that a criminal is owed punishment because to do otherwise would not be according him or her equal respect as a human. However, the punishment should not be used as a means to any other end but retribution. Treatment is not supported by ethical formalism because

QUOTE AND QUERY

Juridical punishment ... can be inflicted on a criminal, never just as instrumental to the achievement of some other good for the criminal himself or for the civil society, but only because he has committed a crime; for a man may never be used just as a means to the end of another person.... Penal law is a categorical imperative, and woe to him who crawls through the serpentine maze of utilitarian theory in order to find an excuse, in some advantage to someone, for releasing the criminal from punishment or any degree of it, in line with the pharisaical proverb "it is better that one man die than that a whole people perish"; for if justice perishes, there is no more value in man living on the earth....What mode and degree of punishment, then, is the principle and standard of public justice? Nothing but the principle of equality....

Thus, whatever undeserved evil you inflict on another person, you inflict on yourself. . . .

Immanuel Kant, quoted in Borchert and Stewart, 1986: 322

Do you understand what Kant was trying to say? Rephrase the passage to make it more simple and current.

---

it uses the offender as a means to protect society. The "Quote and Query" box presents Immanuel Kant's views.

Several arguments support this retributive rationale. First, Mackie (1982) discusses the universal aspects of punishment: The urge to react in a hostile manner to harm is an element inherent in human nature; therefore, one might say that punishment is a natural law. Another supporting argument is found in the principle of forfeiture, which postulates that when one intrudes on an innocent person's rights, one forfeits a proportional amount of one's own rights. By restraining or hurting a victim in some way, the aggressor forfeits his or her own liberty; in other words, he or she forfeits the right to be free from punishment (Bedau, 1982).

ETHICS OF CARE

The ethics of care would probably not support punishment unless it was essential to help the offender become a better person. This ethical system defines good as that which meets everyone's needs—victims and offenders alike. It forms the rationale for punishments that one might find under restorative justice programs, which will be discussed more fully in Chapter 14.

Several authors have discussed the ethics of care in relation to the justice and corrections system. For instance, Heidensohn (1986) and Daly (1989) discuss differences in the perception of justice from a care perspective versus a retributive perspective—as female and male perceptions, respectively. The female care perspective emphasizes needs, motives, and relationships, while the male retributive perspective emphasizes rights, responsibilities, and punishments.

The corrections system, ideally, should be supported by a caring ethic because it takes into account offender needs. Community corrections, especially, emphasizes the relationship of the offender to the community. From this perspective one should help the offender to become a better person because that is what a caring and committed relationship would entail. Retributive punishment and deterrence are not consistent with the ethics of care. However, some say that retribution and a care ethic are not, nor should they be considered, in opposition to each other. Restorative justice might be considered the merger of the two in that this approach views the offender as responsible for the wrong committed, but the responsibility is satisfied by reparation to the victim rather than by punishment and pain.

RAWLSIAN ETHICS

John Rawls presents an alternative to utilitarianism and retributivism. Rawls's defense of punishment starts with Kant's proposition that no one should be treated as a means, and with the idea that each should have an "equal right to the most extensive basic liberty compatible with a similar liberty to others." According to Rawls, a loss of rights should take place only when it is consistent with the best interests of the least advantaged. Rules regarding punishment would be as follows (cited in Hickey and Scharf, 1980: 169):

1. We must punish only to the extent that the loss of liberty would be agreeable were one not to know whether one were to be the criminal, the victim, or a member of the general public [the veil of ignorance].
2. The loss of liberty must be justified as the minimum loss consistent with maintenance of the same liberty among others.

Furthermore, when the advantage shifts—when the offender instead of the victim or society becomes the one with the least advantage—punishment must cease. This theory leaves a lot of unanswered questions. For instance, if victims were chosen carefully (e.g., only those who would not suffer financially or emotionally) and the criminal were from an impoverished background, the criminal would still be at a disadvantage and, thus, not morally accountable for his or her actions. This rationale for punishment promotes the idea that the criminal act creates an imbalance between offender and victim, and that punishment should be concerned with regaining that balance. The utilitarian thread in this proposition is that by having this check-and-balance system in determining punishment, all of society benefits.

PUNISHMENT

We have discarded many punishments that were acceptable in earlier times, such as flogging, hanging, banishment, branding, cutting off limbs, drawing and quartering, and pillories and stocks. Although we still believe that society has the right to punish, what we do in the name of punishment has changed substantially. As a society, we became gradually uncomfortable with inflicting physically painful punishments on offenders, and as these punishments were discarded, imprisonment was used as the substitute.

Inside prison we have only relatively recently abandoned physical punishments as a method of control (at least formally), but that is not to say that prisons are not injurious. In addition to the informal corporal punishments that are inflicted by officers and fellow inmates, prison is painful because it consists of banishment and condemnation; it means separation from loved ones and involves the total loss of freedom. More subtly, it is an assault on one's self-esteem and prevents the individual from almost all forms of self-definition, such as father, mother, professional, and so on. About the only self-definition left is as a prison "tough guy" (or woman)—a stance that destroys the spirit and reduces the individual to a baser form of humanity.

The rate of imprisonment has increased tremendously during the last thirty years. In most states the amount of money directed to justice and corrections has increased while the amount of the budget directed to education and social services has decreased. Some argue that the costs are justified and have resulted in the reduction in crime that we have seen, beginning in the early- to mid-90s and continuing through the mid-2000s; others argue that there does not seem to be a relationship between correctional spending and decreased crime rates, or that the effect is modest and the crime rate has been affected by other social factors (Austin and Fabelo, 2004). Note that it is a utilitarian question as to whether we are now paying "too much" to keep people locked up (comparing the cost to the benefit of reduced crime or incapacitation). Whether all of the two million people in jails and prisons "deserve" to be locked up is a retributive, deontological question.

HUMANE PUNISHMENT

The Eighth Amendment protects all Americans from **cruel and unusual punishment**. Although what is "cruel and unusual" is vague, several tests have been used to define the terms, such as the following, discussed in *Furman v. Georgia*, 408 U.S. 238, 92 S.Ct. 2726, 33 L.Ed.2d 346 (1972):

1. *Unusual* (by frequency): Punishments that are rarely, if ever, used thus become unusual if used against one individual or a group. They become arbitrary punishments because the decision to use them is so infrequent.
2. *Evolving standards of decency*: Civilization is evolving, and punishments considered acceptable in the past century are no longer acceptable in this century.
3. *Shock the conscience*: A yardstick for all punishment is to test it against the public conscience. If people are naturally repelled by the punishment, it must be cruel and unusual by definition.
4. *Excessive or disproportionate*: Any punishment that is excessive to its purpose or disproportionately administered is considered wrong.
5. *Unnecessary*: Again, we are looking at the purpose of the punishment in relation to what is done. If the purpose of punishment is to deter crime, we should administer only an amount necessary to do so. If the purpose is to protect and the offender presents no danger, prison should not be used.

These tests have eliminated the use of the whip and the branding iron, yet some say that we may have done nothing to move toward humane punishment and that, instead, we may have moved away from it. It may be that corporal punishment, at least the less drastic kinds such as whipping, is actually less harmful than a prison sentence. After all, a whipping takes perhaps days or weeks to get over, but a prison sentence may last years and affect all future earnings.

Some sentences given to offenders, especially some conditions attached to a probation sentence, have been criticized as being inhumane. Although typical probation conditions include performing community service, paying court costs and/or restitution, finding employment, and submitting to drug tests, other conditions are more problematic. Someone convicted of driving while intoxicated (DWI) may be required to donate blood to a blood bank, but if he or she has a phobia about needles or is a Jehovah's Witness, this punishment may be worse than jail. So-called "shaming" conditions include DWI offenders' having special license plates that indicate to other drivers that the driver has been convicted of DWI, probation officers putting up signs in the yard or nailing them to the door of convicted sex offenders warning people that a sex offender lives there, announcing to one's church congregation one's criminal conviction and asking for forgiveness, and taking out an advertisement in the town newspaper for the same purpose. These conditions are rarely challenged in court because the offender usually prefers them to a prison sentence. However, there is some question as to the legal authority for such conditions (Book, 1999).

We could also examine these conditions in light of the ethical systems discussed earlier. One real question concerning the "shaming" conditions is the effect that such conditions have on family members of offenders and whether these conditions constitute a type of extra-legal punishment for them without any due-process procedures of trial and conviction. Braithwaite (2000), Karp (1998), and others distinguish between **stigmatizing shaming** and **reintegrative shaming**. The first is a rejection of the individual and has negative effects; the second is only a rejection of the person's behavior and creates a healthier relationship between the individual and his or her community.

All states now have sex offender registries. These are listings of those convicted of sex crimes, and the offender must report his or her address to the registry. Some states' sex offender registries are made public so anyone can find out if any convicted sex offenders live in their neighborhood. The stated purpose of such registries has been to help parents protect their children, but there have been troubling reports of sex offenders being the target of vigilante justice. Many offenders have been harassed and threatened, the house of one was set on fire, and garbage was thrown all over the lawn of another. A sex offender in New Hampshire was stabbed, two were killed in the state of Washington by the same man and, in 2006, a man in Maine evidently targeted sex offenders and killed two before killing himself (Fahrenthold, 2006). This case also illustrates that sex offender registries are inclusive of individuals that may not fit the typical stereotype of a sex offender. One of the victims in the Maine case was a young man who had been convicted of statutory rape because of consensual sex with his teenage girlfriend. Even though no sex offender deserves to die at the hand of an extra-legal gunman, certainly the death of this young man, who was clearly not the predator that most people think of when they hear the term "sex offender," is a tragedy (Fahrenthold, 2006).

CAPITAL PUNISHMENT

What sets capital punishment apart from all other punishments is its quality of irrevocability. This type of punishment leaves no way to correct a mistake. For this reason, some believe that no mortal should have the power to inflict capital punishment because there is no way to guarantee that mistakes won't be made. The growing number of innocent men and women who came perilously close to being executed indicates that we have an imperfect system (Radelet, Bedau, and Putnam, 1992; Christianson, 2004; Associated Press, 2008c).

Public support for capital punishment has swung up and down. Public opinion polls reveal that public support for the death penalty declined gradually through the 1960s, reaching a low of 44 percent in 1966, but has increased over the past 30 years. In the late 1990s, 75–80 percent supported the death penalty (Britt, 1998). Public support seems to be declining in more recent years. In a poll in 2008, only 63 percent of Americans supported capital punishment (Harris Poll, 2008).

Research indicates that certain groups are more likely to favor the use of capital punishment; for instance, support is higher by 20–25 percentage points among whites as compared to blacks. Membership in fundamentalist Protestant churches predicts higher support for the death penalty as well. Political conservativism also predicts support. Interestingly, church activity negatively predicts support (the more active one is in one's church, the less likely one is to support the death penalty). Women are also less likely than men to support the death penalty. In one study, researchers found that Black Protestant fundamentalists showed the least support for the death penalty while white fundamentalists showed the most support (Britt, 1998).

Retentionists (who believe that we should continue to utilize capital punishment) and abolitionists (who believe that we should not execute anyone) both use utilitarianism, ethical formalism, and religion as moral justifications. Retentionists argue that capital punishment is just because it deters others from committing murder and it definitely deters the individual who is executed. This is a utilitarian argument. They also argue that capital punishment is just because murder deserves a proportional punishment. This argument is more consistent with ethical formalism. Finally, they argue that the Bible dictates an "eye for an eye." This is, of course, a (Christian) religious justification for capital punishment.

Abolitionists argue that capital punishment has never been shown to be effective in deterring others from committing murder, and, therefore, the evil of capital punishment far outweighs any potential benefits for society because there is no proof that it actually deters. This is a utilitarian argument. Abolitionists might also utilize the categorical imperative under ethical formalism to argue that deterrence is using the individual as a means to an end (deterrence). Finally, abolitionists would point to the religious command to "turn the other cheek" an argument against any religious (Christian) justification for capital punishment.

The reason why utilitarianism can be used to justify or oppose capital punishment is that the research on deterrence is mixed. Those who have summarized the evidence marshaled on both sides of the deterrence question found little support for the proposition that executions are useful deterrents (Walker, 1985: 79; Kronenwerter, 1993). However, despite the lack of research for general deterrence, many are still convinced that it does deter, at least the individual offender. Ethical formalism supports capital punishment, however, the imperfect nature of the system is problematic. Recall that under the categorical imperative, you should act in a way that you can will it to be a universal law. In this case, knowing that innocent people may be sentenced to death, can you agree that murderers should be executed if you did not know whether you were the victim, the murderer, the judge, or any citizen?

Religion, also, can be and has been used to support and condemn capital punishment. As with other issues, Christians have pointed to different verses in the Bible to justify their position. Kania (1999), for instance, presents a comprehensive religious justification for capital punishment, along with a social contract justification.

The ethical justification of capital punishment presents serious and probably irresolvable problems. It is a telling commentary that for as long as society has used capital punishment to punish wrongdoing, critics have defined it as immoral (R. Johnson, 1991).

Questions also arise about the methods and procedures of capital punishment. Should all murderers be subject to capital punishment, or are some murders less serious than others? Should we allow defenses of age, mental state, or reason? If we do apply capital punishment differentially, doesn't this open the door to bias and misuse? Evidence indicates that capital punishment has been used arbitrarily and discriminatorily in this country. One study, cited by the Supreme Court, indicated that minorities are more likely to be executed when their victims are white; in Georgia, black offenders charged with killing a white were 4.3 times more likely to be sentenced to death than those charged with killing a black. Yet the Supreme Court stated that this evidence of statistically disproportional administration is not enough to invalidate the death penalty (*McClesky v. Kemp*, 481 U.S. 279 [1987]).

Because our justice system is based on rationality, executions of persons with mental illness and mental retardation have been vehemently criticized. The Supreme Court has ruled that executing the mentally ill is cruel and unusual (*Ford v. Wainwright*, 477 U.S. 399 [1986]). Miller and Radelet (1993) present a detailed account of the *Ford* case, describing the mental deterioration of Ford and the long ordeal of appeals before the Supreme Court finally ruled. They also point out the ethical issues involved when psychiatrists, other medical professionals, and psychologists participate in procedures that involve certifying someone as *death ready* and then assist in the administration of the chosen method of execution. These professions have deep and divisive arguments regarding the seeming inconsistency between identifying oneself as a helping professional and then helping someone be put to death.

In June 2002 the Supreme Court decided that it was cruel and unusual to execute a retarded person. In *Atkins v. Virginia*, 536 U.S. 304 (2002), the court held that a man with an IQ of 59 could not be put to death, finding that the evolution of decency and public opinion supported such a decision. The holding does not answer all the questions that it raises, however, in how serious mental retardation must be to serve as a bar to capital punishment.

Until recently, the United States was one of only a few countries that executed those who committed their crimes when they were juveniles. Some have argued that it put the United States in violation of international human rights treaties. In the 2004 term the Supreme Court held that it was unconstitutional to execute those who had committed their murder when they were under the age of eighteen. In *Roper v. Simmons*, 125 S.Ct. 1183 (2005), the Court, in a narrow ruling (5–4), held that juvenile offenders could not be classified as the "worst" offenders;

therefore, allowing death sentences of juveniles violates the Eighth Amendment. The dissent argued that there was no national consensus on the matter. The ruling affected the sentences of seventy-two people on Death Row who had committed their crimes before the age of eighteen. Note that the question of culpability and whether or not the death sentence is a just sentence for mentally ill, retarded, or juvenile offenders is both a legal and a moral question.

Although one would assume that the offender must have had to kill someone to receive a death sentence, that is not the case. In *Tison v. Arizona*, 481 U.S. 137 (1987), the Court ruled that crime partners in a felony that resulted in a death could be executed even if they did not kill the victim and they did not intend a death to occur. The Tison brothers had no criminal records, but they helped their father escape from an Arizona prison. During the escape, their father and a fellow escaped convict killed a family after kidnapping them for their car. The brothers did not participate, but by this point were felons themselves because of their role in the escape. A massive search ensued, and they were separated from their father, who eventually ended up dying of exposure in the desert. (One wonders if the fact that he escaped his punishment was the reason that the brothers were then tried for capital murder.) Responding to their appeal, the Supreme Court affirmed the state's right to execute for felony murder because crime partners become responsible for any murder that occurs in the course of a felony they participate in, regardless of their role in the killing.

The 2006 renewal of the Patriot Act added a provision that applies to death penalty appeals. In effect, Congress changed federal habeas corpus procedures to "speed up" death penalty appeals for states that are qualified. To be qualified, a state has to show that it has competent legal representation; however, it is completely up to the discretion of the U.S. Attorney General as to whether or not a state is qualified. Once qualified, states can "fast track" a death penalty appeal, which means that prisoners have less time to file appeals and federal appellate judges can consider fewer issues (Copp, 2006). Critics argue that, given the woefully inadequate representation of some on Death Row, such a procedure is certain to result in innocent people being executed.

More recently, the Supreme Court ruled on a challenge to the method of execution. Opponents argued that lethal injection is cruel and unusual because the drugs administered do not prevent the sensation of pain, but they do paralyze; therefore, the individual suffers but is unable to scream or otherwise indicate distress. In *Baze v. Rees*, No. 07-5439, decided, April 16, 2008, the Court held that there was no evidence of substantial or an objectively intolerable risk of serious harm (pain). The arguments supporting the current "cocktail" of drugs used to execute prisoners fall into two camps. The first is that offenders should experience pain because, after all, they killed somebody; and, second, that they do not experience pain under these drugs. The first argument is a philosophical one; the second is a factual one.

Unless the Supreme Court revises its current position, which seems unlikely, the legality of executions is not in question. However, the procedures used to arrive at the decision to execute may continue to be challenged. The morality of capital punishment is still very much a topic of debate, and it elicits strong feelings on the part of many people.

PRIVATE CORRECTIONS

In much of the foregoing discussion, we described punishment as a state function. However, the state may delegate the authority to punish. Private prisons are built and then leased to the state or, in some cases, actually run by the private corporation, which bills the state for the service. Many have objected to the profit motive being introduced into corrections and point to a number of ethical issues raised by private "profiteers" (Pollock, 2004). First, there are potential abuses of the bidding process, as in any situation where the government contracts with a company for services or products. Money may change hands to ensure that one organization receives the contract; companies may make informal agreements to "rig" the bids; and other potentially corrupt practices may go on. Legal as well as ethical issues abound when private and public motives are mixed.

In the building phase, private corporations may cut corners and construct buildings without meeting proper standards for safety. Managing the institution also raises the possibility that a private contractor will attempt to maximize profits by ignoring minimum standards of health and safety and will, if necessary to this end, bribe inspectors or monitors to overlook the deficiencies. It has certainly happened in other areas, such as nursing homes, that those who contract with the state government and receive state monies reap large profits by subjecting clients to inhumane conditions. Some believe that punishment and profit are never compatible and that linking the two has led to a variety of historical abuses (such as the contract labor system in the South).

Although the decision to use private corporations is made by legislators, correctional administrators are faced with a variety of ethical dilemmas as a result, such as whether to support the idea, whether to accept a part-time position as a consultant to a private corporation when one has decision-making authority over issues that concern the corporation, whether to take anything of value from the corporation (from a free lunch to a "grant" for personal study), and whether to allow one corporation to have insider information in order to prepare a more favorable bid.

Private corporations argue that some state systems subject them to endless and picayune rules and continually audit them to the point that it appears that state prison officials are trying to find noncompliance in order to cancel contracts. There is probably some truth that some corrections department officials are not happy to have legislators approve the use of private contractors and would like to see them fail.

Private prisons hold about 7.2 percent of all prisoners in the country (Bureau of Justice Statistics, 2006: 3). Corrections Corporation of America and Wackenhut are the largest players in the private prison industry, holding a little more than half of all private prison beds (more than 60,000 beds in the United States alone). In late 1998, Corrections Corporation of America (CCA) merged into the Prison Realty Trust (PRT), an accounting move that allowed the entity to be exempt from tax liability as long as it distributed 95 percent of its earnings to its stockholders (Geis, Mobley, and Shichor, 1999). In 2001, CCA's stock lost 93 percent of its 2000 value (Greene, 2001: 26). This financial meltdown was partly caused by a decline of crime and prisoners, and partly fueled by a rash of scandals that plagued CCA's prison facilities. Account after account of escapes, violence, under-trained officers, and understaffing had plagued CCA for several years (Parenti, 1999: 219).

CCA was also the target of a loosely organized, global organization of students and reformers that sought to persuade college campuses to drop their contracts with Sodexho Marriott Services, a corporation that owned about 48 percent of CCA stock. Students, upset that their money was being used to fund a corporation that "violat[ed] the human rights of prisoners and prison employees by sacrificing health and safety to improve the corporate bottom-line," were successful in getting several large campuses to drop their contracts with Sodexho (Pranis, 2001). The giant corporation bowed to their threat and sold its shares in CCA (Ward, 2001).

Wackenhut has more than 25,000 beds at several dozen facilities across the country and is considered number two among the private prison providers. It holds 11,000 prison beds internationally (57 percent of the international market of private prisons) (Austin and Irwin, 2001: 66; Perez, 2001). It also runs mental health facilities and addiction treatment centers. Wackenhut has had a series of incidents reported in its facilities that have affected its reputation and financial standing (Greene, 2001). Lawsuits and investigations in states concern the use of tear gas (Louisiana), failing to prevent sexual abuse (Texas), paying $3 million to a member of the state's prison policy panel (Florida), and a murder rate that is much higher than that of the state-run institutions (New Mexico) (A. Solomon, 1999; Fecteau, 1999).

In addition to the "big two," more than a dozen smaller companies across the nation are competing for the private prison bids put out by the states. In a process replete with allegations of bribes, sweetheart deals, and other forms of corruption, some critics contend that the private prison industry seems to be characterized by crooks on both sides of the bars. Box 12.2 gives an example of what sometimes happens when profit is the goal.

Proponents argue that private corrections can save the state money. They argue that private corporations are more efficient, they can build faster with less cost and less red tape, and they have economies of scale (they can obtain savings because of their size). It may be true that private prisons can be built faster because private

---

BOX 12.2 | **WHO'S MONITORING THE MONITORS?**

Geo Group, Inc. is a Florida-based private corrections company. A Texas contract was pulled from Geo Group in 2007 when it was discovered that a juvenile facility did not meet basic standards. It was reported that three of the state monitors who were supposed to be checking to make sure that the facility met state standards had worked for the Geo Group and reported no violations. Six state employees were fired and one resigned. In the testimony about the Geo Group before the decision was made to pull its contract, a mother testified about her son who committed suicide while incarcerated in an adult facility run by the Geo Group. She stated that he was held in a solitary cell containing a cot, blanket, and pillow covered in mold and filth.

Source: M. Ward, 2007a, 2007: B1, B3.

corporations are not bound by the restrictions placed on government. For instance, a state would most likely have to go to voters to pass a bond in order to build new prisons; however, the state can contract with a private provider without voter approval. States and local governments are bound by a myriad of bidding and siting restrictions, unlike private corporations. However, a General Accounting Office meta-analysis concluded that private and public institutions cost about the same (General Accounting Office, 1996). Any profits realized by a private entity being "leaner and meaner" are offset by the profit margin that private companies maintain and a regulatory system that the state must put in place to make sure that contract specifications are adhered to.

Some studies have concluded that private prisons produce results equal to those of state institutions for less cost. Bourge (2002) describes a study by Segal and Moore that examined twenty-eight governmental and institutional studies, comparing public and private facilities, and found that twenty-two of the private prisons had cost savings of 5 to 15 percent. They concluded that there is "significant evidence" that private facilities can provide quality comparable to that of state institutions. However, critics argue that studies that look only at costs and ignore higher assault rates in private prisons and other indices of quality of service are flawed.

One of the emerging problems is that low wages prevent the hiring of qualified staff. In one situation a private corrections company, Capital Correctional Resources, was forced to defend the actions of its officers who were videotaped using stun guns and dogs to brutalize inmates. It was later discovered that two of the officers had been fired from the state system for brutality (Langford, 1997). Generally, private corrections pay officers a lower salary than the state does, so officers often transfer to state departments after they are trained. Turnover is high in private corrections and state corrections alike.

There have been issues concerning the evaluators as well. The evaluation by Segal and Moore, for instance, was funded by a libertarian think tank that arguably would be inclined to promote private enterprise over government involvement (Bourge, 2002). The biggest scandal in private prison evaluation research concerned Charles Thomas, a University of Florida professor who published many articles and books as "objective" evaluations of private prisons. Thomas testified before Congress and state legislatures considering private prison contracts. He consistently promoted the effectiveness and efficiency of private prisons, presumably as an independent, objective evaluator. However, his objectivity was called into question when it was discovered that he was a highly paid consultant of Corrections Corporation of America and owned more than $500,000 in CCA stock. He was sanctioned by the state of Florida in 1999 for violating its conflict of interest laws, yet he continues to write articles on private prisons, including evaluations that tout their effectiveness (Geis, Mobley, and Shichor, 1999; Mobley and Geis, 2002).

Ogle (1999) argues that private correctional facilities operate in a Catch 22, where organizational imperatives are contradictory. On the one hand is the corporate imperative of profit; on the other hand is the public service imperative of legitimacy. The two conflict when the most profitable way to run a prison conflicts with the perceived "just" or "humane" way to run a prison. When the private corporation is pursuing profit, it uses adaptations such as compromise and avoidance techniques or defiance and manipulation techniques to circumvent governmental mandates for services and contract fulfillment.

A more abstract and subtle criticism of private corrections is that if people are making money from incarcerating offenders, where is the incentive to correct them? If recidivism were somehow to mysteriously plummet, corporations would show reduced profits and stockholders would lose money. The financial incentive to incarcerate more people for longer periods of time arguably ensures that we will not see a reduction of imprisonment as long as privatization continues to grow. Of course, private corrections officials scoff at this scenario. They point out that their piece of the "corrections pie" is small in comparison to that of the states, that they are closely monitored by staff officials who are unhappy with sharing any amount of resources with them, and that there is plenty of opportunity to expand in other states and even in other countries without somehow conspiring to keep offenders in prison solely for some profit motive.

CONCLUSION

In this chapter we have looked at some of the ethical rationales for punishment. What we do to offenders is influenced by our views on things such as free will and determinism, the capacity for individual change, and the basic nature of humankind. Punishment has always been used against those who hurt other members of society and thus might be considered consistent with natural law. However, the limits of punishment have been subject to the laws and mores of each historical era. Today, our punishments primarily consist of imprisonment or some form of restricted liberty, such as probation or parole. The death penalty continues to be used; however, the controversy surrounding it continues as well.

We have seen a trend where the state delegates its authority to punish. Serious questions have arisen over this practice. Some argue that the profit motive is incompatible with the awesome power of the state to deprive individuals of liberty in the name of punishment.

Key Terms

cruel and unusual
   punishment *400*

determinate
   sentencing *389*

expiation *388*

general deterrence *391*

incapacitation *392*

indeterminate
   sentencing *389*

just deserts model *390*

justice model *390*

new
   rehabilitationists *390*

penal harm *390*

prevention *387*

punishment *385*

reintegrative
   shaming *401*

retribution *387*

specific deterrence *391*

stigmatizing
   shaming *401*

three-strikes laws *393*

treatment *385*

treatment ethic *387*

Review Questions

1. Define punishment, and then discuss the major rationales of punishment.
2. Now defend the rationales of punishment through the use of the ethical systems.

3. What are the three different objectives or approaches to prevention? Explain some issues with each.

4. How would Bentham defend punishment? Contrast that position with Kant's position.

5. What are Mackie's three types of retribution?

6. Support three-strike laws through a retributive rationale, and then through a utilitarian rationale.

7. What are some ethical problems with treatment?

8. What are the ways in which prison is harmful?

9. Support or criticize the use of private corrections, and give your reasons.

10. Discuss imprisonment rates, and defend them using utilitarian and retributive philosophies.

Writing/Discussion Questions

1. Write an essay on (or discuss) the "pains" of different types of punishment for different people, including yourself. Would you rather spend a year in prison or receive a severe whipping? Would you rather spend a year in prison or receive five years of probation with stringent restrictions? Would you rather spend a year in prison or pay a $30,000 fine?

2. Write an essay on (or discuss) your views on the justification for punishment. If you knew for certain that prison did not deter, would you still be in favor of its use? Why? If we could predict future criminals, would you be willing to incapacitate them before they commit a crime in order to protect society? Explain.

3. Write an essay on (or discuss) your views on the justification for treatment. Should we have guidelines for what we do in the name of treatment? If so, what should they be?

4. Write an essay on (or discuss) your views on the use of capital punishment and the reasons for your position. Now take the opposite side, and give the reasons for this view.

Ethical Dilemmas

Situation 1

A legislator has proposed a sweeping new crime and punishment bill with the following provisions for punishment. Decide each issue as if you were being asked to vote on it:

- Mandatory life term with no parole for any crime involving a weapon
- Corporal punishment (using an electrical apparatus that inflicts a shock) for all personal violent crimes
- Mandatory five-year prison sentences for those convicted of DWI
- Public executions
- Abolition of probation, to be replaced with fines and prison sentences for those who are not able to pay or are unwilling to do so

Situation 2

Another legislator has suggested an alternative plan with the following provisions. Vote on these:

- Decriminalization of all drug crimes
- Mandated treatment programs for all offenders who were intoxicated by alcohol or other drugs at the time of the crime
- Restructuring the sentencing statutes to make no sentence longer than five years, except homicide, attempted homicide, robbery, and rape
- Implementation of a restitution program for all victims whereby offenders stay in the community, work, and pay back the victims for the losses and/or injuries they received

Situation 3

Your state is one of the few that allows relatives of homicide victims to witness the execution of the perpetrator. Your brother was killed in a robbery, and the murderer is about to be executed. You receive a letter advising you of the execution date and your right to be present. Would you go? Would you volunteer to be the executioner?

Situation 4

Your house has been burglarized. Your community has a new sentencing program, and the program's directors have asked you to participate along with the offender who burglarized your house. As you understand it, this means that you would be sitting down with representatives from the police department and court system and the offender and his family. The group would discuss and come to an agreement on the appropriate punishment for the crime. Would you do it?

Situation 5

You are a legislator who is part of a committee that is revamping the sentencing system. You are contemplating a return to indeterminate sentencing from the determinate sentencing structure that your state passed in the early 1980s. How would you vote?

Suggested Readings

Bedau, H. 1991. "How to Argue About the Death Penalty." *Israel Law Review* 25, 466–480.

Boonin, D. 2008. *The Problem of Punishment.* Cambridge, UK: Cambridge University Press.

Kania, R. 1999. "The Ethics of the Death Penalty." *The Justice Professional* 12: 145–157.

Kleinig, J. and Smith, M. 2001. *Discretion, Community and Correctional Ethics.* Oxford, England: Rowman & Littlefield Publishers.

Kronenwerter, M. 1993. *Capital Punishment: A Reference Handbook.* Santa Barbara, CA: ABC-CLIO.

Palmer, T. 1994. *A Profile of Correctional Effectiveness and New Directions for Research.* Albany, NY: SUNY Press.

Pollock, J. 2004. *Prisons and Prison Life: Costs and Consequences.* Los Angeles: Roxbury.

Sheldon, R. 2001. *Controlling the Dangerous Classes.* Boston: Allyn and Bacon.

Western, B. 2007. *Punishment and Inequality.* New York: Russell Sage Foundation Press.

ETHICS AND INSTITUTIONAL CORRECTIONS

CHAPTER 13

© Pat Greenhouse/Landov Media

Correctional professionals have extremely difficult jobs in guarding individuals who are antagonistic and may be violent. Their ethical code is somewhat similar to the code of police officers in that the values of the law and public service are emphasized.

CHAPTER OBJECTIVES

1. Become familiar with the role conflict and subculture of correctional officers.

2. Become familiar with the ethical issues for correctional officers.

3. Become familiar with the ethical issues for treatment professionals.

4. Understand some of the unique ethical issues for correctional managers and administrators.

CHAPTER OUTLINE

David Armstrong was feared by inmates in the Bureau of Prison's supermax prison in Florence, Colorado. He was a part of a group of correctional officers (C.O.s) known as the Cowboys, who worked the Special Housing Unit (SHU), the segregation unit of the prison. Allegedly, Armstrong was one of the ringleaders of the group who, after several correctional officers had been injured in 1995, got the green light from their captain to "teach some inmates a lesson" by vicious beatings. At first the group selected defiant, violent inmates for "treatments." The C.O.s would punch, kick, and choke the inmates or drop them, handcuffed, headfirst on the concrete floor. They would then fabricate a story about why they had to use force, even to the point of inflicting injuries on themselves to justify the use of force. From 1995 through 1997, the group conducted these systematic beatings, eventually targeting not only violent inmates but gradually including mouthy and troublesome inmates as well. The Cowboys also expressed threats to officers, at one point promising that any officer who snitched would be taken out to the parking lot and beaten.

The group stuck together. Six of the seven were ex-military; several had gone through the Bureau of Prisons' training academy together and arrived at United States Penitentiary (USP) Florence together. The key phrases were "Lie 'til you die" and "What happens in SHU stays in SHU." A Catholic priest and other staff members heard complaints from inmates and tried to get the warden to listen, but most believed that the inmates were lying because, after all, inmates always lied. The Cowboys eventually broke up. Some, like Armstrong, were promoted and transferred. After he left Colorado and was working in a federal prison in Pennsylvania, he evidently had trouble breaking old habits and was disciplined repeatedly for his treatment of inmates. Then, in 1998, he was visited by an FBI agent who wanted to know what had happened in Colorado.

The ensuing FBI and Department of Justice investigation took five years and resulted in a grand jury indictment that listed more than fifty-five acts of beatings, intimidations, and lies. A nine-week trial with more than sixty witnesses ended with two weeks of jury deliberations. Armstrong was the government's star witness, and on the stand he recited beating after beating, explaining that there were so many that he couldn't remember them all. Why did he violate the "lie 'til you die" command? It may have been the plea bargain that the government offered him in return for his testimony; or, it may have been that he had contracted a terminal cancer and sought some type of redemption for what he had done before his death. On the witness stand he could hardly talk and required an oxygen tank to breathe.

Armstrong might have been remorseful, or he might have been trying to make the best deal for himself, but the seven accused C.O.s denied everything. Despite Armstrong's and other guards' testimony, the jury acquitted three of all charges and convicted three of only some of the charges (Prendergast, 2003). The civil suits are ongoing, and the government will probably end up paying tens of thousands of dollars to inmates for their injuries. Hopefully, at least Armstrong has made peace with himself. The story of the Cowboys is not typical of correctional professionals today, but it does illustrate the difficulties of preventing, monitoring and investigating and responding to correctional officer misconduct. The prison is a closed world and outsiders may never know what happens inside the walls.

Institutional correctional personnel can be divided into two groups: (1) correctional officers and their supervisors, and (2) treatment professionals, a group that includes educators, counselors, psychologists, and all others connected with programming and services. These groups have different jobs and different ethical issues.

We previously discussed how discretion plays a role in each phase of the criminal justice system. In corrections, discretion is involved when a correctional officer chooses whether to write a disciplinary ticket or merely delivers a verbal reprimand; this is similar to the discretion that police have in traffic stops. Discretion is also involved when the disciplinary committee makes a decision to punish an inmate for an infraction: The punishment can be as serious as increasing the length of a sentence through loss of good time or as minor as a temporary loss of privileges. This type of discretion is similar to the discretion of the prosecutor and judge in a criminal trial. Officers also make daily decisions regarding granting inmates' passes, providing supplies, and even answering questions.

As always, when the power of discretion is present, the potential for abuse is also present. Sometimes correctional professionals have the *power* to do things that they don't have the *legal authority* to do. That is, some officers can deny an inmate a pass to go to the doctor even though, according to the prison rules, the inmate has a right to go. When officers exceed their authority, inmates' only recourse is to write a grievance. Professional ethics, as provided in a code of ethics, should guide officers and other staff members in their use of discretion and power, but, as with law enforcement and legal professionals, adhering to a code of ethics is influenced by the occupational subculture and institutional values.

CORRECTIONAL OFFICERS

Correctional officers are similar to police officers in that their uniform represents the authority of the institution quite apart from any personal power of the person wearing it. Some C.O.s are uncomfortable with this authority and do not know how to handle it. Other C.O.s revel in it and misperceive the bounds of authority given to them as a representative of the state. The following statement is a perceptive observation of how some C.O.s misuse the authority they have (Kauffman, 1988: 50):

> [Some officers] don't understand what authority is and what bounds you have within that authority.... I think everyone interprets it to meet their own image of themself. "I'm a corrections officer [slams table]! You sit here! [Slam!] You sit there!" rather than, "I'm a person who has limited authority. So, you know, I'm sorry gentlemen, but you can't sit there. You are going to have to sit over there. That's just the rules," and explaining or something like that the reason why.

This observer obviously recognizes that the uniform bestows the authority of rational and reasonable control, not unbridled domination. The power of the C.O. is limited. In actuality, it is impossible to depend on the authority of the uniform to get tasks accomplished, and one must find personal resources—respect and authority stemming from one's personal reputation—in order to gain cooperation from inmates. Some officers who perceive themselves as powerless in relation to the administration, the courts, and society in general may react to this perceived powerlessness by misusing their little bit of power over inmates. They may abuse their position by humiliating or abusing those in their control.

Thus, in ways somewhat similar to those of police officers, correctional officers have power over offenders. They have the full range of coercive control, including loss of liberty through physical force if necessary. Their power may be misused. Blatant examples are an officer who beats an inmate or coerces sex from an inmate. The possibility for these abuses of power exists because of the powerlessness of the offender relative to the officer. Inmates have even less power against officer abuses than citizens on the street do against police officers' abuses of power. Sensitivity to ethical issues in corrections involves recognition and respect for the inherent powers and concurrent responsibilities of the profession.

During the rehabilitative era of the 1970s, professional security staff in corrections exchanged the old label of *guard* for a new one—**correctional officer**. Crouch (1986) examined how changing goals (from custody to rehabilitation) in the 1970s and 1980s created role conflict and ambiguity for the correctional officer. Also in the 1970s, federal courts recognized an expanding number of prisoner rights, including the rights to exercise religious beliefs, obtain medical care, and enjoy some due process. The disruption in the "old way" of doing things created real chaos, and these decades brought danger, loss of control, and stress for officers. In addition to increasing prisoner rights, the advent of unionization, professionalism, and bureaucratization changed the guard's world (Crouch, 1980, 1986, 1995; Silberman, 1995; and R. Johnson, 2002).

The prisoners' rights era of the 1970s gave way to the "due deference" era of today, where courts are more apt to defer to prison officials. Now, when responding to prisoner challenges, prison officials only have to prove a "rational relationship" between prison policies or procedures and the correctional goal of safety and security (Pollock, 2004). The Prisoner Litigation Rights Act of 1996 (PLRA) drastically curtailed the ability of inmates to file lawsuits and made it nearly impossible for federal courts to order consent decrees or order injunctive relief. It also limited attorney's fees.

Today, the prison is not the same as it was before the "rights and rehabilitation" era of the 1960s and 1970s, and correctional officers probably think that inmates still have too many rights. However, the courts' retreat into "due deference" has arguably led to a new era of "penal harm." When legal rights are limited, professional ethics must step in the breach to guide what is appropriate treatment of those in custody.

The American Correctional Association's Code of Ethics in Box 13.1 outlines formal ethics for correctional professionals. This code and the Law Enforcement Code presented in Chapter 7 have many similarities. For instance, integrity, respect for and protection of individual rights, and service to the public are emphasized in both codes, as are the importance and sanctity of the law. Also, the prohibition against exploiting professional authority for personal gain is stressed in both codes.

In an interesting discussion of implementing an ethics program for correctional officers, Barrier et al. (1999) described how officers presented elements of what they thought were important in an ethics code:

- Acting professionally
- Showing respect for inmates and workers
- Maintaining honesty and integrity
- Being consistent
- Acting impartially
- Being assertive but not aggressive
- Confronting bad behavior but reinforcing good behavior
- Standardizing rule enforcement
- Respecting others
- Practicing the Golden Rule
- Encouraging teamwork
- Using professional language
- Not abusing sick leave
- Telling inmates the truth
- Admitting mistakes

These elements are similar to those expressed in the Law Enforcement Code of Ethics and are consistent with the ethical frameworks.

Another similarity between the corrections field and law enforcement is that sometimes the ideal behavior described in the ethical codes is different from the subcultural norms. Although the ethical code clearly calls for fair and objective treatment, integrity, and high standards of performance, the actual practices of some correctional staffs may be quite different.

| BOX 13.1 | AMERICAN CORRECTIONAL ASSOCIATION CODE OF ETHICS |

Preamble

The American Correctional Association expects of its members unfailing honesty, respect for the dignity and individuality of human beings and a commitment to professional and compassionate service. To this end, we subscribe to the following principles.

Members shall respect and protect the civil and legal rights of all individuals.

Members shall treat every professional situation with concern for the welfare of the individuals involved and with no intent to personal gain.

Members shall maintain relationships with colleagues to promote mutual respect within the profession and improve the quality of service.

Members shall make public criticism of their colleagues or their agencies only when warranted, verifiable, and constructive.

Members shall respect the importance of all disciplines within the criminal justice system and work to improve cooperation with each segment.

Members shall honor the public's right to information and share information with the public to the extent permitted by law subject to individual's right to privacy.

Members shall respect and protect the right of the public to be safeguarded from criminal activity.

Members shall refrain from using their positions to secure personal privileges or advantages.

Members shall refrain from allowing personal interest to impair objectivity in the performance of duty while acting in an official capacity.

Members shall refrain from entering into any formal or informal activity or agreement which presents a conflict of interest or is inconsistent with the conscientious performance of duties.

Members shall refrain from accepting any gifts, service, or favor that is or appears to be improper or implies an obligation inconsistent with the free and objective exercise of professional duties.

Members shall clearly differentiate between personal views/statements and views/statements/positions made on behalf of the agency or Association.

Members shall report to appropriate authorities any corrupt or unethical behaviors in which there is sufficient evidence to justify review.

Members shall refrain from discriminating against any individual because of race, gender, creed, national origin, religious affiliation, age, disability, or any other type of prohibited discrimination.

Members shall preserve the integrity of private information; they shall refrain from seeking information on individuals beyond that which is necessary to implement responsibilities and perform their duties; members shall refrain from revealing nonpublic information unless expressly authorized to do so.

Members shall make all appointments, promotions, and dismissals in accordance with established civil service rules, applicable contract agreements, and individual merit, rather than furtherance of personal interests.

Members shall respect, promote, and contribute to a work place that is safe, healthy, and free of harassment in any form.

Source: Adopted August 1975 at the 105th Congress of Correction. Revised August 1990 at the 120th Congress of Correction. Revised August 1994 at the 124th Congress of Correction. Reprinted with permission of the American Correctional Association, Lanham, MD.

THE CORRECTIONAL OFFICER SUBCULTURE

The correctional officer subculture has not been described as extensively as the police subculture, but some elements are similar. First of all, the inmate may be considered the enemy, along with superiors and society in general. Moreover, the acceptance of the use of force, the preference toward redefining job roles to meet only minimum requirements, and the willingness to use deceit to cover up wrongdoing seem to be evident in both subcultures (R. Johnson, 2002; Crouch, 1980; Grossi and Berg, 1991).

In an excellent study of the officers' world, Kauffman (1988: 85–112) notes the following norms of the correctional officer subculture:

1. *Always go to the aid of another officer.* Similar to law enforcement, the necessity of interdependence ensures that this is a strong and pervasive norm in the correctional officer subculture. Kauffman describes a "slam" in Walpole Prison as when the officer slams a heavy cell door, which reverberates throughout the prison building, bringing a dozen officers to his or her aid in minutes—an obvious parallel to the "officer down" call in law enforcement.

2. *Don't lug drugs.* This prohibition is to ensure the safety of other officers, as is the even stronger prohibition against bringing in weapons for inmates. The following norm against "ratting" on a fellow officer may except informing on an officer who is a known offender of this lugging norm.

3. *Don't rat.* In ways similar to the law enforcement subcultural code and, ironically, the inmate code, correctional officers also hate those who inform on their peers. Kauffman notes two subordinate norms: Never rat out an officer to an inmate, and never cooperate in an investigation or, worse yet, never testify against a fellow officer in regard to that officer's treatment of inmates.

4. *Never make a fellow officer look bad in front of inmates.* This applies regardless of what the officer did, for it jeopardizes the officer's effectiveness and undercuts the appearance of officer solidarity.

5. *Always support an officer in a dispute with an inmate.* Similar to the previous provision, this prescribes behavior. Not only should one not criticize a fellow officer, but one should support him or her against any inmate.

6. *Always support officer sanctions against inmates.* This is a specific version of the previous provision, which includes the use of illegal physical force as well as legal sanctions.

7. *Don't be a white hat.* This prohibition is directed at any behavior, attitude, or expressed opinion that could be interpreted as sympathetic toward inmates. Kauffman also notes that this prohibition is often violated and does not have the strong subcultural sanctions that accompany some of the other norms.

8. *Maintain officer solidarity against all outside groups.* Similar to police officers, correctional officers feel denigrated and despised by society at large. This norm reinforces officer solidarity by making any other group, including the media, administration, or the public, the out-group.

9. *Show positive concern for fellow officers.* This norm promotes good will toward other officers. Two examples are: Never leave another officer a problem, which means don't leave unfinished business at the end of your shift for the next officer to handle; and help your fellow officers with problems outside the institution, which means lending money to injured or sick officers or helping in other ways.

If a C.O. violates the correctional subcultural code, the sanctions are felt perhaps even more acutely than by police officers, because one must work closely with other C.O.s all day long. Whereas police officers cite the importance of being able to trust other officers as backups in violent situations, one could make the argument that C.O.s have to trust each other more completely, more implicitly, and more frequently, given that violence in some institutions is pervasive and unprovoked, and that the C.O. carries no weapon. An officer described to Kauffman (1988: 207) the result of violating peer trust:

> If an incident went down, there was no one to cover my back. That's a very important lesson to learn. You need your back covered and my back wasn't covered there at all. And at one point I was in fear of being set up by guards. I was put in dangerous situations purposely. That really happened to me.

Fear of violating the code of silence is one reason that officers do not report wrongdoing. Loyalty is another reason. C.O.s feel a strong *esprit de corps* similar to the previously discussed loyalty among police. This positive loyalty also results in covering for other officers and not testifying or reporting offenses. McCarthy (1991) discusses how theft, trafficking in contraband, embezzlement, and misuse of authority went unreported by other correctional officers because of loyalty and subcultural prohibitions against "ratting."

A pattern of complicity also prevents reporting. New officers cannot possibly follow all the many rules and regulations that exist in a prison and still adequately deal with inmates on a day-to-day basis. Before long they find themselves involved in activity that could result in disciplinary action. Because others are usually aware of this activity and do not inform supervisors, an implicit conspiracy of silence develops so no one is turned in for anything because each of the others who might witness this wrongdoing has engaged in behavior that could also be sanctioned (Lombardo, 1981: 79).

Hamm (1989) discussed what happened when correctional professionals did come forward. He pointed out that whistleblowers sometimes are pursuing self-interest or personal goals by informing. At times there are minimal costs; however, in instances where the individual goes against the subculture, there may be serious consequences.

A rabble-rouser or **whistleblower** can be defined as someone who finds it impossible to live with knowledge of corruption without doing something about it—usually creating a scandal that exposes the corruption. The term has negative connotations, but it describes someone who is typically responding to a higher ethical code than those whose behavior is exposed.

Tom Murton found his career dramatically altered when he was hired by the Arkansas Department of Correction as its director of corrections. Upon arriving in the Arkansas system, he discovered abuses and inhumane conditions, described later in several writings and immortalized in the movie *Brubaker*. The U.S. Supreme Court case of *Holt v. Sarver*, 442 F.2d 304 (8th Cir. 1971) also documented the abuses. Murton received information that over 100 inmates had disappeared and were listed as escapees. Acting on the information of one informant, he dug up (on the grounds of the prison) two bodies that had injuries exactly as the inmate had described. One had been decapitated, and one had a crushed skull. Opposing testimony at the legislative hearing called in response to his investigation proposed that the bodies were from an old church cemetery. Instead of pursuing the matter further and digging up more bodies or testing them in any way for age and other identifying marks, state officials fired Murton and threatened him with prosecution as a grave robber (Murton, 1976).

A more recent whistleblower, Donald Vodicka, a fifteen-year correctional officer veteran in California, testified in a criminal case that the code of silence was pervasive, especially at the Corcoran and Pelican Bay prisons, and that a whistleblower would not be protected by the Department of Corrections against fellow guards. He described the activities of a group of officers at Salinas Valley Prison called "The Green Wall." The group was formed when inmates who had injured officers in a disturbance were beaten by the officers in turn. Even officers in Internal Affairs were affiliated with the group, using markers such as green armbands, green ink, and lapel pins. One officer was given an engraved green-handled knife upon a promotion. Vodicka was challenged, berated, and threatened by other officers when he provided information about the group. He transferred to another prison, but his supervisors there continued the harassment. He eventually took a stress-related leave (Arax, 2004). The "In the News" box gives another example of a whistleblower—who suffered informal and formal sanctions for exposing wrongdoing.

The correctional officer code, and sanctions against whistleblowers, vary from institution to institution, depending on factors such as permeability, the administration, the level of violence from inmates, architecture, and the demographic profile of officers. Distrust of outsiders, dissatisfaction, and alienation are elements of both the police subculture and the correctional officer subculture. In both professions individuals must work with sometimes unpleasant people who make it clear that the practitioner is not liked or appreciated. Further, there is public antipathy (either real or perceived) toward the profession, which increases the social distance between criminal justice professionals and all others outside the profession. In addition, the working hours, the nature of the job, and the unwillingness to talk about the job to others outside the profession intensify the isolation that workers feel.

One additional point to be made about the occupational subculture is that both law enforcement and corrections have experienced an influx of minorities, the college-educated, and women. This demographic change no doubt has altered the dynamics of the subculture in both fields.

IN THE NEWS | "I SHOULD HAVE KEPT QUIET"

One correctional employee wished he hadn't been a whistleblower. Frank Preston, an education supervisor for a New Jersey prison, filed a formal complaint and also wrote a letter to the governor when he saw two C.O.s use what he considered to be excessive force against an inmate. Preston was fired three weeks later. He also alleged that correctional officers in the prison somehow received a copy of his confidential complaint and copied and distributed it to other officers, necessitating a transfer for his own safety. The allegations are counter to the policy advocated by the Department of Corrections, which encourages staff members to come forward to expose wrongdoing.

How can you tell when someone is fired for whistleblowing as opposed to legitimate reasons?

Source: Hepp, 2005.

It should also be pointed out that some researchers believe that some of the values embedded in the correctional officer subculture may not be shared by most officers—a concept referred to as **pluralistic ignorance**. This refers to the idea that a few outspoken and visible members do not reflect the silent majority's views. In a prison this may mean that a few officers endorse and publicize subcultural values, whereas the majority of officers, who are silent, privately believe in different values (R. Johnson, 1996: 130). Kauffman (1988: 179) found this to be true in attitudes toward the use of force (where the silent majority did not endorse it to the extent of the verbal minority) and toward the value of treatment (which was silently supported).

Relationships with Inmates

One would assume that the general relationship between officers and inmates is one of hatred. That is not necessarily the case. As D. Martin (1993), a prisoner writer, points out, the posturing and vocalization from either side come from a small number, with the majority of inmates and officers living in an uneasy state of truce, hoping that no one goes over the line on either side. The "Quote and Query" box points out the extremes in relationships between convicts and guards.

The majority of guards and inmates prefer to live in peace and understand that they have to treat each other with some modicum of respect in order to get along. Unfortunately, both believe they must take sides when conflict arises. Even though prisoners have come to the aid of officers in physical confrontations, in general, inmates support their fellow inmates and guards support their fellow guards, regardless of how little support the individual deserves. Thus, a brutal guard may be protected by his fellows and a racist guard will not be informally or formally sanctioned. Likewise, an assaultive inmate will not be kept in check by his peer group unless his actions are perceived to hurt their interests.

An officer's ethics and professionalism are seriously threatened when relationships with inmates become personal. Gresham Sykes (cited in Crouch, 1980) discussed the issue of **reciprocity** in supervision: Officers become dependent on inmates for task completion and smooth management of the housing unit; in return, C.O.s may overlook inmate infractions and allow some favoritism to enter their supervision style. An example of a type of reciprocal relationship that may

Quote and Query

Some convicts hate all prison guards. They perceive them as the physical manifestation of their own misery and misfortune. The uniform becomes the man, and they no longer see an individual behind it .... Many guards react in kind. The hatred is returned with the full force of authority. These two factions become the real movers and shakers in the prison world. They aren't a majority in either camp, but the strength of their hatred makes its presence known to all.

D. Martin, 1993: 94–95

How would one reduce the level of hate between these small numbers of prisoners toward guards and guards toward prisoners?

lead to unethical actions is that between an officer and an informant. Several authors have described how rewarding informants sometimes creates tension and trouble in a prison environment even though management often depends on the information (Hassine, 1996; Marquart and Roebuck, 1986).

C.O.s who become personally involved with inmates compromise their professional judgment. Involvement is possible because of proximity and close contact over time, combined with shared feelings of victimization by the administration. Officers may start to think they have more in common with inmates than with the administration, especially now that officers are more likely to come from urban areas, come from minority groups, and be more demographically similar to the inmates they supervise. Identification and friendship may lead to unethical conduct, such as ignoring infractions or doing illegal favors for an inmate. McCarthy (1991) writes of this exchange relationship as an incentive for further corruption. He also points out that lack of training, low visibility, and unfettered discretion contribute to a variety of corrupt behaviors.

An extremely problematic situation arises when the officer becomes sexually involved with an inmate (or inmates). Some research indicates that just as many female officers become involved with male inmates as male officers with female inmates, and there are instances of homosexual relationships between officers and inmates as well (Marquart, Barnhill, and Balshaw-Biddle, 2001). Sexual relationships run a continuum of coercion from "true love" to rape. Regardless of how benign the relationship, these relationships are unethical and, in many states, illegal.

The subcultural norms against sympathizing with or becoming too friendly with inmates, as described by Kauffman (1988), may be seen as preventing officers from becoming personally involved with inmates. An officer who is too close to inmates is seen by other officers as untrustworthy. The officer subculture minimizes this possibility by a view of inmates as animalistic and not worth human sympathy. One of the most pervasive themes of a prison culture is that inmates are unworthy of trust, respect, or even normal human kindness. This treatment is sometimes described by inmates as more painful than any physical deprivations. Kauffman also notes that inmates themselves make it difficult for C.O.s to continue to hold sympathetic or friendly views because of their negative behaviors.

Just as officers may act in unethical ways when they like an inmate, they also may abuse their authority with inmates they do not like. These extra-legal harassments and punishments may include "forgetting" to send an inmate to an appointment, making an inmate stay in "keeplock" longer than necessary, or pretending not to hear someone locked in a cell asking for toilet paper or other necessary items. Lombardo (1981, 1989) noted the practice of putting an inmate in "keeplock" on a Friday even without a supportable charge because the disciplinary committee would not meet until the following Monday to release the inmate; the use of profanity toward inmates even in front of families; not notifying an inmate of a visitor; and losing passes. During the time period she studied, Kauffman (1988) noted that officers sometimes flushed cell toilets to aggravate inmates, dumped good food into the garbage, withheld toilet paper or matches, made up "tips" reporting contraband in a cell that resulted in a shakedown, scratched artwork, and in other innumerable informal ways made the targeted inmate's life miserable.

Because prisoners are in a position of need, having to ask for things as simple as permission to go to the bathroom, officers have the power to make inmates feel even more dependent than necessary, and humiliated because of their dependency. The relative powerlessness of officers in relation to their superiors, the administration, and society in general creates a situation where some take advantage of their only power—that over the inmate. The gulf between the status of guard and guarded is the theme of the "Quote and Query" box.

For officers, the potential of injury or being taken hostage is never far from their mind, and may affect to a certain extent their supervision of inmates, for it is potentially dangerous to be personally disliked. Also, on a day-to-day basis, inmates are not that much different from anyone else. Some are friendly, some are funny, and some are good conversationalists. This strange combination of familiarity and fear results in a pervasive feeling of distrust. Officers insist that "you can be friendly with inmates, but you can never trust them." Mature officers learn to live with this basic inconsistency and are able to differentiate situations in which rules must be followed from those in which rules can be relaxed. Younger and less perceptive officers either take on a defensive attitude of extreme distrust or are manipulated by inmates because they are not able to tell the difference between good will and gaming.

Officers, of course, are individuals, and they respond differently to the demands and job pressures of corrections. However, certain types have been identified by R. Johnson (2002):

1. *The violence-prone,* who use the role of correctional officer to act out an authoritarian role.
2. *Time-servers,* who serve time in prison much the same way as the inmates do, avoiding trouble and hoping that nothing goes wrong on their shift.

QUOTE AND QUERY

I never shake hands with an inmate.... They neither are nor ought to be viewed as equals.

George Beto, administrator of Texas prison system, 1962–1972, quoted in Dilulio, 1987: 177

[T]he Sergeant had succeeded in making me feel even more isolated from the world that existed outside the prison walls. I was no longer so proud to be an American. I was just a convict without rights....

Victor Hassine, inmate 1996: 52

Because legitimate power is so unevenly distributed between the keepers and the kept, left to its own inertia abuses of that power will inevitably creep into any prison without diligent and sensitive oversight.

Patrick McManus, state correctional official, reported in Martin, 1993: 333

Should the attitude of correctional professionals be that inmates are not worthy of a handshake, or does that isolation from the "community of man" create the potential for abuse?

3. *Counselors*, who seek to enlarge their job description and perceive their role as including counseling and helping the inmate rather than merely locking doors and signing passes. This type of officer has been called the **human service officer** and incorporates the tasks of providing goods and services, acting as a referral agent or advocate, and helping with institutional adjustment problems.

Changes over time have taken away many of the service functions that C.O.s used to perform. In his update of an older study, Lombardo (1997) found that in the ten years following his first study, much of the ability of C.O.s to grant favors had been taken away. For instance, telephones in the yard eliminated the need for C.O.s to run interference for inmates and get them a pass to make a phone call. This situation increased the autonomy of inmates, but it reduced the ability of the C.O.s to develop helping relationships with inmates, or, to put a more negative interpretation on their loss, it reduced their ability to create debts from the inmate—favors owed in return for favors given.

C.O.s have much less discretion today, and practically every decision that in the past had been made by a C.O. is now made by sergeants and specialized officers. C.O.s think they have much less power today to grant favors and, thus, have less control over inmates. One type of control they do have is the use of force, albeit one that is and should be restrained by legal and ethical norms.

USE OF FORCE

The use of force is a legal and sometimes necessary element of correctional supervision, and most observers say that the serious abuse that occurred in prisons in the past simply does not take place today. For instance, **"tune-ups"** in the Texas prisons involved "verbal humiliation, profanity, shoves, kicks, and head and body slaps"; "ass-whipping"; and using blackjacks and batons to inflict injury (Crouch and Marquart, 1989: 78). Murton (1976) described a litany of abuses that occurred in Arkansas prison farms, including the **Tucker telephone,** an electrical device that was attached to the genitals of inmates to deliver severe shocks as a form of torture.

One prison warden described "hanging up" inmates on the bars so their feet did not touch the floor and leaving them overnight, or making them stand on a 2-by-4 or a barrel for hours; if they fell off, the time would start again (Glenn, 2001: 25–26). This same warden described a situation in which an inmate tried to escape, was shot, and then was hung on the front gate, bleeding, for the field hoe squads to see as they came back from the fields. This was described by Glenn as an "effective ... object lesson" rather than brutality (2001: 44). Glenn also described a prison captain who played a "game" with inmates whom he believed weren't working hard enough on the hoe squad. The captain had them tied and stripped, and then lowered his pants and threatened to sodomize them (2001: 69).

Ironically, as violence by officers decreased in the late 1970s and 1980s, it opened the door to the violence of inmate gangs and cliques. Inmates in the 1980s had less to fear from guards but more to fear from one another as racial gangs and other powerful cliques or individuals solidified their control over prison black markets. There was a time in the 1970s and 1980s when officers described some prisons as "out of control." There were prisons where guards were afraid to walk into living units and inmates literally controlled some parts of the prison (Carroll, 1998; Taylor, 1993).

Bowker (1980) and other authors who described the victimization of inmates by correctional officers explained the violence by the officers' pervasive sense of fear and a C.O. subculture that tolerated, if not encouraged, such victimization. Crouch and Marquart (1989) and Crouch (1986) also discussed the use of violence as a rite of passage for the correctional officer, a way to prove oneself as competent. Today, illegal uses of force are not pervasive, but they do still exist (Pollock, 2004; Prendergast, 2003). Evidence that beatings still occur can be found in court cases. For instance, in *Hudson v. McMillian* (503 U.S. 1 [1992]) the U.S. Supreme Court dealt with a case involving an inmate who had been forced to sit in a chair while two officers hit him in the head and chest area, with a lieutenant looking on. The state argued that because there was no "serious injury," there was no constitutional violation, because cruel and unusual punishment had to involve serious injury. Although some justices agreed with this logic, the majority held that injuries need not be serious to constitute a constitutional violation if the injury was gratuitous.

As with the use of force in law enforcement, policy definitions of *necessary force* are vague. This may mean that the resort to violence is absolutely the last alternative available, or it may mean that force is used when it is the most convenient way to get something accomplished (Morris and Morris, cited in Crouch, 1980: 253).

In 1999, nine Florida guards were indicted for the murder of an inmate. The inmate died from injuries including broken ribs, swollen testicles, and innumerable cuts and bruises. He was on Death Row for killing a prison guard in a botched escape attempt in 1983. Prosecutors alleged that he was killed because he was planning to go to the media with allegations of widespread abuse in the prison. The accused guards insisted that he killed himself by flinging himself against the concrete wall of his cell or, alternatively, that he was killed by other inmates (Cox, 2000). Three officers were acquitted in the case in February 2002 ("Three Guards Acquitted," 2002).

If the guards did beat the inmate in the Florida case, it is similar to the case involving the prison guards known as the Cowboys, described earlier in the chapter. In both of these cases, one might assume that the officers involved viewed the beatings as utilitarian in that beatings serve as warnings to all inmates that they will receive similar treatment if they attack C.O.s. Thus, the action protects all officers from inmate aggression to some extent. Officers might also defend the action on retributive grounds because the inmate would probably not be punished for the attack through legal channels. However, these retaliations always represent the most brutal and inhumane aspects of incarceration and damage the integrity of all correctional professionals.

CORRUPTION AND ABUSE

Bomse (2001) identifies different types of prisoner abuse as follows:

1. *Malicious or purposeful abuse*: This is the type of abuse inflicted by individual officers intentionally, including excessive use of force; rape and sexual harassment; theft and destruction of personal property; false disciplinary charges;

intentional denial of medical care; failure to protect; racial abuse and harassment; and excessive and humiliating strip searches.

2. *Negligent abuse*: This type of abuse is also inflicted by individual officers, but not intentionally, and includes negligent denial of medical care; failure to protect, lack of responsiveness; and negligent loss of property or mail.

3. *Systemic or budgetary abuse*: This type of abuse is system-wide and refers to policies, including overcrowding; inadequate medical care (systematic budget cutting); failure to protect; elimination of visits or other programs; co-payments and surcharges; and use of isolation units.

In recent years the issue of prison rape has gained greater attention. The Prison Rape Elimination Act (PREA), passed by Congress in 2003, mandated that every state keep a record of prison rapes and allocated money to study the problem and develop solutions. No longer is prison rape seen as a joke; it is defined as an unacceptable risk of prison life, and the responsibility of prison staff and administrators. Ignoring the problem or telling prisoners to fight or submit is not an appropriate or ethical response.

One of the results of this attention to prison rape has also been more attention to staff–inmate sexual relationships. All staff–inmate sex, even consensual, is unethical, may result in being fired, and, in many states, is a felony offense. Interestingly, with female inmates, we have come full circle in this issue. In the seventeenth and eighteenth centuries, female prisoners were housed together with men in jails, with predictable results. Women were raped and sexually exploited, and they sold themselves for food and other goods.

With the development of the Walnut Street Jail and penitentiaries, women were separated from male inmates but still guarded by men, and sexual exploitation continued. Various scandals and exposés of prostitution rings led to women's reform groups pressuring legislatures to build completely separate institutions for women in the late 1800s and early 1900s. These women's prisons were staffed by female matrons. This pattern continued until the mid-1970s, when female officers challenged the hiring patterns of state prison systems that barred them from working in institutions for men. They were successful in achieving the right to work in men's prisons, but the corollary was that men could also work in institutions for women.

In the early 1980s, fairly low percentages of male officers could be found in prisons for women, and the male officers were restricted to public places. Today, male officers are assigned to all posts inside prisons for women, including sleeping and shower areas. In some states more than half of the officers in women's prisons are men. Thus, male officers again are in positions of power over women and, again, abuses are occurring (Amnesty International, 1999).

There are instances in women's prisons where male C.O.s have committed rapes of female prisoners by force, and many more instances where they threatened and intimidated women to engage in sex (Henriques, 2001). Evidently, female inmates who have complained about sexual harassment and abuse have been subject to transfer, solitary confinement, or disciplinary charges. In 2002 one officer was convicted of third-degree rape; the female inmate had an abortion after she learned she was pregnant (Craig, 2003). In the most egregious case, one female inmate was raped in a federal prison when officials sent women to the segregation unit of a

---

IN THE NEWS | "SEX SLAVES" IN OKLAHOMA JAIL

An Oklahoma sheriff was indicted on 35 counts of second-degree rape, forcible oral sod-omy, and bribery by a public official for allegedly coercing and bribing female inmates to have sex with him from 2005 through 2007. In one case he allegedly told a female defendant that she would be sent to prison if she did not have sex with him. Other inmates have come forward and said that jail employees had them engage in wet t-shirt contests and offered cigarettes to those who would expose their breasts.

Do you think the sheriff could have engaged in such behavior over that period of time with no one else knowing about it?

Source: Juozapavicius, 2008.

---

prison for men. Officers took money from male inmates in return for unlocking the women's cell doors so the male inmates could have sex (willingly or unwillingly) with them. When one female inmate fought back and reported her attempted rape, she was attacked again, and raped and viciously beaten by several men (Siegal, 2001). See the "In the News" box for another incident of sexual abuse of inmates.

Some officers use their authority to search inmates as a license to grope; others unnecessarily view women in the showers and while they are using the toilet. Although only a few correctional officers would engage in or support these acts, more allow it to happen by setting the tone of the prison. Staying silent while other officers sexualize prisoners by ribald comments, allowing officers to demean and belit-tle inmates, and participating in conversations where women are referred to by their body parts allow the true predators to victimize. Evidently, some correctional officers think that women in prison do not deserve to be treated as human. A prison culture that disparages and demeans inmates gives the green light to brutal individuals who wear a uniform. This situation is similar to the earlier discussion about rogue police officers who used the message that they could do anything in the name of controlling crime as encouragement to commit crimes against drug dealers.

Prisons have other forms of corruption. McCarthy (1991, 1995) and Souryal (1999a) discuss the major types of corruption by correctional officers and other officials in institutional corrections. Categories include theft, trafficking, embezzle-ment, and misuse of authority. Under misuse of authority McCarthy (1991) details the following:

- Accepting gratuities for special consideration for legitimate purposes
- Accepting gratuities for protection of illicit activities
- Mistreatment/harassment or extortion of inmates
- Mismanagement (e.g., prison industries)
- Miscellaneous abuses

Souryal (1999a), in another typology, describes the types of corruption as fall-ing into the following categories:

- Arbitrary use of power (treating workers or inmates preferentially or in a biased fashion)
- Oppression and failure to demonstrate compassion/caring
- Abusing authority for personal gain (extortion, smuggling, theft)

In the 1990s, investigations in several states uncovered abuses, including sexual abuse of inmates, brutality, and bribery at the highest levels of corrections departments, as well as wide-scale corruption involving smuggling drugs (Carroll, 1998; Houston, 1999). In Pennsylvania, an associate superintendent testified before an investigative committee of the state legislature of confirmed cases where officers had beaten a fellow officer; were caught smuggling contraband, including drugs to inmates; assisted an inmate in beating another inmate; raped an inmate; became sexually involved with an inmate; came to work under the influence of cocaine; embezzled inmates' funds; gambled with inmates; and conducted a "mock lynching" of a black inmate (cited in Hassine, 1996: 149–152).

Also in the 1990s, Corcoran prison guards in California were accused of setting up gladiator-type fights between inmates and encouraging or allowing prisoner rapes. One former guard testified that a "loudmouth" prisoner was placed with a prison rapist known as the "Booty Bandit" (Arax, 1999: A3). Other guards were accused of unlawful use of force by shooting an inmate during one of the gladiator fights. Eventually, several guards received federal indictments and were tried for the killing, as well as the other acts of oppression. Some argue that the officer union "tainted" the jury pool by running television ads before the jury selection, showing officers as tough, brave, and underappreciated. The television ads, with the tagline of "Corcoran officers: They walk the toughest beat in the state," aired only in the Fresno area, where the trial was held (Lewis, 1999). The accused guards were acquitted even though former guards and other experts supported the inmates' allegations ("Three Guards Acquitted," 2000).

California's Department of Corrections has been described as corrupt "from the top down" because investigations of wrongdoing seem to be thwarted by powerful union leaders. There have been allegations that members of the independent Office of Inspector General were fired at the behest of the correctional officer union (Thompson, 2004). During legislative hearings about a Folsom riot that was said by some to have originated through guards conspiring with one of the gangs, one legislator received death threats, and witnesses were put under protective custody (Thompson, 2004). The riot and its cover-up evidently led directly to the suicide of an officer who attempted to thwart the riot but was stopped by a supervisor. He left a message: "My job killed me" (Warren, 2004a). Several wardens and assistant wardens have resigned, have taken early retirement, or were fired over the Folsom Prison riot scandal, and dozens of correctional officers have been fired for wrongdoing (Warren, 2004b).

In Texas, Andy "James" Collins, an ex-director of the Department of Corrections, was investigated for his business association with a Canadian company that made VitaPro, a vegetable-based protein substance that evidently tasted bad and created digestive problems for some people. It was discovered that Collins had locked the state into a multi-year contract with the company and he had received two payments of $10,000 from the company director. Collins resigned as director in 1996 and immediately became a $1,000-a-day consultant to VitaPro. In 2001, he and the director of that company were convicted by a federal jury on charges of bribery, conspiracy, and money laundering. Collins appealed, and in 2008 a federal judge overturned the guilty verdict. Despite the judge's decision to ignore the jury verdict, the scandal resulted in a new ethics code and acquitted the two men of the bribery, money-laundering, and conspiracy charges. Despite the acquittal many years after the fact, the scandal resulted in a new ethics code for prison administrators and a "housecleaning" of the top ranks (M. Ward, 2008).

In 2000, state prison guards faced felony bribery charges after they agreed to launder money for inmates. One received $60,000 with the understanding that he would get $10,000 for his services (Associated Press, 2000: B3). In 2006, in Texas, a prison official pleaded guilty to sexually harassing employees, the personnel chief of the prison school system was arrested for lewd conduct, a correctional officer was accused of raping a male convict, and another officer was accused of smuggling marijuana (M. Ward, 2006a).

Inspector General investigators often make their case from cameras placed strategically throughout prisons, which have recorded a range of unethical behaviors, including a female guard embracing an inmate, a sergeant hitting a guard in the face (to cover an unlawful use of force by the guard), and a guard leading an inmate into a closet to have sex (M. Ward, 2006a). In 2006 there were, in total, 761 arrests of 36,000 Texas correctional employees; these numbers compare to about 297 of 26,700 correctional employees in Florida (Ward, 2006b).

Not all of these arrests involved abuse or corruption related to the job; most (484) were for DWI (Ward, 2006b). Explanations for why arrest numbers are so high include the low salaries (Texas was 47th in correctional officers' salaries), a reduction in the number of Inspector General's Office investigators (cut in half as a budget-reduction move), high turnover, and low standards for hiring (the state will accept applicants convicted of Class A or Class B misdemeanors as long as they are 5 years old) (Ward, 2006b). A Florida news article reported that prison guards were more than twice as likely as police officers to violate state standards of conduct (Kleindienst, 1999). If it is true that correctional officers have a pattern of misconduct that is higher than other public servants, it would be important to identify the cause and remedy the situation.

Correctional officers report that they experience a great deal of stress, and stress-related illnesses such as hypertension are common among officers, as well as social problems such as alcoholism and divorce. Some reports indicate that these problems exist in higher numbers with correctional officers than with police officers. Correctional officers feel criticized and even scorned by many, so it is little wonder that they adapt to their role by sometimes unethical and egoistic patterns of behavior. Yet, it is important to understand the consequences of such a position. Kauffman (1988: 222) talked to officers who reported that they had lost their morality in the prison:

> These officers experienced anguish at the change that was wrought in them by the prison environment: Initially, many attempted to avoid engaging in behavior injurious to inmates.... As their involvement in the prison world grew and their ability to abstain from morally questionable actions within the prison declined, they attempted to neutralize their own feelings of guilt by regarding prisons as separate moral realms with their own distinct set of moral standards or by viewing inmates as individuals outside the protection of moral laws. When such efforts failed, they shut their minds to what others were doing and to what they were doing themselves.

Without a strong moral and ethical code, correctional officers may find themselves drifting into relativistic egoism: Behavior that benefits the individual is considered to be acceptable, despite long-term effects or inconsistencies with their duty and their personal value system. The result is a feeling of disillusionment and anomie, and the side effects can be serious dissatisfaction and depression. To maintain a sense of morality in an inherently coercive environment is no easy task, yet a strong set of individual ethics is probably the best defense against being changed by the negative environment of the prison.

Not surprisingly, C.O.s and inmates tend to agree on a description of a good officer as one who treats all inmates fairly with no favoritism but who does not always follow rules to the letter. Discretion is used judicially; when a good officer makes a decision to bypass rules, all involved tend to agree that it is the right decision. A good officer is not quick to use force, or afraid of force if it becomes necessary. A good officer treats inmates in a professional manner and gives them the respect they deserve as human beings. A good officer treats inmates in the way anyone would like to be treated. If an inmate abuses the officer, that inmate will be punished, but through formal, not informal, channels. In some cases the officer will go far outside regular duties to aid an inmate who is sincerely in need; however, he or she can detect game playing and cannot be manipulated. These traits—consistency, fairness, and flexibility—are confirmed as valuable by research (Johnson, 2002).

JAIL OFFICERS

Little has been written about jail officers, who may be sheriff deputies who must complete their assignment at the jail before they can be "promoted" to street patrol. Sometimes jail officers are street deputies who are transferred back to the jail as punishment. In other situations, jail officers are not deputies and have a separate title and pay scale (usually lower). In all these situations the tasks and skills associated with managing jail inmates are discounted or ignored. There is a need for greater recognition of the profession of jail officer; the position should not merely be a dreaded rite-of-passage assignment, a punishment, or a stepping-stone to deputy status, because the body of knowledge required to perform the job well is different from that which a street deputy needs. Recently there has been an attempt to professionalize the image of jail officers, starting again with a code of ethics. See the "American Jail Association Code of Ethics for Jail Officers" in Box 13.2.

Arguably, the job of jail officer is even more difficult than that of correctional officer because jail officers must deal with a transitory population rather than a fairly stable one. Inmates include truant children, violent criminals, misdemeanants, mentally ill, mentally challenged, and intoxicated. Offenders may come into jail intoxicated, have undiagnosed epilepsy or other diseases, suffer overdoses, or be suicidal. Visitation is more frequent, and family issues are more problematic in jails than prisons. The constant activity and chaotic environment of a jail often create unique ethical dilemmas.

Many jail inmates cannot or will not follow rules, especially those with mental illness. Prisoners and guards alike do not tolerate their irrational behavior very well. Jail officers tend to deal with all troublesome behavior as a discipline issue. Is throwing feces a behavioral problem or an indication of mental illness? Sometimes it is both. When the person is placed in isolation (as in segregation), the situation may bring on hallucinations, anxiety attacks, and distorted thinking (Turner, 2007).

BOX 13.2 | AMERICAN JAIL ASSOCIATION CODE OF ETHICS FOR JAIL OFFICERS

As an officer employed in a detention/correctional capacity, I swear (or affirm) to be a good citizen and a credit to my community, state, and nation at all times. I will abstain from all questionable behavior which might bring disrepute to the agency for which I work, my family, my community, and my associates.

My lifestyle will be above and beyond reproach and I will constantly strive to set an example of a professional who performs his/her duties according to the laws of our country, state, and community and the policies, procedures, written and verbal orders, and regulations of the agency for which I work.

On the job I promise to:

Keep the institution secure so as to safeguard my community and the lives of the staff, inmates, and visitors on the premises.

Work with each individual firmly and fairly without regard to rank, status, or condition.

Maintain a positive demeanor when confronted with stressful situations of scorn, ridicule, danger, and/or chaos.

Report either in writing or by word of mouth to the proper authorities those things which should be reported, and keep silent about matters which are to remain confidential according to the laws and rules of the agency and government.

Manage and supervise the inmates in an even-handed and courteous manner.

Refrain at all times from becoming personally involved in the lives of the inmates and their families.

Treat all visitors to the jail with politeness and respect and do my utmost to ensure that they observe the jail regulations.

Take advantage of all education and training opportunities designed to assist me to become a more competent officer.

Communicate with people in or outside of the jail, whether by phone, written word, or word of mouth, in such a way so as not to reflect in a negative manner upon my agency.

Contribute to a jail environment which will keep the inmate involved in activities designed to improve his/her attitude and character.

Support all activities of a professional nature through membership and participation that will continue to elevate the status of those who operate our nation's jails.

Do my best through word and deed to present an image to the public at large of a jail professional, committed to progress for an improved and enlightened criminal justice system.

Source: Reprinted with permission of the American Jail Association.

Mentally ill inmates are more likely to be charged with rule violations, including physical or verbal assaults on staff members, and more likely to be injured, yet jail officers are not trained to be mental health specialists.

Unfortunately in jails one can find the same type of unethical behavior that one finds with police and correctional officers. Jail officers can be uncaring and insensitive to human needs. Then again, some jail officers may be described as "human service" officers who seek to enrich their job by taking on more of a counseling role with inmates.

TREATMENT STAFF

A number of ethical issues that correctional treatment personnel may be faced with are similar to those experienced in a more general way by all treatment professionals, so available sources dealing with ethics in the helping professions would also be applicable to those who work in the corrections field (see, for instance, Corey, Corey, and Callanan, 1988; Braswell, Miller, and Cabana, 2006).

Although they are hired by the state, treatment specialists may believe that their loyalties are to the offender. The professional goal of all treatment specialists is to help the client, but sometimes helping the client is at odds with the safety and security of the institution. For instance, prison psychologists may be privy to information or confessions that they feel bound to hold in confidence, even though this may jeopardize the security of the prison. Assessing risk also involves mixed loyalties. Any treatment necessarily involves risk. How much risk one is willing to take depends on whether the public should be protected at all costs, in which case few people would ever be released, or whether one thinks the public must risk possible victimization in order to give offenders a chance to prove themselves.

Another dilemma is the administration of treatment programs. If a program has potential, someone must make decisions on who is accepted into the program. Ideally, one would want similar people in the treatment program and in a control group, but it is hard sometimes to justify withholding the program from some people who may sincerely wish to participate. Laypersons have difficulty understanding the concepts of random sampling and control groups. There sometimes is pressure to admit anyone who sincerely wants a chance to participate, despite what this might do to experimental design.

Another, more basic issue is whether to provide treatment to people who do not want it. In particular, psychiatrists and psychologists have to reconcile their professional ethics in two fields—corrections and psychiatry—and at times this is hard to do. Psychiatrists in corrections, for instance, believe at times that they are being used for social control rather than treatment (Tanay, 1982). Disruptive inmates, although needing treatment, pose security risks to prison officials, so intervention, especially the use of antipsychotic drugs and barbiturates, often takes the form of control rather than treatment, as the "Quote and Query" box illustrates.

The practice of using antipsychotic drugs is especially problematic for treatment professionals. Although the Supreme Court has determined that the administration of such drugs to unwilling inmates is not unconstitutional, the practice must be scrutinized and held to due-process protections in order to uphold professional ethical standards. Some allege that psychotropic drugs are used to control inmates, rather than used for legitimate treatment purposes. There are pervasive stories from ex-inmates of inmates being maintained on high dosages of drugs during their prison stay. The problem is that, once released, they may go through withdrawal

QUOTE AND QUERY

As it was, John's illness needed to be controlled, not because he was unhappy with it, but because those around him found it objectionable. What can the psychiatrist do in cases like this?

Discussing an inmate who was not violent but was extremely talkative, loud, and inclined to discuss his delusions, as quoted in Arboleda-Florez, 1983: 52

Should psychiatrists use drugs to quiet an inmate who is not violent?

and have no assistance from community mental health facilities because of governmental cutbacks in services (Martin, 1993).

Psychologists have their own ethical code, and some principles seem especially relevant to corrections. For instance, under the principle of responsibility, psychologists are instructed to prevent the distortion, misuse, or suppression of their psychological findings by the institution or the agency that employs them. This obviously affects institutional psychologists, who may believe that their findings are compromised by custody concerns. For instance, something confessed to in a counseling session may be used in parole reports to prevent release, findings may be used to block transfer, behavior brought out in psychological testing may be punished, and so on ("Ethical Principles," 1981: 633).

Other principles involve the treatment of clients: "In their professional roles, psychologists avoid any action that will violate or diminish the legal and civil rights of clients or of others who may be affected by their actions" ("Ethical Principles," 1981: 634). This principle may be applicable to certain treatment programs in prison that restrict inmates' liberty or choice. For instance, some of the behavior modification programs have been questioned legally and ethically.

Haag (2006) describes some ethical dilemmas of prison psychologists in Canada, which apply to the United States as well. In his discussion, he mentions issues of:

- Confidentiality—the inability to keep prisoners' secrets
- Protection of psychological records—whether or not psychologists should create "shadow files" that are not subject to view by other staff
- Informed consent—whether consent is possible from a coerced population
- Assessment—what the psychologist's role is when assessment is used for correctional purposes
- Corroboration—the importance of not accepting everything the inmate says because the inmates may be engaged in "impression management"
- Refusal of services—whether psychologists should honor an inmate's refusal of psychological services
- Nondiscrimination—treating all inmates equally regardless of group membership or individual characteristics
- Competence—the importance of being aware of the boundaries of one's competence
- Knowledge of legal structure—being aware of the rights of the parties involved
- Accuracy and honesty—making clear the limits of predictive validity of psychological assessments
- Misuses of psychological information—refusing to allow file information to be misused to damage an inmate's interests
- Multiple relationships—avoiding dual roles (such as assessment and treatment), which is problematic and creates confusion for the client

Lichtenberg, Lune, and McManimon (2004) use the 1971 movie *Clockwork Orange* to discuss issues of voluntariness and morality in treatment. The movie is a critical treatment of behavior modification and illustrates the fear that manipulating people's minds through aversive conditioning takes away, in some respects, the essence of what it means to be a free individual. Although the film is a satire, and obviously an extremely drawn portrait of the power of aversive conditioning, the idea that when people have been conditioned, they are not rationally choosing good because they cannot freely choose evil, is relevant and important to our discussions of moral culpability, as well as the ethics of trying to change individuals who do not want to be changed.

What is the ethical responsibility of a counselor when an offender threatens future violence toward a particular victim? As in the legal profession, confidentiality is an issue for psychologists. The ethical principles address this issue:

> Psychologists have a primary obligation to respect the confidentiality of information obtained from persons in the course of their work as psychologists. They reveal such information to others only with the consent of the person or the person's legal representative, except in those unusual circumstances in which not to do so would result in clear danger to the person or to others. Where appropriate, psychologists inform their clients of the legal limits of confidentiality.

> *Source: "Ethical Principles,"1981: 636.*

Treatment and security concerns clash in many instances. The treatment professional must choose between two value systems. To emphasize security concerns puts the psychiatrist or counselor in a role of a custodian with professional training used only to better control inmate behavior. To emphasize treatment concerns puts the professional in an antagonistic role *vis-à-vis* the security staff, and he or she may be in situations where these concerns directly conflict.

For instance, if the superintendent demands to see a client's file to support a disciplinary committee's decision, should the psychiatrist surrender the information that was given in confidence? In answer to this dilemma, the psychiatrist or psychologist should probably have not allowed the inmate to assume that information regarding rule infractions or potential wrongdoing could ever be confidential. However, if inmates believe that counselors and psychologists can offer no confidentiality protections, is there any possibility of a trusting relationship? The issues that confront treatment personnel in prison seem to invariably involve the conflicting goals of punishment and treatment.

Faith-based treatment programs have been supported and encouraged by the White House and are becoming increasingly popular in prison systems. Prison Fellowship Ministries, Inc., a Washington, D.C., group headed by Watergate figure Charles Colson, is one such prison program. The program is Christ-centered, biblically rooted, and values-based, and it emphasizes family, community, and Jesus Christ. Inmates volunteer for the program (M. Ward, 1996). The Innerchange Freedom Initiative, introduced in 1997 in the Texas prison system, has shown reduced recidivism. During the two-year study period, only 8 percent of program participants returned to prison, compared to 20 percent for the control group (Criminal Justice Policy Council, 2003).

Having such programs in prison raises several issues. Some argue that the programs violate the separation of church and state and are an unconstitutional violation of freedom of religion. If a Christian program offers hope for early release or other advantages, Muslims or those following other religions may participate only if they also compromise their faith. Individuals associated with such programs must take care not to intrude upon the religious freedom of inmates and not use the benefits of the program to coerce religious conformity.

Probably the most prevalent issue for treatment professionals is how to maintain one's commitment to a helping profession while being in an environment that does not value the goals and mission of treatment. This dichotomy of treatment versus punishment creates a myriad of ethical issues for treatment professionals.

Another area that must be considered under the general heading of treatment is that of medical services. There have been a number of scandals concerning the level of medical care in prisons around the country (Associated Press, 2002). Court cases and exposés have documented the sometimes deadly consequences when the medical needs of inmates are ignored or not met. Vaughn and Smith (1999) described several different ways in which medical services or, more specifically, the lack of such services created pain and suffering for inmates. Sometimes poor medical care is a result of neglect or lack of resources, but sometimes the medical staff simply did not care, believed that prisoners should suffer, and/or did not believe that inmates were sick or injured. The authors suggest that the medical staff itself sometimes furthers "penal harm" by withholding medical services and justifies such actions by a type of ethical relativism in which inmates aren't seen as deserving the same type of care as others.

Others argue that medical professionals in American prisons have begun to fill roles that may be inconsistent with their allegiance to medical ethics—for instance, assisting in body-cavity searches and testing for drugs. These control activities are not a part of the helping profession of medicine and may interfere with the medical professional–client relationship (Kipnis, 2001).

MANAGING THE ETHICAL PRISON

Similar to law-enforcement leaders, correctional administrators set the tone for the facility. It seems to be the case that in prisons where correctional managers and administrators treat officers fairly and with respect, officers are more likely to treat inmates that way. If administrators play favorites, if they indicate that they don't care about the law or formal policies, if they emphasize the goal of keeping the organization out of the newspapers and minimizing negative publicity, through cover-ups if necessary, the prison will be a very different place.

Barrier and colleagues (1999) discussed an ethics training program with correctional officers, in which part of the training involved having the officers identify important elements of an ethics code. Many of the elements had to do with the practices of management rather than officers:

- Treating all staff fairly and impartially
- Promoting based on true merit
- Showing no prejudice
- Leading by example
- Developing a clear mission statement
- Creating a positive code of ethics (a list of do's, rather than don'ts)
- Creating a culture that promotes performance, not seniority
- Soliciting staff input on new policies
- Being respectful
- Letting the word out that upper management cares about ethics

As discussed earlier, correctional administrators in the 1970s and 1980s had to deal with court decisions that were decided in favor of prisoners. Implementation of court-ordered changes indicated that correctional administrators sometimes barely complied with the letter of a court ruling, much less the spirit of the ruling. In one state system, administrators attempted to ban an attorney from the prison and punished inmates who were involved in a class action suit (*Cruz v. Beto*, Civil No. 71-H-1371[S.D.Tex. 1976]). Not surprisingly, the court took a dim view of these actions. What ethical system would justify such behavior?

The career path of an administrator, with its investment of time and energy and the mandate to be a "company man," often creates an immersion in bureaucratic thinking to the point that an individual loses sight of ethical issues. For instance, protecting the department or the director from scandal or litigation becomes more important than analyzing the behavior that created the potential for scandal in the first place. If decision making becomes influenced solely by short-term gains or by avoiding scandal, decisions may be unsupported by any ethical system.

As an example, two employees at a juvenile detention facility were sexually abusing the boys housed there. The men were taking the boys out of their dorms in the evenings, and various staff members saw them with the youths in darkened offices. Complaints from staff members went to the central state office, and one law enforcement investigation in 2005 concluded that there was abuse going on, but the internal investigator sent from the state youth corrections agency wrote a report stating that the charges were groundless. The county prosecutor had the same information and did nothing.

Despite indications that higher-ups in the capital all the way to the governor's office knew about the charges, nothing was done until a volunteer went to the media and a newspaper series in 2007 exposed the charges. It came out that the law enforcement investigation findings had been available to the prosecutor and the central agency staff for years. In the ensuing scandal, the director of the agency and the director of the facility resigned, several individuals were fired, the governor put a special monitor in charge of the agency, and a complete reorganization was threatened by the legislature (Associated Press, 2007d; Moreno, 2007; M. Ward, 2007a, 2007b). The culture of the agency evidently was such that it was better to try to ignore such behavior rather than admit that it was happening. In addition to hurting the children involved and betraying the trust that taxpayers placed in them, the administrators who let such things go on, in the end created a worse outcome for their organization than what would have happened if they had dealt with the problem in the first place.

Obviously, correctional administrators should take care to hire and train to minimize the possibility of sexual predators in positions of authority. A related issue is sexual harassment. When female correctional officers first entered prisons for men, they often encountered a **hostile work environment** where male C.O.s made sexual references and disparaging comments to them in front of inmates, "set them up" by having inmates masturbate when they were sent down the tier, put up posters with naked women and sexual messages, and engaged in even more serious behaviors such as assaults and attempted rapes.

Today, ironically, there are more male C.O.s in women's prisons than there are female C.O.s in prisons for men, but a hostile work environment may still be an issue. Male and female officers work together long hours and in close proximity; sometimes they engage in sexual relationships; sometimes they marry; sometimes they divorce; sometimes they have affairs with other staff members (or even inmates) while they are married. In some prisons that are in small towns, everyone seems to be related to someone and/or has some type of relationship. While people's personal lives are their own, sometimes the personal lives of correctional officers, like police officers, influence their professional ethics. For instance, if a disciplinary sergeant is married to a C.O. who has written a ticket on an inmate, can that sergeant truly be objective when determining punishment? What happens when an inmate accuses an officer of sexual harassment and the grievance officer is the wife of the officer? Sometimes male and female C.O.s allow a sexually charged atmosphere to develop where sexual joking and innuendos are rampant and the atmosphere encourages officers to engage in the same type of behavior with inmates—obviously an inappropriate and unprofessional interaction.

Administrators are responsible for what happens in their facility, and training, supervision, and careful attention to assignments can avoid many problems, especially if nepotism policies are not feasible. Obviously, administrators and managers themselves should take pains to avoid behavior that may be misconstrued as sexual coercion or be perceived by their employees as offensive. Supervisors have a higher duty than co-workers to set a tone for an office free from sexual innuendo that may lead to a description of the workplace as a hostile work environment. Supervisors have an ethical and legal duty to stop sexual humor, inappropriate touching, and inappropriate behavior before there is a complaint.

It should be noted that in cases where there is a pattern of corruption, whether it be brutality or types of graft, it is hard to believe that administrators were not aware of what was going on. Prisons are smaller than small towns, and like a small town, they do not have secrets unless one is willfully ignorant of them. Top administrators often have an outward orientation because their role is to communicate with legislators, the central office, and the community; however, a good administrator does not ignore his or her own backyard. Management by walking around (MBWA) and having a good sense of what is happening in the institution have been the marks of a good administrator and are also the best defense against having the institution ending up on the front page of the newspaper.

Correctional administrators have increasingly been required to negotiate and deal with correctional unions. So far, unions have been seen by researchers as a force resistant to rehabilitation, and concerned only with individual benefits for members rather than the mission or goal of corrections. Unions provide legal assistance to officers in personnel and the subject of legal attacks and often support officers who, many would argue, have no business working in corrections (see, for instance, Josi and Sechrest, 1998).

Unions have been successful in protecting and improving the position of correctional officers. There is no doubt that states where unions are active are those states where correctional officers receive better pay and working conditions. Because of their advocacy role toward officers, they sometimes place individual officers' needs over what is best for the system or society; in this way, one could see them operating in a way similar to that of defense attorneys who see their role as a pure advocate as well. Part of the conflict between administrators and unions may be the different goals and objectives of each side; however, there are obviously ethical and unethical ways to navigate the negotiations.

THE USE OF SUPERMAX PRISONS

One of the most troubling developments in prison management has been the use of supermax prisons. These facilities hark back to the days of the Eastern State Penitentiary, with twenty-four-hour isolation and no programs of self-improvement to salvage the waste and pain of time served (Pollock, 2004). The criticism of these prisons has been directed both to the conditions and to the criteria and procedures used for transferring prisoners to them. Pelican Island in California, the most notorious supermax facility, was the target of a court case, *Madrid v. Gomez*, 889 F.Supp 1146 (N.D. Cal. 1995), in which the courts held the state responsible for brutality and lack of medical care. The case also exposed the practice of guards covering up for each other and the power of union officials in squelching official investigations (Martin, 2003).

The other problem with the supermax prisons has been who is sent there. There are allegations that the prisons are being used for troublemakers who are not especially dangerous. Some report that mentally ill offenders who cannot control their behavior are sent to supermax prisons and become even more ill because of the isolation and lack of medical services. After a supermax had been built in Ohio, it was found that only half the beds could be filled with those in the prison system who met the original criteria for transfer, so officials moved Death Row inmates to the supermax (*Wilkinson v. Austin*, et al., 125 S.Ct. 2384 [2005]). The supermax in this case was similar to all the other supermaxes in having the following characteristics:

1. Human contact was strictly prohibited.
2. Cell lights were on twenty-four hours a day.
3. Inmate exercise was for only one hour a day and in a small room indoors.
4. The transfer was of indefinite duration and reviewed only annually.
5. Transfer to supermax disqualified the inmate from parole consideration.

These prisons have been described as soul-destroying. They involve horrific deprivations of some of the most basic elements of what most people take for granted, including social support, self-esteem, and hope. If they must be used at all, they should be used with the greatest of care and with the greatest attention to how the environment affects the individuals housed there.

ABU GHRAIB: A PRISON BY ANY OTHER NAME

When the abuse in Iraq's Abu Ghraib prison was exposed, many made comparisons between the behaviors of military prison guards and those of correctional officers in U.S. prisons. The comparisons were hard to ignore because several of the worst abusers were correctional officers in civilian life and the person who helped set up the Abu Ghraib prison was Lane McCotter, an ex-head of the Texas, New Mexico, and Utah prison systems (M. Ward, 2004). It cannot be denied that the very environment of an incarcerative facility brings out the worst in people.

The Zimbardo experiment of the 1970s was one of the experiments that spurred the creation of human-subjects review boards in colleges and universities. In this experiment, college men were arbitrarily assigned to be guards or inmates and a mock prison was set up in the basement of a building on the grounds of Stanford University. The changes in both groups were so profound that the experiment was canceled after six days. Zimbardo (1982) noted that about one-third of the guards became brutal and authoritarian, and prisoners became manipulative and exhibited signs of emotional distress and mental breakdown. If college men who know the experiment is artificial succumb to the temptation to inflict their will on those who are in their power, is it possible that the environment itself causes people to act in ways that they would not otherwise?

Even the recent history of prisons is replete with extreme brutality on the part of guards:

- Gladiator fights in Corcoran Prison
- The "Tucker telephone" in Arkansas
- Using "dog boys" as live quarry for Texas dog handlers
- Beatings and the use of dogs on prisoners (most recently videotaped in Brazoria County, Texas)
- Looking the other way while inmates beat and raped a victim

Allegations of abuse in prisons and jails in the United States include the following abuses similar to what took place in Abu Ghraib (Butterfield, 2004):

- Inmates being forced to wear pink underwear as punishment (Phoenix jail)
- Inmates being stripped as punishment (Pennsylvania)
- Inmates being made to wear black hoods (Virginia)

In all cases of abuse in prison, the reasons seem to be a failure of leadership and lack of discipline, training, and supervision (Ward, 2004). Certainly that seems to be the case in Abu Ghraib, as will be described more fully in Chapter 15. It can also be noted that the worst cases of abuse in civilian prisons occur when prison leaders ignore violations on the part of staff and do not clearly convey that the mission is to run a safe and secure prison without the corrupting presence of extra-legalforce.

Correctional managers can and should generate a strong anti-corruption policy (obviously, managers should not be engaging in corrupt practices themselves). Such a policy would include (McCarthy, 1991):

1. proactive measures such as mechanisms to investigate and detect wrongdoing
2. reduced opportunities for corruption
3. screening of employees using state-of-the-art psychological tools
4. improved working conditions
5. providing good role models in the form of supervisors and administrators who follow the Code of Ethics presented earlier in this chapter

Correctional management has not developed in the way that law enforcement management has; there are fewer texts on correctional management, and those that can be found rarely mention ethics for supervisors and administrators (Wright, 2001).

Also, law enforcement seems to be ahead of corrections in ethics training for its officers.

The "trickle down" theory of ethical management is that officers will treat inmates the way they perceive they are being treated—with fairness, compassion, and respect, or with less than fairness, respect, and compassion, if that is the way they perceive they are treated by management. It becomes easier to justify unethical actions if one feels victimized. Obviously, if employees are expected to be responsible, loyal, and treat each other and inmates with respect, administrators should practice these same behaviors (Houston, 1999; Souryal, 1999a; Wright, 2001). Furthermore, staff members who are coerced to do unethical or illegal actions by management are more likely to behave in unethical and illegal ways by their own initiative.

Wright (2001) offers seven principles as a guide for how administrators and supervisors should treat employees: safety, fair treatment, due process, freedom of expression, privacy, participation in decision making, and information. In regard to fair treatment, not penalizing staff members who do corrupt acts is not treating honest officers fairly. As to privacy, staff members have a right to a private life, but not when the use of drugs, alcohol, or sexual partners interferes with their job performance.

Ironically, the scandal at Abu Ghraib led to a national commission to examine U.S. prison conditions, chaired by a former U.S. Attorney General and a Chief Judge of the Third Circuit. The Commission on Safety and Abuse in America's Prisons spent several years holding hearings and obtaining testimony concerning the state of prisons in this country, and in 2006 issued its Summary and Recommendations. The entire report or an executive summary can be accessed by going to http://www.prisoncommission.org/report.asp. One of the findings was that this nation's prisons suffer from a culture of violence and a lack of positive treatment goals. The Commission also found that better safety inside prisons and jails depends on changing institutional culture. This has to be done by enhancing the corrections profession at all levels, and promoting a culture of mutual respect, grounded in respectful behavior between staff and inmates.

To run a safe and secure prison is consistent with running an ethical prison where officers and staff uphold and respect the rights of prisoners. All ethical systems support the need to respect basic rights and use appropriate and legal force and punishments to control the prison population. Under ethical formalism, violating rights and using illegal force against prisoners violate one's duty and are contrary to the categorical imperative. Under utilitarianism, it seems obvious that if one acts in illegal ways toward inmates, there is very little moral authority to influence them to become law-abiding. Research indicates that the system of punishment and retribution as implemented in our prison system does not engender remorse or guilt among prisoners, who feel that they themselves are the victim of an unethical and illegal system (Presser, 2003).

CONCLUSION

In this chapter we touched on some of the ethical issues that correctional personnel face in institutional corrections. These individuals have much in common with other criminal justice practitioners, especially in the area of discretion, and they are also in a unique position in that they hold power over the most basic aspects of life for confined inmates. This position allows correctional officers either to intensify the humiliation that incarcerated offenders feel or to make the prison experience more tolerable for those who serve time. The difficult decisions for correctional officers arise from the personal relationships that develop with inmates, the trust that is sometimes betrayed, the favors that seem harmless, and the coercive environment that makes violence normal and caring abnormal. Correctional treatment personnel have their own problems in resolving conflicts between loyalty toward clients and toward the system.

To be in a helping profession in a system geared for punishment is a difficult challenge for anyone, and the temptation to retreat into bureaucratic compliance or, worse, egoistic relativism is always present. Although this chapter has discussed officers mistreating inmates and correctional professionals engaging in other unethical conduct, we do not mean to imply that criminal justice workers as a whole are blatantly or pervasively unethical. Arguably, the criminal justice system operates as well as it does only because of the caring, committed, honest people who choose it as a career.

Key Terms

correctional
  officer *414*

hostile work
  environment *435*

human service
  officer *423*

pluralistic
  ignorance *420*

reciprocity *420*

Tucker telephone *423*

"tune-ups" *423*

whistleblower *418*

Review Questions

1. How do C.O.s have discretion similar to police officers and court personnel?
2. Describe the role ambiguity that C.O.s faced in the 1970s and 1980s.
3. Describe the formal ethical code for correctional personnel, and compare it to the law enforcement code.
4. Describe the C.O. subculture.
5. What is pluralistic ignorance? Describe the "good" officer.
6. What are some forms of corruption committed by C.O.s?
7. What are some ways to reduce corruption?
8. What are the two interests that members of the treatment staff have to balance? Give examples of some ethical concerns of treatment personnel.
9. Discuss the ethical issues of super max prisons.
10. What is the Commission on Safety and Abuse in American Prisons and what were some of its findings?

Writing/Discussion Questions

1. Write an essay on (or discuss) how you would implement an anti-corruption strategy in a prison known for brutality and other forms of corruption.
2. Write an essay on (or discuss) the full report of the Commission on Safety and Abuse in American Prisons, after you have downloaded it from the internet and read it.
3. Write an essay on (or discuss) the range of legal rights that you believe prisoners should have. Look to international treaties on human rights, the ACA standards, and other sources before you write your essay.

Ethical Dilemmas

Situation 1

You are a prison guard supervising a tier. One of the inmates comes to you and asks a favor. Because he is a troublemaker, his mail privileges have been taken away. He wants you to mail a letter for him. You figure it's not such a big deal; besides, you know he could make your job easier by keeping the other inmates on the tier in line. What would you tell him?

Situation 2

As a new C.O., you soon realize that a great deal of corruption and graft are taking place in the prison. Guards routinely bring in contraband for inmates in return for money, food bought for the inmates' mess hall finds its way into the trunks of staff cars, and money is being siphoned from inmate accounts. You are not sure how far up the corruption goes. Would you keep your mouth shut? They're just inmates, anyway. Would you go to your supervisors? What if, in exposing the corruption, you implicate yourself? What if you implicate a friend?

Situation 3

You are a prison psychologist, and during the course of your counseling session with one drug offender, he confesses that he has been using drugs. Obviously, this is a serious violation of prison rules. Should you report him? What if he tells you of an impending escape plan?

Situation 4

You are a prison warden, and a new C.O. comes to you and says she has been sexually harassed by the captain. You know that the captain has been with the prison for twenty years and has not had any negative reports in his record. On the one hand, you like him and think he is an excellent captain. On the other hand, this C.O. seems earnest and believable and is quite upset, so you believe something must have happened. What is the ethical course of action? What is the legal course of action?

Situation 5

You are a prison counselor and have a good relationship with the other counselors. You all go out drinking after work sometimes, and in general you like and respect everyone. Recently you've noticed that something seems to be going on with one of the other counselors. Stella is usually outgoing and cheerful, but lately she seems distracted and upset. You see her in the parking lot one evening and ask her what's the matter. She confides to you that she is in love with an inmate. She knows it is wrong, but she says that they had an instant chemistry and that he is like no man she has ever known. She has been slipping him love notes, and he has also been writing her. You tell her that she has to stop it or else quit her job. She tearfully tells you that she can't let him go, she needs her job, and you've got to keep quiet or you'll get her fired. What would you do?

Suggested Readings

Braswell, M., Miller, L., and Cabana, D. 2006. *Human Relations and Corrections*, 6th ed. Prospect Heights, IL: Waveland Press.

Conover, T. 2000. *New Jack: Guarding Sing Sing*. New York: Random House.

Crouch, B. (Ed.). 1980. *Keepers: Prison Guards and Contemporary Corrections*. Springfield, IL: Charles C Thomas.

Johnson, R. 2006. *Hard Time: Understanding and Reforming the Prison*. Pacific Grove, CA: Brooks/Cole.

Juozapavicius, J. 2008. Oklahoma Sheriff charged with Using Inmates as Sex Slaves. Assoicated Press, retrieved 4/26/2008 from http://www.officer.com/publication/printer.jsp?id=41064.

Kauffman, K. 1988. *Prison Officers and Their World*. Cambridge, MA: Harvard University Press.

Lerner, J. 2002. *You've Got Nothing Coming: Notes from a Prison Fish*. New York: Broadway.

Martin, D. 1993. *Committing Journalism: The Prison Writings of Red Hog*. New York: Norton.

Pollock, J. 2004. *Prisons and Prison Life: Costs and Consequences*. Los Angeles: Roxbury.

Santos, M. 2007. *Inside: Life Behind Bars in America*. Boston: St. Martin's Press.

ETHICS AND COMMUNITY CORRECTIONS

Community corrections may be a more humane alterative than prison, but many offenders, such as sex offenders, are not welcome in the community. Legislation requiring sex offender registries and mandatory minimums are illustrations of the antipathy the public feels for these offenders. Should sex offenders serve life terms instead?

© Alden Pellett/AP/Wide World Photos

CHAPTER OBJECTIVES

1. Understand the concept of community corrections.

2. Understand the ethical issues that probation and parole officers might face.

3. Understand the concepts of peacemaking corrections and restorative justice.

4. Understand the ethical issues inherent in the restorative justice approach.

Melinda Wawak put her trust in a man called Bob Johnson, who ran a parole consulting service. Supposedly, in return for thousands of dollars, Johnson and the firm would advocate for her husband, who was serving time in prison. Because of the secrecy of the parole system, relatives and prisoners had virtually no chance themselves of understanding the system or influencing the decisions of the parole board hearing officers who determine whether or not someone would be released. After giving Johnson thousands of dollars, she did some Internet sleuthing on the firm and discovered that Johnson was really Andy Bob Coats, a convicted thief on parole himself. Although he was subsequently prosecuted, many other parole "consultants" who do virtually nothing for the money that desperate families give them are immune from legal sanctions. Critics argue that families would not have to resort to such desperate measures if the process were more open and fair (Ward, 2006c).

In Chapter 13 we focused on institutional corrections; however, the majority of offenders are under some form of community supervision—either probation or parole. The correctional professionals who supervise offenders in the community have different ethical issues than do those who work in an institution.

THE CONCEPT OF COMMUNITY CORRECTIONS

Community corrections has a more positive and helpful image than does institutional corrections. However, even in this subsystem of the criminal justice system, the ideals of justice and care become diluted by bureaucratic mismanagement and personal agendas. Professionals in community corrections do not have the same power as police or correctional officers to use physical force, but they do have a great deal of nonphysical power over the clients they control. Their authority and power can be used wisely and ethically or can become subverted to personal ends.

The concept of community corrections is supported by the ethics of care; it promotes meeting the needs of the offender and the victim (through restitution). A prison sentence is basically a rejection or banishment; however, community supervision represents the concepts of acceptance and integration with the community. Even parole, coming after a prison sentence, originally operated with the philosophy of reintegration.

Utilitarianism also supports community corrections because the benefit to the community by not banishing the offender to prison is both financial and emotional.

QUOTE AND QUERY

[Community corrections] signifies moral concern for the individual, one that is consistent with the natural law ethics of "dignity of man," the constitutional ethics of individualized treatment and perhaps the religious ethics of redemption.

Souryal, 1992: 356

Explain how community corrections is either consistent or inconsistent with the various ethical systems.

Even a retributive philosophy can support community corrections because some crimes are simply not serious enough to justify a prison sentence.

Souryal (1996a) discussed the "mystique" of probation. He described John Augustus, the so-called grandfather of probation, as personifying the concepts of probation, including the belief in redemption. Other principles that are consistent with the mystique include honesty, fidelity and obligation, justice, public service, and self-control. The "Quote and Query" box illustrates the ethical justifications of community corrections.

Community corrections is a term that encompasses halfway houses, work release centers, probation, parole, and any other intermediate sanctions, such as electronic monitoring—either as a condition of probation or as a sentence in itself. Jails are somewhat of a hybrid. They are located in the community but share many characteristics of institutional corrections. We considered jail officers in the last chapter because the dilemmas they face vis-à-vis whistleblowing, the officer subculture, and the use of coercive force against inmates are more similar to the issues faced by correctional officers than the issues faced by probation and parole officers.

Probation and parole sentences involve supervision but also usually require meeting some other conditions. Some of these conditions pose special issues of privacy, liberty, and impact on others. For instance, should conditions specify whom the offender can associate with? Mandate that the offender go to church? Dictate to the offender where he or she can live or what type of job he or she can have? Require the use of contraception?

Electronic monitoring programs, usually using ankle bracelets and a telephone, raise issues of privacy. Such sanctions are said to blur the line between the offender and his or her family. Electronic monitoring sometimes involves a camera connected to the telephone. When the offender calls into a monitoring station, the monitor can see past the offender into the home. Is this a violation of family members' privacy, or do we consider it a consent entry? In general, probation and parole require consent for warrantless searches, but is it really consent when the option is prison? And even if the offender gives consent, can he or she give consent for other family members who are also affected?

Some contend that we are needlessly "widening the net" of corrections by putting more and more people on some form of correctional supervision. Further, the use of surveillance techniques against offender populations is spilling over into other contexts. For instance, drug testing started with probationers and now seems to be common in the workplace. Other forms of surveillance started with correctional populations but then became accepted practices in other applications. For instance, metal detectors are used now in a number of settings, and some workplaces use a polygraph, monitor employees' calls, use video cameras, track e-mails, and in other ways apply the surveillance practices created for lawbreakers to the rest of us (Staples, 1997).

The use of alcohol programs and the threat of punitive sanctions raise issues of personal liberty and freedom. Because alcohol is a legal substance, should we punish convicted felons for drinking while on probation? The argument is that convicted felons do not have to accept conditions of probation that prohibit alcohol—they could choose prison—but is that a legitimate choice? Further, although such conditions may make sense for those convicted of driving while intoxicated, do the technical conditions of "no alcohol" make sense for a burglar who did not attempt to explain or defend his actions by claiming to be drunk at the moment of the crime?

The danger of intermediate sanctions is that because they are typically so innocuous, they are used more frequently for offenders who may not have received any formal system response in years past. Unfortunately, what sometimes happens is that the offender, once in the system, fails because of technical violations and becomes more and more immersed in the system. This problem of **net widening**, which means increasing the types of individuals brought into the corrections system, is problematic not only from an ethical stand but also for purely pragmatic reasons of cost. Can we foresee a time when a large portion of the population is on some type of governmental monitoring status? Some say it is already here. We may be happy to note that tax monies may not be burdened by such monitoring because the trend to charge offenders supervision fees is growing. Still, other than providing employment for the legions of criminal justice students who are graduating from colleges and universities, are there good reasons for the dramatic expansion of the net of corrections?

PROBATION AND PAROLE OFFICERS

Formal ethical guidelines for probation and parole officers are provided by the American Correctional Association code as well as by their own ethics codes (i.e., Federal Probation Officers' Association, see Box 14.1). Probation and parole officers are considered to be more professional than correctional officers.

- They typically have at least a bachelor's degree, if not a graduate degree.
- They are subject to fewer organizational controls in the form of rule books and policies.
- They have a great deal of discretion.

The formal ethics of the profession is summarized by the ideal of service—to the community and to the offender. Whether to emphasize offenders' needs over community needs, or vice versa, is at the heart of a number of ethical dilemmas for the probation and parole officer. Other ethical issues are more similar to those encountered in the other subsystems discussed. They revolve primarily around decisions to substitute personal values and goals for organizational values. Next we will touch on some of the themes of previous chapters—the use of discretion, officer subcultures, and relationships with clients.

BOX 14.1	FEDERAL PROBATION OFFICERS' ASSOCIATION CODE OF ETHICS

As a Federal Probation Officer, I am dedicated to rendering professional service to the courts, the parole authorities, and the community at large in effecting the social adjustment of the offender.

I will conduct my personal life with decorum, will neither accept nor grant favors in connection with my office, and will put loyalty to moral principles above personal consideration.

I will uphold the law with dignity and with complete awareness of the prestige and stature of the judicial system of which I am a part. I will be ever cognizant of my responsibility to the community which I serve.

I will strive to be objective in the performance of my duties, respect the inalienable rights of all persons, appreciate the inherent worth of the individual,

and hold inviolate those confidences which can be reposed in me.

I will cooperate with my fellow workers and related agencies and will continually attempt to improve my professional standards through the seeking of knowledge and understanding.

I recognize my office as a symbol of public faith and I accept it as a public trust to be held as long as I am true to the ethics of the Federal Probation Service. I will constantly strive to achieve these objectives and ideals, dedicating myself to my chosen profession.

Source: Federal Probation Officers' Association;Washington, D.C. Adopted September 1960; revised March 1993. Reprinted with permission. All rights reserved.

THE USE OF DISCRETION

Discretion in probation exists at the point of sentencing: Probation officers make recommendations to judges concerning sentences. Discretion also exists during supervision in the following ways:

- Probation officers decide when to file violation reports.
- They decide what recommendation to make to the judge during revocation hearings.
- They make numerous decisions along the way regarding the people on their caseload.

Parole board members or their designees make decisions regarding release, and parole officers have the same discretion in managing their caseload that probation officers do. What criteria are used for these decisions? Usually, the risk to the public is the primary factor, but other considerations also intrude. Some of these other considerations are ethical; some might not be. How would one evaluate the ethics of the following criteria?

- race
- crime
- family ties
- crowding in institutions
- status of the victim
- judge's preference
- publicity generated by the crime.

Probation officers write pre-sentence reports to help judges decide sentences, but research has found that there may be errors in the information presented and that some officers are not as thorough as others in gathering information. This may not make much difference if it is true, as some have found, that probation officers' recommendations and judges' decisions are determined almost completely by the current offense and prior record (Whitehead, 1991).

Probation and parole officers have the authority and power to recommend revocation. This power is also limited because probation and parole officers' recommendations can be ignored by the judge or the parole hearing officer. Yet the implicit power an officer has over the individuals on his or her caseload must be recognized as an important element of the role, not to be taken lightly or misused.

Some practices in decision making are clearly unethical and illegal. Peter Maas's (1983) book *Marie* details a scheme in Tennessee that involved "selling" paroles to convicts. Other situations are perhaps more difficult to judge as unethical or not. In a controversy in Texas in the early 1990s, ex-parole board members were found to have sold their services as "parole consultants" to inmates and inmates' families in order to help them obtain a favorable release decision. There is at least the possibility that what the inmate was buying was a former parole board member's influence. The situation was brought to light when a serial killer was arrested for yet another murder while out on parole. When how he obtained parole was investigated, it was discovered that one of these former parole board members/"parole consultants" had been hired by the inmate. Whether that had anything to do with a favorable parole decision will never be known, but many allege that there is at least the appearance of impropriety in the arrangement, and steps were taken to eliminate the practice.

Although the practice evidently was not against any state law at the time and those who participated described their help as simply explaining the process and helping the inmate prepare a presentation to the board, many viewed it as unethical. Rules were created that restricted such practices to attorneys, but abuses still occur, as evidenced by the experience of Melinda Wawak described in the first paragraph of this chapter (Ward, 2006c).

THE PROBATION/PAROLE OFFICER SUBCULTURE

The subculture of probation and parole officers has never been documented as extensively as that of police and correctional officers. Because of differences between these professions, the subculture of the former is not as pervasive or strong as that of the latter. On the one hand, probation and parole officers do not feel as isolated as police or correctional officers do. They experience no stigmatization; they have normal working hours; they do not wear a depersonalizing uniform; and they have a less obviously coercive relationship with their clients. These factors reduce the need for a subculture. Still, one can probably identify some norms that might be found in any probation or parole office.

1. *Cynicism.* They have a norm of **cynicism** toward clients. The subculture promotes the idea that clients are inept, deviant, and irredeemable. Probation and parole professionals who express positive attitudes toward clients' capacity for change are seen as naïve and guileless.

2. *Lethargy.* At least in some offices, there is a pervasive subcultural norm of lethargy or minimal work output. This norm is supported by the view that officers are underpaid and overworked.

3. *Individualism.* A norm of individualism can be identified. Although parole and probation officers may seek opinions from other professionals in the office, there is an unspoken rule that each runs his or her own caseload; to offer unsolicited opinions about decisions another person makes regarding his or her client violates this norm of autonomy.

Even though there does not seem to be the "blue curtain of secrecy" to the same extent as is found in policing, there no doubt is a norm against informing on colleagues for unethical or illegal behaviors. This relates somewhat to the norm of individualism but is also part of the pervasive occupational subculture against informing on colleagues. Probation and parole officers may see and hear unethical behaviors and not feel comfortable coming forward with such information. If they work in an office where the norm against exposing such wrongdoing is strong, they may indeed suffer sanctions similar to those of police and correctional officers for exposing others' wrongdoing.

Also, there seems to be the same management tendency that is seen in law enforcement to hide or ignore wrongdoing on the part of individual officers. This may be a misguided utilitarianism in managers who are attempting to protect the organization from public scandal, or it may be simply self-interested egoism from managers who fear that the blame will be directed at them. For whatever reason, there seems to be a tendency to ignore officers who are obviously unable or unwilling to do the job. Some officers even point out that those who are arrested for DWI or other crimes continue to work as probation and parole officers. If this is true, it seems ironic that some probation and parole officers seem to have little moral authority over the clients they supervise.

Probation and parole officers have been described as adopting different roles on the job. Recall that police have been described by the watchman, caretaker, and law enforcer typology. In the same way, probation and parole officers have been described by their orientation to the job and individual adaptation to organizational goals. For instance, Souryal (1992) summarizes other literature in his description of the following types:

1. the punitive law enforcer
2. the welfare/therapeutic practitioner
3. the passive time server
4. the combined model

Different ethical issues can be discussed in relation to each of these types. For instance, the **punitive law enforcer** may need to examine his or her use of authority. This officer may have a tendency to use illegal threats and violate the due-process protections that each client deserves. The **welfare/therapeutic worker** may need to think about natural law rights of privacy and autonomy. These officers have a tendency to infringe on clients' privacy because of their mindset that they are helping the client (and, indeed, they might be), but the client may prefer less help and more privacy. The **passive time server** may violate professional ethics in not performing duties associated with the role.

All of us may have some tendency to be a time server in our respective professions. It is important to continue to take personal inventories and ask whether we are still putting in a "day's work for a day's pay." As is the case for many of the other criminal justice professionals we have discussed in this book, parole and probation officers often have a great deal of flexibility in their day. They leave the office to make field contacts; and they often "trade" weekdays for weekend days because weekends are more conducive to home visits. This flexibility is necessary if they are to do the job, but some abuse it and use the freedom to accomplish personal tasks or spend time at home. Some offices have attempted to prevent this behavior by instituting measures such as time clocks and strict controls on movements, but these controls are inconsistent with professionalism and not conducive to the nature of the task.

Other offices develop norms that accept unethical practices and lethargy. Once this occurs, it becomes a difficult pattern to change. If it is already present, a single officer will have a hard time not falling into the pattern. If all officers feel overwhelmed by their caseloads and their relative lack of power to do anything about failure, the result may be that they throw up their hands and adopt a "who cares?" attitude. If the supervisor does not exhibit a commitment to the goal of the organization, does not encourage workers, treats certain officers with favoritism, or seems more concerned with his or her personal career than with the needs of the office, there is an inevitable deterioration of morale.

Whitehead (1991) discusses workers' frustration over incompetents being promoted, low wages, and high caseloads that lead to burnout. Souryal (1992) notes that low pay, a public view that probation and parole are ineffective, and the politicization of parole and probation are factors in professionals' feeling that their role is ambiguous, contradictory, and politically vulnerable. Disillusionment becomes almost inevitable. Although these issues are present in many organizations, they are especially problematic in a profession that requires a great deal of emotional investment on the part of the practitioner. If the organization does not encourage and support good workers, it is no wonder that what develops is an informal subculture that encourages minimum effort and treats organizational goals with sarcasm and cynicism.

CASELOAD SUPERVISION

Discretion exists not only at the recommendation-to-release stage but also throughout supervision. Officers do not make the decision to revoke, but they do make the decision to file a violation report and make a recommendation to the judge or the parole hearing examiner as to whether to continue on supervision status with perhaps new conditions, or revocation and a prison sentence. Many do not submit violation reports automatically upon discovery of every offender infraction. In this way they are like police officers, who practice selective enforcement of the laws. Like police officers, some of their criteria for decision making are ethical and some are not. Also like police officers, the individual officer may face ethical dilemmas when the law doesn't seem to take into account social realities, such as poverty.

The discretion to decide when to write a violation report is a powerful element in the control the officer has over the offender, but this can obviously be a difficult decision to make at times. If the officer excuses serious violations (e.g., possessing a firearm or continuing drug use) and the decision to do so is based on personal favoritism, fear, or bribery, that officer is putting the community at risk and is unethical in making the decision to do so. Situations in which the officer sincerely believes the offender made a mistake, has extraordinary excuses for such misbehavior, and is a good risk still present a danger to the community. Is the decision any more ethical because of the officer's belief in the offender? Would it be more ethical to conduct oneself "by the book" and always submit violation reports when the offender commits any violation, including a purely technical one?

Probation and parole officers are presented with other dilemmas in their supervision of offenders. For instance, the offender often acquires a job without the employer's knowledge of his or her previous criminality. Is it the duty of the officer to inform the employer and thereby imperil the continued employment of the offender? What about offenders' becoming personally involved with others and refusing to tell them about their past history? Does the probation or parole officer have a duty to the unwary party? The issue of confidentiality vis-à-vis AIDS has emerged. If the probation or parole officer knows or suspects that the offender is HIV-positive and the offender begins an intimate relationship with someone, does the officer have a duty to warn the other party? Most states protect the confidentiality of victims of AIDS, and in these cases the officer has a legal duty *not* to disclose.

The rights of the offender, the rights of unwary innocents, and the responsibilities of society are not well sorted out at this point. What is the probation or parole officer's responsibility to the offender's family? If family members are unwilling to help the offender and perhaps fear his or her presence, should the officer find a reason for revocation? Again, these questions revolve around competing loyalties to public and client. The correctional professional must balance these interests in every decision, and the decisions are often not easy to make.

Similar to the police officer, at times the probation officer's role as a family member or friend conflicts with the professional role. Family members and/or friends may expect special treatment or expect that the officer will use his or her powers for unethical purposes. These are always difficult dilemmas because family and friends may not be sympathetic to the individual's ethical responsibilities to the organization and to society at large. Probation and parole officers are likely to have overlapping circles of acquaintances and family connections with those on their caseloads, especially in small towns. Confidentiality and favoritism are issues that come up frequently.

The officer also has to contend with the issue of gratuities. Again, similar to the police officer, probation or parole officers may be offered special treatment, material goods, or other items of value because of their profession. In most cases the situation is even more clearly unethical for probation and parole officers because the gift is offered by a client over whom decisions are made, as opposed to police officers who may or may not ever be in a position to make a decision regarding a restaurant or convenience store manager.

Probation departments have clear rules against any "business relationships" with probationers, and this makes sense, but probation officers in small towns ask, "How can I avoid a business relationship with a client when the only coffee shop in town is run by one of my clients? Am I never to go there during the years he is on probation?" In the same manner as police, some probation and parole officers believe that the gifts offered are given in the spirit of gratitude or generosity and not to influence decision making.

Some probation or parole officers encounter ethical conflicts when they seek part-time employment at counseling centers. They may have counseling or drug treatment licenses that allow them to run groups and engage in individual counseling to earn extra income. This becomes an ethical issue when their part-time employment may involve working with correctional clients. Because their role as private counselor would conflict with their role as professional correctional supervisor, ethics boards have ruled that such employment is acceptable only when the counselor does not interact with clients.

Because probationers may appear to be similar to the probation or parole officer in socioeconomic status, family background, lifestyle, or personal value systems, they have a greater tendency to feel affinity and friendship for some clients. Some probation officers have been known to have clients baby-sit for them, to rent a room in their house, or to socialize with them and their families. Obviously, these personal relationships hinder the ability to perform one's official function as a protector of the community and enforcer for the legal system. Personal relationships of any type—romantic, platonic, or financial—are simply not appropriate or ethical for the probation and parole professional.

CORRUPTION

No doubt there are some probation recommendations based on bribery or favoritism, or decisions not to violate based on unethical criteria. There may be sexual coercion of clients. Urinalysis testing may be subverted by a corrupt scheme to switch test results. Many correctional professionals will complete their careers and retire without having heard about or being involved in any of the corrupt practices described above. However, it would wise to address such issues in training. Corrupt practices exist because honest people allow them to exist. For instance, in the "In the News" box, is it possible that others knew of this probation officer's misconduct before the formal investigation began?

IN THE NEWS | PROBATION OFFICER SENTENCED

A Florida state probation officer was sentenced in federal court to four months' imprisonment and three years of supervised release for accepting bribes from a probationer in exchange for allowing the probationer to avoid mandatory drug testing and other restrictions. The officer was tried in federal court under Title 18, United States Code, Section 1951 (Hobbs Act).

How often do you think probation officers accept bribes from clients to avoid conditions? Why do we hear about probation officer corruption so much less often than police officer corruption?

Source: United States Department of Justice news release, 2005.

Organizations experience corruption partly because they do not support and nurture ethical workers. It is hoped that the increasing professionalism of each of the subsystems of the criminal justice system will create a situation in which whistleblowers don't have to lose their careers and incur subcultural sanctions because they stand up for what is ethical.

As in law enforcement, a few officers will be "crooks" first and officers second. Many others probably slide into corruption because of a lack of organization support for ethical behavior. Also as in law enforcement, officers who are stressed and burned out may be the most vulnerable to ethical relativism and bad decisions. Burrell (2000) proposes that in order to prevent stress and burnout, probation (and parole), organizations should provide clear direction, manage proactively, establish priorities if there are high workloads, ensure stability and constancy, be consistent in expectations, manage with fairness, enforce accountability, delegate authority, provide proper resources, maintain communication, and allow participative decision making.

PAROLE

We have been discussing probation and parole officers simultaneously above, but there are some important distinctions between the two. First, parolees are perceived to be more of a threat to the community, so the supervision role of parole officers is emphasized much more strongly than in probation, where supervision is balanced with a service/counseling emphasis. Further, paroled offenders are usually older and have a longer criminal record, so the relationship between supervisor and client might be different. The problems faced by parolees are quite different from those faced by probationers.

It is estimated that roughly 600,000 prisoners are reentering our communities each year (King and Mauer, 2002: 3). This is a result of the drastic increase in the number of those incarcerated during the 1980s. Even if the use of parole decreases, the sheer number of those eligible for parole will be swelling the ranks of parole caseloads for decades to come. Most have the same low levels of education and vocational skills that they had going into prison and have not had access to many, if any, rehabilitative programs in prison. Further, many of those newly released will be those who *maxed out*—meaning that they completed their entire sentence with no requirements to be supervised (Talbot, 2003).

Even though these individuals have done their time and are released, they still may suffer from a range of civil disabilities, including having lost their right to vote. At least 47 states deny prisoners the right to vote for some period of time and 14 of them deny the right permanently. Ex-inmates cannot hold public office in 25 states (6 permanently), participate in jury service (45 states; 31 states permanently), or possess firearms (33 states; 28 states permanently). In most states, sex offenders must register with police. In 29 states, imprisonment is grounds for divorce, and in 19 states imprisonment is grounds for parental deprivation proceedings (Hemmons, 2001). Despite these disabilities, we expect ex-inmates to behave flawlessly. Obviously, most don't.

Many of those released from prison return. According to a Justice Department study, 67 percent of released inmates were charged with at least one serious crime within three years. The study tracked 272,111 released inmates in 15 states (K. Murphy, 2002). Other study findings indicated that the recidivism rate of offenders is worse than twenty years ago, not better, despite the longer sentences imposed. Men were more likely than women to recidivate (68 percent compared to 57 percent); blacks were more likely to recidivate than whites (73 percent compared to 63 percent); and young people (under 18) were more likely to recidivate than older offenders (45 and above) (80 percent compared to 45 percent). Offenders with the highest recidivism rates included car thieves, those convicted of receipt of stolen property, burglars, and those convicted of robbery.

Our incarceration rates—currently some of the highest in the world—have had a tremendously negative impact on communities. Entire neighborhoods are affected when a large percentage of their population is sent away for years at a time. Generational effects are obvious; children of inmates are six times as likely to be delinquent (Mauer, Chesney-Lind, and Clear, 2002). More subtle effects exist as well. The economy and the social fabric of a community are also affected when large numbers of young people are removed. Community corrections professionals have some power in this scenario. They can make release recommendations and affect revocation rates. They can help offenders with reentry problems, or they can blindly enforce every bureaucratic rule.

Recall that under ethical formalism, to be an ethical professional, one must do one's duty. What is the parole officer's duty? Some officers believe that they have met their ethical duty by explaining the rules to a parolee and then catching the person if he or she "messes up." Others see a more expanded role wherein the officer has some duty to help the offender readjust to society. This may involve taking some responsibility for counseling the offender, referring him or her to services, acting as a troubleshooter or mediator in conflict with family or others, and acting as an advocate in obtaining help. In other words, this officer takes a proactive approach to the parolee's success. Is filing a violation report a success (because the offender was caught) or a failure (because the offender did not succeed)?

A NEW PARADIGM OF CORRECTIONS?

The high incarceration rate in the United States has made a few people rich and others economically comfortable because of strong unions and/or white-collar jobs in corrections. Many more people have found poorly paid jobs as correctional officers. A huge network of profitable enterprise has sprung up because of the corrections industry. At the American Correctional Association meeting, delegates are enticed to a huge ballroom or conference hall filled from front to back with vendors. Participants pick up freebies of pens, water bottles, candy, and other items. they look at prison wares—everything from riot batons to stainless-steel stools. The field of corrections is indeed big business, and it supports a huge number of ancillary businesses. We have become so inured to the concept of deprivation of liberty that it is hard to think of a different approach—but there might be one.

A relatively recent philosophical approach to crime and punishment has been called *restorative justice*. Reichel (1997) briefly describes the movement toward restitution and community service sentences in the 1970s. Although these innovative sentences were originally touted as rehabilitative, when rehabilitative goals lost favor

| POLICY BOX | RESTORATIVE JUSTICE |

Restorative justice programs are used primarily with juvenile and nonviolent offenders. These programs have been financially supported by the federal government, and they have been widely hailed as a progressive advancement in the justice system. However, critics argue that they take away the victim's right to seek retribution, that they create a net-widening effect, and that there are problems when the formal due process of the justice system is bypassed.

Law: Typically, programs that use different sentences or different sentencing structures must have enabling legislation before they can be put into practice. In some cases, judges promote such programs and use their discretion by allowing some offenders to be diverted from the system into the programs.

Policy: Policies must be established regarding who is eligible for such programs and who will make the decision as to whether an offender is referred or not. Ordinarily, the offender and the victim must give consent for the case to be shifted to an alternative sentencing procedure. Policies must also be established for when an offender "fails" and what happens when he or she does not complete the program successfully. Typically, the case is then sent back for official processing. These policies do not carry the force of law, and they are often changed after the program has been in operation for some period of time. Inevitably, cases arise in which the policies do not seem to result in a fair outcome; then informal policies are often applied that do not carry the force of law or the sanction of formally approved policies.

Individual ethics: The individual decision makers (judge, probation officer, restorative justice staff, attorneys) must apply the law, policy, and their own individual ethics in the decision as to who goes into the program, what the offender is required to do, and what sanctions are given, keeping in mind the needs of the victim, the system, and the offender.

with public sentiment, rationales and justifications were redefined, and restoration or reparation (for the victim) became the philosophical rationale behind such programs (Bazemore and Maloney, 1994). See the Policy Box for a discussion of the law, policy, and ethics of restorative justice.

Whether restitution is to the individual (with compensation paid directly to the victim) or is symbolic (where the community benefits from the offender's labor or payments), the idea of alternative justice is to restore the victim to his or her condition before the victimization event, or if the victim is not easily identifiable, to produce a measurable positive effect for the community. In one program, community service offenders helped rebuild a town ravaged by a tornado. This approach has five goals (Bazemore and Maloney, 1994: 27):

1. The service should meet a clearly defined and obvious need.
2. The service should symbolically link offender and victim, or offender and his or her community.
3. Offenders should be viewed as resources, and outcome measures should be directed to the work itself (rather than the offender's behavior).

4. Offenders should be involved in planning and executing the projects.
5. Included should be a sense of accomplishment, closure, and community recognition.

The historical origins of and analogies to restorative justice can be found throughout recorded history. Early laws demanded victim compensation, and reparation has a much longer history than does penal servitude. Many advocates (see Umbreit, 1994; Umbreit and Carey, 1995; van Ness and Heetderks Strong, 1997; Perry, 2002) now believe that restorative justice appropriately places the emphasis back onto the victims and can be life-affirming and positive for the offender as well. The key is to find a method of restoration that is meaningful and somehow related to the offense instead of merely punitive labor—such as the infamous rock pile, which is devoid of worth to the victim, the offender, or society.

One model under restorative justice is called peacemaking corrections. **Peacemaking corrections** offers an approach of care and of *wholesight,* or looking at what needs to be done with both the heart and the head (Braswell and Gold, 2002). Both restorative justice and peacemaking corrections are consistent with the ethics of care and might be considered "feminine" models of justice because of the emphasis on needs rather than retribution.

It is said that a retributive, punitive orientation results in an offender's perception of unfairness (through denial of victim, denial of injury, or a belief that a more serious victimization was visited upon the offender). A different model may reduce those feelings and force the offender to squarely face his or her own responsibility. Arguably, a restorative justice program directs attention to the injuries of the victim and does not involve stigma, banishment, or exclusion, for the offender would not create the opportunity to generate rationalizations and excuses for the offender's behavior.

- *Peacemaking (or sentencing) circles* or *healing circles* constitute one model of this type of correctional approach. In these circles, adapted from interventions used in Native American and other indigenous cultures, the offender meets with the victim, his or her family, and other interested parties. The goal is to find some resolution, but the problem may not be simply the offender's wrongdoing; it could be the victim's behavior or the family's failings. The orientation is acceptance of the person and rejection of the behavior (Umbreit, Coates, and Vos, 2002). Similar programs involve only the family (family group conferencing).
- *Victim–offender mediation* is another type of program, in which offenders meet with their victims so victims can tell the offender face-to-face how the offense affected them—both monetarily and emotionally. These programs usually have an element of restitution, with the offender and victim agreeing on the amount of restitution the offender will pay.
- *Community reparative boards* represent another form of restorative justice. The board members consist of individuals who are representative of the community and who determine the sentence in a way that attempts to meet the needs of both parties.
- *Victim education programs* are somewhat similar in motive to the victim–offender mediation programs, but they do not match the victim with his or her offender. Instead, volunteer victims meet with offenders either in prison or

community settings and explain to offenders what the effect of victimization has been on them. These programs place more emphasis on education of victim rights and research on victimization. The goal is to create empathy toward victims, and the programs show moderate success (Monahan, Monahan, Gaboury, and Niesyn, 2004).

Reintegrative Shaming Versus Stigmatizing Shaming

As mentioned in Chapter 12, a number of punishments that are inflicted on offenders today incorporate the concept of shame. Judges have made those convicted of DWI use special license plates; sex offenders have had to put signs on their residence; and offenders have had to confess and seek the forgiveness of their community by publishing an advertisement or making a public appearance of some kind.

These types of shaming punishments hark back to the days of the stocks and pillory, when punishment was arguably more effective because of community scorn than the physical pain involved. Some believe that this is not a useful or helpful trend. For instance, one American Civil Liberties Union (ACLU) spokesperson called such punishments "gratuitous humiliation that serves no social purpose" (cited in Book, 1999: 653). Whitman (1998) argued that the use of such penalties is contrary to a sense of dignity and creates an "ugly complicity" between the state and the community by setting the scene for "lynch justice." There is even a question as to whether such punishments are legal because some state laws demand that probation conditions have a "rehabilitative function." In general, however, judges have imposed these punishments without much serious challenge. Legally, they seem to be acceptable, but what about ethically?

The major issue seems to be whether such shaming conditions are reintegrative or stigmatizing. Braithwaite (2000) is the best-known spokesperson for reintegrative shaming. He argues that shame is different from guilt because it comes from one's beliefs about how one's community feels about the crime. He argues that societies that don't have shame attached to certain crimes have a lot of that type of crime. Thus, what is necessary to reduce crime is a return to the concept of shame.

According to Braithwaite (2000), **stigmatization** is disrespectful shaming. In punishments where the offender is treated as a bad person rather than someone who has done a bad act, the society is rejecting the individual, which leads the individual to reject society. Braithwaite points out that some African societies that use reintegrative shaming have low crime rates, as does Japan, which uses techniques of reintegrative shaming with delinquents. These cultures do not reject the individual; rather, they reject only the behavior. Individuals continue to feel a part of their family, school, neighborhood, and community.

Stigmatizing punishments lead to oppositional subcultures; reintegrative interventions do not. It is not a coincidence that communities that are more integrated and have stronger social ties have less crime. These communities are much more likely to be able to employ the concept of reintegrative shaming and, thereby, control their members. The corollary, of course, is that if one feels disenfranchised from society, shaming will not work at all (Karp, 1998). The "Quote and Query" box is Braithwaites' summary of restorative justice.

QUOTE AND QUERY

Key values of restorative justice are healing rather than hurting, respectful dialogue, making amends, caring and participatory community, taking responsibility, remorse, apology, and forgiveness.

Braithwaite, 2000: 300

Do you think that restorative justice principles will ever be widely adopted by the criminal justice system? Why or why not?

Karp (1998) provides an interesting perspective on why restorative justice and reintegrative shaming interventions have received positive responses. The public may not believe that probation or other forms of alternative sanctions have the same moral condemnation that prison does; therefore, these punishments are seen as cheapening or lessening the moral blame of the offender. However, shaming penalties emphasize the individual's responsibility to the victim and society. Such programs instill a strong dose of morality and redemption, and the public seems to respond to that.

Further, Karp emphasizes the difference between stigmatizing and reintegrative shaming. He points out that most of the shaming punishments that have been reported, such as sex offenders being required to post signs on their doors, are stigmatizing shaming punishments. These may lead to unintended results, such as the offender being victimized by the community through vigilante justice. This is what Whitman (1998) finds problematic and distasteful about such punishments.

Recall that Whitman saw the state as setting the scene for "lynch justice," and, in truth, such punishments have led to the community victimizing offenders. **Megan's laws**—those that require registration of sex offenders and allow the publication of such lists—are questioned by some who point out that such laws have led to cases where an offender or his family have been attacked and, in some instances, actually driven from the community. Although the response might be, "So what—he's a sex offender!" it should be noted that in some states, all sex crimes are covered, and this may include a man who was convicted of statutory rape when he was eighteen, because his girlfriend was under the age of consent even though she was only slightly younger than the man. Further, the family members are stigmatized, and, arguably, they are innocent of wrongdoing.

Stigmatizing shaming punishments are ineffective with those who are already "on the margins" of society. One interesting study explored prisoners' feelings of remorse and discovered that most did not feel any guilt or remorse, and when they did, it had little to do with formal punishment (Presser, 2003). This author argues that no matter what one does to an offender, remorse cannot be coerced; it has to come from the internal psyche of the offender and is unlikely unless the person has been socialized to feel guilt. Arguably, this culture does not do a good job of doing that; the individualistic culture of the United States socializes its citizens in such a way that apologies are contrary to self-interest. Other cultures (such as Japan) place more importance on apologies, and this helps victims recover from the "moral insult" of the violation and reaffirms that victim and offender share the same moral order.

Presser (2003) notes that even when offenders indicate remorse, it may be contrived; the offender is really feeling sorry that he or she got caught. Offenders sometimes excuse or neutralize their violence—for instance, blaming a robbery victim who did not do what the offender told him to do. Often the offender neutralizes the harm to the victim by explaining that the victim was also a criminal, or explains the actions as self-defense:

> Fightin' ain't violence...when it's street, anyway. ...If you fight somebody, that's like normal. Ya know from where the streets that I come from. (Presser, 2003: 811)

When they did express remorse, it sometimes related to offenses for which they weren't even caught, and often because of something the victim did, interestingly, when the victims forgave them.

Forgiveness, like mercy, is an interesting concept. When a gunman killed five young girls in an Amish schoolhouse in 2006 before killing himself, the nation was appalled and grieved along with the Amish community. It was a truly horrific event, made all the more so by the gentle nature of the religious community, where violence was such a rarity. In a truly unusual and unique turn of events, the parents of the murdered children and the community immediately forgave the murderer and his family. In the Amish religion and tradition, forgiveness is said to be much more important than anger or revenge. This forgiveness was as newsworthy as the killings themselves and gave rise to many discussions about the nature of forgiveness and how it fits into religion and faith (Draybill, 2006).

Dzur and Wertheimer (2002) discuss how restorative justice can further forgiveness, and they ask the question: Is forgiveness a social good? They also question whether the justice system should be pursuing restoration and forgiveness. They summarize the philosophy of restorative justice, noting that it gives the victim a chance to voice his or her emotions. In this public discourse there is a presence of the victim that is not felt in the professional and objective traditional justice procedures. It is believed that the dialogue and the opportunity to be heard enable forgiveness and that forgiveness is good for the victim.

Those authors then argue against the idea that what is good for the individual victim is also good for everyone else. Using a utilitarian approach, they propose that there could be a greater good in incarcerating offenders who are thought to be likely to re-offend. Note that this is an empirical question because it is a question about consequences: Does restorative justice deter fewer people than traditional punishment?

Also, the authors point out that forgiving offenders may be good for the individual victim but may not be good for the "class of victims" who might have yet to be victimized. Other issues include determining who the victim is in attempted crimes. Should the burden of proof be lowered in restorative justice programs because there is no punishment when finding a person guilty? The basic point is that restorative justice may be good for the individual victim but not result in a greater good for society. Now we turn to other ethical issues in restorative justice.

ETHICAL ISSUES IN RESTORATIVE JUSTICE

Restorative justice seems to be a healthy alternative to prison. However, certain issues merit discussion. First, because such interventions are seen as benign, they have the potential to create net widening, further enlarging the scope of corrections over the citizenry (Roach, 2000). There are also questions of due process and whether restorative justice meets the traditional goals of crime prevention (Dzur and Wertheimer, 2002).

Another issue is the potential privacy issues of the offender and other members who are involved. One of the strengths of restorative justice interventions is the inclusion of a number of parties, including the offender's family, co-workers, and friends, as well as the victim and the victim's support group. But what if some individuals important to the process choose not to participate? If schools even have trouble getting some parents to involve themselves in their children's progress, it is entirely possible that a juvenile who is otherwise qualified for a program would not be able to participate because of unwillingness of family members.

Does this mean that the juvenile would be punished for having uncaring or unwilling parents? It may be that parents are caring but choose not to allow the state to intervene in what is considered "private" family business. Parents and relatives may point out that they have not broken any laws and that the state cannot tell them what to do or demand their presence in the process. Even when the process is seen as a positive intervention, whenever state actors are involved, there is a potential for coercion and some people react strongly to that idea.

Restorative justice programs are looked upon with favor by victims' rights groups because of the idea of restoration and restitution for victims. But what happens when victims do not suffer much and offenders have great needs? The approach is oriented to meeting the needs of victims and offenders, and in some cases it may be that the offender is needier. Would a victim reject such an approach? Should the victim be able to veto this approach and demand traditional punishment? Is it possible for a victim to be too vindictive?

An example of an interesting program that can be labeled restorative is the Texas mediation program. This program allows the family members of homicide victims to meet with the killer, even if the killer is on Death Row. Such meetings are preceded by months of counseling by trained volunteers for both the offender and the victims. The counselors decide when both parties are ready to meet, and the meeting doesn't take place if the victim is seen as too emotionally fragile or too retaliatory, or if the offender is seen as too manipulative or doesn't admit culpability.

In one mediation session (Nowell, 2001), a woman and her teenage granddaughter met with the killer of the woman's daughter and young girl's mother. The father and brothers refused to participate, but the mother and daughter wanted to see and talk to their loved one's killer. The daughter was only five years old when the killing took place, and she wanted to learn more about how her mother died and to see the man who did it. The offender turned out to be a man who had killed the victim when he was fifteen. His childhood was marked by sexual abuse, physical abuse, and abandonment. He and another teenager were high on "speedballs" (cocaine and methamphetamine) when they were picked up by the young mother after their car broke down. They raped and killed her.

In prison, this man came to know the family of a cellmate, who eventually adopted him. This family evidently had been instrumental in changing his life and outlook. His goal for participating in the program was to tell the victim's family how sorry he was for the crime and to ask forgiveness. The mediation between the women and young man continued for most of one day. The counselor guided the discussion. The offender told them what he remembered from the crime, and they told him about the dead woman. At the end of the day, the two women hugged the murderer and had a picture taken with his arms around their shoulders (Nowell, 2001).

While not all, or even most, mediations end with the victims and the offenders hugging, this story is amazing as it illustrates the power of humans to move beyond anger, hate, and grief toward solace and forgiveness. In addition, the women had to face negative reactions from their family members for participating and, especially, for having their picture taken with the murderer. From their point of view, the experience left them with something more than they had before: They got a glimpse of their loved one in her final hours, and some reassurance that the offender was not a monster.

It should be noted that victims' rights groups tend to be cautious about restorative justice programs in general because of the focus on offenders. The anger that victims feel toward the offender and the system that ignores their needs leaves little room for forgiveness. Most groups advocate harsher punishments, not restorative justice; they discuss "rights" rather than "needs" and thus draw their moral legitimacy from retribution rather than the ethics of care. However, other sources also argue that forgiveness and restorative justice are just as beneficial to the victim as the offender (Morris, 2000).

An emerging perspective indicates that the pendulum has swung too far in making the victim feel a part of the process. The **victim satisfaction model** (Stickels, 2003) proposes that Packer's models, first discussed in Chapter 8, of due process or crime control have given way to victim satisfaction. That is, the system and its actors (specifically, prosecutors) attempt to appease the victim in decisions from charging to plea bargaining. This creates a situation wherein the criminal justice system becomes, in effect, a civil system with the victim as plaintiff and the prosecutor a plaintiff's attorney. The implications are diverse and include cost–benefit issues (is it worth prosecuting some cases?) and also justice (does the victim's perspective of just resolution always equal an objective view of a just resolution?). This emerging perspective is contrary to the more established perspective that the system "forgets" the crime victim and is focused solely on the offender.

Does a murderer ever deserve forgiveness? Did the women in the mediation program forgive the offender or simply recognize his humanity? Should the Amish community have forgiven the murderer even though he expressed no remorse for his actions? We can't say that the family members who can't forgive are wrong, so is there ever a good in forgiveness? These questions are at the heart of restorative justice and probably explain why it thus far has been limited largely to nonserious property crimes and to juvenile offenders. However, the questions posed are at the very heart of any discussion of justice and are questions that we've asked in prior chapters. Specifically, do criminals ever deserve forgiveness?

CONCLUSION

In this chapter we looked at two approaches to community corrections. The first approach, probation and parole, is the traditional form of community corrections. We considered the ethical issues of these professionals and noted similarities with other criminal justice professionals in the presence of discretion and the use of ethical and unethical criteria of decision making. The second approach is a paradigm of justice called restorative justice. In this model, rights are replaced with needs and punishment is replaced with restoration. This is a fairly new idea in corrections, and the concepts are still being formed. However, it raises important questions about how best to meet the ends of justice and also presents new ethical issues such as the rights of family members and others connected with the offender. Despite being a benign intervention, issues of privacy and coercion still must be considered.

Key Terms

community corrections *445*

cynicism *448*

Megan's laws *458*

net widening *446*

passive time server *450*

peacemaking corrections *456*

punitive law enforcer *449*

stigmatization *457*

victim satisfaction model *461*

welfare/therapeutic worker *449*

Review Questions

1. Explain the concept and ideology of community corrections.
2. What is the concept of net widening?
3. Describe the discretion of probation and parole officers, and give examples of ethical and unethical applications of discretion.
4. Describe the probation officer subculture.
5. Describe the types of probation officers and ethical issues for each.
6. What are some ethical issues for probation and parole officers? Differentiate these issues.
7. What are the principles of restorative justice? Contrast these with traditional models of justice.
8. What are some examples of programs that use the restorative justice approach.
9. Distinguish between reintegrative shaming and stigmatizing shaming.
10. Explain whether the ethical systems would support restorative justice programs, and discuss some ethical issues that arise in restorative justice programs.

Writing/Discussion Questions

1. Write an essay on (or discuss) an ethical code for probation officers. Now support each element of the code using as a basis either utilitarianism or ethical formalism.
2. Write an essay on (or discuss) forgiveness. Would you want to meet with the murderer of a loved one? What would you want to ask him or her? Would you be able to forgive?
3. Write an essay on (or discuss) restorative justice. Find examples in your state. Do you agree or disagree with the philosophy of restorative justice? Why?

Ethical Dilemmas

Situation 1

You are a probation officer and have a specialized sex-offender caseload. The judge disagrees with a recommendation for a prison sentence and places an offender on probation. This man was convicted of molesting his four-year-old niece. One of the conditions of his probation is that he notify you whenever he is around children. He becomes engaged and moves in with a woman who has three children under the age of twelve. You believe that the man is not repentant and that there is a good chance he will molest these children. Although the woman knows his criminal history, she does not seem to care and even allows him to baby-sit the young girls. The judge has indicated that he will not entertain new conditions or a revocation unless there is evidence of a crime, but you understand from the offender's counselor that the offender continues to be sexually aroused by children. What can you do? What should you do?

Situation 2

You are a probation officer with a DWI probationer who has not been reporting for any of the court-sanctioned programs, and a motion to revoke (MTR) was supposed to be filed. However, a high-ranking administrator in your office tells you not to file the MTR. or take any other negative actions because this person is a personal friend and, anyway, he isn't a "serious criminal." What would you do?

Situation 3

You are a parole officer whose caseload includes a single mother with three hyperactive, attention-deficit-disordered young children. She receives no support from her ex-husband. Her own mother wants nothing to do with her or the children, believing that "God is punishing her." The mother works as a topless dancer but hates it. She continues dancing because it pays the bills so well. You know that she smokes marijuana on a fairly regular basis in an effort to deal with stress. Obviously, this is a violation of probation. However, if you file a violation report on her, she will go back to prison. You know she is doing the best she can with her kids, she is heavily involved with their school, and they are strongly bonded to her. You worry about what will happen to the kids. What would you do?

Situation 4

You are the director of a restorative justice program in your community. It is set up for juvenile offenders and involves circle sentencing, in which the offender meets with family members, school officials, and the victim and the victim's relatives and friends. The circle comes up with what should be done, and often there is no punishment per se but, rather, the juvenile is connected to programs that can help him or her get back in school, get a job, or receive vocational training.

In the case you are reviewing, you suspect that there are real questions as to whether or not the juvenile actually committed the burglary he is accused of. There is no evidence to link the juvenile with the crime, and he and his court-appointed attorney have claimed innocence. They then changed their plea and agreed to the restorative justice program, perhaps because if it is completed successfully, the juvenile will have no criminal record. Should you care whether the juvenile is innocent or not, given that the program is restorative, not punitive?

Situation 5

You have some real concerns about your co-worker's treatment of offenders. You hear him screaming obscenities at them in his office, and one time you saw him pat a female probationer on the rear end and say, "Be sweet to me and I'll keep you out of jail." No one else seems to notice that anything is wrong. Could you have misinterpreted the exchange with the client? Might it have been simply bad taste rather than sexual harassment. Should you do anything?

Suggested Readings

Bazemore, G. and Schiff, M. 2001. *Restorative Community Justice*. Cincinnati, OH: Anderson Publishing.

Braithwaite, J. 2000. "Shame and Criminal Justice." *Canadian Journal of Criminology* 42(3): 281–301.

Braswell, M., McCarthy, B., and McCarthy, B. 2006. *Justice, Crime, and Ethics*. Cincinnati, OH: Anderson Publishing.

Dzur. A., and Wertheimer, A. 2002. "Forgiveness and Public Deliberation: The Practice of Restorative Justice." *Criminal Justice Ethics* 21(1): 3–21.

Mauer, M., Chesney-Lind, M., and Clear, T. 2002. *Invisible Punishment: The Collateral Consequences of Mass Imprisonment*. New York: The Sentencing Project.

Perry, J. (Ed.). 2002. *Repairing Communities Through Restorative Justice*. Lanham, MD: American Correctional Association.

Van Ness, D., and Heetderks Strong, K. 1997. *Restoring Justice*. Cincinnati, OH: Anderson.

ETHICAL CHOICES AND THE "WAR ON TERROR"

CHAPTER **15**

Waterboarding, demonstrated here by protestors at Attorney General Michael Mukasey's confirmation hearing in 2007, is defined by some as torture, but President George W. Bush holds the position that it is "coercive interrogation" and legal. What do you think?

CHAPTER OBJECTIVES

1. Become familiar with the connection between the war on terror and traditional law enforcement.

2. Understand the basic elements of the "just war" debate and the just means discussion.

3. Be familiar with the counter-terrorism measures taken since 9/11, and explain how deontological and utilitarian rationales might be used to justify counter-terrorism measures.

4. Understand the human rights model of policing.

CHAPTER OUTLINE

In this book we have explored ethical issues in each of the subsystems of the criminal justice system. We have discovered certain themes that run through each of the subsystems:

- The presence of authority, power, force, and discretion in each of the subsystems of the criminal justice
- Informal practices and value systems among criminal justice actors that vary from formal principles of behavior
- The importance of ethical leadership
- The tension between deontological ethical systems and teleological or "means–end" ethical analysis

In this final chapter we will reiterate some of these themes and discuss more specifically the most important challenge facing all of us today.

THE THREAT OF TERRORISM

On September 11, 2001, the United States was changed forever. The terrorist attack on the World Trade Center was the single most devastating terrorist attack in this country and, indeed, the world, with more than 3,000 deaths and the complete destruction of two buildings that stood as icons of Western capitalism. Although we had experienced earlier incidents—the 1993 bombing of the World Trade buildings, the Oklahoma City bombing, and numerous attacks on U.S. targets worldwide—nothing prepared the country for the severity of the attack. The event traumatized a city, affected the American psyche, led to U.S. military engagement on foreign soil in two countries, and spurred the dramatic restructuring of federal law enforcement. The long-term effects of this event are still unfolding, but we have already seen pervasive changes in law enforcement at both the federal and the local levels.

We conclude this book with a discussion of the unique challenges that terrorism presents. Terrorists are not garden-variety criminals; therefore, our analyses of the activities of law enforcement, court, and correctional professionals thus far may or may not be applicable. One thing is clear, however: The "war on terror" affects not only the military and federal agencies; every law enforcement and justice agency in the land may have occasion to be involved. Targets of terrorist activity include not only buildings and bridges in big cities but also dams, power plants, schools, government buildings, and farms in the most remote areas.

Terrorism has been defined as the "deliberate, negligent, or reckless use of force against noncombatants, by state or non-state actors for ideological ends and in the absence of a substantively just legal process" (Rodin, 2004: 755). Modern terrorism has included acts by the Irish Republican Army, which attacked civilian targets in England to protest continued British presence in northern Ireland; by the Palestinians, who have targeted Israelis and others across the world in their continued protest over Israeli occupation of what they believe to be the Palestinian homeland; and by Al Qaeda, a fundamentalist Islamic group that is opposed to all Western secular power and is responsible for the attack on the World Trade Center as well as numerous other attacks throughout the world.

Terrorist groups also include groups that are separatists (Tamil Tigers in Indonesia), racial hegemonic groups (Ku Klux Klan), and even environmentalists (Earth Liberation Front) (Rodin, 2004). Terrorism has led to new questions about what is appropriate or ethical in law enforcement investigative techniques, individual rights vis-à-vis the government, and what is legal and ethical in the detention and treatment of prisoners.

"JUST WARS" AND JUST MEANS

When is it appropriate to engage in war? What methods are morally and ethically acceptable in a war? Philosophers have been engaged in the **"just war" debate** since Cicero (McMahan, 2004). The traditional justification of war comes from natural law, and the second comes from positivist law. Classical "just war" theorists such as Hugo Grotius (1583–1645) have held that natural law gives sovereigns the right to use force to uphold the good of the community, when unjust injuries are inflicted on others, and to protect the state (Grotius, 2005; Bellamy, 2004). States are justified to engage in war when any of these events exist; otherwise, the war is unjust and immoral. However, natural law has been criticized as a justification for war because of the likelihood that leaders use moral arguments to justify wars that are, in reality, initiated for other means (e.g., when a sovereign engages in war against another state under the justification of self-defense or protecting a victim group, when the true motivation is a land grab or some other reason.

The second, more recent, justification for war comes from **positivist law**, which is **man-made law**. Increasingly, this is used as the only legitimate justification for war. Specifically, the idea is that legal incursions into the sovereignty of other nations are justified only under the auspices of international law as provided through the United Nations and other multilateral treaties and organizations. The problem with positivist law as the basis for justifying war is that no single authoritative legal body in international relations sits above all sovereigns and it has not been developed enough to include all countries and cover all circumstances (Bellamy, 2004).

Because of the lack of complete coverage of positivist law, natural law justifications for war still exist; the main justifications are either the defense of one's own state or humanitarian reasons, which refers to the justification to engage in war with a sovereign nation to protect its citizens from serious victimization such as genocide. Intrusions in internal conflicts within states have been undertaken by other states when gross humanitarian violations have occurred (such as the ethnic cleansing campaigns in Rwanda and Bosnia). Again, however, the problem in using these "natural law" or moral imperative justifications to engage in war is that they can be abused and misused; therefore, limits on the moral justifications for war have been proposed, including the following (Bellamy, 2004):

- The violations must be knowable to all.
- The violations must be widespread and systematic.
- The force used must save more lives than it injures.

These are not too different from other justifications that have been offered by other writers. For instance, Crank and Gregor (2005: 230) and Hicks (2004) have offered the following justifications for war:

1. The threat must be grave, lasting, and certain.
2. There are no other means to avert the threat.
3. There must be a good probability of success.
4. The means must not create a greater evil than the threat responded to.

These justifications seem to be consistent with a utilitarian system of ethics. They are not inconsistent with ethical formalism either, for ethical formalism includes the principle of forfeiture, which states that someone who impinges on others' rights forfeits his or her rights to the same degree.

Even if a war can be justified by natural or positivist law, there is the second question as to what means are acceptable in fighting a war. Utilitarian ethics and ethical formalism tend to agree, in general, upon the restrictions of what is ethically acceptable in a just war. In determining "just means," the extent of the harm is weighed against the end or injury averted, just as when one asks if the war itself is justified. Ethical formalism may be less accepting than utilitarianism of harming innocents or noncombatants; however, even under ethical formalism, the **principle of double effect** states that if one undertakes an action that is a good, but that also results in a negative end, as long as the negative end was not the intent of the actor, the good action and the good end can be considered a good.

For instance, if one bombs a military target and innocents are harmed during the bombing, the act, if otherwise considered ethical, does not become unethical because of the death of civilians. The bombing of Dresden, the use of the atomic bomb on Hiroshima and Nagasaki, and not warning people in Coventry that the British had cracked the Nazi code and knew that the city was about to be bombed but didn't reveal that they knew the information—all have been discussed as ethical conundrums during World War II. Whether someone concludes that these were ethical actions or not, the analysis is usually an application of utilitarianism (the end of winning the war justified the means, even though the means included the death of many innocent civilians). We continue these same discussions today in debates about the war in Iraq and the means employed in both Iraq and the more amorphous "war on terror."

Although questions concerning the ethics and morals of the Iraq war are outside the scope of this text, the means acceptable to combat terrorism in this country are not. There has been a good deal of argument and analysis over whether traditional "just war" arguments can be applied to the fight against terrorists (Crank and Gregor, 2005; Zohar, 2004). Smilansky (2004) points out that terrorists have no moral justification and they attack democracies partially because the ethos and values of such countries prohibit taking an "any means necessary" response. However, this statement does not seem to be supported by facts, as democratic governments have resorted to a variety of means, in response to terrorist attacks, that are, arguably, inconsistent with democratic values.

In Chapter 9, the "Dirty Harry problem" was presented as a question whether police should use any means necessary to obtain information from a criminal suspect in order to save a life. The Dirty Harry problem can be applied to terrorism: The current Harry Callahan is Jack Baur, the hero from the television show "24." In this show he was confronted with "the ticking bomb scenario," specifically, whether one should use torture to find the location of a bomb that is about to go off and kill many people. While the stakes may be higher, this is the same dilemma that faced the fictional Harry Callahan and, one might add, the same analysis may be applied: Do bad means ever justify a good end?

THE RESPONSE TO 9/11

Since 9/11, we have seen a fundamental shift in the goals and mission of law enforcement and public safety. This shift has included an expansion of the number of law enforcement agencies and personnel, a nationalization of law enforcement, a reduction of civil liberties, and a merging of immigration control and traditional law enforcement. We have seen federal money directed to training law enforcement officers to act as "first responders" to critical events such as terrorist attacks. There has also been more federal money available for hardware purchases. The trend of community or neighborhood policing that sought to forge links between law enforcement and the community it served has been eclipsed by these new initiatives, and federal financial support for community policing has been drastically reduced.

Further, there are increasing links between local law enforcement and immigration and federal law enforcement. Although they are all related, we will discuss the following responses to 9/11 separately:

- detainments and greater governmental secrecy,
- the Patriot Act and the Department of Homeland Security,
- wiretapping and threats to privacy,
- renditions and secret prisons,
- Guantanamo and the Military Commissions, and
- the use of torture.

Detainments and Governmental Secrecy   Immediately after 9/11, hundreds of noncitizens were detained on either immigration charges or material witness warrants. The Patriot Act required that all individuals on visas report to immigration offices and, once there, many were detained for minor violations of their visa. Hundreds were held for months in federal facilities and county jails without hearings. Despite civil liberties groups pressing for the names of the detainees, it took months for the federal government to release even the numbers of individuals detained, much less their names.

The deportation hearings that were held were closed to the public and to the media, despite legal suits to open them. When information finally became available, it was clear that individuals were being deported for extremely minor immigration violations even if they had lived in the United States for thirty years or more, and the detainment of individuals on material witness warrants seemed to be based on rumor, innuendo, and a level of proof that did not even meet reasonable suspicion, much less probable cause (Kreimer, 2007).

Although some individuals believe that nothing like the Japanese internment during World War II could happen again in this country, pundits and some politicians advocated just such a scenario directed to aliens and Americans of Middle East descent, especially those who practiced the Muslim faith (Harris, 2006). Legal experts point out that the Supreme Court case that upheld the internment of 110,000 Japanese, *Korematsu v. U.S.*, 323 U.S. 214 (1944), has not been overturned, even though Congress issued an official apology and voted to make reparations to internees (Harris, 2006).

The separate questions here are whether the initial detainments were legal; whether they were ethical; whether the deportations for minor offenses are ethical (even if they are legal); and whether the federal government should have been more open about what they were doing so that individuals involved could obtain legal assistance. Perhaps as a response to 9/11, there has been a shift in policy so there is less openness in governmental activities. Specific elements, besides the secrecy about the number and names of who was held and where they were held after 9/11, include admonitions by the government to media officials to be careful of what they print, fewer White House briefings, and punishing government employees for giving unclassified information to the press (Crank and Gregor, 2005: 223).

According to Cole (2001), secret proceedings encourage distrust and hatred of the government. Cole points out that in the secret detainments after 9/11 and when government held individuals based on secret evidence, it was discovered later that the evidence was merely innuendo and rumor, and most individuals were released. The reason for openness is that governmental actions and decision making can be vetted in a fair and balanced debate. Although certain information essential to national security should not be subject to public dissemination, the question is: What secrets protect the country, and what secrets protect the government? The "In the News" box points out the government secrecy that characterizes the country today.

The Patriot Act and the Department of Homeland Security   The immediate federal response to the World Trade Center was the passage of the Patriot Act. This legislation included the following elements (D. Wood, 2003):

1. It allowed federal agencies to spy on Americans without probable cause or even reasonable suspicion.
2. It also allowed authorities to share with state prosecutors information obtained via search warrants obtained through the Foreign Intelligence Surveillance Act, which does not require probable cause.
3. It allowed deportation of anyone who financially supports a "terrorist organization," but the definition is so ambiguous that it might be used if a person contributed humanitarian aid.

IN THE NEWS | UNPRECEDENTED GOVERNMENT SECRECY?

More than thirty nonprofit groups have banded together to fight what they call "unprecedented" governmental secrecy. Their website, www.openthegovernment.org, seeks to raise awareness of a growing number of sealed court cases, classified documents, and hidden reports that hinder the people's ability to determine whether governmental officials are truly serving the public good. The media are involved in this coalition, as several cases, such as a reporter having his recording of a speech by Justice Antonin Scalia confiscated, have raised serious questions as to whether federal officials are engaging in oversight that may cross the line into intimidation. Government officials respond that the government is just as open as it has ever been.

Do you think the government is hiding more information than it used to? How would we know?

Source: Carr, 2004: A10.

4. It required all Arab-born citizens to report to immigration offices around the country to be interviewed and registered under the National Security Entry–Exit Registration system.

The Patriot Act was passed swiftly, with little debate. The most controversial portions included the sneak-and-peek provision, Section 213, which allowed federal agents to search someone's residence without telling those who lived there, even after the fact. Also controversial was Section 214, which authorized the issuance of pen register warrants—warrants that allow devices that record outgoing numbers from a telephone—on less than probable cause, and Section 505, which broadened the authority of the FBI to issue **national security letters**—letters requiring a recipient to turn over private information without notifying the target of the request; these are issued without a judge evaluating probable cause.

The Patriot Act reached its sunset provision in December 2005, and Congress extended it by only five months. In March of 2006 the Patriot Act was extended until 2009, but with significant modifications. In one modification, recipients of national security letters may contact attorneys and challenge the letters in court.

One of the most dramatic changes after 9/11 was the creation of the Department of Homeland Security (DHS), an umbrella federal agency that incorporated many federal law enforcement functions. Many observers note that the creation of this mammoth federal agency indicates a move toward the nationalization of our police force. Historically, a national police force has been resisted, going back to the origins of this country and the legacy of distrust of centralized power, yet it seems to be more of a possibility today (Stuntz, 2002). The Department of Homeland Security has absorbed agencies such as the Immigration and Naturalization Service and Customs, and the director is the central coordinator of all information regarding counter-terrorism even though the FBI and the CIA are not formally included under the organization chart of the DHS.

Wiretapping and Threats to Privacy   One of the effects of 9/11 has been the loss of some privacy rights that we enjoyed before the attack. The government, in its counter-terrorism efforts, has aggressively sought to access private information such as emails and telephone calls of large numbers of non-citizens and citizens alike. Along with the passage of the Patriot Act, which allowed expanded powers of federal law enforcement in search and seizure, the Administration pushed for several "data mining" programs that basically sift through large amounts of information, tagging key words for further scrutiny.

For instance, the Total Information Awareness pilot program was an initiative proposed by the government to collect voluminous amounts of information about citizens through the Internet (Kravets, 2003; Moss and Fessenden, 2002). Another proposal—"Operation TIPS"—encouraged citizens to spy on one another and proposed an official identity card. These programs, at least initially, have been rejected by legislators (D. Cole, 2002). However, other incursions into the private lives of Americans have taken place. The Patriot Act included provisions that allowed federal agents to "sneak and peek," and to utilize national security letters to circumvent warrant requirements.

National security letters are letters issued by the Federal Bureau of Investigation (FBI) to access private information without a warrant. Recipients of such a letter, until the modifications of the Patriot Act, could not ever tell anyone of the letter. Thus, a librarian who received a letter demanding all internet records for a particular patron or all patrons or a telecommunications agency that received a similar request could not tell the target of the letter or even discuss the letter with their lawyers (Kreimer, 2007).

Lawsuits by individuals who received the letters were aided by the ACLU and other organizations created to provide legal support against what was perceived as government incursions into the privacy rights of Americans. These lawsuits slowly made their way through the appellate levels of the federal courts, opposed at every step by government lawyers who argued that national security trumped even the right to challenge the letters in court.

Eventually, some information came to light. Freedom of Information Act requests showed that the FBI was issuing more than 30,000 letters a year, and in 2004 the actual number was closer to 65,000. It has also come to light that the FBI's use of such letters often broke the law by what was asked for or the level of proof it had in order to justify the letter. In one random audit of seventy-seven letters, twenty-two involved possible violations of law or policy (Kreimer, 2007: 1185).

Misuse of national security letters prompted an investigation by the Office of Inspector General of the Department of Justice and annual audits. As mentioned, in the latest extension of the Patriot Act, modifications were put in place that gave recipients at least the right to confer with a lawyer upon receipt of a national security letter, and required annual audits of the use of the letters (Kreimer, 2007).

It also has come to light that the President authorized "secret" wiretapping by the National Security Agency. These wiretaps were conducted without warrants from the secret Foreign Intelligence Surveillance Courts, and even without national security letters. Evidently there is (or was) a "Quantico circuit" in a major telecommunications company that was a direct feed of all the information of subscribers (email and telephone) to "somewhere" in Quantico (Devine, 2008).

Critics argue such wiretapping was clearly illegal, while supporters argue that the President was granted by Congress to do anything necessary to protect the country from the threat of terrorism (Lichtblau, 2008a). Information has surfaced that only a few people knew that the wiretapping was being conducted and that it had not received the formal approval of the Justice Department.

John Yoo, a lawyer with the Office of Legal Counsel, wrote a legal memorandum approving of the wiretapping when it involved foreign nationals and had been approved by Attorney General John Ashcroft, but neither approval covered the wiretapping of American citizens (Lichtblau, 2008a). The Justice Department and the Attorney General's position was that this portion of the wiretapping program was illegal, despite strong opposition from the White House. This resulted in the infamous 2004 visit from White House counsel Alberto Gonzales and Andrew Card to Attorney General Ashcroft while he was in intensive care recovering from gallbladder surgery, in an effort to persuade him to approve the wiretapping program (Eggen, 2007).

The Supreme Court refused to hear a legal challenge to the wiretapping, brought forward by civil liberties groups. White House lawyers argued that, first, the ACLU and other civil liberties groups that brought suit had no standing (because they had not been the ones wiretapped) and, second, that under the state secrets privilege the plaintiffs could not get information on who had been wiretapped; therefore, it was impossible to have a court hearing on any wiretapping that might have been done (Savage, 2008). Evidently, the Supreme Court agreed with these arguments.

After the secret wiretapping came to light, in August of 2007, the Protect America Act was passed, which allowed the government to wiretap, without a warrant, anyone suspected of being linked to a terrorist group. In effect, this gave approval to the secret wiretapping program after the fact. In October of 2007, Democrats tried to pass a bill that would require warrants from FISA, although the warrant was a "blanket warrant" that would allow comprehensive wiretapping of a person, group, cell, or government of interest. Republicans blocked the changes to the Protect America law, largely because it did not give immunity to telecommunications companies that had cooperated in the past with the federal government by providing access to subscribers' information without warrants in the President's secret wiretapping program by the national security agency (Nakashima, 2007).

The Protect America Act had an expiration date of February 2008, and, in that month, Democrats and Republicans could not come to terms on the elements of the extension and the Act expired without confirmation. However, in July of 2008, Congress agreed to a bill that included legal immunity for telecommunications companies that cooperated with warrantless wiretapping. The bill also changes some elements of the FISA court, expanding government's powers to invoke emergency wiretapping, and affirms the position that the FISA court is the only legal authority to grant wiretaps (specifically opposing any presidential power in that regard) (Licthtblau, 2008b).

The discussion regarding governmental "spying" on citizens has been consistently framed by a utilitarian rationale. On the one hand, the argument says that a loss of some privacy is necessary in order to protect the country from the terrorist threat. Civil libertarians argue, on the other hand, that giving up basic privacy rights that have always been the bedrock of our form of government is too high a price to pay.

It should be noted that we have had these discussions before. During the antiwar movement of the 1960s and early 1970s, the federal government was involved in a widespread program of wiretapping and infiltrating groups thought to be dangerous to the government. The spying, however, extended far beyond revolutionary groups that advocated violence and included pacifist groups and even individuals such as Martin Luther King, Jr.

Government abuse of this type of power during the Nixon administration was what led to Congress dramatically curtailing "spying powers" of federal law enforcement. The Senate created the Select Committee on Intelligence in 1976, and strengthened the Freedom of Information Act, allowing citizens to gain some government documents by filing a Freedom of Information Request. In 1978 the Foreign Intelligence Surveillance Act (FISA) created a secret court that consisted of seven federal district court judges appointed by the Supreme Court's Chief Justice. Federal agents who wanted to wiretap had to go to this court and show that their target was an agent of a foreign power and that the information sought was in furtherance of counter-intelligence.

FISA originally approved only electronic eavesdropping and wiretapping but was amended in 1994 to include covert physical entries and, later, in 1998, to permit pen/trap orders (which record telephone numbers) and business records. If the target is a U.S. citizen, there must be probable cause that his or her activities may involve espionage. It is believed that the FISA court has never denied a government request for a warrant, and it is this court that was bypassed by the President's secret wiretapping program.

The argument for governmental spying is clearly utilitarian, as is the argument against it. Supporters argue that the government should be able to do anything it has to in order to investigate and prevent terrorist acts. Critics argue that the government should be controlled and limited by due process rights so the power is not misused and abused. They point out that, just as in the 1960s and 1970s, such unfettered power has been misused today in the indiscriminate use of national security letters and spying on groups that have no possible connection to terrorism but are merely left-leaning or are considered to be anti-administration (Harris, 2006).

The idea of a federal government that collects and keeps a great deal of information about individual citizens makes many people nervous—and not just civil liberties advocates. For instance, we are heading toward a centralized DNA data bank that stores not only criminals' DNA but also DNA of members of the military, all government employees, and other citizens who may have had their DNA taken for other reasons. Some point out that once DNA is in a data bank, it may be misused to refuse health insurance or deny jobs to individuals based on their health risks.

Governmental spying has even taken on the quality of science fiction. When large, unusual-looking dragonflies were seen buzzing overhead demonstrators at an anti-war rally in 2007, many in the crowd believed them to be robotic surveillance "insects" created by the CIA. Although the government denied that it had such a device, experts allege that since at least the 1970s, the CIA has been working on insect robots that can take pictures and sound, even experimenting with inserting computer chips into moth pupae to create "cyborg" moths (Weiss, 2007). Thus, the use of "bugs" has entered the twenty-first century, but are the legal and ethical considerations for the use of such devices as advanced? The "Quote and Query" offers an answer by one observer.

QUOTE AND QUERY

We're protecting freedom and democracy, but unfortunately freedom and democracy have to be sacrificed.

Jethro Eisenstein, a New York lawyer, quoted in Moss and Fessenden, 2002: A18

Is this claim overstating the issue?

Renditions and Secret Prisons   Other actions that the United States has taken in response to 9/11 have occurred overseas. Officials in Canada, Sweden, Germany, and Italy have alleged that the CIA has kidnapped individuals in those countries and subjected them to torture to discover what they knew about terrorist activities. The practice, called **rendition**, is usually done with the host country's knowledge, but in some cases no notice was given or permission granted. When this happens, the country's leaders object to the U.S. practice of ignoring the sovereignty of the country and its laws (Whitlock, 2005; Weinstein, 2007).

Italy has alleged that CIA operatives kidnapped a radical Egyptian cleric in February of 2003 and smuggled him out on a U.S. military airplane. In an unusual turn of events, twenty-six CIA agents are being prosecuted in absentia in Milan, Italy, for this kidnapping. In May of 2008, the wife of the kidnapped man testified that, after he was kidnapped by CIA agents, he was taken to an Egyptian prison and held for fourteen months. During those months, he was beaten, shocked over all parts of his body including his genitals, and tortured in other ways. Similar to others who were subjected to rendition, he was released with no explanation of why he had been taken in the first place (Associated Press, 2008d).

In some of the cases, evidently the kidnapped suspects were sent to "secret prisons" run by the CIA in Eastern European countries. The existence of secret prisons run by the United States in formerly Soviet countries is an ironic and sad commentary on recent history. After the existence of such prisons was exposed in 2006, they were allegedly closed, with some of the detainees sent to Guantanamo. Other "ghost prisoners" are still not acknowledged, and there is no accounting of what happened to prisoners who were not sent to Guantanamo (Whitlock, 2007).

Guantanamo and the Military Commissions Act   Soon after the United States military initiated hostilities in Afghanistan, "enemy combatants" were captured and sent to Guantanamo Bay in Cuba, a military installation that is considered American territory. The Iraq war began, and enemy combatants from Iraq were also sent there, along with suspected terrorists captured in other countries. Controversy continues over the legal status of these detainees and what due process rights they should receive.

Remember that due process is to protect against error in the governmental deprivation of life, liberty, or property. In this case, due process would consist of the procedural steps that would evaluate the reason for the individual's detention, and, if there was no good reason, lead to the person's release. The initial arguments by the federal government were that the individuals did not deserve the due process rights granted by the American Constitution because these individuals were not Americans and they were not on American soil; and they did not deserve the due process rights granted by the Geneva Conventions, the agreements made by all the major world powers after WWII as to how to treat war prisoners, because they were not soldiers but, rather, "enemy combatants."

From the beginning of the detainments, various civil libertarian groups challenged them in court and attempted to force the government to provide information as to who the detainees were and why they were being held. In some early cases that finally reached the U.S. Supreme Court, the Court held that the detention practices violated individual rights. In *Hamdi v. Rumsfeld*, 542 U.S. 507 (2004), the Court held that U.S. citizens could not be held indefinitely without charges even if they were labeled "enemy combatants." In *Rasul v. Bush*, 542 U.S. 466 (2004), the Court held that detainees in Guantanamo could challenge their detention in U.S. federal courts. A related case was *Clark v. Martinez*, 125 S.Ct. 716 (2005), which involved Cubans held for years in federal penitentiaries after illegally entering the United States. In this case, the Court held that the government may not indefinitely detain even illegal immigrants without some due process. In *Hamdan v. Rumsfeld*, 125 S.Ct. 972 (2005), the Supreme Court held that the "military commissions," set up as a type of due process for the detainees, were outside the President's power to create and were, therefore, invalid.

After the *Hamdan* case, Congress passed the Military Commissions Act, which set up procedures similar to those struck down by the Supreme Court. Government lawyers argue that because Congress created this due process procedure, it meets legal requirements. Critics argue that the Act strips detainees of habeas corpus rights—basically the right to contest the legality of governmental imprisonment. Habeas corpus rights have been recognized by Western democracies since the Magna Carta in 1215. The Act was widely criticized and was challenged in Court.

In June of 2008, in *Boumediene v. Bush* (No. 06-1195, decided June 12, 2008), the Court rejected the Military Commissions as a due process substitute for federal courts and habeas corpus, and it further held that the Detainee Treatment Act with the provision of some form of appeal over the "enemy combatant" status was also not a substitute for habeas corpus rights. The Court's rationale is that Guantanamo is considered to be a legal territory of the United States and, therefore, is subject to United States law. Dissents by Chief Justice Roberts, and Justices Scalia, Thomas and Alito vigorously opposed the Court's rationale and predicted "devastating" consequences (Greenhouse, 2008, Savage, 2008b).

Box 15.1 gives the timeline of events concerning detainees in Guantanamo. As of 2008, about 350–385 detainees remain in Guantanamo. About half are in the newer section of the camp, built in 2006 along the lines of a federal maximum security prison. The detainees, some of whom have been there for years now, are locked in 8 × 10 foot cells 22 hours a day. They exercise in small wire cages. Some have committed suicide. Several are on hunger strikes and are being force-fed through tubes. They have alleged being tortured and mistreated, especially in the earlier years of confinement before the scandal of Abu Ghraib. They have not been found guilty of any crime by a court of law, although the Military Commissions to evaluate their detention are now under way (Swift, 2007).

Some argue that the only reason that the government has fought so hard to keep the detainees out of the civilian or military justice system is that these legal bodies would never accept what is sometimes the only source of evidence that exists to show their guilt, specifically, information obtained through coercive interrogation techniques—in other words, torture (Swift, 2007).

BOX 15.1 | TIMELINE OF DUE PROCESS AND DETAINEES

2001–2003

- Detainees from Afghanistan and Iraq were sent to Guantanamo.
- Detainees identified as "enemy combatants" and their names and even the number of them was considered classified information.
- President Bush created Military Commissions by Executive Order to provide some due process for detainees.

2004

- *Hamdi v. Rumsfeld*, 542 U.S. 507
- *Rumsfeld v. Padilla*, 542 U.S. 426
- In *Rasul v. Bush* 542 U.S. 466 (2004) the Court held that the reach of federal courts extended to military prison in Cuba; detainees had a statutory right to habeas corpus appeals.

2005

- Congress passed the Detainee Treatment Act, which allowed limited federal court appeal only on the question of whether the person was an enemy combatant (Combatant Status Review Tribunals); did not allow counsel, did not allow detainees to see all the evidence against them, provided only a limited right to appeal, with an annual review of status.
- Federal government continued to oppose Freedom of Information Act (FOIA) requests from civil liberties groups as to even the detainees names.
- *Hamdan v. Rumsfeld*, 125 S.Ct. 972 (2005): In a *5–3 decision*, the Court held that the President had exceeded his authority in creating the Military Commissions.

2006

- On May 15, 2006, the government released a list of all present and former Guantanamo detainees.
- Three terrorists who were alleged to have contributed to the 9/11 plot were moved to Guantanamo from secret prisons in Eastern Europe.
- President Bush asked Congress to pass the Military Commissions Act in order to try these terrorists for their involvement in 9/11.
- On October 17, 2006, Congress passed the Military Commissions Act, establishing a new system of military tribunals. Critics argue that the Act eliminated habeas corpus, a right recognized by all free democracies. Provisions limit access to evidence, permit testimony and evidence obtained by coercion, and provide limited opportunity for review.

2007–2008

- In April, the Supreme Court first declined to hear a case that challenged the Military Commissions Act, but then in June reversed itself and decided to hear the case.
- In December arguments were heard for *Boumediene v. Bush* and *Al Odah v. United States.* In June 2008, the Supreme Court ruled (5-4) that the Military Commissions Act, as created by Congress could not constitutionally strip the detainees of habeas corpus rights and they had a right to access federal courts.
- In August 2008, the Military Commission panel convicted Salim Ahmed Hamdan of "providing material support for terrorists" but acquitted him of conspiracy.

Quote and Query

It is a sad day when the rubber-stamp Congress undercuts our freedoms, assaults our Constitution and lets the terrorists achieve something they could never win on the battlefield.

Senator Patrick Leahy (D-Vt.) in response to the Military Commissions Act, quoted in Fletcher, 2006: A04

Do you believe that Leahy and others overstate the significance of the Act?

The "Quote and Query" box gives one Congressman's response to the Military Commissions Act.

Torture   Many citizens probably would not have believed that the legality and ethics of torture would ever be a topic of discussion in the United States of America, yet it is. After World War II, commanders of the Japanese and German armies were tried for war crimes that included unnecessary killings of civilians, mistreatment of civilians, and the use of torture against captured soldiers. One of the forms of interrogation used by the Japanese that was later the basis for convictions was the "water cure." We know it today as "waterboarding." In the 1940s, judicial officials assessing guilt in war crime trials called it torture and convicted the military officers who ordered it or allowed it to happen; in 2007 and 2008 the President of the United States called it legal and necessary.

Torture is defined as the deliberate infliction of violence and, through violence, severe mental and/or physical suffering upon individuals. Others describe it as any intentional act that causes severe physical or mental pain or suffering. Amnesty International considers all forms of corporal punishment as falling within the definition of torture and prohibited by the United Nations Convention Against Torture (McCready, 2007).

As new information about the government's activities in the wake of 9/11 comes to light, we now know that immediately after 9/11, certain individuals suspected of being involved in the planning of 9/11 or members of Al Qaeda were seized wherever they happened to be and taken to secret locations. At first they were sent to countries such as Egypt, which used torture in interrogation. Later they were taken to "secret prisons" run by the CIA in Eastern Europe. Finally, some were moved to Guantanamo. Evidently by 2002, various forms of coercive interrogation techniques were being used at Guantanamo, as well as Bagram prison in Afghanistan. At these locations, allegedly, the suspects were subjected to extreme forms of coercive interrogations, including the following (Massimino, 2004: 74):

- subjected to loud noises and extreme heat and cold
- deprived of sleep, light, food, and water
- bound or forced to stand in painful positions for long periods of time
- kept naked and hooded
- thrown into walls
- sexually humiliated
- threatened with attack dogs
- shackled to the ceiling

IN THE NEWS | GUANTANAMO BAY

An anonymous source gave information to reporters that a military investigation recommended a reprimand for the former commander of the Guantanamo Bay prison, finding that he failed to oversee interrogations that led to abusive treatment. The report stopped short of defining the abuses as torture. The commander was not reprimanded and was sent to Iraq to supervise interrogations there. The investigation was begun when FBI agents generated internal memoranda complaining about the abusive treatment they witnessed at Guantanamo.

As far back as 2004 and 2005, troubling reports emerged about what was happening at Guantanamo. What do you think happened to the FBI officers who complained about the type of interrogation techniques they saw being used at Guantanamo?

Source: Cloud, 2005: A12.

The "In the News" box describes a military investigation at Guantanamo Bay.

In an ironic twist, it has now been revealed that military interrogators in Guantanamo were trained in the techniques of coercive interrogation techniques with material that was originally from a 1957 Air Force study of Chinese Communist techniques used during the Korean war. The original source detailed a continuum of coercive techniques that were used to obtain false confessions from U.S. soldiers, including practices such as semi-starvation, filthy surroundings, extreme cold, and stress positions. At some point the chart was taken from the original source, which described how such techniques "brainwashed" American soldiers into confessing war crimes, and became included in training materials on how to conduct coercive interrogations to obtain evidence against suspected insurgents (Shane, 2008b).

At the Bagram prison in Afghanistan, a young taxi driver was literally killed by interrogators who suspended him from the ceiling and beat his legs so badly that an autopsy revealed his leg bones were pulverized (see the "Quote and Query" box). It was discovered that Dilawar, the taxi driver, had no association at all with insurgents and that his taxi and the passengers in it had been picked at random by an Afghan guerrilla commander who told the Americans that they were responsible for bombing a U.S. camp. Later it was discovered that the commander himself was responsible for the bombing (Golden, 2005).

QUOTE AND QUERY

It became a kind of running joke, and people kept showing up to give this detainee a common peroneal strike just to hear him scream out "Allah." .... It went on over a 24-hour period, and I would think that it was over 100 strikes.

**Statement by one of the soldiers assigned as a military guard at the prison.
The prisoner subsequently died. Quoted in Golden, 2005: A16**

How does the utilitarian ethical system justify this treatment? Does any ethical system justify it?

There were troubling indications that interrogation techniques being utilized in Guantanamo, starting in 2001 through 2003, were contrary to the *Military Field Manual* and American law. FBI agents who were at Guantanamo to assist in interrogations wrote memoranda to their superiors objecting to what they saw, as did some military lawyers and other officers. The case of Chaplain Yee, described in the "Walking the Walk" box later in the chapter, is illustrative of those who objected to the treatment that the detainees were receiving at Guantanamo.

By the time the Abu Ghraib prison scandal erupted, such techniques had been used in Guantanamo and in Bagram prison in Afghanistan. Far from being the isolated acts of a few sadistic soldiers, these techniques were the subject of memos written and signed by officials in the Office of Legal Counsel and in the Pentagon. The pictures that Sergeant Darby provided to the Army Criminal Investigation Division CID) showed prisoners being subjected to a range of physically painful and psychological traumatizing behaviors. Later investigations documented the following acts (Massimino, 2004):

- Forcing naked prisoners to pose in humiliating, sexually oriented poses
- Forcing hooded prisoners to stand on a box and be attached to electric wires
- Threatening male detainees with rape
- Sodomizing a male detainee with a broomstick
- Threatening detainees with attack dogs
- Pouring chemicals from broken lightbulbs onto detainees

Bagram prison practices included the following:

- Stepping on the neck of a detainee and kicking him in the genitals
- Being forced to roll back and forth on the floor of a cell kissing the feet of the interrogators
- Being made to pick plastic bottle caps out of a drum mixed with excrement and water (Golden, 2005)
- Being stuffed in a sleeping bag, wrapped in electrical cord, and beaten to death (J. White, 2005)

Sometimes these men had been dragged from their beds and taken away to be interrogated based on "tips"; sometimes the tips were obtained by money, and sometimes they were given to get back at enemies. There have been as many as 14,000 detainees in Afghanistan and Iraq. Some were not insurgents or even suspected to be insurgents but, rather, petty criminals accused of stealing from the military. One detainee said, after being tortured and released, "I will hate Americans for the rest of my life" (quoted in Quinn, 2006).

We now know that a legal memorandum authored by lawyers John Yoo and Robert Delahunty from the Office of Legal Counsel had provided a 2002 opinion that the President could authorize waterboarding and other forms of torture, stating that the Geneva Conventions did not apply to the detainees because they weren't POWS or civilians, nor did international laws of war bind the President because it wasn't U.S. law. Yoo also wrote a 2003 memorandum that basically reiterated the justification that the President had the legal right to order torture as long as it did not result in organ failure or death (Shane, 2008a).

Critics today argue that these legal memoranda were shoddy to the point of being unethical and violative of the American Bar Association's Model Rules of Professional Responsibility because they ignored other sources of law, including international treaties such as the Convention Against Torture, which the United States ratified in 1994, that also bar such acts (Gillers, 2004). Subsequent events make it clear that torture techniques were used in Bagram Prison and Guantanamo, and only when they were exposed by the Abu Ghraib pictures was there widespread condemnation. Even now, President Bush publicly supports the use of waterboarding and declares it legal.

Box 15.2 outlines the sequence of events surrounding the use of torture.

BOX 15.2 | TORTURED REASONING

2002

- Colin Powell, Secretary of State, wrote in a January 26, 2002, memo to Alberto Gonzales that denying applicability of the Geneva Conventions in Afghanistan "will reverse over a century of U.S. policy and practice ... and undermine the protections of the law of war for our troops, both in this specific conflict and in general." (Quoted in Gillers, 2004: 65)
- John Yoo, of the Office of Legal Counsel, wrote what is known as the "torture memo," offering a legal analysis that justified the use of torture.
- FBI agents at Guantanamo registered complaints regarding the legality of some practices there.

2003

- John Yoo's second "torture memo" expanded the legal justification for the President's power to order torture.
- A Pentagon "working group" in April 2003 endorsed the use of extremely aggressive tactics but kept the contents of the final report secret from top military lawyers who had objected strenuously to torture.
- Some Justice Advocate General (JAG) officers approached civilian human rights advocates and urged them to investigate and protest standards for detentions and interrogation.

2004

- In January, Sgt. Joseph Darby at Abu Ghraib prison submitted a complaint to the military CID with a CD with pictures of soldiers engaged in a variety of extreme acts.
- Also in January, the Canadian government initiated an investigation into the detention and torture of a Canadian citizen, Maher Arar, by the CIA.
- In March, General Taguba's report of Abu Ghraib detailed sadistic, blatant, and wanton prisoner abuse by guards and apparent collusion and acquiescence by officers.
- In April, the story of Abu Ghraib broke on TV's *60 Minutes* and in the *New Yorker* magazine.
- In October, the government released 6,000 pages of documents in response to FOIA requests, including parts of the classified Taguba report; some showed FBI internal investigations of detention practices at Guantanamo that were similar to the techniques documented at Abu Ghraib.
- A Justice Department memorandum was issued repudiating the Yoo memos, stating that torture is "abhorrent."

(Continued)

2005

- A "secret memorandum" written by Steven Bradbury, Office of Legal Counsel, defined waterboarding and other techniques, such as head slapping and subjecting individuals to hypothermia, as coercive techniques not constituting torture.
- The Defense Department rescinded the 2003 Working Group Report, which authorized coercive interrogations.
- Congress passed Sen. John McCain's bill outlawing torture and prohibiting methods that are outrages on personal dignity, but it applies only to the military and not the CIA. The Senate approved it by a 90–9 vote, and the House with a vote of 308–122. President Bush at first declared that he would veto the bill but then reversed his position and signed it.
- General Hayden, head of the CIA, ordered that tapes of interrogations using coercive techniques be destroyed, despite advice from lawyers and members of Congress on the Intelligence Committee not to do so. In 2007, when the existence of the tapes came to light, he testified that destruction of the tapes was for "national security." Evidently, CIA officials had also lied to the 9/11 Commission about having the tapes.

2006

- A new Army field manual specified new rules of interrogation consistent with the Geneva Convention's Article 3 (outlawing forced nudity, hooding, dogs, waterboarding, stress positions, and sleep deprivation). The military manual asks the soldier to question a method: "If the proposed approach technique were used by the enemy against one of your fellow soldiers, would you believe the soldier had been abused?"
- Congress passed the Military Commissions Act, which, in addition to creating the tribunals, commanded that evidence obtained by torture, defined as treatment intended to cause severe pain, be suppressed; however, in cases where pain is "serious" but not "severe," the tribunal can admit the evidence if it is reliable, probative, and serves the interests of justice. For evidence obtained on or after December 30, 2005, the Military Commission Act instructs the tribunal to admit statements that are reliable, probative, and were not obtained through cruel, unusual, and inhuman treatment that would violate the Fifth, Eighth, and Fourteenth Amendments to the U.S. Constitution; however, another provision allows the President to find that interrogation methods do not meet the definition of torture.

2007

- The President approved new "coercive techniques" that are not defined as torture.
- At the confirmation hearing of Michael Mukasey for Attorney General, legislators questioned Mukasey on his opinion about waterboarding as torture; he refused to answer the questions, arguing that he did not have access to all the facts. He was confirmed.

2008

- In February, President Bush defended the use of waterboarding, admitting that it was used on subjects in 2002 and 2003 and declared that it is legal.
- Congress passed the Senate Intelligence Authorization Bill, which declared waterboarding and similar forms of interrogation techniques as illegal but allowed nineteen less painful or traumatizing techniques. President Bush vetoed the bill. Congress did not have enough votes to override the veto.
- In April, Congress' Senate Intelligence Committee voted to limit the CIA from using waterboarding, expecting another presidential veto.

Sources: Hess, 2008; Associated Press, 2008e; Eggen, 2008; Mazetti, 2007; Margulies, 2006; Douglas, 2005; Shane, 2008; Eggen and Abramowitz, 2007; Kreimer, 2007; Monroe, 2006.

The Abu Ghraib scandal has tarnished America's reputation and, very probably, led to the deaths of American soldiers because it spurred a renewal and resurgence of support for those fighting American forces in Iraq (Monroe, 2006). The entire world was outraged and upset at the images of soldiers engaged in systematic abuse of prisoners. While the Administration's position has always been that these were the acts of a few rogue soldiers, it becomes clear that the techniques were used in other places as well and formed a pattern that began in Bagram and Guantanamo. Interrogators were not necessarily the U.S. military but, rather, may have been CIA or even more shadowy "contractors" who seemed to be responsible to no superiors or law (Monroe, 2006).

Some bitterly criticize the fact that no higher ranking military officers, such as Brigadier General Janis Karpinski and Lt. Colonel Ricardo Sanchez, were ever punished for the Abu Ghraib incident. They argue that under the doctrine of "command responsibility," superiors are responsible for the war crimes committed by their soldiers when they either knew what was happening or should have known. Even though the United States and Allied Forces utilized the concept of command responsibility in war crimes trials after WWII to hold commanders responsible for the acts of others, the Uniform Code of Military Justice does not have a parallel responsibility of American commanders (J. Smith, 2006).

General Taguba's report of Abu Ghraib indicated that the reserve soldiers assigned to be guards in the prison did not have training in the Geneva Convention, nor were there clear directions from the commanding officers as to what was acceptable or not in the treatment of prisoners. The soldiers, including Charles Graner, testified that they were never told not to engage in the abusive acts portrayed in the pictures. Graner said he was complimented on his ability to "soften up" the prisoners for interrogation. However, when the soldiers tried to use a "superior orders defense"—which basically states that they were not guilty because they were following orders—in their court martials, the defense was rejected (J. Smith, 2006).

Others argue that military commanders over Abu Ghraib and other prisons may deserve some blame, but that their position was tenuous because the questioning was often done by the CIA or other contractors. Military investigations and prosecutions now discovered that paramilitary units called Scorpions, which included CIA operatives, special forces, and civilians, used tactics in Afghanistan and Iraq that included beating prisoners (J. White, 2005). The blurred lines of authority, not to mention conflicting legal opinions from the Justice Department and the Pentagon, had led to a situation where abuse was not only possible, but probable (Swift, 2007).

As far as can be determined, many of those who were tortured in Abu Ghraib or even Guantanamo were not insurgents. Some had stolen from military supply trucks, some had engaged in civilian crimes, some had been captured after "tips" that they were involved. Soldiers evidently felt comfortable using interrogation techniques that they knew military interrogators used on all detainees, regardless of whether they were suspected insurgents or not. Once human rights are discarded for one group, it is hard to preserve them for others.

Recall that at the time of the Abu Ghraib scandal, emotions ran high against Iraqi insurgents because some U.S. soldiers and contractors had been killed in gruesome ways, including beheadings. Some Americans responded to the pictures of American soldiers inflicting torture with the response that "they deserve it because 'they' were killing Americans." This form of simplistic retribution is the worst kind of illogical rationalization:

1. There was no evidence that the prisoners being tortured were involved in the killings.
2. There was no evidence that they were even insurgents because the prison was being used to house those who had committed typical crimes such as looting. Thus, the only thing they had in common with the insurgents was that they were Iraqis.
3. If one commits the same atrocities as one's enemies, how can you argue that you are any more moral or right?
4. Such thinking ends up in a cyclical chain of retribution (blood feuds) whereby individuals are killed or injured simply because of their membership in the other group, thereby justifying the next attack by the injured group.

The "Quote and Query" box sums up the message in the above points.

Kleinig (2001) and others, even before the worst abuses were revealed, examined the weak justification for torture and abusive practices during interrogation and also pointed out that it has been used in Northern Ireland, Israel, South Africa, and South America, among many other countries. The so-called "doctrine of necessity" is purely utilitarian, as is the argument of some that there must be secrecy concerning interrogation tactics so they can be more effective. To the contrary, Kleinig (2001: 116) points out that torture dehumanizes both victim and oppressor: "There is a loss of the moral high ground, a compromising of values that supposedly distinguish a society as civilized and worth belonging to."

Whether torture is effective or not is a utilitarian argument. Some argue that it is not effective because people will say anything to stop the torture and interrogators can't tell when someone is lying (Rejali, 2007). Others argue that torture does work in getting information out of individuals. Even those people, however, admit that using torture to interrogate may damage the interrogator as well as the detainee. Individuals may find the dark corners of their soul when they realize that

QUOTE AND QUERY

We take this moral high ground to make sure that if our people fall into enemy hands, we'll have the moral force to say, "You have got to treat them right." If you don't practice what you preach, nobody listens.

Senator Lindsey Graham, in support of an amendment banning torture to military prisoners, quoted in Galloway and Kuhnhenn, 2005: A4

Is this argument against torture a utilitarian argument or an ethical formalist argument?

QUOTE AND QUERY

How do you fight bad guys and stay good? You don't. You can't.

Quoted from former British agent in Blumenfeld, 2007

Do you believe that you have to use "bad means" against "bad guys?"

---

they get excited about inflicting pain on others. They may suffer guilt that destroys their peace of mind and affects them long after the detainee's wounds have healed. It has been reported that some interrogators are suffering post-traumatic stress syndrome (Blumenfeld, 2007). Whether torture is ever justified is asked and answered succinctly by one person in the "Quote and Query" box.

The argument that we should not use torture because our enemies then will feel free to use torture against American soldiers is a utilitarian argument (greatest benefit), but it also has elements of the categorical imperative (act in such a way that you will it to be a universal law) and the religious imperative (do unto others as you would have them do unto you). The "Walking the Walk" box gives the experience of James Yee, an army chaplain, who tried to follow this religious doctrine.

Alan Dershowitz (2004) argues that sometimes the greatest benefit is to torture, but that it should be limited to situations in which the benefit is so great that it overwhelms the harm to the individual. He also proposes, however, that any torture should be done under the auspices of a court or objective hearing body that issues a type of "torture warrant." Others (e.g., McCready, 2007) disputes the feasibility of this proposal, arguing that any need for torture would be immediate and, if there was time to pursue a warrant, there probably would be other ways to get that information.

One of the things that is important to note is that when individuals such as Dershowitz present justifications for torture, they invariably use the most extreme situation—the "ticking bomb" scenario in which one *knows* that the person being tortured has information about a bomb that is going to go off soon, killing many people. Whether one accepts the utilitarian equation for such a scenario does not necessarily justify the actual incidents of torture that have taken place. There is a world of difference between the "ticking bomb" scenario and torturing a suspect accused of stealing from the U.S military, or torturing a suspect to obtain his confession so that he can be punished.

Several sources have documented that some of the detainees tortured in Bagram and Abu Ghraib were petty criminals. Although proponents argue that torture has saved lives, there has been no definitive proof to substantiate it. One of the terrible effects of torturing for information is that the innocent who knows nothing suffers the most pain. Furthermore, there is a vast difference between the justification of torture for saving lives and the justification of torture to obtain evidence against someone to use against them, as is now the case in the Military Commissions tribunals.

WALKING THE WALK

U.S. ARMY CHAPLAIN JAMES YEE

James Yee was raised as a Lutheran in a Chinese-American family in New Jersey. He converted to the Muslim faith after graduating from West Point in 1990. Yee left the Army for a short time, but then came back into the Army as a chaplain. In 2002 he was sent to Guantanamo to minister to the prisoners. For 10 months, from November 2002 to September 2003, he witnessed acts toward the prisoners including beating and humiliation by military police and interrogators. He saw religion used as a weapon. Prisoners were made to bow down in the middle of a satanic circle and profess that Satan was their god, not Allah. Detainees were mocked during prayer, and teased sexually by female soldiers. Detainees begged Yee to take away their Koran because, allegedly, the military police would deface the holy books.

Chaplain Yee began to be known as a prisoner advocate. He ministered to the detainees and tried to intervene to stop the abuse they endured. As he explained, "I was not willing to silently stand by and watch U.S. soldiers abuse the Quran, mock people's religion, and strip men of their dignity—even if those men were prisoners." He advocated openly for the prisoners, especially against the actions that were taken against the religious practices of the Muslim prisoners. His advocacy brought him into conflict with his superiors. "I believed that the hostile environment and animosity toward Islam were so ingrained in the operation that Maj. Gen. Miller and the other camp leaders lost sight of the moral harm we were doing."

He became concerned especially about the young detainees. Boys as young as twelve to fourteen years old, who had been seized as they engaged in hostilities against American soldiers in Afghanistan, were detained at Guantanamo. Once there, they were, or are, being held with no idea as to when they will be released, or even if they will be. They may have been interrogated with coercive measures, and they experience day-to-day treatment by guards that is typical of the worst prisons. How these young men will turn out and what they will think of America were the questions that Yee asked himself. Despite the pervasive attitudes that he experienced that discouraged any attempt to advocate for prisoners, he continued to do so.

On his first leave from Guantanamo, in September of 2003, Yee was arrested at the airport coming back into the United States, and accused of being a spy. He was imprisoned for seventy-six days under conditions of sensory deprivation, and interrogated. Yee's wife and daughter were subjected to interrogation as well.

Eventually the treason and spying charges were dropped. Because Yee was carrying names of detainees and interrogators, he was charged with mishandling classified information. He was also charged with pornography because of pictures on his computer, and with adultery for an affair he had had with another officer. Even those charges were dropped in 2004. General Miller (the superior officer he had criticized at Guanatanamo) was quoted as saying that the reason charges were dropped was that national security would be compromised in any prosecution; however, nothing in the record indicated that Yee was, in any way, a spy. He was never formally exonerated, nor was he ever issued an apology, even though his life had been torn apart by the accusations and he ended up with $260,000 in legal bills.

Yee believes that there was a plan to discredit him (by accusing him of being a spy) in case he exposed the treatment of the Guantanamo detainees. He left the military in 2005, with an honorable discharge, and today continues to speak out against what the United States is doing in Guantanamo.

Sources: Buchholz, 2008: G1, G4; Lewis, 2005; Yee and Molloy, 2005.

CRIME CONTROL AND "MEANS–END" THINKING

Utilitarianism is the ethical justification for all the counter-terrorism measures we've discussed. The "end" of deterring or preventing terrorist attacks outweighs all of the following:

- The privacy rights of individuals (so that government agents can search and wiretap individuals with less oversight than before 9/11).
- Due-process rights (so detainees and aliens are held without charges for extended periods in investigative detentions).
- The First Amendment right to associate (when individuals are deported or, if they are citizens, investigated simply for associating with groups that have been defined by the State Department as terroristic).
- Even the right not to be tortured (if one is believed to have information).

This justification is simply a restatement of the crime control approach discussed in earlier chapters. Instead of police and court practices being justified because of their role in deterring or preventing crime (most specifically, drug-related activity), the new practices are justified as preventing or deterring terrorism.

Our theme in the chapters concerning law enforcement is that the police role in society is either that of crime fighter or public servant. This discussion can be expanded to examine the whole system of public safety and justice, and the shift from the war on drugs to the war on terror. The **crime control approach** is associated with means–end or utilitarian thinking that determines good by the result (crime control). Utilitarian reasoning is employed to analyze tactics. For instance, Cohen (1987: 53) uses a utilitarian approach in the following justification for police action:

1. The end must itself be good.
2. The means must be a plausible way to achieve the end.
3. There must be no alternative—better means to achieve the same end.
4. The means must not undermine some other equal or greater end.

Crank and Caldero (2005) also use utilitarian thinking in their examination of noble-cause corruption. However, they state that those who employ such tactics do not weigh the utility of the acts correctly, arguing that in today's multicultural reality, police will have to negotiate an "end" that takes into account the needs of all groups in society. It cannot be denied that a crime control model may subvert law, policy, or human rights if utilitarian reasoning justifies it. In other words, the end, if important enough, will justify any means.

In the **public service approach**, values and ethics focus on human rights, including the right to due process, and the fundamental duty of all public servants is to protect those rights. In this approach the protection of rights is more important than the end of crime control. Kappeler, Sluder, and Alpert (1994: 243) present the U.S. Department of Justice recommendations for the values of a police department:

1. Preserve and advance the principles of democracy.
2. Place the highest value on preserving human life.
3. Prevent crime as the number-one operational priority.
4. Involve the community in delivering police services.
5. Believe in accountability to the community served.

6. Commit to professionalism in all aspects of operations.
7. Maintain the highest standards of integrity.

A **rights-based model** of policing recognizes police officers as servants of the public good. Although crime control is important, protection of civil liberties is the fundamental mission. A crime control approach is utilitarian, and a rights-based approach is not. Under the rights-based approach, which is deontological, no end would justify taking away human rights. This discussion has become incredibly more pressing in the face of terrorist threats. It is interesting to note that for many who have argued that the "end" of catching criminals does not justify certain means, such as racial profiling, the answer seems to be different when the end is to prevent terrorist attacks.

Thus, although racial profiling has been legally and ethically condemned as a violation of rights when it is used to catch drug dealers, it has been resurrected as an appropriate and justified response to catching terrorists. Our Supreme Court has held that privacy is more important than catching criminals, so wiretaps have been used sparingly and with judicial oversight. However, the prevention of terrorist attacks has changed this balance, and many are willing to give up their privacy rights in order for the government to protect them from terrorism.

Some argue that it is a false argument to weigh privacy or any civil liberty against security. Writing before the attack on the World Trade Center, Alderson (1998: 23) presented a prescient argument against the "end" of security as a justification for taking away liberties:

> I acknowledge that liberty is diminished when people feel afraid to exercise it, but to stress security to unnecessary extremes at the price of fundamental freedoms plays into the hands of would-be high police despots. Such despots are quick to exploit fear in order to secure unlimited power.

Alderson also addressed terrorism directly: "It is important for police to maintain their high ethical standards when facing terrorism, and for their leaders to inspire resistance to any degeneration into counter-terrorism terror" (1998: 71).

Protection of rights can also be framed as a utilitarian argument. In the effort to prevent future terrorism by Al Qaeda or other radical Muslim groups, the greatest ally of law enforcement in any country is the Muslim community. If the Muslim community is cooperative with preventive efforts, it is because this community believes in the legal system and the integrity of those within it. Observers noted that one of the reasons that British police were able to identify the subway bombers so quickly in 2005 was the cooperation of the Muslim community, but that later actions enraged community members and hardened opinion against the police; thus, it is possible that their assistance in identifying future perpetrators may not be forthcoming (Buchholz, 2005; Emling, 2005).

The major problem in the utilitarian ethical system or "means–end thinking" is that we are unable to know the outcome of our actions. Justifying otherwise unethical means by arguing that these means will lead to a good end depends on the ability to know that the means will result in the desired outcome. Unfortunately, this is not possible. In our haste to protect ourselves from terrorists, it is at least conceivable that we may create more terrorists (Bender, 2005). The current generation of Middle Eastern children may identify the United States only as an aggressor. Our actions, if misunderstood, could create many times more terrorists than the number we are trying to control today.

In this country, those of Arab descent who came here for freedom now find that their heritage denies them that precious gift. In detaining Arab American men without the due process that protects most citizens, we may germinate the seeds of future destruction in the children who watch their fathers being taken away. In engaging in renditions, operating secret prisons, and defending the right to torture, we lose allies across the world and, in the process, threaten our future security.

By parceling out human rights for some and not for others, we also weaken civil liberties for all citizens. A few soldiers have committed crimes against Iraqi civilians and typically receive less punishment than soldiers who commit much less serious crimes against other soldiers. In one case, for instance, two soldiers robbed an Iraqi shop owner and his family at gunpoint. Both were found guilty of armed robbery. One was sentenced to five months, but the other was sentenced to only one month of confinement. This contrasts with another punishment case in which a soldier was also imprisoned for six months—but for adultery! In an investigation of a soldier who shot a teenager for stealing a box of food, an investigator noted that the soldier seemed surprised that anyone would care that an Iraqi civilian was shot (Carollo and Kaplow, 2005: A9).

Evidently some who are inclined to abuse and victimize Iraqis feel free to do so because of the deterioration of rights and the belief that Iraqis don't deserve the same rights as Americans. The Iraq situation seems to be parallel to the case of rogue officers who robbed and, in a few instances, killed drug dealers for their money. It is also similar to prosecutors who feel justified in lying about or hiding evidence because they are prosecuting a "guilty" defendant, or correctional officers who believe they can steal from the inmate fund or coerce sex from inmates because they are, after all, "just inmates."

Rogue cops target drug dealers and rogue soldiers target Iraqi civilians or civilian detainees perhaps because they think these individuals are outside the protection offered by systems of justice. Once we start parceling out human rights and justice differentially, it opens the door to those who look for an excuse to abuse and victimize. Once the door is open, however, everyone is less safe, such as the innocent taxi driver who was killed by U.S. soldiers in Afghanistan during an interrogation that involved torture. The "Quote and Query" box gives an opinion by a former military judge.

QUOTE AND QUERY

I think it's an attitude that starts at the very top that these people [insurgents] somehow are beyond the law, and if they are beyond the law, they are essentially fair game.

Ex-military judge and prosecutor quoted in Carollo and Kaplow, 2005: A1, A9

Is it possible that the tendency to believe that our enemies (insurgents) don't deserve justice leads to a deterioration of justice for innocent groups as well (Iraqi victims of criminal soldiers)?

CRIME CONTROL, HUMAN RIGHTS, AND THE WAR ON TERROR

The premise of rights-based law enforcement is that some acts are never justified. No end is so important that governments can stoop to slavery, genocide, or torture. No situation ever justifies sexism, racism, murder, rape, or intimidation. There is a suspicion of state power in rights-based law enforcement and a fear that police will be used to oppress the powerless. The way to avoid this is to place the protection of rights, rather than crime control, as the central theme of policing, because the definition of crime and the identification of who is a criminal may be subverted for political ends. Further, the suspicion of state power leads to a "stacking" of rights on the side of the individual in any actions (such as criminal prosecution) taken by the government against the individual.

Arguably, the individual needs these due-process rights because of the awesome power of the state against the weakness of one individual. So the individual is protected against state power by the Bill of Rights and by case law that identifies even the right to be informed of such rights (e.g., the Miranda ruling). Yes, it is usually the criminals who get to exercise these rights. But the rights exist to protect us all, and if they were not there, arguably, more innocents would be arrested, prosecuted, and imprisoned.

The United Nations Code of Conduct for Law Enforcement Officials illustrates the values and premise of the rights-based approach: "In the performance of their duty, law enforcement officials shall respect and protect human dignity and maintain and uphold the human rights of all persons" (Article 2, reported in Kleinig, 1999).

Neyroud and Beckley (2001: 62) describe the police standards of the United Kingdom as reflecting an emphasis on human rights. Standards include the following provisions:

1. To fulfill the duties imposed on them by the law
2. To respect human dignity and uphold human rights
3. To act with integrity, dignity, and impartiality
4. To use force only when strictly necessary, and then proportionately
5. To maintain confidentiality
6. Not to use torture or use ill-treatment
7. To protect the health of those in their custody
8. Not to commit any act of corruption
9. To respect the law and the code of conduct and oppose violations of them
10. To be personally liable for their acts

Because European police have had a longer history of dealing with terrorism, it is interesting that the trend there evidently has been to move toward a rights-based model of policing. For instance, British police have had their share of noble-cause corruption in dealing with Irish terrorists; Spain has dealt with Basque terrorists; Germany dealt with the Baeder–Meinhoff gang in the 1970s and, more recently, with neo-Nazi groups; and so on. It might be argued that the "end justifies the means" thinking by law enforcers who have dealt with terrorists inevitably have led to violations of civil liberties and to scandal and disgrace. Arguably, there has been a recognition that official oppression leads to more bitterness and disenfranchisement among certain groups of people and, ultimately, more unrest and terror.

Thus, those who have been through the cycle realize that rights are more important than the "end" if the "end" requires the deterioration of rights.

In Chapter 11 we discussed the importance of an independent judiciary. This concept is an essential element of the discussion here as well. It is no coincidence that the United Nations and the European Union both mandate that a country have an independent judiciary in order for that nation to be considered protective of human rights and thus eligible to join the European Union. The way to freedom and democracy is through the recognition of human rights, and the way to protect human rights is through an independent judiciary, with the following elements (Keith, 2002, 196–197):

- guaranteed terms of office
- finality of decisions
- exclusive authority
- ban against exceptional or military courts
- fiscal autonomy
- separation of powers
- enumerated qualifications

Some of the elements are problematic, even in the United States. For example, the Military Commissions would violate the prohibition against exceptional or military courts.

Why are we discussing terrorism and the Iraq war in a book on the criminal justice system? The answer is that the war on terror has replaced the drug war, and the crime control perspective has morphed into a much broader government mandate of national security. In response to that mandate, government's powers of investigation and control were expanded to address terrorism. However, we see that the powers given to government in the "war against terror" have also been used against "garden-variety" criminals. Crank and Gregor (2005) note cases where the arsenal of responses against terror have been used against ordinary criminals, such as a federal law against terroristic threats applied to a lovesick woman who wanted the cruise ship she was on to turn around, the use of a law against weapons of mass destruction against a methamphetamine "cook," and the use of federal subpoena power to investigate members of an anti-war group that sponsored a rally with signs reading "Bring the Iowa Guard Home."

We have also noted cases where torture has been used against petty thieves in Afghanistan and Iraq and the likelihood that many of the detainees in Guantanamo were never tied to insurgent activity. The second Patriot Act was passed with an addendum that removed some of the due process impediments to imposing capital punishment here in the United States. Thus, the "war on terror" has impacted the criminal justice system in many ways.

Extreme measures that were rationalized because of extreme threats have been used against common criminals and citizens engaging in constitutionally protected activities. The U.S. public, in response to fear, submits to ever-increasing predations on liberties. The investigative powers given by the Patriot Act have led to routine partnerships between law enforcement and national security in investigations against U.S. citizens suspected of criminal activity. The preceding chapters have pointed out how noble-cause corruption can pollute due process, and there is no reason to believe that the same tendency will not occur when public servants think they are protecting society from terrorists.

Bayley (2002) argues that in order to reduce the means–end thinking that leads police to violate rights and engage in corruption, police must be shown that such behaviors do not result in effective crime control. The same argument can be made against certain practices in the war on terror. Bayley argues that noble-cause corruption does the following:

1. Contributes marginally to deterrence (e.g., searches through racial profiling are less successful than through other methods)
2. Reduces enforcement effectiveness (because it alienates the public and reduces cooperation)
3. Weakens the authority of law (because the majority of people follow the law because they believe in it; thus, justice professionals must never lose their moral authority)
4. Makes scapegoats of police (if the law can't respond, we shouldn't expect police to respond)
5. Depresses morale and makes police work less satisfying (because it conflicts with individual belief systems)
6. Wastes community resources (through overturned convictions and retrials)
7. Puts police officers at risk (through illegal activities)

These elements can also be applied to the practices and tactics used in the war on terror:

1. Torture contributes marginally to deterrence because it often creates more extreme views among those who are tortured.
2. Torture, illegal detainments, and governmental violation of individual liberties alienate both the target group (terrorists) and ordinary citizens who are caught in the net of investigation and enforcement.
3. These practices definitely weaken the authority of law because public servants are violating laws such as the law against torture and the Geneva Convention.
4. The practices make scapegoats of state and federal law enforcers as well as soldiers who are caught and then punished as public scapegoats for enacting practices that were informally approved.
5. These practices depress morale because of individual moral such as Sgt. Darby's and those described in Box 15.3.
6. The practices waste incredible resources in legal defense and reparative costs to victims.
7. The practices create a situation where we have no moral authority when our soldiers or agents are caught and imprisoned because we have been publicly exposed as engaging in the worst practices of torture against Iraqis, Afghans, and others.

The "Quote and Query" box on page 494 summarizes this thinking applied to the war on terror.

| BOX 15.3 | MORAL DILEMMAS AND DECISIONS IN THE WAR ON TERROR |

Lt. Comm. Charles Swift: As described in the "Walking the Walk" box in Chapter 5, Lt. Commander Swift was the JAG officer assigned to defend Hamdan, the alleged driver of Osama Bin Laden, in the military tribunal system that was created by the President and the Pentagon. Swift and the group of civilian lawyers assigned to the case were successful in challenging the tribunals when the Supreme Court ruled, in *Hamdan v. Rumsfeld*, that their creation exceeded the President's power. Lt. Commander Swift was passed over for promotion and had to leave the military.

Babak Pasdar: Pasdar, a computer security expert, was hired to conduct a security audit of a "major telecommunications carrier" and, in the course of his audit, found a mysterious circuit that others called the "Quantico Circuit," which was sending all information about telephone and email from subscribers to Quantico Virginia. When Pasdar asked about it and objected that it was a threat to the security of the system, he was told to forget that he ever saw it. He could not forget it, though, and, because of his concern, ended up testifying to Congress about what he witnessed and went public in March of 2006. Pasdar is now affiliated with an organization that seeks to protect the privacy of Americans from secret governmental spying.

Source: Devine, 2008: 4A

Cpt. James Yee: Captain Yee was described in the "Walking the Walk" box in this chapter. His efforts to protect the rights of detainees in Guantanamo led to charges of spying and an end to his military career.

Mary McCarthy: McCarthy was a veteran CIA agent who had been in "the company" for more than 20 years. She was fired in 2006, allegedly for revealing that CIA had secret prisons in Eastern Europe. She discovered their existence after she was assigned to Office of the Inspector General, with the responsibility of looking into allegations that the CIA was involved in torture in Iraqi prisons. Allegedly, McCarthy provided information to *Washington Post* writer Dana Priest, who won a Pulitzer Prize for her report of the CIA's secret prisons in eight countries. According to reports, after the story broke, the CIA moved some of the prisoners to Guantanamo, but others have disappeared. They are called "ghost prisoners."

Source: Smith and Linzer, 2006: A01.

Lt. Cmdr. Matthew Diaz: Diaz was a JAG lawyer for the joint military task force at Guantanamo, in charge of holding and interrogating enemy combatants. He supported the 2004 Supreme Court decision *Rasul v. Bush*, granting detainees the right of habeas corpus, and thought they should be allowed lawyers to represent them. He disagreed with the government's refusal to supply the names of the detainees after a civil rights organization had filed a Freedom of Information Act to obtain them. On January 15, 2005, he mailed a list of detainees to the Center for Constitutional Rights in New York.

In 2006, a federal court declared that the list of names was public information and the government released it to the Associated Press, but Diaz was still prosecuted for his disclosure with the government, arguing that he exposed the United States to danger. Diaz was convicted and sentenced in May of 2007 to six months' imprisonment and a dishonorable discharge.

Source: Wiltrout, 2007.

Coleen Rowley: Rowley was the FBI lawyer who made headlines when she publicly reported that officials in Washington ignored reports from the field about Zacarias Moussaoui, who has since admitted conspiring with Al Qaeda. Rowley retired from the FBI in frustration over the bureaucratic practices that punished those who criticized superiors who were not doing their job in sharing and analyzing important information.

Source: Carr, 2005: A1, A6.

General Taguba: Taguba is not strictly a whistleblower, as he merely did his job in preparing a report on Abu Ghraib. However, he was criticized informally, evidently for the comprehensiveness of the report and his strong condemnation of the practices he found there. According to reports, his career was derailed by doing his job too well in investigating and chronicling the abuses at Abu Ghraib and documenting the lack of leadership that lead to the abuses (see Box 15.2)

QUOTE AND QUERY

This war will be won or lost, not on the battlefield, but in the minds of potential supporters who have not yet thrown in their lot with the enemy. If we forfeit our values by signalling that they are negotiable in situations of grave or imminent danger, we drive those undecideds into the arms of the enemy. This way lies defeat, and we are well down the road to it.

Krulak and Hoar, 2007: A11

Do you agree?

CONCLUSION

The World Trade Center attack and other assaults on U.S. targets around the world have created a sense of vulnerability and fear. The response to this fear has been to reduce civil liberties through law, policy, and individual practices. In earlier chapters we discussed the means–end thinking called noble-cause corruption, which justifies ignoring due process requirements and laws in order to catch criminals and protect the public.

This "end justifies the means" thinking is insidious—even more so now that that threat is so much greater. Fear, unfortunately, leads to bad decisions. Fear causes police officers and correctional officers to use illegal force. During World War II, fear caused this country to incarcerate tens of thousands of citizens whose only

crime was being of Asian descent. Fear causes a country's leaders to trample the rights of the very individuals they are sworn to protect and defend. It is also true that some people have stood up for what they believe to be right and suffered the consequences, as Box 15.3 on the previous page illustrates.

In this chapter we took a last look at ethical decision making. The conclusion that many of the methods discussed are misguided may be debated. Such debate is, and should be, taking place all across this country. However, it is important to clearly identify what ethical system might support any contested practice, act, or government policy. If it is utilitarianism, then one must also show what facts exist to prove that the desired

QUOTE AND QUERY

Political liberty, which is one of the greatest gifts people can acquire, is threatened when social order is threatened. It is dismaying to see how ready many people are to turn to strong leaders in hopes that they will end, by adopting strong measures, the disorder that has been the product of failed or fragile commitments. Drug abuse, street crime, and political corruption are the expression of unfettered choices. To end them, rulers, with the warm support of the people, will often adopt measures that threaten true political freedom. The kind of culture that can maintain reasonable human commitments takes centuries to create but only a few generations to destroy.

James Q. Wilson, cited in Cole, 2002: 234

Although Wilson's statement is discussing the sacrifice of due process in the drug war and crime control, it has incredible relevance to the issues of terrorism. Interestingly, it was made by a noted conservative. How do we meet the threat of terrorists?

end will be brought about and that negative side-effects do not outweigh the good that one seeks. Or it may be the case that even a good end cannot justify certain acts. Some human rights belong to everyone—even terrorists. In the crime war, drug war, or war on terror, the most important element of making ethical decisions is to apply ethical reasoning and not succumb to fear. Our final "Quote and Query" box on page 494 makes a case for political liberty.

Key Terms

crime control approach *487*

national security letters *471*

"front-page test" *495*

positivist law/ man-made law *467*

"just war" debate *467*

principle of double effect *468*

public service approach *487*

rendition *475*

rights-based model *488*

terrorism *467*

torture *478*

Review Questions

1. What elements does Cohen identify as justifying police action?
2. What are the most problematic elements of the Patriot Act?
3. What are the holdings of *Hamdi v. Rumsfeld, Rasul v. Bush, Clark v. Martinez* and *Hamdan v. Rumsfeld?*
4. What are some actions the federal government has taken in response to terrorism?
5. What are the arguments in support of torture? What are the arguments against torture?
6. What are some rights recognized by the United Nations and the European Union?
7. What is the relationship between an independent judiciary and human rights? What are the elements of an independent judiciary?
8. Explain why "means–end" thinking leads to criminal actions.
9. What are the two justifications for a "just war?"

Writing/Discussion Questions

1. Write an essay on (or discuss) the most difficult ethical dilemma in this chapter, and try to answer it by considering law, policy, and ethics. Also, use the **"front-page test."** This is a quick ethics test that asks if you would feel comfortable if your action were published on the front page of the newspaper. If you would not want it to be, there may be an ethical problem with your action.
2. Write an essay on (or discuss) an ethical or moral dilemma from your own life. Try to solve it by using any guidelines derived from this book. Be explicit about the procedure you used to arrive at a decision and about the decision itself.
3. Write a code of ethics for yourself.

Ethical Dilemmas

Situation 1

You are a member of Congress, and the Patriot Act is coming up for a vote to renew its provisions. What would you do, and why?

Situation 2

As a soldier in Iraq, you have pictures of fellow soldiers engaging in various acts of abuse and torture. What, if anything, would you do with the pictures?

Situation 3

You are a new police officer and are talking with other officers before roll call. The group is loudly and energetically proposing various gruesome torture techniques to get Al Qaeda operatives to talk. There is some hyperbole in the discussion, but also the sincere belief that torture is justified by the circumstances. What do you think about this position? If you object to torture, would you make your position known?

Situation 4

You live next door to an Arab family, and you hear the husband talking negatively about the United States. Your friends at work tell you that you should report him to the police because he might be a terrorist. What would you do? Why?

Situation 5

You have been sitting in a criminal justice ethics class all semester and disagree with virtually everything the teacher has said. You want to get a good grade, so you think maybe you shouldn't disagree, although the professor has not indicated that she takes disagreement personally or would punish someone for expressing any opinion. However, few people in the class seem to share your opinions, or if they do, they are also keeping quiet. Would you ever express your opinion? Why or why not?

Situation 6

You are the President of the United States, and there has been another terrorist attack using passenger airplanes. One has crashed into the Pentagon again, and another is heading for the White House. You have deployed fighter jets to surround the plane, and whoever is flying it refuses to acknowledge the command to turn around. Your military commanders are advising you to shoot down the plane— an act that would kill the 353 people aboard. What would you do? Would your answer be any different if it was heading toward the Statute of Liberty? Toward an athletic stadium filled to capacity?

Suggested Readings

Albanese, J. 2006. *Professional Ethics in Criminal Justice: Being Ethical when No One Is Looking.* Boston: Allyn & Bacon.

Alderson, J. 1998. *Principled Policing: Protecting the Public with Integrity.* Winchester, MA: Waterside.

Braswell, M., McCarthy, B., and McCarthy, B.2006. *Justice, Crime and Ethics.* Cincinnati, OH: Anderson Publishing Company.

Crank, J., and Gregor, P. 2005. *Counter Terrorism After 9/11: Justice, Security and Ethics Reconsidered.* Cincinnati, OH: Lexis/Nexis Publishing.

Etzioni, A., and Marsh, J., eds. 2003. *Rights Vs. Public Safety After 9/11: America in the Age of Terrorism.* Lanham, MD: Rowman & Littlefield.

Lagouranis, T., and A. Mikaelin. 2007. *Fear Up Harsh.* London, England: NAL Hardcover (Penguin Group).

Yee, J., and Molloy, A. 2005. *For God and Country: Faith and Patriotism Under Fire.* New York: PublicAffairs Press.

Glossary

actus reus an element of a crime constituting the physical act(s) required to be culpable of the crime

act utilitarianism the type of utilitarianism that determines the goodness of a particular act by measuring the utility (good) for all, but only for that specific act and without regard for future actions

age of reason the legal age at which a person is said to have the capacity to reason and, thus, to understand the consequences of his or her action

applied ethics the study of what is right and wrong pertaining to a specific profession or subject

aspirational code a code that sets a high standard of behavior with the knowledge that many employees will not live up to it at all times

asset forfeiture a legal tool used to confiscate property and money associated with organized criminal activity

attorney–client privilege the legal rule by which an attorney cannot disclose confidential information regarding his or her client except for in a very few specified circumstances

authority unquestionable entitlement to be obeyed that comes from fulfilling a specific role

baksheesh graft

blue curtain of secrecy another name for the code of silence or the practice of police officers to remain silent when fellow officers commit unethical actions

bureaucratic justice the approach in which each case is treated as one of many; the actors merely follow the rules and walk through the step;, and the goal is efficiency

burnout the condition in which a worker has abandoned the mission of the organization and is just "going through the motions"

categorical imperatives the concept that some things just must be, with no need for further justification, explanation, or rationalization for why they exist (Kant's categorical imperative refers to the imperative that you should do your duty, act in a way you want everyone else to act, and don't use people)

civil disobedience voluntarily breaking established laws based on one's moral beliefs

civilian review/complaint model the use of an outside agency or board that includes citizens and monitors and/or investigates misconduct complaints against police

code of silence the practice of officers not to come forward when they are aware of the ethical transgressions of other officers

cognitive dissonance psychological term referring to the discomfort that is created when behavior and attitude or belief are inconsistent

community corrections a term that encompasses halfway houses, work-release centers, probation, parole, and any other intermediate sanctions, such as electronic monitoring, either as a condition of probation or as a sentence in itself that takes place in the community rather than prison

community policing a model of law enforcement that creates partnerships with the community and addresses underlying problems rather than simply enforcing the law

commutative justice the component of justice that is concerned with the fairness of contracts and business relations

confirmatory bias fixating on a preconceived notion and ignoring other possibilities, i.e. in regard to a specific suspect during a police investigation

conflict paradigm the idea that groups in society have fundamental differences and that those in power control societal elements, including law

consensus paradigm the idea that most people have similar beliefs, values, and goals and that societal laws reflect the majority view

correctional officer the term that replaced the old label of *guard*, indicating a new role

corrective justice the component of justice that is concerned with punishments and sanctions

crime control approach the law enforcement concept that uses means-end or utilitarian thinking to determine good by the result, which is crime control

criminalistics the profession involved in the application of science to recognize, identify, and evaluate physical evidence in court proceedings

cruel and unusual punishment punishment proscribed by the Eighth Amendment

culpability blameworthiness

cultural relativism the idea that values and behaviors differ from culture to culture and are functional in the culture that holds them

cynicism a trait of those who work in corrections characterized by a pessimistic view of human nature and their ability to change

deontological ethical system the study of duty or moral obligation emphasizing the intent of the actor as the element of morality

determinate sentencing a form of sentencing in which the length of the sentence is determined by the seriousness of the crime

developmental theories approaches to behavior proposing that individuals have normal growth phases in areas such as morality and emotional maturity

Dirty Harry problem the question of whether police should use immoral means to reach a desired moral end (taken from a Clint Eastwood movie)

discretion the authority to make a decision between two or more choices

discrimination the process by which a decision maker treats a group or an individual different from others for no justifiable reason

distributive justice the component of justice that is concerned with allocation of the goods and burdens of society

due process constitutionally mandated procedural steps designed to eliminate error in any governmental deprivation of protected liberty, life, or property

duty(ies) required behaviors or actions; i.e., the responsibilities that are attached to a specific role

egoism the ethical system that defines the pursuit of self-interest as a moral good

enlightened egoism the concept that egoism may appear to be altruistic because it is in one's long-term best interest to help others in order to receive help in return

ethical dilemmas situations in which it is difficult to make a decision, either because the right course of action is not clear or the right course of action carries some negative consequences

ethical formalism the ethical system espoused by Kant that focuses on duty; holds that the only thing truly good is a good will, and that what is good is that which conforms to the categorical imperative

ethical issues difficult social questions that include controversy over the "right" thing to do

ethical system a structured set of principles that defines what is moral

ethics the discipline of determining good and evil and defining moral duties

ethics of care the ethical system that defines good as meeting the needs of others and preserving and enriching relationships

ethics of virtue the ethical system that bases ethics largely upon character and possession of virtues

excessive force use of force that exceeds what is necessary to accomplish a lawful purpose, or when the purpose is not lawful apprehension or self-defense but, rather, personal retaliation or coercion

exclusionary rule court-created rule of evidence that excludes evidence obtained through illegal means, except in certain instances, such as "good faith," "public safety," and "inevitable discovery"

expiation atonement for a wrong to achieve a state of grace

explication a systematic set of principles that are extrapolated from a range of moral judgments that then can be used to resolve other ethical dilemmas

Federal Sentencing Guidelines mandated sentences created by Congress for use by judges when imposing sentence (recent Supreme Court decisions have overturned the mandatory nature of the guidelines)

force the authority to use physical coercion to overcome the will of the individual

"front-page test" a test that asks whether an individual would be comfortable if his or her action was reported on the front page of the newspaper

general deterrence what is done to one person to discourage future crime by anyone

generalization principle the principle that all decisions should be made assuming that the decision would be applied to everyone else in similar circumstances

Good Samaritan laws legislation that prohibits passing by an accident scene or witnessing a crime without rendering assistance

graft any exploitation of one's role, such as accepting bribes, protection money, or kickbacks

grass eaters those who are fairly passive in their deviant practices of taking bribes, gratuities, and unsolicited protection

gratuities items of value received by an individual because of his or her role or position rather than because of a personal relationship with the giver

gray areas of crimes infractions such as prostitution, gambling, and drug use that do not carry the moral opprobrium of other crimes

group think the tendency for similar people in a group to agree with the group's values or beliefs

guidelines suggested or preferred rules of behavior

halo effect the phenomenon in which a person with expertise or status in one area is given deference in all areas

hostile work environment a work situation characterized by one type of sexual harassment whereby sexual innuendo or joking makes the workplace uncomfortable

human service officer the corrections officer who perceives the role to include influencing and interacting with the offender

hypothetical imperatives statements of contingent demand known as if-then statements (if I want something, then I must work for it); usually contrasted with categorical imperatives (statements of "must" with no "ifs")

ideology a set of general and abstract beliefs or assumptions about the correct or proper state of things

imperative principle the concept that all decisions should be made according to absolute rules

imperfect duties moral duties that are not fully explicated or detailed

incapacitation holding an offender until he or she presents no risk of further crime

indeterminate sentencing a sentence that is not specific and can be adjusted to how quickly the prisoner is reformed (usually through parole)

inductive discipline form of discipline that requires the child/student to understand why what he or she did was wrong

informants civilians who are used to obtain information about criminal activity and/or participate in it so evidence can be obtained for an arrest

Innocence Projects organizations staffed by lawyers and law students that reexamine cases and provide legal assistance to convicts when there is a probability that serious errors occurred in their prosecution

integrity testing "sting" operations to test whether or not police officers will make honest choices

intent the highest level of *mens rea*: to intend and plan deliberately for the act and the consequence of the act

internal affairs model a review procedure in which police investigators receive and investigate complaints and resolve the investigations internally

interpretationist an approach to the Constitution that uses a looser reading of the document and reads into it rights that the framers might have recognized or that should be recognized as a result of "evolving standards"

just deserts model Fogel's conceptualization that the punishment of an individual should be limited by the seriousness of the crime, although treatment could be offered

justice the quality of being impartial, fair, and just

justice model von Hirsch's conceptualization that the punishment of the individual should be purely retributive and balanced to the seriousness of the crime

"just war" debate philosophical argument about when war is ethically justified and what methods are ethical

knowing the second level of *mens rea*: to intend to do the act but not necessarily intend the consequence (to intend to shoot, but not intend to kill the victim)

Kohlberg's moral stages the view that moral development is hierarchical; each higher developmental stage is described as moving away from pure egoism toward altruism

laws formal, written rules of society

legal moralism a justification for law that allows for protection and enforcement of societal morals

legal paternalism refers to laws that protect individuals from hurting themselves

McNaughten rule a legal test of insanity

meat eaters deviant officers who engage in shakedowns, "shop" at burglary scenes, and engage in more deviant practices than "grass eaters"

mechanical solidarity Durkheim's concept of societal solidarity as arising from similarities among society's members

Megan's laws legislation requiring sex offenders to register in order to alert law enforcement about their presence in the community

mens rea the level of mental blameworthiness of an offender; intent is the most blameworthy *mens rea* and negligence is the least blameworthy

meta-ethics the discipline of investigating the meaning of ethical terms, including a critical study of how ethical statements can be verified

modeling learning theory concept that people learn behaviors, values, and attitudes through relationships; they identify with another person and want to be like that person and pattern themselves after the "model"

moral pluralism the concept that there are fundamental truths that may dictate different definitions of what is moral in different situations

moral rules prescriptions or proscriptions of behavior that are consistent with an ethical system

morals principles of right and wrong

national security letters a legal requirement for recipients to turn over private information without notifying the target of the request; issued by law enforcement without a judge evaluating probable cause

natural law idea that principles of morals and rights are inherent in nature and not human-made; such laws are discovered by reason but exist apart from humankind

natural right the concept that one has certain rights just by virtue of being born, and these rights are not created by humans although they can be ignored

negligence the condition in which an individual should have known of a risk but didn't, and caused harm

net widening the concept that some intermediate sanctions are used for those who would not have received any formal correctional sanction before, so instead of diverting those who would have been sentenced to harsher sanctions, the program increases the total number under correctional supervision

new rehabilitationists theorists and researchers who believe that evidence shows that rehabilitative programs do result in lower recidivism

noble-cause corruption bad acts that are done for the good end of crime control

normative ethics what people ought to do; defines moral duties

organic solidarity Durkheim's concept of societal solidarity as arising from differences among people, as exemplified by the division of labor

paradigm a schema or organization of knowledge; a way of seeing the world

parens patriae model of the juvenile justice system that describes the state as a substitute for parents

passive time server the type of officer who does the bare minimum on the job to stay out of trouble

peacemaking corrections an approach to corrections that depends on care and *wholesight*, or looking at what needs to be done with both the heart and the head

peacemaking justice an ancient approach to justice that includes the concepts of compassion and care, connectedness and mindfulness

penal harm the idea that the system intentionally inflicts pain on offenders during their imprisonment or punishment, because merely depriving them of liberty is not considered sufficiently painful

persuasion the use of signs, symbols, words, and arguments to induce compliance

plea bargain exchange of a guilty plea for a reduced charge or sentence

pluralistic ignorance the prevalent misperception of the popularity of a belief among a group because of the influence of a vocal minority

pluralist paradigm the concept that there are many groups in society and that they form allegiances and coalitions in a dynamic exchange of power

policies guidelines for action that are derived from organizational goals or objectives

positivist law human-made law

power the right inherent in a role to use any means to overcome resistance

prevention a rationale for punishment that views it as a means rather than an end and embraces any method that can avoid crime, painful or not (includes deterrence, rehabilitation and incapacitation)

principle of double effect the concept that a means taken for a good end results in the good end but also in an inevitable but unintended bad result

principle of forfeiture the idea that one gives up one's right to be treated under the principles of respect for persons to the extent that one has abrogated someone else's rights; for instance, self-defense is acceptable according to the principle of forfeiture

principle of the golden mean Aristotle's concept of moderation, in which one should not err toward excess or deficiency; this principle is associated with the ethics of virtue

procedural justice the component of justice that concerns the steps taken to reach a determination of guilt, punishment, or other conclusion of law

professional ethics applied principles of right and wrong relevant to specific occupations or professions

proximate cause legal cause (when the natural and predictable cause of a harm creates legal culpability)

psychological egoism the concept that humans naturally and inherently seek self-interest, and that we can do nothing else because it is our nature

public servants professionals who are paid by the public and whose jobs entail pursuing the public good

public service approach the law enforcement principle whereby the values

and ethos of law enforcement and justice professionals focus on human rights, including the right to due process, and the fundamental duty of all public servants is to protect those rights

punishment unpleasantness or pain administered by one in lawful authority in response to another's transgression of law or rules

punitive law enforcer the type of officer who perceives the role as one of enforcer, enforces every rule, and goes "by the book"

reciprocity Sykes's term denoting the situation in which officers become indebted to inmates and return favors

recklessness the level of *mens rea* whereby one knows of the risk of an action but does it anyway

recognition measures "paper-and-pencil" tests that measure an individual's ability to recognize and/or agree with moral terms

recuse to excuse oneself from deciding a case because of real or apparent bias

regulations orders issued by the government that have the force of law

reinforcement rewards

reintegrative shaming Braithwaite's idea that certain types of punishment can lead to a reduction of recidivism as long as they do not involve banishment and they induce healthy shame in the individual

religious ethics the ethical system that is based on religious beliefs of good and evil; what is good is that which is God's will

rendition the practice of kidnapping suspected offenders in foreign countries and transporting them to secret locations or back to the United States for questioning and possible prosecution

repressive law Durkheim's view that law controls behavior that is different from the norm (related to mechanical solidarity)

actus reus an element of a crime constituting the physical act(s) required to be culpable of the crime

restitutive law Durkheim's view that law resolves conflicts between equals, as in commutative justice (related to organic solidarity)

restorative justice an approach to corrective justice that focuses on meeting the needs of all concerned

retribution a rationale for punishment that states that punishment is an end in itself and should be balanced to the harm caused

retributive justice the component of justice that concerns the determination and methods of punishment

rights-based model the policing approach that recognizes the police as servants of the public good; although crime control is important, protection of civil liberties is the fundamental mission

rotten-apple argument the proposition that the officer alone is deviant and that it was simply a mistake to hire him or her

rule utilitarianism the type of utilitarianism that determines the goodness of an action by measuring the utility of that action when it is made into a rule for behavior

sanctuary ancient right based on church power; allowed a person respite from punishment as long as he or she was within the confines of church grounds

self-efficacy individuals' feelings of competence and confidence in their own abilities and power, developed by comparing self to others.

shadow jury a panel of people selected by the defense attorney to represent the actual jury; sits through the trial and provides feedback to the attorney on the evidence presented during the trial

situational ethics the philosophical position that although there are a few universal truths, different situations call for different responses; therefore, some action can be right or wrong depending on situational factors

situational model a conceptualization in which lawyers weigh the priorities in each case and decide each case on the particular factors present

social contract theory the concept developed by Hobbes, Rousseau, and Locke in which the state of nature is a "war of all against all" and, thus, individuals give up their liberty to aggress against others in return for safety; the contract is between society, which promises protection, and the individual, who promises to abide by laws

socio-moral reasoning programs programs that help the individual learn how to think better; the individual learns how to identify inappropriate thinking patterns and change them to prosocial patterns of thought

specific deterrence what is done to one person to discourage him or her from committing more crime

standards rules or models to be followed

stigmatization disrespectful shaming

stigmatizing shaming the effect of punishment whereby the offender feels cast aside and abandoned by the community

street justice individual discretion in applying the law

strict constructionist the view that an individual has no rights unless these rights are specified in the Constitution or have been created by some other legal source

substantive justice concerns *just deserts*, in other words, the appropriate amount of punishment for a crime

superogatories actions that are commendable but not required in order for a person to be considered moral

systems model an absolute or legalistic model in that an attorney's behavior would always be considered wrong or right depending on the ethical rule guiding the definition

teleological ethical system an ethical system that is concerned with the consequences or ends of an action to determine goodness

terrorism the "deliberate, negligent, or reckless use of force against noncombatants, by state or non-state actors for ideological ends and in the absence of a substantively just legal process"

three-strikes laws sentencing legislation that imposes extremely long sentences

for repeat offenders, in this case, after three prior felonies

torture the deliberate infliction of violence and, through violence, severe mental and/or physical suffering upon individuals

treatment anything used to induce behavioral change with the goal of eliminating dysfunctional or deviant behavior and encouraging productive and normal behavior patterns

treatment ethic the idea that all criminal acts are symptoms of an underlying pathology

Tucker telephone an electrical device attached to the genitals of inmates that delivered severe shocks as a form of torture; formerly used at an Arkansas prison farm

"tune-ups" "lessons" taught to inmates by Texas prison guards that involved verbal humiliation, profanity, shoves, kicks, and head and body slaps

utilitarianism the ethical system that claims that the greatest good is that which results in the greatest happiness for the greatest number; major proponents are Bentham and Mill

utilitarian justice the type of justice that looks to the greatest good for all as the end

utilitarian principle the principle that all decisions should be made according to what is best for the greatest number

values judgments of desirability, worth, or importance

veil of ignorance Rawls's idea that people will develop fair principles of distribution only if they are ignorant of

their position in society, so in order to get objective judgments, the decision maker must not know how the decision would affect him or her

victim-compensation programs programs in which state funds are used to compensate victims of crime for their medical and financial losses

victim precipitation the victim's part in criminal incident

victimology the study of victims

victim satisfaction model Stickels's concept that the system has shifted too far in the direction of satisfying the victim's need for revenge and retribution

wedding-cake illustration the model of justice in which the largest portion of criminal cases forms the bottom layers of the cake and the few "serious" cases form the top layer; the bottom-layer cases get minimal due process

welfare/therapeutic worker the type of officer who perceives the role as one of counselor to the offender and who helps to effect rehabilitative change

whistleblowers individuals, usually employees, who find it impossible to live with knowledge of corruption or illegality within a government or organization and expose it, usually creating a scandal

wholesight exploring issues with one's heart as well as one's mind

zero-tolerance policy the law enforcement approach whereby small violations and ordinances are enforced to the maximum with the expectation that this will reduce more serious crime

BIBLIOGRAPHY

Adams, V. 1981. "How to Keep `Em Honest." *Psychology Today*, November: 52–53.

Alain, M. 2004. "An Exploratory Study of Quebec's Police Officers' Attitudes Toward Ethical Dilemmas." In *The Contours of Police Integrity*, eds. C. Klockars, S. Ivković, and M. Haberfeld, 40–55. Thousand Oaks, CA: Sage.

Albanese, J. 2006. *Professional Ethics in Criminal Justice: Being Ethical When No One Is Looking*. Boston: Allyn & Bacon.

Albert, E., T. Denise, and S. Peterfreund. 1984. *Great Traditions in Ethics*. Belmont, CA: Wadsworth.

Alderson, J. 1998. *Principled Policing: Protecting the Public with Integrity*. Winchester, MA: Waterside.

Aleixo, P., and C. Norris. 2000. "Personality and Moral Reasoning in Young Offenders." *Personality and Individual Differences* 28(3): 609–623.

Allen, H., and C. Simonsen. 1986. *Corrections in America: An Introduction*. New York: Macmillan.

Allen, M. 2005. "DeLay Wants Panel to Review Role of Courts." April 2, 2005. Retrieved on October 1, 2005, from http://www.washingtonpost.com/ac2/wp-dyn/A19793–2005Apr1?language=printer

Alpert, G., and R. Dunham. 2004. *Understanding Police Use of Force*. New York: Cambridge University Press.

Alpert, G., and J. MacDonald. 2001. "Police Use of Force: An Analysis of Organizational Characteristics." *Justice Quarterly* 18(2): 393–409.

American Bar Association. 2007. *Model Code of Judicial Conduct*. Retrieved on May 12, 2008, from http://www.abanet.org/judicialethics/approved_MCJC.html

American Bar Association. 2008. Standards for Criminal Justice. Retrieved on May 26, 2008 from http://www.abanet.org/crimjust/standards/pinvestigate.html

American Judicature. 2005. "Judicial Independence." Retrieved on August 17, 2005, from http://www.ajs.org/include/story.asp?content_id=418

American Society for Public Administration. 1979. *Professional Standards and Ethics: A Workbook for Public Administrators*. Washington, DC: American Society for Public Administration.

Amnesty International. 1999. "*Not Part of My Sentence*": Violations of the Human Rights of Women in Custody. London: Amnesty International.

Anderson, C. 1989. "DNA Evidence Questioned." *American Bar Association Journal*, October: 18–19.

Anderson, P., and L. T. Winfree. 1987. *Expert Witnesses: Criminologists in the Courtroom*. Albany, NY: SUNY Press.

Arax, M. 1999. "Ex-Guard Says 4 Men Set Up Rape of Inmate." *Los Angeles Times*, October 14: A3.

Arax, M. 2004. "Guard Challenges Code of Silence." LATimes.com, January 20, 2004. Retrieved on January 21, 2004, from http://www.lattimes.com/news/printededition/california/la-me-guard20jan20,1,5834171.story?coll=la-headlines-pe-california

Arboleda-Florez, J. 1983. "The Ethics of Psychiatry in Prison Society." *Canadian Journal of Criminology* 25(1): 47–54.

Arbuthnot, J. 1984. "Moral Reasoning Development Programmes in Prison: Cognitive–Developmental and Critical Reasoning Approaches." *Journal of Moral Education* 13(2): 112–113.

Arbuthnot, J., and D. Gordon. 1988. "Crime and Cognition: Community Applications of Sociomoral Reasoning Development." *Criminal Justice and Behavior* 15(3): 379–393.

Armstrong, K., and M. Possley. 2002. "The Verdict: Dishonor." *Chicago Tribune* Reports, November 11,

2002. Retrieved on November 11, 2002, from http://www.ishipress.com/dishonor.htm

Aronson, R. 1977. "Toward a Rational Resolution of Ethical Dilemmas in the Criminal Justice System." In *Criminal Justice Planning and Development*, ed. A. Cohn, 57–71. Beverly Hills, CA: Sage.

Arrillaga, P. 2006. "Corruption Opens Holes in the Border." Associated Press, in *Austin Statesman*, October 1: A13.

Associated Press. 1997. "After Cash Rains Down in Miami, Finders Remain Quiet Keepers." *Austin American-Statesman,* January 10: A7.

Associated Press. 2000. "Prison Guards Suspected of Money Laundering." *Austin American-Statesman,* January 27: B3.

Associated Press. 2002. "Review of Prison Clinic Stumbles." *Austin American-Statesman,* November 21: A1, A12.

Associated Press. 2004. "Brazill Seeks to be Worthwhile in Jail." *St. Petersburg Times Online.* Retrieved on April 8, 2008, from http://www.sptimes.com/2004/02/09/State/Brazill_seeks_to_be__.shtml

Associated Press, 2005a. "Appeal Denied in Harris Murder Case." FoxNews.com. Retrieved on April 7, 2008, from http://www.foxnews.com/story/0,2933,169419,00.html

Associated Press. 2005b. "Study: Detroit Pays More in Police Misconduct Cases than Other Big Cities." *Officer.com.*, July 15, 2005. Retrieved on April 9, 2008, from http://www.officer.com/publication/printer.jsp?id=24773

Associated Press. 2007a. "Focus Turns to Federal Probe in Hewlett-Packard Spy Scandal." *International Herald Tribune*, March 14, 2007. Retrieved April 16, 2008, from http://www.iht.com/articles/ap/2007/03/15/business/NA-FIN-US-Hewlett-Packard-Directors.php

Associated Press. 2007b. "Faith Based Prison Programs Multiply." CNN.com. Retrieved on March 27, 2008, from http://www.cnn.com/2007/LIVING/wayoflife/10/15/god.behindbars.ap/

Associated Press. 2007c. "Has Zero Tolerance Gone Too Far?" MSNBC, June 15, 2007. Retrieved on April 2,

2008, from www.msnbc.msn.com/id/19249868

Associated Press. 2007d. "Sexual Abuse Alleged at State Juvenile Prison." *Austin American Statesman,* Monday, February 19: B1, B3.

Associated Press. 2008a. "Father of 5 Drowned Children Has New Son." AP Online. Retrieved on April 8, 2008, from http://ap.google.com/article/ALeqM5jogZjxEVjvN-VhxIrwB_NXmSOMCgD8VON4P02

Associated Press. 2008b. "Ireland Appoints Top Official to Field Complaints of Police Corruption, Malpractice." In *International Herald Tribune.* Retrieved on April 9, 2008, from http://www.iht.com/articles/ap/2008/03/11/europe/EU-GEN-Ireland-Police-Corruption.php

Associated Press. 2008c. "Report: Dallas County Inmate Cleared of Rape After 26 Years in Prison." *Austin American-Statesman,* January 3: B3.

Associated Press. 2008d. "Wife Says Cleric Tortured After CIA Captured Him." In *Austin American-Statesman,* May 15: A4.

Associated Press. 2008e. "White House: Waterboard Technique is Legal, Useful." *Austin American-Statesman,* February 7: A7.

Associated Press. 2008f. "Deal to Return Children to Parents Collapses." Reported by MSNBC.com, May 30, 2008. Retrieved on June 11, 2008, from http:www.mdnv.mdn.vom/if/24887140

Attorney General's Commission on Pornography. 1986. *Final Report.* Washington, DC: U.S. Government Printing Office.

Auerhahn, K. 1999. "Selective Incapacitation and the Problem of Prediction." *Criminology* 37(4): 705–734.

Austin, J., and T. Fabelo. 2004. *The Diminishing Returns of Increased Incarceration.* Austin, TX: JFA Institute.

Austin, J., and J. Irwin. 2001. *It's About Time: America's Imprisonment Binge.* Belmont, CA: Wadsworth.

Axtman, K. 2003. "Bungles in Texas Crime Lab Stir Doubt Over DNA." *Christian Science Monitor,* April 18, 2003. Retrieved on April 21, 2003, from http://www.csmonitor.com/2003/0418/p03s01-usgn.html

Babwin, D. 2001. "In Chicago, Allegations Plague Police Department." *Austin American-Statesman,* April 22: A26.

Baelz, P. 1977. *Ethics and Beliefs.* New York: Seabury.

Baker, M. 1985. *Cops: Their Lives in Their Own Words.* New York: Pocket Books.

Bandura, A. 1964. *Principles of Behavior Modification.* New York: Holt, Rinehart & Winston.

Bandura, A. 1969. "Social Learning of Moral Judgments." *Journal of Personality and Social Psychology* 11: 275–279.

Bandura, A. 1971. *Social Learning Theory.* New York: General Learning Press.

Bandura, A. 1990. "Mechanisms of Moral Disengagement in Terrorism." *Origins of Terrorism: Psychologies, Ideologies, Theologies, States of Mind,* ed. W. Reich, 161–191. Cambridge, England: Cambridge University Press.

Bandura, A. 1991. "Social Cognitive Theory of Moral Thought and Action." *Handbook of Moral Behavior and Development*, eds. W. Kurtines and J. Gewirtz, 44–103. Hillsdale, NJ: Lawrence Erlbaum Associates.

Bandura, A. 2002. "Selective Moral Disengagement in the Exercise of Moral Agency." *Journal of Moral Education* 31(2): 101–119.

Barker, T. 1983. "Rookie Police Officers' Perceptions of Police Occupational Deviance." *Police Studies* 6: 30–40.

Barker, T. 2002. "Ethical Police Behavior." In *Policing and Misconduct,* ed. K. Lersch, 1–25. Upper Saddle River, NJ: Prentice-Hall.

Barker, T., and D. Carter. 1991. "Police Lies and Perjury: A Motivation-Based Taxonomy." In *Police Deviance,* 2d Ed., eds. T. Barker and D. Carter. Cincinnati, OH: Anderson Publishing Company.

Barker, T., and D. Carter, eds. 1994. *Police Deviance,* 3rd Ed. Cincinnati, OH: Anderson Publishing Company.

Barnes, R. 2007. "High Court Reaffirms Leeway on Sentencing." *Austin American-Statesman*, December 11: A7.

Barrier, G., M. Stohr, C. Hemmons, and R. Marsh. 1999. "A Practical User's Guide: Idaho's Method for

Implementing Ethical Behavior in a Correctional Setting." *Corrections Compendium* 24(4) (April): 1–3.

Barry, V. 1985. *Applying Ethics: A Text with Readings.* Belmont, CA: Wadsworth.

Bartollas, C., and S. Miller. 2001. *Juvenile Justice in America.* Upper Saddle River, NJ: Prentice-Hall.

Bay City News. 2007. "Three Oakland 'Riders' Still Seeking Arbitration." *East Bay Daily News*, February 6, 2007. Retrieved on March 28, 2008, from http://www.ebdailynews.com/article/2007-2-6-02-06-07-bcn89

Bayley, D. 2002. "Law Enforcement and the Rule of Law: Is There a Tradeoff?" *Criminology and Public Policy* 2(1): 133–154.

Bazemore, G., and D. Maloney. 1994. "Rehabilitating Community Service: Toward Restorative Service Sanctions in a Balanced Justice System." *Federal Probation* 58(1): 24–35.

Bazemore, G., and M. Schiff. 2001. *Restorative Community Justice.* Cincinnati, OH: Anderson Publishing Company.

Beauchamp, T. 1982. *Philosophical Ethics.* New York: McGraw-Hill.

Beccaria, C. 1977. *On Crimes and Punishment*, 6th Ed. Trans. Henry Paolucci. Indianapolis: Bobbs-Merrill.

Bedau, H. 1969. *Civil Disobedience: Theory and Practice.* New York: Pegasus.

Bedau, H. 1982. "Prisoners' Rights." *Criminal Justice Ethics* 1(1): 26–41.

Bedau, H. 1991. "How to Argue About the Death Penalty." *Israel Law Review* 25: 466–480.

Bellamy, A. 2004. "Ethics and Intervention: 'The Humanitarian Exception' and the Problem of Abuse in the Case of Iraq." *Journal of Peace Research* 41: 131–145.

Belluck, P. 2007. "Judge: US Must Pay Millions in Framing of Four Men." *New York Times*, reported in *Austin American-Statesman*, July 27, 2007: A13.

Bender, B. 2005. "War Turning Young Arabs into Terrorists, Studies Say." *Austin American-Statesman*, July 23: A21, A24.

Bentham, J. 1970. "The Rationale of Punishment." In *Ethical Choice: A Case Study Approach*, eds. R. Beck and J. Orr. New York: Free Press. (original work published 1843)

Bloom, M. 2007. "Hays Near Deal in Groping Suit." and "Officer Accused of Fondling Child." *Austin American-Statesman*, July 7: B1, B2.

Bloom, M. 2008a. "Corruption Case Yields Guilty Pleas by Ex-officials." *Austin American-Statesman*, January 23: A1, A7.

Bloom, M. 2008b. "Chief Accused of Using Slurs, Abusing Power." *Austin American-Statesman*, March 18.

Bloom, M. 2008c. "Quit: Man Won't Seek Police Job, Lawyer Says." *Austin American-Statesman*, March 22.

Blumberg, A. 1969. "The Practice of Law as a Confidence Game." In *Sociology of Law*, ed. V. Aubert, 321–331. London: Penguin.

Blumenfeld, L. 2007. "The Tortured Lives of Interrogators." *Washington Post*, June 4: A01.

Blumenthal, R. 2005. "The DeLay Inquiry." *The New York Times*, September 29: A26.

Bohm, R. 1996. "Crime, Criminal, and Crime Control Policy Myths." In *Justice, Crime, and Ethics*, eds. M. Braswell, B. McCarthy, and B. McCarthy, 341–363. Cincinnati, OH: Anderson Publishing Company.

Bomse, A. 2001. "Prison Abuse: Prisoner-Staff Relations." In *Discretion, Community and Correctional Ethics*, eds. J. Kleinig and M. Smith, 79–104. Oxford, England: Rowman & Littlefield Publishers.

Book, A. 1999. "Shame on You: An Analysis of Modern Shame Punishment as an Alternative to Incarceration." *William and Mary Law Review* 40(2): 653–683.

Boonin, D. 2008. *The Problem of Punishment.* Cambridge, England: Cambridge University Press.

Borchert, D., and D. Stewart. 1986. *Exploring Ethics.* New York: Macmillan.

Boss, J. 2001. *Ethics for Life*, 2d Ed. Mountain View, CA: Mayfield Publishing.

Bossard, A. 1981. "Police Ethics and International Police Cooperation." In *The Social Basis of Criminal Justice: Ethical Issues for the 80's*, eds. F. Schamalleger and R. Gustafson, 23–38. Washington, DC: University Press.

Bourge, C. 2002. "Sparks Fly Over Private v. Public Prisons." UPI. Retrieved on February 21, 2002,

from www.upi./com/view.cfm?storyID=20022002–064851–41221

Bouza, A. 2001. *Police Unbound: Corruption, Abuse, and Heroism by the Boys in Blue.* Amherst, NY: Prometheus.

Bowie, N. 1985. *Making Ethical Decisions.* New York: McGraw-Hill.

Bowker, L. 1980. *Prison Victimization.* New York: Elsevier.

Boyce, W., and L. Jensen. 1978. *Moral Reasoning: A Psychological–Philosophical Integration.* Lincoln: University of Nebraska Press.

Boyer, P. 2001. "Bad Cops." *New Yorker*, May 21, 2001. Retrieved on January 17, 2003, from http://www/newyorker.com/printable/?fact/010521fa_FACT

Braithwaite, J. 2000. "Shame and Criminal Justice." *Canadian Journal of Criminology* 42(3): 281–301.

Braithwaite, J. 2002. "Linking Crime Prevention to Restorative Justice." In *Repairing Communities Through Restorative Justice*, ed. J. Perry, 67–83. Lanham, MD: American Correctional Association.

Braswell, M. 1996/2002. "Ethics, Crime, and Justice: An Introductory Note to Students." In *Justice, Crime, and Ethics*, eds. M. Braswell, B. McCarthy, and B. McCarthy, 3–9. Cincinnati: Anderson.

Braswell, M., and J. Gold. 2002. "Peacemaking, Justice, and Ethics." In *Justice, Crime, and Ethics*, eds. M. Braswell, B. McCarthy, and B. McCarthy, 25–43. Cincinnati, OH: Anderson Publishing Company.

Braswell, M., B. McCarthy, and B. McCarthy. 2002/2007. *Justice, Crime and Ethics*, 3rd ed. Cincinnati, OH: Anderson Publishing Company.

Braswell, M., L. Miller, and D. Cabana. 2006. *Human Relations and Corrections*, 6th Ed. Prospect Heights, IL: Waveland Press.

Braswell, M., and J. Whitehead. 1999. "Seeking the Truth: An Alternative to Conservative and Liberal Thinking in Criminology." *Criminal Justice Review* 24(3): 50–63.

Breslin, J. 2008. *The Good Rat.* New York: HarperCollins Publishers.

Britt, C. 1998. "Race, Religion, and Support of the Death Penalty: A Research Note." *Justice Quarterly* 15(1): 175–191.

Brown, B. 2007. "Community Policing in Post-September 11 America: A

Comment on the Concept of Community-Oriented Counterterrorism." *Police Practice & Research*, 8(3): 239–251.

Brown, J., and J. Gaines. 1990. *Justice Denied*. New York: Noble Press.

Brown, M. 1981. *Working the Street*. New York: Russell Sage Foundation.

Buchholz, B. 2005. "Innocents Are Dying, in the Name of Security." *Austin American-Statesman*, September 4: H1.

Buchholz, B. 2008. "Chaplain's Guantanamo Nightmare." *Austin American-Statesman*, March 23, 2008: G1, G4.

Buntin, J. 2007. "William J. Bratton: Solid Brass." Governing.com. Retrieved on April 20, 2008, from http://www.governing.com/poy/2007/bratton.htm

Bureau of Justice Statistics. 1992. *Prosecutors in State Courts, 1990*. Washington, DC: U.S. Department of Justice.

Bureau of Justice Statistics. 2006. *Prison and Jail Inmates at MidYear 2006*. Retrieved on May 26, 2008, from http://www.ojp.usdoj.gov/bjs/abstract/pjim06.htm

Burrell, W. 2000. "How to Prevent PPO Stress and Burnout." *Community Corrections Report* 8(1): 1–2, 13–14.

Buttell, F. 2002. "Exploring Levels of Moral Development Among Sex Offenders Participating in Community-Based Treatment." *Journal of Offender Rehabilitation* 34(4): 85–95.

Butterfield, F. 2004. "Mistreatment of Prisoners Is Called Routine in U.S." NYTimes.com, May 8, 2004. Retrieved on May 12, 2004, from http://www.nytimes.com/2004/05/08/national/08PRIS.html.

Callahan, D. 1982. "Applied Ethics in Criminal Justice." *Criminal Justice Ethics* 1(1): 1, 64.

Cane, P. 2002. *Responsibility in Law and Morality*. Portland, OR: Oxford Press.

Carey, M. 2005. "Social Learning, Social Capital, and Correctional Theories: Seeking an Integrated Model." In *What Works and Why: Effective Approaches to Reentry*, ed. American Correctional Association, 1–33. Lanham, MD: American Correctional Association.

Carollo, R., and L. Kaplow. 2005. "In Iraq, Military Justice in Doubt," *Austin American-Statesman*, October 2: A1, A9.

Carr, R. 2004. "Coalition Fights Unprecedented Government Secrecy." *Austin American-Statesman*, May 13: A10.

Carr, R. 2005. "In Federal Job: Blow Whistle, Get Boot." *Austin American-Statesman*, December 11: A1, A6.

Carr, R. and Herman, H. "Attorney General Apologizes for Handling of Firings but Says He Can Do Job." *Austin American-Statesman*, April 14: A1, A7.

Carroll, L. 1998. *Lawful Order: A Case Study of Correctional Crisis and Reform*. New York: Garland.

Carter, D. 1999. "Drug Use and Drug-Related Corruption of Police Officers." In *Policing Perspectives*, eds. L. Gaines and G. Cordner, 311–324. Los Angeles: Roxbury.

Casey, R. 1996. "Cop Wins One Million in Whistleblower Appeal." *Ethics Roll Call* 4(6), Fall: 1.

Cassidy, R. 2006. "Character and Context: What Virtue Theory Can Teach Us About a Prosecutor's Ethical Duty to 'Seek Justice.'" *Notre Dame Law Review* 82(2): 635–697.

CBS.news. 2007. "Exposing the Truth of Abu Ghraib." CBSnews.com. Retrieved on March 21, 2008, from www.cbsnews.com/stories/2006/12/07/60minutes/main2238188_page4.shtml

CBS.news.com. 2005. "Praise for Iraq Whistleblower." Retrieved on March 21, 2008, from http://www.cbsnews.com/stories/2004/05/10/iraq/main616660.shtml

Chattha, Z., and S. Ivković. 2004. "Police Misconduct: The Pakistani Paradigm." In *The Contours of Police Integrity*, eds. C. Klockars, S. Ivković, and M. Haberfeld, 175–194. Thousand Oaks, CA: Sage.

Chermak, S., E. McGarrell, and J. Gruenewald. 2006. "Media Coverage of Police Misconduct and Attitudes Toward Police." *Policing: An International Journal of Police Strategies & Management*, 29(2): 261–281.

Chevigny, P. 1995. *The Edge of the Knife: Police Violence in the Americas*. New York: New Press.

ChicagoTribune.com. 2008. "Exorcising Officer Abbate." ChicagoTribune.com, March 19, 2008. Retrieved on April 10, 2008, from www.chicagotribune.com/news/chi-0319edit1mar19,0,6591244.story

Christianson, S. 2004. *Innocent: Inside Wrongful Conviction Cases*. New York: New York University Press.

Clear, T. 1996. *Harm in American Penology: Offenders, Victims, and Their Communities*. Albany: SUNY Albany Press.

Close, D., and N. Meier. 1995. *Morality in Criminal Justice*. Belmont, CA: Wadsworth.

Cloud, D. 2005a. "Guantanamo Bay Inquiry Finds Violations." *Austin American-Statesman*, July 13: A12.

Cloud, D. 2005b. "Lynndie England Guilty of Abuses." *Austin American-Statesman*, September 27: A1, A4.

CNN.com. 2001. "Florida Judge Hears Motions in Child Murder Case." CNN.com Law Center, February 23, 2001. Retrieved on February 6, 2003, from http://www.cnn.com/2001/law/02/23/child.killer.hearing

Cohen, E. 1991. "Pure Legal Advocates and Moral Agents: Two Concepts of a Lawyer in an Adversary System." In *Justice, Crime, and Ethics*, eds. M. Braswell, B. McCarthy, and B. McCarthy, 123–163. Cincinnati, OH: Anderson Publishing Company.

Cohen, E. 2002. "Pure Legal Advocates and Moral Agents Revisited: A Reply to Memory and Rose." *Criminal Justice Ethics* 21(1): 39–55.

Cohen, H. 1983. "Searching Police Ethics." *Teaching Philosophy* 6(3): 231–242.

Cohen, H. 1985. "A Dilemma for Discretion." In *Police Ethics: Hard Choices in Law Enforcement*, eds. W. Heffernan and T. Stroup, 69–83. New York: John Jay Press.

Cohen, H. 1986. "Exploiting Police Authority." *Criminal Justice Ethics* 5(2): 23–31.

Cohen, H. 1987. "Overstepping Police Authority." *Criminal Justice Ethics* 6(2): 52–60.

Cohen, H., and M. Feldberg. 1991. *Power and Restraint: The Moral Dimension of Police Work*. New York: Praeger.

Cohen, R. 2001. "How They Sleep at Night: DAs Turned Defenders Talk About Their Work." *American Lawyer: The Legal Intelligence*, April 9.

Cole, D. 1999. *No Equal Justice*. New York: Free Press.

Cole, D. 2001. "Secret Evidence." In *Policing, Security and Democracy: Special Aspects of Democratic Policing*, eds. S. Einstein and M. Amir, 281–295. Huntsville, TX: Office of International Criminal Justice (OICJ), Sam Houston State University.

Cole, D. 2002. "Trading Liberty for Security After September 11." *Foreign Policy in Focus Policy Report*. Retrieved on August 29, 2002, from http://www.foreignpolicy-infocus.Org/papers/post9–11_body.html

Cole, D., and J. Lamberth. 2001. "The Fallacy of Racial Profiling." *The New York Times*, May 13: A19.

Cole, G. 1970. "The Decision to Prosecute." *Law and Society Review* 4, February: 313–343.

Coleman, S. 2004a. "Police, Gratuities, and Professionalism: A Response to Kania." *Criminal Justice Ethics* 23(1): 63–65.

Coleman, S. 2004b. "When Police Should Say 'No!' to Gratuities." *Criminal Justice Ethics* 23(1): 33–44.

Columbia Law School. 2002. "A Broken System, Part II: Why There Is so Much Error in Capital Cases, and What Can Be Done About it." *Columbia Law School Publications*. Retrieved on February 11, 2002, from http://www.law.columbia.edu/brokensystem2/exe_summary.html

Commission on Accreditation for Law Enforcement Agencies (CALEA). 1994. *Standards for Law Enforcement Agencies*. Fairfax, VA: CALEA.

Commission on Obscenity and Pornography. 1970. *Final Report*. New York: Random House.

Conlon, E. 2004. *Blue Blood*. New York: Riverhead.

Conover, T. 2000. *New Jack: Guarding Sing Sing*. New York: Random House.

Conti, N. 2006. "Role Call: Preprofessional Socialization into Police Culture." *Policing and Society* 16(3): 221–242.

Conti, N., and J. Nolan. 2005. "Policing the Platonic Cave: Ethics and Efficacy in Police Training." *Policing and Society* 15(2): 166–186.

Copp, T. 2006. "Renewed Patriot Act Could Limit Appeals." *Austin American Statesman*, March 10: A1, A8.

CopsWritingCops. 2008. Accessed several times through April and June

2008. http://copswritingcops.com/home.php?subaction=showfull&id=1204644103&archive=&start_from=&ucat=9&

Corey, G., M. Corey, and P. Callanan. 1988. *Issues and Ethics in Helping Professions*. Pacific Grove, CA: Brooks/Cole.

Cox, D. 2000. "Grand Jury Inquiry Into Death of Inmate Extended." *Sun-Sentinel* (Ft. Lauderdale), January 5.

Craig, G. 2003. "Suit Alleges Rampant Female-Inmate Abuse." *Rochester Democrat and Chronicle*. Retrieved on January 30, 2003, from http://www.rochesterdandc.com/news/forprint/0129story2_news.shtml

Crank, J. 1998. *Understanding Police Culture*. Cincinnati, OH: Anderson Publishing Company.

Crank, J. 2003. *Imagining Justice*. Cincinnati, OH: Anderson Publishing Company.

Crank, J., and M. Caldero. 2000/2005. *Police Ethics: The Corruption of Noble Cause*. Cincinnati, OH: Anderson Publishing Company.

Crank, J., D. Flaherty, and A. Giacomazzi. 2007. "The Noble Cause: An Empirical Assessment." *Journal of Criminal Justice* 35(1): 103–116.

Crank, J., and P. Gregor. 2005. *Counter Terrorism After 9/11: Justice, Security and Ethics Reconsidered*. Cincinnati, OH: Lexis/Nexis Publishing.

Criminal Justice Policy Council. 2003. "Initial Process and Outcome Evaluation of the Inner Change Freedom Initiative." Available at www.cjpc.state.tx.us

Crouch, B. 1980. *Keepers: Prison Guards and Contemporary Corrections*. Springfield, IL: Charles C Thomas.

Crouch, B. 1986. "Guard Work in Transition." In *The Dilemmas of Corrections*, 3d Ed., eds. K. Haas and G. Alpert, 183–203. Prospect Heights, IL: Waveland.

Crouch, B., and J. Marquart. 1989. *An Appeal to Justice: Litigated Reform in Texas Prisons*. Austin: University of Texas Press.

Cullen, F. 1995. "Assessing the Penal Harm Movement." *Journal of Research in Crime and Delinquency*, 32(3): 338–358.

Curry, M. 2002. "Faulty Drug Cases Draw Police Inquiry." *Dallas Morning News*, February 21: 25A.

Daley, R. 1984. *Prince of the City*. New York: Berkeley.

Daly, K. 1989. "Criminal Justice Ideologies and Practices in Different Voices: Some Feminist Questions About Justice." *International Journal of the Sociology of Law* 17: 1–18.

Dart, B. 2004. "Police Use Taser Guns 'Excessively,' Rights Group Asserts." *Austin American-Statesman*, November 30: A14.

Davies, N. 1991. *White Lies*. London, England: Chatto & Windus.

Davis, M. 1991. "Do Cops Really Need a Code of Ethics?" *Criminal Justice Ethics* 10(2): 14–28.

Davis, M., and F. Elliston. 1986. *Ethics and the Legal Profession*. Buffalo, NY: Prometheus.

Dawson, J. 1992. "Prosecutors in State Courts." *Bureau of Justice Statistics Bulletin*. Washington, DC: U.S. Department of Justice.

DeCarlo, S. 2006. "What the Boss Makes." Forbes.com. Retrieved on March 29, 2008, from http://www.forbes.com/2006/04/20/ceo-pay-options-cz_sw_0420ceopay.html

Delaney, H. 1990. "Toward a Police Professional Ethic." In *Ethics in Criminal Justice*, ed. F. Schmalleger, 78–95. Bristol, IN: Wyndham Hall.

Delattre, E. 1989a. *Character and Cops: Ethics in Policing*. Washington, DC: American Enterprise Institute for Public Policy Research.

Delattre, E. 1989b. "Ethics in Public Service: Higher Standards and Double Standards." *Criminal Justice Ethics* 8(2): 79–83.

DeLeon-Granados, W., and W. Wells. 1998. "Do You Want Extra Police Coverage With Those Fries?" *Police Quarterly* 1(2): 71–85.

Dershowitz, A. 1982. *The Best Defense*. New York: Vintage.

Dershowitz, A. 1994. *The Abuse Excuse and Other Cop-Outs, Sob Stories, and Evasions of Responsibility*. Boston: Little, Brown.

Dershowitz, A. 2004. *Rights From Wrongs: A Secular Theory of the Origins of Rights*. New York: Basic Books, 2004.

Deutsch, L. 2001. "L.A. Police Corruption Probe Set to Wrap Up." *San Jose Mercury News*. Retrieved on November 12, 2001, from http://www.mercurycenter.com/premium/local/docs/rampart08.htm

Devine, T. 2008. "The Need for Privacy." *San Marcos Daily Record*, March 28: 4A

Dewan, D., and B. Goodman. 2007. "Prosecutors Say Corruption in Atlanta Police Dept. is Widespread." *The New York Times*, April 27: A18.

Dilulio, J. 1987. *Governing Prisons: A Comparative Study of Correctional Management*. New York: Free Press.

Dix, G. 1991. "When Government Deception Goes Too Far." *Texas Lawyer* 7(31): 12–13.

Dolan, M. 2005. "High Court Condemns Conduct of Prosecutor." Latimes.com March 4, 2005. Retrieved on March 8, 2005, from http://www.latimes.com/news/local/la-me-prosecute4mar04,1,1197051.story?coll=la-headlines-california&ctrack=1&cset=true

Donn, J. 2003. "Ex-Agents Say FBI Overlooked Informants' Violent Crimes." *Austin American-Statesman*, March 2: A16.

Dorschner, J. 1989. "The Dark Side of the Force." In *Critical Issues in Policing*, 2d Ed., 254–274. Prospect Heights, IL: Waveland.

Douglas, W. 2005. "Torture Ban Wins Bush's Approval." *Austin American-Statesman*, December 16, 2005: A1, A4.

Draybill, D. 2006. "Forgiveness in the Foundation of Amish Faith." *Austin American Statesman*, October 11: A11.

Dunningham, C., and C. Norris. 1999. "The Detective, the Snout, and the Audit Commission: The Real Costs in Using Informants." *Howard Journal of Criminal Justice* 38(1): 67–87.

Durkheim, E. 1969. "Types of Law in Relation to Types of Social Solidarity." In *Sociology of Law*, ed. V. Aubert: 17–29. London: Penguin.

Dwyer, J. 2005. "Videos Challenge Accounts of Convention Unrest." NYTimes.com April 12, 2005. Retrieved on April 19, 2008, from http://www.nytimes.com/2005/04/12/nyregion/12video.html

Dwyer, J. 2007. "New York Police Spied on Protesters." *The New York Times*. Reported in *Austin American-Statesman*, March 25: A11.

Dzur, A., and A. Wertheimer. 2002. "Forgiveness and Public Deliberation: The Practice of

Restorative Justice." *Criminal Justice Ethics* 21(1): 3–20.

Edelbacher, M., and S. Ivković. 2004. "Ethics and the Police: Studying Police Integrity in Austria." In *The Contours of Police Integrity*, eds. C. Klockars, S. Ivković, and M. Haberfeld, 19–39. Thousand Oaks, CA: Sage.

Egelko, B. 2007. "Firing over Web Site of Nude Wife Upheld." SFGate.com, September 6, 2007. Retrieved on April 2, 2008, from http://www.sfgate.com/cgi-bin/article.cgi?f=/c/a/2007/09/06/MN8ORVPD8.DTL

Eggen, D. 2006. "Prosecutor, Agent Indicted in Detroit." *Washington Post*, March 30: A03.

Eggen, D. 2007. "White House Secrecy on Wiretaps Described." *Washington Post*, October 3, 2007: A05.

Eggen, D. 2008. "Senate Passes Ban on Waterboarding, Other Techniques." *Washington Post*, February 14, 2008: A03.

Eggen, D., and Abramowitz, M. 2007. "Democrats Decry Justice Department Torture Policy." *Washington Post*. Reported in *Austin American-Statesman*, October 5: A9.

Einstein, S., and M. Amir. 2001. *Policing, Security and Democracy: Special Aspects of Democratic Policing*. Huntsville, TX: Office of International Criminal Justice (OICJ), Sam Houston State University.

Einstein, S., and M. Amir. 2003. *Police Corruption: Paradigms, Models and Concepts: Challenges for Developing Countries*. Huntsville, TX: Office of International Criminal Justice (OICJ), Sam Houston State University.

Einstein, S., and M. Amir. 2004. *Police Corruption: Challenges for Developed Countries: Comparative Issues and Commissions of Inquiry*. Huntsville, TX: Office of International Criminal Justice (OICJ), Sam Houston State University.

Elias, R. 1986. *The Politics of Victimization*. New York: Oxford University Press.

Ellington, K. 2003. "Justice Tempered with Mercy." *Houston Chronicle*, January 30: 10A.

Elliott, A., and B. Weiser. 2004. "When Prosecutors Err, Others Pay the

Price." NYTimes.com. Retrieved on March 23, 2004, from http://www.nytimes.com/2004/03/21/nyregion/21prosecute.html

Ellis, L., and A. Pontius. 1989. *The Frontal–Limbic–Reticular Network and Variations in Pro-antisociality: A Neurological Based Model of Moral Reasoning and Criminality*. Paper presented at 1989 ASC conference, Reno, NV.

Elliston, F. 1986. "The Ethics of Ethics Tests for Lawyers." In *Ethics and the Legal Profession*, eds. M. Davis and F. Elliston, 50–61. Buffalo, NY: Prometheus.

Elliston, F., and M. Feldberg. 1985. *Moral Issues in Police Work*. Totawa, NJ: Rowman & Allanheld.

Emling, S. 2005. "Terror Crackdown Upsets British Race Relations." *Austin American-Statesman*, August 6: A18.

Engel, R. S., J. Calnon, and T. Bernard. 2002. "Theory and Racial Profiling: Shortcomings and Future Directions in Research." *Justice Quarterly* 19(2): 249–273.

ESPN News Service. 2007. "Genarlow Wilson Released After Georgia Supreme Court decision." ESPN.com October 26, 2007. Retrieved on April 30, 2008, from http://sports.espn.go.com/espn/news/story?id=3080331

"Ethical Principles for Psychologists." 1981. *American Psychologist* 36 (June): 633–638.

Etzioni, A., and J. Marsh. 2003. *Rights v. Public Safety After 9/11: America in the Age of Terrorism*. Lanham, MD: Rowman & Littlefield.

Ewin, R. 1990. "Loyalty and the Police." *Criminal Justice Ethics* 9(2): 3–15.

Faherty, C. 2008. "Judge Grants Release of 3 City Crack Offenders." *New York Sun Online*, March 5, 2008. Retrieved on April 2, 2008, from http://www.2.nysun.com/article/72316

Fahrenthold, D. 2006. "Online Registry or Target List?" *Washington Post*, April 20, 2006: A03.

Farrell, G. 2005. "Sentence's Message: Crime Doesn't Pay." *USA Today*, July 14: B1–B2.

Fattah, G. 2005. "Complaints Against Utah Judges Rise." Desertnews.com. Retrieved on August 11, 2005, from http://desertnews.com/dn/print/1,1442,600154724,00.html

Fecteau, L. 1999. "Private Prisons Warned." *Albuquerque Journal,* August 27, 1999. Retrieved from http://www.albqjournal.com/news/2news08-27-99.html

Feeney, J. 2005. "The Wisdom and Morality of Present-Day Criminal Sentencing." *Akron Law Review* 38: 853–867.

Feibleman, J. 1985. *Justice, Law and Culture.* Boston: Martinus Nijhoff.

Feinberg, J., and H. Gross. 1977. *Justice: Selected Readings.* Princeton, NJ: Princeton University Press.

Felkenes, G. 1984. "Attitudes of Police Officers Towards Their Professional Ethics." *Journal of Criminal Justice* 12: 211–220.

Felkenes, G. 1987. "Ethics in the Graduate Criminal Justice Curriculum." *Teaching Philosophy* 10(1): 23–36.

Feurer, A., and W. Rashbaum. 2005. "Blood Ties: Two Officers' Long Path to Mob Murder Indictments." *The New York Times Online.* Retrieved September 29, 2005, from http://www.ipsn.org/indictments/caracappa_indictment/blodd_ties_2_officers.htm

Fielding, N. 2003. "Integrity Is Non-Negotiable: Cultural, Legal and Organizational Responses to Police Corruption in the United Kingdom." In *Police Corruption: Challenges for Developed Countries,* eds. M. Amir and S. Einstein, 53–74. Huntsville, TX: Office of International Criminal Justice (OICJ), Sam Houston State University.

Fieser, J. 1999. *Metaethics, Normative Ethics, and Applied Ethics: Contemporary and Historical Readings.* Belmont, CA: Wadsworth.

Fink, P. 1977. *Moral Philosophy.* Encino, CA: Dickinson.

Fishbein, D. 2000. *Biobehavioral Perspectives on Criminology.* Belmont, CA: Wadsworth.

Fishman, E. 1994. "'Falling Back' on Natural Law and Prudence: A Reply to Souryal and Potts." *Journal of Criminal Justice Education* 5(2): 189–203.

Fitzgerald, G. 1989. *Report of a Commission of Inquiry Pursuant to Orders in Council.* Brisbane, Australia: Goprint Publishers.

Flanagan, D., and K. Jackson. 1987. "Justice, Care, and Gender: The Kohlberg–Gilligan Debate Revisited." *Ethics* 97: 622–637.

Fletcher, B. 2008. "The Iraq Winter Soldier Hearings: A Cry in Silence?" New America Media, March 31, 2008. Retrieved on April 16, 2008, from http://news.newamericamedia.org/news/view_article.html?article_id=5231b68167c41d025c004fee26d45201

Fletcher, G. 1993. *Loyalty: An Essay on the Morality of Relationships.* New York: Oxford University Press.

Fletcher, M. 2006. "Bush Signs Terrorism Measure." *Washington Post,* October 18: A04.

Fogel, D., 1975. *We Are the Living Proof.* Cincinnati, OH: Anderson Publishing Company.

Fogelson, R. 1977. *Big City Police.* Cambridge, MA: Harvard University Press.

Foot, P. 1982. "Moral Relativism." In *Relativism: Cognitive and Moral,* eds. J. Meiland and M. Krausz, 152–167. Notre Dame, IN: University of Notre Dame Press.

Fountain, J. 2001. "Former Top Chicago Detective Admits to Leading Theft Ring." *The New York Times,* October 26: A16.

Foxnews.com. 2007. "Congressman William Jefferson Indicted on Bribery Charges." June 5, 2007. Retrieved on May 2, 2008, from http://www.foxnews.com/story/0,2933,377774,00.html

Freedman, M. 1986. "Professional Responsibility of the Criminal Defense Lawyer: The Three Hardest Questions." In *Ethics and the Legal Profession,* eds. M. Davis and F. Elliston, 328–339. Buffalo, NY: Prometheus.

Fuller, L. 1969. *The Morality of Law.* New Haven, CT: Yale University Press.

Fyfe, J., and R. Kane. 2006. *Bad Cops: A Study of Career-ending Misconduct Among New York City Police Officers* (Document #215795). Washington, DC: U.S. Department of Justice.

Galloway, J., and J. Kuhnhenn, 2005. "Senators Add Anti-Torture Words to Bill." *Austin American-Statesman,* October 6: A4.

Gallup Poll. 2005. *Gallup Poll online.* Respect For Police. Retrieved on April 20, 2008, from http://www.gallup.com/poll/19783/Confidence-Local-Police-Drops-10Year-Low.aspx#2

Gallup Poll. 2006. *Gallup Poll Online,* May 8, 2008. Retrieved on May 8,

2008, from http://www.gallup.com/poll/25888/Nurses-Top-List-Most-Honest-Ethical-Professions.aspx

Galston, W. 1980. *Justice and the Human Good.* Chicago: University of Chicago Press.

Garay, A. 2007. "Man's Innocence in Gang Rape Affirmed." *Austin American-Statesman,* April 10, 2007:B5.

Gardner, H. 2006. *Multiple Intelligences.* New York: Basic Books.

Gardner, H. 2007. *Five Minds for the Future.* Boston: Harvard Business School.

Gardner, H., Csikszentmihalyi, M., and Damon, W. 2002. *Good Work: When Excellence and Ethics Meet.* New York: Basic Books.

Garland, D. 1990. *Punishment and Modern Society.* Chicago: University of Chicago Press.

Garner, J., C. Maxwell, and C. Heraux. 2002. "Characteristics Associated with the Prevalence and Severity of Force Used by the Police." *Justice Quarterly* 19(4): 705–745.

Gavaghan, M., K. Arnold, and J. Gibbs. 1983. "Moral Judgment in Delinquents and Nondelinquents: Recognition Versus Production Measures." *Journal of Psychology* 114: 267–274.

Gavzer, B. 1997. "Are Jury Consultants Good for Justice?" *Parade,* January 5: 20.

Geis, G., A. Mobley, and D. Shichor. 1999. "Private Prisons, Criminological Research and Conflict of Interest." *Crime and Delinquency* 45(3): 372–388.

General Accounting Office (GAO). 1996. *Private and Public Prisons—Studies Comparing Operational Costs and/or Quality of Service.* Washington, DC: U.S. Government Printing Office.

General Accounting Office (GAO). 1998. *Law Enforcement Information on Drug-Related Police Corruption.* Report to the Honorable Charles B. Rangel, House of Representatives. Washington, DC: U.S. General Accounting Office.

Gershman, B. 1991. "Why Prosecutors Misbehave." In *Justice, Crime, and Ethics,* eds. M. Braswell, B. McCarthy, and B. McCarthy, 163–177. Cincinnati, OH: Anderson Publishing Company.

Gershman, B. 2003. "The Use and Misuse of Forensic Evidence."

Oklahoma City University Law Review 28: 17–45.

Getlin, J. 2002a. "Officer Refuses to Arrest Homeless." *Austin American-Statesman,* November 30: A8.

Getlin, J. 2002b. "DA Suggests Overturning Convictions in Jogger Case." *Austin American-Statesman,* December 6: A16.

Gibbs, J., K. Arnold, H. Ahlborn, and F. Cheesman. 1984. "Facilitation of Sociomoral Reasoning in Delinquents." *Journal of Consulting and Clinical Psychology* 52(1): 37–45.

Gillers, S. 2004. "Tortured Reasoning." *American Lawyer,* July: 65–66.

Gilligan, C. 1982. *In a Different Voice: Psychological Theory and Women's Development.* Cambridge, MA: Harvard University Press.

Gilligan, C. 1987. "Moral Orientation and Moral Development." In *Women and Moral Theory,* eds. E. F. Kittay and D. Meyers, 19–37. Totawa, NJ: Rowman and Littlefield.

Gilmartin, K., and J. Harris. 1998. "Law Enforcement Ethics: The Continuum of Compromise." *Police Chief,* January 1998. Retrieved on March 26, 2008, from http://www .rcmp-learning.org/docs/ecdd1222 .htm

Giradeaux, J. 1949. *The Madwoman of Chaillot,* adapted by Maurice Valency. New York: Random House.

Glaberson, W. 2008. "Panel Convicts bin Laden Driver in Split Verdict." *The New York Times,* August 7.

Glendon, M. 1994. *A Nation Under Lawyers.* New York: Farrar, Straus and Giroux.

Glenn, L. 2001. *Texas Prisons: The Largest Hotel Chain in Texas.* Austin, TX: Eakin.

Glover, S., and M. Lait. 2000. "71 More Cases May Be Voided Due to Rampart." *Los Angeles Times.* Retrieved on April, 20, 2000, from www.latimes.rampart/lat_ rampart000418.html

Golab, J. 2000. "L.A. Confidential." Salon.com. Retrieved on January 17, 2003, from http://dir.salon.com/ news/feature/2000/24/rampart/ index.http

Gold, J., M. Braswell, and B. McCarthy. 1991. "Criminal Justice Ethics: A Survey of Philosophical Theories." In *Justice, Crime, and Ethics,* eds.

M. Braswell, B. McCarthy, and B. McCarthy, 3–25. Cincinnati, OH: Anderson Publishing Company.

Golden, T. 2005. "Cruel and Unusual Punishment." *Austin American-Statesman,* May 21: A16.

Gourevitch, P., and E. Morris. 2008. "Exposed: the Woman Behind the Pictures at Abu Ghraib." *New Yorker.* Retrieved on March 21, 2008, from www.newyorker.com/ reporting/2008/03/24/ 080324fa_fact_gourevitch? currentPage=all

Greene, J. 1999. "Zero Tolerance: A Case Study of Police Policies and Practices in New York City." *Crime and Delinquency* 45(2): 171–187.

Greene, J. 2001. "Bailing Out Private Jails." *American Prospect* 12(16): 23–27.

Greenhouse, L. 2007. Supreme Court Took Big, Small Steps to Right." *Austin American-Statesman,* July 1: A15.

Greenhouse, L. 2008. "Justices, 5-4, Back Detainee Appeals for Guantanamo." *The New York Times,* June 13, 2008. Retrieved from nytimes.com on June 14, 2008, from http://www.nytimes.com/2008/ 06/13/washington/13scotus.html? _r=1&th=&oref=slogin&

Greenwood, P. 1982. *Selective Incapacitation.* Santa Monica, CA: Rand Institute.

Grossi, E., and B. Berg. 1991. "Stress and Job Dissatisfaction Among Correctional Officers: An Unexpected Finding." *International Journal of Offender Therapy and Comparative Criminology* 35(1): 79–110.

Grotius, H. 2005. *The Rights of War and Peace. Book 1,* ed. Richard Tuck. Indianapolis, IN: Liberty Fund.

"Guards Acquitted of Staging Gladiator Fights." 2002. *The New York Times,* June 10: A16.

Haag, A. 2006. "Ethical Dilemmas Faced by Correctional Psychologists in Canada." *Criminal Justice and Behavior* 33: 93–109.

Haberfeld, M. 2006. *Police Leadership.* Upper Saddle River, NJ: Prentice-Hall.

Hafetz, D. 2002. "Their Innocence Proved, Men Sue." *Austin American-Statesman,* November 8: B1.

Hall, H. 2008. "A Sentence Too Close to Death." *L.A. Times,* March 27,

2008, retrieved on March 29, 2008, from http://www.latimes.com/news/ opinion/sunday/commentary/la-oe-hall27mar27,0,3591034.story

Hall, M. 2002. Death Isn't Fair. *Texas Monthly,* December: 124–167.

Hall, M. 2004. "The Worst Court in Texas." *Texas Monthly,* November: 155–263.

Hamm, M. 1989. "Whistleblowing in Corrections." *Sociological Viewpoints* 5(1): 35–45.

Hamm, M. 1995. *The Abandoned Ones.* Boston: Northeastern Press.

Hamm, M. 2005. "The USA Patriot Act and the Politics of Fear." In *Cultural Criminology Unleashed,* ed. J. Ferrell, 287–299. London: Glasshouse.

Hansen, M. 2007. "The Toughest Call." *ABA Journal,* August: 28–29.

Harman, G. and J. Thomson. 1996. *Moral Relativism and Moral Objectivity.* London: Blackwell.

Harmon, T., and Lofquist, W. 2005. "Too Late for Luck: A Comparison of Post-Furman Exonerations and Executions of the Innocent." *Crime & Delinquency* 51(4): 498–520.

Harris, C. 1986. *Applying Moral Theories.* Belmont, CA: Wadsworth.

Harris, D. 2004. "Review Essay/ Profiling: Theory and Practice." *Criminal Justice Ethics* 23(2): 51–57.

Harris, D. 2006. "Do Something Before the Next Attack, But Not This." *Criminal Justice Ethics* 25(2): 46–54.

Harris Poll. 2008. Support for Capital Punishment. Harris Opinion Poll. Retrieved on May 24, 2008, from http://www.pollingreport.com/crime .htm

Hart, H. L. 1961. *The Concept of Law.* London: Oxford.

Hartman, V. 2001. "Implementing an Asset Forfeiture Program." *FBI Law Enforcement Bulletin,* 70(1): 1–7.

Hassine, V. 1996. *Life Without Parole: Living in Prison Today.* Los Angeles: Roxbury.

Hatamyar, P., and K. Simmons. 2002. "Are Women More Ethical Lawyers? An Empirical Study." *Florida State University Law Review* 31: 785–857.

Hays, K. 2005. "Report: Houston Crime Lab Was Long Neglected." *Austin American-Statesman,* July 1: B7.

Hays, T. 2006. "Former NYPD Chief Kerik Pleads Guilty." WashingtonPost.com, June 30,

2006. Retrieved April 6, 2008, from http://www.washingtonpost.com/wp-dyn/content/article/2006/06/30/AR2006063000241_pf.html

Heffernan, W., and J. Kleinig. 2000. *From Social Justice to Criminal Justice: Poverty and the Administration of Criminal Law.* New York: Oxford University Press.

Heffernan, W., and T. Stroup. 1985. *Police Ethics: Hard Choices in Law Enforcement.* New York: John Jay Press.

Heidensohn, F. 1986. "Models of Justice: Portia or Persephone? Some Thoughts on Equality, Fairness and Gender in the Field of Criminal Justice." *International Journal of the Sociology of Law* 14: 287–298.

Hemmons, C. 2001. "The Collateral Consequences of Conviction," *Perspectives* 25, 1: 12–13.

Henriques, Z. 2001. "The Path of Least Resistance: Sexual Exploitation of Female Offenders as an Unethical Corollary to Retributive Ideology and Correctional Practice." In J. Kleinig and M. Smith, *Discretion, Community and Correctional Ethics,* pp. 192–201. Oxford, England: Rowman & Littlefield Publishers.

Hentoff, N. 1999. "Serpico: Nothing Has Changed." VillageVoice.com. Retrieved on November 4, 1999, from http://www.villagevoice.com/issues/9944/hentoff.shtml

Hepp, R. 2005. "Corrections Worker: I Should Have Kept Quiet." NJ.com, May 16, 2005. Retrieved on May 18, 2005, from http://www.nj.com/printer/printer.ssf?/base/news-0/1116293400232240.xml

Herbert, B. 2002. "In Tulia, Justice Has Gone into Hiding," *Austin American-Statesman,* August 13: A9.

Herbert, B. 2003. "Truth Has Been Told About Tulia, But Story Isn't Over Yet." *Austin American-Statesman,* April 29: A9.

Herbert, S. 1996. "Morality in Law Enforcement: Chasing 'Bad Guys' with the Los Angeles Police Department." *Law and Society Review* 30(4): 799–818.

Hersh, F. 1979. *Developing Moral Growth: From Piaget to Kohlberg.* New York: Longman.

Hess, P. 2008. "Senate Panel Makes Second Try at Preventing Waterboarding." Associated Press. Retrieved from Google.Com on

May 16, 2008, from http://ap.google.com/article/ALeqM5iASWS1P4bBULp9TwdMDnotGBi5bQD90BSNB00

Hickey, J., and P. Scharf. 1980. *Toward a Just Correctional System.* San Francisco: Jossey-Bass.

Hickman, M., and B. Reaves. 2006. *Local Police Departments, 2003.* Washington, DC: Bureau of Justice Statistics, U.S. Dept. of Justice.

Hicks, W. 2004. "Constraints in the Police Use of Force: Implications of the Just War Tradition." *American Journal of Criminal Justice* 28(2): 254–270.

Hight, B. 2005. "In Atoning for Tragedy, a Former Navy Captain Finds His Voice." *Austin American-Statesman,* March 11: A11.

Hinman, L. 1998. *Ethics: A Pluralistic Approach to Moral Theory,* 2d Ed. Ft. Worth, TX: Harcourt Brace.

Hobbes, T. 1651/1982. *Leviathan.* New York: Penguin Classics.

Hockstader, L. 2003. "Texas to Toss Drug Convictions Against 38 People." *Washington Post,* April 2: A3.

Hofer, P., K. Blackwell, and R. B. Ruback. 1999. "The Effect of Federal Sentencing Guidelines on Inter-Judge Sentencing Disparity." *Journal of Criminal Law and Criminology* 90(1): 239–321.

Holmes, M. 2000. "Minority Threat and Police Brutality: Determinants of Civil Rights Criminal Complaints in U.S. Municipalities." *Criminology* 38(2): 343–336.

Hook, M. 2001. "How and Why the System Is Failing Victims with Mental Impairments." *Crime Victims Report* 4(6): 81–82.

Hopfe, L. 1983. *Religions of the World.* New York: Macmillan.

Hornum, F., and F. Stavish. 1978. "Criminology Theory and Ideology: Four Analytical Perspectives in the Study of Crime and the Criminal Justice System." In *Essays on the Theory and Practice of Criminal Justice,* ed. R. Rich, 143–161. Washington, DC: University Press.

Houston, J. 1999. *Correctional Management: Functions, Skills, and Systems.* Chicago: Nelson-Hall.

Hsu, S. 2007. "Ex-prosecutor and Security Officer Cleared of All Charges." *Washington Post,* November 1: A03.

Huberts, L., M. Kaptein and K. Lasthuizen. 2007. "A Study of the Impact of Three Leadership Styles on Integrity Violations Committed by Police Officers." *Policing: An International Journal of Police Strategies & Management,* 30(4): 587–607.

Human Rights Watch. 1998. *Shielded from Justice: Police Brutality and Accountability in the U.S.* New York: Human Rights Watch.

Hunter, R. 1999. "Officer Opinions on Police Misconduct." *Journal of Contemporary Criminal Justice* 15(2): 155–170.

Huspek, M., R. Martinez, and L. Jiminez. 2001. "Violations of Human Civil Rights on the U.S.–Mexico Border, 1997–1997: A Report." In *Notable Selections in Criminal Criminology and Criminal Justice,* eds. D. Baker and R. Davin, 183–202. Guilford, CT: McGraw-Hill/Dushkin.

Hylton, W. 2006. "Prisoner of Conscience." GQ.com. Retrieved on March 21, 2008, from www.men.style.com/gq/features/landing?id=content_4785

Institute for Law Enforcement Administration. Ethical Courage Awards. Retrieved on April 15, 2008, from website http://www.cailaw.org/ilea/pastwinners.html

International Association of Chiefs of Police (IACP). 2008 (1999). Ethics Training in Law Enforcement. Available through official website. Retrieved http://www.theiacp.org/documents/index.cfm?fuseaction=document&document_id=99

Ivković, S., and C. Klockars. 2004. "Police Integrity in Croatia." In *The Contours of Police Integrity,* eds. C. Klockars, S. Ivković, and M. Haberfeld, 56–74. Thousand Oaks, CA: Sage.

Jablon, R. 2000. "L.A. Confronts Police Scandal That May Cost Tens of Millions." *Austin American-Statesman,* February 19: A18.

Jacoby, J., L. Mellon, and W. Smith. 1980. *Policy and Prosecution.* Washington, DC: Bureau of Social Science Research.

Jeffrey, D. 2007. "How Prosecutors Go Bad." *Legal Times,* August 6, 2007: 1–2.

Jenson, E., and J. Gerber, 1996. "The Civil Forfeiture of Assets and the

War on Drugs: Expanding Criminal Sanctions While Reducing Due Process Protection." *Crime and Delinquency* 42(3): 421–434.

Johnson, C., and G. Copus. 1981. "Law Enforcement Ethics: A Theoretical Analysis." In *The Social Basis of Criminal Justice: Ethical Issues for the 80's*, eds. F. Schmalleger and R. Gustafson, 39–83. Washington, DC: University Press.

Johnson, D. 2004. "Police Integrity in Japan." In *The Contours of Police Integrity*, eds. C. Klockars, S. Ivković, and M. Haberfeld, 130–160. Thousand Oaks, CA: Sage.

Johnson, L. 1982. "Frustration: The Mold of Judicial Philosophy." *Criminal Justice Ethics* 1(1): 20–26.

Johnson, R. 1991. "A Life for a Life? Opinion and Debate." In *Justice, Crime, and Ethics*, eds. M. Braswell, B. McCarthy, and B. McCarthy, 199–210. Cincinnati, OH: Anderson Publishing Company.

Johnson, R. 1996/2002. *Hard Time: Understanding and Reforming the Prison*. Belmont, CA: Wadsworth.

Johnson, R. 2005. "Whistleblowing and the Police." *Rutgers University Journal of Law and Urban Policy* 1(3): 74–83.

Johnson, R. 2006. *Hard Time: Understanding and Reforming the Prison*. Belmont, CA: Wadsworth.

Johnston, M. 1995. "Police Corruption." In *Morality in Criminal Justice*, eds. D. Close and N. Meier. Belmont, CA: Wadsworth.

Josephson Institute of Ethics. 2005. *Preserving the Public Trust*. Available from website www. josephsoninstitute.org

Josephson Institute of Ethics. 2008. 6 Pillars of Character. Accessed on March 19, 2008, from website http://.org/MED/MED-2sjosephsoninstituteixpillars.html

Josi, D., and D. Sechrest. 1998. *The Changing Career of the Correctional Officer: Policy Implications for the 21st Century*. Boston: Butterworth-Heinemann.

Juozapavicius, J. 2008. Oklahoma Sheriff charged with Using Inmates as Sex Slaves." Associated Press. Retrieved on April 26, 2008, from http://www.officer.com/publication/printer.jsp?id=41064

Kamisar, Y., W. LeFave, and J. Israel. 1980. *Modern Criminal Procedure: Cases, Comments, and Questions*. St. Paul, MN: West.

Kane, R. 2002. "The Social Ecology of Police Misconduct." *Criminology* 40(4): 867–896.

Kane, R. 2005. "Compromised Police Legitimacy as a Predictor of Violent Crime in Structurally Disadvantaged Communities." *Criminology* 43(2): 469–498.

Kania, R. 1988. "Police Acceptance of Gratuities." *Criminal Justice Ethics* 7(2): 37–49.

Kania, R. 1999. "The Ethics of the Death Penalty." *The Justice Professional* 12: 145–157.

Kania, R. 2004. "The Ethical Acceptability of Gratuities: Still Saying 'Yes' After All These Years." *Criminal Justice Ethics* 23(1): 54–63.

Kant, I. 1949. *Critique of Practical Reason*, trans. Lewis White Beck. Chicago: University of Chicago Press.

Kant, I. 1981. "Ethical Duties to Others: Truthfulness." In *Lectures on Ethics*, ed. L. Infield, 224–232. Indianapolis: Hackett.

Kaplan, M. 1976. *Justice, Human Nature and Political Obligation*. New York: Free Press.

Kappeler, V., M. Blumberg, and Potter, G. 2000/2005. *The Mythology of Crime and Justice*. Prospect Heights, IL: Waveland.

Kappeler, V., R. Sluder, and G. Alpert. 1984/1994. *Forces of Deviance: Understanding the Dark Side of Policing*. Prospect Heights, IL: Waveland.

Karmen, A. 1984. *Crime Victims: An Introduction to Victimology*. Pacific Grove, CA: Brooks/Cole.

Karp, D. 1998. "The Judicial and Judicious Use of Shame Penalties." *Crime and Delinquency* 44(2): 277–295.

Kauffman, K. 1988. *Prison Officers and Their World*. Cambridge, MA: Harvard University Press.

Keith, L. 2002. "Judicial Independence and Human Rights Protection Around the World." *Judicature* 84(4): 195–200.

Kessler, G. 1992. *Voices of Wisdom: A Multicultural Philosophy Reader*. Belmont, CA: Wadsworth.

King, R., and M. Mauer. 2001. *Aging Behind Bars: Three Strikes Seven Years Later*. Washington, DC: The Sentencing Project.

King, R., and M. Mauer. 2002. *State Sentencing and Corrections Policy in an Era of Fiscal Restraint*. Washington, DC: The Sentencing Project.

Kipnis, K. 2001. "Health Care in the Corrections Setting: An Ethical Analysis." In J. Kleinig and M. Smith, *Discretion, Community and Correctional Ethics*, pp. 113–124. Lanham, MD: Rowman & Littlefield Publishers.

Kittel, N. 1990. "Criminal Defense Attorneys: Bottom of the Legal Profession's Class." In *Ethics in Criminal Justice*, ed. F. Schmalleger, 42–62. Bristol, IN: Wyndam Hall.

Kleindienst, L. 1999. "Florida Prison Guards Twice as Likely as Police to Commit Violations." *Sun-Sentinel* (Ft. Lauderdale), August 25: A1.

Kleinig, J. 1986. "The Conscientious Advocate and Client Perjury." *Criminal Justice Ethics* 5(2): 3–15.

Kleinig, J. 1999. "Human Dignity and Human Rights: An Emerging Concern in Police Practice." In *Human Dignity and Police: Ethics and Integrity in Police Work*, ed. G. Lynch, 8–40. Springfield, IL: Charles C Thomas.

Kleinig, J. 2001a. "National Security and Police Interrogations: Some Ethical Considerations." In *Policing, Security and Democracy: Special Aspects of Democratic Policing*, eds. S. Einstein and M. Amir, 105–127. Huntsville, TX: Office of International Criminal Justice (OICJ), Sam Houston State University.

Kleinig, J. 2001b. "Professionalizing Incarceration." In *Discretion, Community and Correctional Ethics*, ed. J. Kleinig and M. Smith, 1–17. Oxford, England: Rowman & Littlefield Publishers.

Kleinig, J. and M. Smith. 2001. *Discretion, Community and Correctional Ethics*, Oxford, England: Rowman & Littlefield Publishers.

Klockars, C. 1983. "The Dirty Harry Problem." In *Thinking About Police: Contemporary Readings*, ed. C. Klockars and S. Mastrofski, 428–438. New York: McGraw-Hill.

Klockars, C. 1984. "Blue Lies and Police Placebos." *American Behavioral Scientist* 27(4): 529–544.

Klockars, C., S. Ivković, and M. Haberfeld. 2004. *The Contours of*

Police Integrity. Thousand Oaks, CA: Sage.

Klockars, C., S. Ivković, W. Harver, and M. Haberfeld. 2000. *The Measurement of Police Integrity? NIJ Research in Brief.* Washington, DC: U.S. Department of Justice.

Klotter, J., and J. Pollock. 2007. *Criminal Law.* Cincinnati, OH: Lexis/Nexis.

Knudten, M. 1978. "The Prosecutor's Role in Plea Bargaining: Reasons Related to Actions." In *Essays on the Theory and Practice of Criminal Justice,* ed. R. Rich, 275–295. Washington, DC: University Press.

Kohlberg, L. 1976. "Moral Stages and Moralization." In *Moral Development and Behavior: Theory, Research and Social Issues,* ed. T. Lickona, 31–53. New York: Holt, Rinehart and Winston.

Kohlberg, L. 1983. *Essays in Moral Development, Vol. 2. The Psychology of Moral Development.* New York: Harper & Row.

Kohlberg, L. 1984. *The Psychology of Moral Development.* San Francisco: Harper & Row.

Kohlberg, L., and D. Candel, 1984. "The Relationship of Moral Judgment to Moral Action." In *The Psychology of Moral Development,* ed. L. Kohlberg, 498–582. San Francisco: Harper & Row.

Kottak, C. 1974. *Anthropology: The Exploration of Human Diversity.* New York: Random House.

Kramer, M. 2004. *Where Law and Morality Meet.* New York: Oxford University. Press.

Kramer, R. 1982. "The Debate Over the Definition of Crime: Paradigms, Value Judgments, and Criminological Work." In *Ethics, Public Policy and Criminal Justice,* eds. F. Elliston and N. Bowie, 33–59. Cambridge, MA: Oelgeschlager, Gunn and Hain.

Kraska, P., and V. Kappeler. 1995. "To Serve and Pursue: Exploring Police Sexual Violence Against Women." *Justice Quarterly* 12(1): 85–111.

Kraus, C. 1994. "Poll Finds a Lack of Faith in the Police." *The New York Times,* June 19: A1.

Kravets, D. 2003. "ACLU: Privacy Rights Diminished." Salon.com. Retrieved on January 16, 2003, from http://www.salon.com/tech/wire/2003/01/16/aclu/index.http

Kreimer, S. 2007. "Rays of Sunlight in a Shadow 'War': FOIA, The Abuses of Anti-Terrorism, and the Strategy of Transparency." *Lewis & Clark Law Review* 11(4): 1141–1220.

Kreytak, S. 2008. "No Excess Force Used in Police Beating in Austin." *Austin American-Statesman,* March 28, 2008, A1.

Krisberg, B. 1975. *Crime and Privilege: Toward a New Criminology.* Englewood Cliffs, NJ: Prentice-Hall.

Krogstand, J., and J. Robertson. 1979. "Moral Principles for Ethical Conduct." *Management Horizons* 10(1): 13–24.

Kronenwerter, M. 1993. *Capital Punishment: A Reference Handbook.* Santa Barbara, CA: ABC–CLIO.

Krulak, C., and Hoar, J. 2007. "Torture Betrays Us and Aids Our Enemies." *Washington Post.* Reprinted in *Austin American-Statesman,* May 23: A11.

Lait, M., and S. Glover. 2000. "LAPD Chief Calls for Mass Dismissal of Tainted Cases." LATimes.com. Retrieved on February, 1, 2000, from http://www.latimes.com/news/state/200000127/t000008518.http

Laitinen, A. 2002. *Corruption of the Police: Is It Not at All a Problem in Finland?* Paper presented at ACJS, Anaheim, CA, March.

Laitinen, A. 2004. "Corruption and Policing in Finland." In *Police Corruption: Challenges for Developed Countries,* eds. M. Amir and S. Einstein, 383–413. Huntsville, TX: Office of International Criminal Justice (OICJ), Sam Houston State University.

Lane, C. 2005. "5–4 Supreme Court Abolishes Juvenile Executions." *Washington Post,* March 2: A1.

Lane, C. 2006. "Scalia's Recusal Sought in Key Detainee Case." *Washington Post,* March 28: A06.

Langford, T. 1997. "Company Defends Its Jailers' Conduct." *Austin American-Statesman,* August 22: B3.

Larrabee, M. 1993. *An Ethics of Care: Feminist and Interdisciplinary Perspectives.* New York: Routledge.

Lavoie, D. 2007. "Wives Struggled After Husbands Were Wrongly Convicted of Murder." *Austin American-Statesman,* August 15: A19.

Leahy, R. 1981. "Parental Practices and the Development of Moral Judgment and Self Image Disparity During Adolescence." *Developmental Psychology* 17(5): 580–594.

Lee, H. 2004. "Oakland 'Riders' Lied, Brutalized Man, Ex-Rookie Testifies." SFGate.com December 14, 2004. Retrieved on April 16, 2008, from http://www.sfgate.com/cgi-bin/article.cgi?file=/chronicle/archive/2004/12/14/BAG75ABBIT1.DTL&type=printable

Leighton, P., and Reiman, J. 2001. *Criminal Justice Ethics.* Upper Saddle River, NJ: Prentice-Hall.

Leiser, B. 1986. *Liberty, Justice and Morals.* New York: Macmillan.

Lenz, R. 2007. "Documents Reveal Pattern in Killings by US Soldiers." Associated Press. Reprinted in *Austin American-Statesman,* September 4: A1, A4.

Lerner, J. 2002. *You've Got Nothing Coming: Notes From a Prison Fish.* New York: Broadway.

Lersch, K. (ed.). 2002a. *Policing and Misconduct.* Upper Saddle River, NJ: Prentice-Hall.

Lersch, K. 2002b. "All Is Fair in Love and War." In *Policing and Misconduct,* ed. K. Lersch, 55–85. Upper Saddle River, NJ: Prentice-Hall.

Levine, C., L. Kohlberg, and A. Hewer. 1985. "The Current Formulation of Kohlberg's Theory and Response to Critics." *Human Development* 28: 94–100.

Lewis, D. 1998. *Guilty by Reason of Insanity.* New York: Ivy.

Lewis, M. 1999. "Corcoran Guards Launch Ads." *Fresno Bee,* September 17: A1.

Lewis, N. 2005. "In New Book, Ex-Chaplain at Guantanamo Tells of Abuses." *The New York Times,* October 3, 2005. Retrieved on May 14, 2008, from http://www.nytimes.com/2005/10/03/politics/03yee.html?_r=1&oref=slogin

Lichtblau, E. 2005. "Profiling Leads to a Demotion." *The New York Times,* August 24, 2005. Retrieved on April 4, 2008, from http://www.nytimes.com/2005/08/24/politics/24profiling.html?_r=1&ei=5065&en=80c10916e1504601&ex=1125547200&partner=MYWAY&pagewanted=print&oref=slogin

Lichtblau, E. 2008a. "Debate and Protest at Spy Program's Inception." *The New York Times,* March 30, 2008. Retrieved on March 31, 2008, from http://www.nytimes.com/2008/ 03/30/washington/30nsa.html? _r=1&th=&adxnnl=l&oref

Lichtblau, E. 2008b. "Senate Approves Bill to Broaden Wiretap Powers." *The New York Times.* Retrieved on July 10, 2008 from http://www .nytimes.com/2008/07/10/ washington/10fisa.html? _r=1&th=&oref=slogin&em

Lichtenberg, I., H. Lune, and P. McManimon. 2004. "'Darker Than Any Prison, Hotter Than Any Human Flame': Punishment, Choice, and Culpability in "A Clockwork Orange." *Journal of Criminal Justice Education* 15(2): 429–449.

Lickona, T. 1976. *Moral Development and Behavior: Theory, Research and Social Issues.* New York: Holt, Rinehart and Winston.

Lin, A. 2006. "New York Panel Disbars Defense Lawyer for 14 Actions." *Law.com,* August 14, 2006. Retrieved on March 5, 2007, from http://www.law.com/jsp/article.jsp? id=1155303323211

Lindell, C. 2006a. "When $25,000 is the Limit on a Life." *Austin American-Statesman,* October 30: A1.

Lindell, C. 2006b. "Sloppy Lawyers Failing clients on Death Row." *Austin American-Statesman,* October 29: A1, A8.

Lindell, C. 2006c. "Lawyer's Writs Come Up Short." *Austin American-Statesman,* October 30: A11.

Lindell, C. 2007a. "Judge Grants Request for Testimony Inquiry" *Austin American-Statesman,* October 11: B1, B5.

Lindell, C. 2007b. "Effort to Reform Death Penalty Appeals Falters." *Austin American Statesman,* June 9: A1.

Lindell, C. 2007c. "Criticism Grows For Judge Over Execution." *Austin American- Statesman,* October 11: B1.

Lindquist, C. 1994. "Criminalistics in the Curriculum: Some Views from the Forensic Science Community." *Journal of Criminal Justice Educaion* 5(1): 59–68.

Liptak, A. 2003. "Houston DNA Lab Worst in Country, Experts Say." *Austin American-Statesman,* March 11: B1.

Liptak, A. 2004. "Study Suspects Thousands of False Convictions." NYTimes.com, April 19, 2004.

Retrieved on April 20, 2004, from http://www.nytimes.com/2004/ 04/19/national/19DNA.html? pagewanted=print

Liptak, A. 2005a. "No, Life in Prison Means Exactly That." *Austin American-Statesman,* October 2: A7.

Liptak, A. 2005b. "Date Missed: Court Rebuffs Low IQ Man Facing Death." *Austin American-Statesman,* December 17, 2005: B1.

Liptak, A. 2007. "Study Reveals Gap in performance of Public Defenders." *Austin American-Statesman,* July 14, 2007: A7.

Liptak, A., and R. Blumenthal. 2004. "Death Sentences in Texas Cases Try Supreme Court's Patience." NYTimes.com, December 5, 2004. Retrieved on December 7, 2004, from http://www.nytimes.com/2004/ 12/05/national/05texas.html? oref=login&pagewanted=print

Lombardo, L. 1981. *Guards Imprisoned: Correctional Officers at Work.* New York: Elsevier.

Lombardo, L. 1989. *Guards Imprisoned: Correctional Officers at Work.* Cincinnati, OH: Anderson Publishing Company.

Lombardo, L. 1997. "Guards Imprisoned: Correctional Officers at Work." In *Correctional Contexts,* eds. J. Marquart and J. Sorensen, 189–203. Los Angeles: Roxbury.

Longmire, D. 1983. "Ethical Dilemmas in the Research Setting." *Criminology* 21(3): 333–348.

Loo, R. 2003. "Are Women More Ethical Than Men? Findings from Three Independent Studies." *Women in Management Review* 18(4): 169– 181.

Lord, V., and B. Bjerregaard. 2003. "Ethics Courses: Their Impact on the Values and Ethical Decisions of Criminal Justice Students." *Journal of Criminal Justice Education* 14(2): 191–211.

Lucas, J. 1980. *On Justice.* Oxford, England: Oxford University Press.

Luscombe, B. 2001. "When the Evidence Lies." Time.com, May 13, 2001. Retrieved on April 9, 2008, from http://www.time.com/time/ printout/0,8816,109568,00.html

Lush, T. 2007. "The G-Man and the Snitch." MiamiNewTimes.com, February 8, 2007. Retrieved on April 26, 2008, from http://www. miaminewtimes.com/2007-02-08/ news/the-g-man-and-the-snitch/print

Lutwak, N., and J. Hennessy. 1985. "Interpreting Measures of Moral Development to Individuals." *Measurement and Evaluation in Counseling and Development* 18(1): 26–31.

Lynch, G. (Ed.). 1999. *Human Dignity and the Police: Ethics and Integrity in Police Work.* Springfield, IL: Charles C Thomas.

Maas, P. 1973. *Serpico.* New York: Viking.

Maas, P. 1983. *Marie.* New York: Random House.

MacIntyre, A. 1991. *After Virtue.* South Bend, IN: University of Notre Dame Press.

MacIntyre, A. 1999. *Dependent Rational Animals: Why Human Beings Need the Virtues.* Chicago: Open Ct.

Macintyre, S., and T. Prenzler. 1999. "The Influence of Gratuities and Personal Relationships on Police Use of Discretion." *Policing and Society* 9: 181–201.

Mackie, J. L. 1977. *Ethics: Inventing Right and Wrong.* New York: Penguin.

Mackie, J. L. 1982. "Morality and the Retributive Emotions." *Criminal Justice Ethics* 1(1): 3–10.

Maestri, W. 1982. *Basic Ethics for the Health Care Professional.* Washington, DC: University Press.

Malloy, E. 1982. *The Ethics of Law Enforcement and Criminal Punishment.* Lanham, NY: University Press.

Mankiewicz, J. 2005. "Why Do We Care About Natalee, Laci, Jennifer?" MSNBC, *Dateline NBC.* Retrieved on September 5, 2005, from www .msnbc.msn.com/id/ 8667821.

Manning, P. 1997. *Policework,* 2d Ed. Prospect Heights, IL: Waveland.

Manning, P., and L. Redlinger. 1991. "Invitational Edges." In *Thinking About Police: Contemporary Readings,* eds. C. Klockars and S. Mastrofski, 398–413. New York: McGraw-Hill.

Mappes, T. 1982. *Social Ethics.* New York: McGraw-Hill.

Margolis, J. 1971. *Values and Conduct.* New York: Oxford University Press.

Margulies, P. 2006. "The Military Commissions Act, Coerced Confessions, and the Role of the Courts." *Criminal Justice Ethics* 2: 2–6.

Markon, J., and Dwyer, T. 2006. "Judge Halts Terror Trial."

Washington Post, March 14, 2006: A01.

Marks, F., F. Raymond, and D. Cathcart. 1986. "Discipline Within the Legal Profession." In *Ethics and the Legal Profession*, eds. M. Davis and F. Elliston, 62–105. Buffalo, NY: Prometheus.

Marquart, J., M. Barnhill, and K. Balshaw-Biddle. 2001. "Fatal Attraction: An Analysis of Employee Boundary Violations in a Southern Prison System, 1995–1998." *Justice Quarterly* 18(4): 877–911.

Marquart, J., and J. Roebuck. 1986. "Prison Guards and Snitches." In *The Dilemmas of Corrections: Contemporary Readings*, eds. K. Haus and G. Alpert, 158–176. Prospect Heights, IL: Waveland.

Marquez, J. 2005. "In Los Angeles, Computers Sniff Out Rogue Cops." *Austin-American-Statesman*, July 24: A15.

Martin, D. 1993. *Committing Journalism: The Writings of Red Hog*. New York: Norton.

Martin, M. 2003. "Corrections Director Summoned to Testify: Federal Inquiry Seeks Pelican Bay Answers." SFGate.com Retrieved on November 7, 2003, from www.sfgate.com/article.cgi?file=/c/a/2003/11/03/MNGJJ20R5Q1.DTL

Martinelli, T. 2000. *Combating the Charge of Deliberate Indifference Through Police Ethics Training and a Comprehensive Risk Management Policy*. Paper presented at 2000 Annual Meeting of the Academy of Criminal Justice Sciences, New Orleans, LA.

Martinelli, T. 2007. "Minimizing Risk by Defining Off-Duty Police Misconduct." *Police Chief*, June: 40–45.

Martinez, P., and J. Pollock. 2008. "The Impact of Type of Attorney on Criminal Sentencing." *Criminal Law Bulletin* 5(44): forthcoming.

Martyn, S., L. Fox, L., and W. Wendel. 2008. *The Law Governing Lawyers: 2007–2008 Edition*. New York: Aspen Publishers.

Marx, G. 1985a. "Police Undercover Work: Ethical Deception or Deceptive Ethics?" In *Police Ethics: Hard Choices in Law Enforcement*, eds. W. Heffernan and T. Stroup, 83–117. New York: John Jay Press.

Marx, G. 1985b. "Who Really Gets Stung? Some Issues Raised by the New Police Undercover Work." In *Moral Issues in Police Work*, eds. F. Elliston and M. Feldberg, 99–129. Totawa, NJ: Rowman and Allanheld.

Marx, G. 1991. "The New Police Undercover Work." In *Thinking About Police: Contemporary Readings*, eds. C. Klockars and S. Mastrofski, 240–258. New York: McGraw-Hill.

Marx, G. 1992. "Under-the-Covers Undercover Investigations: Some Reflections on the State's Use of Deception." *Criminal Justice Ethics* 11(1): 13–25.

Massimino, E. 2004. "Leading by Example? U.S. Interrogation of Prisoners in the War on Terror." *Criminal Justice Ethics* 23(1): 2, 74–76.

Mastrofski, S., M. Reisig, and J. McCluskey. 2002. "Police Disrespect Toward the Public: An Encounter-Based Analysis." *Criminology* 40(3): 519–551.

Mather, L. 2003. "Ethics Symposium: What Do Clients Want? What Do Lawyers Do?" *Emory Law Journal* 52: 1065–1088.

Matthews, J., and R. Marshall. 1981. "Some Constraints on Ethical Behavior in Criminal Justice Organizations." In *The Social Basis of Criminal Justice: Ethical Issues for the 80's*, eds. F. Schmalleger and R. Gustafson, 9–22. Washington, DC: University Press.

Mauer, M., M. Chesney-Lind, and T. Clear. 2002. *Invisible Punishment: The Collateral Consequences of Mass Imprisonment*. New York: The Sentencing Project.

Mazetti, M. 2007. "White House, Others Urged CIA to Keep Tapes of Interrogations." *The New York Times*. Reprinted in *Austin American-Statesman*, December 8: A14.

McAnany, P. 1981. "Justice in Search of Fairness." In *Justice as Fairness*, eds. D. Fogel and J. Hudson, 22–51. Cincinnati, OH: Anderson Publishing Company.

McCaffrey, S. 2007. "Release of Sex Video Draws Fire." *Austin American-Statesman*, July 13: A6.

McCarthy, B. 1991. "Keeping an Eye on the Keeper: Prison Corruption and Its Control." In *Justice, Crime, and Ethics*, eds. M. Braswell, B. McCarthy, and B. McCarthy, 239–253. Cincinnati, OH: Anderson Publishing Company.

McCarthy, B. 1995. "Patterns of Prison Corruption." In *Morality in Criminal Justice*, eds. D. Close and N. Meier, 280–285. Belmont, CA: Wadsworth.

McCready, D. 2007. "When is Torture Right?" *Studies in Christian Ethics*, 20: 393–398.

McDonald, C. 2007. "Updated: SAPD Trio Facing Sex Charges." MySA.com December 21, 2007. Retrieved on April 16, 2008, from http://www.mysanantonio.com/news/metro/stories/MYSA122107.01A.officerscharged.28dce2b.html

McGurrin, D., and V. Kappeler. 2002. "Media Accounts of Police Sexual Violence." In *Policing and Misconduct*, ed. K. Lersch, 121–142. Upper Saddle River, NJ: Prentice-Hall.

McKinley, J. 2007. "Mexico Purges 284 Police Commanders in Antidrug Effort." NYTimes.com, June 26, 2007. Retrieved on April 9, 2008, from http://www.nytimes.com/2007/06/26/world/americas/26mexico.html?n=Top/Reference/Times%20Topics/People/C/Calder&pagewanted=all

McMahan, J. 2004. "The Ethics of Killing in War." *Ethics* 114: 693–733.

McRoberts, F., and S. Mills. 2004. "From the Start, a Faulty Science." *Chicago Tribune—Online Edition*. Retrieved on October 19, 2004, from http://www.chicagotribune.com/news/specials/chi-041019 0150oct19,1,2959538,print.story

McRoberts, F., S. Mills, and M. Possley. 2004. "Forensics Under the Microscope." *Chicago Tribune—Online Edition*. Retrieved on October 19, 2004, from http://www.chicagotribune.com/news/specials/chi-0410170393oct17,1,7219383,print.story

Meehan, A., and M. Ponder. 2002. "Race and Place: The Ecology of Racial Profiling African American Motorists." *Justice Quarterly* 19(3): 399–430.

Memory, J., and C. Rose. 2002. "The Attorney as Moral Agent: A Critique of Cohen." *Criminal Justice Ethics* 21(1): 28–39.

Menninger, K. 1973. *Whatever Became of Sin*. New York: Hawthorne Books.

Messner, S., and R. Rosenfeld. 1994. *Crime and the American Dream*. Belmont, CA: Wadsworth.

Metz, H. 1990. "An Ethical Model for Law Enforcement Administrators." In *Ethics in Criminal Justice*, ed. F. Schmalleger, 95–103. Bristol, IN: Wyndam Hall.

Mieczkowski, T. 2002. "Drug Abuse, Corruption, and Officer Drug Testing." In *Policing and Misconduct*, ed. K. Lersch, 157–192. Upper Saddle River, NJ: Prentice-Hall.

Milgram, S. 1963. "Behavioral Study of Obedience." *Journal of Abnormal and Social Psychology* 67: 371–378.

Miller, J., and R. Davis. 2007. "Unpacking Public Attitudes to the Police: Contrasting Perceptions of Misconduct with Traditional Measures of Satisfaction." *International Journal of Police Science and Management*, 10(1): 9–22.

Miller, K., and M. Radelet. 1993. *Executing the Mentally Ill*. Newbury Park, CA: Sage.

Mills, S. 2005. "Texas May Have Put Innocent Man to Death." *Chicago Tribune*, April 20: A7.

Mills, S., and F. McRoberts. 2004. "Critics Tell Experts: Show Us the Science." *Chicago Tribune*, October 17: A18.

Mitchell, J., and S. Banks. 1996. "Once Again, Americans Fall into Racial Rut." *Austin American-Statesman*, February 9: B1.

Mobley, A., and G. Geis. 2002. "The Corrections Corporation of America a.k.a. The Prison Realty Trust, Inc." In *Justice, Crime and Ethics*, eds. M. Braswell, B. McCarthy, and B. McCarthy, 329–349. Cincinnati. OH: Anderson Publishing Company.

Monahan, L., J. Monahan, M. Gaboury, and P. Niesyn. 2004. "Victims' Voices in the Correctional Setting: Cognitive Gains in an Offender Education Program." *Journal of Offender Rehabilitation* 39(3): 21–34.

Monique, J. 2002. *The Origins of Justice: the Evolution of Morality, Human Rights, and Law*. Philadelphia: University of Pennsylvania Press.

Monroe, J. 2006. "Applying the Responsible Corporate Officer and Conscious Avoidance Doctrines in the Context of the Abu Ghraib Prison Scandal." *Iowa Law Review* 91: 1367–1395.

Moore, M. 1997. *Police Integrity: Public Service Without Honor*. Washington, DC: U.S. Department of Justice.

Moore, M. 2008. "Lynndie England Blames Media for Abu Ghraib Photos." Huffington post.com, April 6, 2008. Retrieved on April 6, 2008, from http://www.huffingtonpost.com/2008/03/18/lynndie-england-blame-me_n_92245.html

Moran, J. 2005. "'Blue Walls,' 'Grey areas' and 'Cleanups'": Issues in the Control of Police Corruption in England and Wales." *Crime, Law & Social Change* 43: 57–79.

Moreno, S. 2007. "In Texas, Scandals Rock Juvenile Justice System." *Washington Post*, April 5: A03.

Mores, T. 2002. "Police Misconduct: A Global Problem." *Crime and Justice International*, January: 9–10, 24–26.

Morris, R. 2000. *Stories of Transformative Justice*. Toronto: Canadian Scholars Press.

Moscoso, E. 2007. "Lawmakers Seek Review of 2 Border Agents' Cases." *Austin-American Statesman*, October 17: A7.

Moss, M., and F. Fessenden, 2002. "War Against Terrorism Stirs a Battle Over Privacy." *Austin American-Statesman*, December 11: A17–A19.

Muir, W. 1977. *Police: Streetcorner Politicians*. Chicago: University of Chicago Press.

Muraskin, R., and Muraskin, M. 2001. *Morality and the Law*. Upper Saddle River, NJ: Prentice-Hall.

Murphie, J. 1988. "Forgiveness, Mercy, and the Retributive Emotions." *Criminal Justice Ethics* 7(2): 3–15.

Murphy, C. 2002. "Monitor Gives DC Police Mixed Review." *Washington Post*. Retrieved on August 8, 2002, from www.washingtonpost.com/wp-dyn/articles/A52807– 2002Aug6.http

Murphy, J. 1985/1995. *Punishment and Rehabilitation*. Belmont, CA: Wadsworth.

Murphy, J. 1988. "Forgiveness, Mercy, and the Retributive Emotions." *Criminal Justice Ethics*, 7(2): 3–15.

Murphy, K. 2002. "States Get Grants to Help Ex-Offenders." Stateline.org. Retrieved on July 17, 2002, from www.stateline.org/story.do?storyID=248888

Murphy, P., and D. Caplan. 1989. "Conditions That Breed Corruption." In *Critical Issues in Policing*, eds. R. Dunham and G. Alpert, 304–324. Prospect Heights, IL: Waveland.

Murphy, P., and K. Moran. 1981. "The Continuing Cycle of Systemic Police Corruption." In *The Social Basis of Criminal Justice: Ethical Issues for the 80's*, eds. F. Schmalleger and R. Gustafson, 87–101. Washington, DC: University Press.

Murphy, S., and S. Smalley. 2006. "Hunt is On for Other Police Corruption." Boston.com, July 22, 2006. Retrieved on April 22, 2008, from http://www.boston.com/news/local/articles/2006/07/22/hunt_is_on_for_other_police_corruption/

Murray, J. 2005. "Policing Terrorism: A Threat to Community Policing or Just a Shift in Priorities?" *Police Practice and Research*, 6(4): 347–361.

Murton, T. 1976. *The Dilemma of Prison Reform*. New York: Irvington.

Murton, T., and J. Hyams. 1969. *Accomplices to the Crime: The Arkansas Prison Scandal*. New York: Grove.

Nakashima, E. 2007. "GOP Opposes Attempt to Revise Wiretap Law." *Washington Post*, October 10: A04.

Nash, L. 1981. "Ethics Without the Sermon." *Harvard Business Review*, November–December: 81.

National Institute of Justice. 1992. "Community Policing in the 1990s." *National Institute of Justice Research Bulletin*, August: 2–9.

Nelson, J. 2000. *Police Brutality*. New York: Norton.

Nettler, G. 1978. *Explaining Crime*. New York: McGraw-Hill.

Newman, G. 1978. *The Punishment Response*. New York: Lippincott.

Newsweek. 2001. "A Captain's Story: Scott Waddle's PR Savvy." April 2, 2001. Retrieved on March 19, 2008, from http://www.accessmylibrary.com/coms2/summary_0286-10978509_ITM

New York Times. 1988a. "Police Corruption Trial Under Way in Boston." *The New York Times*, July 1, 1988. Retrieved on April 21, 2008, from http://query.nytimes.com/gst/fullpage.html?

sec=travel&res=940DE4DB153BF 932A35754C0A96E948260.

New York Times. 1988b. "Boston Jurors Convict 7 in Police Corruption Inquiry." *The New York Times,* September 14, 1988. Retrieved on April 21, 2008, from http://query .nytimes.com/gst/fullpage.html? res=940DE4DC1030F937A2575AC 0A96E948260

Neyroud, P., and A. Beckley. 2001. *Policing, Ethics and Human Rights.* Devon, England: Willan.

Nicosia, G. 2008. "Veterans' Testimonies heard at 'Winter Soldier Iraq and Afghanistan.'" *San Francisco Chronicle*/SFGate.com, April 8, 2008. Retrieved on April 6, 2008, from http://www.sfgate.com/ cgi-bin/article.cgi?f=/c/a/2008/04/04/ EDKGVVDTM.DTL

Noddings, N. 1986. *Caring: A Feminine Approach to Ethics and Moral Education.* Berkeley: University of California Press.

Nowell, S. 2001. "Face to Face." *Houston Press,* September 27– October 3.

Ogle, R. 1999. "Prison Privatization: An Environmental Catch 22." *Justice Quarterly* 14(3): 579–600.

O'Hagan, M. 2000. "Putting Police to Honesty Test." *Washington Post,* October 6: B1.

Owens, M. 2008. "Winter-Soldier Again. National Review.com., March 31. Retrieved on April 6, 2008, from http://article .nationalreview.com/print/? q=ZTU3NjMwNTVhNWQ3Y WUwMzRlM2Uz ZmQ4YWQyN2UwNDc=.

Packer, H. 1968. *The Limits of the Criminal Sanction.* Stanford, CA: Stanford University Press.

Palmer, T. 1994. *A Profile of Correctional Effectiveness and New Directions for Research.* Albany, NY: SUNY Press.

Paoline, E., S. Myers, and R. Worden. 2000. "Police Culture, Individualism, and Community Policing: Evidence from Two Police Departments." *Justice Quarterly* 17(3): 575–605.

Papke, D. 1986. "The Legal Profession and Its Ethical Responsibilities: A History." In *Ethics and the Legal Profession,* eds. M. Davis and F. Elliston, 29–49. Buffalo, NY: Prometheus.

Parenti, C. 1999. *Lockdown America: Police and Prisons in the Age of Crisis.* New York: Verso (New Left Books).

Pasztor, D. 2003a. "Lawyer, Ex-Judges Fear Texas About to Kill an Innocent Man." *Austin American-Statesman,* March 6: A1, A11.

Pasztor, D. 2003b. "Rejected Appeals Leave Inmate with Execution Date a Day Away." *Austin American-Statesman,* March 11, 2003: A1.

Payne, D. 2002. *Police Liability: Lawsuits Against the Police.* Durham, NC: Carolina Academic Press.

Pearson, F. 2002. "The Effects of Behavioral/Cognitive–Behavioral Programs on Recidivism." *Crime and Delinquency* 48(3): 476–497.

Pellicotti, J. 1990. "Ethics and the Criminal Defense: A Client's Desire to Testify Untruthfully." In *Ethics and Criminal Justice,* ed. F. Schmalleger, 67–78. Bristol, IN: Wyndam Hall.

Pepinsky, H. 1999. "Peacemaking Criminology and Social Justice." In *Social Justice/Criminal Justice,* ed. B. Arrigo, 51–69. Belmont, CA: Wadsworth.

Perez, E. 2001. "For Profit Prison Firm Wackenhut Tries to Break Shackles to Growth." *Wall Street Journal.* Retrieved May 15, 2001, from www.msnbc.com/news/ 570728.asp?cpi=1

Perry, J. (Ed.). 2002. *Repairing Communities Through Restorative Justice.* Lanham, MD: American Correctional Association.

Piller, C. 2003. "FBI's Crime Scene Bullet Analysis Test Flawed." *Austin American-Statesman,* November 21: A28.

Piller, C., and R. Mejia. 2003. "FBI's Bullet Analysis Method Is Flawed, Studies Suggest." *Austin American-Statesman,* February 4: A8.

Pinkele, C., and W. Louthan. 1985. *Discretion, Justice and Democracy: A Public Policy Perspective.* Ames: Iowa State University Press.

Pistone, J. 1987. *Donnie Brasco: My Undercover Life in the Mafia.* New York: Hudder & Stoughton.

Pistone, J., and C. Brandt. 2007. *Donnie Brasco: Unfinished Business.* New York: Running Press Book Publishers.

Platt, A. 1977. *The Child Savers.* Chicago: University of Chicago Press.

Plohetski, T. 2006. "Consent Searches in Austin Plummet." *Austin American-Statesman,* March 11: A1, A8.

Plohetski, T. 2007. "From Officer's Order to Taser: 45 Seconds." *Austin American-Statesman,* September 30: A1, A6.

Plohetski, T. 2008. "Officer Accused of Filing False Report Not Indicted." *Austin American-Statesman,* March 20: B3.

Pollock, J. 2004. *Prisons and Prison Life: Costs and Consequences.* Los Angeles: Roxbury.

Possley, S. 2004. "Arson Myths Fuel Errors." *Chicago Tribune—Online Edition.* Retrieved October 19, 2004, from http://www .chicagotribune.com/news/specials/ chi0410180222oct18,1, 1517744,print.story

Possley, S., S. Mills, and F. McRoberts. 2004. "Scandal Touches Even Elite Labs." *Chicago Tribune—Online Edition.* Retrieved October 25, 2004, from http://www .chicagotribune.com/technology/ chi-0410210285oct21,1,2398403, print.story

Post, L. 2005. "FBI Bullet Test Misses target: Court Rejects Test." *Whistleblowers.org.* Retrieved on April 16, 2008, from www .whistleblowers.org/hljFjP.htm

Postema, G. 1986. "Moral Responsibility in Professional Ethics." In *Ethics and the Legal Profession,* eds. M. Davis and F. Elliston, 158–179. Buffalo, NY: Prometheus.

Poveda, T. 2001. "Estimating Wrongful Convictions." *Justice Quarterly* 18(3): 689–708.

Power, C., and L. Kohlberg. 1980. "Faith, Morality, and Ego Development." In *Toward Moral and Religious Maturity,* eds. J. Fowler and C. Bursselmans, 311–372. Morristown, NJ: Silver Burdett.

Pranis, K. 2001. "Sodexho to End Support for Right Wing Lobby." News Release. Retrieved on April 20, 2001, from www.nomoreprisons .org

Prendergast, A. 2003. "Cowboy Justice." *Denver Westword,* June 26, 2003. Retrieved on April 1, 2008, from http://www.westword.com/2003-06-26/news/cowboy-justice/4

Prenzler, T. 1995. "Police Gratuities: What the Public Thinks." *Criminal Justice Ethics* 14(1): 15–26.

Prenzler, T. 2000. "Civilian Oversight of Police: A Test of Capture Theory." *British Journal of Criminology* 40: 659–674.

Prenzler, T. 2006. "Senior Police Managers' Views on Integrity Testing, and Drug and Alcohol Testing." *Policing: An International Journal of Police Strategies & Management* 29(3): 394–407.

Prenzler, T., A. Harrison, and A. Ede. 1996. "The Royal Commission into the NSW Police Service." *Current Affairs Bulletin,* April/May: 4–13.

Prenzler, T., and J. Ransley. 2002. *Police Reform: Building Integrity.* Sydney, Australia: Hawkins.

Prenzler, T., and C. Ronken. 2001a. "Police Integrity Testing in Australia." *Criminal Justice* 1(2): 319–342.

Prenzler, T., and C. Ronken. 2001b. "Models of Police Oversight: A Critique." *Policing and Society* 11: 151–180.

Presser, L. 2003. "Remorse and Neutralization Among Violent Male Offenders." *Justice Quarterly* 20(4): 801–825.

Price, A. 2005. "Soldier's Path Winds from Front Lines to Protest Line." *Austin American-Statesman,* September 19: A1, B9.

Prior, W. 1991. "Aristotle's Nicomanchean Ethics." In *From Virtue and Knowledge: An Introduction to Ancient Greek Ethics,* ed. W. Prior, 144–193. New York: Routledge, Kegan Paul.

Puka, B. (Ed.). 1994. *The Great Justice Debate: Kohlberg Criticism.* New York: Garland.

Puonti, A., S. Vuorinen, and S. Ivković, 2004. "Sustaining Police Integrity in Finland." In *The Contours of Police Integrity,* eds. C. Klockars, S. Ivković, and M. Haberfeld, 95–115. Thousand Oaks, CA: Sage.

Putman, Y. 2008. "Retired Navy Officer Reflects on Honesty, Responsibility." *Chattanooga Times Free Press,* February 27. Retrieved on March 19, 2008, from http://timesfreepress.com/news/2008/feb/27/retired-navy-officer-reflects-honesty-responsibility

Quinn, M. 2005. *Walking with the Devil.* Minneapolis: BooksbyQuinn.

Quinn, P. 2006. "Detentions Called Unjust." Associated Press, reported in *Austin American-Statesman,* September 18: A1, A7.

Quinney, R. 1974. *Critique of the Legal Order.* New York: Little, Brown.

Radelet, M., H. Bedau, and C. Putnam. 1992. *In Spite of Innocence: Erroneous Convictions in Capital Cases.* Boston: Northeastern University Press.

Raphael, D. 1980. *Justice and Liberty.* London: Athlone.

Rawls, J. 1957. "Outline of a Decision Procedure for Ethics." *Philosophical Review* 66: 177–197.

Rawls, J. 1971. *A Theory of Justice.* Cambridge, MA: Belknap.

Reasons, C. 1973. "The Politicalization of Crime, the Criminal and the Criminologist." *Journal of Criminal Law, Criminology and Police Science* 64 (March): 471–477.

Reichel, P. 1997. *Corrections.* Minneapolis: West.

Reiman, J. 1990/2004. *Justice and Modern Moral Philosophy.* New Haven, CT: Yale University Press.

Reiman, J. 2005/2007. *The Rich Get Richer and the Poor Get Prison: Ideology, Class, and Criminal Justice.* Boston: Allyn & Bacon.

Reisig, M., J. McCluskey, S. Mastrofski, and W. Terrill. 2004. "Suspect Disrespect Toward the Police." *Justice Quarterly* 21(2): 241–268.

Reisig, M., and R. Parks. 2000. "Experience, Quality of Life, and Neighborhood Context: A Hierarchical Analysis of Satisfaction with Police." *Justice Quarterly* 17 (3): 607–630.

Rejali, D. 2007. "What Torture Tells Us (And What It Doesn't)" *Washington Post.* Reprinted in *Austin American-Statesman,* December 23: G1, G4.

Reuss-Ianni, E. 1983. *Two Cultures of Policing: Street Cops and Management Cops.* New Brunswick, NJ: Transaction.

Rhode, D. 2001. *In the Interests of Justice: Reforming the Legal Profession.* New Haven, CT: Oxford Press.

Rich, R. 1978. *Essays on the Theory and Practice of Criminal Justice.* Washington, DC: University Press.

Riddle, A. 2001. "Recent Murder Trial Sparks Debate." *ABC News.* Retrieved on May 21, 2001, from

http://dailynews.yahoo.com/h/ap/20010518/vs/young_killers/.http

Rimer, S. 2000. "Lawyer Sabotaged Case of a Client on Death Row." *The New York Times,* November 24, 2000. Retrieved on November, 11, 2002, from http://www.againstdp. org/sabotage.http

Roberg, K. 1981. "Management Research in Criminal Justice: Exploring Ethical Issues." *Journal of Criminal Justice* 9: 41–49.

Robinson, C. 2003. "Perry Wants Review of Convictions in 1999 Sting." *Houston Chronicle,* May 14: A02.

Rodin, D. 2004. "Terrorism Without Intention." *Ethics* 114: 752–771.

Rossmo, K. 2008. *Criminal Investigative Failures.* Boca Raton, FL: Taylor & Francis.

Roth, A., and J. Roth. 1989. *Devil's Advocates: The Unnatural History of Lawyers.* Berkeley, CA: Nolo.

Rothbart, M., D. Hanley, and M. Albert. 1986. "Differences in Moral Reasoning." *Sex Roles* 15(11/12): 645–653.

Rothlein, S. 1999. "Policy Agency Efforts to Prevent Abuses." In *Human Dignity and the Police: Ethics and Integrity in Police Work,* ed. G. Lynch, 15–27. Springfield, IL: Charles C Thomas.

Rothwell, G., and J. Baldwin. 2007. "Whistle-Blowing and the Code of Silence in Police Agencies: Policy and Structural Predictors." *Crime & Delinquency* 53(4): 605–632.

Rousseau, J. 1983. *Discourse on the Origins of Inequality.* Indianapolis, IN: Hackett Publishing.

Ruggiero, V. 2001. *Thinking Critically About Ethical Issues* (5th Ed.). New York: McGraw-Hill.

Ruiz, J., and C. Bono. 2004. "At What Price a 'Freebie'? The Real Cost of Police Gratuities." *Criminal Justice Ethics* 23(1): 44–54.

Ryan, J. 2002. "The Appearance of Ethics." *Austin American-Statesman,* November 16: A11.

Sabol, W., T. Minton, and P. Harrison. 2008. *Prison & Jail Inmates at Midyear 2006.* Washington DC: Bureau of Justice Statistics, U.S. Department. of Justice.

San Antonio Express News. 2002. "Lawyers Should Not Aid, Abet Wrongdoers." December 29: 2H.

Santos, M. 2007. *Inside: Life Behind Bars in America.* Boston: St. Martin's Press.

Sapp, A. 1994. "Sexual Misconduct by Police Officers." In *Police Deviance,* 3rd Ed., eds. T. Barker and D. Carter, 187–200. Cincinnati, OH: Anderson Publishing Company.

Saslow, E. 2008. "Congregation Defends Obama's Ex-Pastor." *Washington Post,* March 18: A01.

Savage, D. 2008a. "High Court Won't Hear Surveillance Program Challenge." *Austin American-Statesman,* February 20: A10.

Savage, D. 2008b. "Court: Detainees Have Rights." *Los Angeles Times.* Reprinted in *Austin American Statesman,* June 13 A1, !3.

Schafer, J. 2002. "Community Policing and Police Corruption." In *Policing and Misconduct,* ed. K. Lersch, 193–217. Upper Saddle River, NJ: Prentice-Hall.

Schanberg, S. 2002. "A Journey Through the Tangled Case of the Central Park Jogger." *Village Voice.* Retrieved on September 5, 2005, from www.villagevoice.com/generic/ show_print. php?id=39999&page= schanberg&issue=O

Schaper, D. 2007. "Former Illinois Gov. George Ryan Heading to Prison." *NPR.* Retrieved on March 17, 2008, from www.npr.org/templates/story/ story.php?StoryId=16051850

Schehr, R., and J. Sears. 2005. "Innocence Commissions: Due Process Remedies and Protection for the Innocent." *Critical Criminology* 13(2): 181–209.

Schehr, R., and L. Weathered. 2004. "Should the United States Establish a Criminal Cases Review Commission?" *Judicature* 88(3): 122–145.

Scheingold, S. 1984. *The Politics of Law and Order.* New York: Longman.

Schoeman, F. 1982. "Friendship and Testimonial Privileges." In *Ethics, Public Policy and Criminal Justice,* eds. F. Elliston and N. Bowie, 257–272. Cambridge, MA: Oelgeschlager, Gunn and Hain.

Schoeman, F. 1985. "Privacy and Police Undercover Work." In *Police Ethics: Hard Choices in Law Enforcement,* eds. W. Heffernan and T. Stroup, 133–153. New York: John Jay Press.

Schoeman, F. 1986. "Undercover Operations: Some Moral Questions About S. 804." *Criminal Justice Ethics* 5(2): 16–22.

Schweigert, F. 2002. "Moral and Philosophical Foundations of Restorative Justice," In *Repairing Communities Through Restorative Justice,* ed. J. Perry, 19–37. Lanham, MD: American Correctional Association.

Sellin, T. 1970. "The Conflict of Conduct Norms." In *The Sociology of Crime and Delinquency,* eds. M. Wolfgang, L. Savitz, and N. Johnston, 186–189. New York: Wiley.

Serrano, R., and R. Ostrow. 2000. "Probe of FBI Lab Reviews 3,000 Cases—Affects None." LATimes.com. Retrieved on August 21, 2000, from http://www.latimes .com/ news/front/20000817/ t0000077169.http

Shakespeare, W. 1969. "The Merchant of Venice, Act IV, Scene i," *William Shakespeare: The Complete Works.* Baltimore: Penguin.

Shane, S. 2008a. "Waterboarding Inquiry Focuses on Legal Advice." *Austin American-Statesman,* February 23, 2008: A10.

Shane, S. 2008b. "China Inspired Interrogations at Guantanamo." Retrieved July 2, 2008, from http:// www.nytimes.com/2008/07/02/us/ 02detain.html

Shea, C. 2005. "Disaster Experts Rebut Tales of Looting." *Austin American-Statesman,* September 18: H1, H4.

Sheldon, R. 2001. *Controlling the Dangerous Classes.* Boston: Allyn and Bacon.

Sheley, J. 1985. *Exploring Crime.* Belmont, CA: Wadsworth.

Sherman, L. 1981. *The Teaching of Ethics in Criminology and Criminal Justice.* Washington, DC: Joint Commission on Criminology and Criminal Justice Education and Standards, Law Enforcement Assistance Administration.

Sherman, L. 1982. "Learning Police Ethics." *Criminal Justice Ethics* 1(1): 10–19.

Sherman, L. 1985a. "Becoming Bent: Moral Careers of Corrupt Policemen." In *Moral Issues in Police Work,* eds. F. Elliston and M. Feldberg, 253–273. Totawa, NJ: Rowman and Allanheld.

Sherman, L. 1985b. "Equity Against Truth: Value Choices in Deceptive Investigations." In *Police Ethics: Hard Choices in Law Enforcement,* eds. W. Heffernan and T. Stroup, 117–133. New York: John Jay Press.

Shermer, M. 2004. *The Science of Good and Evil: Why People Cheat, Gossip,* Care, Share, and Follow the Golden Rule. New York: Times Books, Holt & Co.

Shukovsky, P. 2006. "Gitmo Win Likely Cost Navy Lawyer His Career." *Seattle Post-Intelligencer,* July 1, 2006. Retrieved on April 2, 2008, from http://seattlepi.nwsource.com/ printer2/index.asp?ploc=b&refer= http://seattlepi.nwsource.com/ national/276109_swift01.html

Siegal, N. (2001). "Sexual Abuse of Women Inmates is Widespread." In M. Wagner, *How Should Prisons Treat Inmates? Opposing Viewpoints,* ed. M. Wagner. San Diego, CA: Greenhaven Press.

Silberman, M. 1995. *A World of Violence: Corrections in America.* Belmont, CA: Wadsworth.

Simerman, J., D. Ott, and T. Mellnik. 2005. "Early Data Challenge Assumptions About Katrina Victims." *Austin American-Statesman,* December 30: A1, A8.

Simmons, A. 2006. "Immigration Judges' Abusive Antics Prompt Review." *San Antonio Express News,* Sunday, February 12, 2006: 6A.

Simon, W. 1998. *The Practice of Justice: A Theory of Lawyer's Ethics.* Boston: Harvard University Press.

Skolnick, J. 1982. "Deception by Police." *Criminal Justice Ethics* 1(2): 40–54.

Skolnick, J., and J. Fyfe. 1993. *Above the Law: Police and the Excessive Use of Force.* New York: Free Press.

Skolnick, J., and R. Leo. 1992. "Ideology and the Ethics of Crime Control." *Criminal Justice Ethics* 11(1): 3–13.

Slevin, P. 2008. "Affirmative Action Foes push Ballot Question in 5 More States." Boston.com. Retrieved on March 31, 2008, from http://www .boston.com/news/nation/articles/ 2008/03/27/affirmative_action_ foes_push_ballot

Smilansky, S. 2004. "Terrorism, Justification and Illusion." *Ethics* 114: 790–805.

Smith, B., and M. Holmes. 2003. "Community Accountability, Minority Threat, and Police Brutality: An Examination of Civil Rights Criminal Complaints." *Criminology* 41(4): 1035–1063.

Smith, D. 1982. "Ideology and the Ethics of Economic Crime Control."

In *Ethics, Public Policy and Criminal Justice,* eds. F. Elliston and N. Bowie, 133–156. Cambridge, MA: Oelgeschlager, Gunn and Hain.

Smith, J. 2006a. "A Few Good Scapegoats: The Abu Ghraib Courts-Martial and the Failure of the Military Justice System." *Whitter Law Review* 27: 671–720.

Smith, J. 2006b. "God v. Taser: Officer Sues APD." *AustinChronicle.com,* December 29, 2006. Retrieved on April 19, 2008, from http://www .austinchronicle.com/gyrobase/Issue/ print?oid=%3A432110

Smith, M., and G. Alpert. 2002. "Searching for Direction: Courts, Social Science, and the Adjudication of Racial Profiling Claims." *Justice Quarterly* 19(4): 673–703.

Smith, R., and Linzer, D. 2006. "CIA Officer's Job Made Any Leaks More Delicate." *Washington Post,* April 23: A01.

Smith, S., and R. Meyer. 1987. *Law, Behavior, and Mental Health.* New York: New York University Press.

Sniffen, M. 1997. "FBI Suspends Agent Whose Charges Led to Critical Report." *Austin American-Statesman,* January 28: A5.

Solomon, A. 1999. "Wackenhut Detention Ordeal." *Village Voice.* Retrieved on March 5, 1999, from http://www.villagevoice.com/ features/9935/solomon.html

Solomon, J. 2007a. "Former N.C. Chief Justice Takes Up Prisoner's Case." *Washington Post,* November 28, 2007: A07.

Solomon, J. 2007b. "FBI Fails to Tell Convicts of Ruling That Could Help Their Cases, Investigation Finds." *Washington Post,* reprinted in *Austin American-Statesman,* November 18, 2007: A11.

Solomon, R. 2006. *The Big Questions: A Short Introduction to Philosophy.* Belmont, CA: Wadsworth.

Sourcebook of Criminal Justice Statistics. 2007. "Respondents' Ratings of the Honesty and Ethical Standards of Police, Table 2.20." Retrieved on April 23, 2008, from http://www.albany.edu/sourcebook/ pdf/t2202007.pdf

Souryal, S. 1992/2007. *Ethics in Criminal Justice: In Search of the Truth.* Cincinnati, OH: Anderson Publishing Company.

Souryal, S. 1996a. "Probation as Good Faith." *Texas Probation* 11(3): 1–6.

Souryal, S. 1996b. "Personal Loyalty to Superiors in Public Service." *Criminal Justice Ethics,* Summer/ Fall: 44–62.

Souryal, S. 1999a. "Corruption of Prison Personnel." In *Prison and Jail Administration: Practice and Theory,* eds. P. Carlson and J. Garrett, 171–177. Gaithersburg, MD: Aspen.

Souryal, S. 1999b. "Personal Loyalty to Superiors in Criminal Justice Agencies." *Justice Quarterly* 16(4): 871–906.

South, N. 2001. "Police, Security and Information: The Use of Informants and Agents in a Liberal Democracy." In *Policing, Security and Democracy: Special Aspects of Democratic Policing,* eds. S. Einstein and M. Amir, 87–105. Huntsville, TX: Office of International Criminal Justice (OICJ), Sam Houston State University.

Spader, D. 1984. "Rule of Law v. Rule of Man: The Search for the Golden Zigzag Between Conflicting Fundamental Values." *Journal of Criminal Justice* 12: 379–394.

Spence, G. 1989. *With Justice for None.* New York: Penguin.

Stace, W. 1995. "Ethical Relativity and Ethical Absolutism." In *Morality and Criminal Justice,* eds. D. Close and N. Meier, 25–32. Belmont, CA: Wadsworth.

Staples, W. 1997. *The Culture of Surveillance.* New York: St. Martin's.

Stefanic, M. 1981. "Police Ethics in a Changing Society." *The Police Chief,* May: 62–64.

Steptoe, S. 2007. "Can Bratton Survive May Day?" *Time.com,* May 31, 2007. Retrieved on April 20, 2008, from http://www.time.com/time/ nation/article/0,8599,1627076,00 .html

Sterba, J. 1980. *The Demands of Justice.* Notre Dame, IN: University of Notre Dame Press.

Sterngold, J. 2000. "Los Angeles Police Admit a Vast Management Lapse." *New York Times,* March 2: A14.

Stevens, D. 1999. "Corruption Among Narcotics Officers: A Study of Innocence and Integrity." *Journal of Police and Criminal Psychology* 14(2): 1–11.

Stickels, J. 2003. *The Victim Satisfaction Model in Criminal Justice.* Ph.D. dissertation, University of Texas.

Stitt, B., and G. James. 1985. "Entrapment: An Ethical Analysis." In *Moral Issues in Police Work,* eds. F. Elliston and M. Feldberg, 129–147. Totawa, NJ: Rowman and Allanheld.

Stover, R. 1989. *Making It and Breaking It: The Fate of Public Interest Commitment During Law School,* ed. H. Erlanger. Urbana: University of Illinois Press.

Streiffer, R. 2003. *Moral Relativism and Reasons for Action.* New York: Routledge.

Stuntz, W. 2002. "Terrorism, Federalism, and Police Misconduct." *Harvard Journal of Law and Public Policy* 25(2): 665–680.

Swift, C. 2007. "The American Way of Justice." Esquire online, June 26, 2007. Retrieved on April 2, 2008, from http://www.esquire.com/print-this/features/ESQ0307swift

Sykes, G. 1980. "The Defects of Total Power." In *Keepers: Prison Guards and Contemporary Corrections,* ed. B. Crouch. Springfield, IL: Charles C Thomas.

Sykes, G. 1989. "The Functional Nature of Police Reform: The Myth of Controlling the Police." In *Critical Issues in Policing,* eds. R. Dunham and G. Alpert, 292–304. Prospect Heights, IL: Waveland.

Sykes, G. 1996. "How Much Is Our Credibility Worth?" *Ethics Roll Call* 3(1): 5.

Talbot, M. 2003. "Catch and Release." Atlantic online. Retrieved on January 23, 2003, from http://www .thatlantic.com/cgi-bin/send.cgi? page=http%2A//www.theatlantic. com/ issues

Talvi, S. 2002. "The Other War." *The Nation,* December 24.

Tanay, E. 1982. "Psychiatry and the Prison System." *Journal of Forensic Sciences* 27(2): 385–392.

Tanner, R. 2002. "Central Park Case Puts Focus on Confessions." *Austin American-Statesman,* December 7: A9.

Tanner, R. 2006. "Bad Science May Taint Many Arson Convictions." *Austin American Statesman,* May 3: A1, A5.

Tarnoff, S. 2001. "Hard Line on a White Lie." *ABA Journal* 87: 32–33.

Taylor, W. 1993. *Brokered Justice: Race Politics and Mississippi Prisons 1798–1992.* Columbus: Ohio State University Press.

Terrill, W. 2001. *Police Coercion: Application of the Force Continuum.* New York: LFB Scholarly Publishing.

Terrill, W. 2005. "Police Use of Force: A Transactional Approach." *Justice Quarterly*, 22(1): 107–139.

Terrill, W., and S. Mastrofsky. 2002. "Situational and Officer-Based Determinants of Police Coercion." *Justice Quarterly* 19(2): 216–248.

Terrill, W., E. Paoline, and P. Manning. 2003. "Police Culture and Coercion." *Criminology* 41(4): 1003–1034.

Texas Bar Association. 2000. "Muting Gideon's Trumpet: The Crisis in Indigent Defense." Report by the Committee on Legal Services to the Poor in Criminal Matters, Texas State Bar. Retrieved on January 2, 2005, from http://www.uta.edu/pols/moore/indigent

Thevenot, B., and G. Russell. 2005. "No Evidence Supports Tales of Murder, Rape." *Austin American-Statesman,* September 28: A1, A7.

Thiroux, J., and Kraseman, K. 2006. *Ethics: Theory and Practice.* Upper Saddle River, NJ: Prentice Hall.

Thoma, S. 1986. "Estimating Gender Differences in the Comprehension and Preference of Moral Issues." *Developmental Review* 6: 165–180.

Thompson, D. 1980. "Paternalism in Medicine, Law and Public Policy." In *Ethics Teaching in Higher Education,* eds. D. Callahan and S. Bok, 3–20. Hastings, NY: Hastings Center.

Thompson, D. 2004. "Prison System Blasted by Lawmakers, New Administration." Sandiego.com, January 20, 2004. Retrieved on January 22, 2004, from http://signonsandiego.com/news/state/20040120–1658-ca-prisonhearings.html

"Three Guards Acquitted." 2002. *The New York Times,* February 16: A13.

Timerman, J. 1981. *Prisoner Without a Name, Cell Without a Number,* trans. Toby Talbot. New York: Knopf.

Toch, H. 1977. *Living in Prison.* New York: Free Press.

Toch, H. 1997. *Humanistic Corrections.* Guilderland, NY: Harrow and Heston.

Tonry, M. 2005. "The Functions of Sentencing and Sentencing Reform." *Stanford Law Review* 58: 37–67.

Tonry, M., L. Ohlin, and D. Farrington. 1991. *Human Development and Criminal Behavior.* New York: Springer Verlag.

Toohey, M. 2005. "Soldier a Willing Participant, Prosecutors Say." *Austin American-Statesman,* September 23: B1, B3.

Transparency International. 2003. "Annual Report." Retrieved on December 30, 2005, from www.transparency.org/publications

Transparency International. 2008. "Annual Report." Retrieved on March 27, 2008, from http://www.transparency.org/policy_research/surveys_indices/cpi/2007

Trautman, N. 2008. The Ethics Continuum. Available from Ethics Institute website. Retrieved on April 7, 2008, from www.ethicsinstitute.com/pdf/**Corruption**%20Continum.pdf

Turley, J. 2006. "109th Congress Just Can't Resist." *USA Today*, October 19, 2006, 13.

Turner, C. 2007. "Ethical Issues in Criminal Justice Administration." *American Jails* (January/February): 49–53.

Tyler, T. 1990. *Why People Obey the Law.* New Haven, CT: Yale University Press.

Tyler, T., and L. Wakslak. 2004. "Profiling and Police Legitimacy: Procedural Justice, Attributions of Motive, and Acceptance of Police Authority." *Criminology* 42(2): 253–281.

Umbreit, M. 1994. *Victim Meets Offender: The Impact of Restorative Justice and Mediation.* Monsey, NY: Criminal Justice Press.

Umbreit, M., and M. Carey. 1995. "Restorative Justice Implications for Organizational Change." *Federal Probation* 59(1): 47–54.

Umbreit, M., R. Coates, and B. Vos. 2002. "Peacemaking Circles in Minnesota: An Exploratory Study." *Crime Victims Report* 5(6): 81–82.

Uniform Crime Reports (U.C.R.). 2006. *Crime in the United States.* Washington, DC: U.S. Department of Justice, Table 32. Retrieved on April 2, 2008, from www.fbi.gov/ucr/cius2006/data/table_32.html

United States Attorney's Office. 2008. "Boston Police Officer Pleads Guilty to all Charges." (News Release: November 8, 2007.) Boston: U.S.

Dept. of Justice, U.S. Attorney's Office, Michael J. Sullivan.

United States Department of Justice, July 28, 2005. Retrieved on October 7, 2005, from http://www.usdoj.gov/usao/fls/050728-02.html

Van Maanen, J. 1978. "The Asshole." In *Policing: A View From the Street,* eds. P. Manning and J. van Maanen, 221–240. Santa Monica, CA: Goodyear.

Van Natta, D. 2003. "Blurry Line Marks Banned, Acceptable in Interrogations." *Austin American-Statesman,* March 2: A13.

Van Ness, D., and K. Heetderks Strong. 1997. *Restoring Justice.* Cincinnati, OH: Anderson Publishing Company.

Vaughn, M. and L. Smith. 1999. "Practicing Penal Harm Medicine in U.S. Prisons." *Justice Quarterly*, 16(1): 175–231.

Vaznis, J. 2008 "Ex-Officer Gets 18 Years in Drug Plot." Boston.com Retrieved on April 9, 2008, from http://www.boston.com/news/local/articles/2008/03/11/ex_officer_gets_18_years_in_drug_ plot?mode=PF

Vedantam, S. 2007. "If it Feels Good to be Good, It Might be Only Natural." WashingtonPost.com. Retrieved on May 28, 2007 from http://www.washingtonpost.com/wp-dyn/content/article/2007/05/27/AR2007052701056.html

Vogelstein, R. 2003. "Confidentiality vs. Care: Re-evaluating the Duty to Self, Client, and Others." *Georgetown Law Journal* 92: 153–171.

Von Bergen, J. 2006. "Graft Probe Mushrooming in Chicago." *Philadelphia Inquirer,* August 10: A1, A13.

von Hirsch, A. 1976. *Doing Justice.* New York: Hill and Wang.

von Hirsch, A. 1985. *Past or Future Crimes.* New Brunswick, NJ: Rutgers University Press.

von Hirsch, A., and L. Maher. 1992. "Can Penal Rehabilitation Be Revived?" *Criminal Justice Ethics* 11(1): 25–31.

Walker, L. 1986. "Sex Difference in the Development of Moral Reasoning." *Child Development* 57: 522–526.

Walker, S. 1985/2005. *Sense and Nonsense About Crime.* Monterey, CA: Brooks/Cole.

Walker, S. 2001. *Police Accountability: The Role of Citizen Oversight.* Belmont, CA: Wadsworth.

Walker, S. 2007. *Police Accountability: Current Issues and Research Needs.* Paper presented at National Institute of Justice, Policing Research Workshop: Planning for the Future, Washington, DC, November 28–29, 2006. (Available through National Institute of Justice, Washington DC)

Walker, S., and G. Alpert. 2002. "Early Warning Systems as Risk Management for Police." In *Policing and Misconduct,* ed. K. Lersch, 219–230. Upper Saddle River, NJ: Prentice-Hall.

Walker, S., C. Spohn, and M. DeLone. 2000. *The Color of Justice.* Belmont, CA: Wadsworth.

Walsh, A. 1995. *Biosociology: An Emerging Paradigm.* Trenton, NJ: Praeger.

Walsh, A. 2000. "Evolutionary Psychology and the Origins of Justice." *Justice Quarterly* 17(4): 841–864.

Walsh, A. 2001/2002. *Biosocial Criminology: Introduction and Integration.* Cincinnati, OH: Anderson Publishing Company.

Ward, G. 2001. "C.C.A. Majority Shareholder to Sell Stocks." *Tennessean.* Retrieved on May 23, 2001, from www.tennessean.com/business/archives/01/04/05094888.shtml?Element_ID550948

Ward, M. 1996. "State Approves Faith-Based Pre-Release Program for Texas Inmates." *Austin American-Statesman,* November 16: B12.

Ward, M. 2004. "Echoes of Texas' Sordid Past in Iraq Prison Abuse." *Austin American-Statesman,* May 12: B4.

Ward, M. 2006a. "Arrests of Prison Workers Climb." *Austin American Statesman,* April 23: A1, A9.

Ward, M. 2006b. "Prison Workers' Rap Sheets Run Gamut." *Austin American Statesman,* April 28: A1, A12.

Ward, M. 2006c. "Secrecy of Parole Files Opens Door For Abuses." *Austin American Statesman,* March 18: A1, A11.

Ward, M. 2007a. "Privately Run Prisons Come Under More Fire at Capitol." *Austin American Statesman,* October 13: B1, B3.

Ward, M. 2007b. "Inquiries Spring Up in Abuse Scandal." *Austin American Statesman,* March 3: A1, A14.

Ward, M. 2008. "Inquiry: New Trial Had Been Ordered by Federal Appeals Court Last August." *Austin American Statesman,* April 23: A1, A9.

Ward, S. 2007. "Pulse of the Legal Profession." *ABA Journal* (October). Retrieved on May 8, 2008, from http://www.abajournal.com/magazine/pulse_of_the_legal_profession/

Warren, J. 2004a. "Guards Tell of Retaliation for Informing." LATimes.com, January 21, 2004. Retrieved on January 22, 2004, from http://www.latimes.com/news/local/la-me-prison? 1jan21,1,1780985.story?coll=la-headlines-california

Warren, J. 2004b. "State Penal System Is Hammered in Report." LATimes.com. Retrieved on September 19, 2004, from http://www.latimes.com/news/local/la-me-prisons16Jan16,1, 6085723.story?coll5la-home-headlines

Washington Post. 2007. "Ex-New York Police Commissioner Kerik Indicted on Federal Charges." Reported in *Austin American-Statesman,* November 9: A11.

Wasserman, D. and R. Wachbroit. 2001. *Genetics and Criminal Behavior.* New York: Cambridge University Press.

WBZTV.com. 2007. "Boston Cop Pleads Guilty to Drug, Gun Charges." November 8, 2007. Retrieved on April 21, 2008, from http://wbztv.com/topstories/Boston.Police.Department.2.605024.html

Weber, D. 1987. "Still in Good Standing. The Crisis in Attorney Discipline." *American Bar Association Journal,* November: 58–63.

Weinstein, H. 2007. "ACLU: Company Aiding Torture." *Los Angeles Times.* Reprinted in *Austin American-Statesman,* May 31: A8.

Weisburd, D., and R. Greenspan. 2000. *Police Attitudes Toward Abuse of Authority: Findings from a National Study (Research In Brief).* Washington, DC: U.S. Department of Justice.

Weiss, R. 2007. "What's That buzzing Nearby? A Dragonfly or a High-Tech Spy?" *Washington Post,* reprinted in *Austin American-Statesman,* October 19, 2007: A25.

Weitzer, R. 1999. "Citizens' Perceptions of Police Misconduct: Race and Neighborhood Context." *Justice Quarterly* 16(4): 819–846.

Weitzer, R., and S. Tuch. 2000. "Reforming the Police: Racial Differences in Public Support for Change." *Criminology* 38(2): 391–416.

Weitzer, R., and S. Tuch. 2002. "Perceptions of Racial Profiling: Race, Class, and Personal Experience." *Criminology* 40(2): 435–456.

Western, B. 2007. *Punishment and Inequality.* New York: Russell Sage Foundation Press.

Westmorland, L. 2005. "Police Ethics and Integrity: Breaking the Blue Code of Silence." *Policing and Society,* 15(2): 145–165.

Westmorland, L. 2004. "Policing Integrity: Britain's Thin Blue Line." In *The Contours of Police Integrity,* eds. C. Klockars, S. Ivković, and M. Haberfeld, 75–94. Thousand Oaks, CA: Sage.

Whistleblowers Australia. 2007. The Whistle: Newsletter of Whistleblowers Australia, 50, April 2007: 4–10. Also see Government Accountability Project website: http://www.whistleblower.org/template/index.cfm

White, J. 2005. "Documents Tell of Brutal Improvisation by GIs." *Washington Post,* August 3: A1.

White, R. 1999. "Are Women More Ethical? Recent Findings on the Effects of Gender on Moral Development." *Journal of Public Administration Research and Theory* 9: 459–472.

Whitehead, J. 1991. "Ethical Issues in Probation and Parole." In *Justice, Crime, and Ethics,* eds. M. Braswell, B. McCarthy, and B. McCarthy, 253–273. Cincinnati, OH: Anderson Publishing Company.

Whitlock, C. 2005. "CIA Role in Abductions Investigated." *Austin American-Statesman,* March 13: A5.

Whitlock, C. 2007. "Officials Remain Reticent About Fate of 'Ghost Prisoners.'" *Washington Post,* reprinted in *Austin American-Statesman,* October 27, 2007: A3.

Whitman, J. 1998. "What Is Wrong with Inflicting Shame Sanctions?" *Yale Law Journal* 197(4): 1055–1092.

Wiley, L. 1988. "Moral Education in a Correctional Setting: Reaching the Goal by a Different Road." *Journal* of Offender Services and Rehabilitation 12(2): 161–174.

Williams, G. 1984. The Law and Politics of Police Discretion. Westport, CT: Greenwood.

Wilson, J. Q. 1976. Varieties of Police Behavior. New York: Atheneum.

Wilson, J. Q. 1993. The Moral Sense. New York: Free Press.

Wilson, M., and R. Barry Ruback. 2003. "Hate Crimes in Pennsylvania, 1984–1999: Case Characteristics and Police Responses." Justice Quarterly 20(2): 373–398.

Wiltrout, K. 2007. "Naval Officer Sentenced to Six Months in Prison, Discharge." McClatchy-Tribune Information Services, May 18, 2007. Retrieved on March 19, 2008, from http://www.accessmylibrary.com/coms2/summary_0286-30808288_ITM

Witt, A. 2001. "Allegations of Abuses Mar Murder Cases." Washington Post, June 23: A01.

Wolfe, C. 1991. Judicial Activism. Pacific Grove, CA: Brooks/Cole Publishing.

Wood, D. 2003. "Registration for Arabs Draws Fire." FindLaw.com. Retrieved on February 10, 2003, from http://news.findlaw.com/csmonitor/s/20030206/06feb2003104706.http

Wood, J. 1997. Royal Commission into the New South Wales Police Service,

Final Report. Sydney, Australia: Government of the State of N.S.W. (cited in Prenzler and Ronken, 2001b).

Worden, R., and S. Catlin. 2002. "The Use and Abuse of Force by Police." In Policing and Misconduct, ed. K. Lersch, 85–120. Upper Saddle River, NJ: Prentice-Hall.

Worrall, J. 2001. "Addicted to Drug War: The Role of Civil Asset Forfeiture as a Budgetary Necessity in Contemporary Law Enforcement." Journal of Criminal Justice 29(3): 171–187.

Worrall, J. 2002. "If You Build It They Will Come: Consequences of Improved Citizen Complaint Review Procedures." Crime and Delinquency 48(3): 355–379.

Wozencraft, Kim. 1990. Rush. New York: Random House.

Wren, T. 1985. "Whistle-blowing and Loyalty to One's Friends." In Police Ethics: Hard Choices in Law Enforcement, eds. W. Heffernan and T. Stroup, 25–47. New York: John Jay Press.

Wright, K. 2001. "Management-Staff Relations: Issues in Leadership, Ethics, and Values." In Discretion, Community and Correctional Ethics, eds. J. Kleinig and M. Smith: 203–218. Oxford, England: Rowman & Littlefield Publishers.

Yee, J. and Molloy, A. 2005. For God and Country: Faith and Patriotism

Under Fire. New York: Public Affairs Press.

Zamora, J. Lee, H. and van Derbeke, J. 2003. "Ex-Cops Cleared of 8 Counts." SFGate.com, October 1, 2003. Retrieved on April 16, 2008, from http://www.sfgate.com/cgi-bin/article.cgi?file=/c/a/2003/10/01/MN20967.DTL

Zernike, K. 2001. "Crackdown on Threats in Schools Fails a Test." The New York Times. Retrieved on May 17, 2001, from www.nytimes.com/2001/05/17/nyregion/ 17THRE.html

Zhao, J., N. He, and N. Lovrich. 1998. "Individual Value Preferences Among American Police Officers." Policing: An International Journal of Police Strategies and Management 21(1): 22–37.

Zimbardo, P. 1982. "The Prison Game." In Legal Process and Corrections, eds. N. Johnston and L. Savitz, 195–198. New York: Wiley.

Zimring, F., G. Hawkins, and S. Kamin. 2001. Punishment and Democracy: Three Strikes and You're Out in California. Oxford, England: Oxford University Press.

Zitrin, R. and C. Langford. 1999. The Moral Compass of the American Lawyer. New York: Ballantine Books.

Zohar, N. 2004. "Innocence and Complex Threats: Upholding the War Ethic and the Condemnation of Terrorism." Ethics 114: 734–751.

Name Index

Subject Index

A

Abortion, 8, 22
Abscam operation, 271
Absolutism, 53–56
Absolutist system, 34
Abu Ghraib, 165–166, 437–439, 483–484
Abuse excuses, 16–17
Abuse of power, 225–226, 236
Accepted lies, 270–271
ACLU. *See* American Civil Liberties Union (ACLU)
Activism. *See* Judicial activism
Acts, 8–9
    affects others, 10–11
    free will, 10
    human, 9–10
Actus reus, 15
Act utilitarianism, 37–38
Affirmative action, 97–98, 99
Age of reason, 16
Age-related explanations, of corruption, 256
Alcohol, on-duty use, 234–235
Al Qaeda, 467, 478, 488
American Bar Association (ABA), 312
    Model Code, 313, 319, 324
    Model Code of Judicial Conduct, 359, 367
    Model Rules, 313, 314, 316, 324, 339–340
    standards for criminal justice, 333
American Civil Liberties Union (ACLU), 165, 457, 472, 473

American Correctional Association Code of Ethics, 415, 416
American Jail Association Code of Ethics for Jail Officers, 430
Amnesty International, 246
Applied ethics, 7
Arson investigation, 343
Aspirational code, 190
Asset forfeiture, 337–338
Atonement. *See* Expiation
Attorney
    client privilege, 323
    client relationships, 316–319
Audit systems, 298–300

B

Baeder-Meinhoff gang, 490
Baksheesh, 252
Ballistics testing, 343–344
Behavior
    modification, 432
    morality and, 19–20
    prediction from moral beliefs, 76–77
Bill of Rights, 108
Biological criminology, 66
Biological theories, of moral development, 65, 66–68
Bite mark comparison, 345
BJS. *See* Bureau of Justice Statistics (BJS)
Blue curtain of secrecy, 245, 258, 287, 290, 449
Blue lies, 270
Boston's drug cops, 241

Brady motion, 347
Buddhism, 41, 42
Buddy Boys, 239–240
Bureaucratic justice, 356. *See also* Justice
Bureau of Justice Statistics (BJS), 161, 338
Burnout, 175, 186, 450

C

Capitalism, 50
Capital punishment, 401–404. *See also* Death penalty
    public support for (opinion polls), 402
    religion and, 403
    utilitarianism and, 402–403
Care, ethics of, 47–49
Care perspective, morality, 75
Categorical imperative, 34, 38, 46, 57, 126, 138, 232, 324, 338, 402
Causation, crime, 15
CCA. *See* Corrections Corporation of America (CCA)
Central Park jogger case, 134, 285
Christopher Commission, 170, 246, 304
CIA, 285, 471, 474, 475
Circle sentencing, 148
Civil Asset Forfeiture Reform Act, 338
Civil disobedience, 15, 139, 140, 142
Civilian review boards, 298

CASE INDEX

CREDITS

This page constitutes an extension of the copyright page. We have made every effort to trace the ownership of all copyrighted material and to secure permission from copyright holders. In the event of any question arising as to the use of any material, we will be pleased to make the necessary corrections in future printings. Thanks are due to the following authors, publishers, and agents for permission to use the material indicated.

Chapter 1. 6: Josephson Institute of Ethics

Chapter 3. 76: "The Six Stages of Moral Judgement," by Lawrence Kohlberg in "Moral Stages and Maralization: The Cognitive-Developmental Approach," in MORAL DEVELOPMENT AND BEHAVIOR by Thomas Lickona, 1976. Used by permission.

Chapter 4. 94: Used by permission of The Associated Press. **107:** From The Merchant of Venice.

Chapter 5. 141: From Jacobo Timerman, tranls. Toby Talbot, 1981, PRISONER WITHOUT A NAME, CELL WITHOUT A NUMBER, A.A. Knopf, p.51. Used with permission.

Chapter 7. 189: Used by permission of the International Assn. of Chiefs of Police. **193:** Reprinted with the permission of Simon & Schuster from COPS: Their Lives in Their Own Words by Mark Baker. p.286. ©1985 by Mark Baker. **207:** Reprinted by permission of Waveland Press, Inc. from R. Kappeler, et al, FORCES OF DEVIANCE, (Long Grove IL: Waveland Press, Inc., 1998), p.173. All rights reserved.

Chapter 8. 229: From "Should We Tell the Police to say "yes" to Gratiuities?" from Criminal Justice and Ethics, Richard Kania, 1988, pp.37–49. Used by permission of the publisher. **245:** Reprinted with the permission of Simon & Schuster from COPS: Their Lives in Their Own Words by Mark Baker. ©1985 by Mark Baker.

Chapter 9. 276: Reprinted with the permission of Simon & Schuster from COPS: Their Lives in Their Own Words by Mark Baker. pp 139–40. ©1985 by Mark Baker. **281:** Used by permission of John Jay Press from "Ethical Justifications for and Against Undercover Work," from Police Ethics by Gary Marx, pp.83-11 in POLICE ETHICS: Hard Choices in Law Enforcement, 1985, eds. W. Heffernan and T. Stroup.

Chapter 13. 418: Used by permission of the American Correctional Assn. **432:** Reprinted with permission of the American Jail Assn.

Chapter 14. 449: Used by permission of the Federal Probation Officers Assn.